Causality of Psychological Injury

p23 - Greenberg - 5 basic tasks of an eval
+2
27 - Complicating Factors - the litigation process
& 29 & 30

Causality of Psychological Injury

Presenting Evidence in Court

Gerald Young
York University
Toronto, Ontario, Canada

Andrew W. Kane
Wisconsin School of Professional Psychology
and
Andrew W. Kane & Associates, S.C.
Milwaukee, Wisconsin, USA

Keith Nicholson
Toronto Western Hospital
Toronto, Ontario, Canada

With a contribution by
Daniel W. Shuman
Dedman School of Law
Southern Methodist University
Dallas, Texas, USA

Springer

Gerald Young, Ph.D., C. Psych.
Department of Psychology
Glendon College
York University
Toronto, Ontario, M4N 3M6
Canada

Andrew W. Kane, Ph.D.
Clinical, Consulting & Forensic Psychologist
2815 North Summit Ave
Milwaukee, Wisconsin 53211-3439
USA

Keith Nicholson, Ph.D.
Comprehensive Pain Program
Toronto Western Hospital
Room 4F-811
399 Bathurst St.
Toronto, Ontario, M5T 2S8
Canada

Library of Congress Control Number: 2006929451

ISBN-10: 0-387-36435-8
ISBN-13: 978-0-387-36435-3
e-ISBN-10: 0-387-36445-5
e-ISBN-13: 978-0-387-36445-2

Printed on acid-free paper

9 8 7 6 5 4 3 2 1

springer.com

Acknowledgments

The authors wish to thank several reviewers for their feedback when the book was in its proposal stage, especially Bruce Sales and Timothy Moore. Our families and colleagues have provided much encouragement, and our families tolerated our very long hours at the computer writing the book. Natalie Kardasopoulos worked tirelessly on the references and did much to put the book together. Renée Gauthier and Emilie Lavoie contributed many hours to the subject index. Ali Khan and Lisa Dang gave a lot of time putting together the permissions for all citations and use of copyright material. At the publishers, Sharon Panulla, along with Amanda Breccia, have proven to be extremely involved editors, guiding us through all phases of the book. Joseph Quatela and Vidya Jayaprakash had the thankless job of shepherding the book through production. To help in preparing the book, Gerald Young received several internal research grants from Glendon College, York University, Toronto, Ontario. Young wishes to thank several members of the Canadian Academy of Psychological Disability Assessors who made some useful suggestions about the causality factors in Chapter 3, and Jean-Maurice Bellaiche for having reviewed Table 3.1 from the legal perspective, and co-authoring certain sections.

Contents

Section II. Causality in Court: Psychological Considerations

Section III. Malingering in Psychological Injury: TBI, Chronic Pain, and PTSD

Section IV. Causality, Psychology, and Law

About the Authors

Gerald Young, Ph.D., C. Psych., is an Associate Professor in the Department of Psychology at Glendon College, York University, Toronto, Ontario. He teaches Rehabilitation Psychology to senior undergraduates. In addition, he is a licensed psychologist in Ontario and Quebec, practicing in rehabilitation, in particular. He is the author or co-author of four books, and multiple chapters and articles. He is a member of Canadian registers in clinical practice and disability assessment. He has undertaken over 1,000 assessments related to rehabilitation and disability claims for psychological injury, including after referral for medicolegal purposes from attorneys, insurance companies, and assessment companies. He is a member of the college policy and planning committee, having served in this function at the university level, as well. For the field of psychological injury and law, he is organizing (a) the first professional association, (b) the first academic journal, (c) the first graduate-level textbook related to the field, and (d) the first book series.

Andrew W. Kane, Ph.D., ABAP, is a licensed psychologist in private practice in Milwaukee. Dr. Kane is a diplomate of the American Board of Assessment Psychologists. He is a Professor at Wisconsin School of Professional Psychology, an Adjunct Clinical Professor in the Department of Psychology at University of Wisconsin-Milwaukee, and an Associate Clinical Professor in the Department of Psychiatry and Behavioral Medicine at the Medical College of Wisconsin. He is the author or co-author of eight books and some five dozen professional papers and chapters. He served as a member of the Expert Panel on Psychiatric and Psychological Evidence of the Commission on Mental and Physical Disability Law of the American Bar Association, which helped produce the National Benchbook on Psychiatric and Psychological Evidence and Testimony, published by the ABA. He is a former president of the Wisconsin Psychological Association and of its Division of Forensic and Correctional Psychologists. Dr. Kane also served as a member of the board of the Wisconsin Psychological Association's forensic and clinical divisions. He served for ten years as a member of the Ethics Committee of the Wisconsin Psychological Association. Dr. Kane founded the Wisconsin Coalition on Sexual Misconduct by Psychotherapists and Counselors, a national model program. Dr. Kane has served as an expert in more than 3,000 civil cases involving a variety of issues.

Keith Nicholson, Ph.D., C. Psych., has had extensive clinical experience working with many different patient populations. He obtained his Ph.D. in Clinical

Neuropsychology from the University of Victoria and, since then, has worked at the Toronto Western Hospital, now part of the University Health Network in Toronto, Ontario, in addition to working at several community clinics and maintaining a private practice. Dr. Nicholson is now affiliated with the Comprehensive Pain Program at the Toronto Western Hospital, Toronto, Ontario. He has a particular interest in the psychology of chronic pain and clinical neuropsychology and has many publications in these and other areas of interest.

Contributors

Marek J. Celinski, Ph.D., 27 Roncesvalles Ave., Suite 508, Toronto, Ontario, M6R 3B2, marekcelinski1@rogers.com

C. Richard Chapman, Ph.D., Department of Anesthesiology, University of Utah School of Medicine, 615 Arapeen Drive, Suite 200, Salt Lake City, UT 84108, crc20@utah.edu

Jennifer L. Hardy, J.D., Dedman School of Law, Southern Methodist University, 3314 Daniel Ave., Dallas, TX 75275-0116

Andrew W. Kane, Ph.D., 2815 North Summit Avenue, Milwaukee, Wisconsin 53211-3439, awkane@sbcglobal.net

Michael F. Martelli, Ph.D., Concussion Care Centre of Virginia, 10120 West Broad Street, Suite H, Glen Allen, VA 23060, msensorium@yahoo.com

Keith Nicholson, Ph.D., Toronto Western Hospital, Comprehensive Pain Program, Room 4F-811, 399 Bathurst St., Toronto, Ontario, M5T 2S8, keith@uhnres.utoronto.ca

Ronnie Shore, LL.B., 260 Besserer St., # 608, Ottawa Ontario K1N 1J3

J. Douglas Salmon, Jr., Ph.D., 69 Dale Ave., Scarborough, Ontario, M1J 3J7, dr.salmon@rrees.com

Daniel W. Shuman, J.D., Dedman School of Law, Southern Methodist University, PO Box 750116, Dallas, Texas 75275-0116, dshuman@mail.smu.edu

Gerald Young, Ph.D., C. Psych., Department of Psychology, Glendon College, York University, 2275 Bayview Ave., Toronto, Ontario, M4N 3M6, gyoung@glendon.yorku.ca

1

Causality, Psychological Injuries, and Court: Introduction

GERALD YOUNG, ANDREW W. KANE, AND KEITH NICHOLSON

> Having a degree and a license to practice does not demonstrate that the expert is competent to fulfill [her or his] responsibilities. For example, a review of the scientific literature demonstrates that at any given point in time some questions are unanswerable. In addition, an expert's response to answerable questions may be inaccurate unless the expert keeps abreast of the relevant scholarly literature on the topic. (Sales & Shuman, 2005, pp. 134–135)

> The post-*Daubert* world of expert admissibility demands more of the lawyer in understanding scientific methods. To satisfy the demands of *Daubert*, the lawyer must understand the nature of the scientific enterprise, be able to demonstrate that his expert is offering scientifically valid testimony, and be able to challenge the validity of the opposing expert's testimony. (Sales & Shuman, 2005, p. 103)

These two quotes from a book by law professors Bruce Sales and Daniel Shuman on the topic of experts in court illustrate well the goals of our two-book series on causality, psychology, and law, and the need for these books in the field. Our aim in these two books appears timely: we want to educate the lawyer about psychologists and the psychologist about evidence law and about the state of the art in relevant areas of psychological injury—Posttraumatic Stress Disorder (PTSD), chronic pain, and Traumatic Brain Injury (TBI). A broader goal is to promote informed dialogue among professionals in the mental health field and the law. Both law and forensic psychology, the latter defined as "the application of the science and profession of psychology to questions and issues relating to law and the legal system" (American Board of Forensic Psychology, in Archer, 2003, p. 317), often deal with issues of causality, and in many ways causality is central to the evidence psychologists offer to court.

In the companion volume to this book, entitled *Psychological Knowledge in Court: PTSD, Pain, and TBI* (Young, Kane, & Nicholson, 2006), we gathered experts in the field who presented state of the art reviews of the literature pertaining to the three primary areas that are involved in psychological injury cases: PTSD, chronic pain, and TBI. In this book, we continue to explore these themes, but with a focus on causality, evidence law, and psychological assessment, with a particular focus on malingering. We elaborate on factors related to causation, the evidence law pertaining to scientific standards to which psychologists are asked to adhere, and a multicausal explanatory framework.

After this brief introductory chapter, in Section I of this book, Gerald Young and colleagues review causality and related terms from a conceptual point of view, and analyze the literature on psychological injury in PTSD, chronic pain, and mild TBI. Young underscores the need for careful definition of terms and their translation from law to psychology and medicine, and vice versa, partly because there are some differing terms in the field, or because some terms are identical but either are used differently or have different meanings across fields. Young emphasizes the biopsychosocial model: causality is considered multifactorial, with psychological, and environmental contributions. In addition, in establishing causality, the psychological assessor needs to consider roles for preexisting psychological vulnerabilities, including the proverbial "thin" skull, for the trauma itself, and for postevent developments, both related to and independent of the trauma and its consequences. Most important, when addressing causality determinations in mental health assessments, the psychological assessor needs to adopt a scientific approach both with respect to the data gathered on the individual, including information from psychological instruments, and the research literature consulted.

In the second section, Andrew W. Kane presents the context for psychological evaluations, including the United States (*Daubert v. Merrell Dow Pharmaceuticals*, 1993; *General Electric Co. v. Joiner, 1997*; and *Kumho Tire Co. v. Carmichael, 1999*) and Canadian (*R. v. Mohan, 1994*) Supreme Court cases that address the requirements for experts in order to meet the gatekeeping standards of the courts. Psychologists must carefully consider base rates, error rates, diagnosis, learned treatises, and other psychological and legal bases for addressing the forensic issues in a given case. A comprehensive evaluation requires the expert to identify the pre- and posttrauma status of the plaintiff through a combination of historical review, use of psychological tests and other instruments and interviews, and a reasoned and cautious analysis of the data. Numerous recommendations are made and areas for caution are identified. Kane also addresses in detail the requirements for practicing outside of the jurisdiction in which one is licensed.

In the third section of the book, Keith Nicholson and Michael F. Martelli discuss the differential diagnosis of malingering in psychological injury cases, in the context of TBI, chronic pain, and PTSD or other psychoemotional problems. There is now an extensive scientific literature that the expert must be familiar with and numerous techniques for the detection of malingering or other behavior that may be mistaken for malingering. This literature and these techniques are critically reviewed in this section by Nicholson and Martelli.

The first three sections of this book together address the challenge presented by developments in evidence law that specify the need for expert evidence to pass criteria for trustworthiness, reliability, and validity (*Daubert*, 1993; *Mohan*, 1994, and their progeny). In their chapter, Daniel Shuman and Jennifer L. Hardy present the specifics of that challenge to the field, arguing that testimony about causality in mental health assessments requires rigorous standards, grounded in the scientific study of human behavior. The concluding chapter of this book, written by Young, Kane, and Nicholson, addresses the manner to which each of the three sections of the book has succeeded at this daunting task.

Chapter Summaries

Section I: Causality and Psychological Evidence: Concepts, Terms, and Issues

The first chapter in this section (Chapter 2 of this book, written by Young and Kane) briefly presents the *Daubert* trilogy, on rules and regulations governing admissibility of evidence to court. The chapter addresses torts, and how causality is approached in law. Various legal tests are described. It is noted that cases of psychological harm present challenges to the court. The chapter then turns to more psychological considerations, such as forensic mental health assessment, diagnosis, impairment, and disability. As noted in Ackerman and Kane (1998), the *DSM* (*Diagnostic and Statistical Manual of Mental Disorders, Fourth Edition*, American Psychiatric Association; *DSM-IV*, 1994; text revision, *DSM-IV-TR*, 2000) is the standard diagnostic manual of mental disorders in use in North America, and the process followed in the construction of each of its revisions reflects not only knowledge of the research but, also, factors such as political issues and votes by American Psychiatric Association committees.

An especially important topic concerns the psychological approach to catastrophic impairment, as specified in the Ontario Superior Court ruling, *Desbiens v. Mordini* (2004), and the questions it leaves unanswered. We conclude the chapter by emphasizing that in using a biopsychosocial or multifactorial model to guide an assessment, the psychologist improves chances of having testimony admitted into evidence in court.

Chapter 3 provides definitions of basic concepts related to causality and causation, and suggestions for disambiguating and clarifying ideas presented differently in law and psychology. Young provides flow charts illustrating the causality determination process, and describes an ordinal scale of causality to help with individual evaluations. The chapter considers the role of preexisting psychological vulnerabilities in arriving at causality judgments, along with the event and postevent developments. Assessments need to consider "thin" and "crumbling" skulls among the multiple factors that need to be examined in arriving at causality formulations. In addition, the chapter presents a list of possible rationales that may be used to accept or deny causality arguments in evidence offered to court. Young suggests that the mechanism of symptom "exacerbation" may apply to the postevent course of symptom development, whether it concerns PTSD, chronic pain, TBI, or other disorders. Moreover, the source of the exacerbatory stress involved may be pre-, peri-, or postevent. Finally, the concept, as defined, allows a role in the exacerbation process for factors such as conscious or unconscious symptom exaggeration, showing that it is a general concept that may apply either in a more neutral manner or in a more negative manner with respect to an individual's apparent motivation and validity of presentation. Psychologists need to undertake careful and comprehensive evaluations to clarify these various influences and motivations.

In Chapter 4, written with Ronnie Shore, the authors consulted well-known dictionaries and related sources in the fields of law, psychology, and medicine. Young and Shore examined them for similarities and differences in how they define causality, causation, and related terms. All the fields have developed a complex lexis of terms related to these concepts but despite many similarities, differences exist and render translation across the fields difficult and often confusing. Young and Shore make proposals to facilitate better standardization of terminology.

After a comprehensive analysis of the relevant terms in the three fields under review, the authors conclude that the legal field has contributed useful terms dealing with causality and causation, such as *proximate, concurrent, contributing, intervening, material*, and *superseding*. From medicine, we gleaned other useful terms to add, such as *component, exacerbation, predisposing, primary*, and *secondary*. As for psychology, in addition to the terms already listed, we considered relevant terms such as *catalytic, latent, maintaining, mediating*, and *multiple*. Together, these terms allow a more differentiated perspective of multiple causality. Young and Shore suggest that any mental health assessment dealing with a possible chain of causation in temporal terms specify relevant links by referring to initial components, intermediate components, or recent components, rather than using more ambiguous terms such as "immediate" and "remote."

Chapters 5–7 selectively review the literature in the psychological injury areas of PTSD, chronic pain, and mild TBI, presenting an integrated biopsychosocial model and illustrating important concepts related to causality. The biological, psychological, and social components of the model (which includes macrovariables such as culture, socioeconomic status, and ethnicity) are considered to be interactive in causality. The biopsychosocial model assumes that all behavioral and psychological phenomena are multidetermined in a complex manner. The mind and body are intimately connected in a coherent system, for example, in which both parts of the system may need to be treated for therapy to be effective. In their assessments, psychologists take account of biomedical as well as psychological influences, being wary of simplistic mind-body dualism or reductionism of psychological symptoms to medical factors. Currently, the predominant model of psychopathology is an interactive diathesis/stress one, where a predisposition, possibly biological, acts in conjunction with a stressor, or precipitating event, to trigger a cascade leading to a psychological disorder. In establishing the origins of an individual's psychological condition or psychopathology, psychologists are quite aware of the influence of context. Behavior is a function of "person by situation" interaction. The person varies in dimensions related to personality, motivation, coping, cognitions, and so forth. Together, the person and situational variables characterize an individual's psychological resiliency vs. vulnerability.

In Chapter 8, Gerald Young and C. Richard Chapman examine the relationship between chronic pain and affect, illustrating important principles in psychological causality. The chapter is an elaboration of a briefer chapter by Young and Chapman (2006) in the companion volume to this book. These chapters present the argument that pain and associated affect reflects a unified, nonlinear dynamical system. Concepts such as dynamical attractors, the "butterfly" effect, and Complex Adaptive Systems (Kauffman, 1993) may help explain the evolution toward chronic pain and sudden changes in pain, as well as resistance to change in pain. The authors apply a five-step model of change (Young, 1997) to the development of chronic pain, and consider the five-step change model for therapy in its terms. Young and Chapman conclude that the *DSM* should consider a unified category of chronic pain, perhaps calling it "Chronic Pain Complications Disorder."

J. Douglas Salmon, Marek J. Celinski, and Gerald Young conclude this section of the book, in Chapter 9, by examining sequential causality and the need for repeated assessment in the rehabilitation context. Following Gatchel's (1991) model of chronic pain development, they describe a three-phase model of the rehabilitation process, involving a dynamic in which secondary and tertiary effects are possible. They present a model of the recovery process, which includes the patient's subjective recovery strategy, schemas developed, coping skills, and effort to comply with therapy and mitigate losses. Salmon and Celinski have developed an assessment battery that includes the first instrument specifically designed for the tracking of rehabilitation progress and outcome, the Rehabilitation Checklist (RCL, Salmon, 1998).

Section II: Causality in Court: Psychological Considerations

In this section, Andrew W. Kane's four chapters, Chapters 10–13, focus on the interaction of psychology and the law, and, particularly, on what psychologists and attorneys need to know about one another's areas of expertise. In Chapter 10, Kane discusses basic concepts from the perspective of both psychology and law. Because of its emphasis in the U.S. federal courts and in most states, he discusses *Daubert v. Merrell Dow Pharmaceuticals* (1993) at length, as well as other relevant case law. He also discusses *R. v. Mohan* (1994), Canada's similar Supreme Court case on expert testimony. Kane explains critical concepts such as error rates, base rates, diagnosis, bases for expert opinions, learned treatises, and the role of psychological assessments in evaluations for court. Both attorneys and the psychologists that they retain need to be very familiar with these areas if the psychologist's testimony is to be admitted to the court and considered relevant and helpful.

In Chapter 11, Kane presents information regarding the goals and conduct of a psychological assessment for court purposes. The forensic or other psychologist must undertake a comprehensive assessment, beginning with a substantial historical review, including reviewing many types of records, to try to establish the pretrauma and posttrauma psychological status of the individual. The psychological assessment process includes psychological testing, assessment of response style and malingering, utilization of various information-gathering instruments, and a substantial amount of interviewing of both the individual being assessed and collateral sources of information. In this chapter, Kane makes specific recommendations for tests and other instruments that should be used to increase the reliability and validity of assessments undertaken. If the psychologist does not undertake an adequate evaluation, comprehensive in its use of interviews, psychological tests, and relevant records and documentation, as well as careful use of the scientific literature and clear arguments supporting the conclusions offered, including reasons to reject alternative hypotheses, the psychologist will not be able to meet the requirements of *Daubert/Mohan* and their progeny, nor of her or his professional ethics codes and forensic guidelines.

In Chapter 12, Kane discusses other issues that are essential to the psycho-legal assessment process. The forensic expert must be extremely familiar with the professional literature relevant to a given case. Evaluations have limits that must be addressed, and assessments must have ecological, incremental, and other types of validity. Sources of bias are addressed at some length. There is then discussion of the problems associated with a therapist testifying as an expert, because the two roles are very different. The current controversy regarding the Comprehensive System for the Rorschach is discussed at length. The concepts of "thin skulls" and "eggshell personalities" are reviewed. Because many experts accept cases outside of the jurisdiction in which they are licensed or certified, Kane provides information regarding the requirements of every state and province in this regard, and cautions experts to ensure that they are not violating the law in any nonlicensed jurisdiction in which they wish to consult, because they may, at best, not be permitted to testify about an evaluation conducted in that "foreign" jurisdiction, and, at worst, be charged with a felony and/or a breach of the licensing law that could lead to a loss of their license/certification to practice in their home state or province. Because it is at times a major conflict between psychologists and attorneys, there is extensive discussion of the psychologist's duty to protect raw test data and test instruments. These and many other ethical issues are discussed at length.

In Chapter 13, Kane summarizes the key information given in this section of the book and draws conclusions based on its chapters, making practice recommendations. Kane concludes that the best means of meeting *Daubert* or *Mohan* challenges on admissibility of evidence to court is for the psychologist to conduct comprehensive, multimethod assessments that are impartial and thoroughly grounded in scientific and/or clinical methodology.

Section III: Malingering in Psychological Injury: TBI, Chronic Pain, and PTSD

In this section, Keith Nicholson and Michael F. Martelli critically examine malingering and related constructs, focusing upon the differential diagnosis of malingering within the context of TBI, chronic pain, and PTSD or other psychoemotional problems that may be the subject of medicolegal proceedings. Malingering needs to be carefully evaluated in personal injury or other medicolegal cases in which large financial settlements or other compensation may be at stake. There are serious consequences of either failing to identify malingering when a plaintiff is engaging in this, or mistakenly labeling a person as malingering when she or he is not.

The first chapter of this section, Chapter 14, provides an overview of basic concepts important in understanding malingering and related behavior. It begins with a discussion of deception, deceit, and lie-catching in everyday life, noting that deception is common not only in humans but, also, in other primates and that it is generally difficult to catch those who are lying. The chapter reviews the use of various biomedical techniques, some of which are quite promising, in the detection of lying. Next, the chapter provides a brief history of malingering, and examines the controversies about its current *DSM* definition and criteria. The authors proceed to discuss the differential diagnosis between malingering and other diagnoses, especially Factitious Disorder. The concept of malingering is then contrasted with several other concepts and terms, including response bias, response style, illness deception, exaggeration and symptom magnification, effort, and symptom validity.

The authors next discuss methodology used in the research, and the validity of studies on malingering. In particular, they argue that there are very few cases of proven malingering that have been available for study, and that most studies have relied upon simulation of problems by healthy individuals, with their performance contrasted with that of various control groups. The authors stress the need for appropriate control groups in the empirical research on malingering because degree of psychopathology and related problems (e.g., pain, sleep disturbance) might markedly interfere with performance on measures of malingering. The incidence and prevalence of malingering is addressed, noting that estimates vary widely.

In the next chapter of this section, Chapter 15, Nicholson and Martelli examine the effect of compensation status on aspects of presentation by those with TBI, chronic pain, PTSD, or other psychoemotional problems. They find that, although there is some relationship, this is generally moderate and may be explained on the basis of many factors other than malingering.

Chapters 16–18 provide an in-depth presentation of research on malingering in TBI, chronic pain, and PTSD/depression. The chapters critically review specific strategies and techniques used to assess malingering in each of these areas. It is finally concluded that, although a number of techniques may be useful in identifying malingering, none provides unambiguous evidence, and, therefore, the assessor must carefully consider all available information in the determination of whether the person being assessed is malingering.

Section IV: Causation, Psychology, and Law

In Chapter 20, Daniel Shuman and Jennifer L. Hardy present further thoughts on causation, psychology, and the law. Using the anchor question of whether there is psychological order to the universe, the chapter initially presents and analyzes the legal rules that govern demonstration of causation of psychological harm in personal injury actions. It then critically explores other models that the courts have applied for demonstration of psychological harm. The authors review the history of tort claims for psychological harm, focusing on decisions related to Schizophrenia. They indicate the challenges that will be faced by psychologists as evidence law changes in the coming years.

Shuman and Hardy emphasize that when the expert offers a *specific causal attribution*, explicitly linking the defendant's negligent action as the cause in fact and proximate cause of the plaintiff's clinical psychological condition, in order to be admissible, it is necessary that the evidence be based on a reliable scientific foundation. Testimony about cause and effect in psychological assessments must be held to demanding standards, or psychology's claim to be grounded in the scientific study of human behavior will be undermined.

Concluding Chapter

In the conclusions to the book (Chapter 21), Young, Kane, and Nicholson summarize the material presented throughout the book, indicate directions for future conceptualization and research, and anticipate future trends in the law and how psychology must keep its focus in order to satisfy evidentiary standards. The challenge presented by Shuman and Hardy in their chapter is addressed: Is there a psychological order in the universe; does the science of psychology allow for a general understanding of the process of elaboration of psychological harm after events involving psychological injury and the factors that are involved? Further, can this general knowledge be prudently applied in individual cases, explaining causality for court purposes?

We emphasize that the psychologist must adhere to a scientific stance throughout the psychological evaluation, including critical appraisal of the recent literature, selecting instruments with acceptable reliability and validity, gathering all the relevant data, exploring all relevant hypotheses, following appropriate critical reasoning in arriving at conclusions, and knowing which hypotheses are justified in terms of the data and the literature, and which are more tentative. The task of the assessor is to parse out what can be legitimately ascribed to the effects of the index event or to other factors, such as a preexisting personality disorder or psychopathology, concurrent stressors, or even malingering.

Conclusions

Throughout this book, and the companion one by the authors (*Psychological Knowledge in Court: PTSD, Pain and TBI*, 2006), we emphasize that the practitioner needs a sound knowledge of the research on the population at large (nomothetic level), and also must proceed in a careful, comprehensive, and scientific fashion at the individual (idiographic) level, in order to arrive at defensible decisions that meet the requirements of *Daubert* and its progeny in the United States, or *Mohan* and its progeny in Canada. In their forensic and related assessments, psychologists and other mental health professionals should adopt multifactorial causal models, undertake comprehensive assessments of individuals to ascertain causality, and apply the scientific approach, both in terms of consulting state-of-the-art research in the literature and of evaluating carefully all alternative hypotheses about individuals being assessed.

The authors have prepared this book for a broad audience that needs to understand legal and psychological approaches to causality. We make recommendations on understanding causality and assessing it that will be beneficial to all disciplines dealing with the topic. The authors provide an in depth discussion of evidence law, rules, and regulations. Psychologists and other mental health professionals need to know about these matters for court purposes, and lawyers need to know what psychologists should know about these matters. In this book, the authors have striven to adopt a balanced perspective concerning the controversies in the field, and have emphasized the need to remain impartial when facing the implicit pressures from different stakeholders and from the adversarial nature of the legal side of personal injury. To conclude, the authors reaffirm the need for reliable and valid scientifically-informed evidence at all stages in causality assessment in cases of psychological injury. This is the optimal manner of cutting through controversy and moving toward best practice (Schultz, 2005).

References

Ackerman, M. J., & Kane, A. W. (1998). *Psychological experts in personal injury actions* (3rd ed.). New York: Aspen.

American Psychiatric Association. (1994). *Diagnostic and statistical manual of mental disorders* (4th ed.). Washington, DC: Author.

American Psychiatric Association. (2000). *Diagnostic and statistical manual of mental disorders: Text revision* (4th ed.). Washington, DC: Author.

Archer, R. P. (2003). Editor's introduction to a special issue on the topic of forensic assessment. *Assessment, 10*, 317.

Daubert v. Merrell Dow Pharmaceuticals, Inc. 509 U.S. 579, 113 S.Ct. 2786, 125 L.Ed. 2d 469 (1993).

Desbiens v. Mordini, 2004 CanLII 41166 (ON S.C.).

Gatchel, R. J. (1991). Early development of physical and mental deconditioning in painful spinal disorders. In T. G. Mayer, V. Mooney, & R. J. Gatchel (Eds.), *Contemporary conservative care for painful spinal disorders* (pp. 278–289). Philadelphia, PA: Lea & Febiger.

General Electric Co. v. Joiner, 522 U.S. 136, 118 S.Ct. 512 (1997).

Kauffman, S. A. (1993). *The origins of order*. New York: Oxford University Press.

Kumho Tire Co. v. Carmichael, 526 U.S. 137, 119 S.Ct. 1167 (1999).

R. v. Mohan [1994] 2 S.C.R. 9, 1994 CanLII 80 (S.C.C.).

Sales, B. D., & Shuman, D. W. (2005). *Experts in court: Reconciling law, science, and professional knowledge*. Washington, DC: American Psychological Association.

Salmon, J. D., Jr. (1998). *The Rehabilitation Checklist: Technical manual*. Toronto, ON: Multi-Health Systems.

Schultz, I. Z. (2005). Impairment of occupational disability in research and practice. In I. Z. Schultz & R. J. Gatchel (Eds.), *Handbook of complex occupational disability claims: Early risk identification, intervention, and prevention* (pp. 25–41). New York: Springer Science+Business Media.

Young, G. (1997). *Adult development, therapy, and culture: A postmodern synthesis.* New York: Plenum.

Young, G., & Chapman, C. R. (2006). Chronic pain and affect as a nonlinear dynamical system. In G. Young, A. W. Kane, & K. Nicholson (Eds.), *Psychological knowledge in court: PTSD, pain, and TBI* (pp. 181–192). New York: Springer Science+Business Media.

Young, G., Kane, A. W., & Nicholson, K. (Eds.). (2006). *Psychological knowledge in court: PTSD, pain, and TBI.* New York: Springer Science+Business Media.

Section I

Causality and Psychological Evidence: Concepts, Terms, Issues

2

Causality in Psychology and Law

GERALD YOUNG AND ANDREW W. KANE

The study of causality and related terms has its roots in philosophy, and the concept is considered important in many contemporary fields of research. Despite its pervasiveness, there is little agreement in psychology and law about causality's definition, underlying conceptual basis, and implications for legal actions in which psychology is at issue. A comprehensive account of causality and related terms, which can help both fields navigate the difficulties that these concepts present, is direly needed, and this book has been written to fill this void. In the first section of this chapter, we address the area of legal issues and causality, such as evidence law, torts, and how causality is treated in law. Then, in the second section, we turn to more psychological considerations, such as forensic mental health assessment (FMHA), disability, and catastrophic impairment. At the end of the chapter, we present in an appendix the concepts of reliability and validity in psychological assessment.

Legal Issues and Causality

In this section of the chapter, we explain the basic rules and regulations that govern expert psychological evidence presented to the court, concentrating on the American judicial system, with its *Daubert* trilogy and associated Federal Rules of Evidence. Most criteria presently applicable to forensic psychological evaluations and testimony derive from the U.S. legislation and appellate court cases. Other jurisdictions, such as Canada, share many of the same requirements of admissibility of evidence as the American approach. Their shared origin in British common law explains much of the similarity. The next section examines the tort system, in which plaintiffs lodge civil suits against defendants for negligence, personal injury, and so forth. Various legal tests are described. It is noted that cases of psychological harm present challenges to the court. Psychologists often are called upon to offer evidence in such cases, and they face challenges in their own right. The third section examines the concepts of causality and causation in psychological evidence proffered to court. We emphasize that there are no universally accepted conceptualizations, that psychologists must be aware that causality and causation are multiple in origin, and that, in individual cases, a careful application from population-level research to the case at hand is critical. In psychological assessment, complicating factors relate to preevent psychological vulnerabilities (in legal parlance, "thin" and "crumbling" skulls), to postevent individual effort, to partial or full malingering, and so forth.

Rules of Evidence

Forensic assessments by psychologists are undertaken in order to formulate a "scientific opinion" that will assist the judge or jury (the trier of fact) in its deliberations (Van Dorsten, 2002). In the U.S. federal legal ruling, *Frye v. United States* (1923), expert evidence was considered admissible by the court if it had been formulated on principles that had gained "general acceptance" in the field, considering the limits in the discipline involved. The 1962 ruling in *Jenkins v. United States* specifically addressed expert psychological evidence, accepting it when it "probably" could aid the trier of fact in making a determination. The Federal Rules of Evidence (FRE, 2004) now govern the standards of expert testimony and their admissibility. For example, rule 702 indicates that testimony of experts whose evidence would assist the trier of fact in understanding relevant scientific information is admissible.

The U.S. Supreme Court ruling in *Daubert v. Merrell Dow Pharmaceuticals, Inc.* (1993) served as a landmark of contemporary requirements on admitting expert evidence. Along with the subsequent Supreme Court rulings in *Joiner* and in *Kumho* (*General Electric Co. v. Joiner*, 1997; *Kumho Tire Co. v. Carmichael*, 1999; respectively), they are commonly called "the *Daubert* trilogy." (In Chapter 10, Kane specifies the admissibility requirements of the *Daubert* trilogy and the Federal Rules of Evidence in the United States for presenting evidence in court, and their impact on admissibility of psychological evidence).

Daubert underscored that scientific testimony must meet accepted standards of legal reliability (trustworthiness), which, for psychology, means that it must be valid, sound, or grounded in appropriate scientific methods and standards. *Daubert* also specified that scientific testimony must be relevant, that is, applicable to the particular case to which it has been addressed, aiding the trier of fact in evaluating the case. In this regard, any science used in testimony will ideally meet standards for falsifiability (being empirically testable), for having been published after peer review, for having considered error rate (false positives and false negatives), and for following standardized procedures. It has been noted that various social sciences differ in how they define the concepts of scientific reliability and validity, complicating the confusion between the different uses of the terms in legal and psychological fields (Saxe & Ben-Shakhar, 1999).

Joiner added that the standard for appellate review is abuse of discretion, and *Kumho* expanded its application to nonscientific, but nevertheless technical, specialized knowledge. Slovenko (2002a, 2002b, 2002c) noted that a psychologist providing evidence about a particular individual might be considered a technical expert more than a scientific one. Federal Rule of Evidence 702 does not deny admissibility of expert opinion based on appropriate professional knowledge and experience (Brodsky, Caputo, & Domino, 2002; Kane, Chapter 10, this volume). Van Dorsten (2002) noted that, on the one hand, psychologists have been cautioned that the scientific knowledge in psychology is not sufficient to allow them to address certain issues in court and on the other hand, they have been cautioned to arrive at conclusions based on sufficient scientific evidence (See, for example, Melton, Petrilla, Poythress, & Slobogin, 1997).

Shuman (2002, 2003a) discussed whether medical/clinical opinion evidence is admissible in court in light of the *Daubert* trilogy and related Federal Rules of Evidence. Apparently, the federal courts have been divided in their opinion, with some decisions in toxic tort cases arguing that the *Daubert* criteria permit an expert to testify based on clinical experience involving sound application of "clinical medical methodology," whereas other decisions only permit evidence grounded in "hard science." Shuman noted that by following their ethical obligations, psychologists and psychiatrists will stay current in their relevant scientific knowledge and not stray from research-supported opinions, thereby satisfying evidentiary requirements, as well.

Slovenko (2002a, 2002b, 2002c) showed that post-*Daubert* hearings on the admissibility of behavioral and social science evidence have not significantly altered the course of decisions, in that few experts have been prevented from offering evidence. He concluded that it is quite likely that the negative publicity about "junk science" has better prevented it from entering the court system than has *Daubert*.

Similarly, Shuman and Sales (2003) asked whether *Daubert* and its progeny have significantly affected standards of admissibility of scientific evidence in federal courts. They concluded that, overall, there has been little impact on the nature of behavioral and social science evidence admitted to court. They asked whether expert testimony that is clinical rather than scientific, *per se*, needs contextual consideration and less rigorous gatekeeping scrutiny by judges. For example, reliable scientific information evaluates the error rate in normative population research, but individual, clinically based evidence, by definition, cannot examine such an error rate, though it can take into account normative and base-rate data. Moreover, *Daubert* does not specify what error rates are acceptable in court. Indeed, for each aspect of its criteria for admissible science, imprecisions arise. Judicial decisions have not yet led to operationalization of *Daubert*'s criteria. Further, scientific criteria are relative, not absolute, whereas legal needs require definitive decisions and seek hard evidence in support of them.

Relevant scientific support for a clinician's particular testimony may not even exist. Normally, *Daubert* factors require that the scientific basis (reasoning, methodology) underlying evidence is reliable (valid) and relevant; however, it could happen that for a particular testimony there is no research directly on the topic, or "the inferential leap from the research to the issue in the case is significant" (Shuman, 2002, p. 39). However, the *Daubert* criterion of general acceptability may provide support for some clinical testimony.

Nevertheless, one must be prudent in offering testimony, whether scientific or clinical. Shuman and Sales (2003) concluded, "Unfortunately, lawyers are typically happy to have their experts reach conclusions on the witness stand that support their client's position, even if it goes beyond the bounds of the witness's expertise" (p. 178).

Note that in the Canadian context, *Daubert* has been cited in a Supreme Court of Canada case (*R. v. J.-L.J., 2000 SCC 51*) and in some provincial cases. *Daubert*'s expectations of scientific rigor both in proferred evidence of expert witnesses and in the gatekeeping function of judges match the similar requirements of *R. v. Mohan* (Gold, 2003).

In the United Kingdom, reforms have had the same objectives as *Daubert* (Woolf, 1996), to improve the quality of scientific evidence proferred in court, but the manner in accomplishing them has been to assign "neutral" court experts to cases (Faigman, 2003). Trimble (2004) criticized the implementation of this new system in the United Kingdom.

Van Dorsten (2002) noted that "the primary objective of expert witness testimony is to educate about both a specific area of science, and its relevant application to specific circumstance" (p. 7). This quote illustrates the two-tiered function that psychologists usually engage in when offering evidence. That is, when performing assessments for legal purposes, psychologists examine the population-level science applicable to the legal question at hand and then determine its relevance to the particular case at issue. When expert testimony involves only presentation of research relevant to a case, without attempting to link it to the case, it is considered "standard" expert testimony, and when an attempt is made to link a psychological explanation grounded in research to a case at hand, it is considered "concrete" expert testimony (Brodsky et al., 2002). Van Dorsten and James (2002) point out that the pathway in forensic psychological assessment is not from the scientific research to the individual being assessed, but from the individual to the research, in that each individual in a forensic assessment constitutes a "single case study design" to which the applicability of the scientific research varies and thus is at issue.

To conclude, the various gatekeeping rules and regulations concerning the admissibility of evidence to court demand that the highest standards of science be applied to both the psychological research on populations related to court purposes and the psychological assessments of individuals presented to court. At the same time, the court's criteria of good science leaves gaps, and the gray area of clinical testimony about individuals, where both scientific and clinical procedures are used, presents issues that need better resolution.

Torts

According to McLearen, Pietz, and Denney (2004), a tort is a private or civil wrong or injury, such as in negligence or intentional tortious conduct, which a fact finder may decide merits damages. The process of proving a tort must meet four criteria, often referred to as the "4 Ds": duty, dereliction, direct causation, and damages. For a plaintiff to receive damages in a tort case, it must be shown that the defendant committed a derelict act or omission, where a duty was owed to the plaintiff. For example, in negligence, the standard to be met is generally the "reasonable-person test"; in the circumstances in which the defendant found herself or himself, would a reasonable person have engaged in the same behavior (or its lack thereof)? If dereliction of duty is established, then the causal question is broached: Is the dereliction of duty, or the lack thereof, the "proximate cause" of the injury, factually and logically preceding the harm incurred? Again, the reasonable person test is applied—would another individual in the same circumstance have reasonably predicted that the act or the lack thereof would have caused the harm? Citing Daller (2000), McLearen et al. (2004) underscore that proximate cause is defined differently in different jurisdictions. Legal standards are governed by case law that indicates which harms involve a legally protected right or interest that can be pursued for damages.

Gabbay and Alonso (2004) indicate that tort action for mental harm caused by negligent acts derives from three to four rules used by the courts, depending on the jurisdiction involved: the physical contact rule (e.g., loss of limb), the physical consequences rule (e.g., ulcers from mental distress, rather than pathogens), the zone of danger rule (e.g., potential for physical harm), and, sometimes, the bystander rule (witnessing a traumatic event, usually for a close relative).

Campbell and Montigny (2004) elaborate upon the zone of danger and bystander rules, specifying both the common law tests used and their limits with respect to claims and damages. They suggest that the courts have adopted "control mechanisms" to limit flooding the courts with claims of psychological damage. In the "zone of danger" test, the plaintiff must be clearly a participant in the negligent event in question, fearing for her or his safety, because there had been a physical injury or a near miss. Normally, being a passive observer is not sufficient grounds for a legitimate claim. As for the "bystander" test, in many jurisdictions it applies only when a close relative of a victim witnesses a tragedy, realizes the harm occasioned, and reacts with "severe emotional impact." Campbell and Montigny criticize the zone of danger and bystander tests for being too restrictive, thereby denying legitimate claims.

Another important test considered in tort cases involving psychological harm concerns "foreseeability." Given the negligent conduct of the defendant, the legal threshold is whether the psychological harm that had been purportedly caused by the conduct had been reasonably foreseeable. Could the harm have been readily anticipated; for example, had the negligent party foreseen any possible collateral psychological injury from her or his negligent conduct? The test allows that each case is considered for its facts and merits, and can be readily evaluated by the laypersons serving as jurors. The test has been criticized for not being stringent enough and for being open to subjective influence (Campbell & Montigny, 2004).

The "combination" test seeks to determine whether psychological injuries had been both foreseeable and severe enough to permit diagnosis of a recognizable psychiatric disorder. Campbell and Montigny query whether the latter part of the test, "having a recognizable psychiatric illness," is reasonable, given that science may be in the middle of an ongoing debate about the "characterization" of a particular disorder. The debate in the literature about the validity of "Rape Trauma Syndrome" provides one example. Another area of contention about the combination test concerns its requirement that the illness be "serious" enough. The test does not specify what seriousness means in terms of intensity, permanence, and so on.

Finally, Campbell and Montigny proposed a "neutral observer" test, in which if one witnesses a traumatic event involving a person who is a relative, and the resultant psychological injuries are greater than what a neutral observer would be expected to objectively experience, then these injuries would constitute a sufficient basis for legitimate claims of psychological trauma. This test "restricts the scope of psychological harm to those cases which are so serious they eclipse what a person of normal fortitude would be expected to handle" (p. 155). This approach harkens to the hypothetical "reasonable person," often considered as a standard of comparison in court. At the same time, from the psychological point of view, it suffers from imprecision in defining "seriousness" of the injury and "reasonable fortitude" of the nonrelative normative observer. It also disregards the substantial case law regarding "thin skulls" and "eggshell personalities."

The difficulties posed in defining legally relevant terms, such as in the example just considered, constitute a major reason why, traditionally, case law had not accepted strictly psychological damages as an adequate basis for tort claims (Gabbay & Alonso, 2004; McLearen et al., 2004; Shuman & Hardy, Chapter 20, this book). Initially, the courts had found the issue so difficult to resolve that there had been a "physical contact or impact" rule that excluded cases of psychological harm alone. However, the past century witnessed advances in which the presence of physical injury was not necessary for a plaintiff to pursue a defendant for tortious conduct. The zone of danger and bystander or physical proximity rules broadened the range of tort cases. In particular, the California Supreme Court case of *Dillon v. Legg* (1968) allowed greater pragmatic consideration of "all the circumstances" in a claim for psychological harm in arriving at conclusions about cause (Shuman & Hardy, Chapter 20). Nevertheless, strict psychological damages typically are "much more difficult" to ascertain (McLearen et al., 2004), and courts are opting to treat mental harms more stringently than physical harms, and difficult to prove (Gabbay & Alonso, 2004). This is especially true where there are preexisting mental conditions that are involved or are exacerbated.

Both forensic and treating psychologists are called upon to offer evidence in tort claims. The latter should be fact witnesses only, and not provide expert opinion on the ultimate issue facing the trier of fact, that is, whether the plaintiff's alleged psychological harm had been proximally caused by the actions or inactions of the defendant. There are numerous problems when a treating psychologist attempts to be an expert witness (See Kane's Chapter 10). Forensic psychologists should address ultimate issues in their conclusions only if permitted or required to do so by a court or statute. Psychological tests, by themselves, cannot provide data that can directly answer this type of question; a comprehensive assessment is needed (Butcher, 2002).

Causality

Van Dorsten and James (2002) comment on the confusion in legal circles about causality-related terms. "It is somewhat difficult to analyze causation issues, because courts often use the terms and concepts of causation in inconsistent and contradictory ways" (p. 259). For the most part, the approach of the authors of the present book has been to use the term "causality" when either of the terms "causation" or "causality" would fit. Our approach fits with Haynes (1992), whose influential book on psychopathology included the term "causality" rather than "causation" in its title and ensuing discussion.

Ackerman and Kane (1998) addressed the issue of causality in psychological assessment of Posttraumatic Stress Disorder (PTSD) and personal injury. They indicate that cause does not have to be unique or exclusive for liability to be attached to it. They point out that, after arriving at diagnoses, if any, and making recommendations, the psychological evaluator might need to consider causality. "The law of torts indicates that the tortfeasor is liable whether the stressor caused the injury or aggravated a preexisting condition" (p. 578).

With respect to causality assessments or determination, Schultz has presented a comprehensive work (Schultz, 2003a, 2003b; Schultz & Brady, 2003a, 2003b). Schultz (2003b) indicated that "to date, no standards or even guidelines for answering causality questions have been developed" (p. 102). According to her, causality assessment or determination needs to avoid personal belief or judgment, intuition, art, practicing beyond the realm of science, assessing without scientific validation, and so on. Moreover, in the causality determination process, the legal question of causality needs to be appropriately translated into a psychological question. Research in the area "overemphasizes the issues of malingering and secondary gain detection" (p. 104), and may minimize the interaction of preexisting, injury-related, and concurrent factors. Also, causality determination frequently encounters problems and confusion "when the existing literature does not provide a clear scientific basis for the causal connection" (p. 105). She argued that, until there is a uniform process in causality determination, there is too much room for bias and a lack of scientific substantiation of offered evidence.

For Schultz, psychological causation is multifactorial, multifaceted, interactive, and not simply binary (yes or no) or linear (A caused B), contrary to the approach that appears in the legal sphere. Legal causality determination addresses proximate causation, or the degree to which "the *cause of action* constitutes a substantial factor in causing or exacerbating impairment" (p. 106). Temporal sequence by itself is insufficient to imply causation; there must be evidence of a significant or material contribution of event A as part of the multiple factors jointly contributing to result B. Causal determinations are usually retrodictive ("it did"), but also can be potential and predictive.

Schultz (2003b) explains that for the "thin skull" victim, the individual has some "preexisting vulnerabilities, weaknesses, or susceptibilities, which become activated or aggravated" by the event at claim (p. 109). The response severity to a stressor may significantly exceed the expected response of an individual with a "normal skull." In a related concept in the Canadian context, in particular, when the preexisting condition is active beforehand, or when it is latent but degenerative and is accelerated by the event, the concept of "crumbling skull" applies. In the latter cases, the courts consider the defendant only partially responsible and might award damages that reflect only the effect of the event, that is, the degree to which the plaintiff's condition had been worsened by the tortious act. (See the next chapter for a more complete discussion of thin and crumbling skulls.)

Psychological Issues and Causality

In this section, we provide an outline of forensic mental health assessment (FMHA) pertaining to causal determination, introduce the basic psychological injuries usually the subject of legal dispute (PTSD/distress, chronic pain and physical injury, TBI), including complicating factors in these areas such as malingering or the effect of participating in litigation, and address the issue of impairment and ability evaluation. The Canadian legal case of *Desbiens* (2004) has provided an interesting set of guidelines for the evaluation of catastrophic impairment, though, as a Canadian case rather than as an American appellate court case, it does not set a precedent for American cases. We emphasize that by using multifactorial, biopsychosocial models as guides in their assessments, psychologists improve chances for admissibility of the evidence that they offer to court.

Assessment

Heilbrun (2001), Heilbrun, Marczyk, and DeMatteo (2002), Heilbrun et al. (2003) and colleagues' integrative approach to FMHA is important to consider. In particular, it deals with the difference between nomothetic (population level) and idiographic (individual) data, and the manner in which they can be applied to causality assessment. This section also looks at the assessment process and diagnosis. The *DSM-IV* (*Diagnostic and Statistical Manual of Mental Disorders, Fourth Edition*) stands as the primary diagnostic manual, but is it accepted for court purposes, and how should the psychologist proceed in light of its shortcomings?

Forensic Mental Health Assessment

The psychologist must engage in a comprehensive assessment before arriving at any conclusions (Groth-Marnat, 2003). Unlike psychiatrists and other mental health professionals who may undertake analogous assessments, psychologists generally utilize psychometric instruments in their assessments. These instruments include self-report questionnaires addressing mood and personality attributes, and tests addressing intellectual levels, neuropsychological functioning, malingering, and so on, with some of the latter instruments containing scales that evaluate positive or negative impression management or their equivalent, response bias, and other threats to validity. Psychologists integrate the data from these instruments into their assessment formulations and conclusions.

Heilbrun (2001), Heilbrun et al. (2002), Heilbrun et al. (2003) and colleagues have elaborated principles of FMHA that consistently address causality (See also Chapter 10, this text, by Kane). Human behavior is considered multidimensional, and in FMHAs multiple sources of information should be used for each area assessed. Similarly, Schultz (2003b) espouses an integrative, multifactorial psychological causality determination process.

According to Heilbrun and colleagues (2002), in assessing clinical condition, functional abilities, and causal connection, FMHAs should use nomothetic evidence, defined as empirical evidence derived from populations similar to that of the individual being evaluated, using reliable and valid assessment instruments appropriate to the populations, and other appropriate sources of data. Nomothetic research provides scientific data, or an established empirical base, on (a) forensic measuring devices, such as tests and questionnaires, and on (b) base rates, outcomes, and so forth. It provides group norms on pertinent variables, allowing empirically supported bases for opinions about an individual's function or degree of impairment. In addition, research at the population level speaks to prediction of outcome, and how planned interventions can aid in management of symptom course.

In contrast to nomothetic evidence, idiographic evidence pertains to the information collected on a specific individual being assessed. The individual assessment should proceed like a scientific study, leading to the most parsimonious explanation after gathering all relevant data (including data on pre- and postevent capacities and functioning, and possible malingering and response styles such as symptom exaggeration or minimization). After the evaluation is completed and the data are gathered, the forensic assessor must continue to proceed in a scientific manner, considering all reasonably possible explanations in arriving at conclusions. The FMHA identifies the nature of the mental disorder, if any, the legally relevant functional abilities impacted in context, if any, and, just as important from a legal perspective, the strength of the causal connection between the two areas.

Legal standards may be overly broad and lacking in detail, not readily permitting the translation of legal criteria into defined forensic psychological capacities needing evaluation. For example, what exactly is meant by a work-related disability? In such cases, the operationalization of legal standards into psychological capacities to be evaluated should be based on the empirical literature. The use of scientific reasoning in idiographic formulation in an individual case informs the applicability of group level or nomothetic research to the case.

Along similar lines, Schultz (2003b) provides a list of best practice standards that should govern psychological causality determination. She advises (a) application of the biopsychosocial/contextual framework, (b) use of standardized methods, (c) use of multiple sources of information, including standardized instruments, (d) not only seeing the individual for her or his unique attributes, but also seeing population parameters such as base rates, (e) recognition of factors such as iatrogenic (medically generated) and litigation factors, and (f) evaluation of preevent (premorbid) levels.

Caution is advised in determining causality. "Some experts go to considerable lengths to dismiss the accident or event as a causal factor, and others to connect the two, whether warranted or not" (Faust & Heard, 2003b, p. 1729). Similarly, with respect to PTSD, in particular, Koch (2003) cautions against subscribing to myths or beliefs either inconsistent with the scientific literature or never investigated in it.

Greenberg (2003) indicated that the five basic tasks of a forensic psychologist in personal injury cases are to establish the baseline state before the harm occurred, the distress that may have been caused, the injuries and impairments that may result, the "likely psychological cause" of each one, and the treatment needed for each. There may be additional tasks related to liability—for example, whether the individual had reasonably attempted to reduce or mitigate the harm experienced. Is the stressor severe enough to significantly impair the average person, and is the reported impairment clinically consistent with what had been experienced? Greenberg added that a majority of individuals will "probably somewhat exaggerate" their impairments, and that this should not be interpreted as malingering of all claimed damages.

Diagnosis

Goldstein (2003) indicated that in personal injury cases, a *DSM-IV* diagnosis is not mandatory, but in practice Slovenko (2002a) indicated that a *DSM-IV* diagnosis normally is provided. There are primary compendia of psychiatric diagnostic categories: the American Psychiatric Association's diagnostic manual *DSM-IV-TR* (*Diagnostic and Statistical Manual of Mental Disorders, Fourth Edition, Text Revision*, 2000, with nearly all diagnoses identical to those in the *DSM-IV*, 1994) and the *ICD-10* (*International Statistical Classification of Diseases and Related Health Problems, Tenth Revision*, World Health Organization, WHO, 1992). The *DSM* is used in North American jurisdictions (although the *ICD-9-CM* is used for insurance billing purposes in the United States and the *ICD-10* in Canada). The *DSM* consists of a multiaxial system that allows for diagnosis of clinical disorders (Axis I), as well as personality disorders (or mental retardation) (Axis II). The third axis concerns associated medical factors. The remaining two axes permit identification of associated psychosocial and environmental problems and the individual's general level of functioning, respectively (See the next section, by Kane).

Shuman (2003b) points out the quandary faced by forensic practitioners who use the *DSM-IV* (1994, 2000) to render a diagnosis. Its descriptions of diagnoses were designed for clinical use, so there are risks of misunderstanding when it is transposed into the legal setting. Moreover, the deficiencies of the *DSM-IV* are readily challenged, including those concerning its reliability and validity. The dilemma for both psychologists and courts is that, despite its shortcomings, the *DSM-IV* represents the best diagnostic manual available to psychiatric and psychological practitioners.

Faust and Heard (2003a, 2003b) counsel prudence in forensic psychological assessments. Instead of using obtuse terms and language, forensic psychological evaluations should translate any diagnosed disorder or incapacity into objective, observable, functional language, having real-life or external correlates, or specified, concrete outcomes or achievements, which can be tested and verified or disconfirmed.

Three Areas of Psychological Effects of Trauma and Stress

In this section, the three basic psychological conditions considered in this book are introduced in terms of legal concerns and issues (PTSD, chronic pain, TBI; see Chapters 5–7). The area of psychological injury involves "damage or dysfunction in one's thinking, feeling, and behaving" causally related to an event at claim for damages (Schultz & Brady, 2003b). Koch, Douglas, Nicholls, and O'Neill (2006) add that the injury should "impair" both "function" and "well-being." The precursors might be stress, trauma, or real or imagined injuries or threats of injury. The cause is deemed legally compensable, that is, as significantly contributory or materially involved, rather than too far removed or too remote, in the proximate induction of the psychological harm that had resulted. The harm reaches critical thresholds of disturbance of "mental" or "emotional" "tranquility," that is, being put in a meaningfully worse condition requiring legally sanctioned restoration. The individual's degree of preexisting psychological difficulties, in terms of either latent predisposition or symptomatic expression, presents a baseline in establishing whether a meaningful alteration of mental-emotional tranquility had been induced.

Koch et al. (2006) indicated that for thresholds to be met, the claimed psychological injury must be harmful or serious enough. In some jurisdictions, examples serve to define serious psychological injury, for example, the individual has developed a phobia. Other jurisdictions refer to broader principles, diagnoses, and significance level. Yet other jurisdictions seek out behavioral markers of genuineness, for example, being on the verge of tears. This does not refer to the expression "pain and suffering," a manner of summarizing the effects of a tortious conduct for legal purposes but rather, refers to the typical person's ability to cope while attempting to engage in functional activity after having experienced a purportedly negligent or otherwise tortious act. The resulting distress must be "highly unpleasant" or severe. Koch et al. concluded that the term "psychological injury" is still met with skepticism in law, requiring extra burdens of proof.

Koch et al. described three types of psychological injuries: (a) mental or physical-mental ones, such as PTSD or depression due to the loss of part of the body, (b) neuropsychological ones, and (c) pain-related ones. Craig (2005) presented a slightly different typology of psychological injuries, focusing on worker's compensation claims: (a) physical-mental ones, in which there is an actual injury or disease compounded by psychological factors further disabling the individual; (b) mental-physical ones, in which a psychological factor such as excessive stress induces a physical problem; and (c) mental-mental ones, for example, a reaction to a trauma.

However, controversy abounds in the scientific literature in each of the three areas of psychological injury, complicating tort action. For example, PTSD has become a major focus in tort action yet, as a diagnosis, it is sometimes criticized. As for chronic pain, pain experience is not easily documented, nor is it necessarily correlated with known pathological effects. Finally, standardized neuropsychological evaluation does not necessarily address certain aspects of the effects of TBI, such as executive function. In the following, we only discuss some legal issues in the three areas, leaving a more detailed discussion for the literature review in Chapters 5–7.

PTSD

Slovenko (2002a, 2002b, 2003) indicated that the diagnosis of PTSD has spawned a growth industry in compensation and tort action. PTSD is a preferred diagnosis in tort litigation, relative to others like depression, because it is incident-specific, and simplifies the causation argument in the traumatic incident in question. Shuman (2002, 2003a) advised that, in diagnosing PTSD, the psychologist should avoid arguing that the presence of the PTSD "proves" the occurrence of the stressor that reportedly had functioned as its precipitating cause. Similarly, evidence of Rape Trauma Syndrome should not be used to support allegations of a rape having taken place. At the same time, Shuman cited court decisions where, contrary to this stance, evidence of PTSD has been admitted toward proving that a rape had occurred.

Pain

Chronic pain is not simply related to peripheral pathology, is subjectively experienced, and might be dismissed by medical practitioners, psychologists, other mental health professionals, defense attorneys, and even family members when there is little objective evidence consistent with continuing pain complaints. Research indicates that up to 85% of back pain patients have no identifiable pain-producing pathology, and that about 30% of individuals without back pain have significant pathology on scan data that would be expected to induce pain (Cocchiarella & Andersson, 2001). In cases of low back pain after a motor vehicle accident (MVA), Van Dorsten and James (2002) concur that there usually is an absence of physical findings to justify continued pain complaints. They add that healthy asymptomatic adults might show evidence of disc degeneration or disc bulging. Moreover, diagnosis is confounded by comorbidity, for example, if there is concomitant depression or other psychoemotional problems. Craig and Hadjistavropoulos (2004) point out that, although pain is subjectively experienced, this is no reason to dismiss pain reports as having no basis in objective reality, nor to consider them as reflective of a self-serving bias. Nevertheless, forensic assessors need to be especially prudent in evaluating pain chronicity for such undue influences and motivations.

Van Dorsten and James (2002) argue that the research on individuals pursuing financial compensation for the effects of personal injury does not support the argument that compensation-seeking status influences physical complaints and outcome. At the same time, plaintiffs may face disbelief about their complaints, which might act to increase the likelihood that they amplify their complaints in order to demonstrate that their injuries are "real." Van Dorsten and James mention that, in a jurisdiction in which compensation for pain and suffering had been eliminated, a rapid decrease in the number of whiplash claims resulted, and treatment led to improved prognosis (Cassidy et al., 2000; but see Merskey, 2003, and Nicholson and Martelli, this volume, Section III, for a critique of this study). Van Dorsten and James conclude that, in their assessments, psychologists have the ethical responsibility to examine the scientific literature, giving it more weight than they give to clinical opinion when both types of data are available.

How is it possible that physical injury and tissue damage, when objectively measured, do not predict pain experience in a dose-response relationship? Contemporary study of pain provides some answers. Melzack and Katz (2004) describe the gate control theory, which emphasizes (a) not only modulating gating mechanisms in the spinal cord but, also, (b) central control processes, or downward inhibitory influences from the brain to the spinal cord, and thus a dynamic, integral role for psychology in the pain experience. Melzack's work on phantom limb pain led to the "neuromatrix" model of pain, in which neural networks dynamically shape pain experience. Pain is multiply determined, including effects of stress on pain perception.

Mild Traumatic Brain Injury

Hartlage and Patch (2003) estimate that 1.5 million individuals each year in the United States experience brain injury residua, mostly from mild traumatic brain injury (mTBI). Van Dorsten and James (2002) note the difficulty in establishing valid base rates of premorbid neuropsychologically related abilities. At the same time, neuropsychological testing is limited in showing relations between specific test findings and postinjury behavioral abilities or inabilities (e.g., in self-care, child care, home care, socializing, and work aspects). Goodyear and Umetsu (2002) deal with the definition of mTBI, noting certain problems like the difficulty in evaluating retrospectively the duration of loss of consciousness and post-traumatic amnesia. [For a comprehensive discussion of definitional issues related to mTBI and related concepts such as postconcussive syndrome (PCS), see Barth, Ruff and Espe-Pfeifer (2006).]

For Goodyear and Umetsu (2002), when PCS is persistent, that is, when there is severe impairment after one year, psychosocial and related factors, including possible secondary gain, constitute the salient reason for that persistence. However, Hartlage and Patch (2003) argue that behavioral evidence indicates that there may be legitimate long-term residua due to effects of mTBI in a minority of victims. They suggest that the long-term damage in the brain is especially likely to be frontal in location, and involves progressive neuronal loss. Bigler (2003a) reviews the role of neuroimaging in forensic neuropsychological evaluation. New techniques are being developed that can trace objective, reproducible, and irrefutable evidence of lesions. These lesions can be related to neurobehavioral data in individual cases so that structure and function can be evaluated simultaneously. Neuroimaging has been subject to *Daubert* challenges but according to Bigler, has been accepted into evidence. When an individual sustains a brain injury documented by neuroimaging, defense neuropsychologists will often dispute the relevance of neuroimaging evidence.

Our own view is that it may be impossible to isolate the significance of any neurobiological evidence associated with persistent PCS from complicating factors such as depression, headaches, and job loss, and that such evidence is still in the experimental stage at the population level. As with others in the field, we call for more research.

Note that some areas in neuropsychological assessment are difficult to evaluate by standardized instruments. In frontal lobe dysfunction, it is difficult to obtain standardized instrument scores on executive dysfunction, which includes planning deficits, behavioral disinhibition, and apathy (Williams, 2003). Therefore, when evaluating frontal lobe dysfunction, the use of behavioral decision rules based on observation, and supported by knowledge of the literature, may be more important than data from psychometric test results.

Biopsychosocial Model

In all three areas under review, that of PTSD, chronic pain, and TBI, it is generally accepted that a multifactorial model of causality applies, whether it be in terms of considering preevent, event, and postevent factors, biological and environmental factors, vulnerabilities and stressors, and so on. Weissman and DeBow (2003) conclude that in psychology the biopsychosocial model is both conceptually grounded and empirically sound, so that it would qualify for admissibility under legal rules. The biopsychosocial model considers multiple interactive bases in causation at the biological, psychological, and social levels, rather than adopting a single factor approach. The framework is generally accepted, useful for elucidating specific causal factors, has acquired an acceptable scientific base, and thus is more likely to provide "reliable and probative bases" for opinions in psycholegal evidence. For example, it can help explain how acute low back pain can evolve into chronic back pain. This model is the one emphasized throughout this book.

Schultz and Gatchel (2005a, 2005b, 2005c) also adopt the biopsychosocial model in their handbook on disability, and even refer to "biopsychosocial disabilities" for injuries such as PTSD, chronic pain, and TBI, the areas most dealt with in our book. Schultz, Joy, Crook, and Fraser (2005) contrast the biopsychosocial model with the biomedical, psychiatric, labor relations, and insurance models of musculoskeletal pain-related disability. Each model has its advantages and limitations. As for the biopsychosocial model, despite its theoretical sophistication, Schultz and Gatchel maintain that it may be too complex to apply to simpler cases and may lead to a too broad scope of treatment. The needs of the individual must be determined on the basis of the specific parameters of her or his case.

Complicating Factors

The temporal course of a psychological injury that has been attributed to an index event may be influenced by the process of pursuing tort action. The litigation process might act to heighten felt symptoms. The complainant might engage in unconscious symptom amplification. The assessor might determine that there is outright conscious malingering. The litigation process functions as a double-edged sword, because it offers its own stresses beyond any induced by the index event in question, serving to exacerbate symptoms. Moreover, these stresses can relate to the inappropriate denial of claims as much as to self-induced symptom amplification for secondary financial gain.

Malingering

Halligan, Bass, and Oakley (2003a) have written an important book on malingering and illness deception. In their introductory chapter (Halligan, Bass, & Oakley, 2003b), they remind that standard psychiatric diagnostic classification systems do not consider malingering as a valid diagnostic disorder, only as an auxiliary code (in the *DSM-IV*, as a V-code). The authors define malingering as the intentional production of false or exaggerated symptoms by individuals motivated by external incentives. They present a sociolegal model of malingering in which malingering is considered as embedded in a broader phenomenon of willful deception in society. They provide the example of a disproportionate increase in work-related disability benefits in most countries with such systems available over the last 30 years, despite objective indicators that people's health has improved over the same time period. Because malingering cannot always be detected, psychological assessors need to consider the broader issue of illness deception, which may take place due to conscious choice and intent, through social deviance, through lack of morals, through subterfuge, or for monetary and other gain. Aylward (2003) indicates that the biopsychosocial model of disability does not sufficiently consider cases of conscious intent to deceive the system.

Rogers and Neumann (2003) concur that it is difficult to diagnose malingering, *per se*, and the behavior involved is quite similar to feigning, for example, in both one finds extremeness in presentation. Malingering appears to be part of a general adaptational stance to a difficult adversarial circumstance that includes a cost-benefit analysis. Faust (2003) argues that the search for an elusive "gold standard" in the assessment of malingering may be less fruitful than finding a less exact "silver standard." Sharpe (2003) advises to search for a range of inconsistencies in presentation to check for possible malingering and related motivations, although specification of intent to malinger remains "probably impossible." For example, the patient should be allowed to describe exhaustively her or his symptoms through open-ended questions rather than checklists. Main (2003) recommends that malingering should be determined by the court, not by the expert assessor. Exaggeration is not uncommon in pain patients and, therefore, interpretation is "particularly difficult." He distinguishes exaggeration with the intent to convince from the intent to deceive. He reviews various terms associated with the detection of malingering; even ones such as "low effort" need to be used with caution because of its association with terms such as malingering.

Zasler and Martelli (2003) report that numerous studies show a high incidence of response bias in medicolegal evaluations, where response bias concerns not only malingering but any "less than fully truthful, accurate or valid symptom report and presentation, whether deliberate or unconscious" (p. 34). For example, an individual may express undue sensitization to distress from mild, subtle, negligible, or benign symptoms. In symptom magnification, an individual may consciously or unconsciously exaggerate symptoms, for example, for psychological needs, financial reward, or as a "cry for help." Zasler and Martelli advise that, especially in medicolegal settings, assessment of response bias is critical.

Ferguson (2004) and Bordini, Chaknis, Ekman-Turner, and Perna (2002) have examined malingering in the context of neuropsychological evaluations. Malingering refers to the deliberate fabrication or gross exaggeration of symptoms, but it does not refer to adopting the sick role, nor does it refer to any nonintentional symptom/deficit production.

According to the *DSM-IV*, two or more of four features need to be present for malingering to be strongly suspected: referral by an attorney, marked discrepancies in test data and presentation, little effort/cooperation, and Antisocial Personality Disorder. Unfortunately, as they are presently described, the *DSM* criteria may lead the forensic assessor to attribute malingering to a client with legitimate reasons for poor effort and for attorney referral, for example. Rogers and Bender (2003) also criticize the *DSM-IV* for its lack of accurate criteria for the classification of malingering.

Iverson (2005) discusses the detection of malingering in civil forensic neuropsychological evaluations. According to Iverson, the *DSM-IV* defines malingering in an unsatisfactory way compared to the proposal in his chapter, first presented in Slick, Sherman, and Iverson (1999). Criteria are proposed for definite, probable, and possible malingering of cognitive dysfunction, and assessment methods are reviewed. Iverson notes that there is no one test that can assess malingering well, and, therefore, when malingering is diagnosed, it is a diagnosis of exclusion [See the section by Nicholson and Martelli for a critique of Iverson's approach to diagnosing malingering].

McLearen et al. (2004) cite evidence that in civil litigation involving neuropsychological-related assessment, the base rate of malingering may be as high as 40% (Larrabee, 2003). Malingering levels in neuropsychological assessment have been estimated to range from 2% to as high as 64%. Unfortunately, with different definitions of malingering, different samples studied, and different objectives of the research, comparing rates of malingering across studies is difficult.

Rogers and Bender (2003) consider that a defensive attitude brings denial or symptom minimization, which stands at the opposite end of the spectrum of malingering. Other response styles concern irrelevant responding, suboptimal effort, feigning, and dissimulation. The authors dispel the myth that malingering is common, yet at the same time suggest that it is not rare, with prevalence estimates around 15%, in general, but with variation across settings.

Malingering assessment strategies include detection of purported rare symptoms, improbable symptoms, rare symptom combinations, or too many severe symptoms, and also indiscriminant symptom endorsement, overendorsement of obvious symptoms of mental disorder, the display of erroneous stereotypes of mental disorder, and discrepancies between verbally reported and clinically observed symptoms. Measures of malingering may be embedded in larger psychometric instruments such as the MMPI-2 (Minnesota Multiphasic Personality Inventory, Second Edition; Butcher, Dahlstrom, Graham, Tellegen, & Kaemmer, 1989), or may stand alone, such as with the SIRS (Structured Interview of Reported Symptoms; Rogers, Bagby, & Dickens, 1992), which uses items related to all the above detection strategies, except for the one regarding erroneous stereotypes. Bryant (2003) concludes after his review of malingering in PTSD in personal injury that there is "little" empirical support for the many guidelines and techniques available. However, the standard of practice for forensic evaluators is to include at least one instrument to address both response style and the possibility of malingering, and many evaluators utilize more than one. The validity scales of the MMPI-2 are probably the most-utilized scales for this purpose.

Bush et al. (2005) presented the National Academy of Neuropsychology's position paper on symptom validity assessment, which includes malingering detection. According to them, symptom exaggeration or symptom fabrication takes place in a "sizeable minority" of neuropsychological assessments, with "greater" prevalence in forensic evaluations and, therefore, they must be adequately addressed. (a) "Symptom validity" refers to accuracy or truthfulness, (b) "response bias" to "attempt to mislead," (c) effort to "investment in performing," (d) malingering to "volitional production of false or exaggerated symptoms," and (e) dissimulation to "intentional misrepresentation or falsification of symptoms." The authors maintain that neuropsychological assessments in the forensic context performed without careful consideration of "motivation" are incomplete. [See the discussion of malingering in Nicholson and Martelli's, Section III, and Kane's chapters, Section II, in this book. The chapter by Iverson and Lange (2006) in Koch et al. (2006) is another useful source.]

Litigation

Call (2003) discusses the stressful nature of the legal process on personal injury claims. Kennedy (1946, p. 20) had written that "compensation neurosis is a state of mind, born out of fear, kept alive by avarice, stimulated by lawyers, and cured by verdict" (as cited in Call, 2003, p. 53). However, the bulk of the evidence disputes the claim that psychiatric symptoms improve after completion of the litigation process. Bryant and Harvey (2003) found that litigation status has little effect on the maintenance of PTSD, return to work, and so on. Nevertheless, Frueh et al. (2003) found that compensation-seeking veterans overreport or exaggerate their symptoms. Call (2003) argues that litigation does contribute to and maintain emotional trauma; it is "jurisogenic" or "critogenic," a term akin to "iatrogenic," which refers to harm caused by the medical process. We add that the whole insurance process, from starting a claim and treatment to going to multiple medical and other assessments to passing through tort action to potentially going to court, could be considered both a cardinal risk for symptom exacerbation due to stress and an additional traumatizing factor. (See the discussion of litigations factors in Sections II and III, this volume.)

Impairments and Disability

In this section, we address the crux of causality determination. The forensic assessor is confronted with the need to consider the impact of psychological effects of index events on the individual's functional roles, for example, in terms of work.

Psychological Injury

Schultz (2003a) calls the area of psychological injury a confused minefield or quagmire, with no clear guidelines, with myths, misconceptions, second-guessing, speculation, arbitrariness, tradition, and with an absence of scientific substantiation. For example, according to Schultz, the most widely used forensic definitions of impairment and disability are presented in the *Guidelines to the Evaluation of Permanent Impairment of the American Medical Association* (Fourth Edition; Cocchiarella, 1993; Fifth Edition; Cocchiarella & Andersson, 2001), but they "have not been specifically designed to describe the sequelae of psychological injury" (Schultz, 2003a, p. 66). Typically, then, psychological impairment is considered a "loss of, loss of use of or disturbance of psychological function." A disability concerns a present or future "alteration of an individual's capacity to meet personal, social, or occupational demands or statutory or regulatory requirements because of an impairment" (Cocchiarella & Andersson, 2001, p. 8). (Note. The terms "handicap" and "disability" had been used interchangeably, but the former term is being replaced by the latter.) Schultz (2005) describes that the AMA Guides' approach to disability relates it to the environment or context in which it is functionally expressed.

Peterson (2005) described the WHO's (2001) initiative of developing an *International Classification of Functioning, Disability, and Health (ICF)*, which attempts to clarify the meaning of the terms impairment, disability, and functioning. Impairment "represents a deviation from certain generally accepted population standards" of functioning (WHO, p. 12). Notice that this definition, as presented in the article, appears to refer to a comparison of the individual to population parameters, whereas the AMA approach implies a pre-post comparison in establishing the presence of impairment. In the forensic context, the AMA approach appears more appropriate, although, most probably, the two approaches should be blended in future approaches to definition and to research. Similarly, the WHO approach to the definition of disability may be too broad for the forensic context. "*Disability*, then, refers to any impairments, activity limitations, or participation restrictions or to 'the outcome or result of a complex relationship between an individual's health condition and personal factors, and of the external factors that represent the circumstances in which the individual lives' (WHO, p. 17)" (Peterson,

p. 106). Although the latter part of the definition is excellent, notice the difficulty of having included impairment as an example of a disability. Peterson (2005) describes that different degrees of activity limitations and participation restrictions are possible (mild, moderate, severe, complete, or 5–24, 25–49, 50–94, 95–100%, respectively). However, he does not specify which ones constitute critical alterations, because lower levels do not necessarily constitute disabilities. To conclude, Peterson contends that diagnostic information is of limited value in specifying functional outcome. Scherer and Glueckauf (2005) describe well the comprehensive nature of functional outcome that should be evaluated, including contextual, environmental, and personal factors as they interact with one's activities and participations. At the same time, Schultz (2005) offers the opinion that without a substantial body of research evidence, relevant definitions and methodologies in disability determinations of persons claiming disabilities will lack sufficient "relevance, reliability, and validity," thereby affecting "fairness."

Work Disability and Impairment

Schultz (2003a, 2003b) further addressed the relationship among psychological impairment, occupational disability, and causality determination. Schultz (2003a) remarked that psychological distress or cognitive disturbance, even if accompanied by a diagnostic clinical label, does not in and of itself specify impairment. "For an impairment to be identified, it must be behaviorally described in terms of dysfunction" (Schultz, 2003a, p. 67). When an impairment or behavioral dysfunction translates into functional limitations at work, an individual is disabled from the work to the extent that the limitation prescribes. One could be clinically depressed, for example, and still be able to discharge work performance responsibilities, so that there is no disability. Yet one could have a relatively minor psychological impairment, such as phobia of heights, which is not relevant to most vocational contexts, but for some others would be disabling (e.g., for a construction worker).

Perusal of the 2001 AMA Guides (Cocchiarella & Andersson, 2001) indicates that the mediating variable that translates an impairment into a disability is the degree to which the impairment induces functional limitations. We conclude that all sources ask the psychological assessor to clearly specify the functional limitations that obtain as a result of psychological symptoms, impairments, disorders, and so on, and clarify the reasons why the limitations constitute a disability, should that be the opinion offered. However, the task is fraught with complexity and difficulty, requiring the utmost prudence in disability assessment, along with sound knowledge of the scientific literature to buttress all arguments made in the formulation.

The 2001 AMA Guides (Cocchiarella & Andersson, 2001) speak to the issue of evaluating permanent psychological impairment. Four areas of functioning need to be assessed: activities of daily living, social functioning, concentration/persistence/pace, and deterioration/decompensation, or repeated failure to adapt to stressful work or work-like settings. Each of the areas needs to be evaluated for independence, appropriateness, and effectiveness. Psychological impairments are evaluated for severity, from mild to extreme. "Extreme" impairments (class 5) "preclude" useful function, and at the next level "marked" ones (class 4) "significantly impede" them. Schultz (2003b) suggests that the AMA should construct one rating system of psychological impairment for both psychological and neuropsychological conditions, because at present there are different (although very similar) systems in these two areas (We address this suggestion below).

Schultz (2005) adds that, because the AMA has blurred the distinction between impairment and disability, and the four areas of possible disability functioning are "not sufficiently defined," the reliable and valid assessment of possible disability is jeopardized. She argues that the practice of using ratings of disability impairment to estimate degree of disability is inappropriate. Rather, in evaluating work disability, one needs to consider preexisting and residual work capacity, coping skills, work motivation, work place characteristics and demands, possible need for work modification, accommodation, and change, and the predicted long-term capacity to persist in a return to work. We would add that the difficulty in obtaining work at a new company or in a new field, if this is necessary, would be especially difficult for an injured or once-disabled worker, in part because there may be implicit or even explicit employer prejudice against injured and once-disabled workers.

Catastrophic Impairment

The AMA Guides define a permanent physical impairment as one reaching "maximum medical improvement" "where it is well stabilized and unlikely to change substantially in the next year with or without medical treatment" (Cocchiarella & Andersson, 2001, p. 2). In the Guides, the criterion for permanent impairment is that the individual should have suffered a whole body impairment of 55% or a higher percentage. Specific criteria are provided for losses of physical function for each body part or system. Note that the definitions of physical impairments are not adjusted for psychological impairment. However, the Guides address evaluation of pain-related impairment. When the diagnosis is uncertain, pain-related impairment should not be rated. Otherwise, where the individual appears credible pain-related impairment can add up to 3% to the physically derived total body impairment.

A recent Ontario Superior Court decision has addressed the lack of specific guidelines in the AMA Guides for determining permanent psychological impairment, or a contribution of psychological impairment to permanent whole-body impairment (*Desbiens v. Mordini*, 2004, CanLII 41166 (ON S.C.)). The overview of the decision begins with the statement that the "gods of good fortune" had not been "kind" to the complainant. Desbiens had already been paraplegic before the MVA in question due to a spinal cord injury sustained in a fall from a roof. In his unfortunate MVA, while in his wheel-chair on the sidewalk, he was struck by a car that led to the wheel-chair being thrown 10 feet. Desbiens sustained a fractured right femur and other right-side injuries. The effects of the accident had deprived him of his relatively independent lifestyle. The plaintiff's position held that he was "catastrophically" impaired because (a) there had been an impairment of "55% or more," when the "whole body" is considered, as per the 1993 version of the AMA Guides, or (b) there had been a marked or extreme (class 4 or 5) "mental or physical disability." (The 55% level, and the definition of the classes are the same in the 1993 and 2001 editions of the Guides.) The justice noted that the Guides do not address quandaries presented by superimposition of acquired injuries on preexisting injuries, yet allow discretion in arriving at impairment percentages that "accurately reflect" real functional impairments.

In the case of the complainant, Mr. Desbiens, his whole-person percentage impairment was judged to have been 40% at the musculoskeletal level; however, the justice considered his preexisting paraplegia in determining that the superimposition of 40% had "grave" consequences for his real functional impairments, so that when considering the full picture, the catastrophic threshold of 55% was attained. Although the court had not addressed whether preexisting *psychological* impairments can be superimposed on preexisting ones, we suggest that the same logic should apply. This conclusion is strengthened by examination of the following analysis of the appropriate percentages for degrees of psychological impairment.

The fourth and fifth editions of the Guides do not ascribe percentages for degree of psychological impairment. However, in *Desbiens*, Allan Finlayson, a neuropsychologist, noted that the 1984 second edition of the Guides had provided estimates of ranges for degrees of psychological impairments: mild = 10–20%; moderate 25–50%; moderately severe 55–75%; and severe 75% or more. A related range is given in the fourth edition for emotional and behavioral disturbance due to dysfunction of the brain or central nervous system (CNS): mild = 0–14%; moderate 15–29%; severe 30–49%; and severe for all daily functions 50–70%. Finlayson had argued that, first, the qualification of the degrees of mental and behavioral disorders without CNS involvement uses similar adjectives (mild, moderate, marked, extreme; See above), and that, second, the psychological effects of brain and CNS dysfunctions refer to mental and behavior disorders. Therefore, the percentages applicable to the brain/CNS categories (0+, 15+, 30+, 50+ percent) should apply to the mental/behavioral ones. The justice accepted this logic, determining that Mr. Desbien's psychological impairments, which had been evaluated as moderate, had contributed another 25% to the whole-body impairment evaluation. That is, whole-body impairment should consider combined physical and psychological consequences, and the latter can be estimated.

Desbiens is an important court decision, because it more clearly specifies what is catastrophic impairment, what are degrees of psychological impairment, and what are their associated percentages of impairment. Further, it confirms that estimates of physical and psychological impairment percentages can be added together to arrive at evaluations of percentage of whole body impairment, and that preexisting factors need to be considered in arriving at estimates of whole-body impairment percentage.

Note that in *Desbiens* no estimate of the psychological contribution to functional limitations is offered for the mild, moderate, marked (severe), or extreme levels. Therefore, we propose on the basis of this that the percentages of impairment for brain/CNS dysfunction can function as appropriate anchor points not only in determining degree of psychological impairments in causality evaluations but, also, of psychologically-based functional limitations. Therefore, conservative estimates would be that in terms of estimated percentages of psychological impairments, the mild level can be as low as 0%, the marked level can never be at 55% or higher, the threshold level, and the extreme level may be lower than 55%, depending on its degree. That is, when psychological impairments alone are responsible for real functional limitations, the burden of proof on the plaintiff should be to demonstrate that more than a minimal degree of extreme impairment is evident. Finally, by evaluating the degree of psychological impairment that may have been present before the event in question, the evaluating psychologist can determine the manner in which postevent impairments have been superimposed on any preexisting ones, and whether the final combined state of preexisting and postevent impairments reach the grave, catastrophic threshold. A factor to consider is that, for any one plaintiff, the preexisting degree of psychological impairment may have been so high that any added postevent impairments needed to exceed the 55% level is minimal, reducing damages greatly, and perhaps to zero after consideration of contingencies or deductibles in the legislation involved.

Despite our suggested percentages of psychological impairment and psychological functional limitations for the mild to extreme levels, the critical question remains whether psychologists can effectively evaluate degree of psychological impairments/limitations and moreover, can they specify an exact percent in these regards. Also, can they arrive at these determinations with a degree of certainty sufficient for court purposes. To solidify the use of these percentages in court, it is recommended that guidelines be written demonstrating their reliability and validity, which will require an active research program.

Disability

In their evaluations, psychologists have difficulties with the accurate prediction of future strengths and weaknesses in abilities and behavior. "Thus, clinicians are faced with the issue of how to measure the degree or permanence of a mental disability, and this can be very difficult to quantify" (McLearen et al., 2004, p. 275). This difficulty is especially important for evaluation of future work capacity.

Occupational disability does not have one commonly accepted definition; it has been linked to inability to return to preevent employment, impaired work performance, duration absent from work, lack of employability, loss of earning capacity, and so on, as well as consideration of need for work-site corrections, modifications, or accommodations such as flexible hours (Schultz, 2003b). Occupational disability evaluation needs to include information about the individual's education, training, work history, transferable skills, adaptability, coping, motivation, job satisfaction, work-place factors, work demands, personal requirements, work modifications, and so forth.

Bryant (2003) added that even if an individual does not meet criteria for a psychological disorder, she or he might still be evaluated as impaired in functioning in any of a range of domains. Conversely, an individual evaluated as having a psychological disorder might still be able to function quite ably. Thus, as indicated throughout this book, it is the individual in context that must be evaluated, and recommendations must be based on that individual and her or his context.

Returning to Schultz (2003a), psychological tests generally have not been constructed with ecological validity, or applicability of findings for individuals to their particular real-life work sites (Sbordone, 2000). Positive motivation is difficult to measure, is especially context-dependent, and cannot be easily operationalized; moreover, the measures of its inverse, suboptimal effort, "often are incorrectly equated to detection of malingering" (Schultz, 2003a, p. 79). Overall, psychologists do not yet have precise disability assessment instruments. There are no commonly accepted measures of psychological work dysfunction. Also, it is difficult to tease out occupational disability due to pain vs. mental-based injury, depression, and related factors, which is problematic in jurisdictions and legal contexts that do not recognize the former as a basis for compensation in full or in part.

In terms of research on the relationship between mental disorder and occupational performance, there is a clear absence of well-designed scientific research (Schultz, 2003a). The forensic assessor has to extrapolate from this limited research base and hypothesize about the individual being assessed, thus potentially being at a "disadvantage in the context of the *Daubert* standard of admissibility of scientific evidence" (Schultz, 2003a, p. 74). Depending on the task undertaken by a forensic psychologist, she or he may need to coordinate with vocational experts and/or forensic economists.

We suggest that if the forensic psychologist undertakes a comprehensive, impartial assessment, can identify pre- and postfunctioning levels with respect to vocation, and can attribute the current, decreased, level to the incident or accident in question, not only may causal statements be presented but, also, reasoned predictions about future work capacity may be formulated. However, the psychologist needs to remain within the bounds of scientific knowledge after ascertaining that the individual being assessed has valid psychological dysfunctions.

In adducing evidence of disability from the research in the field, it is a truism that population-level investigations never capture the idiosyncratic intricacies of the individual case, including at the level of specific mechanism. More important, there are large gaps in the research that has been published in terms of what is needed for court purposes. This especially applies to insufficient prospective, well-controlled research of a long-term nature on functional impairment and outcome. The informed assessor will proceed cautiously at all these levels in determining disability. Koch et al. (2006) note that the assessor must logically demonstrate or trace a causal link or pathway between a deficit and the focus of the case, whether occupational, educational, social, or recreational functioning.

Dillman (2003) suggested that in cases of personal injury, occupational functioning might be affected in the domains of memory, concentration, social interaction, and adaptation to change (as summarized by Koch et al., 2006). Koch et al. (2006) add the domains of motivation/energy, decreased stress tolerance, and phobic avoidance (e.g., driving to work) to this list of what to consider in mediators of occupational functioning. We would add that where psychological injuries include Pain Disorder or pain conditions, physical limits become involved. Also, where job loss has taken place or vocation has to be changed, the psychological assessor needs to consider the capacity for retraining, succeeding at interviews once trained, keeping a job once hired, adjusting to less income (should that apply), and dealing with possible employer prejudice against injured or once-disabled workers.

Conclusions

Law and Psychology. In terms of causality assessment, the law and psychology exist in a collaborative but potentially tense relationship due to their differing training, regulations, ethics, and professional guidelines. Attorneys function in an adversarial system with the obligation to present the best case possible for their clients, whereas psychologists function in terms of adequately finding and describing the most parsimonious explanation of an individual's symptoms, irrespective of the side that has retained them in a legal dispute. Inevitably, the psychologist is exposed to biases, and the best manner in dealing with them is to conduct an impartial, comprehensive assessment in which she or he evaluates all reasonably likely factors that can influence conclusions offered to the court.

Haney and Smith (2003) differentiate between law and psychology. For example, law is authoritarian and conservative, but psychology is creative and empirical (data-driven). In seeking facts/truths, the methodology of psychology is scientific, but for the law it is adversarial. Psychologists are trained to be objective, but lawyers, in their adversarial stance, function from a built-in biased perspective. Law emphasizes certainty, predictability, and finality; psychology deals in probability, and attaching qualifiers and conditionals to statements. To better deal with legal matters, psychologists need to adhere to the standards and norms of their discipline, "not the dictates of the court" (Haney & Smith, 2003, p. 198). Miller (2003) concurs that psychologists may be subject to the biases of the side that retains their services.

Rogers and Shuman (2005) noted that the law assumes that people should be held accountable when they do not exercise sufficient control over their behavior as it relates to moral and legal thresholds. In contrast, psychology's theory of behavior is more "deterministic," "multi-determined," and geared to individual differences, which is a major theme of this book.

Other important differences between law and psychology relate to statistics and statistical concepts such as reliability and validity. (See below and Kane's discussion of these factors in Section II.) In psychology, reliability has a very specific meaning, relating to the degree of consistency of measurement by psychometric instruments (Groth-Marnat, 2003). For example, does an individual obtain similar scores on separate administrations of a test, or do two scorers arrive at similar results when scoring an individual's answers to a test. In contrast, for the law, reliability is akin to psychology's concept of validity. For example, in *Daubert*, reliability is defined as "trustworthiness" (See Chapter 10 by Kane, this volume). For psychology, validity refers to whether a psychometric instrument is accurate, measuring what it is intended to measure (Groth-Marnat, 2003). Other examples of differing conceptions for the same term in law and psychology indicate that we need to be alert to exact definitions of terms in the two professions, and care is needed in using them, especially when communicating across the professions (See Chapter 4 for presentation of an extensive dictionary of terms in the two professions, and suggestions for dealing with them).

Statistics are used in different ways in the two professions. Scientific experiments never *prove* a hypothesis; they can only support it or not support it. In a research study in science, if there are significant results in the empirical data, the "experimental" hypothesis that there is a significant difference across different conditions, groups, levels, and so on, is not directly accepted. Rather, the "null" hypothesis, that there is no difference across different conditions, groups, levels, and so on, is considered inapplicable, that is, it is rejected. Moreover, there is always an element of doubt or uncertainty about any significant result in the statistics presented in a scientific study. This relates to the "alpha level," or significance level, characterizing the results of a statistical test applied to the data to test the acceptability of a null hypothesis. Normally, psychologists choose an alpha level of .05, which specifies that for results found significant by application of statistical tests there is only a 5% or lower probability that the results obtained are due to chance rather than due to any direct effect in the study. That is, to simplify, in psychology a significant statistical result deriving from a study appears on the surface to have a 95% degree of certainty. When greater certainty is warranted, psychologists may consider that a result is significant only if it is likely to have been obtained by chance at a 1% level or less. This indicates that the convention of what should be considered significant according to statistics in a scientific study varies with the needs, that the alpha level chosen is not purely a mathematical decision.

In contrast, Greenberg (2003), Goldstein (2003), and Weissman and DeBow (2003) address the level of certainty that a *forensic* psychologist should consider in assessments of individuals, especially for personal injury cases, as opposed to evaluation of statistics applied to data gathered on a sample of subjects in a research study. They argue that, in arriving at conclusions about an individual in a psychological assessment, the preponderance of the evidence should support the conclusions offered; this is called "the more likely than not" standard, and the percentage of certainty that reflects it is anything greater than 50%. This is a far cry from the typical alpha levels of statistical significance in a scientific study (e.g., .05), but, nevertheless, the 50+% "more likely than not" level is the standard for personal injury cases in the legal system.

Overall Conclusions. Law and psychology form a system in which change in one profession affects the other. Psychologists improve their science and develop a stable fund of knowledge as they continue to expand it. The law expects that psychologists accrue ever-increasing knowledge through their population-level research but, at the same time, asks psychologists to apply this ever-changing fund of knowledge to arrive at definitive judgments in assessments of individuals, in terms of their impairments, disabilities, diagnoses, and so on. The law seeks to identify one proximate cause, or its absence, among the multifactorial determinants of behavior, whereas psychologists undertake multifactorial comprehensive assessments of all the behavior and test results needed to understand the individuals being assessed in effort to answer a referral question, and often they arrive at complex judgments of causality.

Psychologists become part of an adversarial legal system, offering evidence for or against the argument that an alleged event had fully or partly caused a psychological injury. They need to attempt to remain impartial, evidence-based, and scientific in their reasoning and methodology, despite the pushes and pulls from attorneys and a host of other biasing factors. Moreover, the law is not static, and psychologists need to keep abreast of its developments. For example, evidence law changed with *Daubert* (in 1993) and its progeny and consequent amendments to Federal Rules of Evidence. Psychologists should continue to provide input into the legal system in order to promote a better understanding of science and human nature and in order to assist triers of fact in their deliberations.

The following chapters of this section of the book explore the concepts of causality, causation, and related terms pertaining to psychological injury after exposure to a stressor or potentially traumatic event, and some recent research on the psychological knowledge that has accrued in the three areas crucial to forensic psychological assessments, those of PTSD/distress, chronic pain, and mTBI. Psychologists need to be familiar with both (a) the psychological literature in these areas and their legal implications, and (b) how to properly evaluate individuals reporting these types of psychological injury.

Appendix 1

Reliability and Validity in Assessment

Reliability. Groth-Marnat (2003) described the full range of reliability and validity concepts and indicators that are used in psychological instrument construction, and we present a brief overview. Psychological instruments vary from self-report questionnaires, to administered tests, such as for intellectual evaluation, to batteries comprised of many tests, such as used in neuropsychological assessment. In general, psychological instruments, tests, and self-report questionnaires that are standardized are first given to a normative, large, or relatively large sample that is representative of the population to which the instrument/test/self-report questionnaires are meant to be applied. The reliability of an instrument, test, or questionnaire refers its degree of stability, consistency, predictability, and accuracy. That is, will a score obtained by a person on a particular test be the same when it is readministered, or can two scorers agree on the score that should be assigned to a respondent's answers? There is a range of error, error of measurement, or range of random fluctuation, that can underlie a score on any test. There may be a certain degree of error or "noise" due to factors such as errors in reading, deviations from standardized administration, or respondent variation in mood, motivation, and so on. If the degree of measurement error is reduced, any difference in respondent scores on successive administration of an instrument will better reflect a "true difference." However, for tests that address emotions such as anxiety, respondents are more prone to variation across successive administrations. Moreover, psychological tests attempt to measure concepts that are often hard to operationalize. Therefore, some testing error is inevitable, but the goal is to minimize it.

Test reliability is indicated by correlational statistics, such as the Pearson product-moment correlation coefficient [*r*], which can range in value from −1 to +1 (e.g., an *r* of 1 indicates a perfect, positive correlation). Urbina (2004) indicates that estimates of reliability below 0.7 are considered "low" and, normally, in its construction with a standardized population, a test needs to have scores with a reliability correlation of 0.8 or more to be considered "trustworthy." Urbina indicates that "a reliability coefficient might be described as the correlation of the test with itself … such as two administrations of the same test, two versions of the same test, inter-item correlations, and so on—that *ought to be* highly consistent" (p. 137, italics in original). According to Groth-Marnat (2003), there are four primary ways of obtaining reliability estimates of a test—(a) test-retest: ascertains whether individuals obtain consistent results on successive administrations; (b) alternate forms: do individuals obtain similar results on different but comparable, parallel versions of the same test; (c) split half: are results internally consistent when the test is divided, for example, as in odd vs. even items; and (d) interscorer reliability: can scorers agree on which scores to assign to an individual's responses.

The amount of error associated with a test is estimated by a statistic called the "standard error of measurement" (*SEM*). Test scores consist of true and error components. The *SEM* estimates the range of the error. The higher a test's reliability, the less is its range of error. Theoretically, the *SEM* is a statistical index of the likely distribution of repeated scores of a test, were an individual to undertake such repeated administrations. It provides a range of scores, indicating the percent of times that an individual's obtained score has a chance of being lower or higher by the *SEM* value from the estimated true score. The error band is also called the "confidence interval."

Validity. Validity refers to whether a test measures what it is intended to measure, is accurate, and produces "useful" information. In developing a test, it must have a sound theoretical base, and its items must represent well the constructs to which they are aimed. For example, does a measure of intelligence quotient (IQ) correlate with school performance and, if so, does this permit us to say that IQ represents intelligence? There are three major methods of establishing validity.

(a) In *content* validity, the test constructor attempts to ensure the "representativeness and relevance" of the instrument with respect to the underlying construct. Items are selected by experts in a way that all major aspects of the needed content areas are covered, while respecting the different proportions of the areas. (b) *Criterion* validity concerns comparing test scores with a relevant "outside" measure. In the type of criterion validity termed *concurrent* validity, the outside measure is given at about the same time as the test of interest. In *predictive* validity, the outside measure is given at a time clearly after the test of interest. For example, with an intelligence test, an academic achievement test can be given at the same time or at the end of the year, depending on which type of validity is being measured. (c) In *construct* validity, the degree to which a test measures its underlying theoretical construct or trait is evaluated. For example, a test of anxiety should give results that correlate highly with behavior in an anxiety-provoking situation but not with behavior in a situation unrelated to anxiety. Or it should correlate with a similar test of anxiety (Note that this example does not refer to criterion validity, which concerns measures more removed than another measure of the same construct).

Factor analysis is a statistic used to assess construct validity, for it serves to find statistical groupings of items based on positive correlations of similar items, or to find items that clearly do not belong to specified groups, showing negative correlations with them. If the factors make sense, for example, a researcher finds that factors of anxiety and depression seem to emerge from a factor analysis of a test of psychopathology, the test is considered to possess *factorial* validity. Another method of establishing validity is to correlate subtest scores of a test with total scores, seeking "internal consistency." (In *face* validity, the items that had been selected by experts appear valid in the judgment of test users.)

Finally, by using *convergent* and *discriminant* validity checks, the test constructor establishes to what degree a test correlates positively with similar measures and poorly or negatively with dissimilar measures; for example, a test of reading comprehension should strongly correlate with a test of vocabulary but not a test of mathematics. Related to convergent and discriminant validity are the concepts of *specificity* and *sensitivity*. Test constructors address to what degree a test genuinely detects "true negatives" and "true positives," respectively. There is no simple formula for establishing a test's validity, but a variety of methodological and empirical steps need to be taken before it obtains results that can be respected as valid. Other validity techniques include discriminant analysis, and other validity types include *ecological* validity, where the degree of correlation with everyday, real-world function is established. For a more detailed analysis of psychological testing, the reader is referred to Anastasi and Urbina (1997), Groth-Marnat (2003), and Urbina (2004).

Instruments. To conclude, we mention several common psychological instruments. The first three relate to self-report questionnaires of common clinical symptoms encountered in this book, that of depression (Beck Depression Inventory, BDI-II; Beck, Steer, & Brown, 1996), posttraumatic stress (Detailed Assessment of Posttraumatic Stress, DAPS; Briere, 2001), and pain (Multidimensional Pain Inventory, MPI; Kerns, Turk, & Rudy, 1985). The next two concern the two most commonly used personality inventories, the MMPI-2 (Minnesota Multiphasic Personality Inventory, Second Edition; Butcher et al., 1989) and the MCMI-III (Millon Clinical Multiaxial Inventory-III; Millon et al.,

1994). (See discussion of these two tests by Kane, Chapter 10, this volume). Finally, two most common cognitive tests are the Wechsler intelligence and memory tests (the WAIS-III and the WMS-III; Wechsler Adult Intelligence Scale, Third Edition, Wechsler, 1997a; and the Wechsler Memory Scale, Third Edition, Wechsler, 1997b, respectively). The assessor should be on constant vigil about the reliability and validity of all such instruments; for example, for the WMS-III, according to the test manual, reliability and validity are considered adequate; however, results with closed head injury patients have shown unexpected memory patterns with lower visual memory indices than auditory ones (Wechsler, 1997c, p. 156). In Section II of this book, Kane further explores these issues.

References

Ackerman, M. J., & Kane, A. W. (1998). *Psychological experts in personal injury actions* (3rd ed.). New York: Aspen Law and Business.

American Psychiatric Association. (1994). *Diagnostic and statistical manual of mental disorders* (4th ed.). Washington, DC: Author.

American Psychiatric Association. (2000). *Diagnostic and statistical manual of mental disorders: Text revision* (4th ed.). Washington, DC: Author.

Anastasi, A., & Urbina, S. (1997). *Psychological testing* (7th ed.). Upper Saddle River, NJ: Prentice-Hall.

Aylward, M. (2003). Origins, practice, and limitations of disability assessment medicine. In P. W. Halligan, C. Bass, & D. A. Oakley (Eds.), *Malingering and illness deception* (pp. 287–300). New York: Oxford University Press.

Barth, J., Ruff, R., & Espe-Pfeifer, P. (2006). Mild traumatic brain injury: Definitions. In G. Young, A. W. Kane, & K. Nicholson (Eds.), *Psychological knowledge in court: PTSD, pain, and TBI* (pp. 271–278). New York: Springer Science+Business Media.

Beck, A. T., Steer, R. A., & Brown, G. K. (1996). *Beck Depression Inventory: Manual* (2nd ed.). San Antonio, TX: Harcourt Brace.

Bigler, E. D. (2003a). Neuroimaging in forensic neuropsychology. In A. M. Horton Jr. & L. C. Hartlage (Eds), *Handbook of forensic neuropsychology* (pp. 195–213). New York: Springer Science+Business Media.

Bigler, E. D. (2003b). Neurobiology and neuropathology underlie the neuropsychological deficits associated with traumatic brain injury. *Archives of Clinical Neuropsychology, 18*, 595–621.

Bordini, E. J., Chaknis, M. M., Ekman-Turner, R. M., & Perna, R. B. (2002). Advances and issues in the diagnostic differential of malingering vs. brain injury. *NeuroRehabilitation, 17*, 93–104.

Briere, J. (2001). *Detailed Assessment of Posttraumatic Stress: Professional manual*. Odessa, FL: Psychological Assessment Resources.

Brodsky, S. L., Caputo, A. A., & Domino, M. L. (2002). The mental health professional in court: Legal issues, research foundations, and effective testimony. In B. Van Dorsten (Ed.), *Forensic psychology: From classroom to courtroom* (pp. 17–33). New York: Kluwer Academic/Plenum.

Bryant, R. A. (2003). Assessing individuals for compensation. In D. Carson & R. Bull (Eds.), *Handbook of psychology in legal contexts* (pp. 89–107). Chichester, UK: Wiley.

Bryant, R. A., & Harvey, A. G. (2003). The influence of litigation on maintenance of Post-traumatic Stress Disorder. *The Journal of Nervous and Mental Disease, 191*, 191–193.

Bush, S. S., Ruff, R. M., Tröster, A. I., Barth, J. T., Koffler, S. P., Pliskin, N. H., Reynolds, C. R., & Silver, C. H. (2005). Symptom validity assessment: Practice issues and medical necessity. *Archives of Clinical Neuropsychology, 20*, 419–426.

Butcher, J. N. (2002). Assessment in forensic practice: An objective approach. In B. Van Dorsten (Ed.), *Forensic psychology: From classroom to courtroom* (pp. 65–81). New York: Kluwer Academic/Plenum.

Butcher, J. N., Dahlstrom, W. G., Graham, J. R., Tellegen, A., & Kaemmer, B. (1989). *Minnesota Multiphasic Personality Inventory-2 (MMPI-2): Manual for administration and scoring*. Minneapolis, MN: University of Minnesota Press.

Call, J. A. (2003). Liability for psychological injury: History of the concept. In I. Z. Schultz & D. O. Brady (Eds.), *Psychological injuries at trial* (pp. 40–64). Chicago, IL: American Bar Association.

Campbell, D. S., & Montigny, C. (2004). Psychological harm and tort law: Reassessing the legal test for liability. In T. Archibald & M. Cochrane (Eds.), *Annual review of civil litigation: 2003* (pp. 133–155). Toronto, ON: Thomson/Carswell.

Cassidy, J. D., Carroll, L. J., Côté, P., Lemstra, M., Berglund, A., & Nygren, A. (2000). Effect of eliminating compensation for pain and suffering on the outcome of insurance claims for whiplash injury. *New England Journal of Medicine, 342*, 1179–1186.

Cocchiarella, L. (Ed.) (1993). *Guides to the evaluation of permanent impairment* (4th ed.). Chicago, IL: American Medical Association.

Cocchiarella, L., & Andersson, G. B. J. (Eds.). (2001). *Guides to the evaluation of permanent impairment* (5th ed.). Chicago, IL: American Medical Association.

Craig, K. D., & Hadjistavropoulos, T. (2004). Psychological perspective on pain: Controversies. In T. Hadjistavropoulos & K. D. Craig (Eds.), *Pain: Psychological perspectives* (pp. 303–326). Mahwah, NJ: Erlbaum.

Craig, R. J. (2005). *Personality-guided forensic psychology*. Washington, DC: American Psychological Association.

Daller, M. F. (2000). *Tort law desk reference: A fifty state compendium*. New York: Aspen Law and Business.

Daubert v. Merrell Dow Pharmaceuticals, Inc. 509 U.S. 579, 113 S.Ct. 2786, 125 L.Ed. 2d 469 (1993).

Desbiens v. Mordini, 2004 CanLII 41166 (ON S.C.).

Dillman, E. G. (2003). Impairment to earning capacity based on psychological findings. In I. Z. Schultz & D. O. Brady (Eds.), *Psychological injuries at trial* (pp. 342–356). Washington, DC: American Bar Association.

Dillon v. Legg, 441 P.2d 912 (Cal. 1968).

Faigman, D. L. (2003). Expert evidence: The rules and the rationality the law applies (or should apply) to psychological expertise. In D. Carson & R. Bull (Eds.), *Handbook of psychology in legal contexts* (pp. 367–400). Chichester, UK: Wiley.

Faust, D. (2003). Alternatives to four clinical and research traditions in malingering detection. In P. W. Halligan, C. Bass, & D. A. Oakley (Eds.), *Malingering and illness deception* (pp. 107–121). New York: Oxford University Press.

Faust, D., & Heard, K. V. (2003a). Objectifying subjective injury claims. In I. Z. Schultz & D. O. Brady (Eds.), *Psychological injuries at trial* (pp. 1686–1705). Chicago, IL: American Bar Association.

Faust, D., & Heard, K. V. (2003b). Biased experts: Some practical suggestions for identifying and demonstrating unfair practices. In I. Z. Schultz & D. O. Brady (Eds.), *Psychological injuries at trial* (pp. 1706–1739). Chicago, IL: American Bar Association.

Federal Rules of Evidence. (2004). Washington, DC: U.S. Government Printing Office. Retrieved January 18, 2005, from http://www.house.gov/judiciary/evid2004.pdf.

Ferguson, K. E. (2004). Detecting malingering in forensic neuropsychological evaluations in litigants with mild traumatic brain injury. In W. T. O. Donohue & E. R. Levensky (Eds.), *Handbook of forensic psychology* (pp. 301–314). Amsterdam: Elsevier.

Frueh, B. C., Elhai, J. D., Gold, P. B., Monnier, J., Magruder, K. M., Keane, T. M., & Arana, A. (2003). Disability compensation seeking among veterans evaluated for Posttraumatic Stress Disorder. *Psychiatric Services, 54*, 84–91.

Frye v. United States, 293 F. 1013, 34 ALR 145 (D. C. Cir. 1923).

Gabbay, V., & Alonso, C.M. (2004). Legal aspects related to PTSD in children and adolescents. In R. R. Silva (Ed.), *Posttraumatic Stress Disorder in children and adolescents: Handbook* (pp. 60–82). New York: Norton.

General Electric Co. v. Joiner, 522 U.S. 136, 118 S.Ct. 512 (1997).

Gold, A. D. (2003). *Expert evidence in criminal law: The scientific approach*. Toronto, ON: Irwin Law.

Goldstein, A. M. (2003). Overview of forensic psychology. In I. B. Weiner (Series Ed.) & A. M. Goldstein (Vol. Ed.), *Handbook of psychology: Vol. 11, Forensic psychology* (pp. 3–20). Hoboken, NJ: Wiley.

Goodyear, B., & Umetsu, D. (2002). Selected issues in forensic neuropsychology. In B. Van Dorsten (Ed.), *Forensic psychology: From classroom to courtroom* (pp. 283– 313). New York: Kluwer Academic/Plenum.

Greenberg, S. A. (2003). Personal injury examinations in torts for emotional distress. In I. B. Weiner (Series Ed.) & A. M. Goldstein (Vol. Ed.), *Handbook of psychology: Vol. 11, Forensic psychology* (pp. 233–257). Hoboken, NJ: Wiley.

Groth-Marnat, G. (2003). *Handbook of psychological assessment* (4th ed.). Hoboken, NJ: Wiley.

Halligan, P. W., Bass, C., & Oakley, D. A. (Eds.). (2003a). *Malingering and illness deception*. New York: Oxford University Press.

Halligan, P. W., Bass, C., & Oakley, D. A. (2003b). Willful deception as illness behaviour. In P. W. Halligan, C. Bass, & D. A. Oakley (Eds.), *Malingering and illness deception* (pp. 3–28). New York: Oxford University Press.

Haney, C., & Smith, A. (2003). Science, law, and psychological injury: The *Daubert* standards and beyond. In I. Z. Schultz & D. O. Brady (Eds.), *Psychological injuries at trial* (pp. 184–210). Chicago, IL: American Bar Association.

Hartlage, L. C., & Patch, P. C. (2003). Epidemiology of traumatic brain injury. In A. M. Horton Jr. & L. C. Hartlage (Eds.), *Handbook of forensic neuropsychology* (pp. 181– 193). New York: Springer Science+Business Media.

Haynes, S. N. (1992). *Models of causality in psychopathology: Toward dynamic, synthetic and nonlinear models of behavior disorders*. New York: Macmillan.

Heilbrun, K. (2001). *Principles of forensic mental health assessment*. New York: Kluwer Academic/Plenum.

Heilbrun, K., Marczyk, G. R., & DeMatteo, D. (Eds.). (2002). *Forensic mental health assessment: A casebook*. New York: Oxford University Press.

Heilbrun, K., Marczyk, G. R., DeMatteo, D., Zillmer, E. A., Harris, J., & Jennings, T. (2003). Principles of forensic mental health assessment: Implications for neuropsychological assessment in forensic contexts. *Assessment, 10*, 329–343.

Iverson, G. L. (2005). Outcome from mild traumatic brain injury. *Journal of Neuropsychiatry, 18*, 301–317.

Iverson, G. L., & Lange, R. T. (2006). Detecting exaggeration and malingering in psychological injury claims. In W. J. Koch, K. S. Douglas, T. L. Nicholls, & M. L. O'Neill (Eds.), *Psychological injuries: Forensic assessment, treatment, and law* (pp. 76–112). Oxford, UK: Oxford University Press.

Jenkins v. United States, 307 F.2d 637 (D.C. Cir. 1962).

Kennedy, F. (1946). The mind of the injured worker: Its effects on disability periods. *Compensation Medicine, 1*, 19.

Kerns, R. D., Turk, D. C., & Rudy, T. E. (1985). The Westhaven-Yale Multidimensional Pain Inventory (WHYMPI). *Pain, 23*, 345–356.

Koch, W. J. (2003). Posttraumatic Stress Disorder following motor vehicle accidents: Clinical forensic guidelines. In I. Z. Schultz & D. O. Brady (Eds.), *Psychological injuries at trial* (pp. 794–819). Chicago, IL: American Bar Association.

Koch, W. J., Douglas, K. S., Nicholls, T. L., & O'Neill, M. L (2006). *Psychological injuries: Forensic assessment, treatment, and law.* Oxford, UK: Oxford University Press.

Kumho Tire Co. v. Carmichael, 526 U.S. 137, 119 S.Ct. 1167 (1999).

Larrabee, G. J. (2003). Detection of malingering using neuropsychologically atypical performance patterns on standard neuropsychological tests. *Clinical Neuropsychologist. 17*(3), 410–425.

Main, C. J. (2003). The nature of chronic pain: A clinical and legal challenge. In P. W. Halligan, C. Bass, & D. A. Oakley (Eds.), *Malingering and illness deception* (pp. 171–183). New York: Oxford University Press.

McLearen, A. M., Pietz, C. A., & Denney, R. L. (2004). Evaluation of psychological damages. In W. T. O'Donohue & E. R. Levensky (Eds.), *Handbook of forensic psychology: Resource for mental health and legal professionals* (pp. 267–299). New York: Elsevier.

Melton, G. B., Petrilla, J., Poythress, N. G., & Slobogin, C. (1997). Law and the mental health professions: An uneasy alliance. *Psychological evaluations for the courts.* New York: Guilford.

Melzack, R., & Katz, J. (2004). The gate control theory: Reaching for the brain. In T. Hadjistavropoulos & K. D. Craig (Eds.), *Pain: Psychological perspectives* (pp. 13–34). Mahwah, NJ: Erlbaum.

Melzack, R., & Wall, P. D. (1965). Pain mechanisms: A new theory. *Science, 150*, 971–979.

Merskey, H. (2003). Research paradigms in psychosomatic medicine with special emphasis on whiplash-Cervical Hyperextension Flexion Injury (CHFI). *Pain Research & Management, 8*, 13–18.

Miller, M. W. (2003). Personality and the etiology and expression of PTSD: A three-factor model perspective. *Clinical Psychology: Science and Practice, 10*, 373–393.

Millon, T., Millon, C., & Davis, R. (1994). *Millon Clinical Multiaxial Inventory-III: Manual.* Minneapolis, MN: National Computer Systems.

Nicholson, K., & Martelli, M. F. (2006). The confounding effects of pain, psychoemotional problems or psychiatric disorder, premorbid ability structure, and motivational or other factor on neuropsychological test performance. In G. Young, A. W. Kane, & K. Nicholson (Eds.), *Psychological knowledge in court: PTSD, pain, and TBI* (pp. 335–351). New York: Springer Science+Business Media.

Peterson, D. B. (2005). International classification of functioning, disability, and health: An introduction for rehabilitation psychologists. *Rehabilitation Psychology, 50*, 105–112.

Rogers, R., Bagby, R. M., & Dickens, S. E. (1992). *Structured Interview of Reported Symptoms: Professional manual.* Lutz, FL: Psychological Assessment Resources.

Rogers, R., & Bender, S. D. (2003). Evaluation of malingering and deception. In I. B. Weiner (Series Ed.) & A. M. Goldstein (Vol. Ed.), *Handbook of psychology: Vol. 11, Forensic psychology* (pp. 109–129). Hoboken, NJ: Wiley.

Rogers, R., & Neumann, C. S. (2003). Conceptual issues and explanatory models of malingering. In P. W. Halligan, C. Bass, & D. A. Oakley (Eds.), *Malingering and illness deception* (pp. 71–82). New York: Oxford University Press.

Rogers, R., & Shuman, D. W. (2005). *Fundamentals of forensic practice: Mental health and criminal law*. New York: Springer Science+Business Media.

R. v J-L.J. [2000] 2 S.C.R. 600, 2000 SCC 51 (CanLII).

R. v. Mohan [1994] 2 S.C.R. 9, 1994 CanLII 80 (S.C.C.).

Saxe, L., & Ben-Shakhar, G. (1999). Admissibility of polygraph tests: The application of scientific standards post-*Daubert*. *Psychology, Public Policy, and Law, 5*, 203–223.

Sbordone, R. J. (2000). The executive functions of the brain. In G. Groth-Marnat (Ed.), *Neuropsychological assessment in clinical practice: A practice guide to test interpretation and integration* (pp. 437–456). New York: Wiley.

Scherer, M. J., & Glueckauf, R. (2005). Assessing the benefits of assistive technologies for activities and participation. *Rehabilitation Psychology, 50*, 132–141.

Schultz, I. Z. (2003a). The relationship between psychological impairment and occupational disability. In I. Z. Schultz & D. O. Brady (Eds.), *Psychological injuries at trial* (pp. 65–101). Chicago, IL: American Bar Association.

Schultz, I. Z. (2003b). Psychological causality determination in personal injury and workers' compensation contexts. In I. Z. Schultz & D. O. Brady (Eds.), *Psychological injuries at trial* (pp. 102–125). Chicago, IL: American Bar Association.

Schultz, I. Z. (2005). Impairment of occupational disability in research and practice. In I. Z. Schultz & R. J. Gatchel (Eds.), *Handbook of complex occupational disability claims: Early risk identification, intervention, and prevention* (pp. 25–41). New York: Springer Science+Business Media.

Schultz, I. Z., & Brady, D. O. (Eds.). (2003a). *Psychological injuries at trial*. Chicago, IL: American Bar Association.

Schultz, I. Z., & Brady, D. O. (2003b). Preface: Definition and introduction to psychological injuries. In I. Z. Schultz & D. O. Brady (Eds.), *Psychological injuries at trial* (pp. 13–17). Chicago, IL: American Bar Association.

Schultz, I. Z., & Gatchel, R. J. (Eds.). (2005a). *Handbook of complex occupational disability claims: Early risk identification, intervention, and prevention*. New York: Springer Science+Business Media.

Schultz, I. Z., & Gatchel, R. J. (2005b). Introduction. In I. Z. Schultz & R. J. Gatchel (Eds.), *Handbook of complex occupational disability claims: Early risk identification, intervention, and prevention* (pp. 1–3). New York: Springer Science+Business Media.

Schultz, I. Z., & Gatchel, R. J. (2005c). Research and practice directions in risk for disability prediction and early intervention. In I. Z. Schultz & R. J. Gatchel (Eds.), *Handbook of complex occupational disability claims: Early risk identification, intervention, and prevention* (pp. 523–539). New York: Springer Science+Business Media.

Schultz, I. Z., Joy, P. W., Crook, J., & Fraser, K. (2005). Models of diagnosis and rehabilitation in musculoskeletal pain-related occupational disability. In I. Z. Schultz & R. J. Gatchel (Eds.), *Handbook of complex occupational disability claims: Early risk identification, intervention, and prevention* (pp. 43–65). New York: Springer Science+Business Media.

Sharpe, M. (2003). Distinguishing malingering from psychiatric disorders. In P. W. Halligan, C. Bass, & D. A. Oakley (Eds.), *Malingering and illness deception* (pp. 156–170). New York: Oxford University Press.

Shuman, D. W. (2002). Retrospective assessment of mental states and the law. In R. I. Simon & D. W. Shuman (Eds.), *Retrospective assessment of mental states in litigation: Predicting the past* (pp. 21–45). Washington, DC: American Psychiatric Association.

Shuman, D. W. (2003a). Persistent re-experiences in psychiatry and law: Current and future trends for the role of PTSD in litigation. In R. I. Simon (Ed.), *Posttraumatic Stress Disorder in litigation* (2nd ed., pp. 1–18). Washington, DC: American Psychiatric Publishing.

Shuman, D. W. (1994, 2003 supplement (2003b)). *Psychiatric and psychological evidence* (2nd ed.). New York: Thomson West.

Shuman, D. W., & Sales, B. D. (2003). The impact of *Daubert* and its progeny on the admissibility of behavioral and social science evidence. In I. Z. Schultz & D. O. Brady (Eds.), *Psychological injuries at trial* (pp. 168–183). Chicago, IL: American Bar Association.

Slick, D. J., Sherman, E. M. S., & Iverson, G. L. (1999). Diagnostic criteria for malingering neurocognitive dysfunction: Proposed standards for clinical practice and research. *Clinical Neuropsychologist, 13*, 545–561.

Slovenko, R. (2002a). *Psychiatry in law/law in psychiatry: Law in psychiatry*. New York: Brunner-Routledge.

Slovenko, R. (2002b). *Psychiatry in law/law in psychiatry: Psychiatry in law*. New York: Brunner-Routledge.

Slovenko, R. (2002c). Causation in law and psychiatry. In I. Freckelton & D. Mendelson (Eds.), *Causation in law and medicine* (pp. 357–378). Burlington, VT: Ashgate/Dartmouth.

Slovenko, R. (2003). Introduction. In R. I. Simon (Ed.), *Posttraumatic Stress Disorder in litigation: Guidelines for forensic assessment* (2nd ed., pp. ixx–xxiv). Washington, DC: American Psychiatric Publishing.

Trimble, M. (2004). *Somatoform disorders: A medicolegal guide*. New York: Cambridge University Press.

Urbina, S. (2004). *Essentials of psychological testing*. Hoboken, NJ: Wiley.

Van Dorsten, B. (2002). Forensic psychology: Decades of progress and controversy. In B. Van Dorsten (Ed.), *Forensic psychology: From classroom to courtroom* (pp. 1– 16). New York: Kluwer Academic/Plenum.

Van Dorsten, B., & James, L. B. (2002). Forensic medical psychology: Personal injury litigation. In B. Van Dorsten (Ed.), *Forensic psychology: From classroom to* courtroom (pp. 247–282). New York: Kluwer Academic/Plenum.

Wechsler, D. (1997a). *Wechsler Adult Intelligence Scale-III: Administration and scoring manual*. San Antonio, TX: The Psychological Corporation.

Wechsler, D. (1997b). *Wechsler Memory Scale—Third Edition: Administration and scoring manual*. San Antonio, TX: The Psychological Corporation.

Wechsler, D. (1997c). *Wechsler Adult Intelligence Scale-III, Wechsler Memory Scale: Technical manual*. San Antonio, TX: The Psychological Corporation.

Weissman, H. N., & DeBow, D. M. (2003). Ethical principles and professional competencies. In I. B. Weiner (Series Ed.) & A. M. Goldstein (Vol. Ed.), *Handbook of psychology: Vol. 11, Forensic psychology* (pp. 33–53). Hoboken, NJ: Wiley.

Williams, A. D. (2003). Diagnostic decision making in neuropsychology. In A. M. Horton Jr. & L. C. Hartlage (Eds.), *Handbook of forensic neuropsychology* (pp. 113–136). New York: Springer Science+Business Media.

Woolf, Rt Hon. Lord (1996). *Access to justice: Final report*. London: HMSO.

World Health Organization. (1992). *International classification of diseases. Mental and behavioral disorders (including disorders of psychological development)*, clinical descriptions and diagnostic guidelines (10th rev.). Geneva, Switzerland: Author.

World Health Organization. (2001). *International classification of functioning, disability, and health (ICF)*. Geneva, Switzerland: Author.

Zasler, N. D., & Martelli, M. F. (2003). Mild traumatic brain injury: Impairment and disability assessment caveats. *Neuropsychological Rehabilitation, 13*, 31–41.

3

Causality: Concepts, Issues, and Recommendations

GERALD YOUNG

Civil law seeks to determine responsibility for wrongdoing and appropriate compensation for individuals who have been wronged. It considers psychology an adjunct profession in this endeavor, with psychologists offering evidence to help the trier of fact arrive at just decisions. The law treats causality and causation from the perspective of this overall orientation. When a defendant is accused of wrongfully causing a certain outcome, the legal system marshals its resources to either prove causality or defend against the accusations. In terms of civil (tort) cases, this usually refers to personal injury, negligence, or malpractice, and there may be judgments of liability and subsequent awards for damages and compensation. Romano (1999) underscores that causation is intrinsic to virtually every case that an attorney will ever handle. Freckelton (2002) concurs, even indicating that causation is central to most litigation: "Proof of causation lies at the very heart of the resolution of most civil and criminal litigation" (p. 478).

The terms "causality" and "causation" are defined similarly in the lay dictionary, with "causality" defined in a more general way as the relationship between cause and effect, whereas "causation" is defined as the act or process of causing (Oxford; Jewell & Abate, 2001; Merriam-Webster, 2003). However, in common usage, the legal professions and mental health professionals interchange the terms, and do not keep the implied distinction that one should be used more as a product and the other as a process. In this chapter, I examine the concept of causality as it is treated in philosophy, the law, medicine, and psychology. I also present the concepts of "thin" and "crumbling" skulls, because they allow a bridge between law and psychology. The chapter terminates with suggestions, including how to standardize terminology, and presents a causality scale and a list of 25 causality factors for consideration in arriving at conclusions in evidence offered in court.

Causality and Causation in Different Disciplines

Causality and Causation in Philosophy

The ancients considered behavior as beyond human control, although causality has been a concern from the earliest writings, as evidenced by the Biblical stories of original sin, Adam, Eve, the apple, and the snake (Pearl, 2000). In Western philosophy, the Greeks were first to consider the issue of causality. Aristotle described four causes: material, formal, efficient, and final. Efficient causes refer to those external agents held responsible for a particular event or phenomenon (Haynes, 1992). The types of efficient cause that have been suggested include those that are sufficient, insufficient, necessary, necessary and sufficient, first (in a chain), principal (primary), immediate (no other intervenes), and mediate (a cause that works only through another). To make a valid inference of causality, conditions such as covariation, temporal precedence, logical connection, and whether there is an equally plausible explanation need to be considered.

The study of causality in philosophy is marked by inconsistency as much as if not more than in the legal and psychological fields. Aristotle criticized Plato for having a restricted view of causality (Cocchiarella & Lord, 2001). Flew and Priest (2002) argue that only efficient causality (defined as the agency producing the result) among the four causes in Aristotle's doctrine directly concerns causality. In contrast, Craig (1998) argues that the four causes all play roles in causal explanation. Haynes (1992) stated that for centuries the concept of causality in philosophy was subject to divergent opinion, discourse, and "impassioned debate." Different schools exist with respect to understanding causal connections, from those that argue that, because they are inferred from perceptions they can always be invalidated, to those that are more realist and positivist, indicating that the connections exist beyond any perception and we need to find the best ways of observing and measuring them (Haynes, 1992). Blackburn (1994) points out that some philosophers deny causation, because of ambiguity in the concept of link (e.g., Hume). This tradition continued into the past century, where Russell (1910, 1918, 1950) labeled the law of causality a "relic" (Psillos, 2002). Pearl (2000) points out that "causality is a notion shrouded in mystery, controversy, and caution, because scientists and philosophers have had difficulty defining when one event *truly causes* another" (p. 331). The law, however, requires that causality be identified, so that responsibility can be assigned to a wrongdoer.

Schultz (2003b) argues that the definition of causality that best applies to the forensic context is not clear. She indicates that three philosophical views of causality may apply to the medicolegal context. First, Aristotle's concept of efficient cause indicates that one event necessitates the other, in a cause and effect relation. Second, causes may exist in the plural, as sets of conditions that jointly necessitate an outcome. Third, in the counterfactual definition, cause is inferred by arguing that the effect would not occur if the causal event had not taken place. Haack (2005), writing on the philosophy of science implicit in the *Daubert* trilogy (*Daubert v. Merrill Dow Pharmaceuticals, Inc., 1993*; see the next section, by

Kane), indicates that evidence proferred to court is interrelated, interlocked, and intersected in a whole greater than the sum of the parts, presaging our discussion of the importance of having a multifactorial model of causality.

Epistemology is a branch of philosophy dealing with ways of knowing. Ozonoff (2005a) indicates that the rational, formal, essential view of knowledge acquisition is a "top-down" one, in which positivist, objective inquiry, observation, testing, and experimentation may lead to pure truth and to support of a hypothesis. In contrast, a "bottom-up" view of knowledge views it more as the pragmatic outgrowth of naturalistic, transactional processes in the world. This debate in the philosophy of science has leaned more to the rationalist position in contemporary evidence law, with *Daubert* (1993) as a prime example. In court, expert witnesses presenting testimony need to demonstrate the reliability, trustworthiness, and validity of the data gathered on individuals and of the scientific literature used to support conclusions (see the next section, by Kane).

Confusions in Causality and Causation

This section of the chapter addresses various definitions of key terms, and points out different ways that the same term may be used differently in the mental health and legal professions, or how different terms are used for the same concept in the different professions. Without clarification, the fields are destined to have continuing difficulty both communicating and translating terms and concepts from one to the other.

In legal dictionaries, causality is generally defined as the relation between cause and effect, whereas causation generally refers to the producing of an effect (Garner, 1995, 2004). Garner (1995) indicates the confusion between use of the terms causality and causation in the legal field relative to common usage. "In law, *causation* has long been given the additional sense the relation of cause and effect, a sense best reserved to *causality* in nonlegal contexts" (Garner, 1995, p. 138). Garner (1995) suggests, "There are few words in the English vocabulary that have given rise to more legal problems than the words *cause* and *causing*" (p. 138). Slovenko (2002a, p. 361) echoes his concerns, stating that terms such as "causal connection" and "causal factor" used by legislatures and the courts are "unsatisfying and impenetrable."

Despite their central importance to the legal process, the concepts of causality and causation are not clearly presented in the field of law. Rather, they subsume a network of related and sometimes confusing terms such as "proximate cause," "remote cause," and "superseding cause." The assumption is that the necessary and sufficient condition(s) that have acted as agents in altering an individual's physical and/or psychological state after a putative causal event can be isolated and examined for their legal consequences, in a tort action. If there is joint cause, the primary one can be differentiated; that is, the original precipitating one may not be considered the most important one to an individual's eventual medical or psychological outcome.

The network of terms subsumed under causality and causation vary in detail in the legal, medical, and psychological fields. For example, legal ones, such as "superseding" cause, are not found in the other two areas; medical ones, such as "inciting" cause, are not found in its counterparts. Psychology also has its own unique language to describe causality; for example, "triggering" cause and "latent" cause (see below) are specific to psychology. In addition, psychology often emphasizes dicta such as correlation not offering a sufficient basis to establish causation. Psychologists maintain that a statistical linkage between two variables reveals an association or correlation, but this does not mean that there is an underlying causation because for example, the correlation may be explained by a third variable influencing the other two variables.

In the legal arena, the term "proximate" cause (causation or causality) is the most relevant. It is also called the legal or direct cause. It is the dominant specific, identifiable, responsible component of the negligent event in question that is considered necessary and sufficient to have produced the altered condition. It is "[a] cause that is legally sufficient to result in liability" (Garner, 2004, p. 234).

Ozonoff (2005b) examined the concepts of legal causation and responsibility for causing harm. He indicated that in the legal arena, "legal cause" consists of the interrelated components "scientific" causality, or "cause-in-fact," and legal "responsibility" for negligent action, or "proximate cause." Ozonoff cited Dobbs (2000) to indicate the confusion generated by these terms. "Proximate cause" is often used to stand for "legal cause," and this term itself may be used to refer both to cause-in-fact and legal responsibility. Therefore, Ozonoff maintained that the concept of proximate cause, in its limited sense, does not really concern cause in the scientific or fact sense. I would note that when it is used to replace the term legal cause, confusingly, it comes to include this latter aspect of the term.

In addition, it is worth noting that outside of the legal profession the term "proximate cause" appears to be understood in the sense of cause-in-fact as used by the legal profession. That is, in mental health fields, the term proximate cause most often is used to refer to the scientific basis for arriving at a judgment that there is a factual cause that is responsible for the outcome involved. Note that the concept of legal liability, or financial and related responsibility for the outcome involved, lies outside the scope of practice of mental health professionals. For example, Rothman and Greenland (2005) remark that in the law, proximate causes are component causes "implying a more direct connection or responsibility" (p. S145) for effects of negligent actions. Finally, note that in the legal setting, the word "responsibility" may be used without clarification both to define the cause-in-fact component of the definition of proximate cause and to refer to the scope of liability component, possibly adding to the confusion about the term proximate cause.

Consistent with Ozonoff (2005), Van Dorsten and James (2002) comment that the concept of "proximate cause" should be used in the sense of "legal cause," where there is not only physical harm suffered by a plaintiff but also liability attached to the actions of the defendant. Thus, its scope is quite specific and limited, with the goal of seeking certainty in legal attribution of liable cause.

To simplify, in the legal field, there are two components to the definition of proximate cause—first, an act is considered responsible for an effect, and second, it leads to compensable consequences, that is, an individual or other entity is held legally liable for the effect.

The question then becomes which of the legal tests and criteria will be used to establish cause-in-fact? For example, would the injuries sustained in an accident have developed without the negligent act having occurred? This is called the "but-for" test (the counterfactual argument), which refers to "[a] cause that directly produces an event and without which the event would not have occurred" (Garner, 2004, p. 234). Other tests relate to "material" cause or contribution, or whether the event in question had any causal impact on the psychological effects ascribed to the victim.

Proximate cause is treated in two ways in the psychological literature. In psychology, proximate cause is used in the legal sense being discussed (Corsini, 2002), but also in a biological one (Alcock, 2001). It has a quite different meaning from the legal one in the field of animal behavior, one quite unrelated to it. Alcock (2001) refers to genetic, physiological, developmental, and sensorimotor mechanisms as components of proximate cause. He also separates these mechanisms from "ultimate" ones, which refer to both evolutionary history and Darwinian adaptive function. Thus, the term "proximate cause" has a quite different meaning in animal behavior and psychology compared to the traditional legal one.

The next example illustrates that law and psychology may use the same term with respect to causality, but with opposite perspectives. The term "recovery" refers to very different concepts in these disciplines. For law, recovery refers to the award of compensation to an individual (a plaintiff) against a defendant because of a harmful (tortious) act. In contrast, for psychology, recovery refers to the rehabilitation of a complainant after she or he had experienced a harmful act. Therefore, it is paradoxical that the *more* the "recovery" in a psychological sense by an individual due to the effective therapy provided by a psychologist, the *less* the amount of "recovery" in the monetary sense obtained by the individual's lawyer! Typically, psychologists and lawyers want more "recovery," but of different kinds and for different reasons.

Another example illustrates that when psychologists and lawyers are addressing the same or similar issues, the terms used may differ. When the psychological effects of a harmful act are marked, psychologists use qualifiers such as serious, severe, and significant, whereas lawyers ask psychologists to address the language of legal tests and thresholds. Psychologists, then, are required to translate their conclusions into legal language, for example, to what extent an evaluated individual's psychological status reflects substantial, important, or catastrophic effects, a translation that, although must be accomplished, presents difficulties. In another example, both professions address vocational and other disabilities, but they do so from different perspectives. In this regard, if an evaluation establishes that an individual cannot work, from a psychological perspective, at her or his prior employment, the psychologist determines whether there are residual and transferable skills. The psychologist may also be asked to speak to legal questions regarding whether the new employment being considered is consistent with past training, experience, and work history, will any training for the job be successful, will the individual be able to obtain work once trained, given the psychological disability involved, and then be able to keep the job, if obtained, and so on. These questions are not typical ones dealt with by the psychological procedures and instruments that have been developed in the profession.

In a final example, I consider the question of reliability and validity. Although the concepts do not relate directly to causality, they have far reaching consequences for causality, whether in the legal or psychological spheres. Moreover, consistent with the ambiguities that have been shown for other terms, these two terms also differ across the two domains of psychology and law. In psychology, reliability refers to whether a measurement or judgment, for example, a diagnosis, is consistent and sufficiently free from error, or is reproducible or replicable (Urbina, 2004). In psychology, validity concerns whether a measurement or judgment is conceptually or theoretically sound, or adequate and appropriate, in understanding an issue, or, at the applied level, whether a measurement or judgment is measuring what it is supposed to measure, the intended purpose (Urbina, 2004). In law, validity addresses, as indicated in *Daubert*, trustworthiness. Evidence needs to be relevant and reliable. Relevant evidence is helpful to the trier of fact, and is applicable to the particular case. "Reliable" evidence is trustworthy, meaning that it is "valid" evidence in the psychological sense. Validity in law also refers to the quality of the arguments rendered in court or elsewhere (Garner, 2004, p. 1586). Therefore, "reliability" in law is like "validity" in psychology, though reliability and validity are very different concepts in psychology. Any psychologist wanting to work in the legal arena *must* learn the legal terminology in order to ethically pursue forensic and other court-related work. I discuss again this issue in Chapter 4, which presents a dictionary of terms.

Causality and Causation in Law

Faieta (2005) describes the general principles of causation in tort law, as outlined by the Canadian Supreme Court in *Athey v. Leonati* (1996). He lists eight points: (1) In the first one, cause is defined in terms of "contribution" to the injury, and the level of certainty needed refers to a "balance of probabilities." (2) Next, the general, although not conclusive, test in establishing causation is the "but-for" test. (3) Where the "but-for" test does not apply, the "material contribution" test applies, for example, it asks had the defendant "materially contributed" to the plaintiff's personal injury through her or his tortious conduct. (4) A material contribution may be involved as long as it contributes beyond the minimal range ("de minimus"). (5) There must be proof of the alleged cause. (I would add that in science, one can never prove anything, but only offer data in support of a hypothesis, theory, or model, while simultaneously reducing the probability that alternate explanations may apply; also see point 7 below.) (6) "The causation test need not be applied too rigidly. Causation need not be determined by scientific precision. It is essentially a practical question of fact which can be answered by ordinary common sense" (p. 34). (7) Causation may be inferred "without positive scientific proof" (p. 34). (8) If the causation is multiple, with other factors not involving the defendant, the defendant is still considered liable as long as she or he has "helped produce the harm" (p. 34). In this regard, depending on the jurisdiction, there may be no basis for reducing liability when causation is only partly due to the plaintiff's negligence.

It is important to note that, for tort law, in terms of the *Athey* decision in Canada, causation does not reside in only one proximate factor nor does it lie in absolute certainty. Rather, causation may be multiple, as long as the defendant has contributed materially to the injury or harm. Moreover, causation should be determined by both (a) using common sense, without too much rigidity, and, (b) as much as possible, via positive scientific evidence.

Feehan and Tinkler (2005) trace the development of *Athey*, and decisions that followed it, with respect to medical malpractice. In the Canadian Supreme Court decision *Snell v. Farrell* (1990), Justice Sopinka described a "less onerous standard" of proof of causation, one that is more robust and pragmatic, when there is absence of evidence to the contrary. In *Scott (Crick) v. Mohan* (1993), the court adduced that medical testimony may not be precise and it is rarely unanimous in disputed cases. In *Stevens v. Okrainec* (1997), the eight *Athey* causation principles were summarized into six points. Point five mentions that, in some instances, causation may be inferred from the evidence presented despite a lack of scientific proof. Point six mentions that a material contributing cause may still be held liable in multiple causation where other factors are not legally responsible for the injury or harm, even when the cause alone was "not enough" to cause the injury or harm. In the end, legal cause revolves around the concept of proximate cause, which includes whether a putative cause had not been too remote to have materially contributed to the outcome in dispute.

Ozonoff (2005b) noted that, historically, the tests in place today addressing whether legal liability attaches to negligent conduct developed in response to social, political, and moral issues. For example, prior to the development of the "foreseeability" doctrine, that a defendant should have foreseen the danger in the negligence at issue, there were more objective, formal rules that were applied in an arbitrary, mechanical fashion.

Sales and Shuman (2005) provide 11 reasons to doubt that current evidence law (the *Daubert* trilogy and their progeny; *Daubert v. Merrill Dow Pharmaceuticals, Inc., 1993*; see the section by Kane) inevitably leads to accurate evidence. Consistent with *Athey*'s more relaxed standards of proof of causation, Sales and Shuman begin by stating that scientists do not always agree on what is scientifically demonstrated. In deciding on appropriate interpretation, researchers may realize that critical experiments have yet to be undertaken, or different researchers may have different evaluations of the significance of research already undertaken. This ambiguity is compounded when research is entered into an adversarial system, such as in the civil litigation arena. In a system that uses adversarial, retained experts, questions will always arise "about the completeness of the information presented" (Sales & Shuman, 2005, p. 57).

Moreover, in their gatekeeping function on the reliability and validity of scientific evidence presented to court, judges cannot turn to specific criteria on the matter found in the *Daubert* trilogy, because the criteria do not articulate clear guidelines. The criteria are not ordered in importance nor are they meant to be exclusive. Compounding the problem, judges typically lack scientific acumen. They may also have their own policy goals.

Finally, much evidence in personal injury cases concerns clinical testimony and, due to its individual basis, it reflects the clinician's view or judgment as "influenced by his or her professional experiences that have not been scientifically studied" (Sales & Shuman, 2005, p. 78). This applies even when science is used in formulating clinical opinion. "Thus, as with pure clinical opinion, the interpretation of *Daubert* to permit the use of clinical opinion to draw inferences from the science to the facts of a particular case leaves us with limited confidence that this approach advances the goal of truth as accuracy" (p. 79).

According to Sales and Shuman (2005), one trial court has enunciated formal criteria to determine whether clinical assessments can be presented as reliable evidence to establish causal linkage (*Antoine-Tubbs v. Local 513 Air Transp. Div.*, U.S. Federal District Court, 1998). These criteria include: (a) personal examination of the patient, (b) detailed history, (c) differential diagnosis/etiology, (d) review of documentation, (e) review of other reasonable facts/data, (f) reference to medical literature, and (g) the clinician's training and experience. However, Sales and Shuman (2005) take these criteria to task, because subjective, nonscientific information may be used in unspecified ways. They conclude that where there is no science available to guide them, clinicians may arrive at incorrect conclusions about causation even when using accepted clinical methods and procedures. Nevertheless, a clinician's clinical opinion may be entered as evidence, in the absence of any scientific basis for the clinician's conclusions because, in the adversarial system, evaluation of the value of clinical opinion in the case at hand resides with the fact-finder. Judge or jury may give little or great weight, or anything in between, to a clinician's testimony. Therefore, Sales and Shuman (2005) conclude that the *Daubert* trilogy has had "minimal impact" in altering the admissibility of clinical opinion evidence. Moreover, the body of scientific knowledge in any area is always "imperfect," so that basing causality decisions especially on current scientific knowledge in and of itself does not represent the ideal solution.

Taking a different approach, Faigman and Monahan (2005) ask whether clinical testimony meets Daubertian criteria, given the latter's evidence-based requirements. Faigman and Monahan maintain that *Daubert* has "largely changed" how psychology will conceive of itself. They maintain that many areas of psychology relevant to the decision-making process in law "lack robust research traditions" (p. 633). Moreover, the science of psychology is quite complex.

The U.S. appellate courts have not established a consistent framework for the degree of rigorous proof necessary with respect to causation that can be determined from clinical judgment. In *Heller v. Shaw* (1999), the court adopted a "relatively lenient" approach, permitting a good deal of clinical judgment in the case, leaving the degree of weight that should be given to the evidence to the fact-finder. However, another decision called for "substantial" research on the question, being much more rigorous in this regard (*Black v. Food Lion, Inc.*, 1999). Faigman and Monahan conclude that the U.S. Supreme Court will likely have to deal with these differing appellate court decisions, potentially impacting evidence presented by psychological experts.

Faigman and Monahan maintain that despite the difficulty in studying human behavior, psychology needs to be as rigorous in research as other areas that fare well in court despite their difficulties, such as epidemiology. For example, those using unvalidated assessment techniques may find their resultant testimony inadmissible, or given little weight, in court. "For psychologists, *Daubert* stands as a guardian at the courtroom door, warmly welcoming those with relevant and valid scientific evidence, and brusquely sending others on their way" (Faigman & Monahan, 2005, p. 656).

Causality and Causation in Medicine

Medical dictionaries attempt to differentiate cause into constituent types. However, the plethora of medical terms in this regard are not defined in consistent ways, both across the dictionaries and with respect to their equivalent legal terms.

For example, according to Dorland's medical dictionary, an "exciting" cause is a direct, provoking, precipitating trigger, and an "immediate" cause is the beginning one in a series of causal links (Dorland & Newman, 2003, p. 311). However, other dictionaries addressing medical terms indicate that "immediate" cause is also termed the exciting, inciting, or precipitating cause (e.g., Bailey, 1998) and, moreover, it need not be the first or the last but the primary one, if there is a chain. To conclude, with respect to the temporal chain of causal components to which the term "immediate" cause applies, the legal definition refers to the most recent, last component of the chain, whereas, in a primary reference source, Dorland's, immediate cause refers to the beginning of the chain!

In another example of inconsistency in definition across professions, "remote" cause is defined legally as the first, beginning, original, or initial component cause of a chain. However, in legal practice, the term "remote" cause can be used in the sense of a possible cause being too remote or too removed from a chain of factors to have had any causal effect. The medical definition also includes variations, but different ones. Dorland and Newman (2003, p. 311) consider remote cause as not immediate, which is fine, but its examples give it wide latitude; it can be predisposing or secondary, as well as "ultimate" in the sense of being first.

In a third example, note that in law, the "ultimate" issue is a cardinal concept, referring to the matter being adjudicated by the trier of fact. This should not be confused with the concept of "ultimate" or initial cause, as used in medicine. (To add further confusion, and to underscore the need for the current attempt to disambiguate these terms in the three disciplines under discussion, note the quite different use of the term "ultimate" in the psychological/animal behavioral field, as we have seen above.)

In Chapter 4, which presents a dictionary of terms, Young and Shore make specific suggestions on how to deal with the confusion in the terminology across the three disciplines under discussion. We now move on to how the field of medicine considers the manner in which causality determinations should proceed.

Henifin, Kipen, and Poulter (2000) have written a reference guide to medical testimony for the Federal Judicial Center. First, the authors delve into the different terminology in the medical and legal fields, or how the same term has different meanings in the two fields. For example, in the medical field, "differential diagnosis" refers to the process of establishing which disease is causing an individual's symptoms. According to Henifin et al. (2000), legally the term refers to identification of external cause(s), or negligent action(s), in particular. Faigman (2003) makes the same distinction, to illustrate that the courts "stumble" in translating terms from other fields, and in this case the use of the term "differential diagnosis" in law should be rephrased as "differential etiology."

Henefin et al. (2000) continue that physicians consider both "internal" and "external" causation of medical conditions, whereas the courts focus on the latter, determining whether a defendant or other responsible party can be held accountable for a negligent act inducing a psychological harm. Moreover, courts have borrowed the epidemiological distinction between "general" and "specific" causation, where the former refers to what the scientific and medical literature informs about exposure to a toxic substance and the probability that it results in a disease, and the latter refers to establishing whether a particular exposure had resulted in a particular disease in a particular individual.

Physicians explore the chain of causation, how one level of abnormality may substantially lead to abnormality in the next highest level. They arrive at a diagnosis, but "[m]edical diagnosis is not an exact science. ... [P]hysicians make probabilistic judgments" (Henifin et al., 2000, p. 465), or use "probabilistic reasoning," for example, about prevalence rate of the diagnosis in question. In addition, in a separate step, in order to clarify the relationship between any diagnosis and any putative causal agent, they use "causal reasoning" to seek cause-and-effect relationships, analyzing how bodily systems react to external stressors and environmental factors, while keeping in mind prior medical and other modifying factors such as individual susceptibility. They examine synergistic interactions among factors, multiplicative interactions, incremental effects, and so on, considering all possible causal possibilities. Opinions on causality cannot be reduced to mathematical formulae, so that in the end "clinical judgment is critical to opinions on diagnosis and causation for the individual patient even when the scientific population basis for general causation may be quite strong" (p. 478).

Rothman and Greenland (2005) also underscore the multifactorial nature of causality in medicine. More than one mechanism may cause a given disease. Every causal mechanism involves multiple interacting components, including genetic and environmental components in nearly every case. The components may have stronger or weaker effects, or they may vary with time. The multiple interactive components may need to be present collectively in order to be sufficient to produce disease. For example, "causes" are events, conditions, or characteristics that precede disease, and, when their presence is sufficient, they inevitably lead to the disease in question.

Cocchiarella and Andersson (2001) have authored the American Medical Association's *Guides to the Evaluation of Permanent Impairment, (Fifth Edition)*, and there is an accompanying text on *Mastering the Guides* (Cocchiarella & Lord, 2001). In this supplement, the authors wrote an excellent chapter on evaluating causation, which is oriented especially toward epidemiological cases. Causation in epidemiological terms refers to an event, condition, or characteristic that plays an important role in occurrence of disease. Models of causality in epidemiology are used to separate and analyze multiple factors for their interaction, and in epidemiology they function more like values than rules because they change depending on study and circumstances, and so do not require conformity in order that causal criteria are met.

The Guides recommend 10 steps in arriving at conclusions concerning causation: (1) Identify any diagnoses and permanent impairments; (2) Research the literature to identify all factors and social practices that may function as component causes; (3) Investigate uncertain risk factors, focusing on the strength of the association, temporality, consistency among studies, and biological plausibility; (4) Identify the individual's known or associated risk factors, through medical records, history, and clinical evaluation; (5) Determine the temporal relationship in the individual between the risk factors and the condition (e.g., did the risk factors precede the condition); (6) Identify probable component causes and sufficient causes; (7) Identify temporal relationships across component causes and sufficient causes; (8) Specify the degree of certainty about whether any component causes are proximal or major in causal outcome, for example, a probability of "more likely than not"; (9) If feasible, assign apportionment of causation to any risk factors; and (10) Discuss the contributing role played by any risk factor in the chain of causal events.

Rothman and Greenland (2005) caution that these epidemiological criteria of causation should not be used as hard and fast rules of causal evidence, or a checklist of aids of inference on causation, because they are marked by reservations and exceptions. Instead they should be used as deductive tests, in which "crucial" observations and data are used to evaluate competing causal explanations.

The medical approach recommended by the Guides to establish causation is consistent with the psychological approach. Like the psychological approach, the recommended medical approach gravitates between the individual and the literature, the effects and the risk factors, the strength of the causes and the strength of the conclusions that the causes had been involved, and apportionment of causation across the primary and secondary risk factors, implying the presence of multiple causation.

Causality and Causation in Psychology

Psychological dictionaries indicate that causality is more of a philosophical term, and that causation is the more frequent one used in psychology (Corsini, 2002;

Reber & Reber, 2001). However, the one psychology book with the title clearly on the topic is entitled "Models of Causality in Psychopathology" (Haynes, 1992). Causality refers to an abstract quality in contingent or actualizing linkage, whereas causation refers to an empirical transition where there is a condition preceding an effect. Multiple or joint causation, where there is more than one causal factor, is typical in the social sciences (Reber & Reber, 2001).

Multiple Cause. Haynes (1992) indicates that psychopathological models of causality are moving away from unidirectional, linear models to complex, dynamic, and synthetic ones. He maintains that one can never know with certainty all the causes of behavior or the individual impact of a relevant factor on behavior. Haynes (1992) lists the classes or types of causal variables. *Original* causes are the first functional components in a causal chain. *Intermediate* effects and mechanisms constitute ensuing components in a causal chain. *Maintaining* causes are those that best explain current manifestations in a causal chain. *Triggering* causes constitute a subset of maintaining causes, and function as immediate precipitants to behavior. *Latent* causal variables are specific dormant causal mechanisms embedded in a causal chain that can act to trigger behavior in the right context.

The complexity of the causal process, as exemplified by these concepts, illustrates the need for psychologists to be careful in assigning cause in their individual assessments. Psychologists need to be wary of simplified, unilateral, or incomplete explanations of causality and, instead, should favor using integrated, comprehensive, and interactional perspectives on determinant factors and processes. Thus, for psycholegal questions, such as whether a single index event can induce a purported psychological condition, psychologists need to be especially prudent.

Schools and Systems. Psychology is a discipline about the study of behavior, and, therefore, its scope covers fundamental issues about the nature of human behavior. It can be argued that schools of psychology have arisen especially to decipher cause. Briefly, Freudian thought attributed behavior to conscious and unconscious determinants, with the unconscious ones deriving from intrapsychic conflict, in particular. Behaviorism espoused a quite direct causal model, denying any unconscious influence. Behavior was considered as responses to stimuli, with stimulus-response connections altered by reinforcement contingencies in the environment and by learning. More complex psychological schools of thought emerged with time, increasingly integrating biological, environmental, and personal factors in determination of behavior (e.g., the ecological model). Cognitive and related dimensions took on increasing importance; the cognitive-behavioral and related schools became prominent. These approaches emphasize cognitive schemas or filters, how they can become distorted and maladaptive, and the role of individual differences in attention, motivation, and other processes that influence the schemas' contents.

The dynamic systems perspective is an increasingly influential one (Haynes, 1992). It indicates that through multiple interactions among the elements of a system, the whole emerges as greater than the sum of its parts, and continually evolves its pattern in self-organization. "Dynamic systems, with its view of multiple causality and levels of interactions, encompasses a wide variety of kinds of causes" (Smith & Samuelson, 2003, p. 436). Therefore, behavior can be "emergent" in context and not predictable even from knowledge of all the constituent parts in the system. "Causality, as a linear change of precedent and antecedent events, cannot be singularly assigned to any agency within or surrounding the organism" (Smith & Thelen, 1993, p. xiv). Context is as critical as is the organism in understanding behavior, and causality lies in the pattern of interactions of constituent elements, which include biological, social, and personal factors, along with context. Therefore, in a systems perspective, causality can never reside in any one element.

Causal Levels. Causal models vary in level (Haynes, 1992). For example, at the molecular level, a stimulus, either alone or in concert with others, can causally effect change in behavior and its organization in the ongoing person-environment interaction. At the molar level, behavior reflects the causal interaction of a larger number of causal variables, ones that are more broadly conceived, for example, the environment includes work and society. A more differentiated perspective includes in this biological-environmental interaction the organism or person, with her or his individual differences in goals, personalities, motivation, learning history, strengths and weaknesses, coping skills, perceptions, and so on. In short, causality is a process involving the interactive, multifactorial, and developing dynamic in all these components.

Individual Differences. Haynes (1992) emphasizes that because there are multiple causal variables, weights, paths, and so on, there are "important" individual differences in causal relationships. "Individuals exhibiting the same behavior problem may differ in the causal variables affecting that behavior problem, the mechanisms through which the causal relationships operate, and the importance of the various causal variables and paths" (p. 108). Individual differences constitute a cornerstone of psychology, so that one causal model cannot fit all, although general models can be helpful. Psychology studies population-level phenomena but, also, individual variations across groups, gender, cultures, age, intellectual status, different skill levels, and so on. In addition, psychology examines what makes individuals unique, special, a whole person, different from others, and so on. Finally, psychology may even study one individual at a time, in case studies. Psychologists gravitate between normative, population-wide data, and individual data, or between the nomothetic level and the idiographic level. Ultimately, for court purposes, psychologists need to know the general scientific literature about populations but, also, the literature about individual differences in the populations. In parallel, they need to know well their individual assessees, how the literature applies to them, and what are the gaps in the literature that they have to bridge in understanding any individual being assessed.

Thin and Crumbling Skulls

Despite attorneys' goals of finding simplified theories of their cases, of finding isolated, unique causes that can be readily litigated or defended against, closer inspection reveals that the law has adopted a model of causality that is implicitly multicausal and, therefore, similar to the psychological approach. In any one individual case, the law may seek to isolate the primary or singular legal cause but, when necessary, the law distils it out of a nexus of causal factors. Moreover, it has an elaborate terminology to specify the different types of secondary causes and to clarify the relationship of the primary cause to the others. Two difficult concepts with which to deal in this legal causal nexus concern the concepts of "thin skulls" and "crumbling skulls" (which are also called thin, or "eggshell," and crumbling "psyches," or "personalities").

Douglas, Huss, Murdoch, Washington, and Koch (1999) specify that these legal constructs have implications for determining causality; both refer to preexisting conditions. The "thin skull" doctrine applies to individuals who are fragile, or who are predisposed to develop a particular condition, but who had been asymptomatic prior to the index event (Canadian decisions; *Athey v. Leonati*, 1996, S.C.C; *Janiak v. Ippolito*, 1985, S.C.R.; American decisions; for example, *Padget v. Gray*, 1987, Texas Ct. App.; *Theriault v. Swan*, 1989, Maine Sup. Jud. Ct.). The "crumbling" skull doctrine applies when an injured party's expressed preexisting symptoms are worsened or aggravated by an index event. Therefore, in causality determination, the court establishes the extent to which an individual has experienced an index event that acts on preexisting conditions. These may be severe enough to be fully or partly responsible for any changes in psychological condition observed after the event (crumbling skull). Or, the preexisting conditions may be latent but predispose the individual to a psychological response to the event out of proportion to the expected norm because of their contributing vulnerabilities (thin skull).

According to Douglas et al. (1999) thin skull cases are common in the United States and Canada, whereas crumbling skull cases are primarily found in Canada. In the legal realm, defendants must take plaintiffs as they are found. In terms of compensation, "if a defendant's tortious conduct aggravates a preexisting condition, the defendant is liable to the extent of the aggravation" (*Miramon v. Bradley*, 1997; La. App. 1st Cir.), although this rule is not universal. Therefore, for the crumbling skull case, often damages awarded to the plaintiff are matched to the degree of injury added to the injuries or conditions present before those sustained because of the defendant's actions. This is consistent with the legal formula that when there are multiple, joint causes, the proportion of fault for each is distributed. "Some courts … impose liability only for such damage as could have been foreseen …" (Slovenko, 2002b, p. 459).

To conclude, despite often stated major discrepancies in the approach of law and psychology to causality determination, the network of concepts in both fields allows for a differentiated, fair, understanding of the multiple factors potentially involved. The law may seek to reduce causal complexity to a simplified account for its adversarial purposes, and psychology may have difficulty translating some legal terms into its familiar language, but the basis for a cooperative understanding of causality is present, although continued conceptualization, such as in this chapter, is needed.

Recommendations

In the following, I present several models and lists aimed at providing a common framework in the dialogue between psychology and the law pertaining to issues in causality. First, I present a standardized figure of the causality process. For example, where does the typical psychological evaluation fit in the process? Second, I indicate what is involved in the typical assessment procedure, with the critical issues given but, at the same time, I suggest using standardized terminology, such as use of the terms "complainant" and "index event." Third, I introduce the concept of "symptom exacerbation" in order to complement the term of "symptom magnification" because of criticisms related to the latter term. Similarly, I offer suggestions with respect to criticism of the concept of secondary gain. Fourth, I propose a five-point ordinal causality scale for use in psychological evaluations, a scale that affords estimation of the degree of causality attributable to an index event or stressor for a reported resultant psychological condition. The concepts of thin and crumbling skulls have been embedded in the scale. Fifth, I offer a list of possible factors to consider in the rationales, considerations, or explanations used by psychologists and other mental health professionals in arriving at their conclusions and formulations about causality.

The Causality Process

Table 3.1 illustrates the steps involved in the causality process from referral to court decision. First, the psychologist receives a referral, to evaluate whether an index event has induced a clinically significant or legally relevant psychological reaction. The psychologist ensures that she or he is competent to address each component of the referral question. In the second step, once the complainant is engaged in a psychological evaluation, the psychologist requests records or documentation from the referring source that address relevant issues in the evaluation. This may include police, hospital, therapy, and/or other records. The psychologist is ethically obligated to request needed records. If these records are not made available, the psychologist may not be able to draw conclusions to a reasonable degree of certainty. In certain cases, the requested documents may cast doubt on whether the index event actually happened as described. Bryant (2003) underscores the importance of independently verifying the individual's account of the index event to the degree reasonably possible. For example, in the case of reported Posttraumatic Stress Disorder (PTSD) due to purported intense military combat or a severe accident, the psychologist might attempt to check military records for actual combat, or verify the alleged severity

TABLE 3.1. Steps in the Causality Process

Process				
(1) Complaint lodged (tort); Referral made to psychologist; Referral question addresses theory of the case	**(2) Psychologist checks whether: Index event really took place; Is there a discredited diagnosis; inappropriate therapy, etc.?**	**(3) Psychologist proceeds to causal analysis in a comprehensive, impartial assessment (Did index event A cause reported condition B?)**	**(4) Legal gatekeeper function: Judge determines expert's qualifications and evidence's admissibility**	**(5) Legal deliberation: Psychologist's evidence included in legal decision making process**
The referral question	*Verification by psychologist*	*Psychological assessment*	*Level of court*	*Evidence*
– to determine whether index event A caused reported condition B:	(to the degree possible, and without having an investigative role):	– comprehensive, impartial – undertaken of symptoms, impairments, diagnoses, disorders, disabilities, possible malingering, etc. which addresses:	Federal State Provincial etc.	Report Testimony Deposition etc.
Index event (A)	*Of index event* (A)	*Causation process*	*Regulation/rule in jurisdiction*	*Trier of fact*
– is it proximate, psychological cause of a clinically significant, functionally relevant effect or reported condition	– is it possible, plausible – is it documented *Of reported condition* (B) – in other documents(s), does the diagnosis fit the person and event	Two-tiered process: (a) what is normative expectation in research evidence (nomothetic) (b) applying this to individual case (idiographic)	*Frye* *Daubert* *Kumho/Joiner* FREs *Mohan* etc.	Judge Jury *Thresholds/tests* Disability Functional impairment Degree Permanency etc. (varies with jurisdiction)
Reported condition (B) – reported symptoms may constitute impairments, disorders, diagnoses, disability, etc., which are serious, severe, etc.	– in the professional opinion of the psychologist, is PTSD, or any disorder or syndrome, even possible, given the nature of the event – has a diagnosed disorder or syndrome been deemed valid in the literature	*Causation product* Two decisions possible: (a) causation evident (A caused B) (full, partial) (b) causation absent	*Admissibility* Yes, No *Attorney's role* – initiate tort/ defend – retain expert – adhere to rules	*Compensation* Two decisions possible: (a) liability: Yes, No (b) damages: based on factfinder's judgment of degree of harm

Context				
– Psychologist must be competent to address each component of the referral question – Referral source/side—defense or plaintiff; or by court appointment	– Psychologist may believe, for example, that: (a) an MVA had been staged, (b) a child's testimony had been elicited inappropriately, (c) Battered Women's Syndrome is valid	– Court decisions on "crumbling" skull, "thin" skull, etc. – For example, is a complainant with a "thin" skull eligible for psychological therapy and/or for compensation, and, if so, to what degree	– Regulations/ rules vary according to jurisdiction – Regulations/ rules are not uniformly interpreted/ applied – Variable knowledge of psychology, science	– How are legal tests and thresholds different from psychological ones – Dialogue between law and psychology – e.g., on how disability is defined psychologically and legally

of the impact in an accident. Or, the psychologist verifies the ambulance and emergency room hospital records about a claimed serious traumatic brain injury (TBI) to ascertain whether there had been a loss of consciousness, disorientation, and so on. In all cases, collateral information is checked carefully to identify all information relevant to assessing the alleged injuries of the complainant.

When the psychologist has little or no doubt about whether an index event had taken place, such as with a documented serious accident or assault where there are appropriate police reports, witness accounts, and so on, the psychologist proceeds to the next step of a comprehensive causal analysis, determining whether there is any evident link between the index event and its purported psychological consequences, symptoms, impairments, diagnoses, functional outcomes, and so on. The causal process is two-tiered. First, based on knowledge of the literature, the psychologist addresses the normative, population level, nomothetic, scientific expectation for the complainant, given the nature of the index event, the context, any past psychological difficulties, relevant base rates, if any, and so on. At the individual, idiographic level, the psychologist undertakes a comprehensive assessment of all components of the referral question, using appropriate interview techniques with the individual, using standardized, psychometrically sound psychological instruments, using collateral sources of information and prior records and reports, and so forth. [In this regard, Bryant (2003) advised that, at first, interviews should be open-ended, before becoming more directed.] Then, the psychologist arrives at a conclusion regarding, for the individual complainant, whether proximate psychological causation of a clinically significant or legally relevant nature has derived from the index event. The psychologist specifies the individual's compliance with treatment recommendations in order to mitigate her or his losses, the functional implications, the prognosis, and the apparent severity, permanency, and so on, of any impairment, disorder, or disability. In addition, the psychologist addresses the extent to which there are preexisting vulnerabilities, preexisting psychopathology, and so on, altering the material contribution of the index event relative to other factors, thus addressing the concepts of "thin" and "crumbling" skulls, or their equivalent.

In the next step in the causality determination process, the legal system engages in its gatekeeping function. In the United States, since 1993 when *Daubert* was promulgated, in the jurisdictions where it or the equivalent state or Federal Rule of Evidence (2004) is applicable, judges have been assigned the role of vetting the scientific validity underlying psychological and other evidence, that is, in legal terms, whether it is "reliable" (trustworthy). However, the evidence needs to be relevant to the specific case, and more probative than prejudicial in aiding the trier of fact (judge or jury) to arrive at its decisions. In the last step of the causality process, if the offered evidence has been judged admissible, it is available to assist the trier of fact in its deliberations. Compensation is awarded if the defendant is deemed responsible for the damages to the plaintiff. The same process occurs in Canadian courts on the basis of *R. v. Mohan* (1994).

Neutral Terminology

In an effort to control possible bias with respect to terms used in causal analysis, for example, in the connotative meaning implied in the terms "claimant" and "alleged assault," it is suggested that more neutral terms be adopted (see Table 3.2).

Index Event. The proximate event, with its particular psychologically relevant mechanism and its associated context, constitutes the index event. The proximate event denotes the larger event, such as an MVA or an assault, whereas the proximate mechanism refers to the particular details of the event that may render it psychologically relevant. For example, medically, physicians query the mechanical forces in a motor vehicle accident in an MVA and the subsequent physical forces, how the body is projected, and so on, including forces that could be responsible for a closed head injury. At the psychological level, the parallel would refer to the exact nature of the traumatic components of an event such as an MVA, assault, or a rape, what occurred and is recalled by all the senses.

Complainant. The victim and the plaintiff. Psychologists should avoid using the term "claimant," because it is inexact with reference to their relationship to the individual being assessed; that is, it refers to the relation between the subject individual and the third party, and not the relationship between the subject individual and the psychological assessor. By using the term "claimant," the psychologist inadvertently adopts the stance of the third party payor to which the claim is being made. Are there other terms that may be better? The term "plaintiff" is too limited; it refers to the suing individual in a tort action. However, causality determinations are made not only for plaintiffs in court cases but also for individual complainants in worker compensation cases, rehabilitation cases, and so on. Therefore, the term "complainant" appears a satisfactory one. (The following terms do not reflect any contentious issue, but are provided to suggest a consistent framework for discussion.)

TABLE 3.2. Multifactorial Causal Framework

Precausal/preexisting state	Causal event	Caused condition
	Process	
Functional status	*Index event at possible proximate cause*	*Impairments/disorders*
for example,	for example,	for example,
– Health status, work/school status – Personal/family/relational status – Life role satisfaction – Leisure activity/ social status	– MVA – Rape – TBI in accident	– Symptom/impairments – Course – Diagnosis/disorder(s) – Normative expectation – Prognosis
Psychological status	*Causal mechanism*	*Disability/handicap*
for example,	for example,	for example,
– Personality – Psychopathology – Psychological vulnerability – History of prior stressors/ their perception – Coping skills	Traumatic aspects of: – MVA – Rape – TBI in accident	– Functional limitations – Outcome – Catastrophic injury – Quality of life – Suffering – Permanency – Barriers to recovery
	Context	
for example,	for example,	for example,
– Social support – History of life successes/their perception	– Loved one killed – Child hurt in MVA – Job requires skills affected by TBI	– Iatrogenic therapy – Treatment compliance – Positive motivation – Secondary gain – Malingering

Preexisting Status. The levels of functional and psychological integrity of a complainant prior to the index event together constitute the individual's preexisting state and degree of predisposing psychological vulnerability.

Reported Condition. The psychologist evaluates the complainant's psychological status, symptoms/impairments, diagnoses/disorders, handicaps/disabilities, traumatic brain injury status, possible catastrophic injury, altered quality of life/ functional status, change from preexisting psychological state, degree of permanency/ seriousness, outcome/prognosis, possible malingering, etc.

Context. Each of the three points in the process model being described, that of the preexisting state, index event experienced, and reported condition, exist in context. For example, what are the complainant's degree of social support, coping resources, barriers to recovery, treatment compliance, work/educational/caregiving stresses, financial losses, and so on.

Symptom Exacerbation and Secondary Gain

Although there is a need to remain vigilant to subtle biases in evaluating complainants' psychological condition after an index event, the psychological assessor must also remain vigilant to the possibility of malingering and/or symptom exaggeration in complainants' presentation. In this regard, Rogers and colleagues (Rogers & Bender, 2003; Rogers & Shuman, 2005; Rogers & Vitacco, 2002) criticize the concept of "symptom magnification," or symptom overreporting. Rogers argues that the concept of symptom magnification is ill-defined, has an unwarranted connotation to malingering, and is hard to operationalize in terms of degree.

Because of the negative connotation associated with the term of "symptom magnification," I suggest that at the descriptive level, wherever appropriate, the terms symptom "exaggeration" or perhaps symptom "amplification" be used instead. These terms appear more descriptive, rather than implying a deceptive or related cause.

Moreover, in terms of hypothesized mechanism underlying an evident symptom exaggeration or amplification, I suggest that assessors refer to the concept of "symptom exacerbation." This concept derives from the manner of the elaboration of acute pain into chronic pain. In the *DSM-IV* (APA, 1994, 2000), chronic Pain Disorder involves psychological factors in full or in part that help to initiate, maintain, worsen, or otherwise contribute to pain experience, to the point that it is pervasive, persistent, and so on. By definition, chronic Pain Disorder is understood to have symptom exacerbatory components. However, in the current approach to symptom exacerbation, I am considering it not only as a mechanism applicable to chronic pain but, also, as a mechanism that can play a role in any psychological condition.

That is, in the current scheme, symptom exacerbation is understood as a psychological mechanism that can help explain how psychological symptoms become prolonged beyond their expected course (or at least toward the upper end of the expected course), or even indefinitely, due to the interactive effects of perceived stress and concomitant factors. The sources of the stress and related factors can be derived from any combination of three time periods relative to the moment of onset of the symptom exaggeration. First, there may be preexisting stressors or vulnerabilities that act to exacerbate the symptoms. Second, the stressors may be related directly to the moment of onset of the symptoms, as with traumatic MVAs and sexual assaults. Third, the relevant stressors may concern postevent stressors, such as job loss directly attributable to an index event, or mourning the death of a family member in that event. Individual differences characterize these stressors. In addition, there may be corollary or concurrent postevent stressors unrelated to the index event (as with one's workplace going bankrupt), but which interact with it and therefore are part of the legally-relevant factors to consider in evaluating the effect of an event on an individual's psychological reaction to it. Finally, the symptom exacerbation may be generated by any of somatization factors, unconscious wishes to prolong the symptoms for purposes of secondary gain, conscious malingering for financial gain, and so on.

"Secondary gain" is another problematic term according to Rogers and colleagues. It is a concept used in the area of causality assessment to indicate that individuals may express symptom prolongation or worsening due to the effect of nonmonetary external incentives, such as receiving care. Rogers indicates that the attribution of secondary gain as a motive for symptom continuation is convenient, simplistic, and unsubstantiated. Similar concepts have been proposed in the neuropsychological literature, including that of suboptimal or incomplete effort (Rogers & Bender, 2003), or insufficient or inadequate effort (King, Sweet, Sherer, Curtiss, & Vanderploeg, 2002). Rogers and Bender (2003) advise not to label suboptimal effort as poor motivation, for the term is too ambiguous. Lack of effort may or may not be the product of conscious or intentional motives (King et al., 2002).

To cover the full range of these various terms, it is suggested that psychologists use the neutral and descriptive term "apparent effort." Then, the quality of the effort expressed by an individual can be seen to vary on a continuum from positive, optimal, and so on, to negative, suboptimal, and so on. When the data support it, the assessing psychologist can refer to the negative end of the spectrum in terms of the nature of any hypothesized reason for the behavior, even referring to conscious malingering when it is evident. Clearly, better psychometric instruments and forensic tools need to be developed in this area, ones that can disambiguate the neutral description of apparent effort with the more complex question of the reasons behind its differing degrees. Moreover, the diverse types of unconscious influence on symptom exaggeration and exacerbation need to be arranged in a more conceptually coherent fashion, which would afford them better validity.

The type of unconscious influences/psychological conflicts that amplify pain experience may follow a developmental level or hierarchical level of complexity, such as progression from the physical to the emotional to the cognitive. For example, at the beginning of the progression, and thus quite deeply ingrained, we may find there is (a) illness behavior or a fear of pain, and resultant physical deconditioning, all of which may be seen as more physically related. These factors may serve to increase somatization, sensitization, vicious circles in pain experience, and so on. (b) Then as we move toward more advanced levels, dependency or a "cry for help" may be at play, which may be seen as more emotionally related. Next, different cognitive levels may be found. (c) Catastrophizing or a call for attention may be at work, and reflect basic thinking or cognition that is not well reasoned. (d) If the conflict is more complex cognitively, for example, with partial clear reasoning having unconscious components, it may be related to feeling overwhelmed by responsibilities, rejecting responsibility/blaming anyone or anything other than oneself, and so on. (e) Finally, the cognitive conflict may be quite existential, abstract, or spiritual, reflecting more advanced conscious or unconscious conflicts, and as a result, social withdrawal and isolation may obtain more than would normally happen. Concepts involving an ordering such as this one, from the physical to the emotional to the cognitive, may help organize into a coherent framework the multiple ways that pain experience may be unconsciously exaggerated. It would complement work on direct malingering or other apparently conscious reasons for symptom exaggeration.

An Ordinal Scale of Degree of Causality and Causation

In the following, we turn to a different type of ordering, analyzing an ordinal scale of degree of causality and causation, created to help psychological assessors formulate their overall conclusions in individual cases after they have considered all the data in a case, including factors such as those just discussed. The scale has been formulated to help the mental health assessor qualify the degree of causality or causation that can be attributed to an index event for any subsequent psychological effects deriving from it. The scale is presented in a general way, so that it can apply to any stressor, including the gradual onset of physical illness or work harassment.

Ebaugh and Benjamin (1937; in Call, 2003, and in Melton, Petrilla, Poythress, & Slobogin, 1997; also summarized in Schultz, 2003b, but with reference to Bisbing, 1992) present a five-step analytic structure to guide forensic psychologists' formulation with respect to cause. The five steps consist of the following: (1) The index event is the "sole cause" of the resulting condition. There are no manifest or latent signs evident in the preevent state. The psychological result would not have occurred either in the present or later on had the event in question not occurred (Call, 2003, p. 56). (2) The event is the major "precipitating" factor or cause. An emotional disorder had been present in latent or potential form, but would not have manifested but for the effects of the event. (3) The event is an "aggravating" factor; some emotional disorder had been clinically evident, but the event adversely affected the condition. (4) The event is a "minor" factor. An emotional disorder had been well-developed prior to the event, which contributed to only a small degree to the disorder's intensity. (5) The event is unrelated to any emotional disorder.

The five statements can be seen to constitute an ordinal scale of degree of causality in which the relative balance of preexisting, event-related, and postevent psychological conditions are weighed. With respect to the validity of the five points, I query Ebaugh and Benjamin's contention that the only type of case in which an event can be the sole cause of a resultant disorder concerns head injury. This type of conjecture fit the times when it had been formulated, in 1937, but is no longer applicable. In addition, the third and fourth terms should be altered to reflect the concepts of thin and crumbling skulls, to which they are clearly related. Moreover, the second and third terms should be changed in terminology to reflect degree of cause (e.g., preponderant or predominant) rather than type of cause (e.g., precipitating). Therefore, the scale should be modified to read as follows—*Sole Cause, Preponderant Cause, Partial Cause, Minor Cause, or Absent Cause* (see Appendix I).

As I present in detail the scale points in Appendix I, note that the concepts of thin and crumbling skulls, which represent different degrees of preevent vulnerabilities, are largely embedded in scale points 3 and 4. Also, general recommendations for psychotherapy are offered at each scale point in order to make the scale applicable to rehabilitation as well as forensic contexts. In this regard, Samra and Connolly (2004) point out that when a trauma victim with an "eggshell" personality takes longer to recover or never recovers (e.g., from PTSD) due to a preexisting unconscious psychological personality "flaw," the defendant is fully liable, nevertheless, and the victim must be returned to the position in which she or he would have been had there been no trauma, obtaining all needed therapy even if it takes longer than typically expected.

This chapter began by pointing out the confusion in the fields of law, medicine, and psychology related to the terms of causality and causation. It now provides a suggestion for a scale that may render more rigorous the process of arriving at conclusions about causality in individual psychological assessments. The scale should be seen as a qualitative instrument, much like the five-level one for prognosis—positive, fair, guarded, poor, and grim. The proposed causality scale needs to be researched for its reliability and validity, although its predecessor by Ebaugh and Benjamin is considered classic even without this refinement.

Multiple Factors to Consider in Conclusions Pertaining to Causality and Causation

Psychologists and other mental health professionals (e.g., psychiatrists) often are required to consider whether an event or stressor in question, such as an accident, a work-injury, an assault, being victim of a crime, or witnessing community violence or trauma, contributes in a significant way to a complainant's psychological condition, and whether that condition reaches thresholds of impairment, disorder, or disability, requiring psychological and/or other treatment. In these type of cases, assessors need to justify conclusions offered about causality, causation, and their consequences found in their reports, or other forms of evidence that are presented to court, to third party payors, or other referral sources. In such cases, there is a range of factors to consider in formulating explanations of causality. That is, does the event or stressor in question explain, in full or in part, or materially contribute to, the complainant's ongoing psychological and related condition, or is there an increase in reported psychological and related difficulties being experienced by the complainant due to other factors?

The causality scale that has just been described in the last section can help the mental health assessor specify the degree of causality or causation attributable to an index event or stressor. However, it does not provide the rationale, justifications, arguments, explanations, and factors that can help the assessor arrive at conclusions about which level of causality is most appropriate in a particular case. Therefore, this section presents a list of multiple factors to consider in arriving at conclusions about causality, and the degree to which an index event or stressor materially contributes to an individual's assessed functional and psychological status. In ruling in or ruling out an index event or any subject stressor as at least partly responsible for a complainant's psychological and related impairment(s), disorder(s) and/or disability(ies), I underscore that multiple rationales, justifications, arguments, explanations, and factors need careful evaluation to help the mental health professional arrive at valid conclusions as to whether the event or stressor in question had contributed causally to the individual's psychological and functional presentation.

I propose a list of 25 such factors to consider in causality explanations, and present it in a manner that highlights some crucial "dos" and "don'ts." The list is not meant to be inclusive, formulaic, or a replacement for comprehensive and sound assessments. The list is general enough to apply to forensic purposes or rehabilitation purposes, for initial assessments or later ones, for MVA or worker's insurance claims, for sexual assaults or other types of traumatic incidents, and for consequences of physical injury/tissue damage, and psychological injury such as PTSD or TBI.

The list that I have constructed, with its 25 possible causality factors, recognizes that for individual assessments, the weighting is case-specific, and that many categories may not apply. As such, individual, case-specific interpretation is necessary. Before an assessor attributes full or partial causality to any one factor in any one assessment, the assessor must be able to support the conclusion offered, both in terms of having undertaken a comprehensive and relevant evaluation of the complainant and having obtained comprehensive knowledge of the pertinent research literature at the time of the assessment. Relevant supporting evidence is always needed to establish the validity of any factor under consideration as a causal explanation. This requirement places the onus on the assessor to be especially prudent, and to consider all factors from among the multiple factors possible in arriving at conclusions about causality, fitting the predominant theme of this book.

To summarize, each of the 25 possible causality factors that I have proposed may explain a complainant's range of psychological symptoms in full or in part. In contrast, each causality factor listed may not apply to or explain the complainant's psychological symptoms (e.g., a personality disorder may be present and may have no role or the specific disorder evident may not be applicable, or no personality disorder may be present).

[Note. If assessors use this list to guide them in arriving at conclusions in their individual assessments, they may want to indicate whether each factor had been relevant, in what direction (for or against), and to what degree (e.g., not applicable, minor relevance, moderate relevance, major relevance, sole factor involved).]

These 25 possible causality arguments can be grouped into five clusters related to: (1) the complainant's condition, (2) malingering, (3) other factors concerning the complainant, (4) the context, and (5) extra-complainant information. We review each of these clusters, in turn.

(1) *The complainant's condition.* The primary consideration in assessing a complainant usually lies in the information gathered about the complainant's behaviors, symptoms, history, and course, and in response to instruments administered.

(a–b) The first two items of the list query whether the complainant had been noticeably inconsistent in verbal report or in nonverbal behavior in interview.

(a) When noticeable inconsistency is found, at the verbal level, complainants may be poor or confused historians, or (b) at the nonverbal level, they may exhibit distressed physical signs of mood difficulties or pain behavior. However, an assessor may find that a complainant presents as only mildly inconsistent and/or as not excessively emotionally distressed or pain-focused (without excessive pain behavior or fear of pain), and these characteristics will be considered part of a generally valid profile. Note that Sharpe (2003) emphasized that the astute assessor of illness deception and malingering searches for inconsistency in the totality of the evidence available.

(c–d) The third and fourth items address whether preexisting factors are sufficient to partially or fully explain a complainant's psychological condition.

(c) Had there been a preexisting psychopathology or overwhelming history of psychological vulnerabilities, or too many prior psychological and other vulnerabilities/disorders/psychopathology, which may prevent attributing the alleged event or stressor as having causal responsibility for a complainant's psychological presentation? In legal parlance, as we have seen in earlier sections of this chapter, this refers to whether the complainant manifests an extreme "eggshell psyche" or "crumbling skull," such that the complainant's underlying, ongoing condition would have obtained even absent the alleged causal event/ stressor. For example, because of the degree of preexisting psychopathology, it may be extremely difficult to differentiate pre- and post-conditions. Alternatively, there may be evidence that, for example, prior psychological or other vulnerabilities/disorders/psychopathology may be insufficient to fully explain an individual's condition. In legal terminology, there is a "thin skull" or "crumbling skull," where at least some of the complainant's psychological condition can be causally related to the index event or stressor at issue.

(d) The next item relates to individuals engaging in multiple, demanding roles. It is possible that a complainant has had many prior psychological stressors and/or responsibilities related to work, school, home, chores, and/or children, or had been working at two jobs, or had been both working and studying, and so on. There had been no room in the life of the individual for the event or stressor in question, and its effects, which then had served to trigger the complainant's psychological condition. In extreme cases, any event/stressor, no matter how minimal, might have done the same — overwhelm the individual psychologically. For example, a complainant may have been so stressed prior to an accident that he or she lacked the ability to cope with it, having had no room for an event such as an accident and its effects. Therefore, any little extra stress and/or responsibility, no matter how small, would have caused an equally disproportionate psychological decline as that found after the event in question. Of course, the opposite may obtain. A complainant may have been managing well her or his myriad daily responsibilities, and could have handled even a substantial additional amount of stress including experiencing an event such as the one in question. In this case, an accident and its effects may constitute sufficient extra material stress and/or responsibility relative to the complainant's preexisting status.

(e) Psychologists and other mental health professionals administer psychological instruments that assess for negative impression management, symptom overreporting, symptom magnification, or "faking bad" with respect to postevent/stressor symptoms. [These instruments are discussed in Kane's and in Nicholson and Martelli's sections of this book.] A complainant may verbally report in interview a host of symptoms, the report of which might be subject to unconscious biases or even conscious manipulation, including beyond the question of malingering (see point "j"). However, comprehensive assessments should include psychological and related instruments that check for response biases, such as impression management and other confounding factors or threats to validity, utilizing well-researched, reliable and valid scales to provide data regarding the likelihood that the person had not been forthright in her or his responses. The assessor may find that the complainant has passed the validity checks on administered psychological and related instruments. Second, in contrast, the assessor may discover clear or unambiguous evidence of a failure to pass validity checks. Third, the assessor may find that the complainant did not pass the validity checks, but the overall pattern of results indicate a "cry for help" (catastrophizing; desperately seeking recognition of, or attention for, perceived serious mental health and/or physical problems) rather than symptom exaggeration for financial gain (or malingering). Finally, it could be that the complainant had not passed the validity checks due to a need to engage in "sick role behavior" and receive misplaced social support and sympathy (See points "l–n" below). Although there is a total of 25 items on this list of 25 factors to consider in causality estimation, this item especially requires good supporting evidence, and much caution is needed before conclusions relating to it are offered.

(f) The assessor may conclude that there is an absence of clinical-level symptoms. However, this may obtain because of symptom minimization detected by the psychological instruments administered to verify the complainant's validity in presentation. For postevent or poststressor symptoms, rather than finding negative impression management, symptom magnification, or faking bad, the assessor may find positive impression management, symptom minimization, underreporting, or "faking good." However, confounds may lie in finding trends such as these for preevent/stressor symptoms; for example, a complainant may minimize common human frailties that should be evident, in general, and, in contrast, magnify postevent/stressor symptoms. It should be noted that when symptom minimization is found to derive from motivations such as trying to continue on despite everything that has happened posttrauma, adopting the attitude of a "stiff upper lip," symptoms may wax and wane in moments when defenses and coping skills give out.

(g) A complainant may express symptoms that lie on the border of clinical significance, without any confounding factors. These cases are difficult to evaluate because of the gray areas involved. Does the complainant arrive at the legal threshold at which psychotherapy, financial compensation, and so forth, are required, or fall just below threshold? What are the standards that psychologists should use in such cases? Does the complainant or the third party payor, the plaintiff or the defendant, get some benefit of doubt? Is the conclusion that "more likely than not" there is a clinically significant condition, given that more rigorous evidence has not been obtained, or more rigorous criteria do not apply?

(h–i) A complainant may have received a typical course of psychotherapy.

(h) She or he may have received an adequate course of psychotherapy or other therapy, for the statistically average or typical person in her or his situation, with her or his injuries. Moreover, the psychotherapy or other therapy might have been successful in reducing to subclinical levels all previously clinically significant psychological symptoms due to the event/stressor in question, and continuation of the therapy is not needed. Or psychotherapy may have helped resolve all outstanding psychological issues. Alternatively, a complainant may still have residual, clinically significant symptoms. The psychotherapy or other therapy had not been successful in reducing all previously clinically significant psychological symptoms to subclinical levels, and continuation of the therapy is needed.

(i) A complainant may have reached the "maximum" psychological recovery of which she or he is capable, but is left with permanent or relatively permanent clinically-significant symptoms despite the therapy, and so on. Even in cases such as this, the question arises about the need for further psychotherapy. For example, further treatment may be warranted for prevention of deterioration, maintenance of gain, crisis management, and/or ongoing support. Nevertheless, when therapy is long term, the issue of encouraging dependency in the complainant needs to be recognized.

(2) *Malingering.* (j) There may be clear evidence of malingering, or outright, conscious illness deception for fraudulent, financial, or other reasons. Often, this evidence is most difficult to obtain (Sharpe, 2003), and seldom do assessors arrive at clear-cut conclusions related to the presence of malingering. The sociolegal consequences of malingering, illness deception, excessive subjective health complaints, unexplained medical symptoms, and so on, are described in Halligan, Bass, and Oakley (2003). Their collective cost to society requires that assessors remain vigilant about willful deception and related motivations. Although each possible causality factor listed in this section requires careful argumentation and good supporting evidence, much caution is needed before conclusions related to malingering are offered. For example, evidence of malingering may be partial, and some legitimate, clinically significant symptoms may be present in the complainant due to the event/stressor in question. [See point "e" above on negative impression management.] When reliable and valid instruments are used, such as the MMPI-2 (Minnesota Multiphasic Personality Inventory, Second Edition, Butcher, Dahlstrom, Graham, Tellegen, & Kaemmer, 1989), and evidence for malingering is found, the assessor needs to examine the multiple array of data gathered on the individual in order to rule out alternative explanations before arriving at a conclusion that malingering is a reasonable possibility.

(3) *Factors related to the complainant.* There are a variety of ways that assessors may deem that a complainant is manifesting postevent/stressor symptoms that are more related to preexisting factors inherent in the individual and/or to postevent/stressor factors clearly beyond the effects of the event/stressor.

(k) The complainant may be evaluated to have one or more types of personality disorder that can fully or partially explain her or his ongoing symptoms clearly outside of any event/stressor-related and/or postevent/stressor-related developments. The assessor must be extremely prudent in arriving at such conclusions, and must establish that the personality pattern involved can clearly contribute to the complainant's symptoms. It may be impossible to show that the pattern can explain all the symptoms involved. As an example, the complainant may be excessively antisocial and aggressive, but may still have valid symptoms attributable to the event/stressor in question.

(l) The complainant may be engaging in unconscious desire for secondary gain, such as getting sympathy or avoiding work, which serves to prolong symptoms through over-focusing, exaggerating, sensitization, somatization, and like processes. These factors may contribute to explaining the complainant's presentation, but the difficult question remains whether a desire for secondary gain can fully explain her or his symptoms, and assessors who put forth such conclusions should be prepared to defend them in court with appropriate case-specific and research evidence. For example, an assessor may find that there is some evidence of excessive somatization that is out of awareness (unconscious), which appears to be for secondary gain, but there is still sufficient evidence in the complainant's presentation that any psychopathology identified had been primarily or exclusively, and adequately, a result of the effect of the subject event/stressor.

(m) The complainant may be using the symptoms to somehow attempt to satisfy preexisting unconscious conflicts, unmet needs, issues, or behavioral habits and patterns of a maladaptive nature, such as being overly dependent or needing attention. As with the above, any conclusions offered for or against this type of argument need appropriate supporting evidence.

(n) Significant others, such as close family members, may unwittingly reinforce "illness behavior" by being overly solicitious, discouraging functional activity, and so on, and the complainant does not attempt to counter this behavior, creating in her or him a passive attitude with little effort. There may be an unconscious desire to engage in sick role behavior, thereby getting sympathy, and so on, compounding this familial attitude (See points "e," "l," and "m" above.) Although this pattern of interactive behavior is explained by learning theory models proposed by Fordyce (Flor & Hermann, 2004), it would need careful documentation in any case to which it is applied.

(o) In other ways, the complainant may avoid undertaking activities related to legal issues at hand, such as engaging in work-hardening (therapy preparing the individual for work, for example, by building up physical treatment and engaging in exercise for considerable hours per week), or attempting a return to work on modified duties or reduced load. In such cases, there is no apparent effort to mitigate losses, despite the complainant being psychologically capable of engaging in the work function/responsibility at issue. In this regard, the complainant may shirk other normal daily functions or activities, such as leisure, family life, social life, and sexual activity. Of course, the assessor may conclude that there is genuine loss of the psychological capacity to undertake the pertinent responsibility, whether at work, at home, or in other spheres. Again, irrespective of the direction of the argument, it would need careful supporting evidence.

(p) The complainant may avoid potentially beneficial psychotherapy, or possesses a personality and psychological structure that renders her or him unlikely to profit from it, perhaps as suggested by results on psychometric tests. There is no apparent effort to mitigate losses by complying with therapy or other treatment. In contrast, of course, the assessor may find that the complainant had demonstrated throughout good effort and full participation in all phases of treatment. As with the above, any aspect of this argument would need to be carefully documented.

(4) *The context.* Psychologists examine context and extraneous factors in an effort to understand the whole person. These variables may be crucial in understanding causality. Complainants are subject to myriad stressors after an alleged causal event/stressor that together need consideration.

(q) Aside from a complainant's symptom onset and course at the physical, emotional, and cognitive levels, because vocational capacity may be affected, income may decrease substantially, even after benefits are paid. A complainant may lose her or his job due to employer prejudice against injured workers, or fear of increased worker disability insurance premiums.

(r) A complainant may be subject to repeated insurer- and/or attorney-prompted medical/physical and/or psychological/psychiatric evaluations. The insurance and litigation process and procedures may be even more distressing and frustrating than the original event, injuries, and course. A complainant may be coached by an attorney, dissuaded inappropriately by an insurer, experience acts of bad faith, and otherwise be a victim of the adversarial process.

(s) Corollary, postevent stressors may be unrelated to the event/stressor in question and its purported consequences. A complainant may lose her or his job due to factory closure, for example, or a family member may pass away. Of course, the assessor needs to examine the degree to which residual coping mechanisms for such stressors has been reduced by the effects of the event/stressor at issue; the assessor determines whether the added perceived stress from such apparently unrelated stressors has contributed indirectly to the complainant's total perceived life stress beyond the direct effects of event/stressor in question. That is, even putatively unrelated stressors may need to be considered for their interactive effects on the complainant's clinical presentation.

(5) *Extra-complainant information.* In the last category of collateral and supplementary information about a complainant, the assessor must identify and evaluate the documentation, information provided by significant others, and the scientific literature that are relevant in determining causality.

(t) The ambulance call, emergency record, treating physician clinical notes both before and after the event/stressor, assessment reports on the personal injury in question, childhood and adolescent school records, military records, work performance records, and so on, might provide valuable information to the assessor. That is, documentation written both before and after the event/stressor (not by a psychologist or other mental health professional) might address issues pertinent to psychological or related impairments, disorders, and/or disabilities due to an event/stressor.

(u) Information gathered from significant others might prove helpful to the assessor. For example, collateral information from significant others (family, coworkers, and treating physician) might support the complainant.

(v) Additionally, the assessor needs to know well the scientific literature. To what degree does population-level, nomothetic research speak to the case at hand,

and facilitate an understanding of the causality involved for the particular complainant? The scientific literature might support the conclusion that a psychological or related impairment, disorder, and/or disability due to the event/stressor in question is possible in the case under consideration.

(w–y) Finally, other psychological and related mental health evaluations undertaken with the individual after the event should be carefully analyzed for the quality of their assessments, including whether the conclusions about causality were informed by enough evidence in terms of clinical interviews, collateral information, instruments/tests, documents reviewed, and other data.

(w) In examining prior mental health assessment(s), it may become evident that perhaps an incorrect process was followed by other mental health professional(s) who had offered an opinion different from the conclusion that the assessor is prepared to offer, in that some aspects of the interview or the psychological or related instruments and tests used with the complainant were not comprehensive/appropriate and reliable/valid.

(x) Also, perhaps some aspects of the other types of data gathered (e.g., collateral information, the assessor's analysis of prior documentation) may or may not have been comprehensive/appropriate and reliable/valid.

(y) Finally, some aspects of the process followed in arriving at conclusions may or may not have been comprehensive/appropriate and reliable/valid. For example, were attempts made to rule out all competing, plausible explanations of a complainant's psychological presentation?

Conclusions

Practice. We advise that for the mental health assessment of any one complainant, independent of whether the final decision is to support or deny the claim of harm due to the alleged negligent event/stressor, psychologists and other mental health professionals should consider the full range of possible arguments in their conclusions, for example, in terms of the 25 factors suggested in this section. In addition, attorneys may find it advisable to consult this list or a similar list, in order to determine to what degree alternative explanations to the ones offered in reports, testimony, and other forms of evidence may apply.

We emphasize that in one way or another, in their conclusions to individual assessments, and in evaluating the origins of clinically significant psychological symptoms, assessors should consider a multifactorial approach before attributing cause to the subject index event or stressor. We cannot envision that one simple explanation would be sufficient to explain causality or its lack in most cases. We maintain that the mental health assessor who uses a too-simplified explanation of causality acts to increase the chances of a successful *Daubert* challenge on the admissibility to her or his testimony, not to mention queries of whether the assessor has addressed the standard of practice required by his or her professional license or registration.

With respect to our list of 25 possible causality factors, we note that certain terms may need more conceptualization in order to clarify their standing (e.g., the concept of "secondary gain," in accord with the criticisms of Rogers, see above). Nevertheless, these terms are included because they are still used in the field, although in using them the assessor should be aware of their limitations.

Some items on the presented list should never be used alone as justifications for conclusions about causality. For example, a psychologist should never argue for or against causality on the basis solely of another assessor about the claim. Also, malingering should be specified only when extremely strong supporting evidence is available.

Some explanations offered in individual testimony are too vague and should not be used without supporting evidence. Both sides of the adversarial divide are equally guilty, for example, by using preferred catchwords or phrases with multiple implications that explain little because no or little supporting evidence is offered. In this regard, assessors should avoid using terms such as "poor historian," or "major inconsistency" without supporting evidence. As converse examples, assessors should avoid describing an examinee as having a "permanent," "serious" impairment of an "important psychological function" or "substantial impairment" without, for example, carefully delineating the mechanism from deficit to functional outcome, without comment on sufficiency of attempts at mitigating loss, or without offering typical course and prognosis in the base rates of the population-level research.

In addition, some terms often offered in testimony appear to address relevant mechanisms, but are essentially vague. For example, as we have seen, Rogers and colleagues point out that the term "symptom magnification" is vague as typically used. I have suggested that, when warranted, psychologists use the term "symptom exaggeration" but also that they should specify what is involved in the process, such as providing an evidence-supported interpretation in terms of malingering or a "cry for help." Another example relates to the term "somatization," which is limited when its use does not specify the source of psychological factors contributing to any psychophysiological or "psychosomatic" condition involved. For example, in terms of the adversarial divide, more than any intrapersonal factor, contributing stressors may relate to the initial effects of an injury, poor coping mechanisms, poor social support, subsequent job loss, or, to the contrary, they may relate to a bellicose attitude, misattributing blame for all preexisting psychological difficulties and life stresses uniquely to the event in question, conscious wish for a large settlement out of proportion to the injury, and so on. In this regard, Craig (2005) cites Vendrig (2000), who noted that some chronic pain patients may be "channeling" their emotional difficulties into somatic pain reactions, although this tendency may be a response to living in pain rather than an impetus in causing the pain.

Ultimately, any conclusion about causality offered in forensic and other assessments, such as in rehabilitation, need to be carefully crafted in light of supporting evidence, both in terms of the data gathered on the individual and the scientific literature related to the complainant's purported psychological and functional status.

Finally, we point out that the availability of this list of 25 factors to consider in determining causality increases the chances of effective cross-examination of statements made in testimony, because the list provides attorneys knowledge of the range of possible justifications, rationales, and explanations that could have been used but were not. Therefore, the list reminds that assessors need to consider all reasonably possible alternative explanations in their conclusions, and not slip into facile explanations one way or the other. Thus, we hope that the list helps serve an important educational function both for mental health professionals and attorneys, protecting the right of complainants, third party payors, and parties involved in tort action.

Overall Conclusions. For court purposes, the task of the plaintiff is to establish that the index event in the causal nexus to which she or he had been exposed is the necessary and sufficient cause for her or his ongoing complaints. Generally, unlike psychologists, attorneys attempt to distil out of the multiple causes that may be involved in their client's case, one allegedly responsible cause. Attorneys identify a "theory of the case," and seek linear, predominant, or sole proximate cause to their client's symptoms. The plaintiff's attorney will maximize the impact of the alleged tortious event, while the defendant's attorney will build up factors such as the plaintiff's preexisting stressors or psychopathology, the plaintiff's other problems and any personality disorders, or the plaintiff's inconsistencies or alleged symptom magnification/malingering.

After events such as personal injuries, the adversarial nature of the legal system pressures forensic and other psychologists to seek simplified explanations for individuals' psychological complaints; for instance, that the event in question caused "everything" subsequent to it or, at the other extreme, that every symptom is an expression of malingering. However, psychologists understand that comprehensive evaluations may reveal multiple causal elements that interact with the effects of a purported causal event, to the point of creating a psychological impairment, disorder, or disability. Psychologists understand that it may be too difficult to single out as primary one causal factor or another.

There is no standard system that allows law and psychology to bridge these different emphases, to speak the same language with respect to causality and causation. The present chapter attempts to provide a psychological perspective needed to build toward such a language, and offers practical suggestions to follow in evaluating causality. In the chapter, I suggest using terminology that is neutral with respect to causality, propose that patients may exaggerate their symptoms due to an exacerbation process that does not involve malingering present an ordinal causality scale on the degree of material contribution of an index event to patient presentation, and offer a list of 25 causality factors applicable to causality formulations, ones that mental health professionals may want to consider in constructing the evidence offered to court. The latter two applications allow for conclusions with respect to possible malingering and related processes, but only careful evaluation of any one patient can determine the presence of such conscious exaggeration of symptoms for financial incentives.

Appendix I

An Ordinal Scale of Degree of Causality and Causation

After an index event such as a motor vehicle accident, sexual assault, or physical impact to the head, mental health assessors may need to estimate the degree of responsibility of the event in eliciting an individual's subsequent psychological symptoms relative to other factors such as preexisting state and unrelated stressors. The following scale is proposed to assist in attributing cause in such evaluations. It is comprised of five scale points, ordinal in nature: Sole cause, Preponderant cause, Partial cause, Minor cause, and Absent cause. It should be used only after comprehensive assessment and consideration of all the data gathered.

(1) *Sole Cause.* The current postevent psychological and functional status of the complainant is fully caused by the event or stressor under review. There may have been some relatively minor preevent psychological considerations, but these in no way constitute a predisposing factor to the psychological reaction that the complainant experienced due to the event. The complainant's postevent psychological and functional status have been altered uniquely by the event, and it is reasonable and necessary that psychotherapy and/or other rehabilitation is required to help return the complainant to or toward her or his preevent status.

(2) *Preponderant Cause.* The complainant had experienced, in her or his past, stressors that had created psychological vulnerabilities on which the index event or stressor has acted. But, clearly, the preponderant proportion of the current psychological and functional status of the complainant is directly related to the event at issue. In no way can the prior psychological vulnerabilities account in full for the current postevent condition of the complainant. The complainant had been functioning adequately prior to the event, and psychotherapy or other rehabilitation is deemed reasonable and necessary in order to help return the complainant to or toward prior psychological and functional levels of daily adaptation. It is conceivable that, in these cases, psychotherapeutic needs are prolonged compared to uncomplicated cases.

(3) *Partial Cause.* The complainant had experienced before the index event significant prestressor psychological vulnerabilities/weaknesses/susceptibilities, but without having experienced any actual preevent clinical psychological condition (thus, in legal parlance, the complainant had a "thin skull" or "eggshell personality"). The individual's current psychological status and any functional impairment can be directly related to the subject event via an interaction/activation/aggravation effect. That is, prior vulnerabilities contribute to the complainant's current psychological status, but not in unique or preponderant ways, and only in conjunction with the subject event, in an interactive or multiplicative fashion. Thus, the index event constitutes an important and material agent in the complainant's current psychological condition, even if the complainant's prior psychological vulnerabilities hastened, deepened, or otherwise contributed to this condition, in a compounding, cumulative effect. "Crumbling skull" cases involve

a preexisting active condition worsened by an event at issue, or a latent but degenerative condition accelerated by an event. Typically, such cases should be treated in scale point 4, which concerns minor cause. However, one type of crumbling skull case should be treated in the current scale point 3. That is, when a complainant had suffered marked psychological difficulties before occurrence of an event (having a "crumbling skull"), and then experienced an event that contributed to the activation of a new clinical psychological condition unrelated to the preexisting condition, as evaluated by the assessor, she or he should be judged to have experienced an event constituting a partial cause. Or a milder preexisting or latent condition was exacerbated by the event. In these various cases, consistent with the argument made in presenting scale point 2, psychotherapy and/or other rehabilitation needs may be prolonged.

(4) *Minor Cause.* The complainant's preevent psychological status had been very fragile, and if outright psychological problems had not already been manifested, the individual had been close to experiencing them before the event. The index event has exacerbated her or his condition, either by putting the individual over the edge from a quite fragile state, or by worsening a preexisting clinical-level psychological condition. In either case, the worsening of the individual's psychological condition would likely have manifested, although not as quickly, even without the index event having taken place (the "crumbling skull" case). In all these types of cases, everything else being equal, the index event should be considered only a minimal or minor causal factor of the complainant's current psychological status; there is only a mild contribution by the index event in question. It is judged to have not appreciably altered or accelerated the ongoing preevent dynamic being experienced by the complainant, although it functioned as the last psychological "straw that broke the camel's back," as a precipitating agent. Nevertheless, despite its relatively minor nature, it is judged that the event ultimately represents a contributing material, causative agent exacerbating the complainant's current psychological condition. Some psychological rehabilitation would be considered reasonable and necessary in such cases. Moreover, depending on which regulations and rules governing the case at hand apply, greater rehabilitation needs may be permitted, for example, to bring the complainant back to her or his prior psychological state and functional status, that is, toward how she or he had been found.

(5) *Absent Cause.* This category brings together several situations in which no cause can be attributed to the index event or stressor in question, either because there has been no increase in clinical-level psychological symptoms (5a–b), or because clear evidence of malingering has been found (5c). (5a) The complainant's preevent psychological vulnerabilities had been pronounced enough that the index event did not materially contribute in any way to the complainant's current psychological condition, not even in a minimal, minor way, because a psychological dynamic had been set in place prior to the event that the event did not alter or accelerate in any evident way (it is not true that the dynamic would not have happened but for the event). (5b) Currently, despite the possible presence of some nonclinical-level psychological symptoms, the complainant is not experiencing

any significant psychological symptoms. The complainant may report difficulties to varying degrees, but the overall psychological profile suggests that these are not at a threshold level at which the present psychological condition is compromised, nor is there interference with the complainant's functional activities. (5c) Finally, a complainant may report numerous symptoms and functional effects due to the index event, but she or he is judged to be malingering all complaints on the basis of reliable and valid data collected by the assessor. It is strongly advised that malingering should not be identified as an issue without detailing the data and arguments leading to the conclusion. When the malingering is judged to be only partial, or when there are signs of valid symptoms despite the presence of symptom exaggeration or exacerbation or otherwise misattributing symptoms to the event in question, the assessor must determine to what degree the other scale points (1–4, 5a–b) legitimately apply. Finally, for scale points 5a–b, some psychotherapy may be reasonable and necessary in a prophylactic, preventative sense.

References

Alcock, J. (2001). *Animal behavior: An evolutionary approach* (7th ed.). Sutherland, MA: Sinauer.

American Psychiatric Association. (1994). *Diagnostic and statistical manual of mental disorders* (4th ed.). Washington, DC: Author.

American Psychiatric Association. (2000). *Diagnostic and statistical manual of mental disorders: Text revision* (4th ed.). Washington, DC: Author.

Antoine-Tubbs v. Local 513 Air Transp. Div., 50 F. Supp. 2d 601 (N.D. Tex. 1998).

Athey v. Leonati [1996] 3 S.C.R. 458.

Bailey, J. A., II. (1998). *The concise dictionary of medical-legal terms*. New York: Parthenon.

Bisbing, S. B. (1992, November). *The psychological injury claim in worker's compensation: Unraveling one of the industry's most vexing challenges*. Paper presented at the Second APA & NIOSH Conference on Occupational Stress, Washington, DC.

Black v. Food Lion, Inc. 171 F.3d 308 (5th Cir. 1999).

Blackburn, S. (1994). *The Oxford dictionary of philosophy*. New York: Oxford University Press.

Bryant, R. A. (2003). Assessing individuals for compensation. In D. Carson & R. Bull (Eds.), *Handbook of psychology in legal contexts* (pp. 89–107). Chichester, UK: Wiley.

Butcher, J. N., Dahlstrom, W. G., Graham, J. R., Tellegen, A., & Kaemmer, B. (1989). *Minnesota Multiphasic Personality Inventory-2 (MMPI-2): Manual for administration and scoring*. Minneapolis, MN: University of Minnesota Press.

Call, J. A. (2003). Liability for psychological injury: History of the concept. In I. Z. Schultz & D. O. Brady (Eds.), *Psychological injuries at trial* (pp. 40–64). Chicago, IL: American Bar Association.

Cocchiarella, L., & Andersson, G. B. J. (Eds.). (2001). *Guides to the evaluation of permanent impairment* (5th ed.). Chicago, IL: American Medical Association.

Cocchiarella, L., & Lord, S. J. (Eds.). (2001). *Master the AMA Guides Fifth* (5th ed., pp. 327–341). Chicago, IL: American Medical Association.

Corsini, R. J. (2002). *The dictionary of psychology*. New York: Brunner-Routledge.

Craig, E. (Ed.). (1998). *Routledge encyclopedia of philosophy*. New York: Routledge.

Crick v. Mohan (sub nom.) [1993] 142 A.R. 281 (Q.B.).
Daubert v. Merrell Dow Pharmaceuticals, Inc. 509 U.S. 579, 113 S.Ct. 2786, 125 L.Ed. 2d 469 (1993).
Dobbs, D. B. (2000). *The law of torts*. St. Paul, MN: West Group.
Dorland, I., & Newman, W. A. (2003). *Dorland's illustrated medical dictionary* (30th ed.). Amsterdam: Elsevier.
Douglas, K. S., Huss, M. T., Murdoch, L. L., Washington, D. O., & Koch, W. J. (1999). Posttraumatic Stress Disorder stemming from motor vehicle accidents: Legal issues in Canada and the United States. In E. J. Hickling & E. B. Blanchard (Eds.), *The international handbook of road traffic accidents and psychological trauma: Current understanding, treatment and law* (pp. 271–289). New York: Elsevier Science.
Ebaugh, F., & Benjamin, J. (1937). Trauma and disease 56. As cited in J. A. Call (2003). Liability for psychological injury: History of the concept. In I. Z. Schultz & D. O. Brady (Eds.), *Psychological injuries at trial* (pp. 40–64). Chicago, IL: American Bar Association.
Faieta, M. (2005). Civil liability for environmental torts. In T. Archibald & M. Cochrane (Eds.), *Annual review of civil litigation: 2004* (pp. 21–58). Toronto, ON: Thomson/ Carswell.
Faigman, D. L. (2003). Expert evidence: The rules and the rationality the law applies (or should apply) to psychological expertise. In D. Carson & R. Bull (Eds.), *Handbook of psychology in legal contexts* (pp. 367–400). Chichester, UK: Wiley.
Faigman, D. L., & Monahan, J. (2005). Psychological evidence at the dawn of the law's scientific age. *Annual Review of Psychology, 56*, 631–659.
Federal Rules of Evidence. (2004). Washington, DC: U.S. Government Printing Office. Retrieved January 18, 2005, from http://www.house.gov/judiciary/evid2004.pdf.
Feehan, K. P., & Tinkler, P. S. (2005). Medical malpractice litigation: The pure application of the principles of negligence. In T. Archibald & M. Cochrane (Eds.), *Annual review of civil litigation: 2004* (pp. 59–104). Toronto, ON: Thomson/Carswell.
Flew, A., & Priest, S. (Eds.). (2002). *A dictionary of philosophy*. London: Pan Books.
Flor, H., & Hermann, C. (2004). Biopsychosocial models of pain. In R. H. Dworkin & W. S. Breitbart (Eds.), *Psychological aspects of pain: A handbook for health care providers* (pp. 47–75). Seattle, WA: IASP Press.
Freckelton, I. (2002). Epilogue: Dilemmas in proof of causation. In I. Freckelton & D. Mendelson (Eds.), *Causation in law and medicine* (pp. 429–481). Burlington, VT: Ashgate/Dartmouth.
Frye v. United States, 293 F. 1013, 34 ALR 145 (D. C. Cir. 1923).
Garner, B. A. (Ed.). (1995). *A dictionary of modern legal usage* (2nd ed.). New York: Oxford University Press.
Garner, B. A. (Ed.). (2004). *Black's law dictionary* (8th ed.). St. Paul, MN: West Group.
General Electric Co. v. Joiner, 522 U.S. 136, 118 S.Ct. 512 (1997).
Haack, S. (2005). Trial and error: The Supreme Court's philosophy of science. *American Journal of Public Health, 95* (Suppl. 1), 566–573.
Halligan, P. W., Bass, C., & Oakley, D. A. (2003). Wilful deception as illness behavior. In P. W. Halligan, C. Bass, & D. A. Oakley (Eds.), *Malingering and illness deception* (pp. 3–28). New York: Oxford University Press.
Haynes, S. N. (1992). *Models of causality in psychopathology: Toward dynamic, synthetic and nonlinear models of behavior disorders*. New York: Macmillan.
Heller v. Shaw, 167 F.3d 146 (3d Cir. 1999).
Henifin, M. S., Kipen, H. M., & Poulter, S. R. (2000). Reference guide on medical testimony. In Federal Judicial Center, *Reference manual on scientific evidence* (2nd ed., pp. 39–484). Washington, DC: Author.

Janiak v. Ippolito [1985] 1 S.C.R. 146, 1985 CanLII 62 (S.C.C.).

Jewell, E. J., & Abate, F. (Eds.). (2001). *The new Oxford American dictionary*. New York: Oxford University Press.

King, J. H., Sweet, J. J., Sherer, M., Curtiss, G., & Vanderploeg, R. D. (2002). Validity indicators within the Wisconsin Card Sorting Test: Application of new and previously researched multivariate procedures in multiple traumatic brain injury samples. *Clinical Neuropsychologist, 16*, 506–523.

Kumho Tire Co. v. Carmichael, 526 U.S. 137, 119 S.Ct. 1167 (1999).

Melton, G. B., Petrilla, J., Poythress, N. G., & Slobogin, C. (1997). Law and the mental health professions: An uneasy alliance. *Psychological evaluations for the courts*. New York: Guilford Press.

Merriam-Webster's collegiate dictionary (11th ed.). (2003). Springfield, MA: Merriam-Webster.

Miramon v. Bradley, 701 So.2d 475 (La. App. 1 Cir. 1997).

Ozonoff, D. (2005a). Legal causation and responsibility for causing harm. *American Journal of Public Health, 95* (Suppl. 1), 35–38.

Ozonoff, D. (2005b). Epistemology in the courtroom: A little "knowledge" is a dangerous thing. *American Journal of Public Health, 95* (Suppl. 1), 513–515.

Padget v. Gray, 727 S.W.2d 706 (Tex. App. 1987).

Pearl, J. (2000). *Causality: Models, reasoning, and interference*. New York: Cambridge University Press.

Psillos, S. (Ed.). (2002). *Causation and explanation*. Montreal: McGill-Queen's University Press.

Reber, A. S., & Reber, E. S. (2001). *The Penguin dictionary of psychology* (3rd ed.). London: Penguin Books.

Rogers, R., & Bender, S. D. (2003). Evaluation of malingering and deception. In I. B. Weiner (Series Ed.) & A. M. Goldstein (Vol. Ed.), *Handbook of psychology: Vol. 11, Forensic psychology* (pp. 109–129). Hoboken, NJ: Wiley.

Rogers, R., & Shuman, D. W. (2005). *Fundamentals of forensic practice: Mental health and criminal law*. New York: Springer Science+Business Media.

Rogers, R., & Vitacco, M. J. (2002). Forensic assessment of malingering and related response styles. In B. Van Dorsten (Ed.), *Forensic psychology: From classroom to courtroom* (pp. 83–104). New York: Kluwer Academic/Plenum.

Romano, J. F. (1999). Cause yourself to understand the intricacies of causation. *Trial Lawyer, 22*, 101–103.

Rothman, K. J., & Greenland, S. (2005). Causation and causal inference in epidemiology. *American Journal of Public Health, 95*, 5144–5150.

Russell, B. (1910). *Philosophical essays* (3rd Imp.). London: Allen & Unwin.

Russell, B. (1918). *Mysticism and logic*. London: Allen & Unwin.

Russell, B. (1950). *Mysticism and logic: And other essays* (9th Imp.). London: Allen & Unwin.

R. v. Mohan [1994] 2 S.C.R. 9, 1994 CanLII 80 (S.C.C.).

Sales, B. D., & Shuman, D. W. (2005). *Experts in court: Reconciling law, science, and professional knowledge*. Washington, DC: American Psychological Association.

Samra, J., & Connolly, D. A. (2004). Legal compensability of symptoms associated with Posttraumatic Stress Disorder: A Canadian perspective. *International Journal of Forensic Mental Health, 3*, 55–66.

Schultz, I. Z. (2003b). Psychological causality determination in personal injury and workers' compensation contexts. In I. Z. Schultz & D. O. Brady (Eds.), *Psychological injuries at trial* (pp. 102–125). Chicago, IL: American Bar Association.

Sharpe, M. (2003). Distinguishing malingering from psychiatric disorders. In P. W. Halligan, C. Bass, & D. A. Oakley (Eds.), *Malingering and illness deception* (pp. 156–170). New York: Oxford University Press.

Slovenko, R. (2002a). Causation in law and psychiatry. In I. Freckelton & D. Mendelson (Eds.), *Causation in law and medicine* (pp. 357–378). Burlington, VT: Ashgate/ Dartmouth.

Slovenko, R. (2002b). *Psychiatry in law/law in psychiatry: Psychiatry in law*. New York: Brunner-Routledge.

Smith, L. B., & Samuelson, L. K. (2003). Different is good: Connectionism and dynamic systems theory are complementary emergentist approaches to development. *Developmental Science, 6*, 343–439.

Smith, L. B., & Thelen, E. (Eds.). (1993). *A dynamic systems approach to development: Applications*. Cambridge, MA: The MIT Press/Bradford Book.

Snell v. Farrell [1990] 2 S.C.R. 311, 1990 CanLII 70 (S.C.C.).

Stevens v. Okrainec [1997] 210 A.R. 161 (Alta. Q.B.).

Theriault v. Swan, 588 A.2d 369 (Me. 1989).

Urbina, S. (2004). *Essentials of psychological testing*. New York: Wiley.

Van Dorsten, B., & James, L. B. (2002). Forensic medical psychology: Personal injury litigation. In B. Van Dorsten (Ed.), *Forensic psychology: From classroom to courtroom* (pp. 247–282). New York: Kluwer Academic/Plenum.

Vendrig, A. A. (2000). The Minnesota Multiphasic Personality Inventory and chronic pain: A conceptual analysis of a long-standing but complicated relationship. *Clinical Psychology Review*, 20, 533–559.

4

Dictionary of Terms Related to Causality, Causation, Law, and Psychology

Gerald Young and Ronnie Shore

The dictionary of terms presented in this chapter concerns the specific terms of "causality" and "causation," key terms related to these terms, and auxiliary terms such as "expert witness" and "trier of fact." For straightforward terms, often, we give only one definition is given and it is derived from a standard source, such as a law dictionary or a psychology dictionary. However, for variation, the definition may be taken from a different source. For important terms, where dictionaries clearly differ in definition, or are complementary, we may provide several definitions, a procedure which facilitates grasping the differences. In addition, this approach also helps prepare discussion of clear differences in definition for the same term across domains, for example, in psychology and in law.

In this chapter, first, key legal terms are defined, in particular, according to standard legal dictionaries (especially Garner, 1995, 2004). Then, auxiliary legal terms are introduced. The chapter moves on to definitions found in medicine, psychology, and philosophy. Where appropriate, comments and notes applicable to terms are included after they are defined. The conclusions to this dictionary include a list of key terms with respect to "causality" and "causation" in the various disciplines. It is hoped that the list will help lead to clearer use of the terms concerning causality, causation, and related ones, both within and across the various disciplines in which they are essential.

Key Legal Terms Related to Causality and Causation

The law has established a complex network of terms related to causality and causation. However, the terms are not always defined consistently, used consistently, or consistent with definitions of the same term in other disciplines. Commentators have bemoaned the confusion. More so than in the ensuing sections on medicine, psychology, and philosophy, we comment on the terms as they are presented. We used *Black's Law Dictionary*, in particular (Garner, 2004), as the primary source of legal definitions. At times, we referenced the previous edition in 1999, if it provided supplementary information. Garner has edited another dictionary (Garner, 1995, for Oxford University Press), which we also consulted, as needed.

Causa. This term is the Latin one from which the terms causality and causation have evolved. The following quotes illustrate the confusion associated with these terms in legal circles, complicating the task of other professionals needing to establish equivalence or translation into their field.
Definition. The Latin term "causa" refers to "cause" (Garner, 2004, p. 232).
Comment/Note. Garner (2004) refers to the term causa as "[o]ne of the vaguest terms of the Roman juristic language" (Berger, 1953; in Garner, 2004, p. 232). Garner (1995) specifies that the words "cause" and "causing" have produced more legal problems than most words in the English language (p. 138). He adds that the term "cause" in legal circles has a specific meaning beyond those relevant to other professions dealing with complainants. For Garner, legal terminology indicates that courts are concerned with determining "cause" from the perspective of attaching liability, not of determining causes related to the physical or medical areas (Garner, 1995, p. 139). Garner (2004) specifies further that where cause is sequential, "the cause of the cause" should also be considered. "Causa causae est causa causati … [Latin «the cause of the cause is the cause of the thing caused»] … The principle that the cause of the cause (rather than only the immediate cause) should also be considered as the cause of the effect" (p. 233).

Causa scientiae. *Definition*. "Cause of knowledge" (Garner, 2004, p. 233). *Comment/Note*. "… a witness's basis for drawing a particular conclusion, esp. in a case involving scientific expertise" (Garner, 2004, p. 233). This quote illustrates the central subject matter of this book, and shows that it has roots as a question in the Latin origins of law.

Causal. The legal and common dictionaries concur in their definitions. *Definition*. "1. Of, relating to, or involving causation" … 2. "Arising from a cause …" (Garner, 2004, p. 233). (Garner, 1995) adds that the term "causal" relates to expressing or indicating cause (p. 138). In addition, in reference to the term "causal," *Merriam-Webster's Collegiate Dictionary* (2003) employs the concept of "constituting" cause (p. 196).
Comment/Note. Garner (2004) adds that the term is used to denote a legally actionable index event. "A causal link exists between the defendant's action and the plaintiff's injury" (Garner, 2004, p. 233). Slovenko (2002) specifies that all causal terminology involves concepts such as product, result, connection, because, and causative factor (Slovenko, 2002, p. 361).

Causality. The legal and common dictionaries agree on their definitions, but cross-reference causality to causation.

Definition. "The principle of causal relationship; the relation between cause and effect" (Garner, 2004, p. 233). Garner makes explicit reference to the term "causation" as a term for "causality" (Garner, 2004, p. 233). Garner (1995) has a very similar definition for causality (p. 138). The *New Oxford American Dictionary* (Jewell & Abate, 2001) refers to the relationship between cause and effect, but adds a more philosophical notion, the principle that everything can be explained in terms of cause (p. 273). *Merriam-Webster Collegiate Dictionary* (2003) provides a fine definition, adding two elements not yet mentioned: "1: a causal quality or agency 2: the relation between a cause and its effect or between regularly correlated events or phenomena" (p. 196). The first definition refers to the philosophical notion of causality, but without indicating its universal application to "everything" having to have a cause. The second definition refers to the standard concept of relationship, but adds that it may involve observed correlations or associations. Garner (2004) adds a legal argument that causality involves the "foreseeability" test, along with duty (p. 233; these concepts are elaborated below).
Comment/Note. Beyond conceptual confusion about the two terms of causality and causation, we found that in our reading both in the law and psychology, the terms often are used interchangeably, and this may occur even within one source. However, for Garner (1995, p. 138), the terms causality and causation were seen to have a fine distinction in law. The latter term denotes the additional meaning "the relation of cause and effect." However, for Garner, in nonlegal contexts, this is best reserved to the former term. Moreover, the concept of causality will never be easy to specify, observe, or differentiate, even if in the future it should be clearly defined. In this regard, Pearl (2000) has indicated that although the concept of causality is fundamental to human thought, it is embedded in mystery and controversy, given the difficulty in establishing when an agent "truly" causes an effect (p. 331).

Causation. The dictionaries seem to agree on definition, but as with causality, there is a cross-reference to the related term, that is, to causality.
Definition. "1. The causing or producing of an effect ... 2. CAUSALITY." (Garner, 2004, p. 233). In a technical sense, it refers to anything that contributes to a given outcome (Garner, 1995, p. 138). Garner adds that causation refers to all the factors that contribute to an effect but, from a legal standpoint, what matters is liability, or whether an individual's actions had played a role in eliciting an actionable outcome. Romano (1999) specifies that the negligent factors may be inactions as well as actions (p. 101). At the outset of their definitions, the common dictionaries refer to acts or actions, as well as to the related term of causality: "the action of causing something" ... "the relationship between cause and effect; causality" (*New Oxford American Dictionary*; Jewell & Abate, 2001, p. 273). "1a: the act or process of causing b: the act or agency which produces an effect 2. CAUSALITY" (*Merriam-Webster's Collegiate Dictionary*, 2003, p. 196).
Comment/Note. Garner (2004, p. 234) refers to Cardozo (1928), who refers to the "key" in the legal treatment of causation. One needs to ask: what is the "dominant" cause of the legal consequences related to an event in dispute? Koocher (1998)

adds the relevance of causation to tort action. There needs to be a "connection" between an act or its omission and a subsequent injury suffered by an individual. For example, "harm" must be shown to have resulted "proximately" from negligence (p. 509). Romano (1999) underscores the ubiquity of the concept of causation [and causality] in law. He maintains that "[c]ausation is an intricate part of virtually every case a trial advocate or litigation specialist will ever handle …" (p. 101). Garner (1995) clarifies that the legal term, causation, should not be used when the more general term, cause, is the one meant (p. 138).

[Different types of causation exist; they are enumerated below for the most part, except where similar terms exist under the heading of "Cause."]

-factual causation. See: "but-for" cause.

-general causation. Toxic tort cases require epidemiological experts. They provide evidence with respect to both general and specific causation.
Definition. General causation refers to whether the "exposure" to the alleged toxic substance (or other event or alleged cause, e.g., a motor vehicle accident (MVA)) is capable of inducing the alleged "disease or injury" (See, 2000, p. 478).

-medical causation. In the following, note how "mental or emotional" condition is subsumed under "medical causation," which might ring true for psychiatrists but not for psychologists.
Definition. "A physical, physiological, mental, or emotional condition in a person caused by trauma or some other happening or event which is medically responsible for the final condition in the person" (Romano, 1999, p. 102).

-proof of causation. The ambiguities in defining causation are compounded by difficulties in establishing its legal relevance. In attempting to establish legal reliability or validity of evidence, the expert needs to provide support for the inferences drawn to a sufficient degree of certainty.
Definition. "Causation, whether it be legal or medical, is virtually always proved through circumstantial evidence." The effects are "inferred," "because the actual result having been caused cannot be 'perceived' by the senses (or by direct evidence). Accordingly, circumstantial evidence is the key" (Romano, 1999, p. 102).
Comment/Note. Proof of causation lay in the evidence gathered. "Proof of causation raises evidentiary questions that are, at least theoretically, independent of legal policy or precedent. If the plaintiff cannot prove on the balance of probabilities that the defendant's negligent act was a cause of her injury, then her claim will fail." (Solomon et al., 1996, p. 349).

-proximate causation. This term is the most important legal one.
Definition. Proximate causation refers to the "essential" or "dominant and responsible" cause. Where other causes occur, the proximate one "necessarily" sets the others in operation. A proximate cause may be "a natural and continuous sequence," with other factors not intervening or breaking the chain (Koocher, 1998, p. 512). (In this sense, the term "intervening" refers to "superseding" or replacing.)

-specific causation. In cases in which general causation applies, there may also be specific causation.
Definition. Had the MVA, other event, or "exposure or substance" at issue "actually caused" the purported "disease or injury" in the case at hand (See, 2000, p. 478).

Causative. Straightforward.
Definition. Effective, expressive, or operative as a cause; producing a result (Garner, 1995, p. 138; Garner, 2004, p. 234).

Cause. The common dictionaries are quite good.
Definition. "1. Something that produces an effect or result … 2. A ground for legal action … 3. A law suit; a case …" (Garner, 2004, pp. 234, 235). "1 a person or thing that gives rise to an action, phenomenon, or condition … 3 a matter to be resolved in a court of law" (*New Oxford American Dictionary*; Jewell & Abate, 2001, p. 273). "1a: a reason for an action or condition: MOTIVE b: something that brings about an effect or a result c: a person or thing that is the occasion of an action or state; esp.: an agent that brings something about d: sufficient reason … 2a: a ground of legal action 3: a matter or question to be decided …" (*Merriam-Webster's Collegiate Dictionary*, 2003, p. 196).
Comment/Note. These definitions of the term "cause" reiterate the major themes expressed in discussing the terms causa, causation, and causality. However, they add the question of motive and whether the reasons or grounds are sufficient to have produced the effect, result, action, phenomenon, condition, or state.

-but-for cause. One way of defining cause is roundabout.
Definition. Black's legal dictionary refers to "but-for" cause as a necessary cause; "the cause without which the event could not have occurred" (Garner, 2004, p. 234). The "but-for" cause is related to the "but-for" legal test: "Causation can sometimes be as simple as a 'but for' test, in which a condition would not have existed "but for" the occurrence of a certain event" (Cocchiarella & Lord, 2001, p. 328). Also termed *actual cause; cause in fact; factual cause* (Garner, 2004, p. 234).
Comment/Note. The "but-for" test is judged with respect to a balance of probabilities in the evidence. "Causation in both Canada (*Athey v. Leonati*, 1996, S.C.C.) and the United States (*Chaney v. Smithkline Beckman Corp.*, 1985; U.S. 8th Circuit Ct.) is proved through use of the 'but-for' test. … If it can be answered that on a balance of probabilities, the injury would not have occurred *but for* the negligence of the defendant, then causation is made out" (Douglas, Huss, Murdoch, Washington, & Koch, 1999, p. 276).

-cause in fact. Legal cause goes by many names.
Definition. "The principle that the tortfeasor's action must have had a factual cause, that is, a material cause, in bringing about the defendant's misfortune" (*Tort Law Dictionary*, 2003, p. 1).

-concurrent cause. Here we see that concurrent cause has two quite different meanings. The first refers to the situation where two potential causes together reach a threshold of cause, where neither alone would have been sufficient. The second definition resembles joint cause, with one of the causes dominant and with the secondary one being considered "concurrent."
Definition. In the prior edition of Black's, Garner (1999) defines concurrent cause as, "One of two or more causes that simultaneously create a condition that no single cause would have brought about" (p. 212). However, concurrent cause can also mean "one of two or more causes that simultaneously create a condition that any one cause could have created alone" (Garner, 1999, p. 212). In the most recent version of Black's, Garner (2004) simplifies these definitions to "One of two or more causes that simultaneously produce a result" (p. 234).

-contributing cause. When several factors are involved in a causal nexus, the ones considered secondary and not primary are labeled as "contributing."
Definition. "A factor that—though not the primary cause—plays a part in producing a result" (Garner, 2004, p. 234).
Comment/Note. According to the definition of the term "contributing" offered in a general dictionary (*Merriam-Webster's Collegiate Dictionary*, 2003, p. 272), when a factor is labeled as "contributing" in a causal network, it is not necessarily secondary. The general dictionary definition of the term "contributing" specifies that the factor involved should be important or significant, and not necessarily secondary. Here we see that the legal profession has limited a common term to a particular usage that may be confusing to others exposed to the legal system, who might have different understandings of the term, such as jurors evaluating testimony.

-direct cause. Ultimately, the courts establish whether or not there is legal cause that is tortious. Legal cause goes by many names, with "proximate cause" the most widespread. All specify the existence of liable, direct cause, such as an event, incident, or accident, that is dominant or primary, and necessary and sufficient, even if not exclusive, in causation, and that produces a specific and identifiable effect, result, condition, or injury.
Definition. A cause acting directly to produce an effect. If there is a chain, it is a "natural," "continuous" series, uninterrupted by another "independent" cause. Absent the said cause, the index injury would not have happened (Garner, 1995, p. 139). Also termed *legal cause* (Garner, 1995, p. 139).

-good cause. "Good cause" does not deal with causality or causation, *per se.*
Definition. Garner (2004) defines "good cause" as a reason that is sufficient from a legal perspective (p. 235). Also termed *good cause shown; just cause; lawful cause; sufficient cause* (Garner, 2004, p. 235).

-immediate cause. When cause involves a sequence of factors, the most recent or immediate one prior to the effect in question is called the "last" one, which we find potentially confusing.

Definition. "The last event in a chain of events, though not necessarily the proximate cause of what follows" (Garner, 2004, p. 234). Where there is a chain of causation, it is the "last link" (Garner, 1995, p. 139). Also termed *effective cause* (Garner, 1995, p. 139).

-intervening cause. When a causal sequence is initiated, events can transpire that alter ("intervening") or even replace ("superseding") the previously primary component of the chain.
Definition. "An event that comes between the initial event in the sequence and the end result, thereby altering the natural course of events that might have connected a wrongful act to an injury" (Garner, 2004, p. 234). Also termed *efficient intervening cause; intervening act; intervening agency; intervening force; independent intervening cause; supervening cause; novus actus interveniens; nova causa interveniens* (Garner, 2004, pp. 212–213).
Comment/Note. In intervening causation, the causal chain is not broken, but in superseding cause, the sequence is sufficiently interrupted to relieve the potential wrongdoer of any liability. "If the intervening cause is strong enough to relieve the wrongdoer of any liability, it becomes a *superseding cause*" (Garner, 2004, p. 234).

-dependent intervening cause. *Definition*. "… not an act and is never a superseding cause" (Garner, 2004, p. 234).

-independent intervening cause. *Definition*. "… operates on a condition produced by an antecedent cause but in no way resulted from that cause" (Garner, 2004, p. 234).

-material cause. Material cause can refer to the sole legal cause or a factor that is part of it (a contribution).
Definition. "… necessary and sufficient cause …" (*Tort Law Dictionary*, 2003, p. 1).
Comment/Note. "Sometimes the but-for test is not appropriate. Courts have then employed a *material contribution* test. If the MVA can be viewed as a material contribution to the development of PTSD [Posttraumatic Stress Disorder], despite the presence of other causal factors, then causation may be found" (Douglas et al., 1999, p. 276).

-necessary cause. A primary element in cause, even when there is a chain or sequence.
Definition. "The cause without which the thing cannot be or the event would not have occurred" (Garner, 2004, p. 234). Also termed *Causa sine qua non* (Garner, 2004, p. 234).
Comment/Note. Hart and Honoré (1985) indicated that the better test of causation is not the but-for test; but the "NESS" test (necessary element in a sufficient set).

-proximate cause. Is there an act of omission or commission? Does the act result in an injury? Is there a sequence of events involved and, if so, is it interrupted and, if not, which is dominant, primary, producing, moving, substantial, or considered to have directly precipitated the injury more than the others, being so closely connected to it so that without it the injury would not have occurred? Does the act meet legal, compensable thresholds?

Definition. "1. A cause that is legally sufficient to result in liability; an act or omission that is considered in law to result in a consequence, so that liability can be imposed on the actor." … 2. "A cause that directly produces an event and without which the event would not have occurred. …" (Garner, 2004, p. 234). "The immediate or latest cause" (Garner, 2004, p. 233). Also termed *direct cause; direct and proximate cause; efficient proximate cause; efficient cause; efficient adequate cause; first cause; initial cause; legal cause; producing cause; primary cause; jural cause* (Garner, 2004, p. 234). "Act of commission or omission that through an uninterrupted sequence of events directly results in an injury that otherwise would not have occurred or else becomes a substantial factor in causing an injury" (Koocher, 1998, p. 512).

Comment/Note. The concept of primate cause/causality/causation has been given a cardinal place in tort law. According to Garner, (1995, p. 139), the term has become "indispensable." But the courts are not sufficiently clear in the use of the concept of proximate cause. "The distinction between causation and remoteness has been blurred by the courts' use of the term 'proximate cause' to refer to both issues. Thus, a proximate cause is a cause which, as a matter of law, is not too remote to justify denying liability" (Solomon et al., 1996, p. 349). Similarly, Slovenko noted the distinction between proximate cause as being "responsible" of cause and as being within the scope of proximity as cause, not being too remote to deny liability. However, he added that concepts such as "responsible" cause have their own difficulties. "The term proximate has connotations of nearness in time, but that is not its meaning in law. *Legal cause* and *responsible cause* are more appropriate terms, but those terms also leave much room for vagaries in decision making" (Slovenko, 2003, p. xxiv). Moreover, in establishing proximate cause as responsible cause, the "causal connection cannot be contingent, speculative, or merely possible" (Wecht, 1995, p. 73). Nevertheless, the usual guideline is that the cause seems natural and probable. "There is no litmus test for determining proximity … . Some courts use a foreseeability test, but usually the test is the *natural and probable* cause-and-effect relationship" (Slovenko, 2003, p. xxiii). In addition, proximate cause can be single or multiple, complicating matters. Moreover, multiple cause can involve factors that override the index event in question. The putative causal factor may not contribute to injuries, whether physical or psychological, if these had been present beforehand, beyond their ongoing degenerative course. "In assessing causation, there is the well-known expression, 'The tortfeasor must take his victim as he finds him', so that peculiar vulnerability to harm does not excuse. However, it may be argued, sometimes successfully, that 'the straw that broke the camel's back' is not a proximate cause" (Slovenko, 2003, p. xxiv).

To repeat, the term "proximate cause" refers not only to cause-effect relations but also to scope or extent of liability (Page, 2003); that is, when does responsibility for a harm cease to apply because the chain of causation cannot be extended to include the alleged negligent act (it is too "remote"). Because of the difficulties in establishing responsibility in slippery scenarios and the confusion between the two different concepts referred to by the term, "[t]he phrase 'proximate cause' has generated near universal distaste … ever since courts first coined the expression" (p. vii).

-remote cause. This term is a confusing one in law, for it can refer to events that are distant in a causal chain yet still causal, or it can refer to events that are too distant to be causal.
Definition. "[A] cause that does not necessarily or immediately produce an event or injury" (Garner, 2004, p. 234). "… indirect cause" (Garner, 2004, p. 233).
Comment/Note. "Even if the defendant caused the plaintiff's loss, she will not be held liable if the causal connection between her negligent act and the plaintiff's loss is too tenuous or remote to justify imposing liability" (Solomon et al., 1996, p. 349).

-sole cause. *Definition*. "The only cause that, from a legal viewpoint, produces an event or injury" (Garner, 2004, p. 234).
Comment/Note. "If it comes between a defendant's action and the event or injury at issue, it is treated as a *superseding cause*" (Garner, 2004, p. 234). "It is not necessary for the plaintiff to show that the defendant's negligence is the sole cause of the plaintiff's injury" (Wecht, 1995, p. 73). Therefore, the term "sole cause" does not refer to a cause with a single defining event or act; rather, it refers to the one considered responsible by the court.

-superseding cause. Overriding cause that breaks the chain of causation, replacing one or more other events or acts considered as possible primary or contributing causes.
Definition. "An intervening act or force that the law considers sufficient to override the cause for which the original tortfeasor was responsible, thereby exonerating that tortfeasor from liability" (Garner, 2004, p. 235). Also termed *sole cause* (Garner, 2004, p. 235).

-sufficient cause. As we have seen, legal definitions often are circular, using terms needing definition themselves.
Definition. Necessary and proximate. (*Tort Law Dictionary*, 2003, p. 1).
Comment/ Note. "When a cause is both necessary … (*sina qua non*) and proximate, that is, sufficient, … then a tort will exist in common law" (*Tort Law Dictionary*, 2003, p. 1). The common dictionaries define "sufficient" in terms of having enough for or being adequate to the actual situation or proposed outcome (*Merriam-Webster's Collegiate Dictionary*, 2003, p. 1248).

Cause of action. A theory of the case set out in as simple a scenario as possible, in terms of facts, acts, situations, or events, either for or against the legal claim.
Definition. "1. A group of operative facts giving rise to one or more bases for suing; a factual situation that entitles one person to obtain remedy in court from

another person; CLAIM .... 2. A legal theory of a lawsuit ... 3. loosely, a law suit ..." (Garner, 2004, p. 235). Also termed *right of action; ground of action* (Garner, 2004, p. 235). A set of "operative facts" considered "harmful" that lead to the "right" to pursue legal action (Garner, 1995, p. 140). "Set of facts that give rise to a legal right to redress at law" (Koocher, 1998, p. 509).

Auxiliary Legal Terms Associated with Causality and Causation

These auxiliary terms are presented in order to describe the legal context in which causality and causation are considered. The terms treat the protagonists involved (from the plaintiff and defendant to the triers of fact, and their roles, e.g., judges' gatekeeping), the situations amenable to causal determination (e.g., assault and accidents), the legal subtleties and issues (such as what is appropriate scientific evidence), and the possible outcomes of legal action (compensation, damages, grounds for pain and suffering, and so forth). The terms also deal with the tricky issue of "thin" vs. "crumbling" skulls. Note that the key legal term of "reliability" is defined in a very different way compared to the equivalent psychological term.

Admissible evidence. *Definition.* Refers to evidence relevant to the case at hand, such that it is not prejudicial in an unfair manner, nor based on hearsay, nor considered privileged in nature (Garner, 2004, p. 595).

Admissibility (according to *Daubert*). Prior to *Daubert*, the most common legal standard for admissibility of evidence lay in *Frye*, which addressed the general acceptance of the methods and procedures in the relevant professional community. *Daubert* altered the scientific criteria that trial judges needed to consider and, moreover, emphasized their role as gatekeepers of the evidence.
Definition. "The U.S. Supreme Court in *Daubert* suggested criteria to aid the trial judge in determining both the evidentiary reliability (or scientific validity) of expert scientific testimony and the admissibility of expert scientific testimony ... The pragmatic considerations include: (a) whether the proffered scientific evidence is testable and has been tested; (b) ... has been published and subject to peer review; (c) ... is generally accepted within the appropriate scientific community (which is similar to the 'general acceptance' test that was originally announced in *Frye* to determine the admissibility of novel scientific evidence); (d) ... has a known error rate and whether there is a probability that using the evidence will result in an error; and (e) whether the court should include any other factors in its assessment ..." (Krauss & Sales, 2003, p. 551).
Comment/Note. Despite these criteria, the courts remain uncertain of how to carefully evaluate scientific evidence. "Unfortunately, the court did not provide guidelines on how these criteria should be used by a trial judge to determine admissibility of scientific evidence, how many of these considerations need to

be met for scientific evidence to be admitted, how these considerations should be weighed in reaching a decision, nor how these considerations should be applied to the evidence presented in the original *Daubert* case … . Not surprisingly, the application and use of *Daubert's* pragmatic considerations might lead to varying admissibility decisions even when applied to research judged to be reliable, relevant, and helpful" (Krauss & Sales, 2003, p. 551). Moreover, *Daubert* scientific standards apply with difficulty to clinical testimony, which is often the nature of the evidence furnished by psychologists to the court. "[I]t is difficult to nearly impossible to directly translate some of the *Daubert* pragmatic considerations to clinical testimony" (Krauss & Sales, 2003, p. 554). *Daubert* also made it clear that the Supreme Court's list of criteria is neither mandatory nor exhaustive, leaving each judge to identify the relevant criteria in a specific case.

Bystander proximity rule. The courts used to consider only physical injury as tortious, but this gradually expanded to emotional injury and, as this rule demonstrates, the injury need not be directly experienced.
Definition. "Recovery for emotional injury allowed even if plaintiff not in zone of danger, was close to the zone, observed the accident, and was closely related to the victim" (Walker & Shapiro, 2003, p. 165).

Compensation. *Definition*. Compensation involves legally determined payment of damages or other means of helping injured parties return toward their prior condition or make them whole (Garner, 2004, p. 301).

Complaint. The contents of the tort claim.
Definition. "The initiatory pleading on the part of the plaintiff in filing a civil lawsuit. Its purpose is to give the defendant notice of the general alleged fact constituting the cause of action" (Koocher, 1998, p. 510).

Contributory negligence or comparative negligence. Joint cause may involve the complainant being liable, in part, herself or himself, for alleged damages subsequent to an injury.
Definition. "[T]he plaintiff's concurrent negligence contributed to his or her own injury, even though the defendant's actions may also have been responsible for the injury" (Koocher, 1998, p. 510).

Crumbling-skull rule. Canadian case law recognizes preexisting vulnerabilities on which effects of events in question may act and which may reduce liability, depending on their severity. "Crumbling skull" cases refer to greater preexisting vulnerabilities than "thin" skull cases, and, at their extreme, crumbling skull cases have preexisting vulnerabilities that leave no room for additional effects of any sort due to an event in question. We have not identified use of this term in the United States to date, though a Louisiana case involved the principle without actual use of the term (Douglas et al., 1999, pp. 278–279).

Definition. "If … a plaintiff was experiencing symptoms that were worsened or aggravated by an accident, the 'crumbling skull' doctrine applies. … These doctrines have evolved from the principle that the plaintiff ought to be returned to the position he or she would have been in if the accident had not occurred …" (Douglas et al., 1999, pp. 278–279).
Comment/Note. "In the case of a crumbling skull plaintiff, the defendant is … liable for all losses flowing from the tortious act, with the caveat that the defendant need not place the plaintiff in a position better than his original position, taking into account any preexisting problems inherent in the plaintiff's original position" (Bogoroch & Chandler, 2002, p. 12).

Damages. Harm, impairment, or loss suffered because of a negligent act may call for monetary compensation. When psychological damage occurs, the law permits compensatory damages. In this case, unlike the case for the term "recovery," as we shall see below, there is similarity in the meaning of the terms across law and psychology. Compensation may include special damages, such as for psychotherapy needs.
Definition. "Money received through judicial order by a plaintiff sustaining harm, impairment, or loss to his or her person or property as the result of the accidental, intentional, or negligent act of another" (Koocher, 1998, p. 510). Types of damage include "past and future loss of earning capacity, past and future medical and other care costs, as well as past and future pain and suffering" (Douglas et al., 1999, p. 285).

-general damages. *Definition.* "[R]efer to more immediate, direct, and proximate results of the wrongdoing, and may consist of any form of direct economic loss such as medical bills, lost wages, property damage, and so forth" (Douglas et al., 1999, p. 281). "*General damages* in Canadian law refer to *non-pecuniary damages* (damages that are not quantifiable), and include pain and suffering" (Douglas et al., 1999, p. 281).

-future damages. *Definition.* "Plaintiffs can recover *future damages* for the future effects of an injury, including loss of capacity to work, future pain and suffering, and future medical expenses" (Douglas et al., 1999, p. 281).

-pecuniary damages. *Definition.* "*Pecuniary* damages, which can be either general or special, refer to losses that can be estimated financially and compensated with money" (Douglas et al., 1999, p. 281).

-special damages. *Definition.* "In the United States, 'special damages' are those damages that arise from the injury, but do so in a manner that is peculiar or special to the case. They reflect natural and actual, though not necessary, results of the case, and may include any economic losses or expenses that have occurred as a result of the accident or that will accrue in the future" (Douglas et al., 1999, p. 281). In Canada, "*Special damages*, also called *pecuniary damages*, are those that can be quantified, and essentially include out-of-pocket expenses up to the time of trial (such as medical expenses, loss of earning capacity and past wages, and pretrial care)" (Douglas et al., 1999, pp. 281–282).

Comment/Note. "In law, the term *damage* is used to describe the harm, and *damages* or *recovery* is used to indicate the reward" (Slovenko, 2003, p. xxiii). "Causal issues in the damages context—did the defendant cause the full extent of harm underlying plaintiff's damages claim?—are often subjected to standards of proof less demanding than those required for causal issues concerning liability—did the defendant tortiously cause any harm to the plaintiff? A relaxed evidentiary standard for damages can be justified, according to the U.S. Supreme Court, '[w]here the tort itself is of such a nature as to preclude the ascertainment of the amount of damages with certainty,' because in these cases 'it would be a perversion of fundamental principles of justice to deny all relief to the injured person, and thereby relieve the wrongdoer from making any amend for his acts' " (Geistfeld, 2001, p. 1022).

Defendant. Complainants are termed plaintiffs in tort action, and the alleged wrongdoer is the defendant.

Definition. "The person against whom a civil or criminal action is brought" (Koocher, 1998, p. 510).

Deliberation. Civil court cases are deliberated by triers of fact.

Definition. Deliberation involves triers of fact arriving at decisions by carefully dealing with issues and options through analysis and weighing the evidence (Garner, 2004, p. 459).

Deposition. The American system, but not the Canadian, allows for depositions.

Definition. "1. A witness's out-of-court testimony that is reduced to writing (usu. by a court reporter) for later use in court or for discovery purposes. … 2. The session at which such testimony is recorded" (Garner, 2004, p. 472). "The testimony of a witness or party taken before trial, consisting of an oral, sworn, out-of-court statement" (Koocher, 1998, p. 510)

Deterrence. *Definition.* Legal procedures, including those involving intimidation, aimed at discouraging specified undesirable behavior, which, in the case of personal injury, refers to unsafe or negligent conduct (Garner, 2004, p. 481).

Directed verdict. *Definition.* "… the judge can determine that the party with the burden of proof has failed to present a sufficient prima facie case to proceed to jury consideration" (Greenberg, 2003, p. 238).

Evidence. Among other factors, the quality of the evidence proferred governs outcome of cases.

Definition. Items such as testimony, documents, exhibits, and tangible objects submitted to court in an attempt to prove or disprove an issue at hand (Garner, 2004, p. 595).

Comment/Note. Hearsay evidence is judged inadmissible (Garner, 2004, p. 595), although cases involving allegations of sexual abuse of a child may admit it, for example, in Canada according to *Mohan* (1994). However, experts may rely on hearsay, "if of a type reasonably relied upon by experts in the particular field in forming opinions or inferences upon the subject" (Federal Rule of Evidence, 703) (2004).

Expert witness. A specialized or professional degree does not in and of itself confer expert status.
Definition. An individual with special training, knowledge, skill, or experience in a relevant area of a legal case, so that the evidence offered in court may be admitted (Koocher, 1998, p. 510). "If scientific, technical, or other specialized knowledge will assist the trier of fact to understand the evidence or to determine a fact in issue, a witness qualified as an expert by knowledge, skill, experience, training, or education, may testify thereto in the form of an opinion or otherwise, if (1) the testimony is based upon sufficient facts or data, (2) the testimony is the product of reliable principles and methods, and (3) the witness has applied the principles and methods reliably to the facts of the case" (Federal Rule of Evidence 702) (2004).
Comment/Note. "The forensic expert should not be the litigant's advocate, but may argue for his or her (i.e., the expert's) opinions" (Reid, 1999, p. 167).

Fault. *Definition.* An individual is considered at fault when she or he fails to maintain a standard of conduct, whether by accident or intention, resulting in harm to another individual (Garner, 2004, p. 641).

Fit. *Definition.* Whether "the expert testimony effectively links the scientific evidence to the facts in the case in such a way that it aids the jury in its decision-making" (Krauss & Sales, 2003, p. 549).
Comment/Note. "Fit" addresses the helpfulness standard, whether evidence reliably addresses the legal question at hand, or is valid for that purpose (Krauss & Sales, 2003, p. 549). " 'Fit' is not always obvious, and scientific validity for one purpose is not necessarily scientific validity for other, unrelated purposes" (Brixen & Meis, 2000, p. 702).

Foreseeability test. *Definition.* An action may be determined as negligent only when the negligent party should have anticipated the injurious consequences (Reid, 1999, p. 176).

Full recovery rule. In law, recovery refers to compensation after damages, quite different from the concept in medicine and psychology.
Definition. "Recovery for infliction of severe emotional distress, if a normally constituted reasonable person would be so affected by the trauma" (Walker & Shapiro, 2003, p. 165).

Gatekeeping controls. Trial judges have been instructed by *Daubert* and *Mohan* to keep out unqualified experts who may promote "junk" science.

Comment/Note. "Noteworthy here are the *legal gatekeeping controls* historically articulated in *Daubert* and its progeny and now applied in the new FRE 702. A major purpose of the rule is to prevent unqualified experts from testifying in the courtroom on the basis of irrelevant or inadequate evidence. Noteworthy also are the corresponding *psychological gatekeeping controls* articulated in psychology's ethical principles ... and forensic guidelines" (Weissman & DeBow, 2003, p. 47).

Harassment. Harassment may include grounds for legal action due to personal injury, for example, at work.
Definition. Harassment is constituted by groundless and substantially annoying, alarming, or emotionally distressing words, conduct, or action, often repeated or persistent, aimed at a specific person (Garner, 2004, p. 733).

Liability. The liable person pays the compensation, often through a third party. Joint liability reflects joint responsibility, by two or more individuals or entities.
Definition. Being in a state of legal obligation, accountability, or responsibility after judgment in a civil proceeding (Garner, 2004, p. 933).

Litigant. *Definition.* An individual who launches a lawsuit (Garner, 2004, p. 952).

Malpractice. A class of tortious conduct.
Definition. "Professional negligence. Failure to meet a professional standard of care resulting in harm to another" (Koocher, 1998, p. 511).

Mitigation-of-damages doctrine. Tort action usually is undertaken after the complainant has had enough time to attempt to alleviate her or his postevent condition by appropriate remedial intervention.
Definition. The plaintiff who has experienced an injury or a breach of contract must take reasonable steps to alleviate the effects that ensue (Garner, 2004, p. 1024), or to avoid aggravating the injury and thereby increasing damages (Reid, 1999, p. 179).
Comment/Note. Where plaintiffs fail to reasonably attempt to mitigate losses, damages may be reduced (Garner, 2004, p. 1024), or denied.

Negligence. Another class of tortious conduct.
Definition. "Legal cause of action involving the failure to exercise the degree of diligence and care that a reasonably and ordinarily prudent person would exercise under the same or similar circumstances; the result is the breach of a legal duty, which proximately causes an injury which the law recognizes as deserving of compensation" (Koocher, 1998, p. 511).
Comment/Note. In providing evidence of negligent action, main elements include showing causal connection between (1) the defendant's breach of duty of care, or breach of the responsibility not to expose the plaintiff to foreseeable harm by acting differently from the way a reasonable person would in similar

circumstances, resulting in unreasonable risk to the plaintiff, and (2) the plaintiff's subsequent injury and damages (Douglas et al., 1999, p. 273).

Pain and suffering. An important component of a tort action; it is capped in jurisdictions in Canada but not necessarily in the United States.
Definition. "Element of 'compensatory' nonpecuniary damages that allows recovery for the mental anguish and/or physical pain endured by the plaintiff as a result of injury for which the plaintiff seeks redress" (Koocher, 1998, pp. 511–512).

Physical impact rule. *Definition*. "Emotional injury directly linked to physical injury" (Walker & Shapiro, 2003, p. 164).

Plaintiff. *Definition*. An individual who initiates civil action seeking monetary or other redress for damages (Koocher, 1998, p. 512).

Prejudicial. *Definition*. A biased judgment without factual justification (Garner, 2004, p. 1218).

Preponderance of the evidence. *Definition*. The standard that the proferred evidence "more likely than not" is convincing, credible, reasonable, and probable, outweighing the evidence against it. "This standard is basically considered to be a majority of the evidence, or said another way, more evidence than would be merely reasonable to some persons but less than would be clear and convincing to most persons" (Greenberg, 2003, p. 237).
Comment/Note. "The concept of preponderance of evidence plays a central role in expert witness testimony. For an expert's opinion to be admissible, the expert must also testify that the opinion is supported by a preponderance of the evidence that the expert has considered and relied on" (Greenberg, 2003, p. 237).

Probative. *Definition*. A helpful judgment with factual justification, and without preconceived elements (Garner, 2004, p. 1240).
Comment/Note. "Courts can exclude relevant evidence if its probative value is substantially outweighed by the danger of unfair prejudice" (Garner, 2004, p. 1240).

Prognosis. Prognosis varies on a continuum, from positive to grim.
Definition. An estimate of the projected course, duration, severity, and/or outcome of an individual's medical or psychological condition (Corsini, 2002, p. 766; VandenBos, 2007, p. 738).

Reasonable medical certainty. Legal certainty in civil cases refers to preponderance, or a percent of evidence favoring an outcome at a level just greater than 50%, that is, at a level "more likely than not."
Definition. "As used in personal injury lawsuits, a term implying more than mere conjecture, possibility, consistency with, or speculation; similar to a probability, more likely than not, 50.1%, but an overwhelming likelihood or scientific

certainty is not required" (Koocher, 1998, p. 512). Also termed *reasonable psychological certainty* (Koocher, 1998, p. 512).
Comment/Note. "The credibility and probative value of expert testimony are assisted further by identifying and discussing alternative hypotheses for one's data. The reasonable medical/scientific standard is enhanced further by expert testimony that expresses the degree of conviction attached to different opinions with well-reasoned bases for opinions proffered" (Weissman & DeBow, 2003, p. 37).

Reasonable person. *Definition.* The hypothetical standard person used as a legal standard, to which defendants are sometimes compared. The reasonable person is considered to act sensibly, take appropriate precautions, and so on (Garner, 2004, p. 1294). In sexual harassment cases, the usual standard is the reasonable woman.

Recovery. This term varies in meaning in law and psychology. The health professional aims for a client's health recovery, and the *more* health recovery facilitated by the health professional, the *less* monetary recovery obtained by the legal professional in a tort claim.
Definition. An amount of money awarded as part of a legal judgment or decree (Garner, 2004, p. 1302).

Relevance. Relevance concerns whether evidence is applicable to a particular case.
Definition. "[T]hat the testimony offered be relevant to the legal issues at hand and assist the trier of fact in resolving the legal question" (Brodsky, Caputo, & Domino, 2002, p. 18). "Relevant evidence is any evidence that makes a fact in issue more or less probable" (Krauss & Sales, 2003, p. 548).

Reliability. The equivalent concept of legal "reliability" in psychology is "validity," and not "reliability," which has a different meaning in psychology than validity. These different meanings for the same term across the two fields can be rather confusing to the uninformed.
Definition. "… that the information presented be grounded in scientific standards and methodology over time" (Brodsky et al., 2002, p. 18). "*Daubert* requires federal courts to determine 'whether the *reasoning or methodology* underlying the expert testimony is scientifically valid and whether that reasoning properly can be applied to the facts in issue' " (from *Daubert*, 1993, p. 2796; in Greenberg, 2003, p. 250). "[R]eliability means that the expert testimony is 'properly grounded, well-reasoned and not speculative' " (Brixen & Meis, 2000, p. 702). According to *Daubert* (1993; footnote 9), whereas scientists "distinguish between 'validity' … and 'reliability' … . our reference here is to evidentiary reliability—that is, trustworthiness."
Comment/Note. Gatekeeping guidelines on the quality of scientific evidence speak to the criterion of legal reliability. Legal reliability applies not only to the general science behind a particular case but, also, to the specifics of a particular case, in a two-tiered function. If one of the attorneys involved in a case challenges

the proposed testimony, "the trial judge is required to make a two-prong preliminary admissibility determination prior to the presentation of the expert testimony at trial. The judge must determine whether the *reasoning or methodology* underlying the expert testimony is scientifically valid (i.e., evidentiary reliable) and whether that *reasoning or methodology* can be applied to the facts of the case (i.e., relevant)" (Krauss & Sales, 2003, p. 549). See *Reliability* under "psychological terms" (this chapter, p. 124).

Settlement. *Definition*. "Agreement made between the parties to a lawsuit, which resolves their dispute" (Koocher, 1998, p. 512).

Sexual harassment. *Definition*. "[U]nwelcome sexual advances, requests for sexual favors, and other verbal or physical conduct of a sexual nature [when] (1) submission to such conduct is made either explicitly or implicitly a term or condition of an individual's employment, (2) submission to or rejection of such conduct by an individual is used as the basis for employment decisions affecting such an individual, or (3) such conduct has the purpose or effect of unreasonably interfering with an individual's work performance or creating an intimidating, hostile, or offensive work environment" (U.S. Equal Employment Opportunities Commission (EEOC) 29 C.F.R. §1604.11(a) (1990)).

Sufficiency. *Definition*. "[R]equirement that the expert have an adequate quantity of information to permit reasonable conclusions in the case at bar" (Brixen & Meis, 2000, p. 702). "[T]he *legal sufficiency of expert evidence* (e.g., is the evidence more probative than prejudicial)" (Douglas et al., 1999, p. 288).

Testimony. *Definition*. Evidence provided at trial, in an affidavit, or in a deposition, by a witness deemed competent, while under oath or affirmation (Garner, 2004, p. 1514).

Theory of the case. *Definition*. A theory proposed as the cause of the plaintiff's injuries; usually, it simplifies the typical multiple causes involved to the event in question and its consequences, or to an absence of any relevant effect and liable cause. *Comment/Note*. "The attorney and his or her injured client are content to search for a causal theory; for example, the trauma inflicted by the defendant. The attorney then directs his or her proof only to that 'cause'" (Wecht, 1995, p. 69).

Thin-skull rule. A "crumbling skull" case usually reduces liability, a "thin skull" case does not. An injured individual having a putative "thin skull" before the injury had taken place already had a latent, preexisting condition or vulnerability on which the injury acted, or which complicated it. A thin skull case conceivably can increase overall cost relative to a "normal skull" case, because in such cases preexisting vulnerability exacerbates event-induced symptom severity, the need for treatment, the degree of disability, and so on, and the defendant must take the complainant as she or he had been before the causal event.

Definition. "The principle that a defendant is liable for a plaintiff's unforeseeable and uncommon reactions to the defendant's negligent or intentional act" ("eggshell-skull rule," Garner, 2004, p. 555). Also termed *eggshell-plaintiff rule; special-sensitivity rule; old-soldier' rule.* In *Athey v. Leonati*, 1996, the Supreme Court of Canada "states that thin-skull rule 'makes the tortfeasor liable for the plaintiff's injuries even if the injuries are unexpectedly severe owing to a preexisting condition. The tortfeasor must take his or her victim as the tortfeasor finds the victim, and is therefore liable even though the plaintiff's losses are more dramatic than they would be for the average person.' The thin-skull rule applies to make the defendant fully liable for all of the damages flowing from the tortious act, notwithstanding that the consequences of the tortious act are greater than they would have been had the plaintiff not suffered from a thin skull" (Bogoroch & Chandler, 2002, p. 11). "This doctrine has been expanded to cover predisposition to psychological injury, under the unflattering term of the 'eggshell personality' doctrine" (Douglas et al., 1999, p. 278).
Comment/Note. "Thin skulls" are contrasted with "crumbling skulls" in terms of compensation liable for negligent acts or inaction. "The idea, then, is that there are some characteristics which predispose some persons to suffer more than others upon receiving certain types of injury for which they should not have to bear the costs. Thus in this context, the idea is tied to the logic of corrective justice" (Klimchuk, 1998, p. 131). "The examiner may also be asked if the plaintiff was especially vulnerable to certain kinds of stressors; if so, this might establish the plaintiff as being what is referred to as an 'eggshell' plaintiff ... Such plaintiffs usually are held to be entitled to compensation for all the damage suffered and not only that which would have been experienced by the average person suffering the same experience" (Greenberg, 2003, p. 244). "... for example, if one person negligently scrapes another who turns out to be a hemophiliac, the negligent defendant is liable for the full extent of the plaintiff's injuries even though the harm to another plaintiff would have been minor" ("eggshell-skull rule," Garner, 2004, p. 555). "Jurisdictions in the United States vary in the degree to which preexisting sensitivity to emotional injuries preclude a claim for negligent infliction of emotional distress. In Texas, it would appear that courts are willing to compensate persons with 'eggshell psyches' (*Padget v.* Gray, 1987; Tex. Ct. App.), whereas in other jurisdictions, courts are reluctant to compensate persons who are more than ordinarily sensitive (*Theriault v. Swan*, 1987; Maine Sup. Jud. Ct.)" (Douglas et al., 1999, p. 278). But can thin and crumbling skulls be clearly differentiated? "This move toward thin skull awards for crumbling skull plaintiffs results in over-compensation of plaintiffs and a high level of liability on defendants and is contrary to the principles established by the Supreme Court of Canada" in *Athey* (Bogoroch & Chandler, 2002, p. 36; *Athey* refers to (*Athey v. Leonati*, 1996, S.C.C.)). See *Crumbling-skull rule*.

Tort. *Definition.* "Civil wrong in which a person has breached a duty to another, which requires proof of the following: that a legal duty was owed to the plaintiff by the defendant; that the defendant breached the duty; and that the plaintiff was injured as a [result of a] proximate cause of action, such as negligence" (Koocher, 1998, p. 513). "[Old French: harm, wrong; from Latin *tortus*, twisted or crooked]" (Greenberg, 2003, p. 234).

Trier of fact. *Definition*. "One or more persons—such as jurors in a trial or administrative-law judges in a hearing—who hear testimony and review evidence to rule on a factual issue." Also termed *Fact-finder* (Garner, 2004, p. 629).

Ultimate issue. Experts should provide opinion on such matters only when allowed by the law, and only after weighing all the evidence from a comprehensive assessment.
Definition. "[T]he specific question before the trier of fact" (Ewing, 2003, p. 62).
Comment/Note. "Traditionally, until mid-twentieth century, courts generally proscribed expert opinions that went to what the courts called the ultimate issue: the specific question before the trier of fact. ... [N]ow ... most jurisdictions allow ultimate opinion testimony" (Ewing, 2003, p. 62). "[T]he law allows for such 'ultimate issue' testimony by psychologists in all cases but insanity" (Krauss & Sales, 2003, p. 546). "[T]hey should avoid doing so unless they can be confident in their conclusion" (Krauss & Sales, 2003, p. 556).

Wanton. *Definition*. "Conduct that by its grossly negligent, malicious, or reckless nature evinces a disregard for the consequences or for the rights or safety of others" (Koocher, 1998, p. 513).

Willful. *Definition*. "Term descriptive of conduct that encompasses the continuum from intentional to reckless" (Koocher, 1998, p. 513).

Zone of danger. *Definition*. "Emotional injury occurs to someone who was in area where they could have been injured, but were not actually physically injured" (Walker & Shapiro, 2003, p. 164).

Key Medical Terms Related to Causality and Causation

Only some of the types of medical terms pertaining to causality overlap with the legal ones provided above; they are repeated for comparison purposes, with only one contradiction evident, concerning "immediate cause." In addition, "remote cause" is defined in a more general way compared to the legal term, and the medical term "ultimate cause" should not be confused with the legal term "ultimate issue." In general, the type of causal event considered in medicine differs from the one relevant to law; that is, the law considers any proximate cause pertaining to a tortious act, and these may have medical consequences. In contrast, medicine considers any disease or illness in terms of its various levels, and these may have legal consequences.

Causal. *Definition*. "[P]ertaining to a cause; directed against a cause" (Dorland & Newman, 2003, p. 311).

Causal treatment. *Definition*. "Treatment which aims to eliminate the cause of the disease (as opposed to the treatment of the symptoms)" (Schmidt, 2002, p. C-119).

Causality. *Definition*. "The relating of causes to the effects they produce; the pathogenesis of disease, and epidemiology, are largely concerned with causality" (Stedman, 2000, p. 303).

Causation. *Definition*. In epidemiologic terms, causation is "an event, condition, or characteristic" that has an "essential role" in "producing" "disease" (Cocchiarella & Lord, 2001, p. 331).

Cause. *Definition*. "[T]hat which brings about any condition or produces any effect" (Dorland & Newman, 2003, p. 311). "[T]hat which produces an effect or condition; that by which a morbid change or disease is brought about" (Stedman, 2000, p. 303).

-component cause. *Definition*. "Each sufficient cause is made up of a constellation of component causes" (Cocchiarella & Lord, 2001, p. 335).
Comment/Note. "Component causes interact with each other to produce disease" (Cocchiarella & Lord, 2001, p. 335).

-constitutional cause. *Definition*. "[O]ne acting within the body that is not restricted to a specific site, but is systematic or has a genetic basis" (Dorland & Newman, 2003, p. 311). "[A]cting from within or through some systematic process or inborn error" (Stedman, 2000, p. 303).

-exciting cause. *Definition*. "[O]ne that leads directly to a specific condition" (Dorland & Newman, 2003, p. 311). "[T]he direct provoking cause of a condition" (Stedman, 2000, p. 303).
Comment/Note. The term "eliciting" is synonymous.

-immediate cause. *Definition*. "[A] cause that is operative at the beginning of the specific effect" (Dorland & Newman, 2003, p. 311). Also termed *precipitating cause* (Dorland & Newman, 2003, p. 311). Also termed *primary or inciting cause* (Bailey, 1998, p. 18). Also termed *exciting cause* (Schmidt, 2002, p. C-119).
Comment/Note. The definition given stands in direct contrast to the legal definition, where "immediate cause" refers to a temporally recent causal component in a chain. In the medical definition, the term refers to an initial, or original, first component.

-local cause. *Definition*. "[O]ne that is not general or constitutional, but is confined to the site where the effect is produced" (Dorland & Newman, 2003, p. 311).

-necessary cause. *Definition*. "[A]n etiologic factor without which a result in question will not occur; the occurrence of the result is proof that the factor is operating" (Stedman, 2000, p. 303).

-precipitating cause. *Definition*. "[A] factor that brings on the onset of manifestations of a disease process" (Stedman, 2000, p. 303). "… are those conditioning factors which permit the immediate cause to act, as when a vehicle accident results in the blow on the head" (Bailey, 1998, p. 18).

-predisposing cause. *Definition*. "[A]nything that renders a person more liable to a specific condition without actually producing it" (Dorland & Newman, 2003, p. 311). "[A]nything that produces a susceptibility or disposition to a condition without actually causing it" (Stedman, 2000, p. 304).
Comment/Note. "… such as a 'drunk driver' in the vehicle accident or malnutrition in the case of pneumonia" (Bailey, 1998, p. 18).

-primary cause. *Definition*. "[T]he principal factor contributing to the production of a specific result" (Dorland & Newman, 2003, p. 311). "… this is the trigger factor which initiates the disease …" (Bailey, 1998, p. 18). Also termed *immediate or inciting cause* (Bailey, 1998, p. 18).
Comment/Note. "Examples of primary cause include genetic, congenital and acquired diseases or injuries. They can be easily remember[ed] by remembering the acronym 'MINT', where M is malformation, I is infection or inflammation, N is neoplasms and T is trauma" (Bailey, 1998, p. 18).

-proximate cause. *Definition*. "[T]hat which immediately precedes and produces an effect" (Dorland & Newman, 2003, p. 311). "[T]he immediate cause that precipitates a condition" (Stedman, 2000, p. 304).

-remote cause. *Definition*. "[A]ny cause that does not immediately precede and produce a specific condition; a predisposing, secondary, or ultimate cause" (Dorland & Newman, 2003, p. 311).

-secondary cause. *Definition*. "[O]ne that is supplemental to the primary cause" (Dorland & Newman, 2003, p. 311).

-specific cause. *Definition*. "[O]ne that produces a special or specific effect" (Dorland & Newman, 2003, p. 311). "[A] cause the action of which can definitely produce the condition in question" (Stedman, 2000, p. 304).

-sufficient cause. *Definition*. "[A]n etiologic factor that guarantees that a result in question will occur; non-occurrence of the result is proof that the factor is not operating" (Stedman, 2000, p. 304). "[A] set of minimal conditions and events that inevitably produces disease" (Cocchiarella & Lord, 2001, p. 335).
Comment/ Note. " '[M]inimal' implies that none of the conditions or events is superfluous. The completion of a sufficient cause may be considered equivalent to

the onset of a disease. ... The sufficient cause can represent the underlying mechanism of the condition" (Cocchiarella & Lord, 2001, p. 335).

-ultimate cause. *Definition*. "[T]he earliest factor, in point of time, that has contributed to production of a specific result" (Dorland & Newman, 2003, p. 311). "The first or most remote cause of a series of events which terminate in a particular condition or illness" (Schmidt, 2002, p. U-11).

Exacerbation. *Definition*. "Increase in the severity of a disease or any of its symptoms" (Dorland & Newman, 2003, p. 651).

Hill's Causation Criteria (Epidemiology). *Definition*. "1. strength of the association 2. temporality 3. consistency among studies 4. biological gradient 5. experimental evidence 6. plausibility of a biologic mechanism 7. coherence of evidence 8. analogy to a similar effect produced by a similar agent 9. specificity of outcome" (Cocchiarella & Lord, 2001, p. 332).
Comment/Note. "A major limitation of Hill's criteria is that they do not provide a framework in which to analyze the multifactorial nature of injury and disease and the relative contributions of multiple causes that commonly interact, producing additive or synergistic effects" (Cocchiarella & Lord, 2001, p. 335).

Pathogenesis. *Definition*. "Refers to the mechanism by which the causative agent(s) brings about the ailment" (Bailey, 1998, p. 97).

Auxiliary Medical Terms Associated with Causality and Causation

Most of the terms in this section relate to medical terms such as symptom, diagnosis, disorder, and disability. In general, a tort claim needs to establish not only that the symptoms caused by a proximate event constitute a diagnosable disorder but, also, that there has been an impairment, or functional impact, on the legally relevant roles of concern, such as work, study, or childcare.

Diagnosis. *Definition*. On the basis of appropriate evidence (signs, symptoms, tests, and examinations), determination of an individual's specific disorder(s) or abnormality (Corsini, 2002, p. 274; VandenBos, 2007, p. 277). Refers to the process of diagnosing or the product of the classification. *See DSM-IV*.
Comment/Note. "In clinical psychology, psychiatric diagnosis serves a major function in treatment strategy. ... In forensic psychology, the role of psychiatric diagnosis is generally less critical an issue. Diagnoses are *not* required in many legal issues (e.g., child custody, *Miranda* rights waivers, personal injury)" (Goldstein, 2003, p. 5).

Disorder. *Definition*. A group of signs, symptoms, or impairments, exhibiting an intelligible relationship with one another, and indicating physiological or behavioral abnormality, persistent or intense distress, or dysfunction (Corsini, 2002, p. 285; VandenBos, 2007, p. 288).

Disability. *Definition*. "[A]n alteration of an individual's capacity to meet personal, social, or occupational demands or statutory or regulatory requirements because of an impairment" (Cocchiarella & Andersson, 2001, p. 8). An enduring physical or mental impairment that noticeably interferes with function in core areas of life, such as self-care, mobility, communication, social interaction, sexual activity, studying, parenting, or employment (Corsini, 2002, p. 282; VandenBos, 2007, p. 285).
Comment/Note. "[T]he term disability has historically referred to a broad category of individuals with diverse limitations in the ability to meet social or occupational demands. However, it is more accurate to refer to the specific activity or role the 'disabled' individual is unable to perform. Several organizations are moving away from the term *disability* and instead are referring to specific *activity limitations* to encourage an emphasis on the specific activities the individual can perform and to identify how the environment can be altered to enable the individual to perform the activities associated with various social or occupational roles. ... Disability is content-specific, not inherent in the individual, but a function of the interaction of the individual and the environment ... The change in terminology arose for several reasons: to choose terminology without an associated stigma, to avoid labeling, and to emphasize the person's residual ability" (Cocchiarella & Andersson, 2001, p. 8). "Medical impairments are not related to disability in a linear fashion. An individual with a medical impairment can have no disability for some occupations, yet be very disabled for others. For example, severe degenerative disc disease may impair the functioning of the spine of both a licensed practical nurse and a bank president in a similar fashion when performing their activities of daily living. However, in terms of occupation, the bank president is less likely to be disabled by this impairment than the licensed practical nurse" (Cocchiarella & Andersson, p. 9).

DSM-IV (Diagnostic and Statistical Manual of Mental Disorders) (1994, 2000).
Definition. A manual published by the American Psychiatric Association that organizes, defines, and further describes a wide range of mental and behavioral disorders on the basis of specific symptoms without regard to etiology. The manual is revised periodically, based on the work of committees. Classificatory categories often are considered all or none, and often are based on polythetic criteria, or lists for which an individual must meet a threshold number of symptoms rather than all of them. The manual allows for diagnosis on five axes, involving clinical disorders, personality disorders/mental retardation, medical factors to consider, psychosocial and environmental factors to consider, and general level of adaptive functioning (Corsini, 2002, p. 274; VandenBos, 2007, p. 303).

Etiology. *Definition*. "... cause is the initiation of lesions, while etiology studies the various causes that can give rise to the lesion" (Bailey, 1998, p. 46).

Functional limitation. *Definition*. "Limit in the ability to perform basic activities of daily living" (Cocchiarella & Andersson, 2001, p. 8).

Handicap. *Definition*. A physical or emotional hindrance, obstacle, or impairment that stops, interferes with, or otherwise alters normal daily-living activities in the physical, social, or functional realms, for example, occupationally (Corsini, 2002, p. 434; VandenBos, 2007, p. 428). Often, a handicap is understood in terms of social and cultural perceptions and expectations.
Comment/Note. "Though the term continues to be used, generally it is being replaced with the preferred term *disability*" (Cocchiarella & Andersson, 2001, p. 9).

***ICD-9* (and *ICD-10*)**. The World Health Organization's *International Classification of Diseases*. The clinical modification of the ninth edition (*ICD-9-CM*) is still used in the United States for billing and insurance-related purposes; however, the tenth edition (1992) is used in Canada and most countries for these functions.
Comment/Note. Typically, the *DSM-IV* is used for diagnostic purposes in both countries, because it is considered a better system than the *ICD*. "We recognize that the *ICD-9*'s reliance on a classification system that separates disorders by their 'psychogenic' vs. 'organic' status is inimical to the biopsychosocial model that underlies health psychology as a science and as a profession" (Johnson, Perry, & Rozensky, 2002, p. 4).

Impairment. *Definition*. "Loss, loss of use, derangement of body part, organ system, or organ function" (Cocchiarella & Andersson, 2001, p. 8).

Science. *Definition*. Organized or systematic collection of reproducible data or evidence, enabling laws and principles to be formed, and based on an accumulating body of empirical observations (Corsini, 2002, p. 867; VandenBos, 2007, p. 818).

Symptom. *Definition*. A deviation from normal function as part of a pattern indicating a disorder or the need for therapy (Corsini, 2002, p. 970; VandenBos, 2007, p. 916).

Syndrome. *Definition*. A set of symptoms and signs indicative of a recognized illness, disease, or disorder, even if not included in standard diagnostic manuals (Corsini, 2002, p. 971; VandenBos, 2007, p. 917).
Comment/Note. Typically, *DSM* diagnoses are recognized by the courts. However, some syndromes are usually rejected, or considered to have not met *Daubert* requirements, such as "Child Sexual Abuse Accommodation Syndrome."

Key Psychological Terms Related to Causality and Causation

Compared to the legal and medical approaches to causality and causation, the psychological approach is more differentiated, because it elaborates concepts related to multiple cause. Statistics are essential to research in psychology and, inevitably, our understanding of causality and causation relates to statistical concepts. Nevertheless, psychology is conceptual before it is statistical, and psychologists have developed a refined network of concepts on causality and causation in behavior.

Catalytic variable. Similar to one meaning of the legal term "concurrent cause." *Definition*. "A variable that is necessary for the causal relationship between two other variables. It 'enables' such a relationship" (Haynes, 1992, p. 216).

Causal. *Definition*. Relating to physical and/or logical necessity (Corsini, 2002, p. 146).

-causal ambiguity. Inability to determine whether A and B are correlated, whether A caused B, whether B caused A, or whether A and B are causally unrelated but reflect a common cause C (Corsini, 2002, p. 146). VandenBos (2007) adds that in causal ambiguity an effect appears evident, but that the cause is indeterminate, and that controlled empirical research may help resolve the issue (p. 154).

-causal chain. *Definition*. A series of events reflective of sequential causation (Corsini, 2002, p. 146). VandenBos (2007) provides a more detailed definition in terms of a sequence of conditions or events that result in the particular effect. Moreover, the conditions and events may be empirically-derived or hypothetical. Finally, the relationship between neighboring conditions and events is transitive (p. 154).

-causal connection. *Definition*. A nexus between phenomena that implicates causation (VandenBos, 2007, p. 154).
Comment/Note. "Is the person's legally relevant behavior caused by or the product of mental disorder rather than the product of the person's free choice" (Morse, 1978a, b; in Heilbrun, 2001, p. 84).

-causal discontinuity. *Definition*. "Variation in the strength or form of a causal relationship between two variables" (Haynes, 1992, p. 213).

-causal explanation. *Definition*. An explication of phenomena in terms of their determinants, ranging from simple and direct to complex and multi-stage (Corsini, 2002, p. 146).

-causal explanations of human behaviors. *Definition*. Postulates formulated to explicate the determinants of human actions, thoughts, emotions, and related physiological and nervous system activity (Corsini, 2002, p. 146).

-causal latency. *Definition*. A cause and its effect are temporally separated (VandenBos, 2007, p. 154). "The time between a causal event (or a change in a causal variable) and its effect" (Haynes, 1992, p. 213).
Comment/Note. VandenBos (2007) specifies that not all causes have immediate effects, and that the interval involved may be lengthy, especially when multiple factors are involved. For example, some causes remain latent, delayed, or remote until the correct factors or conditions manifest.

-causal law. *Definition*. 1. A proposition that there is a necessary connection between certain events (e.g., A, B) such that one, A, always causes the other, B. 2. A law based on reproducible empirical findings of cause and effect (Corsini, 2002, p. 146). In causal laws, there is consistency or invariance because of the causal connection between phenomena (VandenBos, 2007, p. 154).

-causal mechanism. *Definition*. The process by which an effect is produced, explaining why the event A caused the outcome B (Corsini, 2002, p. 146). "[R]efers to the means through which a causal effect occurs …" (Haynes, 1992, p. 29), "… is produced" (Haynes, p. 213).
Comment/Note. "Causal mechanisms answer the question of 'how' one event causes another or 'why' there is a causal relationship between two events" (Haynes, 1992, pp. 29–30). VandenBos (2007, p. 154) points out that although one may be able to specify the most immediate, physical means effecting a result, there may be other causal factors to consider.

-causal model (of behavior disorders). This concept lies at the heart of the psychological approach to causality. It emphasizes the multifactorial and complex nature of causality, and its system influences.
Definition. "A qualitative and/or quantitative description of the variables hypothesized to be associated with the variance in a behavior disorder. It emphasizes controllable causal variables and depicts the form, strength, and direction of causal and noncausal (correlational) relationships" (Haynes, 1992, p. 213).
Comment/Note. "Causal models of behavior disorders indicate which events may operate as causal agents for particular behaviors and the nature, strength, and boundaries of those causal relationships" (Haynes, 1992, p. 4). "[C]ausal models of behavior disorders are becoming more complex, nonlinear, and lower level. They are becoming more dynamic … [T]hey acknowledge the impact of multiple variables, complex interactions among variables, and multiple levels of analysis" (Haynes, p. xi).

-causal nexus. *Definition*. A relation across two or more serial events, or across two or more successive phenomena (Corsini, 2002, p. 146).

-causal ordering. *Definition.* When a causal connection specifies that a cause must always temporally precede its effect, then the principle of "causal ordering" is being invoked (VandenBos, 2007, p. 154).

-causal path. *Definition.* Any number of preceding events may differentially influence a particular event that follows (Corsini, 2002, p. 147).
Comment/Note. VandenBos (2007, p. 154) indicates that in statistically testing causal paths, one can ascertain only the relative probable or likely causal sequence, involving which variables play a role and which order makes sense, from presumed cause to presumed effect.

-causal relation. *Definition.* Elements A and B are related in a manner wherein changes in one induce change in the other (Corsini, 2002, p. 147).

-causal texture. *Definition.* A philosophical term borrowed by psychologists (VandenBos, 2007, p. 154). It refers to the numerous, probabilistic, ever-changing interdependencies among events that constitute the "fabric of reality."

-causal variable. *Definition.* A variable that controls a proportion of the variance in another variable (Haynes, 1992, p. 213).
Comment/Note. "[C]ausal variables precede and are correlated with their effects, have a logical connection with their effects, and the association between the causal variable and the effect cannot be wholly attributed to a common effect of another variable" (Haynes, 1992, p. 213).

Causality. *Definition.* "A mental concept that everything that exists, whether static or dynamic, from stones to ideas, was actualized by some prior event. The causal approach contrasts with the purely descriptive approach of statistical research, and with the introspective method" (Corsini, 2002, p. 146).
Comment/Note. Derived from philosophy, the term indicates that all events have causes, being the consequences of preceding events (VandenBos, 2007, p. 154). "Because the term is philosophical and refers to an abstract relation, it is sometimes distinguished from CAUSATION, which is preferred in psychological parlance" (Reber & Reber, 2001, p. 110). [But a key psychology book directly on the topic, that of Haynes (1992), uses the term "causality" in its title.]

Causation. *Definition.* "A basically empirical principle which states that for whatever effects are observed there was a cause that preceded them" (Reber & Reber, 2001, p. 110). VandenBos (2007, p. 154) gives a similar definition, involving the empirical relation between two events/states where one brings about the other in a cause-effect relationship. Corsini (2002) elaborates further: "1. An act or process that generates an effect. 2. A process of transition or transformation of phenomena, objects, events, and so on, when the earlier stages are regarded as the conditions of the later stages; that is, if in the absence of the earlier phenomena, or their equivalents, the later phenomena never occur. 3. The conditioning of a

present event by factors which surround that event both in space and in time" (Corsini, p. 147).
Comment/Note. "The principle of causation (or cause and effect) is asymmetric and unidirectional" (Reber & Reber, 2001, p. 110).

-causation and correlation. Psychologists are conservative about establishing causal relationships, and are very wary of putative associations and correlations that can be explained in any of multiple ways.
Definition. "A positive correlation between two sets of data does not, of itself, indicate a causal relationship. ... Two or more items can covary due to the presence of a third factor. ... Critical elements in determining causation include: (a) factors must be correlated; (b) factors must be temporally related so that the cause precedes the effect; and (c) the potential causal factor remains as the most plausible cause" (Corsini, 2002, p. 147).

-multiple causation. In discussing causation of PTSD, Bloom (1999) refers to the complex "multicausal" web. Flor and Hermann (2004) describe a complex causal model of PTSD. We adopt a similar multicausal model of PTSD (Young & Yehuda, 2006). In discussing causation in traumatic brain injury (TBI), Kay (1999) described an "interaction" of contributing factors (e.g., neurological, physical, psychological), in functional outcome after mild TBI (mTBI). See Vanderploeg, Curtiss, and Belanger (2005) for a recent multicausal model of the long-term effects of mTBI. As for multicausality in the etiology of chronic pain, recent research universally supports the multifactorial biopsychosocial model (Dworkin & Breitbart, 2004; Gatchel, 2005; Hadjistavropoulos & Craig, 2004; Young & Chapman, 2006, and this volume).
Definition. "[S]everal distinguishable causal factors for a particular observed effect" (Reber & Reber, 2001, p. 110).
Comment/Note. "[I]n *multiple* causation, ... the issues of sufficiency and necessity are weakened. Multiple causation is the modal case in the social sciences" (Reber & Reber, 2001, p. 110). Also see "Reciprocal causality" and "Nonexclusive causal relationship" in Haynes (1992, pp. 42–44).

-simple causation. *Definition.* "[S]ingle known or knowable cause" (Reber & Reber, 2001, p. 110).
Comment/Note. "In *simple* causation, where there is a single known or knowable cause, it functions as the necessary and sufficient conditions of the effect observed" (Reber & Reber, 2001, p. 110).

Cause. *Definition.* An object or phenomenon, or a group of such, related in a manner to a simultaneous or succeeding one that absent the former or its equivalent the latter does not appear (Corsini, 2002, p. 147). An event or a state acting to "bring about" another one (an effect) (Vandenbos, 2007, p. 155).
Comment/Note. "Hypotheses about the causes of behavior disorders are often the most important determinants of the focus and methods of assessment, therapy, and research in psychopathology" (Haynes, 1992, p. xi).

-cause and effect. *Definition.* A lawful relationship wherein a certain action achieves a certain result or, conversely, a certain result is the product of a certain action (Corsini, 2002, p. 147).

-efficient cause. *Definition.* "[T]hose 'external' agents responsible for a particular phenomenon or event" [from Aristotle] (Haynes, 1992, p. 25).
Comment/Note. "In the behavioral sciences, efficient causes are often hypothetical constructs (e.g., 'need for achievement') as well as physical and physiological events" (Haynes, 1992, p. 26).

-false cause. "… (non causa pro causa), which involves presuming the reality of a causal connection that does not exist. A common variety of false cause is post hoc ergo propter hoc" (after this, therefore because of this). "This error of reasoning is frequent in evaluations of mild traumatic brain injury" (Williams, 2003, p. 117).

-latent cause. *Definition.* "… [D]ormant until preceded by another specific causal variable" (Haynes, 1992, p. 92).

-intermediate effect (cause). *Definition.* "The time gap between original causes and the identified behavior problem appears to be bridged …" (Haynes, 1992, p. 92).

-maintaining cause. *Definition.* "Maintaining causes are those variables that explain the current parameters of a behavior problem and are often different from those causal events responsible for its early development" (Haynes, 1992, p. 92).
Comment/Note. "Perpetuating" is a synonymous term.

-original cause. *Definition.* "Original causes are the first elements of a causal chain, are often single events, are relatively independent of other elements in the chain, and often precede the targeted behavior by a significant period of time" (Haynes, 1992, pp. 91–92).

-remote cause. *Definition.* In a chain of related events, a distant event that, to a certain degree, influenced the outcome (Corsini, 2002, p. 828).
Comment/Note. This is an example of how the same term in different disciplines can have different meanings; in law, remoteness may refer to an aspect of a chain too distant in unfolding events to participate in causation.

-triggering cause. *Definition.* "Triggering causes are a subset of maintaining causes and are associated with the immediate onset of a behavior disorder" (Haynes, 1992, p. 92).

Determinant. *Definition.* "Any causal or antecedent condition or agent" (Reber & Reber, 2001, p. 193).

Exacerbation. *Definition.* An environmental or other agent acts to increase the symptoms or manifestations of a disorder (Corsini, 2002, p. 347).
Comment/Note. Exacerbation refers to a worsening of symptoms after an index event. The symptoms may already be of clinical significance when the agent impacts the individual, or they may be subclinical.

Functional relationship. *Definition.* "[I]nvolve[s] contiguity between variables, reliable precedence of one variable, absence of an identified third variable that explains the relationship, the implication that manipulation of one variable will lead to a change in the other, a logical causal connection between the variables, and domains for operation of the causal relationship" (Haynes, 1992, p. 32).
Comment/Note. "Therefore, functional relationships do not necessarily, but can, meet the requirements of a 'causal' relationship" (Haynes, 1992, p. 32).

Mediating variable. *Definition.* "A variable that can influence the strength of relationship between two or more other variables" (Haynes, 1992, p. 215).
Comment/Note. "A mediating variable can strengthen or weaken the relationship between two other variables. A 'moderating' … variable weakens another causal relationship" (Haynes, 1992, p. 122). The legal concept of "mitigation" may be somewhat analogous.

Necessary condition. *Definition.* "Essentially, four conditions are necessary for inferring causal relationships for behavior disorders: (1) covariation between variables, (2) temporal precedence of the causal variable, (3) the absence of alternative explanations for the covariance, and (4) a logical connection between the variables" (Haynes, 1992, pp. 35–36).

Necessary causal variable. *Definition.* "[N]ecessary causal variables are those that must occur if the effect is to occur" (Haynes, 1992, p. 45).
Comment/Note. "[F]ew causal variables appear to be 'necessary' for the occurrence of behavior disorders" (Haynes, 1992, p. 45).

Proximate cause. First, the psychological/biological definition is given, and then the legal one as applied to psychology is given.
Definition. (a) "An immediate underlying cause based on the operation of internal mechanisms possessed by an individual" (Alcock, 2001, p. 493). (b) "Act of commission or omission that through an uninterrupted sequence of events directly results in an injury that otherwise would not have occurred or else becomes a substantial factor in causing an injury" (Koocher, 1998, p. 512). In a chain of events, the final one having the most direct effect (Corsini, 2002, p. 771).

Risk factor. *Definition.* An element either directly or indirectly causally associated with a disease, abnormality, or dysfunction (Corsini, 2002, p. 848). "Variables statistically associated with variance in the parameter of a behavior disorder" (Haynes, 1992, p. 92).

Vulnerability. *Definition*. "The degree to which an individual is susceptible to developing a behavior disorder given the occurrence of particular causal events" (Haynes, 1992, p. 216).
Comment/Note. "A 'vulnerable' person is one with a relatively higher probability of developing a disorder when exposed to specific conditions" (Haynes, 1992, p. 216).

Auxiliary Psychological Terms Associated with Causality and Causation

In this section, we present conceptual models of causality and causation, in particular. The biopsychosocial model has gained favor in law and psychology, and can meet *Daubert* admissibility challenges. It is an integrative one, reflecting the zeitgeist in psychology that behavior is a product of multiple, interacting factors. There are variants to this model, such as the diathesis–thesis one, and associated models, such as the person-situation transactional one. The traditional theories of psychology pertaining to causality and causation are the cognitive-behavioral, learning, information processing, psychodynamic, and biological (or medical) models. The psychodynamic model has more historical than contemporary relevance, although the concept of unconscious influence still has important currency. The biological model has moved from its strictly medical and reductionist approach to one that is more interactive, as in behavior genetics. More recent models are especially multiple, interactive, and context-sensitive, such as the dynamic and ecological models. Psychology concerns not only general models of behavior but also attempts at specific understanding of individuals. It is a science of individual differences in behavior. The nomothetic approach is concerned with population trends, whereas the idiographic approach concerns individual cases. Other important definitions in this section of the chapter concern reliability and validity.

Biopsychosocial model. *Definition*. "The biopsychosocial model maintains that health and illness are caused by multiple factors, and the operation of biological, psychological, and social processes must be considered simultaneously in terms of etiology and treatment" (Thompson & Van Loon, 2002, p. 144). "[P]rovides a systems perspective … . Changes in one part of the system can produce changes in another part of the system. For example, increases in disease activity (a biological change) can lead to increases in anxiety and depression (psychological changes) and decreases in the ability to work or perform household chores (social changes), both of which, in turn, can increase pain and disability. Alternatively, improvements in a person's self-efficacy about controlling … symptoms (a psychological change) can lead to enhanced compliance with medications (producing biological changes) or increased interaction with supportive friends and family (a social change)" (Keefe et al., 2002, p. 641).
Comment/Note. "A relevant example of a conceptually grounded and empirically sound framework that would qualify under legal rules (i.e., FRE, [Federal Rules of Evidence] state court rules of evidence, other statutes, case law) and under

psychological rules (i.e., ethical principles, forensic guidelines) is the biopsychosocial frame of reference. … A psycholegal formulation that involves multiple interactive causative factors (i.e., biopsychosocial) vs. a formulation that involves merely a single explanatory factor is more likely to have gained general acceptance in the scientific community, to have acquired a greater scientific basis, and to be more capable of providing reliable and probative bases for psycholegal opinions" (Weissman & DeBow, 2003, p. 49).

Cognitive-behavior model. *Definition*. "Cognitive-behavior theory" is defined in Corsini, (2002), as "a combination of cognition and behaviorism" that emphasizes the role of not only appropriate reinforcements and environmental contingencies but also perceptions and interpretations of events as sources of behavior (p. 179). As for cognitive-behavioral therapy (CBT), "[c]ognitive behavior therapy is an approach designed to change mental images, thoughts, and thought patterns so as to help patients overcome emotional and behavioral problems. It is based on the theory that behaviors and emotions are caused in part by cognitions and cognitive processes which one can learn to change" (Craighead & Nemeroff, 2001, p. 308). "[C]ognitive factors such as expectancies, attributions, and self-talk are targeted along with behaviors such as avoidance in efforts to correct, predict, and understand behavioral and emotional dysfunction" (Kazdin, 2000, p. 135).
Comment/Note. In addition to its cognitive component, the behavioral component of the therapy is quite relevant, and includes the teaching of breathing exercises, visualization, muscle relaxation, and so on. Although cognitive-behavioral therapy is generally considered to have the "most empirical support" and is considered by many to be the "psychotherapy of choice" (Taylor, 2006) for chronic pain disorders and many chronic illnesses, and to be the "main efficacious" treatment for long-term PTSD (Koch, Douglas, Nichols, & O'Neill, 2006), in the area of psychological injury it is important to consider other aspects of therapy, as well. That is, in psychological treatment of psychological injuries due to traumatic events, in addition to using the cognitive-behavioral approach, the literature points to the need for appreciation of psychosocial variables, the biopsychosocial model, neurobiological variables, interpersonal factors, psychoeducation, psychological support, family/system factors, emotions, positive psychology, religion and spirituality, individual differences, treatment matching, and so on.

With respect to therapy, see Brewin (2005), for PTSD; Robinson, Gatchel, and Whitfill (2005) for chronic pain; and McAllister (2005) for mTBI and persistent postconcussive syndrome, for which cognitive rehabilitation may become an important component of treatment, as well. The August, 2005, issue of the journal of *Rehabilitation Psychology* includes articles on rehabilitation therapy involving positive psychology (Dunn & Dougherty, 2005), and religion/spirituality (Rippentrop, 2005).

To conclude, despite the many authors lauding treatment with cognitive-behavior therapy, it is but one important consideration in therapy in the rehabilitation context. Moreover, there are other therapies used successfully in rehabilitation, such as interpersonal psychotherapy and family/systemic therapy. Therefore, continued research is needed to specify the multimodal means needed to treat each patient, and how to tailor treatment to their individual profiles and characteristics (Norcross, Beutler, & Levant, 2006).

Diathesis-stress model. *Definition*. "[A]ll forms of psychopathology can be best explained within the framework of a diathesis-personality-stress-model. The diathesis is the biological predisposition in terms of the biological traits, which create a disposition or vulnerability to the development of psychopathology. Personality is a mediating factor, out of which psychopathology could develop. Biological or environmental stressors may contribute to the development of a disorder or may be the proximal trigger for the episodes of the disorder" (Zuckerman, 1999, p. 417). "[T]he *diathesis-stress hypothesis* refers to a predisposition to develop a particular disorder … as a result of interaction between stressful demands and personal traits" (Roeckelein, 1998, p. 421).

Dynamical systems. *Definition*. "[A]n approach variously called nonlinear dynamical systems theory (or dynamic systems theory, for short), complex systems theory, or chaos theory. … Systems in nature are characterized by interactions among many components, whether molecules in a fluid, cells in a body or brain, organisms in an ecosystem, or individuals in a society. … The interactions among the elements of complex systems are reciprocal, with constituents influencing each other simultaneously, and they recur over time, as systems continue to evolve or perpetuate their own stability. … The most important and dramatic result of this kind of system dynamics is the emergence of novel forms at higher levels of organization. This process is called self-organization. In the sciences at large, self-organization refers to the emergence of order from disorder, and in particular the emergence of coherent, higher-order forms from the interactions of many lower-order components" (Lewis & Granic, 2000, pp. 1–2).
Comment/Note. "Central to all dynamic formulations is the assumption that behavior and its change over time are the result of emergent, rather than prescribed processes. Regularity and pattern … does not require the preexistence of a program, schema, code, clock, or otherwise iconic representation of the form … The behavior—a condensation of these many possible degrees of freedom—shows pattern in time and space that is not contained in any of the components alone. … Because the state of the system depends on the organism within its total context, there can be no logical distinction made between the organism and the environment as the cause of behavior and its change. Causality, as a linear chain of precedent and antecedent events, cannot be singularly assigned to any agency within or surrounding the organism. Rather, [it] is determined by all the collective activity of those components. … [T]he distinction between the 'biological' and the 'environmental', including the cultural and social context, is not tenable, nor is partitioning behavior into these dichotomous categories" (Smith & Thelen, 1993, pp. xiii–xiv).

Determinism. *Definition*. "[T]he doctrine that assumes that every event has causes" (Reber & Reber, 2001, p. 194).

Comment/Note. "[I]t is presumed that behavior disorders are *determined*, which, in turn, implies *lawful* causal relationships. ... [T]he assumption of determinacy does not imply that a behavior disorder has a single or unique cause, is always the result of the same causes, or is readily predicted by easily identifiable causes. ... Consequently, our predictions will always remain imperfect and *probabilistic*" (Haynes, 1992, p. 29). "Causal models are guaranteed to be probabilistic because of the operation of multiple and interacting causal variables, chance occurrence of causal variables, reciprocal determinism in causal relationships, and the dynamic, unstable nature of causal relationships" (Haynes, p. 35).

Ecological model. *Definition.* Considers "individual behavior as inseparable from its context, including the interpersonal, social, and physical aspects" (Craighead & Nemeroff, 2001, p. 476).

Experiment. *Definition.* "The manipulation of one or more independent variables conducted under controlled conditions to test one or more hypotheses, especially for making inferences of a cause-and-effect character. Involves the measurement of one or more dependent variables" (Craighead & Nemeroff, 2001, p. 351).

Free will. *Definition.* A philosophical concept that humans are not ruled by external sources alone, but have the capacity or power to formulate their own independent choices and decisions in a process of self-direction (Corsini, 2002, p. 392; VandenBos, 2007, p. 389).

Freedom of will. *Definition.* "Conscious volition," the ability to choose freely, without influence by others or the context, one's attitude or action (Corsini, 2002, p. 392).
Comment/Note. "The question is really whether there is some 'thing' called *free* will which stands outside scientific analysis of cause and effect or whether it is (merely?) a particular mental/affective state which itself plays a role in the causation of behavior" (Reber & Reber, 2001, p. 194).

Habilitation. *Definition.* The process of maximizing an individual's functioning through treatment or training, and maintaining the individual at that fit level (Corsini, 2002, p. 431; In Matter of Athans, 107 Wis. 2d 331, 320 N.W. 2d 30, Ct. App. 1982).
Comment/Note. Contrast with the term "rehabilitation."

Idiographic. *Definition.* Pertaining to the description or understanding of an individual person or of an individual case. Indicates assessment procedures and data gathered in them that are not necessarily generalizable to the population level or toward the formulation of more general laws applicable to the average person or case (Corsini, 2002, p. 470; VandenBos, 2007, p. 465).

Individual differences. *Definition.* "Individuals exhibiting the same behavior problem may differ in the causal variables affecting that behavior problem, the

mechanisms through which the causal relationships operate, and the importance of the various causal variables and paths" (Haynes, 1992, p. 108).
Comment/Note. "The idea that causal variables can differ in strength across individuals with the same behavior disorder has been supported in thousands of studies and acknowledged in hundreds of review articles and chapters" (Haynes, 1992, p. 108).

Information-processing model. *Definition.* "In general, *information-processing theory* is concerned with the way organisms attend to, select, and internalize information and how the information is subsequently used to make decisions and direct their behavior" (Roeckelein, 1998, p. 69).

Interaction. *Definition.* A relationship across two or more elements such as systems, individuals, or groups, results in mutual or reciprocal influence (Corsini, 2002, p. 486; VandenBos, 2007, p. 489).

Interactionism. *Definition.* Behavior is considered a function of continuous, multidirectional interaction (feedback) between an individual and her or his context, in which context influences individuals who, in turn, influence context (Corsini, 2002, p. 496).

Learning theory. *Definition.* "Learning principles provide explanations of current behavior and predictors of future behavior within the limits of uncertainty about future environments" (Craighead & Nemeroff, 2001, p. 875).
Comment/Note. Social learning theory is a contemporary offshoot.

Level of proof. *Definition.* "Empirical studies must demonstrate statistical significance to be considered interpretable; this level is typically set at the .05 level of probability. That is, the investigator must be 95% certain that the results of the study are attributable to the variables under investigation rather than to chance" (Goldstein, 2003, pp. 5–6).
Comment/Note. "Standards of proof differ in psychology and law, which can cause serious interdisciplinary misunderstandings. For example, the confidence limits in the behavioral sciences are set at higher levels (i.e., … .05 or .01) than those inherent in certain legal probative standards (i.e., … .51 in most civil areas). This difference potentially affects whether a piece of evidence is interpreted by the expert as 'significant' or not" (Weissman & DeBow, 2003, p. 37). *See reasonable degree of psychological certainty.*

Mechanistic approach. *Definition.* Psychological behaviors and processes can be reduced to the activity of underlying physiological activity and processes; for example, perception reflects especially chemical and electrical nervous system activities and processes (Corsini, 2002, p. 578; VandenBos, 2007, p. 562).

Mechanical causality. *Definition.* Behavior involves direct physical relationships across interacting elements (Corsini, 2002, p. 578).

Medical model in psychology. *Definition*. "[T]he medical model presupposes that a patient's report of disturbed mood, problematic thoughts, and/or aberrant behavior are caused by the disruption of internal physiological processes such as neurochemical abnormalities or central nervous system damage" (Craighead & Nemeroff, 2001, p. 933).

Mind/body problem. *Definition*. "[S]cholars have made three major approaches to defining mind in a different manner. The first is one of extreme reductionism. From this point of view, mind *per se* does not exist: … The second approach tries in some way to relate the qualitatively unlike mind and body by learning about the former from empirical knowledge of the latter. … [In] [t]he third approach … the human being is viewed as a single composite of mind and body, neither of which has existence without the other" (Craighead & Nemeroff, 2001, p. 962).

Nomothetic. *Definition*. Relating to the formulation of general laws applicable to populations as the goal of the scientific process, in contrast to the study of the individual person or case; investigation aimed at discovering general or universally valid laws or principles of behavior that characterize the average person or case (Corsini, 2002, p. 646; VandenBos, 2007, p. 627).

Organismic. *Definition*. Relating to the organism as a whole rather than to any particular part(s). In terms of behavior, it is understood as a coordinated and integrated function of the cumulative interacting whole of the organism (Corsini, 2002, p. 675; VandenBos, 2007, p. 654).

Person-environment transactions. *Definition*. "Reactive transactions occur when different individuals exposed to the same environment experience it, interpret it, and react to it differently. Evocative transactions occur when an individual's personality evokes distinctive responses from others. Proactive transactions occur when individuals select or create environments of their own" (Caspi & Roberts, 1999, p. 314).

Positivism. *Definition*. "[F]or the positivists, all knowledge is contained within the boundaries of science, and only those questions answerable from the application of the scientific method can be approached" (Reber & Reber, 2001, p. 549).

Reasonable degree of psychological certainty. *Definition*. "[A]s expert witness[es], forensic psychologists typically are asked whether they were able to reach an opinion 'to a reasonable degree of psychological certainty' … " (Goldstein, 2003, p. 6). See *Reasonable medical certainty*.

Recovery. *Definition*. 1. Recuperation. 2. The progress toward recuperative or normal functioning of an injured, ill, or otherwise incapacitated individual (Corsini, 2002, p. 814; VandenBos, 2007, p. 777).

Reductionism. *Definition*. "[A] philosophical point of view which maintains that complex phenomena are best understood by a componential analysis which breaks down the phenomena into their fundamental, elementary aspects" (Reber & Reber, 2001, p. 609).

Rehabilitation. *Definition*. Rehabilitation is defined as an integrated program of interventions, including the psychosocial, which empowers individuals presenting with disability to achieve "personally fulfilling, socially meaningful, and functionally effective interaction" in their daily contexts (Maki & Riggar, 2004, p. 1). The definition acknowledges that rehabilitation does not necessarily concern return to full functioning but to movement toward optimal residual levels in all affected areas, considering the scope of the symptoms, impairments, disorders, and disabilities involved. This is also implied in Corsini (2002), in which rehabilitation is defined as, "correction … toward a prior … level of functioning" or "restoration … to … fullest possible functioning" (Corsini, 2002, p. 822). Similarly, for VandenBos (2007, p. 782), rehabilitation involves, to the fullest possible degree, restoration through redevelopment and compensation, by providing appropriate resources, treatment, and training, the individual's independence, functional activity, and well-being.

Reliability. Note that the definitions of the term "reliability" in the psychological and legal spheres are quite different.
Definition. "The reliability of a test refers to its degree of stability, consistency, predictability, and accuracy. It addresses the extent to which scores obtained by a person are the same if the person is reexamined by the same test on different occasions" (Groth-Marnat, 2003, pp. 12–13). "Reliability concerns inferences made about consistency of measurement. Consistency is defined by tradition as a family of relationships: temporal stability, similarity among tests proposed to be equivalent, homogeneity within a single test, and comparability of assessments made by raters" (Craighead & Nemeroff, 2001, p. 1314).

Sensitivity. *Definition*. "[R]efers to the percentage of true positives that the instrument has identified" (Groth-Marnat, 2003, p. 22).

Specificity. *Definition*. Refers to "the relative percentage of true negatives" that the instrument has identified (Groth-Marnat, 2003, p. 22).
Comment/Note. "A structured clinical interview might be quite sensitive in that it [might] accurately identify 90% of schizophrenics in an admitting ward of a hospital. However, it may not be sufficiently specific in that 30% of schizophrenics [might] be incorrectly classified as either normal or having some other diagnosis" (Groth-Marnat, 2003, p. 22).

Systems theory. *Definition*. "[V]iews human behavior as a product of complex interactions between persons and their environments. Instead of focusing on either internal psychological processes or external forces, systems theory highlights the fluid process of mutual influence between individuals in relationships and between individuals and their environmental contexts" (Kazdin, 2000, p. 536).

Ultimate cause. Note that definitions of the term "ultimate cause" in the psychological/biological and legal spheres are quite different.
Definition. "The evolutionary, historical reason why something is the way it is" (Alcock, 2001, p. 494).
Comment/Note. " 'Why questions' require answers about the *ultimate* causes of behavior: Why have certain genes and certain proximate mechanisms persisted to the present, and why has evolution followed one path instead of another?" (Alcock, 2001, p. 19).

Validity. Note that in law the term "reliability" refers to validity as defined in psychology.
Definition. "The most crucial issue in test construction is validity. Whereas reliability addresses issues of consistency, validity assesses what the test is to be accurate about. … a valid test is one that accurately measures the variable it is intended to measure" (Groth-Marnat, 2003, p. 17). "The degree to which accumulated evidence and theory support specific interpretations of test scores entailed by proposed uses of a test" (American Educational Research Association, American Psychological Association, National Council on Measurement in Education, 1999, p. 184).

Philosophical Terms

Philosophers raise pertinent issues about causality.

Aristotle's four causes: material, formal, efficient, and final. *Definition*. "Aristotle … distinguished four senses of "cause": the material out of which things come; the form which things eventually have when they are perfected; that which brings about this completion, the moving cause; and finally the purpose or function of such things, the final cause" (Wiener, 1973, p. 272). "Several types of efficient causes have been suggested and are outlined as follows: *Sufficient cause*: *Y* occurs whenever *X* occurs; therefore, *X* is sufficient to cause *Y*. *Insufficient cause*. That cause that *by itself*, is insufficient to produce the effect, but can function as a causal variable in combination with other causal variables. *Necessary cause*: *Y* never occurs without *X*. *Necessary and sufficient cause*: *Y* occurs whenever *X* occurs, and *Y* never occurs without *X*. *First cause*: That cause upon which all others depend—the earliest event in a causal chain. *Principal cause*: That cause upon which the effect primarily depends. *Immediate cause*: That cause which produces the effect without any intervening events. *Mediate cause*: A cause that produces its effect only through another cause" (Haynes, 1992, p. 26).
Comment/Note. "Aristotle criticized Plato and others for maintaining confined and restricted views about the nature and types of causes" (Cocchiarella & Lord, 2001, p. 329). "Some have claimed that Aristotle's 'four causes' are not really causes at all … When explanations of changes are being sought, however, Aristotle seems to provide recognizably causal explanations. … [F]or this reason, the label 'four causes' gives a reasonably accurate impression of Aristotle's doctrine" (Craig, 1998, p. 419). "These distinctions are known collectively as

Aristotle's doctrine of the four causes. The description is unfortunate, because in English the word 'cause' would by anyone quite untouched by Aristotelian influences be applied only to the third" (Flew & Priest, 2002, p. 66).

Causal law. *Definition*. "A regular and invariant connection between one kind of events or states—called causes—and another kind—called effects." They need not follow one after another, there may be delays ("succession") or be simultaneous ("coexistence"). They may occur in series ("chains") (Iannone, 2001, p. 94). *Comment/Note*. Chains can go "wayward," for example, not following what is prescribed by their antecedents. They can be "probabilistic," or "statistical," not "denoting an invariant connection between kinds of events or states" (Iannone, 2001, p. 95).

Causal nexus. *Definition*. "The bonding or link between a cause and its effect" (Blackburn, 1994, p. 58).

Causation. *Definition*. "[T]he relation between causes and effects" (Iannone, 2001, p. 95).

Denier of causation. *Comment/Note*. "Perhaps the most famous denier of causation was Bertrand Russell (1918), who actually thought that the concept of causation was incoherent ... ": for "there are no such things." Here is his famous dictum: "The law of causality, I believe, like much that passes muster among philosophers, is a relic of a bygone age, surviving, like the monarchy, only because it is erroneously supposed to do no harm" [Russell (1910), reprinted in 1918, p. 208] (Psillos, 2002, p. 3).

Determinism. *Definition*. "[T]o set bounds or limits" (Iannone, 2001, p. 147). *Comment/Note*. There are various forms of determinism. "One form is *scientific determinism*, the view that *every event has a cause* and that the event is bound to occur given the occurrence of the cause, plus the standing conditions of laws of nature. So, given the past, only one future is possible. In addition, knowledge of all antecedent conditions and laws of nature would make it possible to predict the entire future. In other words, determinism excludes chance" (Iannone, 2001, p. 147).

Etiology. *Definition*. "The study of causality" (Iannone, 2001, p. 96).

Conclusions

Causality, causation, and related terms are used widely in the legal, medical, psychological, and philosophical disciplines and, indeed, represent the essence of intellectual endeavor in most academic and professional domains. Despite this ubiquity, the survey of the definitions of these terms in the four disciplines of focus in the current review (especially law, medicine, psychology) illustrates that there is no consensus on their denotative and connotative meanings, especially when one field is compared carefully to another. Although some terms are defined in an equivalent manner in the various disciplines, others are not equivalent in the different disciplines or even provide definitions that are exact *opposites*, such as with the term "immediate cause."

Other examples involving conflicting definitions across disciplines include terms less directly related to causality and causation, such as "recovery," or ones with meanings related both to cause and other issues, such as "ultimate." In law, "recovery" refers to monetary compensation because of a lack of health recovery, whereas in psychology it refers to health recovery, and the more of it that takes place, the less the legal monetary recovery. With respect to ultimate cause, in medicine it refers to a remote, initial, first, or original cause, but in psychology and biology it concerns evolutionary and adaptational issues. In law, the word "ultimate" is not used causally, but refers to the issue being adjudicated by the trier of fact, for example, whether a party has been negligent, causing compensable physical or psychological injury.

However, some terms are unique to a discipline, despite other common ones across the disciplines. For example, the term "local" cause is found only in medicine, and the term "catalytic" in psychology stands apart from those in the other disciplines under discussion.

In order to facilitate mutual understanding and translation from one discipline to another, reciprocal awareness of ongoing use of the terms needs to develop. It is hoped that the current dictionary functions as a first step in these regards. Furthermore, we offer a table of terms that compares and contrasts key terms with respect to causality and causation across the various disciplines being considered (see Table 4.1).

The table suggests which causality/causation terms are common to the areas under review and are the same or similar in definition, which ones are different in definition across the areas, and which ones are unique to one discipline or the other. In addition, it helps specify where the disciplines entertain similar definitions, but use different labels for them.

Table 4.1 is structured such that key legal terms are presented first, then additional ones are presented in the disciplines of medicine, psychology, and philosophy. We

TABLE 4.1A. Key Terms Related to Causality and Causation in Law

Term	Meaning (simplified)
Concurrent	Joint
Contributing	Secondary
Immediate	Most recent
Intervening	Added
Joint	Multiple
Material	Part of joint
Proximate	Dominant (Direct)
Remote	Initial, too far removed
Superseding	Replacing dominant

TABLE 4.1B. Key Terms Related to Causality and Causation in Medicine

Term	Meaning (simplified)
Component	Part of multiple
Exacerbation	Worsening
Exciting	Direct
Immediate	Beginning, Initial
Predisposing	Susceptible
Primary	Principle
Remote	Predisposing, Secondary
Secondary	Not principle
Ultimate	Remote

TABLE 4.1C. Key Terms Related to Causality and Causation in Psychology

Term	Meaning (simplified)
Catalytic	Facilitative
Latent	Delayed
Maintaining	Current
Mediating	Intervening
Multiple	Multifactorial
Original	Remote, Initial
Remote	Initial
Triggering	Immediate

TABLE 4.1D. Key Terms Related to Causality and Causation in Philosophy

Term	Meaning (simplified)
First	Remote
Immediate	Last
Principle	Primary

start with law, for even if psychologists would consider their network of terms as coherent in understanding causality and causation, in forensics, psychologists need to work from the existing legal framework.

There appear to be nine important causality-related legal terms that we abstracted from the dictionary of terms developed in this text, with the principle one being *proximate*, and the eight others being—*concurrent, contributing, immediate, intervening, joint, material, remote, and superseding.*

These terms demonstrate that the law has created some refined concepts with respect to causality and causation, despite some shortcomings with respect to the temporal terms of "immediate" and "remote." Although the law has not dealt effectively in terms of the temporal aspect of causal chains, using ambiguous wording, the table suggests, nevertheless, that there is a range of useful terms. For example, in chains of causation, the law prescribes terms involving multiple or joint causation, in which there are concurrent causes, more important proximate ones, secondary contributing ones, material causes, and intervening and even superseding ones that displace proximate ones.

These terms constitute an important nexus of interrelated concepts dealing with causality and causation in the law. Nevertheless, the other disciplines add to understanding of the terms related to causality and causation.

The discipline of medicine is considered next, supporting our conclusion that the terms related to causality and causation in law can be supplemented by analysis of other relevant disciplines. We examine the discipline of medicine before that of psychology, because in the legal arena it has a much greater role to play with respect to causality and causation compared to psychology. Instead of repeating the whole nexus of terms in medicine relating to causality and causation, we only list those terms that have not been mentioned in the legal terms. This process yielded a list of nine additional terms to consider in medicine with respect to causality and causation—*component, exacerbation, exciting, immediate, predisposing, primary, remote, secondary, and ultimate.* (Note that "primary cause" in law refers to proximate cause, and not uniquely principle cause, so that "primary cause" is listed here as a new term in medicine in the sense that its meaning in medicine is new. The same logic leads to the inclusion of the term "immediate" in both lists; that is, the term is the same, but the definition varies across the two disciplines. The term "remote" is included in these two lists and the following one on psychological terms because it varies in definition across the three disciplines.)

In the same manner, we examined the psychological terms related to causality and causation in the dictionary of terms in this text, seeking new terms beyond the terms provided by similar analyses of the disciplines of law and medicine. Eight terms emerged that could be helpful to understanding causality and causation beyond the ones already listed. They are—*catalytic, latent, maintaining, mediating, multiple, original, remote, and triggering.*

Finally, perusal of the list of causal terms in the discipline of philosophy yielded two terms not mentioned in the three disciplines already analyzed—*first and principle.*

The table of 29 terms that we have extracted about causality and causation in the four disciplines under review provides a simplified network of terms that eliminates many of the contradictions, opposite meanings, gaps, ambiguities, and translation difficulties inherent in the lists of terms within the disciplines. However, the network of 29 terms on causality and causation so far presented in this chapter can be reduced to an even tighter network, with little inconsistency, overlap, and contradiction. In our opinion, the most important causal terms that the legal field has contributed include: *proximate, concurrent, contributing, intervening, material*, and *superseding*. Other useful terms that have been added from medicine include: *component, exacerbation, predisposing, primary*, and *secondary*. Beyond these terms from law and medicine, from psychology, we can add the terms: *catalytic, latent, maintaining, mediating*, and *multiple*. The extra terms provided by philosophy are covered in one way or another in the other three disciplines. Together, these 16 critical terms, taken from law, psychology, and medicine, permit an integrated understanding of multiple causality.

In addition to presenting the terms relevant to understanding causality and causation in the four disciplines under review, Table 4.1 also reviews the basic meaning underlying each of the terms. By doing so, the table illustrates the areas of agreement and disagreement across the various disciplines being considered with respect to the conceptualization of causality and causation. For example, the four disciplines have shared understanding of the concept of proximate cause, or its equivalent, in terms of seeking a dominant, responsible cause of an outcome, even if the factor is not unique. They all speak to whether a necessary and sufficient cause can be isolated from the forces impinging on the person in order to explain her or his immediate reactions to an event and the effects of those reactions, although philosophy debates whether causes can legitimately be sought.

Moreover, the four disciplines acknowledge the multiplicity of forces in causality and causation. The law defines not only proximate cause but, also, terms that help differentiate the causal forces in chains of cause or in joint cause, such as the concepts of "contributing" or "material" cause.

At the same time, it is these complex scenarios of multiple, chained, and joint cause that give the law its greatest difficulties, because there is an inherent tension present in this field that is not present in the others with respect to causality and causation. Because, in the end, unlike in the other disciplines under discussion, in order to construct a "theory of the case" that is readily presentable in a tort claim or is readily defendable against such a claim, the law normally seeks to isolate the one cause that is most responsible for a complainant's physical or psychological condition, or both. The law also tends to minimize the other contributing causes that may affect a complainant's condition.

Moreover, the disciplines have a frank confusion about the terms needed to describe the temporally first and last, or initial and most recent components, of a causal chain. Therefore, we recommend that all professionals, in dealing with a possible chain of causation in temporal terms, specify whether they are referring to temporally "initial" components, temporally "intermediate" components, or temporally "more recent" components, rather than using more ambiguous terms such as "immediate" and "remote." Note that the temporal dimension in relation to causality and causation specifies the time lines involved, and does not deal directly with the more important dimension concerning primacy, importance, or relevance of cause. Logically speaking, any of the initial, intermediate, and most recent temporal components of a causal chain may be the legal, proximate, or most important component in cause.

To summarize, in determining causality and causation in a forensic or related case, it appears that there are several major dimensions to consider. Is there an identifiable proximate cause to a complainant's physical condition? Is it the same one for her/his psychological condition? Does the cause consist of a specific, isolated component, or are there multiple components? If present, do the multiple components align sequentially in a chain, or is this less clear? If multiple, can a primary cause be isolated as important and, if so, is this the one that is legally relevant? In examining the nexus of legal terms that deal with causality and causation, it is clear that they allow the legal profession to cover evaluation of these basic dimensions dealing with cause. At the same time, the other three disciplines contribute to a fuller understanding of cause along these dimensions through the supplementary terms that they contribute.

Overall, our analysis of the terms on causality and causation that have been assembled in this dictionary of terms has proved to be a fruitful endeavor. We have shown that the law has created a network of terms sufficient to provide an adequate grasp of the concepts involved. At the same time, the medical and psychological disciplines, in particular, have added to the network of terms by expanding the scope of concepts implicated, through their emphases on predisposing and multiple causality and causation, in particular. At the same time, the terms on causality and causation presented in this chapter are not meant to be inclusive; for example, we do not list medical terms such as "closed head injury" and psychological terms such as "unconscious".

Psychology eschews simplistic explanations in its scientific approach to understanding human behavior, yet the law seeks simplicity in its positions on causality and causation in civil cases. The law presents arguments for or against proximate cause in the various cases with which it deals, too often depending on which side of the adversarial chasm its representatives find themselves. Forensic psychologists and others dealing with law and the courts need to traverse this divide with a clear understanding of the concepts involved, facilitating their impartial use in comprehensive assessments of individuals being assessed, and a ready translation of the concepts across the mental health and legal disciplines. The cross-discipline analysis undertaken in this chapter of terms related to causality and causation in the fields of law, medicine, psychology, and philosophy, and the consequent synthesis of a dictionary or table of terms presented in this chapter, may be helpful in this task, allowing psychologists and lawyers to better bridge some of their differences.

References

Alcock, J. (2001). *Animal Behavior: An evolutionary approach* (7th ed.). Sutherland, MA: Sinauer.

American Educational Research Association, American Psychological Association, & National Council on Measurement in Education. (1999). *Standards for educational and psychological testing*. Washington, DC: Author.

American Psychiatric Association. (1994). *Diagnostic and statistical manual of mental disorders* (4th ed.). Washington, DC: Author.

American Psychiatric Association. (2000). *Diagnostic and statistical manual of mental disorders: Text revision* (4th ed.). Washington, DC: Author.

Athey v. Leonati [1996] 3 S.C.R. 458.

Bailey, J. A., II. (1998). *The concise dictionary of medical-legal terms*. New York: Parthenon.

Berger, A. (1953). Encyclopedic dictionary of Roman law. As cited in B. A. Garner (Ed.). (2004). *Black's law dictionary* (8th ed., p. 233). St. Paul, MN: West Group.

Blackburn, S. (1994). *The Oxford dictionary of philosophy*. New York: Oxford University Press.

Bloom, S. L. (1999). The complex web of causation: Motor vehicle accidents, comorbidity and PTSD. In E. J. Hickling & E. B. Blanchard (Eds.), *The international handbook of road traffic accidents and psychological trauma: Current understanding, treatment and law* (pp. 157–184). Amsterdam: Elsevier.

Bogoroch, R. M., & Chandler, T. S. (2002). *How Canadian courts have turned "Thin Skull" damages into "Crumbling Skulls" damages: What are the implications?* (Available from the Canadian Institute Advanced Forum on Litigating Damages: Bogoroch & Associates, 150 King Street West, Suite 1707, Toronto, ON M5H 1J9).

Brewin, C. R. (2005). Encoding and retrieval of traumatic memories. In J. J. Vasterling & C. R. Brewin (Eds.), *Neuropsychology of PTSD: Biological, cognitive, and clinical perspectives* (pp. 131–150). New York: Guilford Press.

Brixen, C. E., & Meis, C.E. (2000). Codifying the "*Daubert* trilogy": The amendment to Federal Rule of Evidence 702. *Jurimetrics, 40*, 527–536.

Brodsky, S. L., Caputo, A. A., & Domino, M. L. (2002). The mental health professional in court: Legal issues, research foundations, and effective testimony. In B. Van Dorsten (Ed.), *Forensic psychology: From classroom to courtroom* (pp. 17–33). New York: Kluwer Academic/Plenum.

Cardozo, B. (1928). The paradoxes of legal science. As cited in B. A. Garner (Ed.). (2004). *Black's law dictionary* (8th ed., p. 233). St. Paul, MN: West Group.

Caspi, A., & Roberts, B. W. (1999). Personality continuity and change across the life course. In L. A. Pervin, & O. P. John (Eds.), *Handbook of personality: Theory and research* (2nd ed., pp. 300–326). New York: Guilford Press.

Chaney v. Smithkline Beckman Corp., 764 F.2d 527 (8th Cir. 1985).

Cocchiarella, L., & Andersson, G. B. J. (Eds.). (2001). *Guides to the evaluation of permanent impairment* (5th ed.). Chicago, IL: American Medical Association.

Cocchiarella, L., & Lord, S. J. (Eds.). (2001). *Master the AMA Guides Fifth* (5th ed., pp. 327–341). Chicago, IL: American Medical Association.

Corsini, R. J. (2002). *The dictionary of psychology*. New York: Brunner-Routledge.

Craig, E. (Ed.). (1998). *Routledge encyclopedia of philosophy*. New York: Routledge.

Craighead, W. E., & Nemeroff, C. B. (Eds.). (2001). *The Corsini encyclopedia of psychology and behavioral science* (3rd ed.). New York: Wiley.

Daubert v. Merrell Dow Pharmaceuticals, Inc. 509 U.S. 579, 113 S.Ct. 2786, 125 L.Ed. 2d 469 (1993).

Dorland, I., & Newman, W. A. (2003). *Dorland's illustrated medical dictionary* (30th ed.). Amsterdam: Elsevier.

Douglas, K. S., Huss, M. T., Murdoch, L. L., Washington, D. O., & Koch, W. J. (1999). Posttraumatic Stress Disorder stemming from motor vehicle accidents: Legal issues in Canada and the United States. In E. J. Hickling & E. B. Blanchard (Eds.), *The international handbook of road traffic accidents and psychological trauma: Current understanding, treatment and law* (pp. 271–289). New York: Elsevier Science.

Dunn, D. S., & Dougherty, S. B. (2005). Prospects for a positive psychology of rehabilitation. *Rehabilitation Psychology, 50*, 305–311.

Dworkin, R. H., & Breitbart, W. S. (Eds.). (2004). *Psychological aspects of pain: A handbook for health care providers*. Seattle, WA: IASP Press.

Ewing, C. P. (2003). Expert testimony: Law and practice. In I. B. Weiner (Series Ed.) & A. M. Goldstein (Vol. Ed.), *Handbook of psychology: Vol. 11, Forensic psychology* (pp. 55–66). Hoboken, NJ: Wiley.

Flew, A., & Priest, S. (Eds.). (2002). *A dictionary of philosophy*. London: Pan Books.

Flor, H., & Hermann, C. (2004). Biopsychosocial models of pain. In R. H. Dworkin & W. S. Breitbart (Eds.), *Psychological aspects of pain: A handbook for health care providers* (pp. 47–75). Seattle, WA: IASP Press.

Frye v. United States, 293 F. 1013, 34 ALR 145 (D. C. Cir. 1923).

Garner, B. A. (Ed.). (1995). *A dictionary of modern legal usage* (2nd ed.). New York: Oxford University Press.

Garner, B. A. (Ed.). (1999). *Black's law dictionary* (7th ed.). St. Paul, MN: West Group.

Garner, B. A. (Ed.). (2004). *Black's law dictionary* (8th ed.). St. Paul, MN: West Group.

Gatchel, R. J. (2005). *Clinical essentials of pain management*. Washington, DC: American Psychological Association.

Geistfeld, M. (2001). Scientific uncertainty and causation in tort law. *Vanderbilt Law Review, 54*, 1011–1037.

Goldstein, A. M. (2003). Overview of forensic psychology. In I. B. Weiner (Series Ed.) & A. M. Goldstein (Vol. Ed.), *Handbook of psychology: Vol. 11, Forensic psychology* (pp. 3–20). Hoboken, NJ: Wiley.

Greenberg, S. A. (2003). Personal injury examinations in torts for emotional distress. In I. B. Weiner (Series Ed.) & A. M. Goldstein (Vol. Ed.), *Handbook of psychology: Vol. 11, Forensic psychology* (pp. 233–257). Hoboken, NJ: Wiley.

Groth-Marnat, G. (2003). *Handbook of psychological assessment* (4th ed.). Hoboken, NJ: Wiley.

Hadjistavropoulos, T., & Craig, K. D. (Eds.). (2004). *Pain: Psychological perspectives*. Mahwah, NJ: Erlbaum.

Hart, H. L. A., & Honoré, T. (1985). *Causation in the law* (2nd ed.). Oxford: Oxford/Clarendon Press.

Haynes, S. N. (1992). *Models of causality in psychopathology: Toward dynamic, synthetic and nonlinear models of behavior disorders*. New York: Macmillan.

Heilbrun, K. (2001). *Principles of forensic mental health assessment*. New York: Kluwer Academic/Plenum.

Iannone, A. P. (2001). *Dictionary of world philosophy*. New York: Routledge.

In Matter of Athans, (1982) 107 Wis. 2d 331, 230 N.W. 2d 30 (Ct. App.).

Jewell, E. J., & Abate, F. (Eds.). (2001). *The new Oxford American dictionary*. New York: Oxford University Press.

Johnson, S. B., Perry, N. W., Jr., & Rozensky, R. H. (2002). Introduction to volume 1: Medical disorders and behavioral applications. In T. J. Boll (Series Ed.), S. B. Johnson, N. W. Perry Jr., & R. H. Rozensky (Vol. Eds.), *Handbook of clinical health psychology: Vol. 1. Medical disorders and behavioral applications* (pp. 4–5). Washington, DC: American Psychological Association.

Kay, T. (1999). Interpreting apparent neuropsychological deficits: What is really wrong? In J. J. Sweet (Ed.), *Forensic neuropsychology: Fundamentals and practice* (pp. 145–183). Lisse, The Netherlands: Swets & Zeitlinger.

Kazdin, A. E. (Ed.). (2000). *Encyclopedia of psychology*. (Vol. 2). Washington, DC: American Psychological Association & Oxford: Oxford University Press.

Keefe, F. J., Smith, S. J., Buffington, A. L. H., Gibson, J., Studts, J. L., & Caldwell, D. S. (2002). Recent advances and future directions in the biopsychosocial assessment and treatment of arthritis. *Journal of Consulting and Clinical Psychology, 70*, 640–655.

Klimchuk, D. (1998). Causation, thin skulls and equality. *Canadian Journal of Law and Jurisprudence, 11*, 115–141.

Koch, W. J., Douglas, K. S., Nicholls, T. L., & O'Neill, M. L. (Eds.). (2006). *Psychological injuries: Forensic assessment, treatment, and law*. Oxford, UK: Oxford University Press.

Koocher, G. P. (1998). Glossary of legal terms of special interest in mental health practice. In G. P. Koocher, J. C. Norcross, & S. S. Hill III (Eds.), *Psychologist's desk reference* (pp. 509–513). New York: Oxford University Press.

Krauss, D. A., & Sales, B. D. (2003). Forensic psychology, public policy, and the law. In I. B. Weiner (Series Ed.) & A. M. Goldstein (Vol. Ed.), *Handbook of psychology: Vol. 11, Forensic psychology* (pp. 543–560). Hoboken, NJ: Wiley.

Lewis, M. D., & Granic, I. (2000). Introduction: A new approach to the study of emotional development. In M. D. Lewis & I. Granic (Eds.), *Emotion, development, and self-organization: Dynamic systems approaches to emotional development* (pp. 1–12). Cambridge, UK: Cambridge University Press.

Maki, D. R., & Riggar, T. F. (2004). Concepts and paradigms. In T. F. Riggar & D. R. Maki (Eds.), *The handbook of rehabilitation counseling: Issues and methods* (pp. 1– 24). New York: Springer Science+Business Media.

McAllister, T. W. (2005). Mild brain injury and the postconcussion syndrome. In J. M. Silver, T. W. McAllister, & S. C. Yudofsky (Eds.), *Textbook of traumatic brain injury* (pp. 279–308). Washington, DC: American Psychiatric.

Merriam-Webster's collegiate dictionary (11th ed.). (2003). Springfield, MA: Merriam- Webster.

Morse, S. (1978a). Crazy behavior, morals, and science: An analysis of mental health law. *Southern California Law Review, 51*, 527–654.

Morse, S. (1978b). Law and mental health professionals: The limits of expertise. *Professional Psychology*, *9*, 389–399.

Norcross, J. C., Beutler, L. E., & Levant, R. F. (Eds.). (2006). *Evidence-based practices in mental health: Debate and dialogue on fundamental questions*. Washington, DC: American Psychological Association.

Padget v. Gray, 727 S.W.2d 706 (Tex. App. 1987).

Page, J. A. (2003). *Torts: Proximate cause*. New York: Thomas/West.

Pearl, J. (2000). *Causality: Models, reasoning, and interference*. New York: Cambridge University Press.

Psillos, S. (Ed.). (2002). *Causation and explanation*. Montreal: McGill-Queen's University Press.

Reber, A. S., & Reber, E. S. (2001). *The Penguin dictionary of psychology* (3rd ed.). London: Penguin Books.

Reid, W. H. (1999). *A clinician's guide to legal issues in psychotherapy: Or proceed with caution*. Phoenix, AZ: Zeig Tucker

Rippentrop, A. E. (2005). A review of the role of religion and spirituality in chronic pain populations. *Rehabilitation Psychology, 50*, 278–284.

Robinson, R. C., Gatchel, R. J., & Whitfill, T. (2005). Tailoring psychosocial treatment for patients with occupational disability. In I. Z. Schultz & R. J. Gatchel (Eds.), *Handbook of complex occupational disability claims: Early risk identification, intervention, and prevention* (pp. 151–165). New York: Springer Science+Business Media.

Roeckelein, J. E. (1998). *Dictionary of theories, laws, and concepts in psychology*. London: Greenwood Press.

Romano, J. F. (1999). Cause yourself to understand the intricacies of causation. *Trial Lawyer, 22*, 101–103.

Russell, B. (1910). *Philosophical essays* (3rd Imp.). London: Allen & Unwin.

Russell, B. (1918). *Mysticism and logic*. London: Allen & Unwin.

R. v. Mohan, [1994] 2 S.C.R. 9.

Schmidt, J. E. (2002). *Attorney's dictionary of medicine and word finder* (Vol. 1). New York: Matthew Bender & Company.

See, A. (2000). Use of human epidemiology: Studies improving causation. *Defense Counsel Journal, 67*, 478–487.

Slovenko, R. (2002). Causation in law and psychiatry. In I. Freckelton & D. Mendelson (Eds.), *Causation in law and medicine* (pp. 357–378). Burlington, VT: Ashgate/ Dartmouth.

Slovenko, R. I. (2003). Introduction. In R. I. Simon (Ed.), *Posttraumatic Stress Disorder in litigation: Guidelines for forensic assessment* (2nd ed., pp. ixx–xxiv). Washington, DC: American Psychiatric Publishing.

Smith, L. B., & Thelen, E. (Eds.). (1993). *A dynamic systems approach to development: Applications*. Cambridge, MA: The MIT Press/Bradford Book.

Solomon, R. M., Feldthusen, D. P., & Kostal, R. W. (1996). *Cases and materials on the law of torts* (4th ed.). Toronto, ON: Thomson/Carswell.

Stedman, T. L. (2000). *Stedman's medical dictionary* (27th ed.). New York: Lippincott Williams & Wilkins.

Taylor, R. R. (2006). *Cognitive behavioral therapy for chronic illness and disability*. New York: Springer Science+Business Media.

Theriault v. Swan, 588 A.2d 369 (Me. 1989).

Thompson, R. J. Jr., & Van Loon, K. J. (2002). Mental disorders. In T. J. Boll (Series Ed.) S. B. Johnson, N. W. Perry Jr., & R. H. Rozensky (Vol. Eds.). *Handbook of clinical health psychology: Vol. 1. Medical disorders and behavioral applications* (pp. 143–172). Washington, DC: American Psychological Association.

Tort law dictionary. (n.d.). Retrieved July 2, 2003, from http://lexnet.bravepages.com/tortdict.htm

U.S. Equal Employment Opportunities Commission (1990). (EEOC) 29 C.F.R. §1604.11(a).

VandenBos, G. B. (Ed.). (2007). *APA dictionary of psychology*. Washington, DC: American Psychological Association.

Vanderploeg, R. D., Curtiss, G., & Belanger, H. G. (2005). Long-term neuropsychological outcomes following mild traumatic brain injury. *Journal of the International Neuropsychological Society, 11*, 228–236.

Walker, L. E. A., & Shapiro, D. L. (2003). *Introduction to forensic psychology: Clinical and social psychological perspectives*. New York: Kluwer Academic/Plenum.

Wecht, C. H. (1995). Medicolegal causation: The heart of medicolegal litigation. *Trauma, 37*, 69–78.

Weissman, H. N., & DeBow, D. M. (2003). Ethical principles and professional competencies. In I. B. Weiner (Series Ed.) & A. M. Goldstein (Vol. Ed.), *Handbook of psychology: Vol. 11, Forensic psychology* (pp. 33–53). Hoboken, NJ: Wiley.

Wiener, P. P. (Ed.). (1973). *Dictionary of the history of ideas: Studies of selected pivotal ideas: Vol. 1. Abstraction in the formation of concepts to design argument*. New York: Scribner.

Williams, A. D. (2003). Diagnostic decision making in neuropsychology. In A. M. Horton Jr., & L. C. Hartlage (Eds.), *Handbook of forensic neuropsychology* (pp. 113– 136). New York: Springer Science+Business Media.

World Health Organization. (1992). *International classification of diseases. Mental and behavioral disorders (including disorders of psychological development)*, clinical descriptions and diagnostic guidelines (10th rev.). Geneva, Switzerland: Author.

Young, G., & Yehuda, R. (2006). Understanding PTSD: Implications for court. In G. Young, A. W. Kane, & K. Nicholson (Eds.), *Psychological knowledge in court: PTSD, pain, and TBI* (pp. 55–69). New York: Springer Science+Business Media.

Zuckerman, M. (1999). *Vulnerability to psychopathology: A biosocial model*. Washington, DC: American Psychological Association.

5

Multicausal Perspectives on Psychological Injury I: PTSD and MTBI

GERALD YOUNG

In this chapter and the next, I review recent literature in the three predominant areas of psychological injury presented in the book—Posttraumatic Stress Disorder (PTSD), chronic pain, and Mild Traumatic Brain Injury (mTBI). To my knowledge, this review represents the first time that the three areas are reviewed in depth in one article, chapter, or source. The review builds toward a biopsychosocial model across the three areas, with stress considered as a factor common to all three of them (this model is presented in Chapter 7, following the literature review of the three areas). The literature review includes summaries of the main points of the chapters written in the companion volume by Young, Kane, and Nicholson (2006), and adds work published since they were written, in order to give a state of the art perspective of the three areas. I concentrate on articles and chapters published in 2003 to 2005, citing almost two hundred of these, while acknowledging that there are numerous articles and chapters published monthly on these topics. Moreover, I review controversies and confounds associated with the three areas, such as litigation distress, symptom exaggeration, and malingering.

In Chapter 7, I conclude that for all three areas under review, causality is best understood as complex and multicausal. It is often difficult to apply findings derived from the nomothetic (i.e., group) scientific studies to the individual case being evaluated (the idiographic), or even to determine what is the relevant scientific literature applicable to individual cases. Nevertheless, psychologists can meet the reliability and validity requirements needed in the evidence that they offer to court by conducting comprehensive assessments that are based on current scientific procedures, using the most appropriate psychological instruments and that are consistent with the most up to date knowledge of the scientific literature.

I emphasize that the biopsychosocial model offers a sound footing for better understanding the disorders in question and any causal relationships involved. The biopsychosocial model postulates that all behavioral and psychological phenomena are multidetermined. In their assessments, psychologists need to take into account both biomedical and psychosocial influences, avoiding mind-body dualism or reductionism to a medical (disease) model. Psychopathology is broadly conceived as a product of an interaction of vulnerability and stress; behavior is also a function of an interaction of personal factors, such as coping mechanisms or their lack, and situational factors, such as social support or its lack.

Literature Review: PTSD, MTBI, and Chronic Pain

Posttraumatic Stress Disorder

Introduction. For a diagnosis of PTSD to be made (*Diagnostic and Statistical Manual of Mental Disorders, Fourth Edition*, 1994; *Text Revision*, 2000; *DSM-IV-TR*; American Psychiatric Association), the victim of a trauma must evidence a cluster of symptoms for at least one month—reexperiencing, avoidance/numbing, and arousal—and the disturbance must cause "clinically significant distress or impairment" in important areas of function. The traumatic event needs to have involved a response of "intense fear, helplessness, or horror" to "actual or threatened death or serious injury, or a threat to the physical integrity of self or others" (p. 467). Trauma types include disasters, mass violence against noncombatants, transportation accidents, other accidents, emergency worker exposure to trauma, war, rape and sexual assault, intimate partner violence, stalking, torture, life-threatening illness, child abuse, and so on (Briere, 2004). Duke and Vasterling (2005) indicated that the three most frequent traumatic categories involve (a) witnessing a bad injury/death, (b) fire/flood/natural disasters, and (c) life-threatening accidents. It should be noted that an American epidemiological study indicated that a majority of the population has been exposed to traumatic stressors over the lifetime, yet only a small percentage develop PTSD (Kessler, Sonega, Bromet, Hughes, & Nelson, 1995). Duke and Vasterling's (2005) review of the literature indicated that up to 90% of Americans are exposed over their lifetime to trauma (Breslau & Kessler, 2001). However, outcome varies with the type of trauma; Yehuda (2002) reported a majority of women developed PTSD after a rape assault.

Moreover, PTSD is not the only clinically significant response to trauma that can be manifested. Among others, victims may experience Acute Stress Disorder in the first month before PTSD can be diagnosed, Brief Psychotic Disorder with Marked Stressors, Dissociative Disorders, Adjustment Disorder, posttraumatic depression or grief, assault syndromes, Panic Disorder, Conversion Disorder, Somatization Disorder, and cultural-specific disorders (Briere, 2004; Young & Yehuda, 2006).

Wilson (2004; Wilson & Moran, 2004) emphasized that PTSD involves complex, long-term stress-related responses, and consists of clusters beyond the traditional three ones (reexperiencing, avoidance/numbing, and arousal), including ones on self and social impairments. Asmundson et al. (2000) reported a confirmatory factor analysis showing four factors rather than three factors that best fit the data about their PTSD subjects, because avoidance and numbing appeared as separate factors, not combined. In their most recent research on the topic, McWilliams, Cox, and Asmundson (2005) examined the symptom structure of PTSD in a nationally representative sample of Americans. They used data from the National Comorbidity Survey (NCS), a largescale, community sample, epidemiological study (Kessler et al., 1995). McWilliams et al. (2005) found 429 participants with a lifetime history of PTSD. They had been diagnosed according to *DSM-III-R* criteria (American Psychiatric Association, 1987). The most common index traumas for males involved combat experience, witnessing bad injury/death, and having a life-threatening accident. For females, the most common traumas involved rape, sexual molestation, being threatened/abducted, and childhood physical abuse. Principal component analyses were applied to the PTSD data, seeking goodness of fit to the factor structure models. A four-factor solution emerged; the factors were labeled: dysphoria, cued reexperiencing with avoidance, uncued reexperiencing and hyperarousal, and rumination. The study needs replication, but we note that (a) the first and fourth factors appear unique to the study, (b) reexperiencing is included as part of two factors, (c) avoidance and hyperarousal do not appear by themselves as separate factors, and (d) numbing does not appear as part of any factor. These results raise questions about the organization of symptom clusters of PTSD in the *DSM*.

Polusny and Arbisi (2006) examined the psychological effects of sexual assault. Psychological reactions to sexual assault are different in certain ways from other types of trauma. Victims may evidence PTSD, substance abuse, depression, and other psychopathology, although there are resilience and risk factors involved, and the traditional PTSD diagnosis may not capture the complexity of victims' responses to the assault.

Koch, O'Neill, and Douglas (2005) query whether PTSD is best diagnosed as a category. They indicate that a binary categorical classification approach (PTSD or not) could be supplemented by obtaining scores on relevant dimensions, such as of number of symptoms, severity of symptoms, and scores on measures of psychological distress. Moreover, I recommend that psychologists keep up to date on the literature about the various symptoms and their cluster organization, and should it be necessary, they may be able to supplement the PTSD diagnosis given to any one individual with details about how her or his symptoms relate to the various clusters emerging in the literature.

Prevalence. Koch et al. (2005) reviewed the literature on prevalence, and concluded that the most optimistic research suggests that about 10% of individuals who initially develop PTSD continue presenting with PTSD 1 year after their trauma. In this regard, they cited Blanchard, Jones-Alexander, Buckley, and Forneris (1996), in a study of motor vehicle accident (MVA) survivors. Duke and Vasterling (2005) reported a similar rate (9%) in their review with respect to community samples (follow-up time period unspecified), but indicated that the rate varies with type of trauma. Koch et al. (2005) noted that Mayou, Ehlers, and Bryant (2002) reported a 3-year follow-up study of MVA victims, and found that 11% still were diagnosed as having PTSD. Therefore, it appears that about 10% of the population is at risk for PTSD after trauma exposure, even several years posttrauma. Lower estimates of prevalence of PTSD are found, but often these concern secondary participants to trauma. For example, Yehuda and Bierer (2005) describe Galea et al's. (2002) research showing that 6 months after the terrorist attack of September 11, 2001, surveys revealed a gradual reduction of PTSD to just over 1% in Manhattan residents, including those not living near the World Trade Center.

In terms of retention of diagnosis, Duke and Vasterling (2005) indicated that in many survivors who have been diagnosed with PTSD, the condition persisted for at least 3 months, with the estimate for 1-year retention around 70%. These data indicate that for the minority of trauma-exposed individuals diagnosed with PTSD, the condition for a majority remains diagnosable for a period of at least 1 year.

In general, it has been shown that most trauma-exposed individuals do not develop PTSD. The relatively low estimates of prevalence rate of PTSD in the literature reviewed, all indicating about 10%, are concordant with those of O'Donnell, Creamer, Bryant, Schnyder, and Shalev (2006), whose review of the literature showed a variable prevalence rate for PTSD after injury, with a range of 9 to 39% at 3 to 6 months, and 2 to 45% at 12 months. However, as in the Duke and Vasterling review, many survivors, up to 57% of those so diagnosed, retained their PTSD diagnosis from 1 to 4 years postaccident.

O'Donnell, Creamer, Pattison, and Atkin (2004) undertook their own research on the question of prevalence of PTSD following an MVA, instituting rigorous methodological controls. They examined prevalence rates of various psychiatric diagnoses following consecutive admissions to an Australian trauma service, with 75% of victims involved in MVAs, and with 64% of the sample having a moderate to severe physical injury. The longitudinal design included assessment by structured clinical interviews, in particular. PTSD was the most common diagnosis at 12 months, at the level of 10%. Therefore, the figures on prevalence obtained by O'Donnell et al. (2004) concord with the estimate provided by Koch et al. (2005) and the others at the beginning of this section.

O'Donnell et al. (2004) provided a wider perspective on the effects of MVAs on survivors. Major Depressive Disorder also was commonly diagnosed at 12 months, at the level of 10%. Considering both PTSD and Major Depression together, over 20% of their study participants were diagnosed with at least one of these psychiatric conditions at 12 months. Moreover, the prevalence results are likely an underestimate according to the authors. In addition, chronic Pain Disorder was not assessed in the study. The psychiatric prevalence rate would have been even higher had it been a focus. The authors conclude that "[h]ealth care systems targeted at traumatically injured populations have a responsibility to adopt an evidence-based approach both to early identification of high risk individuals and to early psychiatric intervention" (pp. 512–513).

Predictors. Ozer, Best, Lipsey, and Weiss (2003) performed a meta-analysis of prior research on predictors of PTSD, statistically analyzing trends over the studies. Across studies, compared to pretrauma and other variables, peritraumatic dissociation emerged as the best predictor of PTSD, although all seven predictors distilled from the literature were found to predict PTSD outcome. Weiss and Ozer (2006) compared their meta-analysis with that of Brewin, Andrews, and Valentine (2000). In both meta-analyses, the most telling risk factors concerned proximal and subjective links, such as peritraumatic dissociation and subsequent social support, compared to more distal links or general psychological vulnerabilities, such as history of prior trauma or education level. Ozer et al. (2003) found that type of traumatic event moderated most of the predictor results in their meta-analysis, and, therefore, different events are not interchangeable in their effects.

Although research with different populations and methods may be difficult to compare, recent research supports the tenet proposed by Ozer et al. (2003) that peritraumatic variables are primary predictors of who will develop PTSD. Halligan, Michael, Clark, and Ehlers (2003) found that in assault victims, beyond any measure of stressor severity, peritraumatic cognitive processing was related to the development of disorganized memories and PTSD, whereas PTSD maintenance was served by ongoing dissociation and negative appraisal. Delahanty and colleagues (Delahanty, Raimonde, Spoonster, & Cullado, 2003a; Delahanty, Royer, Raimonde, & Spoonster, 2003b) reported an association between peritraumatic dissociation and subsequent development of PTSD in MVA victims, with lowered cortisol levels serving as a possible mediating variable. Creamer, O'Donnell, and Pattison (2004) and Schell, Marshall, and Jaycox (2004) emphasized the predictive power of hyperarousal with respect to the development of PTSD. Gershuny, Cloitre, and Otto (2003) reported research that the cognitive aspects of panic (fear of death, fear of losing control) are involved. A review of the research literature with children (Fletcher, 2003) has found that peritraumatic variables are consistent predictors of PTSD (Udwin, Boyle, Yule, Bolton, & O'Ryan, 2000). (Also see Birmes et al., 2003.) In addition, Hembree, Street, Riggs, and Foa (2004) found that assault-related variables during an assault of adults, even after initial PTSD severity was controlled, were predictive of greater symptoms of PTSD after treatment.

However, other research poses challenges to the viewpoint that peritraumatic variables are the most powerful predictors of PTSD. For example, McNally, Bryant, and Ehlers (2003) point out that other research that includes preexisting cognitive ability finds that this variable is at least as great as dissociation in its predictive power of PTSD. Bowman and Yehuda (2004) review research showing that PTSD risk factors include a history of trauma, personality traits, coping styles, psychiatric history, personality disorders, low intelligence, preevent beliefs and attributions, and biological and genetic factors. There may be subsets of risk factors for different routes to the disorder. They conclude that preevent risk factors have been found to predict PTSD more reliably than event characteristics. This conclusion represents a contrast to the one offered by Ozer et al. (2003). As we have seen, Ozer et al. (2003) emphasize peritraumatic dissociation as the most telling predictive factor of PTSD. Although Bryant (2004) concurs with this conclusion, he cites some contradictory data, and suggests that the explanation of the association remains to be determined.

One important pretrauma variable to consider is personality. Miller (2003) argues that high negative emotionality is a risk factor for the onset of PTSD to trauma (also see Miller, Kaloupek, Dillon, & Keane, 2004). In support of this model, Cox, MacPherson, Enns, and McWilliams (2004) found that the psychological trait of neuroticism is associated with PTSD. Malta, Blanchard, Taylor, Hickling, and Freidenberg (2002) found that MVA victims with a preexisting personality disorder were more likely to be diagnosed with PTSD one year after the event.

Despite some positive findings on the relationship between personality variables and PTSD, little credence can be given to any claim that pretrauma factors can account in full for PTSD development and expression after trauma. On the one hand, critical prospective research, with adequate measurement of personality and postPTSD course and with other appropriate methodological controls, needs to be undertaken. Moreover, the research that has been undertaken does not fully support Miller's (2003) model. For example, van den Hout and Engelhard (2004) found that negative appraisal of symptoms predict PTSD symptoms independently of neuroticism. Golier et al. (2003) found little causal relationship among childhood abuse, Borderline Personality Disorder, and PTSD.

In agreement with Miller (2003), Koch et al. (2005) posit that PTSD is an extreme state of negative emotionality comprised of preexisting superordinate negative emotionality, exacerbation of the negative emotionality by the stress of an index event, and "unique dysfunctional characteristics" related to PTSD. They conclude that it may be that "PTSD may reflect nothing more than general negative affectivity" (p. 127).

In contrast, after considering the data presented by Ozer et al. (2003) and the related research on the question, I support a multicausal perspective on the development of PTSD, involving preexisting, peritraumatic, and posttraumatic factors, with legal issues, malingering, and so forth, needing careful evaluation. Similarly, McKeever and Huff (2003) present a diathesis-stress model of PTSD. In their model, residual stress from trauma has variable effects, depending on preexisting and concurrent ecological and biological factors.

Ozer et al. (2003) concluded that peritraumatic factors may be powerful predictors of future PTSD because they overwhelm resilience mechanisms. However, their view is quite multicausal, as we have seen. Recall that in their meta-analysis all seven predictors distilled from the literature were found to predict PTSD outcome. In addition, they noted that in their meta-analysis a large proportion of the variability of response was not explained by any of the predictors, so that factors unique to the person in combination with the event may be especially determinant in understanding which trauma victims express resilience and which do not.

Prognosis. Koch et al. (2005) reviewed the literature on prognosis in PTSD. Their review indicates that a "sizeable" minority of trauma survivors had continued to suffer PTSD for many years following onset. For example, Schnurr et al. (2000) found that 32% of WWII veterans who had been exposed to mustard gas experiments during the war still met the criteria for PTSD 50 years later. Moreover, an additional 10% met the criteria for subsyndromal PTSD. Duke and Vasterling (2005) review other research with veterans, such as the NCS by Kessler et al. (1995), which reported a similar percentage, with one-third of the sample still experiencing PTSD 10 or more years after diagnosis, even with treatment.

In terms of prognosis with treatment, Koch et al. (2005) describe that in Blanchard et al. (2003), 30% of patients failed to remit with cognitive behavioral therapy. They state that this level is the best one in the studies of which they are aware. This figure is consistent with the data on course, or remittance, as described above, where up to 70% of survivors appear to persist in their PTSD, as well as with the data just cited from the NCS.

Duke and Vasterling (2005) point out that the pattern of PTSD symptom expression varies over course, complicating estimates of outcome. For example, anniversaries of trauma and ongoing life stresses accentuate PTSD symptomology.

In terms of long-term outcome, Koch et al. (2005) contend that psychological science cannot yet specify adequately for court purposes reliable estimates of functional disability outcome. They note that posttraumatic stress is generally associated with impairments in economic functioning, but that, at the same time, in one study personality characteristics were more predictive of work leave than PTSD symptoms themselves (Regehr, Goldberg, Glancy, & Knott, 2002). Therefore, these authors suggest that when assessors comment upon the effect of PTSD on occupational disability, they are largely speculating. They add that it is not the diagnosis of PTSD that affects work, but that return to work is affected by behavioral sequelae of a maladaptive response to trauma that research has yet to address adequately. Similarly, Polusny and Arbisi (2006) indicate that there are no standardized assessment instruments of functional outcome appropriate to PTSD.

Koch et al. (2005) advise that in the realm of PTSD assessments in personal injury claims, triers of fact should carefully examine the methods used by assessors to establish causal links between PTSD and functional limitations. Nevertheless, they recommend that, in determining occupational disability, the assessor should apply the usual approach of integrating specific knowledge of the literature (actuarial and epidemiological data) with evaluation of individual presentation or characteristics. This type of conclusion is standard in forensic and related work.

Physiology. The research consistently shows that PTSD is accompanied by neurobiologic changes, although not in all study participants, limiting application of the research for court purposes. Nutt and Malizia (2004) reviewed neuroimaging studies implicating three areas of the brain in PTSD—the hippocampus (involved in memory), the amygdala (involved in emotions), and the medial frontal cortex (involved in executive functions). The authors posit that lowered dampening or inhibitory control of the amygdala by higher brain regions, such as in the hippocampus and the frontal cortex, may help explain the cardinal symptoms of PTSD, including flashbacks and excessive startle. Shin, Rauch, and Pitman (2005;

Rauch, Shin, Whalen, & Pitman, 1998) present a similar model, in which the amygdala becomes hyperreactive because of a lack of effective top-down governance by the hippocampus and medial prefrontal cortex. Winter and Irle (2004) performed an MRI study on burn victims, examining the issue whether reduced hippocampal volume is a risk factor, preexisting in PTSD patients. The participants included trauma victims with and without PTSD, as well as controls. The results showed that, in their sample, smaller hippocampal size derived from exposure to traumatic stress, suggesting that it did not constitute a risk factor for PTSD.

Lanius and colleagues (2003, 2004, 2005) performed an fMRI investigation of recall of emotional states (sad, anxious, traumatic) of trauma victims with or without PTSD. The former showed less activation of the thalamus and the anterior cingulate gyrus, implicating these areas of the brain in PTSD. In addition, the two groups differed in hemispheric connectivity, with the PTSD group demonstrating left hemisphere correlation in their data and the non-PTSD group demonstrating right hemisphere correlation. These differences may account for the greater nonverbal nature of traumatic memory in PTSD victims. [Also see Brewin and Holmes (2003), in this regard. See Metzger et al. (2004) with respect to right-sided parietal activation and PTSD.]

Yehuda (2004) explored the role of neuroendocrine changes, such as lowered cortisol and alterations in the HPA (hypothalamic-pituitary-adrenal) axis, in relation to PTSD [See Young and Yehuda (2006) for details of the pathways]. Yehuda concluded that PTSD may leave long-lasting physiological changes as much as more overtly organic injuries such as pain experience due to physical injury or TBI. Schnurr and Green (2004) proposed a model in which PTSD and its associated biological alterations and psychological effects are considered the primary pathway through which traumatic experience leads to poor health outcomes. Supporting Schnurr and Green, Boscarino (2004) documented the risks presented by chronic PTSD for inflammatory disorders such as cardiovascular disease and autoimmune diseases.

In perhaps the most complex neurobiological model of PTSD, Southwick, Rasmusson, Barron, and Arnsten (2005) attempt to integrate the research on the areas of the brain that have been implicated in PTSD research and the research on three neurotransmitter/neurohormonal systems. In terms of brain regions, they add to the regions already mentioned (the prefrontal cortex, the amygdala, and the hippocampus) as foci of PTSD localization, the regions of the dorsal raphe nucleus, the locus coeruleus, and the orbitofrontal cortex. The first two of these regions are related to fear and the last one to cognitive evaluation of social/emotional stimuli. In their model, the three neurotransmitter/neurohormonal systems involve the noradrenergic system, the serotonergic system, and the HPA axis, only the last of which has been mentioned in the above. For example, PTSD is associated with elevated norepinephrine, reduced serotonin, and elevated cortisol, all of which would contribute to reducing the inhibitory control by the prefrontal cortex of the amygdala, increasing its activation. According to the authors' neurobiological model of PTSD, other brain regions and neuroendocrine pathways are involved, as well.

Comorbidity. Brown, Campbell, Lehman, Grisham, and Mancill (2001) examined current and lifetime comorbidity of *DSM-IV* anxiety and mood disorders. Participants were 1,127 patients presenting for assessment and treatment at two anxiety disorder clinics. They were administered a semi-structured interview. A small proportion had PTSD as principal diagnosis, but the portion may have been underestimated in the sample. They found that 92% of participants with PTSD as their principal diagnosis had a second ongoing mental health diagnosis, and, tellingly, lifetime comorbidity was at 100%. The authors conclude that in study, the comorbidity was associated with PTSD was "strikingly" elevated. [Also see the comorbidity study by Oquendo et al. (2005).]

O'Donnell et al. (2006) explored the relationship between injury and subsequent PTSD. In MVA victims with PTSD, comorbidity often involved depression and anxiety disorders; for example, one study found comorbid depression in 59% of cases, and comorbidity in general at 70%, with substance abuse/dependence a particular problem. O'Donnell, Creamer, and Pattison (2004) speculated that a general chronic traumatic stress factor can help explain the link between depression and PTSD.

Malingering and Litigation. On the other side of the coin, research on malingering and related phenomena in relation to PTSD is also taking place. Military claimants of PTSD have been known to fake their history of trauma exposure (Burkett & Whitley, 1998). Guriel and Fremouw (2003) reviewed the parameters needed in critical research on the question of malingering in PTSD, and found that basic design procedures, such as using appropriate control groups, are lacking. They emphasize that there is no gold standard instrument that can assess malingering. However, an example of a psychometrically sound instrument to measure PTSD, one which include scales for evaluating positive and negative impression management, is Briere's (2001; Detailed Assessment of Posttraumatic Stress, DAPS). More research is needed to establish its value in detecting malingering and other response biases in cases of purported PTSD.

Frueh, Elhai, and Kaloupek (2004) describe the Infrequency-PTSD scale (*Fptsd*) as a promising measure for the use with the MMPI-2 (Minnesota Multiphasic Personality Inventory, Second Edition; Butcher, Dahlstrom, Graham, Tellegen, & Kaemmer, 1989) in detecting malingering of PTSD. They conclude that a "key unresolved question is the base-rate for malingering" with respect to assessments of PTSD (p. 74).

Rogers, Sewell, Martin, and Vitacco (2003) performed a meta-analysis across research studies on the MMPI-2 in relation to PTSD. They found that Arbisi and Ben-Porath's (1995) *Fp* rare-symptom feigning index was the most effective in discriminating simulators and genuine patients. This was true even for "problematic" disorders such as PTSD but, nevertheless, the value of *Fp* as a malingering detection metric was not as high for other types of patients. Rogers et al. (2003) also examined whether patients in litigation would manifest different results. They found that litigation status had only a modest affect on the results. The assumption that litigation is a context that "substantially" increases the likelihood of feigning is not supported by the data. Other researchers promote different indices of malingering PTSD. See Greiffenstein, Baker, Axelrod, Peck, and Gervais (2004) for a study presenting evidence favoring the *FBS*, Fake Bad Scale, relative to other MMPI-2 validity scales, in predicting implausible psychological trauma claims in an applied setting.

Koch (2003) also examined the relationship between litigation status and PTSD. Although some research reveals a relationship between litigation status and PTSD diagnosis or symptom expression, the relationship has not always been confirmed, patients improve despite litigation, and so on. There is a substantial literature indicating that, in general, patients do not suddenly get better when the lawsuit ends, being "cured" by the verdict (Tait, 2004).

Briere (2004) underscored that, in assessing trauma victims, the assessor needs to consider all types of overreporting and its possible reasons. Overreporting may be caused by reasons other than malingering. For example, forensic and other assessors should consider possible "cries for help," amplification of symptoms because of worry of being ignored, and overreporting due to chronicity. The assessor must rule out all possible explanations other than malingering and related response biases before concluding that they are significant factors.

Questions about PTSD. McNally (2003, 2004; McNally et al., 2003) found controversies in a literature review of PTSD. For example, McNally asked whether PTSD is a valid response to traumatic events. Also, he showed that PTSD is being criticized in terms of its specific diagnostic criteria. Our approach to these criticisms is that the assessor needs to specify carefully the exact symptoms that the individual had experienced during the trauma, just after it, and throughout the course since the trauma in order to make a reasoned argument that the individual had been traumatized, rather than trying to fit the individual to a list of preestablished criteria that may not be broad enough, nuanced enough, flexible enough, or individualized enough. Any diagnosis that may be given should be supported by comprehensive assessment involving a thorough interview and appropriate tests, instruments, and procedures. The assessor needs to provide evidence for the diagnosis offered, or for any reasonable emerging concepts and criteria related to a diagnosis being discussed in the literature.

Note that the construct of PTSD is being questioned in other ways. For example, problems have arisen in its explanation as a dissociative phenomenon (Lynn, Knox, Fassler, Lilienfeld, & Loftus, 2004; McNally, 2003, 2004; Zoellner & Bittenger, 2004). To simplify, if the mind dissociates during a trauma, clouding memory of the event, might this not compromise the possibility of experiencing horror in the event, having flashbacks, and so on, invalidating the diagnosis of PTSD? A recent study by Gil, Caspi, Ben-Ari, Koren, and Klein (2005) addressed this issue. They examined 120 trauma victims with mTBI, mostly due to MVAs, up to 6 months after the event. Participants with memory of the event, which had been evaluated in the first day, were more likely to develop PTSD, as evaluated by standardized interview and self-report instruments. They concluded that immediately forgetting the trauma may be a protective factor. It is interesting to note that some participants without memory of the event still went on to develop PTSD. Their memories may be more implicit and nonverbal than explicit and verbal. Or, PTSD may still develop in such patients with respect to memories of hospital procedures or other sequelae of the trauma. However, the authors explain that they had not evaluated preexisting trauma, so that they could not evaluate whether there had been a "more generalized pretraumatic vulnerability factor that relates to one's autobiographical memory in general" (p. 968).

In terms of the contexts that can evoke PTSD, one also encounters issues. According to McNally (2004), the traumatic stressor criterion has been broadened to include indirect exposure to trauma and childhood molestation. Even sexual harassment of an apparently relatively minor nature may qualify. In this regard, McNally refers to "conceptual bracket creep." He argues that any putative PTSD elicited by such situations would be due to appraisal processes and to the influence of preexisting vulnerability factors, rather than to the horror of the trauma, *per se*.

Gold, Marx, Soler-Baillo, and Sloan (2005) also suggest that the current definition of PTSD is too inclusive. Their study of college students concerned the difference in the association of PTSD with a general life stress and more specific traumatic stress. They found that more students met the criteria for PTSD if they were classified in the former category compared to the latter. Similarly, Mol et al. (2005) reported that, surprisingly, a survey of stressful life events revealed higher PTSD scores for worst-ever events in the past 30 years that did not reach criterion for being traumatic stressors compared to those that did. These two studies call for further research on what should constitute the threshold for traumatic stressors and what types of events elicit PTSDlike symptoms that do and do not reach threshold. They suggest that the *DSM-IV* approach to the definition of PTSD requires careful consideration.

In addition, research does not uniformly support the dose-response model, where degree of traumatic response is supposed to be related to degree of objective stressor quality. For example, not all victims evidence the same psychobiologic mechanisms in response to traumatic events. Many individuals with PTSD do not show heightened reactivity to cues reminiscent of the precipitating traumatic event (See Orr, McNally, Rosen, and Shalev (2004); about 40% do not).

Controversies about PTSD. McNally queries whether PTSD is a valid diagnostic entity after trauma because at least some of its symptoms may be mimicked by fantasized trauma. He and his colleagues undertook a study of nonpsychotic individuals who believed that they have been abducted by space aliens. When tested while listening to audiotaped descriptions of their traumatic abduction memories, they reported some PTSDlike symptoms; participants with such experiences displayed heightened psychophysiologic reactivity (McNally et al., 2004).

The most contentious area of research in PTSD is on the accuracy of recovered childhood memories of childhood sexual abuse (CSA) that had been "repressed"

(McNally, 2003). For example, hypnosis cannot enhance memory accuracy in such recollection, unlike what is often claimed. A related topic concerns whether accurate description of current psychological symptoms of alleged victims of CSA can be used in post hoc reasoning to diagnose the accuracy of any claim that the abuse had transpired. According to McNally (2003, 2004; McNally et al., 2003), another controversial area concerns whether there are always long-term psychological correlates of CSA. After a meta-analysis of the literature, Rind, Tromovitch, and Bauserman (1998, 2001) defended the view that there may be few adverse consequences for many children. McNally indicated that some adverse consequences of CSA are being reported in the literature (Tyler, 2002). Moreover, as O'Neill (2004) indicated, independent of any scientific issue, Rind et al. (1998) had written that sexual contact with minors continues to be illegal and is widely viewed as immoral and unacceptable.

Bias. Bowman (2003) attempted to analyze the biases that can skew assessments with respect to PTSD. The list of biases that she offers is well-founded; however, in presenting them she sets up the "straw man" that all clinicians seemingly are subject to the biases, rather than only *potentially* subject to them. For example, she writes, "Clinicians generally have greater confidence in their judgments than is justified" (p. 838). She also writes, "Outside clinical practice, the ways in which people act … has been the subject of thoughtful research" (p. 833). A false opposition is created between clinicians and research.

Conclusion. Rosen (2004a) concluded that nearly every assumption and theoretical underpinning of PTSD has been found to lack empirical support or is under attack. Rosen (2004b) added the complication that some PTSD cases have been documented to reflect coaching by attorneys. Rosen concluded that the outcome may be that psychologists abandon the diagnosis of PTSD.

I take a more pragmatic view. The *DSM* category of PTSD serves an important heuristic, functioning as a simplified communication device to the court about the nature of an individual's range of clinical symptoms related to an event perceived as traumatic. By careful description of the actual symptoms being expressed in the context of a comprehensive assessment, the psychologist mitigates any pitfalls associated with the summary label of PTSD and will be able to respond to challenges in court on its validity.

Moreover, we are learning that individual variability, or unique, individual pathways, may mark course after trauma (Young & Yehuda, 2006). Therefore, adopting a uniform approach to the diagnosis, etiology, causality, trajectory, and treatment of PTSD does not do justice to the research or the individual. In order to understand PTSD, a multicausal perspective needs to be adopted.

There are gaps in the scientific knowledge of PTSD, especially in terms of long-term functional and psychological outcome. Nevertheless, comprehensive assessment of individuals, that consider the scientific literature and that analyze the scientifically gathered data from a multicausal and individualized perspective facilitate meeting validity and reliability requirements of evidence proferred to court.

Mild Traumatic Brain Injury

Introduction. The area of persistent postconcussion symptoms, or Postconcussive Syndrome (PCS) after mTBI, represents a controversial topic, because of the opposing interpretations of its causality and the consequent claims for damages that can accompany it. PCS persists in a "miserable minority" after mTBI (Barth, Ruff, & Espe-Pfeifer, 2006), typically estimated to be about 15%. Iverson (2005) specifies that the percentage may be more toward 5%, indicating that the higher figure is based on misconception. PCS is one possible outcome of mTBI, and there are multiple terms used in the area, compounding confusion.

Barth et al. (2006) and McAllister (2005) indicate that despite a lack of consensus on definition, there are several cardinal symptoms in mTBI, such as a loss of consciousness (LOC) that does not exceed 30 minutes, a posttraumatic amnesia (self-reported, PTA) that is less than 24 hours, and an initial Glasgow Coma Scale (GCS) score that is 13–15 out of 15. von Holst and Cassidy (2004) arrive at a similar working definition for the World Health Organization (WHO) Task Force on mTBI. Hall, Hall, and Chapman (2005) point out that different sets of criteria exist, for instance, for neurologists compared to emergency room specialists. Ruff (2005) and Bigler (2006) suggest that mTBI should be subclassified according to grade of severity, because a case involving a 30-minute LOC, a 24-hour PTA, and a positive CT scan is quite different than a case with little or no LOC and PTA, and negative scan results. Also, see McAllister (2005) in this regard.

Typically, PCS effects after mTBI include (a) physical symptoms, such as headache, dizziness, and fatigue, (b) cognitive symptoms, such as concentration difficulties and memory difficulties, and (c) emotional symptoms, such as irritability, depression, and anxiety (Schretlen & Shapiro, 2003). Barth et al. (2006) indicate that the mechanics of the injury include acceleration-deceleration and rotational forces, shear-strain effects on axonal fibers, pathophysiological effects that may take days to appear, and, in general, diffuse physiological and metabolic disruption, termed diffuse axonal injury.

However, the validity of the PCS syndrome is debated, because of a lack of objective data, a lack of generally accepted outcome measures, and the variability among individuals in physiological and psychological symptoms; for example, the validity of cognitive deficits persisting so long has been questioned (Barth et al., 2006; Schretlen & Shapiro, 2003).

Multifactorial Model. Ryan and Warden (2003) maintain that most investigators currently argue that causality of PCS after mTBI is multifactorial, rather than uniquely physiogenic, physiological, neuropathological, or neurological as some claim, or uniquely psychogenic, psychological, or motivational, as do others. A combination of premorbid, morbid, and postmorbid factors contributes to etiology. PCS after mTBI may develop in nonlitigants and is not related to litigation, refuting the "compensation neurosis" hypothesis. According to Ryan and Warden, physiological evidence has been reported by Chen, Kareken, Fastenau,

Trexler, and Hutchins (2003), who found that PCS patients, compared to controls, exhibited less right prefrontal cortical blood flow on a working memory task.

Ruff and colleagues (Evered, Ruff, Baldo, & Isomura, 2003; Ruff & Richardson, 1999) refer to the multifactorial model as a cumulative one. After mTBI, cumulative stressors exacerbate premorbid factors. The stressors relate to combined physical, emotional, cognitive, psychosocial, vocational, financial, and recreational setbacks. Premorbid emotional risk factors include personality pathology and depression. The authors reported results in favor of the model, and also address the issue of litigation effects, of which there were little, consistent with Ryan and Warden's (2003) lack of support for the "compensation neurosis" model. McAllister and Arciniegas (2002) also support an integrated model of PCS, and also address the litigation issue, arguing that litigation brings stresses that may worsen symptoms, but that this does not mean that there is no "real injury" or that there is malingering.

Vanderploeg, Belanger, and Curtiss (2006; also see Vanderploeg, Curtiss, & Belanger, 2005; Belanger, Curtiss, Demery, Lebowitz, & Vanderploeg, 2005) described research in support of a multifactorial model of PCS. Despite an absence of positive results on a standard neuropsychological test battery, they found mild difficulties in veterans' 8-year postinjury performance on subtle, yet complex tasks of attention and working memory (Paced Auditory Serial Addition Test, PASAT, continuation rate; and California Verbal Learning Test, CVLT, proactive interference, PI; respectively), which were associated with distinct neurological external correlates (left-sided visual imperceptions and impaired tandem gate, respectively). They also found adverse, long-term mental health and psychosocial outcomes, related to depression, anxiety, postconcussion symptom complex, work status, being unmarried, disability, and so forth. Modulating variables in prediction included intelligence, preexisting problems, and an altered period of consciousness at the time of the mTBI. Belanger et al. (2005) undertook a meta-analytic review of the literature, involving 39 studies. By 3 months, for the mTBI population at large, full recovery was evident, but clinic-based and litigation samples did not reveal such recovery and, indeed, litigation samples even worsened with time. The underlying cause for these results was not clear. For long-term PCS, the literature review and research conducted by Vanderploeg and colleagues together suggest a multifactorial model involving the interaction of predisposing, precipitating, and perpetuating factors in a nonlinear, systemic manner. This may include subtle, ongoing brain dysfunction and a direct effect of the initial mTBI in poorer postinjury outcomes.

Bigler (2003) articulated the position that neurological, neurobiological, and neuropathological bases underlie neuropsychological deficits associated with mTBI. However, Lees-Haley and colleagues query the validity of the neurological approach to neuropsychological effects of mTBI (Fox & Allen, 2003; Lees-Haley, Green, Rohling, Fox, & Allen, 2003). Klonoff and Dawson (2004) advocate an integrated perspective, where both the neurobiological and the psychological views are considered part of the multiplicity of factors in long-term subjective and objective complaints in mTBI. They adopt a multimodal, complex, interactive, holistic perspective on causal agents in mTBI. All pertinent variables need to be weighed for their relative contributions in this syndrome.

The argument made by Klonoff and Dawson about the multicausal nature of persistent mTBI effects is consistent with the one offered by Ryan and Warden (2003). At the same time, research is now addressing the presence or absence of certain genetic markers as risk factors for severity of damage of TBI (Hannay, Howieson, Loring, Fischer, & Lezak, 2004).

I would add that inherent in the multicausal position of mTBI is that the relative weighting for any putative neurobiological causal agent in any one case may be overtly nil, or it may be impossible to isolate because of the multiplicity of interacting factors involved. That is, the possibility that there are multiple factors involved in the evolution of persistent PCS according to the literature should not automatically be taken as a reason to conclude that, for any one individual case, neurobiological factors must be at work. Nevertheless, PCS may still be quite disabling. Kay (1999) indicated that even when TBI damage is minimal or absent, there still may be "disabling psychological reactions" to the trauma (p. 152). That is, mTBI may set up cascade and synergistic reactions, in concert with preexisting vulnerabilities and postTBI psychological effects, which lead to disabling outcomes even after all physiological impacts have equilibrated.

Bonne and colleagues present neurological scan data on the relationship between brain function and neuropsychological performance in PCS patients (Bonne et al., 2003). They found that, in patients relative to controls, cerebral blood flow was reduced in frontal, prefrontal, and temporal cortices, as well as in subcortical structures. Neuropsychological test performance led to categorizing patients according to the presumed location of their deficits, and results revealed relevant associations across most deficits and particular regions of brain flow reduction. The authors conclude that "[t]he results of the present SPECT investigation support the presence of residual organic brain damage following even slight craniocerebral injury in carefully chosen symptomatic subjects" (p. 150). These findings support that persistent postconcussive symptoms are associated with corresponding cerebral brain damage, and that, moreover, the type of neuropsychological deficit involved is associated with particular localized brain damage. However, the authors remind that such results cannot speak to individual diagnosis, although they believe that research like theirs "will aid in lending credibility" to complaints of PCS.

McAllister (2005) cautioned that despite the improvements in the newer functional imaging and related techniques, information derived from these techniques should not be used, at this point in time, as part of routine clinical evaluation from a neurodiagnostic standpoint. For example, a patient may obtain normal results and still be shown in other ways to be brain-injured. However, results from such studies may be integrated into the full diagnostic evaluation.

In related research, Thornton (2003), in an electrophysiological study of the effects of mTBI on auditory memory functioning, found frontal lobe effects, and a right hemisphere shift in the temporal lobe. Umile, Sandel, Alavi, Terry, and Plotkin (2002) also found temporal lobe effects in PCS patients, using dynamic imaging.

Bigler (2006) acknowledged that most cases of mTBI resolve, but for a minority of individuals, symptoms persist, especially in complicated cases. There is a heterogeneity of outcome in mTBI, partly related to preexisting factors, and more research is needed to establish the full range of long-term consequences. Animal models of mTBI demonstrate clearly that white matter in the brain is adversely affected. Speed of processing is affected by white matter damage, and such speed is diminished in mTBI, according to research with patients in Bigler's laboratory, on neuropsychological reaction-time tasks measuring integrated, interhemispheric communication.

In analyzing the spectrum of data available in cases of mTBI, there is one golden rule—that everything must make sense (Stuss, 1995; as cited by Bigler). For example, comprehensive assessments should include documentation of the original symptoms, finding symptoms proportional to the injury, and finding gradual improvement with time. Establishment of disability outcome and of permanent impairment after mTBI is an area in need of better criteria and assessment instruments. Moreover, because of litigation and compensation, explicit incentives, conscious or not, may influence mTBI presentation.

Psychological Consequences. The "miserable minority" with persistent PCS should be carefully scrutinized for the functional effects of their symptoms, and analyzed carefully for any neuropsychological deficits, both in areas amenable to formal testing and in areas harder to test formally, such as with frontal lobe based executive capacities. Research is showing that mTBI is marked by subtle cognitive and related deficits (Barrow et al., 2003; Borgaro, Prigatano, Kwasnica, & Rexer, 2003; Chan, Hussain, Lee, Fan, & Fong, 2003; Mathias, Beall, & Bigler, 2004), but the degree to which they persist after the initial few months and the degree to which they reflect variables such as pain, stress, depression, and preexisting factors is debated (McAllister, 2005; Rapoport, McCullagh, Streiner, & Feinstein, 2003; Rees, 2003; Ruttan & Heinrichs, 2003; Smith-Seemiller, Fow, Kant, & Franzen, 2003; Vanderploeg, Curtiss, Duchnick, & Luis, 2003; See the chapter by Nicholson and Martelli, 2006).

One recent comprehensive review (Carroll et al., 2004) found that for adults most studies indicated that recovery from the psychological effects of mTBI occurs within 1 to 3 months, and when symptoms persist compensation/litigation is likely to be a factor. Other possible predictors showed little consistent findings, although prior health, age, and lifetime stressors also emerged as determinants of poorer outcome. [But see McKerral et al. (2005) for a critique of this review. On the other hand, see Frencham, Fox, and Maybery (2005) for a meta-analysis giving results similar to those of Carroll et al. (2004).]

One recent study found few acute neurobehavioral symptoms in mTBI patients who were compared to orthopaedic controls (in using a neurobehavioral functioning inventory; Rush, Malec, Moessner, & Brown, 2004). Another study showed that when mTBI persists, these patients may have a set to overfocus on their symptoms and their cause in the original injury, and expect that they persist (Uomoto & Fann, 2004). Iverson (2005) lists a gamut of factors that could explain the persistence of symptoms in mTBI, such as having comorbid problems like depression and pain.

At the same time, he indicates that complicated cases of mTBI should be more prone to have biological consequences associated with increased risk of poor outcome, for example, in cases like an mTBI due to a high speed MVA involving 10 minutes of LOC, a GCS score of 13 or 14, and 18 hours of PTA. See McAllister (2005) for a review of the literature examining the multiple factors and outcomes in individuals who develop PCS after mTBI, including the role of litigation/compensation and malingering.

Malingering. Sreenivasan, Eth, Kirkish, and Garrick (2003) advise that neuropsychologists should evaluate malingering and "symptom amplification," for example, in cases of an mTBI among civil litigants. Malingering refers to a volitional production of symptoms for the purpose of external rewards. This is different from symptom amplification, which is a broader concept involving exaggeration of deficits beyond those expected by the nature of the injury, whether consciously or unconsciously. There are quite different estimates of base rates of persistent cognitive deficits after mTBI.

Sreenivasan et al. (2003) suggest that, in conducting assessments, neuropsychologists should follow guidelines for the detecting malingering/symptom amplification. These include the evaluation of (a) testing issues (base rates of brain damage, consistency of results with injury severity, performance on motivational/effort instruments); (b) consistency or congruence issues (test data consistent with observed behavior in testing, serial testing consistent with central nervous system (CNS) processes, test data consistent with medical documentation and with occupational or school functioning); (c) congruence of symptoms/signs with clinical data (patient interview, patient course, past records, physical exam, lab results, collateral data, surveillance, expected response to medication, and social/occupational/school functioning); (d) nonclinical factors (including having reasonable expectations for recovery); (e) comorbidity (e.g., clinical disorder, personality disorder, substance abuse, medications, prior mTBI); and (f) miscellaneous factors (e.g., prior criminality).

For a detailed discussion of malingering in the context of mTBI assessments, refer to the chapters by Nicholson and Martelli (this book).

Conclusion. Even though long-term PCS may develop in a small minority of mTBI patients, and neurophysiological data are beginning to suggest neuropathophysiological concomitants at a population level, the neuropsychologist must be wary when offering expert testimony in individual cases. This is especially true because of the relatively high rates of secondary confounding factors serving to propagate mTBI symptoms beyond their expected healing time, and the possible role of factors such as response bias, symptom exaggeration, possible malingering, and motivations for secondary gain.

Nicholson and Martelli (2006) review the confounding effects on neuropsychological test performance in TBI due to pain, sleep disturbance, psychoemotional distress and psychiatric disorder, and motivational factors, including malingering. In particular, headache often is considered the primary problem in PCS. However, its etiology is poorly understood, and it is more common in mTBI than in more severe head injury. In addition, neck and back pain may be more prominent in mTBI. Pain may interfere significantly with cognitive performance both in pain-challenged controls and in clinical pain patients without brain damage, although individual differences are evident. The cognitive processes of attention, concentration, memory, and processing speed appear the most affected in this research, complicating any simple answer about the cognitive effects of mTBI. Moreover, the presence of sleep disturbance in such patients, given the research on the negative effects of poor sleep on cognition, further complicates simplistic interpretations of causality. Other complicating factors include somatic preoccupation, stress, and depression. Pain, or even its anticipation, may alter actual brain function, in another layer in confounds acting to complicate understanding of the cognitive effects of mTBI. In short, there is a serious problem of symptom overlap in persistent PCS and patients with pain but without brain damage.

Nicholson and Martelli also review how psychoemotional problems and psychiatric disorders, such as depression, PTSD, and substance abuse, are associated with cognitive deficits and brain function abnormalities. In terms of complicating premorbid factors, it is difficult to estimate adequately premorbid intellectual functions, and personality and psychosocial history (e.g., early depression and anxiety, coping deficits, preexisting pain, limited social support) affect variability in neuropsychological assessment. Furthermore, with respect to malingering, in a review of the literature, Binder, Kelly, Villaneuva, and Winslow (2003) found that, in the medicolegal context, malingering may be a factor in greater than 50% of mTBI patients, suggesting a role for pressures for financial incentive. However, one factor to consider is that litigating patients may be worse off to begin with.

Nicholson and Martelli call for improved neuropsychological techniques to help address outstanding issues. They conclude that complicating factors in persistent PCS often are prominent and may account in full for symptom expression, as well as contributing to symptoms in more serious brain injury.

I conclude, further, that all the models that have been proposed to explain the persistent cases of cognitive and related deficit in mTBI appear ambiguous with respect to specifics, and seem difficult to apply to individual cases. Multicausal explanations of mTBI may be the most elegant but, at the same time, for any one individual, multiple factors are difficult to disentangle, leading to difficulty in terms of ascertaining which of the components in the explanation are primary. Therefore, assessments need to be comprehensive in order to permit conclusions about causality, but the neuropsychologist should arrive at particular conclusions with careful scientific reasoning and with a broad knowledge of the current literature applicable to the case at hand and conclusions offered.

Bigler (2003) maintains that there are similar mechanisms, or shared communalities across mTBI, PTSD, chronic pain, and other comorbid disorders that are sequelae to the injury and stress of events such as accidents. This conjecture fits with our own perspective that an integrative, biopsychosocial model is needed across the three areas of psychological injury being considered, especially in terms of their causal determinants. In the next chapter, I conclude my literature review of the three major areas of psychological injury, by reviewing chronic pain, and then, in the chapter that follows, I describe an integrated biopsychosocial model of psychological injury.

References

American Psychiatric Association. (1987). *Diagnostic and statistical manual of mental disorders* (3rd ed.). Washington, DC: Author.

American Psychiatric Association. (1994). *Diagnostic and statistical manual of mental disorders* (4th ed.). Washington, DC: Author.

American Psychiatric Association. (2000). *Diagnostic and statistical manual of mental disorders: Text revision* (4th ed.). Washington, DC: Author.

Arbisi, P. A., & Ben-Porath, Y. S. (1995). On MMPI-2 infrequent response scale for use with psychopathological populations: The Infrequency Psychopathology Scale F(p). *Psychological Assessment, 7*, 424–431.

Asmundson, G. J. G., Frombach, I., McQuaid, J., Pedrelli, P., Lenox, R., & Stein, M. B. (2000). Dimensionality of posttraumatic stress symptoms: A confirmatory factor analysis of DSM-IV symptom clusters and other symptom models. *Behaviour Research and Therapy, 38*, 203–214.

Barrow, I. M., Hough, M., Rastatter, M. P., Walker, M., Holbert, D., & Rotondo, M. F. (2003). Can within-category naming identify subtle cognitive deficits in the mild traumatic brain-injured patient? *The Journal of Trauma, Injury, Infection, and Critical Care, 54*, 888–897.

Barth, J., Ruff, R., & Espe-Pfeifer, P. (2006). Mild Traumatic Brain Injury: Definitions. In G. Young, A. W. Kane, & K. Nicholson (Eds.), *Psychological knowledge in court: PTSD, pain, and TBI* (pp. 271–278). New York: Springer Science+Business Media.

Belanger, H. G., Curtiss, G., Demery, J. A., Lebowitz, B. K., & Vanderploeg, R. D. (2005). Factors moderating neuropsychological outcomes following mild traumatic brain injury: A meta-analysis. *Journal of the International Neuropsychological Society, 11*, 215–227.

Bigler, E. D. (2003). Neurobiology and neuropathology underlie the neuropsychological deficits associated with traumatic brain injury. *Archives of Clinical Neuropsychology, 18*, 595–621.

Bigler, E. D. (2006). Mild Traumatic Brain Injury (mTBI): Causality considerations from a neuroimagining and neuropathology perspective. In G. Young, A. W. Kane, & K. Nicholson (Eds.), *Psychological knowledge in court: PTSD, pain, and TBI* (pp. 308–334). New York: Springer Science+Business Media.

Binder, L. M., Kelly, M. P., Villaneuva, M. R., & Winslow, M. M. (2003). Motivation and neuropsychological test performance following mild head injury. *Journal of Clinical and Experimental Neuropsychology, 25*, 420–430.

Birmes, P., Brunet, A., Carreras, D., Ducasse, J., Charlet, J., Lauque, D., Sztulman, H., & Schmitt, L. (2003). The predictive power of peritraumatic dissociation and acute stress symptoms for posttraumatic stress symptoms: A three-month prospective study. *American Journal of Psychiatry, 160*, 1337–1338.

Blanchard, E. B., Hickling, E. J., Devineni, T., Veazey, C. H., Galovski, T. E., Mundy, E., Malta, L. S., & Buckley, T. C. (2003). A controlled evaluation of cognitive behavioral therapy for posttraumatic stress in motor vehicle accident survivors. *Behaviour Research and Therapy, 41*, 79–96.

Blanchard, E. B., Jones-Alexander, J., Buckley, T. C., & Forneris, C. A. (1996). Psychometric properties of the PTSD Checklist (PCL). *Behaviour Research and Therapy, 34*, 669–673.

Bonne, O., Gilboa, A., Louzoun, Y., Kempf-Sharf, O., Katz, M., Fishman, Y., Ben-Nahum, Z., Krausz, Y., Bocher, M., Lester, H., Chisin, R., & Lerer, B. (2003). Cerebral blood flow in chronic symptomatic mild traumatic brain injury. *Psychiatry Research: Neuroimaging, 124*, 141–152.

Borgaro, S. R., Prigatano, G. P., Kwasnica, C., & Rexer, J. L. (2003). Cognitive and affective sequelae in complicated and uncomplicated mild traumatic brain injury. *Brain Injury, 17*, 189–198.

Boscarino, J. A. (2004). Posttraumatic Stress Disorder and physical illness: Results from clinical and epidemiological studies. *Annals of the New York Academy of Sciences, 1032*, 141–153.

Bowman, M. (2003). Problems inherent to the diagnosis of Posttraumatic Stress Disorder. In I. Z. Schultz & D. O. Brady (Eds.), *Psychological injuries at trial* (pp. 820–849). Chicago, IL: American Bar Association.

Bowman, M. L., & Yehuda, R. (2004). Risk factors and the adversity-stress model. In G. M. Rosen (Ed.), *Posttraumatic Stress Disorder: Issues and controversies* (pp. 15–38). Chichester, UK: Wiley.

Breslau, N., & Kessler, R. C. (2001). The stressor criterion in DSM-IV Posttraumatic Stress Disorder: An empirical investigation. *Biological Psychiatry, 50*, 699–704.

Brewin, C. R., Andrews, B., & Valentine, J. D. (2000). Meta-analysis of risk factors for Posttraumatic Stress Disorder in trauma-exposed adults. *Journal of Consulting and Clinical Psychology, 68*, 748–766.

Brewin, C. R., & Holmes, E. A. (2003). Psychological theories of Posttraumatic Stress Disorder. *Clinical Psychology Review, 23*, 339–376.

Briere, J. (2001). *Detailed assessment of posttraumatic stress: Professional manual.* Odessa, FL: Psychological Assessment Resources.

Briere, J. (2004). *Psychological assessment of adult posttraumatic states: Phenomenology, diagnosis, and measurement* (2nd ed.). Washington, DC: American Psychological Association.

Brown, T. A., Campbell, L. A., Lehman, C. L., Grisham, J. R., & Mancill, R. B. (2001). Current and lifetime comorbidity of the DSM-IV anxiety and mood disorders in a large clinical sample. *Journal of Abnormal Psychology, 110*, 585–599.

Bryant, R. A. (2004). In the aftermath of trauma: Normative reactions and early interventions. In G. M. Rosen (Ed.), *Posttraumatic Stress Disorder: Issues and controversies* (pp. 187–212). Chichester, UK: Wiley.

Burkett, B. G., & Whitley, G. (1998). *Stolen valor: How the Vietnam generation was robbed of its heroes and its history*. Dallas, TX: Verity Press.

Butcher, J. N., Dahlstrom, W. G., Graham, J. R., Tellegen, A., & Kaemmer, B. (1989). *Minnesota Multiphasic Personality Inventory-2 (MMPI-2): Manual for administration and scoring*. Minneapolis, MN: University of Minnesota Press.

Carroll, L. J., Cassidy, J. D., Peloso, P. M., Borg, J., von Holst, H., Holm, L., Paniak, C., & Pépin, M. (2004). Prognosis for mild traumatic brain injury: Results of the WHO collaborating centre task force on mild traumatic brain injury. *Journal of Rehabilitation Medicine, Supplement 43*, 84–105.

Chan, R. C. K., Hussain, R., Lee, T. M. C., Fan, Y. W., & Fong, D. (2003). Are there subtypes of attentional deficits in patients with persisting post-concussive symptoms? A cluster analytical study. *Brain Injury, 17*, 131–148.

Chen, S. H. A., Kareken, D. A., Fastenau, P. S., Trexter, L. E., & Hutchins, G. D. (2003). A study of persistent post-concussion symptoms in mild head trauma using position emission tomography. *Journal of Neurology, Neurosurgery, and Psychiatry, 74*, 326–332.

Cox, B. J., MacPherson, P. S. R., Enns, M. W., & McWilliams, L. A. (2004). Neuroticism and self-criticism associated with Posttraumatic Stress Disorder. *Behaviour Research and Therapy, 42*, 105–114.

Creamer, M., O'Donnell, M., & Pattison, P. (2004). The relationship between Acute Stress Disorder and Posttraumatic Stress Disorder in severely injured trauma survivors. *Behaviour Research and Therapy, 42*, 315–328.

Delahanty, D. L., Raimonde, A. J., Spoonster, E., & Cullado, M. (2003a). Injury severity, prior trauma history, urinary cortisol levels, and acute PTSD in motor vehicle accident victims. *Anxiety Disorders, 17*, 149–164.

Delahanty, D. L., Royer, D. K., Raimonde, A. J., & Spoonster, E. (2003b). Peritraumatic dissociation is inversely related to catecholamine levels in initial urine samples of motor vehicle accident victims. *Journal of Trauma and Dissociation, 4*, 65–80.

Duke, L. M., & Vasterling, J. J. (2005). Epidemiological and methodological issues in neuropsychological research on PTSD. In J. J. Vasterling & C. R. Brewin (Eds.), *Neuropsychology of PTSD: Biological, cognitive, and clinical perspectives* (pp. 3–24). New York: Guilford Press.

Evered, L., Ruff, R., Baldo, J., & Isomura, A. (2003). Emotional risk factors and postconcussional disorder. *Assessment, 10*, 420–427.

Fletcher, K. E. (2003). Childhood Posttraumatic Stress Disorder. In E. J. Mash & R. A. Barkley (Eds.), *Child psychopathology* (2nd ed., pp. 330–371). New York: Guilford Press.

Fox, D. D., & Allen, L. M., III. (2003). Rebuttal to Bigler's response to our commentary on the lesion(s) in traumatic brain injury: Let's stick to science. *Archives of Clinical Neuropsychology, 18*, 623–624.

Frencham, K. A. R., Fox, A. M., & Maybery, M. T. (2005). Neuropsychological studies of Mild Traumatic Brain Injury: A meta-analytic review of research since 1995. *Journal of Clinical and Experimental Neuropsychology, 27*, 334–351.

Frueh, C., Elhai, J. D., & Kaloupek, D. G. (2004). Unresolved issues in the assessment of trauma exposure and posttraumatic reactions. In G. M. Rosen (Ed.), *Posttraumatic Stress Disorder: Issues and controversies* (pp. 63–84). Chichester, UK: Wiley.

Galea, S., Ahern, J., Resnick, H., Kilpatrick, D., Bucuvalas, M., Gold, J., & Vlahov, D. (2002). Psychological sequelae of the September 11 terrorist attacks. *New England Journal of Medicine, 346*, 982–987.

Gershuny, B. S., Cloitre, M., & Otto, M. W. (2003). Peritraumatic dissociation and PTSD severity: Do event-related fears about death and control mediate their relation? *Behavior Research and Therapy, 41*, 157–166.

Gil, S., Caspi, Y., Ben-Ari, I. Z., Koren, D., & Klein, E. (2005). Does memory of a traumatic event increase the risk of Posttraumatic Stress Disorder in patients with traumatic brain injury: A prospective study. *American Journal of Psychiatry, 162*, 963–969.

Gold, S. D., Marx, B. P., Soler-Baillo, J. M., & Sloan, D. M. (2005). Is life stress more traumatic than traumatic stress? *Journal of Anxiety Disorders, 19*, 687–698.

Golier, J. A., Yehuda, R., Bierer, L. M., Mitropoulou, V., New, A. S., & Schmeidler, J. (2003). The relationship of Borderline Personality Disorder to Posttraumatic Stress Disorder and traumatic events. *American Journal of Psychiatry, 160*, 18–24.

Greiffenstein, M. F., Baker, W. J., Axelrod, B., Peck, E. A., & Gervais, R. (2004). The fake bad scale and MMPI-2 f-family in detection of implausible psychological trauma claims. *The Clinical Neuropsychologist, 18*, 573–590.

Guriel, J., & Fremouw, W. (2003). Assessing malingering Posttraumatic Stress Disorder: A critical review. *Clinical Psychology Review, 23*, 881–904.

Hall, R. C. W., Hall, R. C. W., & Chapman, M. J. (2005). Definition, diagnosis, and forensic implications of postconcussional syndrome. *Psychosomatics, 46*, 195–202.

Halligan, S. L., Michael, T., Clark, D. M., & Ehlers, A. (2003). Posttraumatic Stress Disorder following assault: The role of cognitive processing, trauma memory, and appraisals. *Journal of Consulting and Clinical Psychology, 71*, 419–431.

Hannay, H. J., Howieson, D. B., Loring, D. W., Fischer, J. S., & Lezak, M. D. (2004). Neuropathology for neuropsychologists. In M. D. Lezak, D. B. Howieson, & D. W. Loring (Eds.). *Neuropsychological assessment* (4th ed., pp. 157–194). New York: Springer Science+Business Media.

Hembree, E. A., Street, G. P., Riggs, D. S., & Foa, E. B. (2004). Do assault-related variables predict response to cognitive behavioral treatment for PTSD. *Journal of Consulting and Clinical Psychology, 72*, 531–534.

Iverson, G. L. (2005). Outcome from mild traumatic brain injury. *Current Opinion in Psychiatry, 18*, 301–317.

Kay, T. (1999). Interpreting apparent neuropsychological deficits: What is really wrong? In J. J. Sweet (Ed.), *Forensic neuropsychology: Fundamentals and practice* (pp.145–183). Lisse, The Netherlands: Swets & Zeitlinger.

Kessler, R. C., Sonnega, A., Bromet, E., Hughes, M., & Nelson, C. B. (1995). Posttraumatic Stress Disorder in the National Comorbidity Survey. *Archives of General Psychiatry, 52*, 1048–1060.

Klonoff, P. S., & Dawson, L. K. (2004). Commentary-neuropsychological evaluation of patients with traumatic brain injury: Polarization vs. holistic integration. *Archives of Clinical Neuropsychology*, 19, 1095–1101.

Koch, W. (2003). Posttraumatic Stress Disorder following motor vehicle accidents: Clinical forensic guidelines. In I. Z. Schultz & D. O. Brady (Eds.), *Psychological injuries at trial* (pp. 794–819). Chicago, IL: American Bar Association.

Koch, W. J., O'Neill, M., & Douglas, K. S. (2005). Empirical limits for the forensic assessment of PTSD litigants. *Law and Human Behavior, 29*, 121–149.

Lanius, R. A., Williamson, P. C., Bluhm, R. L., Densmore, M., Boksman, K., Neufeld, R. W., Gati, J. S., & Menon, R. S. (2005). Functional connectivity of dissociative responses in Posttraumatic Stress Disorder: A functional magnetic resonance imaging investigation. *Biological Psychiatry, 57*, 873–874.

Lanius, R. A., Williamson, P. C., Densmore, M., Boksman, K., Neufeld, R. W., & Gati, J. S., & Menon, R. S. (2004). The nature of traumatic memories: A 4-T fMRI functional connectivity analysis. *American Journal of Psychiatry, 161*, 36–44.

Lanius, R. A., Williamson, P. C., Hopper, J., Densmore, M., Boksman, K., Gupta, M. A., Neufeld, R. J. W., Gati, J. S., & Menon, R. S. (2003). Recall of emotional states in Posttraumatic Stress Disorder: A functional MRI investigation. *Biological Psychiatry, 53*, 204–210.

Lees-Haley, P. R., Green, P., Rohling, M. L., Fox, D. D., & Allen, L. M., III. (2003). The lesion(s) in traumatic brain injury: Implications for clinical neuropsychology. *Archives of Clinical Neuropsychology, 18*, 585–594.

Lynn, S. A., Knox, J. A., Fassler, O., Lilienfeld, S., & Loftus, E.F. (2004). Memory, trauma, and dissociation. In G. M. Rosen (Ed.), *Posttraumatic Stress Disorder: Issues and controversies* (pp. 163–186). Chichester, UK: Wiley.

Malta, L. S., Blanchard, E. B., Taylor, A. E., Hickling, E. J., & Freidenberg, B. M. (2002). Personality disorders and Posttraumatic Stress Disorder in motor vehicle accident survivors. *Journal of Nervous and Mental Disease, 190*, 767–774.

Mathias, J. L., Beall, J. A., & Bigler, E. D. (2004). Neuropsychological and information processing deficits following mild traumatic brain injury. *Journal of the International Neuropsychological Society, 10*, 286–297.

Mayou, R. A., Ehlers, A., & Bryant, B. (2002). Posttraumatic Stress Disorder after motor vehicle accidents: three-year follow-up of a prospective longitudinal study. *Behavior Research and Therapy, 40*, 665–675.

McAllister, T. W. (2005). Mild brain injury and the postconcussion syndrome. In J. M. Silver, T. W. McAllister, & S. C. Yudofsky (Eds.), *Textbook of traumatic brain injury* (1st ed., pp. 279–308). Washington, DC: American Psychiatric.

McAllister, T. W., & Arciniegas, D. (2002). Evaluation and treatment of postconcussive symptoms. *NeuroRehabilitation, 17*, 265–283.

McKeever, V. M., & Huff, M. E. (2003). A diatheses-stress model of Posttraumatic Stress Disorder: Ecological, biological, and residual stress pathways. *Review of General Psychology, 7*, 237–250.

McKerral, M., Guérin, F., Kennepohl, S., Dominique, A., Honoré, W., Léveillé, G., & Brière, N. (2005). Comments on the task force report on mild traumatic brain injury: Journal of rehabilitation medicine supplement 43. *Journal of Rehabilitation Medicine, 37*, 61–62.

McNally, R. J. (2003). Progress and controversy in the study of Posttraumatic Stress Disorder. *Annual Review of Psychology, 54*, 229–252.

McNally, R. J. (2004). Conceptual problems with the DSM-IV criteria for Posttraumatic Stress Disorder. In G. M. Rosen (Ed.), *Posttraumatic Stress Disorder: Issues and controversies* (pp. 1–14). Chichester, UK: Wiley.

McNally, R. J., Bryant, R. A., & Ehlers, A. (2003). Does early psychological intervention promote recovery from posttraumatic stress? *Psychological Science in the Public Interest, 4*, 45–79.

McNally, R. J., Lasko, N. B., Clancy, S. A., Macklin, M. L., Pitman, R. K., & Orr, S. P. (2004). Psychological responding during script-driven imagery in people reporting abduction by space aliens. *Psychological Science, 15*, 493–497.

McWilliams, L. A., Cox, B. J., & Asmundson, G. J. G. (2005). Symptom structure of Posttraumatic Stress Disorder in a nationally representative sample. *Journal of Anxiety Disorders, 19*, 626–641.

Metzger, L. J., Paige, S. R., Carson, M. A., Lasko, N. B., Paulus, L. A., Pitman, R. K., & Orr, S. P. (2004). PTSD arousal and depression symptoms associated with increased right-sided parietal EEG asymmetry. *Journal of Abnormal Psychology, 113*, 324–329.

Miller, M. W. (2003). Personality and the etiology and expression of PTSD: A three-factor model perspective. *Clinical Psychology: Science and Practice, 10*, 373–393.

Miller, M. W., Kaloupek, D. G., Dillon, A. L., & Keane, T. M. (2004). Externalizing and internalizing subtypes of combat-related PTSD: A replication and extension using the PSY-5 scales. *Journal of Abnormal Psychology, 113*, 636–645.

Mol, S. S. L., Arntz, A., Metsemakers, J. F. M., Dinant, G., Vilters-Van Montfort, P. A. P., & Knottnerus, J. A. (2005). Symptoms of Posttraumatic Stress Disorder after non-traumatic events: Evidence from an open population study. *British Journal of Psychiatry, 186*, 494–499.

Nicholson, K., & Martelli, M. F. (2006). The confounding effects of pain, psychoemotional problems or psychiatric disorder, premorbid ability structure, and motivational or other factor on neuropsychological test performance. In G. Young, A. W. Kane, & K. Nicholson (Eds.), *Psychological knowledge in court: PTSD, pain, and TBI* (pp. 335–351). New York: Springer Science+Business Media.

Nutt, D. J., & Malizia, A. L. (2004). Structural and functional brain changes in Posttraumatic Stress Disorder. *Journal of Clinical Psychiatry, 65*, 11–17.

O'Donnell, M. L., Creamer, M., Bryant, R. A., Schnyder, U., & Shalev, A. (2006). Posttraumatic disorder following injury: Assessment and other methodological considerations. In G. Young, A. W. Kane, & K. Nicholson (Eds.), *Psychological knowledge in court: PTSD, pain, and TBI* (pp. 70–84). New York: Springer Science+Business Media.

O'Donnell, M. L., Creamer, M., & Pattison, P. (2004). Posttraumatic stress disorder and depression following trauma: Understanding comorbidity. *American Journal of Psychiatry, 161*, 1390–1396.

O'Donnell, M. L., Creamer, M., Pattison, P., & Atkin, C. (2004). Psychiatric morbidity following injury. *American Journal of Psychiatry, 161*, 507–514.

O'Neill, P. (2004). Étudier l'impact des contacts sexuels précoces: Commentaire sur l'article de Forouzan at Van Gijseghem. [Studying the impact of early sexual contact: Commentary on the article by Forouzan and Van Gijseghem]. *Canadian Psychologist, 45*, 81–82.

Oquendo, M., Brent, D. A., Birmaher, B., Greenhill, L., Kolko, D., Stanley, B., Zelazny, J., Burke, A. K., Firinciogullari, S., Ellis, S. P., & Mann, J. (2005). Posttraumatic Stress Disorder comorbid with major depression: Factors mediating the association with suicidal behavior. *American Journal of Psychiatry, 162*, 560–566.

Orr, S. C., McNally, R. J., Rosen, G. M., & Shalev, A.Y. (2004). Psychophysiologic reactivity: Implications for conceptualizing PTSD. In G. M. Rosen (Ed.), *Posttraumatic Stress Disorder: Issues and controversies* (pp. 101–126). Chichester, UK: Wiley.

Ozer, E. J., Best, S. R., Lipsey, T. L., & Weiss, D. S. (2003). Predictors of Posttraumatic Stress Disorder and symptoms in adults: A meta-analysis. *Psychological Bulletin, 129*, 52–73.

Polusny, M., & Arbisi, P. (2006). Assessment of psychological distress and disability after sexual assault in adults. In G. Young, A. W. Kane, & K. Nicholson (Eds.), *Psychological knowledge in court: PTSD, pain, and TBI* (pp. 97–125). New York: Springer Science+ Business Media.

Rapoport, M. J., McCullagh, S., Streiner, D., & Feinstein, A. (2003). The clinical significance of major depression following mild traumatic brain injury. *Psychosomatics, 44*, 31–37.

Rauch, S. L., Shin, L. M., Whalen, P. J., & Pitman, R. K. (1998). Neuroimaging and the neuroanatomy of PTSD. *CNS Spectrums: The International Journal of Neuropsychiatric Medicine, 3* (Suppl. 2), 30–41.

Rees, P. M. (2003). Contemporary issues in mild traumatic brain injury. *Archives of Physical Medical and Rehabilitation, 84*, 1885–1894.

Regehr, C., Goldberg, G., Glancy, G. D., & Knott, T. (2002). Posttraumatic symptoms and disability in paramedics. *Canadian Journal of Psychiatry, 47*, 953–958.

Rind, B., Tromovitch, P., & Bauserman, R. (1998). A metal-analytic examination of assumed properties of child sexual abuse using college samples. *Psychological Bulletin, 124*, 22–53.

Rind, B., Tromovitch, P., & Bauserman, R. (2001). The validity and appropriateness of methods, analyses, and conclusions in Rind et al. (1998): A rebuttal of victimological critique from Ondersma et al. (2001) and Dallam et al. (2001). *Psychological Bulletin, 127*, 734–758.

Rogers, R., Sewell, K. W., Martin, M. A., & Vitacco, M. J. (2003). Detection of feigned mental disorders: A meta-analysis of the MMPI-2 and malingering. *Assessment, 10*, 160–177.

Rosen, G. M. (2004a). Preface. In G. M. Rosen (Ed.), *Posttraumatic Stress Disorder: Issues and controversies* (pp. xi–xii). Chichester, UK: Wiley.

Rosen, G. M. (2004b). Malingering and the PTSD data base. In G. M. Rosen (Ed.), *Posttraumatic Stress Disorder: Issues and controversies* (pp. 85–100). Chichester, UK: Wiley.

Ruff, R. (2005). Two decades of advances in understanding of mild traumatic brain injury. *The Journal of Head Trauma Rehabilitation, 20*, 5–14.

Ruff, R. M., & Richardson, A. M. (1999). Mild traumatic brain injury. In J. J. Sweet (Ed.), *Forensic neuropsychology: Fundamentals and practice* (pp. 313–338). Lisse, The Netherlands: Swets & Zeitlinger.

Rush, B. K., Malec, J. F., Moessner, A., M., & Brown, A. W. (2004). Preinjury personality traits and the prediction of early neurobehavioral symptoms following mild traumatic brain injury. *Rehabilitation Psychology, 49*, 275–281.

Ruttan, L. A., & Heinrichs, R. W. (2003). Depression and neurocognitive functioning in mild traumatic brain injury patients referred for assessment. *Journal of Clinical and Experimental Neuropsychology, 25*, 407–419.

Ryan, L. M., & Warden, D. L. (2003). Post concussion syndrome. *International Review of Psychiatry, 15*, 310–316.

Schell, T. L., Marshall, G. N., & Jaycox, L. H. (2004). All symptoms are not created equal: The prominent role of hyperarousal in the natural course of posttraumatic psychological distress. *Journal of Abnormal Psychology, 113*, 189–197.

Schnurr, P. P., Ford, J. D., Friedman, M. J., Green, B. L., Dain, B. J., & Sengupta, J. (2000). A descriptive analysis of PTSD chronicity in Vietnam veterans. *Journal of Traumatic Stress, 16*, 545–553.

Schnurr, P. P., & Green, B. L. (2004). Understanding relationships among trauma, Posttraumatic Stress Disorder, and health outcomes. In P. P. Schnurr & B. L. Green (Eds.), *Trauma and health: Physical health consequences of exposure to extreme stress* (pp. 247–275). Washington, DC: American Psychological Association.

Schretlen, D. J., & Shapiro, A. M. (2003). A quantitative review of the effects of traumatic brain injury on cognitive functioning. *International Review of Psychiatry, 15*, 341–349.

Shin, L. M., Rauch, S. L., & Pitman, R. K. (2005). Structural and functional anatomy of PTSD: Findings from neuroimaging research. In J. J. Vasterling & C. R. Brewin (Eds.), *Neuropsychology of PTSD: Biological, cognitive, and clinical perspectives* (pp. 59–82). New York: Guilford Press.

Smith-Seemiller, L., Fow, N. R., Kant, R., & Franzen, M. D. (2003). Presence of post-concussion syndrome symptoms in patients with chronic pain vs. mild traumatic brain injury. *Brain Injury, 17*, 199–206.

Southwick, S. M., Rasmusson, A., Barron, J., & Arnsten, A. (2005). Neurobiological and neurocognitive alterations in PTSD: A focus on norepinephrine, serotonin, and the hypothalamic-pituitary-adrenal axis. In J. J. Vasterling & C. R. Brewin (Eds.), *Neuropsychology of PTSD: Biological, cognitive, and clinical perspectives* (pp. 27– 58). New York: Guilford Press.

Sreenivasan, S., Eth, S., Kirkish, P., & Garrick, T. (2003). A practical method for the evaluation of symptom exaggeration in minor head trauma among civil litigants. *Journal of the American Academy of Psychiatry and the Law, 31*, 220–231.

Stuss, D. T. (1995). A sensible approach to mild traumatic brain injury. *Neurology, 45*, 1251–1252.

Tait, R. C. (2004). Compensation claims for chronic pain: Effects on evaluation and treatment. In R. H. Dworkin & W. S. Breitbart (Eds.), *Psychological aspects of pain: A handbook for health care providers* (pp. 547–569). Seattle, WA: IASP Press.

Thornton, K. (2003). The electrophysiological effects of a brain injury on auditory memory functioning: The QEEG correlates of impaired memory. *Archives of Clinical Neuropsychology, 18*, 363–378.

Tyler, K. A. (2002). Social and emotional outcomes of childhood sexual abuse: A review of recent research. *Aggression and Violent Behaviour, 7*, 567–589.

Udwin, O., Boyle, S., Yule, W., Bolton, D., & O'Ryan, D. (2000). Risk factors for long-term psychological effects of a disaster experienced in adolescence. Predictors of Posttraumatic Stress Disorder. *Journal of Child Psychology and Psychiatry, 41*, 969– 979.

Umile, E. M., Sandel, M. E., Alavi, A., Terry, C. M., & Plotkin, R. C. (2002). Dynamic imaging in mild traumatic brain injury: Support for the theory of medial temporal vulnerability. *Archives of Physical and Medical Rehabilitation, 83*, 1506–1513.

Uomoto, J. M., & Fann, J. R. (2004). Explanatory style and perception of recovery in symptomatic mild traumatic brain injury. *Rehabilitation Psychology, 49*, 334–337.

van den Hout, M. A., & Engelhard, I. M. (2004). Pretrauma neuroticism, negative appraisals of intrusions, and severity of PTSD symptoms. *Journal of Psychopathology and Behavioral Assessment, 26*, 181–183.

Vanderploeg, R. D., Belanger, H., & Curtiss, G. (2006). Mild Traumatic Brain Injury: Medical and neuropsychological causality modeling. In G. Young, A. W. Kane, & K. Nicholson (Eds.), *Psychological knowledge in court: PTSD, pain, and TBI* (pp. 279–307). New York: Springer Science+Business Media.

Vanderploeg, R. D., Curtiss, G., & Belanger, H. G. (2005). Long-term neuropsychological outcomes following mild traumatic brain injury. *Journal of the International Neuropsychological Society, 11*, 228–236.

Vanderploeg, R. D., Curtiss, G., Duchnick, J. J., & Luis, C. A. (2003). Demographic, medical, and psychiatric factors in work and marital status after mild head injury. *Journal of Head Trauma Rehabilitation, 18*, 148–163.

von Holst, H., & Cassidy, J. D. (2004). Mandate of the WHO Collaboration Centre Task Force on mild traumatic brain injury. *Journal of Rehabilitation Medicine, Supplement 43*, 8–10.

Weiss, D., & Ozer, E. (2006). Predicting who will develop Posttraumatic Stress Disorder. In G. Young, A. W. Kane, & K. Nicholson (Eds.), *Psychological knowledge in court: PTSD, pain, and TBI* (pp. 85–96). New York: Springer Science+Business Media.

Wilson, J. P. (2004). PTSD and complex PTSD: Symptoms, syndromes, and diagnosis. In J. P. Wilson & T. M. Keane (Eds.), *Assessing psychological trauma and PTSD* (2nd ed., pp. 7–44). New York: Guilford.

Wilson, J. P., & Moran, T. A. (2004). Forensic/clinical assessment of psychological trauma and PTSD in legal settings. In J. P. Wilson & T. M. Keane (Eds.), *Assessing psychological trauma and PTSD* (2nd ed., pp. 603–636). New York: Guilford.

Winter, H., & Irle, E. (2004). Hippocampal volume in adult burn patients with and without Posttraumatic Stress Disorder. *American Journal of Psychiatry, 161*, 2194–2200.

Yehuda, R. (2002). Post-traumatic Stress Disorder. *New England Journal of Medicine, 346*, 108–114.

Yehuda, R. (2004). Risk and resilience in Posttraumatic Stress Disorder. *Journal of Clinical Psychiatry, 65*, 29–36.

Yehuda, R., & Bierer, L. M. (2005). Re-evaluating the link between disasters and psychopathology. In J. J. Lopez-Ibor, G. Christodoulou, M. Maj, N. Sartorius, & A. Okasha (Eds.), *Disasters and mental health* (pp. 65–80). New York: Wiley.

Young, G., Kane, A.W., & Nicholson, K. (Eds.). (2006). *Psychological knowledge in court: PTSD, pain, and TBI*. New York: Springer Science+Business Media.

Young, G., & Yehuda, R. (2006). Understanding PTSD: Implications for court. In G. Young, A. W. Kane, & K. Nicholson (Eds.), *Psychological knowledge in court: PTSD, pain, and TBI* (pp. 55–69). New York: Springer Science+Business Media.

Zoellner, L. A., & Bittenger, J. N. (2004). On the uniqueness of trauma memories in PTSD. In G. M. Rosen (Ed.), *Posttraumatic Stress Disorder: Issues and controversies* (pp. 147–162). Chichester, UK: Wiley.

6

Multicausal Perspectives on Psychological Injury II: Chronic Pain

GERALD YOUNG

In this chapter, I continue to review recent literature in the three predominant areas of psychological injury presented in the book—Posttraumatic Stress Disorder (PTSD), chronic pain, and mild Traumatic Brain Injury (mTBI)—concentrating on pain. Then, in the chapter that ensues, I proceed to the conclusions about the review.

Pain

Introduction

Craig and Hadjistavropoulos (2004, pp. 306–307) reviewed standard definitions on pain. In 1979, the International Association for the Study of Pain defined pain as, "[a]n unpleasant sensory and emotional experience associated with actual or potential tissue damage, or described in terms of such damage." In 2001, the IASP acknowledged that an inability to communicate verbally does not negate the possible presence of pain experience. It added in its notes that, "Pain is always subjective."

Although progress has been made in giving an adequate definition of acute pain, the same cannot be said about attempts to define chronic pain. Often, chronic pain is dismissed because of an absence of correlated pathophysiological findings. However, Melzack and Katz (2006) maintain that we should not presume that emotional distress and psychological disturbance inevitably are at the root of chronic pain. For example, the *DSM-IV* category of Pain Disorder allows for attribution of pain to medical factors, psychological factors, or both. They point out that psychological factors are not defined, and the threshold for their inclusion is not given. Moreover, the concept is dualistic, because pain is never one or the other, "psychogenic," (attributable to psychological factors; pejoratively, self-generated), or not. Pain can be triggered by psychological factors in otherwise healthy individuals. In addition, for Melzack and Katz, the diagnosis of Pain Disorder has a negative connotation, and they imply that it should be reconsidered as belonging in a manual of mental disorders. The danger of having the condition entered in a psychiatric or psychological diagnostic classification system is that the assessor will gravitate to this diagnosis when pain continues beyond what the physical findings suggest, unfairly labeling, victimizing, or blaming the individual. Pain is a multidimensional experience produced by multiple influences.

Young and Chapman (2006; in this volume) have recommended that one way of dealing with the difficulties presented by the diagnosis of chronic Pain Disorder is to refer to it as *Chronic Pain Complications Disorder*, so that the psychological factors associated with it become the focus. For any one individual, the complications propagating the pain should be specified in detail, whether they relate to the individual through the affect of the pain on the person's life, or whether they relate to confounding factors, such as preexisting psychopathology, symptom exaggeration, litigation distress, malingering, and so on.

In terms of theory, Keefe, Abernathy, and Campbell (2005) contrast biomedical and psychosocial models of pain. The biomedical model of pain views pain as a symptom of a disease, or a product of injury or tissue damage, in which pain experience is proportional to the degree of the disease/tissue damage, in a dose-response relationship, and for which successful treatment of the disease/tissue damage inevitably abolishes or significantly reduces the pain experience. However, Keefe et al. contend that the biomedical model ignores or minimizes the role of psychological factors in pain experience. They maintain that each of the assumptions of the biomedical model is problematic. They refer to the gate control theory of Melzack and Wall (1965) as a pain theory that has incorporated both biological and psychological perspectives.

Gate Control Theory and the Neuromatrix

Turk (2003; Turk & Okifugi, 2003) emphasizes that the classic gate control theory of pain, formulated by Melzack and Wall (1965), constituted the first integrative, multimodal model of pain. Gate control theory postulates that central control factors, for example, attention/distraction and mood, can act downward on spinal cord nociceptive, receptive gating mechanisms, "opening" or "closing" them. Thus, cognitive and emotional factors processed in the brain can alter linear tissue damage and related transmission signals from the periphery to the brain, so that there is not a one-to-one, dose-response correspondence between stimulus intensity at the periphery and pain experience registered centrally. Blood flow and functional neuroimaging studies confirm that multiple brain regions are involved in a distributed fashion in pain activation, supporting the theory (Coderre, Mogil, & Bushnell, 2003).

Melzack and Katz (2006) ascribed an increased importance to the perception of pain by central processing. The phenomenon of phantom limb pain illustrates the multidimensionality of pain, and even the possibility of independence from peripheral input because, in phantom pain, such as after amputation, the pain is experienced despite the physical removal of the painful area. They concluded that central generating mechanisms must be involved in ongoing pain experience perceived as deriving from an absent limb. In support of this conclusion, Hanley et al. (2004) studied lower-limb amputees for up to two years postamputation. The participants completed measures of phantom pain limb intensity, as well as cognitive (e.g., catastrophizing), coping (e.g., pain contingent rest), social (e.g., support), and functional measures. After controlling for pain intensity, the psychosocial measures at one month accounted for about one-quarter of the variance in the functional measures of pain interference and of depression at two years. Melzack and Katz propose that central factors organize action patterns, as well; for example, the experience of clenched phantom fists produces painful fatigue despite the physical absence of the fist.

Melzack and Katz (2006) make it clear that there is no one pain center in the brain. Rather, there are neural networks, central neural processes, and related factors, producing hypothesized "neurosignatures" from a "neuromatrix." The neuromatrix is postulated as a mechanism wherein there is constant cycling of input, organizing output, and creation of a stream of awareness, including perception of a unified "body-self." Qualities of pain experience are generated by this template of the whole, and are not peripheral in origin. Genetic and experiential factors influence its development. Phantom experiences in people born without limbs indicate its congenital presence.

For Melzack and Katz, the role of psychological factors in pain is shown by the influence of stress, cognitive events, the meaning ascribed to pain, the individual's affect, and so on. Stress may even affect the stress regulation system to the point of facilitating the acquisition of chronic pain, through its role in damaging already injured and other tissue (Melzack, 1999a). The chapter continues with the topics of pain, neuroplasticity, and hypersensitivity, both peripherally and centrally. Therefore, pain presumed to be related to alleged psychopathology now can be explained by neurophysiological mechanisms. Examples are provided that "most clinicians would never have imagined possible."

Other Models of Pain

Gatchel and colleagues (Dersh, Polatin, & Gatchel, 2002; Gatchel, 1991, 1999; see Gatchel & Kishino, 2006) have developed a diathesis-stress model on the interaction of personality variables and pain experience. Diatheses are preexisting, semi-dormant characteristics activated and exacerbated by stress, such as from chronic pain experience and its consequences, facilitating the development of psychopathology. The model has been applied to the development of depression in relation to chronic pain. Gatchel cites the work of Fishbain, who had reviewed the literature on the temporal relationship between pain onset and depression, and found that depression does not precede, but rather follows, pain onset (Fishbain, Cutler, Rosamoff, & Rosomoff, 1999). Gallagher and Verma (2004) reviewed the literature, and arrived at the same conclusion. Although no one model can apply in all cases, Gatchel's diathesis-stress model specifies that there are reciprocal effects, for example, with psychopathology and pain dynamically intensifying and interconnecting with each other. For any one individual case, the assessor needs to carefully evaluate the presence of premorbid psychological factors, such as depression, that might influence pain experience, the approach needed in its treatment, return to work issues, and related issues.

Turk (2003; Turk & Okifuji, 2003) proposed a similar model of chronic pain, in which predisposing factors interact with an instigating event, setting in motion a cascade of cognitive and behavioral effects that maintain disability. "Anxiety sensitivity" (see below in this chapter, p. 175) constitutes one predisposing factor, and fear of pain/injury and catastrophizing are examples of postincident cognitive factors that impede recovery. Both Gatchel and Turk describe their models of chronic pain as biopsychosocial ones, but caution that a unified model is needed.

Pincus (2006; Pincus & Morley, 2001) speaks to these issues, in a cognitive model of pain involving schematic enmeshment. Her research suggests that chronic pain patients selectively process or are biased in information processing of pain stimuli and related stimuli, for example, in recall of pain-related adjectives encoded in reference to the self. Normally, when individuals are without pain, one finds separate internal schemas, or cognitive representations, related to self, pain, and illness. The illness schema contains information about the behavioral and emotional consequences of illness, for example, related to frustration of functional goal attainment and quality of life. When chronic pain develops, the different schemas become enmeshed, as schemas of disability, helplessness, and threat are enmeshed with those of self and pain, and heightened distress results. Sensory-intensity information is selectively processed, acting to exacerbate and maintain distress and illness behavior. As with Turk and Gatchel, Pincus adopts a multifactorial model of pain, in this case showing how it becomes entrenched through cognitive and emotional factors that alter daily adaptation and sense of self. Pincus calls for more research on the specific cognitions that act to maintain enmeshment of schemas in chronic pain patients.

Asmundson and Wright (2004) reviewed biopsychosocial approaches to pain. Historically, the biomedical model espoused a reductionist framework, wherein physical pathology in the body produced noxious receptor or nociceptor stimulation, resulting in pain, with any influence of the mind and of psychological factors excluded from the process. In contrast, but in another linear model, the psychodynamic model contended that psychological factors, such as unconscious emotional conflicts, are converted psychogenically to pain, especially in the pain-prone personality.

After the proposal of gate control theory, which posited mechanisms of integration of physiological and psychological mechanisms in pain, other biopsychosocial models of pain were developed, emphasizing illness rather than disease, and social reinforcement of illness behavior, deconditioning, fear avoidance, pain avoidance, and so forth. In their own integrative model, Asmundson and Wright underscore the vicious circles that develop in pain experience, which are self-reinforcing and which reciprocally influence psychological distress and functional disability. Importantly, at the physiological level, nociceptive triggers to pain shift to autonomic nervous system triggers and to muscular activation triggers. They conclude that simplistic "somatogenic" and "psychogenetic" models of pain are obsolete.

Reinforcing this conclusion, Chapman (2004) describes the emotional aspect of pain, and the somatic markers that serve as symbolic or cognitive representations after the initial pain event. Also, Gatchel (2005) offers a comprehensive account of various theories of pain, emphasizing the value of the biopsychosocial approach.

Young and Chapman (2006, and this volume) relate chronic pain to concepts within nonlinear dynamical systems theory, such as dynamical attractors. Pain experience is constantly built out of the multiple interactions of the components of the nonlinear dynamical system in which they are embedded. Young and Chapman further relate chronic pain to concepts such as the "butterfly effect" and Complex Adaptive Systems (Kauffman, 1993). Systems theory may help explain sudden changes of state in pain experience; for example, a small input may greatly influence a pain state that is unstable because it lies at the cusp of change.

Physiology

Zasler, Martelli, and Nicholson (2005) describe the primary afferents in tissue damage signaling. There are two primary afferent fibers. A-delta fibers mediate pain experience involving fast transmission, resulting in felt pain that is sharp, localized, and well-defined, because the fibers are small, thin, myelinated, have small receptive fields, and are modality-specific (e.g., mechanoresponsive). C-fibers mediate pain experience involving slower transmission, with the pain felt as diffuse, poorly localized, burning, thawing, or gnawing. The fibers are smaller, narrower, and slower than the A-delta ones, and are polymodal and unmyelinated.

Coderre et al. (2003) and Lidbeck (2002) both review the biological psychology of pain. For example, chronic low back pain may reflect abnormalities in central nervous system pain modulation. Neurons in the dorsal horn of the spinal cord become sensitized, or hyperexcitable, as do other parts of the somatosensory pathway. Dysfunctional descending inhibition from the brain plays a role. In addition, structural reorganization takes place, where new connections mediating pain are formed without correspondence to tissue damage. Giesecke et al. (2004) described augmented central pain processing (in the somatosensory cortices, inferior parietal lobule, and cerebellum). Flor and Hermann (2004) described the cortical reorganization that takes place in back patients; their back representation expands, facilitating increased sensitivity and stress-induced hyperreactivity. Apkarian et al. (2004) found neocortical gray matter atrophy in the dorsolateral prefrontal cortex and in the right thalamus, using MRI brain scan data on chronic back pain patients and controls. In a twin study, MacGregor, Andrew, Sambrook, and Spector (2004) explored genetic contributions to pain.

Nicholson and Martelli (2004; Zasler et al., 2005) examined associated pain pathways, describing the lateral and medial pain systems. The lateral system sends inputs into the thalamus and the somatosensory cortex from the lateral spinothalamic tract. It may be more involved in acute pain processing. The medial system involves projections from the medial thalamic nuclei to the forebrain, especially to portions of the anterior cingulate cortex (ACC), an integrative center. The ACC is part of the "limbic cortex," and its connections descend to the medial thalamic nuclei and the peri-acqueductal gray (PAG) in the brain stem. The medial system may be more involved in chronic pain processing. [Chapman and Okifuji (2004) provide details of other pain-related tracts, which the interested reader should consult.] The lateral and medial systems generally represent, respectively, the sensory-discriminative and motivation-affective/cognitive-evaluative dimensions of pain, but they are quite interconnected. This indicates the complex, multidimensional, biopsychosocial, and interactive (e.g., diathesis-vulnerability × stress) aspects of pain. Many studies document that psychological/psychosocial variables may help predict outcome better than medical variables. The authors advise, however, that the importance of such variables does not mean that pain is "psychogenic" as opposed to "organic," and that pain is not "all in the mind," that psychological processes in pain are not uniquely causal of it.

Watkins and Maier's (2003) research provides physiological clues that chronic pain may originate beyond traditional hypersensitization sites in sensory, neuronal, and central pathways, and associated generated structural dysfunctions. They have found that extraneuronal cells in the spinal chord (glia), which outnumber the neuronal cells by a factor of 20 to one, play an important role in the onset and maintenance of pathological pain. For example, the glial cells permit waves of excitation to distant sites, which may account for "impossible" sensations. They release substances that amplify pain (pro-inflammatory cytokines), and they are activated by substances released from neurons within the classic pain pathways. Thus, consistent with Nicholson and Martelli (2004), physiological mechanisms are being found that argue against models of chronic pain that posit that it is all "in the head," "psychogenic," "nonorganic," the product of "psychological overlay," and so forth. In this regard, Ferrari (2004) emphasized "symptom amplification" as a psychological mechanism underlying chronic pain in whiplash victims, whereas Sterling, Jull, Vicenzino, and Kenardy (2003) viewed the chronicity as a more complex condition.

Curatolo, Arendt-Nielsen, and Petersen-Felix (2004) focus their literature review on central hypersensitivity in chronic pain after whiplash. I provide much of their argument because it is focused on a germane type of psychological injury. Moreover, it provides a link to the next section on psychological factors in pain experience.

Research reveals that peripheral tissue injury unleashes a cascade of physiological changes in the inflammatory response, including the release of potassium ions, substance P, bradykinin, and prostaglandins. This mixture may serve as sensitizers of peripheral receptors, or even activate normally "silent" nociceptors. Additional peripheral receptors may be generated, contributing to the peripheral sensitization process. Tissue damage signaling fibers may induce receptive field alterations that contribute to the sensitization.

If prolonged, increased peripheral nociceptive stimulation may lead to increased central sensitization, including of the whole spinal cord and of supraspinal centers. Central sensitization may lead to generalized hypersensitivity to peripheral stimulation, accounting for pain sites distant from the original injury. Dorsal horn neurons in the spinal cord may expand their receptive fields, and their activation may trigger adjacent dorsal horn neuron activity. Glial cell activation may also be involved, as Watkins and Maier (2003) have shown. If the injury involves destruction of inhibitory interneurons, spinal cord hyperexcitability augments even further.

Plasticity in higher brain centers allow for modulation of pain experience, for example, descending pathways are influenced by learning and memory mechanisms, and not only by factors such as endogenous opioids. In pain, the brain's cortical body map reorganizes, helping explain phantom limb pain; but at the same time, these changes may be reversible. In general, more research is needed to determine whether central hypersensitivity outlasts peripheral sensitivity.

Curatolo et al. (2004) present research evidence with whiplash patients and controls that support the model that central sensitization can account for pain chronicity. Sheather Reid and Cohen (1998) found lower pain thresholds in whiplash patients to cutaneous neck stimulation. Koelbaek Johansen, Graven-Nielsen, Schou Olesen, and Arendt-Nielsen (1999) showed that intramuscular injection of hypertonic saline caused higher pain and related ratings, including those of referred and radiated pain. Curatolo et al. (2001) found that whiplash patients displayed lower pain thresholds to cutaneous and muscular electrical stimulation to the neck and leg. Moog, Quintner, Hall, and Zusman (2002) applied nonpainful stimuli, such as vibration, to nondamaged tissue, and whiplash patients reported more pain. The authors' research group (Banic et al., 2004) examined spinal hypersensitivity using an electrophysiological method, stimulation of the innervation area of the sural nerve, and electromyographical recording of the bicep femoris muscle, which serve to detect the nociceptive withdrawal reflex response (i.e., if the response takes place within 150 ms). Whiplash patients demonstrated lower reflex thresholds, providing objective electrophysiological evidence for generalized hypersensitivity in the spinal cord.

In this research, the authors found it "very unlikely" that personality disorders could explain exaggerated responses to sensory stimulation in whiplash patients, because they found that altered pain thresholds were not associated with personality traits. Nevertheless, the patients did present with psychological "distress," which may, therefore, have a role in generating central hypersensitivity. They concluded that a purely "psychogenic" origin for central hypersensitivity cannot be ruled out, but that the research evidence provides almost no support for this hypothesis. Whiplash patients are a heterogeneous group, with variations in central hypersensitivity and psychological distress contributing to variable amplification of pain. It is possible that central hypersensitivity may persist after complete healing of tissue damage, accounting for continuation of chronic pain in whiplash patients beyond the expected normal course.

Although Curatolo et al. (2004) present persuasive evidence for central hypersensitivity of chronic pain in whiplash patients, and attribute importance to psychological factors in propagating the pain beyond expected time frames, they do not fully explore the psychological mechanisms that may contribute to the psychological distress experienced by patients. It is conceivable that preexisting factors are involved, or that a multicausal analysis shows that personality variables are involved in a complex system with other factors. It would be too simplistic to attribute the psychological distress of pain patients only to distress at their pain and its consequences, or to generalize from this study that personality disorders, or malingering and related threats to validity, are not important factors to consider in evaluating chronic pain patients.

Psychological Influences

Pain experience unleashes a range of psychological reactions, and these may come to influence outcome of tissue damage/injury more than any other variable, including physical ones. Sullivan, Stanish, Sullivan, and Tripp (2002) examined the capacity of psychological variables to predict pain ratings in litigating, mild whiplash victims of rear-end motor vehicle accident (MVA) collisions (attending a pain clinic; mean = 13 months after the accidents). Psychological variables accounted for 18% of the variance in pain ratings (in particular, variation on a catastrophic magnification subscale, for example, "I become afraid that the pain will become worse"). Psychological variables accounted for 37% of the variance in perceived disability scores, and remained significant even after statistical control of pain intensity. Therefore, psychological variables emerged as the most important predictors of disability, even more than pain intensity itself. Although all patients were in litigation, psychological factors still accounted for a significant portion in pain and disability rating variance. The authors concluded by suggesting, "it is important to look beyond litigation issues to understand fully the factors that contribute to pain and disability following whiplash injury" (p. 73).

There is much research such as this one being undertaken on the interrelationship of physical and psychological factors in pain experience; for example, for musculoskeletal and related pain, consult Gheldof, Vinck, Vlaeyen, Hidding, and Crombez (2005), Hendriks et al. (2005), MacGregor et al. (2004), McCracken (2005), Peters, Vlaeyen, and Weber (2005), Ramírez-Maestre, Martínez, and Zarazaga (2004), Richter et al. (2004), Schultz et al. (2004), Severeijns, Vlaeyen, van den Hout, and Picavet (2004a, 2004b), Sterling, Jull, Vicenzo, Kenardy, and Darnell (2005), Sullivan, Lynch, and Clark (2005), von Korff et al. (2005), and Waters, Keefe, and Strauman (2004).

For a review of the relationship between pain and affect, see the chapter by Young and Chapman (Chapter 8) in this volume. A recent study by Karp et al. (2005) demonstrated that in the treatment of recurrent depression in the acute phase, prior pain experience (as reported on the Hopkins Symptom Checklist, especially for headaches and muscle soreness) significantly predicted an increased need for treatment. The value of the study lay in the measurement of pain experience prior to treatment and the statistical control of the variable of somatization, a procedure which, nevertheless, produced the indicated relationship between preexisting pain experience and difficult response to treatment. The results suggest that patients having comorbid pain and an emotional disorder may require more "aggressive" treatment.

Personality Influences

The work on the relationship between physical and psychological influences on pain experience includes study of preexisting personality factors. Applegate et al. (2005) found a relationship between MMPI profiles at college entry and reported chronic pain conditions 30 years later at midlife. In this longitudinal study, the hypochondrias and hysteria scales were most predictive. Similarly, Guéz, Brännström, Nyberg, Toolanen, and Hildingsson (2005) found that MMPI-2 profiles were associated with chronic whiplash pain (The most recent version of the MMPI is the MMPI-2; Minnesota Multiphasic Personality Inventory, Second Edition; Butcher, Dahlstrom, Graham, Tellegen, & Kaemmer, 1989). Again, the hypochondrias and hysteria scales were elevated in these patients, along with the depression scale. This pattern conforms to the classic "Conversion V" configuration, and suggests that somatization may be part of what is involved in pain experience in chronic pain patients. Craig's (2005) review of MMPI-2 results with chronic pain patients confirms this pattern as the predominant one in the literature, although litigating/compensation-seeking patients "did not differ" in MMPI results when compared to appropriate control groups (p. 131; but also see different conclusions related to this issue on p. 133, where litigation is considered in some research cited to be a strong "mediating variable" on MMPI data). Applegate et al. describe possible genetic polymorphisms associated with pain. Nevertheless, the amount of variance in pain experience that can be attributed to preexisting personality and genetic variables leaves room for a robust influence of pain-onset and postpain-onset stress and of psychological factors on ongoing pain experience. A fully elaborated biopsychosocial model of pain experience remains the most powerful model to explain its origins and its persistence into chronicity.

Although recent research with the MMPI/MMPI-2 has implicated specific personality variables related to somatization in the development of chronic pain, and other research is suggesting a role for the personality variable of neuroticism (Geisser, 2004), Gatchel and Kishino (2006) stated that the concept of a "pain-prone personality" is outdated, and suggested that the appropriate question concerns the relative role of various personality characteristics in the pain perception process. There is a greater prevalence of psychiatric disorders in patients with chronic pain than in those with acute pain. Chronic pain is associated with depression, anxiety, substance abuse, and suicide. Risk factors for chronic pain include preexisting abnormal personality/psychosocial structure. There may be more diagnoses of personality disorder in chronic pain, but there is not one type that is more frequent. Models that can account for these findings include the diatheses-stress model and the biopsychosocial model. In these models, psychosocial and stress factors can perpetuate and worsen pain experience. Moreover, pain experience is influenced by multiple factors that may vary from individual to individual, so that individuals experience pain in unique ways.

Cognitive Influences

Two recent articles have addressed functional neuroimaging in relation to pain experience, illustrating that psychological and cognitive effects on the latter lead to neural substrate alteration. In the first study, Wager et al. (2004) found that placebo-induced analgesia led to decreased brain activity in pain-related areas, such as the thalamus, and that the anticipation of pain led to increased activity in the prefrontal cortex. Singer et al. (2004) found that empathy for pain activated the affective regions of the pain network, especially in the bilateral anterior insula and the ACC. Koyama, McHaffie, Laurienti, and Coghill (2005) also demonstrated the power of expectation to manipulate the subjective experience of pain, using healthy volunteers. Some of the areas of overlap in nociception processing and expectation of pain included the anterior insula and the ACC, like in Singer et al. These studies illustrate the power of mental processes to amplify and even create pain-related brain activation. Therefore, it could be argued that in chronic pain, contributing factors lie in somatization processes beyond injury-related ones. In this regard, Brown (2004) provides an integrative model of how psychological mechanisms can explain the development of dissociation, conversion, and somatization, for example, through "rogue" representations. I conclude that although pain symptoms may be exacerbated by such processes, it is a far cry from saying that they are produced by any conscious amplification processes or that all chronic pain experiences in all chronic pain sufferers can be fully accounted for through unconscious processes.

Social Influences

MacDonald and Leary (2005a, 2005b) review common pathways underlying physical and social pain. They argue that social rejection is a phenomenon mediated by aspects of the physical pain system. Animal research indicates that the social attachment system evolved from more primitive systems, including those involved in an endorphin-based pain network (Panksepp, 2005). Social pain and physical pain share common physiological mechanisms, including pathways involving the ACC, the PAG, neuroendocrine opioids, and the neuropeptide, oxycontin. Pain affect, but not pain intensity, is associated with the ACC. This common physiological basis of physical and social pain may help explain, in chronic pain, the relationship between tissue damage and psychosocial factors and emotions, such as depression and anxiety, and the importance of social support in helping chronic pain patients. The model of cooccurrence in mechanism of physical and social pain also includes a role for defensive reactions, through the fight-flight-freeze system (Corr, 2005). The latter system is mediated by cerebral areas, such as the prefrontal cortex and the PAG.

Pain and PTSD

An increasing amount of research is examining the interaction of PTSD and physical injury or pain experience. O'Donnell, Creamer, Bryant, Schnyder, and Shalev (2003, 2006) showed that, with respect to this interaction, discrepancies exist in the literature, and that there are confounds in the research, such as participant patients having associated organic symptoms, needing narcotic analgesia, expressing comorbid conditions, and sustaining concurrent brain injury. Their follow-up study of MVA survivors has been described in Chapter 5 (this volume), and it showed that about 10% of the seriously injured went on to develop PTSD at 12 months.

Otis, Keane, and Kerns (2003) described possible models of the interaction of PTSD and chronic pain. They cite research that the estimate of PTSD in MVA victims having concurrent pain ranges from 30 to 50%. The conditions reciprocally maintain each other, and the authors review mechanisms through which this may occur. Sharp and Harvey (2001) had suggested a mutual maintenance model of PTSD and chronic pain (see also Sharp, 2004). Asmundson, Coons, Taylor, and Katz (2002) had suggested that a common vulnerability to PTSD and chronic pain may be the tendency to respond with fear to physical symptoms of anxiety, a concept termed "anxiety sensitivity." Otis et al. (2003) supported a variation of the "triple vulnerability" model, which includes a biological factor, an early psychological factor, and particular ongoing psychological factors, especially when pain experience induces a sense of uncontrollability. Otis, Pincus, and Keane (2006) stated that both PTSD and chronic pain develop as a result of multiple biological and psychosocial factors. In general, comorbidity leads to greater pain, affective distress, life interference, and disability. Beck, Gudmundsdottir, and Shipherd (2003) classified survivors of serious MVAs, according to their Multidimensional Pain Inventory (MPI) results, as Dysfunctional, Interpersonally Distressed, or Adaptive Copers (Kerns, Turk, & Rudy, 1985). The former groups were more at risk for PTSD problems.

Blanchard and Hickling (2004) have undertaken a comprehensive study of MVA victims, updating their 1997 classic book on the topic (Blanchard & Hickling, 1997; See also Freidenberg, Hickling, Blanchard, Malta, 2006). In their research, a follow-up survey about 2 years after the initial accident revealed that up to 25% of MVA survivors were still "noticeably symptomatic" for PTSD. Although the percentage in other research usually is less marked, results vary with the criteria and instruments used. In the Blanchard and Hickling research, primary associated effects included mood disorders and phobic conditions. This is a common finding in the literature. Their data on the relationship between physical healing and psychological healing were mixed, although a chi-square analysis, using self-reported whiplash remission at 6 months and clinical improvement in diagnosed PTSD status, found a concurrent relationship between the two types of healing. Consistent with the general trend in past research, Blanchard and Hickling found little influence of litigation status on the psychological effect of MVAs. The authors concluded that, "long-lasting, nagging injuries, especially the soft tissue injuries of whiplash, seem to impede psychological recovery" (p. 179).

Duckworth and Iezzi (2005) examined a convenience sample of consecutive chronic pain patients referred for psycholegal assessment after MVAs, on average about 30 months after the accidents. They divided the sample according to the median split on the MMPI-2 *PK [PTSD]* scale. The latter consists of 18 symptoms, but is not fully compatible with the *DSM IV* category of PTSD, so that the upper end group was designated the "posttraumatic stress symptoms" (PTSS) group. A total of 160 patients were interviewed with a semi-structured format and administered a battery of psychological instruments, including the MMPI-2 and the MPI. Although all of the patients were litigating, the high PTSS group, compared to the low PTSS group, obtained results indicating more physical impairment, psychological distress, maladaptive pain coping strategies, antidepressant use, nonpain medication use, and psychological "management" (undefined). The authors concluded that MVA-traumatized patients with chronic pain likely need more physical and psychological treatment, given their physical-psychological comorbidity. Similarly, Linnell and Easton (2004) examined the relationship between travel phobia and the physical symptoms of whiplash injury. In a 6-month longitudinal study, they found that higher scores on an accident fear questionnaire concerning phobic anxiety were related to scores on self-report measures of physical symptoms of whiplash (number of symptoms of whiplash, degree of pain disability). In both studies (Duckworth & Iezzi, 2005; Linnell & Easton, 2004), control groups without ongoing pain were not considered. The field needs further research with appropriate designs that can tease out the interactive effects of chronic pain and traumatic factors.

Asmundson and Taylor (2006) addressed the issue of comorbid pain and PTSD. They concluded that difficulty in establishing the exact nature of the PTSD-pain linkage, and difficulty in treating clients having the conditions comorbidly, complicate determining causality in any one individual case.

Young and Chapman (2006, in this volume) examined the relationship between chronic pain and affect. This well-studied area indicates that pain and negative emotion often cooccur and can reciprocally influence each other. Chronic pain may develop especially via the affective dimension of pain. But pain and affect are not separate entities that may interact or not. Rather, they appear to form a unified, nonlinear dynamical system.

In the conclusions to their chapter, Young and Chapman indicate that stress mechanisms may be a mediating variable in the interconnection of pain, posttraumatic reactions, and, if applicable, TBI. They cite the critically important work of Melzack (1999a) in this regard, who described the parallel mechanisms involved in pain and stress. Duckworth and Iezzi (2005) cite a similar publication by Melzack (1999b), by which they indicate that pain and PTSD share a common neurophysiological substrate, with both conditions activating stress-regulating systems.

Malingering

With respect to the evaluation of exaggeration and malingering of pain, and other response biases, the psychological practitioner is faced with a most difficult task. Sherman and Ohrbach (2006) make clear that there is no one psychometric instrument or technique that can mark such behavior. Turk, Monarch, and Williams (2004) reinforce this view, advising that the detection of deception remains somewhat intuitive, and that one should not assume that all pain patients claiming disability will exaggerate their condition. The psychological assessor must proceed with caution before diagnosing malingering but, at the same time, must carefully evaluate for its presence and that of other response biases. The chapters by Nicholson and Martelli and by Kane in this volume address this issue in more detail. For example, the former authors review the special series on pain deception and malingering in the *Clinical Journal of Pain* (2004; Arbisi & Butcher, 2004; Bogduk, 2004; Craig & Badali, 2004; Fishbain, Cutler, Rosomoff, & Rosomoff, 2004; Hill & Craig, 2004; Mendelson & Mendelson, 2004; Robinson & Dannecker, 2004; Sullivan, 2004). Craig and Badali (2004), in introducing the series, indicate that there is an urgent need to improve our capacity to detect complainants' misrepresentation of pain but, at the same time, they caution that false accusations are especially unfair.

Conclusion

The scientific study of pain increasingly has shown that psychological factors play a major role in its determination. What predisposing psychological factors serve to maintain, worsen, and prolong acute pain into a chronic condition, and can these be controlled? How much of a role does the original tissue damage, physical injury, or disease contribute to any eventual clinical psychological condition and an individual's functional outcome in terms of work disability and/or incapacity to discharge other daily responsibilities, and can these be moderated? What ongoing psychosocial factors and stressors typically exacerbate the pain, and can these be controlled? Which therapies for pain work best? Is it appreciated that the central pathways involved in pain experience also mediate stress experience and social factors in pain, and, at the same time, that there is no one pain center in the brain?

Pain does not reflect a one-to-one relationship with the original physical cause, in a dose-response relationship, because of myriad biological, psychological, and social factors. Research pertaining to the needs of forensic mental health professionals and the court needs to consider the multifactorial complexity of pain and its biopsychosocial origins, simultaneously considering its reciprocally interacting factors. Nonlinear dynamical systems theory may provide additional insight into the cascading unfolding of chronic pain. Sensitivity to the multicausality in pain may provide better understanding of reported pain experiences that do not fit standard biomedical models. At the same time, at the other extreme, part of the psychological factors in reported pain experience may refer to illness deception, symptom exaggeration, malingering, and so on, and psychological and related assessors need to be aware of and carefully evaluate these complications.

In terms of assessment of chronic pain patients, Sherman and Ohrbach (2006) emphasize that pain experience needs to be measured at the level of subjective impression, thoughts, and emotions, and not only at the level of anatomy, biology, or physiology, consistent with the biopsychosocial model. Physical signs do not discriminate well between patients with "organic" compared to "nonorganic" pain (e.g., Waddell signs). Often, they are inconsistent with or cannot explain subjective pain reports. The experience of pain can never be verified with certainty by the external observer. Therefore, a comprehensive psychological evaluation of the pain patient is needed.

Applications

The field of psychological injury and law needs to develop chronic pain assessment instruments that facilitate rigorous assessment of areas of pain that have few or no measures. For example, the field needs better instruments that measure (a) the validity of pain complaints of patients, (b) the degree of chronicity of the pain being reported, and (c) the complicating preexisting pain history of individuals complaining of chronic pain. (d) In addition, a scale is needed to determine the exacerbatory effect of stress on pain (Young, 2006).

For example, in the state of the art reviews of the literature of the field of psychological injury and law provided in Young, Kane, and Nicholson (2006, in this volume), there is no mention of any available forensic or rehabilitation instrument to measure pain that contains validity checks, including assessment of positive and negative impression management, and of possible malingering detection. The PAB (Pain Assessment Battery, and related tests), by Eimer and Freeman (1998), is an instrument that purports to accomplish this goal but, apparently, it is not used frequently by assessors. Moreover, none of its questions follow the model of the type of malingering questions that one should use, as presented by Rogers, Bagby, and Dickens (1992), in their malingering assessment instrument, the Structured Interview of Reported Symptoms (SIRS). An equivalent questionnaire for pain would include items that ask patients to indicate to what extent both possible and impossible symptoms characterize their pain experience. The items that reflect impossible symptoms may not be sensitive to the sly malingerer and, in this sense, once developed, the instrument should not be used alone for assessing malingering. Attributions of malingering need to be made carefully after considering all the data gathered in a comprehensive assessment, including sufficient interviewing, testing, and verification of other information. Moreover, attributions of malingering are almost always made on a rule-out basis, with the assessor considering all possible explanations of the data. For example, in explaining the pattern of data in any one instrument and in the assessment as a whole, the assessor needs to ascertain any role for confounds, such as careless responding, an undue influence of poor attention due to pain, headaches, poor sleep, a "cry for help," an effect of personality variables and prior psychopathology, and so on. (See the section by Nicholson and Martelli for an extensive discussion of this issue.)

To my knowledge, there are no instruments on the history of pain that are comprehensive, in the sense of asking particular questions about pain experience in each past time period, such as pain previously in the current year, in childhood, and so forth. Therefore, I suggest that the field needs to develop a "history of pain" questionnaire. Existing instruments that ask about pain history query general health history, the course of pain after its onset, or general questions about past pain. None go into the degree of detail needed about pain history, *per se*.

Another pain instrument that should be developed concerns the degree of penetration of pain in the daily life of patients, which may be taken as an index of chronicity, or its stage of development. We need an instrument that is practical, yet reflects a theoretical understanding of the development of chronic pain, for example, through the five-stage model presented in the chapter by Young and Chapman (which elaborates the three-stage model of Gatchel, 2005). In effect, Young and Chapman have proposed three transition stages in the development of chronic pain, rather than one. They suggest that, first, the chronic pain takes hold, then it systematizes, and then it spreads in its affect on the individual. Instruments need to be developed that allow such differentiation of the transition from acute to chronic pain.

A fourth pain assessment instrument that I propose is aimed at determining individuals' perception of the role of stress in augmenting their pain experience, and the source of the stress in this role (Melzack, 1999a). As indicated in the next chapter, stress provides the glue that coheres the common mechanisms underlying the development of chronicity in the three areas of psychological injury being treated in this book—chronic pain, PTSD, and mTBI.

The four pain instruments that are proposed to complement existing instruments would be well-suited for the task of helping to elaborate, (a) the validity of presentation of chronic pain in patients, (b) the degree of preexisting pain experience that may complicate the presentation, (c) the relative degree, level, or stage of development of the chronic pain, and (d) the role of various sources of stress in possible relation to the pain. Once completed and standardized with appropriate normative populations, the four instruments should help the pain assessor undertake comprehensive evaluations, with adequate reliability and adequate validity, in keeping with court and professional requirements of practice.

To conclude, I have proposed that the field needs to develop four pain instruments, and together they would allow a more global understanding of chronic pain beyond the question of its (a) intensity, duration, sensory-discriminative aspects, and so on, (b) its associated psychosocial and affective-motivational (e.g., interpersonal distress, fear of pain) aspects, and so on, and (c) its underlying cognitive processes, beliefs, and so on (e.g., catastrophizing). (For an examination of pain assessment instruments, consult Turk and Melzack, 2001). Once pain instruments such as these are developed, forensic and related work in the area of pain assessment will be facilitated.

References

Apkarian, A. V., Sosa, Y., Sonty, S., Levy, R. M., Harden, R. N., Parrish, T. B., & Gitelman, D. R. (2004). Chronic back pain is associated with decreased prefrontal and thalamic gray matter density. *Journal of Neuroscience, 24*, 10410–10415.

Applegate, K. L., Keefe, F. J., Siegler, I. C., Bradley, L. A., McKee, D. C., Cooper, K. S., & Riordan, P. (2005). Does personality at college entry predict number of reported pain conditions at mid-life: A longitudinal study. *The Journal of Pain, 6*, 92–97.

Arbisi, P. A., & Butcher, J. N. (2004). Psychometric perspectives on detection of malingering of pain: Use of the Minnesota Multiphasic Personality Inventory-2. *Clinical Journal of Pain, 20*, 383–391.

Asmundson, G. J. G., Coons, M. J., Taylor, S., & Katz, J. (2002). PTSD and the experience of pain: Research and clinical implications of shared vulnerability and mutual maintenance models. *Canadian Journal of Psychiatry, 47*, 930–937.

Asmundson, G. J. G., & Taylor, S. (2006). PTSD and chronic pain: Cognitive-behavioral perspectives and practical implications. In G. Young, A. W. Kane, & K. Nicholson (Eds.), *Psychological knowledge in court: PTSD, pain, and TBI* (pp. 225–241). New York: Springer Science+Business Media.

Asmundson, G. J. G., & Wright, K. D. (2004). Biopsychosocial approaches to pain. In T. Hadjistavropoulos & K. D. Craig (Eds.), *Pain: Psychological perspectives* (pp. 35–57). Mahwah, NJ: Erlbaum.

Banic, B., Petersen-Felix, S., Andersen, O. K., Radanov, B. P., Villiger, P. M., Arendt-Nielsen, L., & Curatolo, M. (2004). Evidence for spinal cord hypersensitivity in chronic pain after whiplash injury and in fibromyalgia. *Pain, 107*, 7–15.

Beck, J. G., Gudmundsdottir, B., & Shipherd, J. C. (2003). PTSD and emotional distress symptoms measured after motor vehicle accident: Relationships with pain coping profiles. *Journal of Psychopathology and Behavioral Assessment, 25*, 219–227.

Blanchard, E. B., & Hickling, E. J. (1997). *After the crash: Assessment and treatment of motor vehicle accident survivors*. Washington, DC: American Psychological Association.

Blanchard, E. B., & Hickling, E. J. (2004). *After the crash: Psychological assessment and treatment of survivors of motor vehicle accidents* (2nd ed.). Washington, DC: American Psychological Association.

Bogduk, N. (2004). Diagnostic blocks. *Clinical Journal of Pain, 20*, 409–414.

Brown, R. J. (2004). Psychological mechanisms of medically unexplained symptoms: An integrative conceptual model. *Psychological Bulletin, 130*, 793–812.

Butcher, J. N., Dahlstrom, W. G., Graham, J. R., Tellegen, A., & Kaemmer, B. (1989). *Minnesota Multiphasic Personality Inventory-2 (MMPI-2): Manual for administration and scoring*. Minneapolis, MN: University of Minnesota Press.

Chapman, C. R. (2004). Pain perception, affective mechanisms, and conscious experience. In T. Hadjistavropoulos & K. D. Craig (Eds.), *Pain: Psychological perspectives* (pp. 59–85). Mahwah, NJ: Erlbaum.

Chapman, C. R., & Okifuji, A. (2004). Pain: Basic mechanisms and conscious experience. In R. H. Dworkin & W. S. Breitbart (Eds.), *Psychological aspects of pain: A handbook for health care providers* (pp. 3–27). Seattle, WA: IASP Press.

Coderre, T. J., Mogil, J. S., & Bushnell, M. C. (2003). The biological psychology of pain. In I. B. Weiner (Series Ed.), M. Gallagher, & R. J. Nelson (Vol. Eds.), *Handbook of psychology: Biological psychology* (Vol. 3, pp. 237–268). Hoboken, NJ: Wiley.

Corr, P. J. (2005). Social exclusion and the hierarchical defense system: Comment on MacDonald and Leary (2005). *Psychological Bulletin, 131*, 231–236.

Craig, K. D., & Badali, M. A. (2004). Introduction to the special series on pain deception and malingering. *Clinical Journal of Pain, 20*, 377–382.

Craig, K. D., & Hadjistavropoulos, T. (2004). Psychological perspective on pain: Controversies. In T. Hadjistavropoulos & K. D. Craig (Eds.), *Pain: Psychological perspectives* (pp. 303–326). Mahwah, NJ: Erlbaum.

Craig, R. J. (2005). *Personality-guided forensic psychology*. Washington, DC: American Psychological Association.

Curatolo, M., Arendt-Nielsen, L., & Peterson-Felix, S. (2004). Evidence, mechanisms, and clinical implications of central hypersensitivity in chronic pain after whiplash injury. *Clinical Journal of Pain, 20*, 469–476.

Curatolo, M., Petersen-Felix, S., Arendt-Nielsen, L., Giani, C., Zbinden, A. M., & Radanov, B. P. (2001). Central hypersensitivity in chronic pain after whiplash injury. *Clinical Journal of Pain, 17*, 306–315.

Dersh, J., Polatin, P. B., & Gatchel, R. J. (2002). Chronic pain and psychopathology: Research findings and theoretical considerations. *Psychosomatic Medicine, 64*, 773–386.

Duckworth, M. P., & Iezzi, T. (2005). Chronic pain and posttraumatic stress symptoms in litigating motor vehicle accident victims. *Clinical Journal of Pain, 21*, 251–261.

Eimer, B. N., & Freeman, A. (1998). *Pain management psychotherapy: A practical guide*. New York: Wiley.

Ferrari, R. (2004). The clinical relevance of symptom amplification. *Pain, 107*, 276.

Fishbain, D. A., Cutler, R. B., Rosomoff, H. L., & Rosomoff, R. S. (1999). Chronic pain disability exaggeration/malingering and submaximal effort research. *Clinical Journal of Pain, 15*, 244–274.

Fishbain, D. A., Cutler, R. B., Rosomoff, H. L., & Rosomoff, R. S. (2004). Is there a relationship between nonorganic physical findings (Waddell signs) and secondary gain/malingering? *Clinical Journal of Pain, 20*, 399–408.

Flor, H., & Hermann, C. (2004). Biopsychosocial models of pain. In R. H. Dworkin & W. S. Breitbart (Eds.), *Psychological aspects of pain: A handbook for health care providers* (pp. 47–75). Seattle, WA: IASP Press.

Freidenberg, B. M., Hickling, E. J., Blanchard, E. B., & Malta, L. S. (2006). Posttraumatic Stress Disorder and whiplash after motor vehicle accidents. In G. Young, A. W. Kane, & K. Nicholson (Eds.), *Psychological knowledge in court: PTSD, pain, and TBI* (pp. 215–224). New York: Springer Science+Business Media.

Gallagher, R. M., & Verma, S. (2004). Mood and anxiety disorders in chronic pain. In R. H. Dworkin & W. S. Breitbart (Eds.), *Psychological aspects of pain: A handbook for health care providers* (pp. 139–178). Seattle, WA: IASP Press.

Gatchel, R. J. (1991). Early development of physical and mental deconditioning in painful spinal disorders. In T. G. Mayer, V. Mooney, & R. J. Gatchel (Eds.), *Contemporary conservative care for painful spinal disorders* (pp. 278–289). Philadelphia, PA: Lea & Febiger.

Gatchel, R. J. (1999). Perspectives on pain: A historical overview. In R. J. Gatchel & D. C. Turk (Eds.), *Psychosocial factors in pain: Critical perspectives* (pp. 3–17). New York: Guilford Press.

Gatchel, R. J. (2005). *Clinical essentials of pain management*. Washington, DC: American Psychological Association.

Gatchel, R., & Kishino, N. (2006). The influence of personality characteristics on pain patients: Implications for causality in pain. In G. Young, A. W. Kane, & K. Nicholson (Eds.), *Psychological knowledge in court: PTSD, pain, and TBI* (pp. 149–162). New York: Springer Science+Business Media.

Geisser, M. E. (2004). The influence of coping styles and personality trains on pain. In R. H. Dworkin & W. S. Breitbart (Eds.), *Psychological aspects of pain: A handbook for health care providers* (pp. 521–545). Seattle, WA: IASP Press.

Gheldof, E. L. M., Vinck, J., Vlaeyen, J. W. S., Hidding, A., & Crombez, G. (2005). The differential role of pain, work characteristics and pain-related fear in explaining back pain and sick leave in occupational settings. *Pain, 113*, 71–81.

Giesecke, T., Gracely, R. H., Grant, M. A., Nachemson, A., Petzke, F., & Williams, D. A., & Clauw, D. J. (2004). Evidence of augmented central pain processing in idiopathic chronic low back pain. *Arthritis & Rheumatism, 50*, 613–623.

Guéz, M., Brännström, R., Nyberg, L., Toolanen, G., & Hildingsson, C. (2005). Neuropsychological functioning and MMPI-2 profiles in chronic neck pain: A comparison of whiplash and non-traumatic groups. *Journal of Clinical and Experimental Neuropsychology, 27*, 151–163.

Hanley, M. A., Jensen, M. P., Ehde, D. M., Hoffman, A. J., Patterson, D. R., & Robinson, L. R. (2004). Psychosocial predictors of long-term adjustment to lower-limb amputation and phantom limb pain. *Disability and Rehabilitation, 26*, 882–893.

Hendriks, E. J. M., Scholten-Peeters, G. G. M., van der Windt, A. A. W. M., Neeleman-van der Steen, C. W. M., Oostendorp, R. A. B., & Verhagen, A. P. (2005). Prognostic factors for poor recovery in acute whiplash patients. *Pain, 114*, 408–416.

Hill, M. L., & Craig, K. D. (2004). Detecting deception in facial expressions of pain: Accuracy and training. *Clinical Journal of Pain, 20*, 415–422.

Karp, J. F., Scott, J., Houck, P., Reynolds, C. F., III, Kupfer, D. J., & Frank, E. (2005). Pain predicts longer time of remission during treatment of recurrent depression. *Journal of Clinical Psychiatry, 66*, 591–597.

Kauffman, S. A. (1993). *The origins of order*. New York: Oxford University Press.

Keefe, F. J., Abernethy, A. P., & Campbell, L. C. (2005). Psychological approaches to understanding and treating disease-related pain. *Annual Review of Psychology, 56*, 601–630.

Kerns, R. D., Turk, D. C., & Rudy, T. E. (1985). The Westhaven-Yale Multidimensional Pain Inventory (WHYMPI). *Pain, 23*, 345–356.

Koelbaek Johansen, M., Graven-Nielson, T., Schou Olesen, A., & Arendt-Nielsen, L. (1999). Generalized muscular hyperalgesia in chronic whiplash syndrome. *Pain, 83*, 229–234.

Koyama, T., McHaffie, J. G., Laurienti, P. J., & Coghill, R. C. (2005, September 6). The subjective experience of pain: Where expectations become reality. *Proceedings of the National Academy of Sciences of the United States of America, 102*, 12950–12955.

Lidbeck, J. (2002). Central hyperexcitability in chronic musculoskeletal pain: A conceptual breakthrough with multiple clinical implications. *Pain Research & Management, 7*, 81–92.

Linnell, M., & Easton, S. (2004). The relationship between phobic travel anxiety and the physical symptoms of whiplash injury. *Rehabilitation Psychology, 49*, 317–320.

MacDonald, G., & Leary, M. R. (2005a). Roles of social pain and defense mechanisms in response to social exclusion: Reply to Panksepp (2005) and Corr (2005). *Psychological Bulletin, 131*, 237–240.

MacDonald, G., & Leary, M. R. (2005b). Why does social exclusion hurt? The relationship between social and physical pain. *Psychological Bulletin, 131*, 202–223.

MacGregor, A. J., Andrew, T., Sambrook, P. N., & Spector, T. D. (2004). Structural, psychological, and genetic influences on low back and neck pain: A study of adult female twins. *Arthritis & Rheumatism, 51*, 160–167.

McCracken, L. M. (2005). Social context and acceptance of chronic pain: The role of solicitous and punishing responses. *Pain, 113*, 155–159.

Melzack, R. (1999a). Pain and stress: A new perspective. In R. J. Gatchel & D. C. Turk (Eds.), *Psychosocial factors in pain: Critical perspectives* (pp. 89–106). New York: Guilford Press.

Melzack, R. (1999b). From the gate to the neuromatrix. *Pain, 82* (Suppl. 6), 121–126.

Melzack, R., & Katz, J. (2006). Pain in the 21st century: The neuromatrix and beyond. In G. Young, A. W. Kane, & K. Nicholson (Eds.), *Psychological knowledge in court: PTSD, pain, and TBI* (pp. 129–148). New York: Springer Science+Business Media.

Melzack, R., & Wall, P. D. (1965). Pain mechanisms: A new theory. *Science, 150*, 971–979.

Mendelson, G., & Mendelson, D. (2004). Malingering pain in the medicolegal context. *Clinical Journal of Pain, 20*, 423–432.

Moog, M., Quintner, J., Hall, T., & Zusman, M. (2002). The later whiplash syndrome: A psychophysical study. *European Journal of Pain, 6*, 283–294.

Nicholson, K., & Martelli, M. F. (2004). The problem of pain. *Journal of Head Trauma Rehabilitation, 19*, 2–9.

O'Donnell, M. L., Creamer, M., Bryant, R. A., Schnyder, U., & Shalev, A. (2003). Posttraumatic disorders following injury: An empirical and methodological review. *Clinical Psychology Review, 23*, 587–603.

O'Donnell, M. L., Creamer, M., Bryant, R. A., Schnyder, U., & Shalev, A. (2006). Posttraumatic disorder following injury: Assessment and other methodological considerations. In G. Young, A. W. Kane, & K. Nicholson (Eds.), *Psychological knowledge in court: PTSD, pain, and TBI* (pp. 70–84). New York: Springer Science+Business Media.

Otis, J. D., Keane, T. M., & Kerns, R. D. (2003). An examination of the relationship between chronic pain and Posttraumatic Stress Disorder. *Journal of Rehabilitation Research and Development, 40*, 397–406.

Otis, J. D., Pincus, D., & Keane, T. M. (2006). Comorbid chronic pain and Posttraumatic Stress Disorder across the lifespan: A review of theoretical models. In G. Young, A. W. Kane, & K. Nicholson (Eds.), *Psychological knowledge in court: PTSD, pain, and TBI* (pp. 242–268). New York: Springer Science+Business Media.

Panksepp, J. (2005). Why does separation distress hurt: Comment on MacDonald and Leary (2005). *Psychological Bulletin, 131*, 224–230.

Peters, M. L., Vlaeyen, J. W. S., & Weber, W. E. J. (2005). The joint contribution of physical pathology, pain-related fear and catastrophizing to chronic back pain disability. *Pain, 113*, 45–50.

Pincus, T. (2006). The effect of cognition on pain experience and pain behavior: Diatheses-stress and the causal conundrum. In G. Young, A. W. Kane, & K. Nicholson (Eds.), *Psychological knowledge in court: PTSD, pain, and TBI* (pp. 163–180). New York: Springer Science+Business Media.

Pincus, T., & Morley, S. (2001). Cognitive-processing bias in chronic pain: A review and integration. *Psychological Bulletin, 127*, 599–617.

Ramírez-Maestre, C., Martínez, A. E. L., & Zarazaga, R. E. (2004). Personality characteristics as differential variables of the pain experience. *Journal of Behavioral Medicine, 27*, 147–165.

Richter, M., Ferrari, R., Otte, D., Kuensebeck, H. W., Blauth, M., & Krettek, C. (2004). Correlation of clinical findings, collision parameters, and psychological factors in the outcome of whiplash associated disorders. *Journal of Neurology, Neurosurgery & Psychiatry, 75*, 758–764.

Robinson, M. E., & Dannecker, E. A. (2004). Critical issues in the use of muscle testing for the determination of sincerity of effort. *Clinical Journal of Pain, 20*, 392–398.

Rogers, R., Bagby, R. M., & Dickens, S. E. (1992). *Structured Interview of Reported Symptoms (SIRS) and Professional Manual*. Lutz, FL: Psychological Assessment Resources.

Schultz, I. Z., Crook, J., Meloche, G. R., Berkowitz, J., Milner, R., & Zuberbier, O. A. et al. (2004). Psychosocial factors predictive of occupational low back disability: Towards development of a return-to-work model. *Pain, 107*, 77–85.

Severeijns, R., Vlaeyen, J. W., van den Hout, M. A., & Picavet, H. S. (2004a). Pain catastrophizing is associated with health indices in musculoskeletal pain: A cross-sectional study in the Dutch community. *Health Psychology, 23*, 49–57.

Severeijns, R., Vlaeyen, J. W., van den Hout, M. A., & Picavet, H. S. (2004b). Pain catastrophizing and consequences of musculoskeletal pain: A prospective study in the Dutch community. *The Journal of Pain, 6*, 125–132.

Sharp, T. J. (2004). The prevalence of Posttraumatic Stress Disorder in chronic pain patients. *Current Pain and Headache Reports, 8*, 111–115.

Sharp, T. J., & Harvey, A. G. (2001). Chronic pain and Posttraumatic Stress Disorder: Mutual maintenance? *Clinical Psychology Review, 24*, 857–877.

Sheather Reid, R. B., & Cohen, M. L. (1998). Psychological evidence for a neuropathic component of chronic neck pain. *Pain, 75*, 341–347.

Sherman, F., & Ohrbach, R. (2006). Objective and subjective measurement of pain: Current approaches for forensic applications. In G. Young, A. W. Kane, & K. Nicholson (Eds.), *Psychological knowledge in court: PTSD, pain, and TBI* (pp. 193–211). New York: Springer Science+Business Media.

Singer, T., Seymour, B., O'Doherty, J., Kaube, H., Dolan, R. J., & Frith, C. D. (2004). Empathy for pain involves the affective but not sensory components of pain. *Science, 303*, 1157–1162.

Sterling, M., Jull, G., Vicenzino, B., & Kenardy, J. (2003). Sensory hypersensitivity occurs soon after whiplash injury and is associated with poor recovery. *Pain, 104*, 509–517.

Sterling, M., Jull, G., Vicenzino, B., Kenardy, J., & Darnell, R. (2005). Physical and psychological factors predict outcome following whiplash injury. *Pain, 114*, 141–148.

Sullivan, M. J. L., Lynch, M. E., & Clark, A. J. (2005). Dimensions of catastrophic thinking associated with pain experience and disability in patients with neuropathic pain conditions. *Pain, 113*, 310–315.

Sullivan, M. J. L., Stanish, W., Sullivan, M. E., & Tripp, D. (2002). Differential predictors of pain and disability in patients with whiplash injuries. *Pain Research & Management, 7*, 68–73.

Sullivan, M. (2004). Exaggerated pain behavior: By what standard? *Clinical Journal of Pain, 20*, 433–439.

Turk, D. C. (2003). Chronic pain and whiplash associated disorders: Rehabilitation and secondary prevention. *Pain Research & Management, 8*, 40–43.

Turk, D. C., & Melzack, R. (Eds.). (2001). *Handbook of pain assessment.* New York: Guilford Press.

Turk, D. C., Monarch, E. S., & Williams, A. D. (2004). Assessment of chronic pain sufferers. In T. Hadjistavropoulos & K. D. Craig (Eds.), *Pain: Psychological perspectives* (pp. 209–243). Mahwah, NJ: Erlbaum.

Turk, D. C., & Okifuji, A. (2003). Pain management. In I. B. Weiner (Series Ed.), A. M. Nezu, C. M. Nezu, & P. A. Geller (Vol. Eds.), *Handbook of psychology: Health psychology* (Vol. 9, pp. 293–315). Hoboken, NJ: Wiley.

von Korff, M., Crane, P., Lane, M., Miglioretti, D. L., Simon, G., Saunders, K., Stang, P., Brandenburg, N., & Kessler, R. (2005). Chronic spinal pain and physical-mental comorbidity in the United States; Results from the national comorbidity survey replication. *Pain, 113*, 331–339.

Wager, T. D., Rilling, J. K., Smith, E. E., Sokolik, A., Casey, K. L., Davidson, R. J., Kosslyn, S. M., Rose, R. M., & Cohen, J. D. (2004). Placebo-induced changes in fMRI in the anticipation and experience of pain. *Science, 303*, 1162–1167.

Waters, S. J., Keefe, F. J., & Strauman, T. J. (2004). Self-discrepancy in chronic low back pain: Relation to pain, depression, psychological distress. *Journal of Pain Symptom Management, 27*, 251–259.

Watkins, L. R., & Maier, S. F. (2003). When good pain turns bad. *Current Directions in Psychological Science, 12*, 232–236.

Young, G. (2006). *Pain assessment complement kit: Four proposed pain assessment instruments.* Presented internally at York University, Toronto, May 8.

Young, G., & Chapman, C. R. (2006). Chronic pain and affect as a nonlinear dynamical system. In G. Young, A. W. Kane, & K. Nicholson (Eds.), *Psychological knowledge in court: PTSD, pain, and TBI* (pp. 181–192). New York: Springer Science+Business Media.

Zasler, N. D., Martelli, M. F., & Nicholson, K. (2005). Chronic pain. In J. M. Silver, T. W. McAllister, & S. C. Yudofsky (Eds.), *Textbook of traumatic brain injury* (pp. 419–436). Arlington, VA: American Psychiatric.

7

Multicausal Perspectives on Psychological Injury III: Conclusions

GERALD YOUNG

In the previous two chapters, I have reviewed recent literature in the three predominant areas of psychological injury presented in the book—Posttraumatic Stress Disorder (PTSD), chronic pain, and mild Traumatic Brain Injury (mTBI). Now I proceed to the conclusions about the review, describing an integrative model.

Integrative Biopsychosocial Model of PTSD, Chronic Pain, and mTBI

Preamble

Ogloff (2002) insists that psychology must develop a theoretical foundation in its work in the legal area, and that the search to understand causal relationships in this regard is cardinal. "Only by applying psychological theory to the law in an attempt to explain causal relationships between the law and human behavior will we be able to advocate valid legal reforms, and to finally have a meaningful impact on the law" (p. 20). The statement is directed to work on sexual harassment, in particular, and to jurisprudence, in general, but applies quite well to the subject matter of the current book.

In this chapter, I attempt to build an integrative model of causality in psychological injury, for PTSD, chronic pain, and mTBI. Typically, psychologists are trained to adopt a multifactorial perspective concerning causality, for example, through models such as the biopsychosocial one. However, the adversarial nature of the court system channels professional opinion toward simplistic, linear, unidimensional, and absolute answers to the complex questions of psychological causality, instead of toward a more integrative, biopsychosocial approach. In order to arrive at fair outcomes in its deliberations about psychological injury cases and tort claims, both the court and mental health professionals offering evidence to it need a firm database derived from scientific research on the neurobiological and psychological mechanisms of the three conditions under review, on the one hand, and a more precise model of how the mechanisms lead to disorders involving the three areas, on the other hand. In addition, research should be undertaken to help specify long-term impairments, disabilities, and functional incapacities that derive from the three conditions. Moreover, a metamodel that englobes all three areas would help, making it easier to explain to the court the causality process when conditions related to these areas are involved.

Assumptions

Suls and Rothman (2004) describe well the biopsychosocial model for court purposes. They indicate that the biological, the psychological, and the social (along with macro variables, such as culture, SES, and ethnicity), are integrally involved in physical illness, and are interactive. They are nested and connected as subsystems. They are multiple, multilevel, and multivariate. They are reciprocal, feedback-linked, and correlated. They cascade in complex, systemic effects over time. Schultz, Joy, Cook, and Fraser (2005) and Schultz and Gatchel (2005a, 2005b, 2005c) describe the biopsychosocial model as hierarchical, dynamic, interactive, and integrated. It is about the whole person, and the impaired individual should be encouraged to be an active participant in managing her/his difficulties. Individuals bring to the mix their perceptions of the injury or event, and their cognitions about the recovery or lack of recovery, as well as their preinjury or preevent status, vulnerabilities, and risks.

In the following, I attempt to parse this general description of the biopsychosocial model into its basic tenets.

(a) All behavioral and psychological phenomena are considered multidetermined or complexly determined; that is, multiple sources interact to causally influence behavior. Causation rarely is linear (A causes B); more than likely, a set of factors consisting of variables related to the past (e.g., vulnerabilities), present (e.g., a traumatic event, a closed head injury), and future (e.g., interrupted goals) coalesce synergistically to facilitate psychological symptom initiation, exacerbation, maintenance, and stabilization.

(b) Psychologists recognize the intimate connection between mind and body. Although the separation of the physical and the psychological is a common heuristic, it does not take into account their essential unity.

(c) Psychologists recognize the superordinate system governing mind and body, that influencing only one part of the system toward the better may not be enough to have a positive effect. For example, psychologists recognize that after trauma, attempts at rehabilitating one problem area (reported pain) should be accompanied by attempts to address the others involved (e.g., psychosocial factors).

(d) Thus, in their assessments of individuals, psychologists take account of both biomedical and psychological influences, being wary of simplistic mind-body dualism or reductionism to a disease model. The disease model especially seeks physical causes for illness, such as from trauma, pathogenesis, and organ degeneration, minimizing a role for psychological factors.

(e) The predominant model of psychopathology is an interactive one, in which a predisposition, possibly biological, acts in conjunction with a stressor, such as pain due to a motor vehicle accident (MVA), to trigger a cascade leading to a psychological disorder (diathesis/stress model; Roeckelein, 1998; Zuckerman, 1999).

(f) In establishing the origins of an individual's psychological condition or psychopathology, psychologists are keenly aware of the influence of context. Context varies from the immediate stimulus environment to more general structures, such as work, school, culture, and society (Corsini, 2002).

(g) Behavior is a function of a person by situation interaction. Individuals do not express their long-present traits in the same way in all circumstances; rather, they express them with conditional variation (e.g., the extrovert often knows when to be more controlled).

(h) The person varies in dimensions related to personality, motivation, intellectual and social resources, coping mechanisms, perceptions/schemas/cognitions/beliefs, and so forth. Psychology is as much about individual differences as group commonalities.

(i) Together, the person's individual differences characterize her/his psychological resiliency and her/his coping skills vs. her/his vulnerability and risk, which varies with particular context. In general, people have less resistance to external stresses when their vulnerabilities/risks are accentuated.

Christopher (2004) modified the biopsychosocial label, referring to the "bio-psycho-sociocultural evolutionary perspective." This label captures the ecological aspect of the person's environment as well as the evolutionary history of our species. For the model to address the cascading physical and psychological effects of events such as accidents, it also can be described as dynamic. There is also the developmental history of the person. Considering all these suggestions, a better term for the model may be the "*biopersonalsocial* model." This terminology embraces the person as the active site of integration of the influencing variables derived from biology and the environment. Nevertheless, the term "biopsychosocial" has gained widespread currency, and it is kept in the present work for heuristic purposes.

Integrative Model

Figure 7.1 provides an integrative biopsychosocial model of causality applicable to the three major areas of psychological injury—PTSD, chronic pain, and mTBI. The figure specifies how preexisting, peritraumatic, and postevent stressors may affect the individual's ongoing adaptation in daily life, leading to possible psychological deterioration and poor functional outcome through effects on the body, brain, behavior, cognition, and emotions. Moreover, it takes into account complicating and confounding factors that may influence the expression of psychological effects after injury, including possible malingering. The model emphasizes that the individual is an important mediator in determining the outcome of any impacting event, through factors such as coping mechanisms, perception of the event, personality, and motivation.

(A) Event and associated stressors

Content: Pre- ⇄ Peri- ⇄ Post-event and stressors

Process: Perception of event and stressors

(B) Acts on lifespan system

Content:
- –Risk factors
- –Developmental stage or level
- –Ongoing ecological adaptation and ecological alteration in daily life (Equilibrium)
- –Adaptation to family, work, school, institutions, neighbourhood, community
- –Health

Process:

Bio ⇄	Psycho ⇄	Social
Genetic	Individual Differences	Environment
Physiological	Personal Attributes	Experience
Organic	Organismic	Significant Others
Chromosomes	Coping	Culture
Innate/Prepared	Personality	Place
Evolutionary	Self/Ego	Ecology/Niche
Hereditary	Hope/Optimism	History/Political Influences
Maturational	Motivation	Context/Milieu
Nature	Need/Desire	Nurture

(C) Areas vulnerable in psychological status/functional outcome/functionality

Content:
- –Body–Brain–Injury–Pain–Trauma
- –Behavior–Actions–Activity–Life roles–Quality of life
- –Emotions–Affect–Feelings–Mood–Self-Regulation
- –Cognition–Thinking–Alertness–Mind–Reason
- –Complicating/Confounding factors–Symptom Exaggeration/Minimization–Malingering

Process: Integrative ⇄ (Dis)equilibrium ⇄ Disintegrative

FIGURE 7.1. Biopsychosocial model of multifactorial causality

For PTSD, chronic pain, and mTBI, there may be common underlying physiological mechanisms and not separate ones. Moreover, Bigler (2003) argues that these three conditions share much in common. I emphasize that an important common factor in psychological injury relates to stress mechanisms. Integrative models across the three conditions may facilitate better research and help dispel some of the controversies and issues in the field. Science needs to lead the way at the population level, so that forensic and related psychological assessment at the individual level includes its findings.

Stress and the Model

In the model being proposed, stress provides the glue that coheres the common mechanisms underlying the three areas of psychological injury under study, those of PTSD, chronic pain, and mTBI. All of these conditions dysregulate the stress system, serving to exacerbate the initial presenting symptoms in the acute stage. Young and Yehuda (2006) described that the typical stress reaction involved increases cortisol production. Initially, cortisol is released in the stress response, and serves an adaptive function, for example, facilitating the fight or flight response. However, in a chronic state, cortisol release is maladaptive and destructive. Similarly, if cortisol is underproduced initially, as in many cases of PTSD, this is equally maladaptive because the regular feedback cycles in which it is involved in order to control its overproduction is not activated. Note that the typical cortisol inhibition that takes place in PTSD does not apply to all individuals with this disorder. Physiological research is showing that a little under half of PTSD patients do not express the responses of the majority of PTSD patients on various physiological measures (Orr, McNally, Rosen, & Shalev, 2004).

Young and Yehuda (2006) explore the effects of initial underproduction of cortisol in trauma, for example, due to preexisting stressors. Normally, cortisol inhibits its own release through negative feedback at various levels of the neuroendocrine system, especially the pituitary gland and the hypothalamus. Therefore, in PTSD, when there is lower production of cortisol, it may disrupt or delay the process of recovering physiologically from stress, by failing to inhibit the activation of the HPA axis (hypothalamic-pituitary-adrenal axis). In the next step, CRF (corticotrophin releasing factor) production is stimulated, in concert with other neuropeptides, resulting in increased ACTH (adrenocorticotrophin hormone). As the vicious cycle continues, this may further stimulate the sympathetic nervous system, in general. Moreover, individuals manifesting relatively low levels of circulating cortisol may experience longer norepinephrine availability at synapses both peripherally and centrally, because glucocorticoids act to inhibit the release of norepinephrine from sympathetic system nerve terminals. This exacerbates neurohormonal cascade effects that may accompany PTSD. The presence of pretrauma variables, which are often found, represents a complicating factor in this cascade effect of trauma on physiological functioning. For example, not only may the adaptive negative feedback on continued production of cortisol at the beginning of the stress cycle be inhibited by cumulative stress but, also, in an exacerbation of the risk represented by the PTSD reaction itself to trauma, there may be enhanced negative feedback inhibition contributing to dysregulated ACTH and cortisol suppression.

Melzack (1999) described the complicated interactions of pain and stress serving to exacerbate and maintain chronic pain, a process that may even lead to destruction of healthy tissue when there is runaway cortisol production occasioned in the chronic stress response. Selye (1950, 1951) had described the General Adaptation Syndrome to stress in terms of acute, chronic, and exhaustive stages, with the latter facilitating disease. Stress involves homeostatic disruption of sensitive physiological systems, such as blood sugar level, thereby activating programs aimed at reinstating homeostasis. When injury occurs, the stress system participates in homeostatic regulatory attempts. Inflammatory-mediating cytokines are released within seconds, and penetrate the hypothalamus, activating the HPA axis; leading to CRF, ACTH, and cortisol release, as per above. In the acute stage, cortisol participates in a negative feedback loop, as described, and the system returns to homeostasis. However, when stress is chronic—and we should appreciate that pain is considered a stressor—cortisol secretion continues at dysregulatory levels, and the HPA system does not stabilize. Moreover, a second channel of stress-generated physiological reactivity is set in motion. The LC-NE (locus coeruleus-norepinephrine, or noradrenaline) sympathetic system in the brainstem is activated. Both systems interact with a wide range of CNS and stress-related mechanisms, such as in the opioid system, the limbic system, and cortical systems. The immune system is suppressed, facilitating concomitant disease-processes.

The processes involved in the pain-perception and stress systems demonstrate that the systems possess overlapping mechanisms, or regions and pathways. Given that glucose is important for the stress system's fight or flight response, "cortisol is potentially a highly destructive substance because, to ensure a high level of glucose, it breaks down the protein in muscle and ... may produce destruction of muscle, bone, and neural tissue and produce the conditions for many kinds of chronic pain" (Melzack, 1999, p. 92). For example, the sites of strain, sprain, or spasm could become the focus of cortisol-mediated muscle destruction. Melzack concludes that, "[I]t is possible that stress alone can become a cause of chronic pain" (p. 101).

Chapman and colleagues arrive at similar conclusions about the overlap of processes and mechanisms of pain and stress (Chapman & Gavrin, 1999; Chapman & Okifuji, 2004). They emphasize that "chronic nociception may cause a sustained, maladaptive stress response" in chronic pain patients (Chapman & Okifuji, 2004, p. 18). Thus, the emotions associated with persistent pain may contribute "heavily" to resultant disability.

Flor and Hermann (2004) present a biopsychosocial model of pain in which stress plays a prominent role. "Predisposing" factors may include physiological variables as well as prior trauma and social learning experiences. "Eliciting" stimuli may include pain-related stimuli or "other stressors" with negative interpretations, such as family conflict and work pressures. These can activate the sympathetic nervous system, muscle tension, or "other nociception-inducing processes," triggering pain experience and pain behaviors. Elicited responses may reflect an inadequate, maladaptive coping and cognitive repertoire, further inducing, exacerbating, or maintaining pain experience. "Maintaining" processes involve learning and the development of "powerful *pain memories* at all levels of the nervous system. Over time, such memories can maintain pain in the absence of peripheral nociceptive input" (p. 49), supported by central sensitization processes, in particular. Uncontrollable stressors in chronic pain patients play a "major" role in their pain. Moreover, pain can develop unrelated to trauma, in overreaction to stressful stimulation, and as vicious circles.

Dworkin and colleagues (Dworkin & Banks, 1999; Poleshuck & Dworkin, 2004) further emphasize that stress can serve as an important risk factor and enhancer in the development of chronic pain. In their model, psychosocial stress, defined in terms of life events and social supports in the months preceding and at the time of injury or illness, either helps protect against or facilitates the development of chronic pain, in conjunction with other factors.

The literature review that we have undertaken in the prior two chapters clearly points out regions of the brain common to two or more of pain perception, stress, PTSD, and socioemotions. These include the amygdala, portions of the frontal lobe, portions of the parietal lobe, the hippocampus, the thalamus, the anterior cingulate cortical area (ACC), and the limbic system. When systems such as the opioid and immune systems are factored in, we see that much of the CNS, the sympathetic nervous system, and the neurohumoral system share a wide-ranging common biological substrate to both biological and psychological insults to the organism.

Pain may be stimulated even by stress alone, or by social rejection without injury, or by its anticipation, as we have seen. This illustrates the biopsychosocial nature of pain. In terms of PTSD, the same applies; this disorder is without physical injury yet may still mimic many of the gamut of psychological symptoms that accompany chronic pain, including bodily related ones. Additionally, for mTBI, it may be initiated by physical forces but, if the postconcussive symptoms persist, the best explanation may be that the original pathophysiological effects have dissipated and psychological factors account for the persistence involved. For example, the stress engendered by a traumatic event may account for long-term headaches associated with mTBI more than any alleged neuropathophysiological residua. Note that in situations where purely psychological factors are considered the perpetuating factors of persistence of symptoms following an mTBI rather than the original pathophysiological neuronal impacts, the symptoms may not be any less impairing, chronic, or disabling, if Melzack's analysis applies here, as well, and there is nothing to suspect that it does not.

Finally, the continued presence of symptoms after a trauma may not relate uniquely to peritraumatic and posttraumatic factors. We need to keep in mind that preevent stressors may account in part or in full for the stress variables impinging on the psychological injury victim, accounting in part or in full for the continuation of posttraumatic stress, pain, and postconcussive symptoms into chronicity. Of course, confounds, such as malingering and other threats to validity, may be involved, as well.

Conclusions

To conclude, the biopsychosocial model provides a powerful means of explaining the persistent nature of different types of psychological injury. However, the model lends itself to understanding any of these injury types as products of preevent factors as well as event and postevent ones. We consider causality multifactorial not only in terms of its various components, such as the biological, the psychological, and the social but, also, in terms of preevent, event, and postevent time periods. Indeed, the prudent forensic assessor will consider chronicity of psychological injury possibly in terms of preevent factors alone. In this regard, the American Surgeon General's Report (U.S. Department of Health and Human Services, 1999) indicated, after a literature review (e.g., Kessler, Sonnega, Bromet, Hughes, & Nelson, 1995), that the one-year prevalence rate of "mental illness" for both adults and children is about 20%. For adults, if one examines mental illness and substance abuse together, the percentage rises to about 30%. Kessler et al. (2005) confirmed these figures in their National Comorbidity Survey, using interviews as recent as 2003. If one considers lifetime prevalence, the rate is significantly higher, although exact estimates are difficult to obtain when they involve years well into the past.

McLean, Clauw, Abelson, and Liberzon (2005) have presented a biopsychosocial model of symptomology after trauma that is very similar to ours. In the development of comorbid chronic pain and psychological conditions, such as PTSD (e.g., after MVAs), as sequelae of motor vehicle accidents, they argue for an important common role of centrally controlled stress response systems. In an expanded biopsychosocial model in their figure 1, they show that injury and pain after a traumatic event activate the acute stress response system (increasing CRF, LC-NE, and cortisol activation). Depending on the individual's resilience, and her/his coping mechanisms, genetics, previous life history, sociocultural experience, and vulnerabilities, the activation of the stress system may become exaggerated, producing biochemical dysregulation and aberrant pain and emotional processing. In addition, descending pain modulation pathways facilitate hypersensitivity, and the limbic, paralimbic, and prefrontal regions function maladaptively. Stress response system dysregulation interacts with cognitive-behavioral-emotional factors, including pain-related fear, avoidance, inactivity, disuse, and withdrawal, in amplified reverberations that become self-sustaining. The authors suggest that psychopharmacological interventions that modulate initial injury and pain-related acute stress responses (e.g., propanolol, hydrocortisone), may act to inhibit the development of chronic pain and related stress conditions. In comparison to their model, among other things, my comparable biopsychosocial model includes mention of TBI, and that we need to consider confounds, such as possible malingering, in assessing the persistence of symptoms in psychological injury.

Research begins with observation, model-building, and empirical exploration, with occasional paradigmatic shifts that present relatively novel perspectives so that the cycle of careful data gathering and theoretical refinement can begin anew, with each such step serving to increasingly reduce uncertainty in the field involved. In the case of the currently proposed integrated biopsychosocial model across the three areas of PTSD, chronic pain, and mTBI, and its relation to stress, the field may be ready to expand and move toward such a paradigm shift, helping psychological assessors and the court in their evaluations and deliberations.

References

Bigler, E. D. (2003). Neurobiology and neuropathology underlie the neuropsychological deficits associated with traumatic brain injury. *Archives of Clinical Neuropsychology, 18*, 595–621.

Chapman, C. R., & Gavrin, J. (1999). Suffering the contributions of persisting pain. *Lancet, 353*, 2233–2237.

Chapman, C. R., & Okifuji, A. (2004). Pain: Basic mechanisms and conscious experience. In R. H. Dworkin & W. S. Breitbart (Eds.), *Psychological aspects of pain: A handbook for health care providers* (pp. 3–27). Seattle, WA: IASP Press.

Christopher, M. (2004). A broader view of trauma: A biopsychosocial-evolutionary view of the role of the traumatic stress response in the emergence of pathology and/or growth. *Clinical Psychology Review, 24*, 75–98.

Corsini, R. J. (2002). *The dictionary of psychology*. New York: Brunner-Routledge.

Dworkin, R. H., & Banks, S. M. (1999). A vulnerability-diathesis-stress model of chronic pain: Herpes zoster and the development of postherpetic neuralgia. In R. J. Gatchel & D. C. Turk (Eds.), *Psychosocial factors in pain: Critical perspectives* (pp. 247–269). New York: Guilford Press.

Flor, H., & Hermann, C. (2004). Biopsychosocial models of pain. In R. H. Dworkin & W. S. Breitbart (Eds.), *Psychological aspects of pain: A handbook for health care providers* (pp. 47–75). Seattle, WA: IASP Press.

Kessler, R. C., Demler, O., Frank, R. G., Olfson, M., Pincus, H. A., Walters, E. E., Wang, P., Wells, K. B., & Zaslavsky, A. M. (2005). Prevalence and treatment of mental disorders, from 1990 to 2003. *The New England Journal of Medicine, 352*, 2515–2523.

Kessler, R. C., Sonnega, A., Bromet, E., Hughes, M., & Nelson, C. B. (1995). Posttraumatic Stress Disorder in the national comorbidity survey. *Archives of General Psychiatry, 52*, 1048–1060.

McLean, S. A., Clauw, D. J., Abelson, J. L., & Liberzon, I. (2005). The development of persistent pain and psychological morbidity after motor vehicle collision: Integrating the potential role of stress response systems into a biopsychosocial model. *Psychosomatic Medicine, 67*, 783–790.

Melzack, R. (1999). Pain and stress: A new perspective. In R. J. Gatchel & D. C. Turk (Eds.), *Psychosocial factors in pain: Critical perspectives* (pp. 89–106). New York: Guilford Press.

Ogloff, J. R. P. (Ed.). (2002). Two steps forward and one step back: The laws and psychology movement(s) in the 20th century. In J. R. P. Ogloff (Ed.), *Taking psychology and law into the Twenty-First Century* (pp. 1–33). New York: Kluwer/Plenum.

Orr, S. C., McNally, R. J., Rosen, G. M., & Shalev, A.Y. (2004). Psychophysiologic reactivity: Implications for conceptualizing PTSD. In G. M. Rosen (Ed.), *Posttraumatic Stress Disorder: Issues and controversies* (pp. 101–126). Chichester, UK: Wiley.

Poleshuck, E. L., & Dworkin, R. H. (2004). Risk factors for chronic pain in patients with acute pain and their implications for prevention. In R. H. Dworkin & W. S. Breitbart (Eds.), *Psychological aspects of pain: A handbook for health care providers* (pp. 589–606). Seattle, WA: IASP Press.

Roeckelein, J. E. (1998). *Dictionary of theories, laws, and concepts in psychology*. London: Greenwood Press.

Schultz, I. Z., & Gatchel, R. J. (Eds.). (2005a). *Handbook of complex occupational disability claims: Early risk identification, intervention, and prevention*. New York: Springer Science+Business Media.

Schultz, I. Z., & Gatchel, R. J. (2005b). Introduction. In I. Z. Schultz & R. J. Gatchel (Eds.), *Handbook of complex occupational disability claims: Early risk identification, intervention, and prevention* (pp. 1–3). New York: Springer Science+Business Media.

Schultz, I. Z., & Gatchel, R. J. (2005c). Research and practice directions in risk for disability prediction and early intervention. In I. Z. Schultz & R. J. Gatchel (Eds.),

Handbook of complex occupational disability claims: Early risk identification, intervention, and prevention (pp. 523–539). New York: Springer Science+Business Media.

Schultz, I. Z., Joy, P. W., Crook, J., & Fraser, K. (2005). Models of diagnosis and rehabilitation in musculoskeletal pain-related occupational disability. In I. Z. Schultz & R. J. Gatchel (Eds.), *Handbook of complex occupational disability claims: Early risk identification, intervention, and prevention* (pp. 43–65). New York: Springer Science+Business Media. (Reprinted from *Journal of Occupational Rehabilitation, 10*, 271–293, 2001.)

Selye, H. (1950). *Stress*. Montreal: Acta Medical Publisher.

Selye, H. (1951). The general adaptation syndrome and the gastrointestinal diseases of adaptation. *American Journal of Proctology, 2*, 167–184; *303*, 1157–1162.

Suls, J., & Rothman, A. (2004). Evolution of the biopsychosocial model: Prospects and challenges for health psychology. *Health Psychology, 23*, 119–125.

U.S. Department of Health and Human Services. (1999). *Mental Health: A Report of the Surgeon General—Executive Summary*. Rockville, MD: U.S. Department of Health and Human Services, Substance Abuse and Mental Health Services Administration, Center for Mental Health Services, National Institutes of Health, National Institute of Mental Health.

Young, G., & Yehuda, R. (2006). Understanding PTSD: Implications for court. In G. Young, A. W. Kane, & K. Nicholson (Eds.), *Psychological knowledge in court: PTSD, pain, and TBI* (pp. 55–69). New York: Springer Science+Business Media.

Zuckerman, M. (1999). *Vulnerability to psychopathology: A biosocial model*. Washington, DC: American Psychological Association.

8

Pain, Affect, Nonlinear Dynamical Systems, and Chronic Pain: Bringing Order to Disorder

GERALD YOUNG AND C. RICHARD CHAPMAN

In this chapter, we offer a nonlinear dynamical systems perspective on the development of chronic pain (see also Young and Chapman, 2006). We incorporate the simpler understanding of systems, as "the whole being greater than the sum of the parts," into contemporary systems theory. We consider systems theory both in terms of its original expression as chaos theory and more advanced versions related to complexity theory. By framing chronic pain within the perspective of nonlinear dynamical systems theory, a transdisciplinary model, some phenomena that are difficult to explain in terms of other models become more transparent, revealing the multifactorial nature of pain. We grant that nonlinear dynamical systems theory is not easy to understand in its details, although systems theory in general has an intuitive appeal. Therefore, theorists, assessors, and practitioners alike need to study and integrate this approach into their work with chronic pain patients. Moreover, the model is consistent with the theme of this book, and with forensic psychology, in general, because it provides a multicausal understanding of chronic pain. Williams and Arrigo (2002) have applied chaos and complexity theory to forensic psychology, examining areas such as dangerousness and its prediction, civil commitment, and the right to refuse mental health treatment. However, the work does not address specific conditions such as chronic pain.

For an introduction to nonlinear dynamical systems theory, chaos theory, related models, and their application in psychology, see Abraham and Gilgen (1995), Boom (2004), Freeman (1995a), Gleick (1987), Guastello (1995), Heath (2000), Howe and Lewis (2005), Lewis and Granic (2000), Masterpasqua and Perna (1997), Robertson and Combs (1995), Thelen and Smith (1994), Vallacher, Read, and Nowak (2002), and Ward (2002). For an introduction to complexity theory, see Kauffman (1990, 1991, 1993) and Lansing (2003). Also, refer to Livneh and Parker (2005) on the application of catastrophe theory, chaos theory, and complexity theory to the issue of psychosocial adaptation to disability. For the application of nonlinear dynamical systems to other relevant areas of psychology, refer to Granic and Patterson (2006) with respect to antisocial development and Fredrickson and Losada (2005) with respect to positive psychology. Although these authors refer to the concept of attractors, like us, they do not apply the concept directly to "illness attractors" and "pain attractors," in contrast to ourselves. Zautra, Johnson, and Davis (2005) present a dynamical model of affect and chronic pain, but without nonlinear elements.

We examine the dynamical quality of pain from two time frames. First, we present a model indicating that ongoing pain experience at any one moment of time is constructed from the multifactorial interaction of the components in the system from which pain experience emerges. This happens continuously throughout the course of pain experience. Second, we explore long-term patterns in chronic pain.

We introduce a five-stage model in the development of chronic pain from the acute stage, based on the work of Gatchel (2005), who proposed a three-step model. Gatchel (2005) has shown how the development of chronic pain is entwined with emotional factors. We relate the transition points in our five-step model to different nonlinear dynamical system configurations.

Witkiewitz, Marlatt, and colleagues (Hufford, Witkiewitz, Shields, Kodya, & Caruso, 2003; Witkiewitz & Marlatt, 2004) provide a similar perspective on the need to consider both ongoing and long-term patterns in health behavior. Specifically, they present a "dynamic" model of relapse and of relapse prevention for alcohol and other drug problems. The model interdigitates tonic and phasic processes. Tonic processes concern chronic vulnerabilities to relapse. Phasic processes are constituted by situational cognitive, emotional, and physical states, as well as coping skill use. Phasic responses stand at the "cusp," or catastrophic turning point, and can either lead to sudden relapse or effective coping. Clients need to learn to assess continually their own relapse vulnerability or, as Witkiewitz and Marlatt (2004) state, in terms of Kauffman's (1990) complexity theory, clients must tune into the ever evolving complexity of the internal world that they use to guide themselves in their interaction with the external world.

Francis (1995) examined psychophysiological self-regulation from the perspective of chaos theory. He described health and illness attractors, referring to chronic pain and stress-related disorders, in particular. As his chapter proceeded, he did not elaborate on his brief mention of chronic pain, considering only the general condition of illness. His approach is different from ours, for he did not refer to complexity theory, and he did not distinguish between the moment-to-moment construction of patterns in a system and its long-term trajectory. Nevertheless, because of its historical importance, at appropriate junctures, we review Francis's application of chaos theory to health and illness.

The nonlinear dynamical systems model of pain that we develop is consistent with contemporary views of pain, such as the biopsychosocial model of pain (Gatchel, 2005; Turk & Monarch, 2002; Young, Kane, & Nicholson, 2006). The biopsychosocial model describes that sensory, cognitive, affective, and behavioral factors interact in generating pain experience. The dynamical model of pain presented in this chapter also is consistent with the gate control and neuromatrix models of pain (Melzack & Wall, 1965; Melzack & Katz, 2006). We present a figure that illustrates the relationship among these theories.

In the second part of the chapter, we address an issue raised by Melzack and Katz, who imply that the next version of the *DSM (Diagnostic and Statistical Manual of Mental Disorders, DSM-IV* and *DSM-IV-TR*; American Psychiatric Association, 1994, 2000), should evaluate whether chronic Pain Disorder should be included in its catalogue of mental disorders. In response, we suggest that, perhaps, a category such as "Chronic Pain Complications Disorder" may be appropriate to include as a disorder in the *DSM*.

A key topic in our chapter concerns the relationship between pain and affect, and we explore the relationship between the two from a dynamical perspective. In addition, we suggest that Posttraumatic Stress Disorder (PTSD) and pain often cooccur because they may form a superordinate system.

Acute and Chronic Pain

Pain and Affect. Pain and affect are intimately related, and negative affect and pain may mutually coexist and worsen each other, in vicious circles. It is important to understand how this plays out in the individual case, because such understanding can lead to more effective pain management and can help protect against the progression from acute pain to chronic pain. Moreover, concepts in the systems perspective facilitate understanding pain as multifactorial, functioning simultaneously at many physical, psychological, and social levels and, moreover, these concepts provide perspectives on how to understand some puzzling phenomena in individuals experiencing pain.

Until the twentieth century and the advent of sensory neurophysiology, scholars regarded pain as an emotion rather than a sensory process. Aristotle, for example, described pain as a "passion of the soul." Scholars prior to the twentieth century recognized that emotions are complex experiential and behavioral states of the person, involving both physiological arousal and heightened cognition. After decades of focusing narrowly on the sensory mechanisms of pain in the twentieth century, science is now moving toward an integration of sensory mechanisms with the mechanisms of emotional states. Studies of pain involving functional brain imaging (Porro, 2003) provide compelling evidence that the experience of pain is intrinsically emotional by demonstrating activity in multiple limbic structures in response to sensory signals of tissue damage (nociception).

Although pain can be considered like an emotion in its own right, it always occurs against a background of preexisting affect that can amplify or dampen its intensity or shape its meaning. An injury or a flare of chronic disease occurring against a background of negative feelings and thoughts is likely to involve more anguish than a similar injury or flare occurring against a background of positive feelings and thoughts.

Research. The relationship between pain and emotions has received extensive attention (Robinson & Riley, 1999), in part, because pain appears to have a bi-directional causal relationship with negative affective states. People with chronic pain tend to manifest more negative affect and negative cognition. Severely depressed patients (Ward, Bloom, & Friedel, 1979) and individuals with a tendency to experience anger (Burns, Bruehl, & Caceres, 2004) tend to have more severe acute and chronic pain compared to others. Moreover, somatic anxiety is higher in chronic pain patients than in controls (Fishbain, Turner, Rosomoff, & Rosomoff, 2001), and state, or reactive, anxiety predicts pain in older patients (Feeney, 2004). Pain exists comorbidly with depression, anxiety, anger, and PTSD (Krueger, Tackett, & Markon, 2004; Von Korff et al., 2005). The causal mechanisms that link pain with negative affective states are a puzzle that has attracted hypotheses at multiple levels of scientific inquiry, from molecular mechanisms to personality theory. Although the conceptual basis for understanding the exact relationship between pain and affect is still incompletely elaborated, a reliable cooccurrence of pain and negative affective states clearly exists in multiple contexts.

Acute vs. Chronic Pain. Pain control remains a significant problem in medicine, in part, because acute pain and chronic pain differ, and require different management strategies. Acute pain occurs in response to the tissue damage, injury, or disease onset. It resolves with tissue healing. Although intense negative emotion may accompany it, depending on its meaning for the patient and the extent of the arousal that the nociceptive messaging elicits, acute pain can have important diagnostic value for the clinician.

Physicians diagnosing patients who present with pain often wish to brush aside the patient's emotions in order to get at the sensory message underneath, because this may inform about possible physical pathology. This is a continuing dilemma for emergency medicine physicians. A middle-aged man presenting with chest pain in an emergency department may have suffered a heart attack or, more simply, he may have pain secondary to hyperventilation syndrome caused by anxiety. In the next room, an anxious woman with a history of cancer may present with a severe headache that may be more physically based, or the woman may be having a stress-related migraine headache. In such cases, the affective states associated with acute pain can complicate medical evaluation.

When pain is chronic, the physician faces a different situation. Chronic pain is that which persists indefinitely after healing of an injury or recovery from disease, or pain that accompanies a nonhealing pathological process, such as arthritis, other degenerative changes, or nerve damage. From a diagnostic perspective, the pain is pervasive and persistent, and the patient presenting with it wants better relief or relief from a flare-up or exacerbation. The aversiveness of the chronic pain and hence, an increase in pain expression, may accelerate in response to: economic, social, interpersonal, or family stresses; or personal loss and grief, or with exacerbations of various cooccurring disorders such as depression or anger, or with physical disease that increases pro-inflammatory cytokines. In such cases, brushing aside the affective state of the patient to get at the information in the sensory message of tissue damage can be counterproductive. The affective aspect of pain, and its reciprocal causal relationship with other negative affects, should be a key focus in effective chronic pain management.

A common dilemma of managing pain in everyday medicine involves discerning whether a patient is presenting with acute or chronic pain. People with chronic pain also develop acute pains and, in such cases, the chronic pain is yet another negative emotional feature of the background affective state of the patient that shapes how she or he experiences the acute pain. However, it is sometimes hard to determine when an acute pain has progressed to become a chronic pain. Tendon injuries, for example, take many months to heal. Finally, chronic progressing diseases can generate acute pains in the presence of a chronic pain. For example, a cancer patient with long-standing chronic pain from an aggressive surgery to remove a tumor may develop painful bone metastasis as the disease progresses. This much seems clear—chronic pain management is not about caring for injured or diseased tissues that are generating unpleasant neural signals. Rather, it is about caring for the whole person, including at the affective level.

Steps in Acute Pain. Examination of the physiology of emotions suggests that the affective dimension of pain involves two stages (Chapman, 2004). First, there is a hypervigilant response to injury, subjectively akin to threat. However, once the afferent messages of tissue damage reach higher centers, efferent messages from the hypothalamus, amygdala, and other limbic structures together activate the autonomic nervous system. In turn, this alters cardiac function, respiratory rate, muscle tension, trembling, and visceral activity. Awareness of the altered, aroused bodily state creates a strong negative subjective experience. Damasio (1994) has argued that when autonomic nervous system activation alters bodily states, this creates "somatic markers" or images. These markers represent the threat that brought on the changes. As bodily states, such markers are subject to the influence of associations, cognitions, and emotions. Nociception can also elicit a sickness response, because it directly or indirectly increases the production of pro-inflammatory cytokines (Watkins & Maier, 2005; Weiseler-Frank, Maier, & Watkins, 2005). These substances produce a sickness experience that typically involves fatigue, malaise, dysphoria, general myalgia, and social withdrawal (Vollmer-Conna et al., 2004).

In reaction to nociception, the body expresses a highly organized protective response—the defense response (Chapman, 2004). This involves stress-related systems, such as the autonomic nervous system, the hypothalamic-pituitary-adrenocortical (HPA) axis, and the immune system, which together act directly and indirectly to generate negative feelings in subjective awareness. Pain patients report poor sleep, lessened appetite, fatigue, poor concentration, and general myalgia. These changes impair function and contribute to the chronicity of the pain, accounting for its persistent, debilitating nature. Acute pain may progress to chronic pain largely through the affective dimension (Chapman, 2004), by way of the physiological sympathetic reactions accompanying it, or psychological learning mechanisms, or both. The evaluation of, and intervention for, chronic pain should incorporate rather than work around the affective dimension.

Pain typically begins with nociception, but in some chronic pain conditions, such as phantom limb pain and poststroke pain, a patient may experience pain in the absence of nociceptive input (See Melzack & Katz, 2006). When nociception is present, there is often a poor correspondence between the severity of a wound or pathological condition and the intensity of the pain, as reflected in the subjective report. This occurs, on the one hand, because physiological processes modulate nociception at various levels of the neuraxis, and, on the other hand, because emotional and cognitive states contribute heavily to the pain experience at the level of the brain. A linear computational sequence of events linking tissue damage to pain does not provide a good description of how pain occurs in response to injury. We submit that pain is an inherently nonlinear, dynamic, and emergent property of the brain, for which nociception is normally necessary but not sufficient.

Gatchel's Stage Model in the Development of Chronic Pain

Gatchel (1991, 1996, 2005) presents a stage model of how acute pain can develop into chronic pain. Gatchel has shown how the development of chronic pain is entwined with emotional factors. In the first phase of acute pain, normal affective distress reactions develop, such as worry, anxiety, and fear. Physical deconditioning compounds the problem. By about 2 to 4 months, in the second phase, behavioral and psychological difficulties exacerbate. For example, the patient develops depression, demoralization, learned helplessness, anger, frustration, distrust, and various psychological disorders, compounded by legal and related issues, such as a sense of entitlement. Preexisting personality, psychosocial, and social and economic issues often influence the degree of the exacerbation. Somatization and symptom exaggeration, or symptom magnification, may develop. The ongoing stress of attempting to cope with the pain may exacerbate predisposing characteristics. In the transition to chronic pain, physical processes play a role; the pain is not "psychogenic" or "all in the head." In stage 3, the pain becomes chronic, creating additional stress. Complex physical, psychological, and social processes are involved. The patient adopts a pain-focused lifestyle, takes on a sick role, and avoids responsibility.

Gatchel has presented an important model of the evolution in pain condition experienced by patients. However, the middle stage of transition is described as a gradual one, and later in our chapter we propose a five-stage model of the development of chronic pain, which includes three transition steps rather than one.

Toward A Dynamical Model of Chronic Pain

Chapman and colleagues (Chapman, 2004; Chapman, Nakamura, & Flores, 1999) have suggested a nonlinear dynamical systems approach to chronic pain, viewing it as an emergent, constructed, conscious experience. In this chapter, we undertake further elaboration of nonlinear dynamical systems theory in terms of attractors and complexity, helping to explicate further the reciprocal causal processes linking pain with other affective states. We introduce the concept of systems, and how systems emerge on a moment-to-moment basis. Later on, we examine patterns of change in system states over time, especially when this process is dynamical and nonlinear.

Systems. A system can be defined as a set or network of related elements or component processes, together with their relationships or linkages, which are liable to change over time. When collections are not systems, there elements may be independent and have an infinite range of ways of combining. In contrast, the elements of systems are interrelated, interdependent, and interactive, producing patterned forms the whole of which is greater than the sum of the parts. In addition, an element of any system cannot be fully understood without reference to the whole. Changing one element of a system, or adding or subtracting an element, risks changing the whole. At the same time, the whole constitutes a global, "top-down" influence that acts to maintain stability in systems when they are perturbed by local, "bottom-up" factors. Systems may exhibit tension, transition, or turbulent alternation between stability and instability, integration and disintegration, evolution and dissolution, and so on. But even if a system enters a transitional turbulent phase, the new form it takes may be quite stable, and resistant to change, until the next round of tension transpires within its organization.

Dynamical systems constitute a variant of the general concept of a system, because they can autonomously generate form and complexity and, if they are nonlinear, their emergent form is discontinuous, abrupt, quite distinct from the preceding one, and so on. Even quite minor inputs can effect disproportionate change in a system, as in the so-called "butterfly effect," where sensitivity to initial conditions can produce marked effects in a system trajectory or pathway of successive forms or states.

Levels. A complete picture of a system includes context-related interactions, and contexts vary in level and complexity. Moreover, an important feature of systems is that simpler systems nest within more complex systems. Systems function at several hierarchically arranged strata, which interact mutually or reciprocally and, moreover, there may be subsystems involved. When a system changes its pattern, configuration, or state, all the levels and subsystems are affected, and this happens simultaneously, not linearly or sequentially, because systems function as wholes and change as wholes. Thus, a child belongs to a family system that is nested within a larger social system and, in another example, within the developing human, there are multiple systems ranging from psychological states to processes within the single cell. These different levels of a system interact with each other.

Primary changes in systems especially occur at lower levels, through interactions of elements. These interactions are termed "coupling," or "cooperativity" across the elements. In systems, lower-order interactions often are termed "bottom-up"; they act to produce higher-level reorganization, which then influences lower levels by "top-down" processes (Granic & Patterson, 2006). Over time, the same constraining effect can be seen—as lower-order, real-time, or moment-to-moment interactions lead to system reorganization, the system develops particular overall patterns that constrain it. Another way of describing this canalization is that, over time, macro time processes, as opposed to micro time ones, "compress" the system, and it loses "degrees of freedom." In any system, habitual modes created in system landscapes function like rivulets of water running downhill that etch deeper, and, therefore, more predictable streams or pathways. When cascades of real-time microchanges take place, for example, through reciprocal, recursive, and interconnected element interactions, the effect of each successive outcome of the cascade process is to limit the range of change possible at the macropattern level. Ultimately, the system experiences loss of possibility, rigidity, and flexibility.

Self-Organization. System dynamics constitute natural organizational processes with efficient, graceful, flexible, and adaptive characteristics. They possess self-organizational properties, both within and across levels, that is, systems reorganize without preprogrammed patterns of organization. New forms or system states assemble out of the matrix of ongoing system interactions, without external or internal instruction. The presence of preprogrammed patterns would prove inefficient for systems, because they need flexibility for optimal functional adaptation to all possible contextual configurations in which the systems might become embedded. Therefore, fixing all the necessary programs within such systems before the systems deploy would require too many such fixed patterns. Systems function most flexibility when they can self-organize online in context.

Emergence. The capability for self-organization is essential for optimal adaptation and emergence. Self-organization allows the spontaneous emergence of coherent patterns and order in a system from the nonlinear interactions of component parts, within the contexts in which it must adapt. When a whole has a property not predictable from the sum of the parts, the new feature is an emergent property. Therefore, emergence is the self-organization of patterns with new properties not predictable uniquely from the local interactions of the system elements from which they arise. For example, mixing hydrogen and oxygen gases at room temperature will produce liquidity (water), an emergent property not predictable from the properties of the parts. In another example, subjective awareness, including somatic awareness, appears to be an emergent property of brain activity. Therefore, it is considered dynamic, changing, multiple in origin, sensitive to context, and independent of preprogrammed modules. Such processes can be multidirectional, involve feedback cycles, and they respond to changes in other, related systems.

States. Self-organization activity produces the states of systems, which are sometimes called phases or phase spaces. States may reflect patterns that had been configured previously out of the array of elements constituting a system, or they may be new patterns that emerge because they are the most adaptive in context, given the ongoing adaptive efforts of the system. Nevertheless, the ensemble of constituent elements and the typical contexts that they inhabit constrain systems, and they have self-preserving, self-correcting, or self-righting, auto-equilibrating internal forces that tend to conserve existing state patterns or states. Therefore, a system often has a limited number of possible states, so that when impinged upon by powerful external forces, or perhaps even when there are miniscule impacts when the system is poised for change, such as with the so-called "butterfly effect," the system may tend to jump abruptly from one state to another. Normally, a system resists change in response to perturbations, especially if these are minor, thus preserving stability, and yet it will spring abruptly into another state when the pressures can no longer be resisted. For example, the states of water and ice alternate at the critical temperature threshold of zero centigrade, but do not do so immediately when the threshold is attained.

Perturbations. Typically, the state-shift jumps that we have been describing, often called phase transitions, or bifurcations, occur in response to some perturbation, or trigger. Perturbations act on complete system organization over system elements, rather than on isolated parts of systems. Perturbations influence systems when they move critical variables beyond thresholds of change, although the thresholds can vary with context. The trigger can be tiny, as in the "butterfly effect," if it sufficiently approaches parameters of change. A familiar example is the response of the body, largely through the immune system, to invasion by the influenza virus. Thus, the person encountering the influenza virus undergoes a phase transition from a healthy state to a disease-resisting or eventually a sick state in response to immunological and pathogen-induced changes. A parallel example relates to the response of the body to tissue damage or wounds, which, at first, elicits the changes associated with acute pain and, then, if the changes become chronic in impact, they may elicit a phase transition from acute pain to chronic pain.

Energy. Systems are considered "open" when they permit energy to enter and potentially galvanize change. Normally, systems exist in equilibrium with the contextual energy about them and in the inflow and outflow of that energy, as they transform incoming energy into increasing self-organized patterns, and manage its dissipation and disordering potential. Although we find many examples related to the inflow and outflow of energy, *per se*, in human systems, according to many adherents of nonlinear dynamical of systems theory, often, at the psychological level, the equivalent of energy flow as the driving force behind self-organizational system dynamics is information flow. In psychology, often, information replaces energy as system energizer. In this regard, Livneh and Parker (2005, p. 20) characterize an open system as one involving the exchange of "energy, material, and information" with the immediate context.

Far from Equilibrium. Humans are complex systems existing "far from equilibrium"; they self-organize, or incorporate incoming energy into complex states far from the equilibrium and system complexity that may otherwise be expected. However, they need continual energy entering their open system in order for their complex self-organization to be maintained. Humans draw in the energy, use it in system workings, lose some, and exchange some, in a dissipative process that needs renewal. For example, locomotion in the toddler is an energetic activity that needs energetic fuel to continue in the short term and improve in the long term. As new states emerge or coalesce from the confluence of system interactions, they need continual energy to avoid regression, loss of transitional gains, and increase in system disorder.

Dynamical Systems in More Depth: Attractors and Complexity

In this section, we articulate a more formal presentation of dynamical systems, keeping it as simple as possible. First, we redefine the concepts of systems and self-organization in dynamical terms, and then introduce the concept of attractors.

Systems. Nonlinear dynamical systems are systems that continuously move toward equilibrium, and they transition naturally between equilibrium points through environmental adaptation and self-organization. Whereas conventional systems are static and have predetermined features, such as preconfigured thresholds of change in critical elements or variables, called "control parameters," which result in preconfigured order, nonlinear dynamical systems are continually evolving and adapting, with control and order changing, emerging out of the properties of the interaction of the system with its context; control does not lie in inflexible, or prefigured, central command, but in flexible, contextual sensitivity (Thelen & Smith, 1994; Waldrop, 1992). Consequently, nonlinear dynamical systems models are useful for describing very complex phenomena that are exquisitely responsive to context, yet attempt to preserve equilibrium in the face of change until the patterns reconfigure when pushed to the "cusp of change," such as in the cases of weather, economies, cultures, and psychological states. In a telling example, Freeman (1995a) asserted that human brains function like complex nonlinear dynamical systems that exist in relationships of continuous adaptation to not only to the external environment but also, to the bodies that they inhabit and to other brains.

A system is comprised of a set of connected variables that interact and change over time. In a dynamical system, the system's present state among its variables is influenced by the system's prior state. If the dynamical system is deterministic, its present state is completely dependent on the prior state. If it is linear, a combination of linear equations can specify all dependence. In a nonlinear dynamical system, linear equations cannot account adequately for its dependence. Stochastic systems have a random term added to their equations (Boom, 2004). Despite their primacy in understanding systems, the mathematical underpinning to systems theory lies beyond the scope of the present chapter (see Appendix 1).

Iteration and Feedback. Williams and Arrigo (2002) indicate that nonlinear dynamical systems have a propensity to behave as a feedback loop, recursively and repetitively self-reinforcing interactions. A system can express either negative or positive feedback (Granic & Patterson, 2006). In the latter, system element interactions amplify certain variations, leading to system change. In the former, change is damped through preservation of existing element linkages, and minimization of new variation, perpetuating stability. In positive feedback, cascades of change may develop as each new variation feeds into system restructuration, propulsing the system toward increasing overall reorganization, to the point of creating instability and novel overall structure.

Self-Organization. For Thelen and Smith (1994), systems are constrained by their organization, and they arrive at their manifest states through self-organization rather than through fixed control mechanisms, either internal to the system or external to it. By self-organization, systems "compress" into lower "dimensional" dynamics, thereby increasing their "degrees of freedom," or optimizing their flexibility to adapt to new contextual demands. Schore (2000) underscores that nonlinear dynamical systems use energy to facilitate the development of emergent forms through self-organization. When systems are open to energy flow and use, they "incorporate" the energy into themselves, facilitating movement away from equilibrium, toward conditions "far from equilibrium," where discontinuous change even to minor perturbations is possible. Given the right conditions, slow or minor change in a variable can lead to abrupt emergence of new discontinuous patterns within the system without external planning or prespecification. Systems stabilize in equilibrium, destabilize, and restabilize through self-organization and reorganization.

Attractors. When system dynamics that describe the movement of a system in its multiple state spaces repeatedly end at the same place in the system's trajectories, the system can be described as characterized by attractors that have gravitated to attractor basins in its state space. Imagine a child's ball rolling into a ditch and going up and down the sides until it stops moving. The trajectory of the ball on the sides of the ditch may serve as a metaphor for the repeated differing trajectories of a system's path as it moves in its basin and eventually settles into an attractor state, in this case of no movement at the bottom of the ditch, or zero velocity, and at equilibrium.

Attractors govern a system when the system almost always gravitates over time to certain fixed values, or to an oscillation among several values, irrespective of its initial value and later perturbations. Mathematical models can represent the movement of systems in state space. This movement refers to the manner in which the data generated by the system's movement can be graphed in time. Attractors, then, are mathematical structures that describe certain classes of motion of objects in space. Mathematically, an attractor exists within a phase space or vector field that has a neighborhood in which every point stays nearby and approaches the attractor as time goes to infinity, except under certain conditions. The graph of a system's trajectories in the neighborhoods or basins of one or more attractors is called its phase portrait.

An attractor is like a magnet or center of gravity in mathematical space, for it pulls the system toward it from many different layouts in its state space, even when perturbed. Therefore, attractors constitute stabilities in system behavior. More simply, an attractor represents a point in phase space in which the system settles down, and ceases to change, at least momentarily. When a system settles into an attractor, with its stable properties, the system has entered a stable state.

Living systems are typically multistable, with several coexisting attractors (Granic & Patterson, 2006). As young infants develop their leg movement skills, the data suggest that they function from an initial attractor state of repetitions of springlike, alternating flexions and extensions (Thelen & Smith, 1994). But the system is "soft-assembled," or prone to instability as other elements in the motor system are acquired in development, allowing system exploration of more complex attractors corresponding to walking. This example suggests that rigid attractor system stability is not adaptive in the long term. Attractors are always stable, at least in the short term, reaching equilibrium. However, inherent in any system pattern or organization are the seeds of renewed, more complex self-reorganization, as additional energy, information, acquisitions, or contextual demands impact the system. In general, attractors assemble out of the elements in a system as adaptive configurations, and contain attributes that lend themselves to potential evolution to different configurations that are further adaptive to the system. Moreover, in the process of reaching equilibrium, the system may cycle between different poles. As we shall see, pain patients may alternate between poles involved in health and sickness. Nevertheless, their ongoing system structure may be preparatory to discontinuous change, such as when individuals improve in therapy.

Attractor Types. There are several kinds of attractors in terms of mathematical description. For example, in point or fixed attractors, the system gravitates to a steady state or a constant value after perturbation, as when a pendulum returns to its resting point after perturbation (Abraham, 1995; Francis, 1995; Williams & Arrigo, 2002). In cyclical or periodic attractors, the system gravitates periodically between two different locations in its state space, as in the movement of a pendulum. Another type of attractor integrates two oscillatory ones, taking a torus or donut shape in trajectory pattern; think of a loosened pendulum that moves forward and back as well as to the sides. It is well known that one class of attractors are called "chaotic" or "strange," but it needs to be pointed out that chaotic attractors are not chaotic in the common meaning of the word. Rather, when seen globally, they are ordered structures; mathematically, they are ordered data pattern generators in state space. However, at another level, chaotic attractors are not ordered; if graphed over time, it can be seen that the states of the system never return exactly to the same particular pathways, so they are considered aperiodic or locally unpredictable. So what to make of the chaos of chaotic attractors? We must keep in mind that the plot of their trajectory defines relatively clear pattern, so that it is considered globally determined and predictable and, in this sense, chaotic attractors are ordered and are not "chaotic" in the traditional sense. Kauffman (1993) suggests that, therefore, chaotic attractors are "anti-chaotic." Even though chaotic attractors are comprised of trajectories that do not repeat themselves, giving them an apparently unpredictable or chaotic attribute in terms of system behavior, at the mathematical level, even if stochastic, chaotic attractors are reflected by simple deterministic equations, usually coupled in one way or another (Guastello, 1995; Boom, 2004; see Appendix 1).

Chaos and Change. Even if stable at the global level in the mathematical sense, at the behavioral level, a chaotic attractor, in its dynamical sense, is a state configuration far from equilibrium that lends itself to further state space exploration through the tension it shares with genuinely disordered elements in its system organization. Thus, we can characterize a chaotic attractor as "a deliberately disordered state from which order springs" (Freeman, 1995b, p. 28). Chaotic attractors, then, may reach a threshold of change, and gravitate to new system patterns. This inherent potential for change within chaotic attractors is facilitated by its "sensitivity to initial conditions," meaning that the system's dynamic configuration of its elements plays an important role as the ongoing system responds to perturbations over time, even in terms of the apparently minor details of its initial organization. Nevertheless, once nonlinear transformation in a far-from-equilibrium system takes place because of its sensitivity, initially or otherwise, the attractor finds and functions in equilibrium. To repeat, at the global level of a system's dynamics, in terms of an attractor's mathematical operation, one finds stability. In contrast, within the attractor, instability is characteristic through the unpredictability of individual trajectories of the system's movements, which never exactly repeat themselves, and which are even liable to abrupt change for seemingly minor perturbations.

In chaotic system organization, then, we encounter a quasi-stable state with simultaneous stable and unstable elements that may be susceptible to abrupt change in state if its counterbalancing stabilizing components are not resilient enough to disruptive perturbations. Minor fluctuations or perturbations normally do not produce major amplifications in a system if the system is buttressed by adequate stabilizing components. However, change manifests when a system is unbalanced toward instability, especially when it is quite unstable, that is, when it does not inherently de-amplify perturbations, or when it becomes governed by destabilizing attributes or rules.

Bifurcation. Bifurcation points mark system pathway splits or transformations (Guastello, 1995). They are "critical junctions of instability" within a system's operating space, deriving from a system's quantitative movement from instability through a crisis point in a shift toward stability, where the system emerges with new forms different from the original (Livneh & Parker, 2005, p. 20). Bifurcation points are governed at crisis or threshold points by critical values in "control parameters," which are variables that, when at bifurcation points, influence system behavior toward splitting. Attractors may diverge noticeably after splitting, or the resultant attractors, more simply, may alter form.

Control parameters may change due to system behavior, and as with any element of a system, they are responsive components to the configuration of the whole and its subsystems and levels. [Nevertheless, there are limits in this regard; think of the transition from water to ice, and vice versa, where the system's internal control parameter is quite fixed, corresponding to the external temperature of zero degrees centigrade.]

Bifurcations may mark instabilities in system dynamics, but they are part of the process of system reconfiguration toward increasing adaptation. After a critical point is reached in a system dynamic, and transformation occurs, the system regains stability, albeit in different ways from the stable state beforehand (Williams & Arrigo, 2002, p. 63). In another way of looking at it, because living systems generally take in energy, information, and so on, relative to what is given out, bifurcations and resultant multi-attractor configurations help living systems reduce the ever increasing energetic and informational entropy in the system to manageable proportions. Through attractor splitting, each of the smaller resultant topologies has lower entropy. In attractor formation, system splitting may accelerate exponentially, in a bifurcation cascade, or a runaway process of "period doubling," before stability is reattained (Williams & Arrigo, 2002).

Fractals. Fractals represent an interesting serial or multiple bifurcation patterning across different levels of a system. Structural similarity or equivalent shape is evident across multiple levels of magnification or scale of a system (Livneh & Parker, 2005, p. 21). There is self-similarity in pattern of geometric form over different strata of the system, yet they vary immensely in mathematical scale. Mathematical scale differs across levels in terms of fractional equivalents or dimensional complexity, rendering the patterns similar across the levels. As an example of a fractal, with self-similarity at different levels, from the microscopic to the macroscopic, think of the form of a bay on a map and the equivalent pattern of the shore as it laps at one's feet at the beach. Williams and Arrigo (2002) point out that fractals represent iterations that build not on themselves but "off of" themselves. As a system branches within, to smaller regions, only to repeat its basic pattern, it has more room for growth, complexity, stability, and adaptation. Because the iteration can be endless, there is unlimited local freedom in system dynamics despite a limiting global order, as the iterative pattern is repeated at increasingly lower levels.

Complexity. Kauffman (1993) has formulated an extension of nonlinear dynamical systems theory that addresses how systems change. Complex systems lie at the interface of cyclic or periodic and chaotic attractors (Kauffman, 1993; Lansing, 2003). As systems self-organize, when conditions are right, they gravitate to increasingly complex regimes, or system reorganization. Chaotic attractors provide the system the ground for advance in system organization in terms of complexity, especially when they compete with organization that is less complex, such as with cyclical attractors.

Living systems are characterized by multi-attractor assemblies (Granic & Patterson, 2006). Complex multi-attractor assemblies can be considered a special case of complexity organization, as the integrated system accommodating them takes on its own adaptive quality. In this sense, integrated complex systems are referred to as "Complex Adaptive Systems." In our conceptualization, we reserve this term exclusively to the processes involved in the formation of integrated, multiple attractor assemblies, avoiding its use when referring to complexly organized systems, in general. Perhaps, we need to distinguish between different degrees of complexity of Complex Adaptive Systems.

Kauffman considered the study of complex systems as the study of "anti-chaos," "because it is concerned with the spontaneous appearance of order in dynamical systems" (Lansing, 2003, p. 192). Complexity theory emphasizes the way systems inherently self-organize toward more complexly ordered structures in order to maximize adaptation. Nonetheless, each new complex structure manifests simplicity in its order relative to the organization of the structures from which it derives. In certain conditions, systems may tend toward disorder, for example, to more fragmented, less stable states. However, instead of tending to disorder, when energy or information is available, incorporated, and used, the natural tendency of systems is to gravitate to more systemized, complex states. In terms of psychological states, normally this would refer to an increasing organizational complexity in information processing, allowing a freeing up of resources for further informational processing and organizational improvement.

As mentioned, complexity processes lead to the emergence of more general behavioral examples of Complex Adaptive Systems, Lansing (2003) gives the example of the terraced water irrigation systems across villages created by the Balinese, a complex system that emerged spontaneously because it facilitated adaptation, taking place without a preordained master plan. Global control of terrace ecology emerged from the actions of local actors balancing constraints in context.

Systems may stand at the "cusp of change," or remain poised at the transition or boundary between stability and instability. In fact, systems may seek out this dynamic region between constancy and self-organized change, because being in this region facilitates movement toward changes involving increasing complexity, which normally maximizes adaptation. In other words, systems may live on "the edge of chaos" (or at the edge of order-disorder), because systems living on cusps of possible change increase the probability of undergoing change to increased complexity, which is normally beneficial.

To conclude, systems gravitate to regions in their state space where movement toward increasing order and complexity is facilitated. However, there can also be movement toward instability and disorder. In terms of system organization, not all system change toward increased complexity is psychologically adaptive; for example, there are many examples of degenerating system organization in the case of human behavior and its organization, *qua* organization. Furthermore, behavioral systems may become increasingly complex from the point of view of system organization, *qua* organization, stabilizing at a self-organized higher-order level but, from the point of view of psychological adaptation, there may be entrenchment in maladaptive disorder.

Steps in the Evolution of Complexity. In effect, complexity theory describes a two-phase process of complex system formation. First, systems tend to hover on the edge of order and disorder on the cusp of change, because stability alone can lead to a loss of flexibility. Second, when contextual factors are optimal, the system self-organizes toward more complex forms. This happens through local rather than global processes of contextual adaptation, bottom-up rather than top-down but, nevertheless, with top-down, holistic, self-organizational processes at play. The process typically described in adaptive change toward increasing complexity is a two-phase one. However, it is possible that the phases in a system's evolution toward increasing complexity involve processes more complex than a dual, state space transition to Complex Adaptive Systems, given that long-term processes are involved and different orders of complexity may obtain, as mentioned above. In this regard, I proceed to describe a four-step transition to integrated Complex Adaptive Systems.

Systems may manifest evolving and dissolving attractor patterns over time (Thelen & Smith, 1994), a concept that appears related to Abraham's (1995) "dynamic schemes," or changing system behavior. Movement through system state space is dynamical. Before a system can gravitate to a region between order and disorder, it may have already produced ordered and/or chaotic attractor formations, and these, in turn, may have passed through less organized system configurations, such as cyclical attractors. In this respect, system change at any given moment builds on preceding system change patterns.

In complexity theory, dynamic schemes are usually progressive, are self-organized, and tend to move toward increased system complexity. The transition of attractors at the edge of chaos, and from there to Complex Adaptive Systems, suggests a powerful model of change processes in system behavior, involving multiple steps. Such change can originate from several earlier, less complex configurations in the system's behavior, such as the presence of cyclical attractors, or even less complex attractors.

The pattern of system change evident in typical progress toward Complex Adaptive Systems suggests the following four-stage model. With adequate energy input and use, systems may inherently self-organize to traverse through the processes of (a) cyclic attractors, (b) chaotic attractors, (c) gravitating to the region between order and disorder, or the cusp of change, and (d) Complex Adaptive Systems. There are many possible dynamic schemes, and this suggested four-step model may self-organize especially under optimal conditions, facilitating increasing system complexity and adaptability. Similar models may involve the insertion of a torus attractor before the chaotic one, and/or dual/multiple, but not yet integrated, attractors after it. Note that in terms of the concept of fractals, there may be iterative repetitions of evolution of complexity at different levels of a system, within nested systems, or within different subsystems, so that multiple repetitions of complexity formation processes may be taking place within an overall system. (We return to this four-step model of nonlinear dynamical system evolution when we discuss the stages in the development of chronic pain.)

Illness and Health Attractors

The concept of attractors can facilitate our understanding of human behavior and its change over time. System behavior changes in mathematically specifiable ways, and for nonlinear dynamical systems, aspects of its behavior seem to be chaotic and unpredictable. However, concepts within dynamical systems theory, such as the attractor concepts, can stimulate new ways of looking at the behavior of living systems, helping to understand that although system behavior may appear unpredictable, to the contrary, it may be governed by increasingly self-organized, complex, and adaptive configurations.

In this regard, according to Francis (1995), a cyclical attractor can represent acute illness, with health and illness behavior as the two regions involved in the dual state space of concern. Additionally, Francis speculates that chaotic attractors potentially can represent improvement in patients with chronic illness. He contends that especially with appropriate therapy, chronically ill individuals may follow trajectories into unpredictable behavior, or challenges to growth, bringing the illness system beyond the threshold of change, allowing the possibility of healthier ways of living to emerge.

In Francis' work, we see that he applied the concept of attractors to the constructive evolution in health behavior from an illness lifestyle to a more adaptive one, at a higher level of integration through therapy. In the following, we see that the concept of attractors can also be used to represent a system tending toward instability rather than stability.

Gottman (1991) has described negative family dynamics in terms of attractors. Systems have energy balance points, which are fixed if they are regulated or unfixed if they are chaotic. In family systems, the energy ratio is defined by anabolic (energy conserving, restoring) emotions (e.g., affection) and catabolic (energy expending) emotions (e.g., anger). According to the empirical research, the threshold for distinguishing regulated families and unregulated, chaotic families obeys a mathematical ratio, which is about 4 to 1 in favor of anabolic, positive emotions. The presence of chronic family inability to resolve conflicts in a manner that promotes family cohesion can lead to runaway negativity in family emotions. Translated into the language of systems theory, the family, then, becomes governed by an attractor with movement toward zero seconds between negative episodes. Every disagreement may be the catalyst leading to chaotic instability, decreased predictability, and increased variance in the system, and even to family dissolution.

Gottman's work suggests that a maladaptive behavioral system functions like an attractor, gravitating to an entrenched basin, or collection of trajectory pathways in its state space, even though the qualitative nature of the attractor is negative rather than positive. That is, systems, in general, may evolve to increased complexity without regard to their underlying constructive or destructive quality. Therefore, a chronically dysfunctional behavioral system may end up governed by an attractor with poor adaptive psychological flexibility, where escape from trajectories of negative behavior that it reflects is not possible. In this regard, although the system may evidence stable far-from-equilibrium properties, nevertheless, from a psychological perspective, they constitute qualitatively maladaptive characteristics.

Application of Dynamical Concepts to Moment-to-Moment Pain, Affect, and Networks

In the following, we explore how pain experience both at the ongoing, moment-to-moment level and at the longer term, chronic level over time, can be explained in terms of nonlinear dynamic systems theory. We describe the ongoing construction of pain experience in more general terms, and then proceed to describe chronic pain in specific terms related to chaotic attractors and complexity theory.

Moment-to-Moment Dynamic Pain. Pain can change rapidly, being continually constructed in a self-organized fashion. It is emergent, or assembled *de novo*, out of the array of complex physical, emotional, and cognitive components at any one moment in consciousness, in patterns the form of which cannot be predicted from knowledge of the parts. Like all systems, the system in which pain is involved is susceptible to change at any moment, especially if it is quasi-stable or unstable in state. Pain always reflects the ongoing behavior of its home system, and the influence of past states, but it is always constructed anew on a moment by moment basis. By using the term "construction," we are not referring to social construction; that is, we are not saying that pain is a social convention, or the like. Instead, pain is conceived as a biopsychosocial product of a dynamic system that constructs pain only in the sense that patterns emerge from the system at each moment. Similarly, Freeman (1995a) suggests that the brain constructs awareness, moment by moment, in its continuous adaptation to the surrounding environment, the body it inhabits, and the brains of others around it. Pain is the potentially ever-changing pattern that emerges over time in the interactions of the system from which it emanates. In the pain system, as in any system, patterns may constantly reassemble, and reform in response to changing conditions.

The system governing pain may appear stable despite its ever-changing construction of pain experience, because the nature of the ensembles that continually emerge out of the confluence of its components may be relatively invariant. In terms of systems dynamics, systems may continually provide the same economical, emergent solution or graceful, ongoing accommodation to its interacting elements. An example from memory research illustrates this concept (McNally, 2003). Contemporary models of memory emphasize that autobiographical memory is a reconstructive process, because the brain does not store memories of every personal event, idea, and so on, that emerges in the course of the day; in terms of memory, the brain does not operate like a videorecorder. Rather, the research indicates that "[r]ecollection entails reassembly of encoded elements of experience that are distributed throughout the brain" (McNally, 2003, p. 77). This obtains because, otherwise, the brain would be quickly overwhelmed in its storage capacity. Autobiographical memories, then, are dynamically constructed when the cognitive system needs to generate them, and their ongoing form is subject to the individual's experiences after their initial formation up until the time of their current reconstruction. Like pain, memories are not static, and many factors shape each reconstruction.

Moment-to-Moment Dynamic Affect. We have contended that pain has a dynamic quality and, in terms of one theme of the chapter, this dynamic aspect of pain applies to the relationship of pain and affect. Pain becomes affective, not mechanically in response to tissue damage, but as part of the multiple, distributed-processing dynamically configured in its expression. Lower-order nociception has no primacy in pain despite its intimate link to tissue damage, because all parts of the system contribute to pain experience, so that higher-order affect is equally important. Pain is a perturbation of an ongoing equilibrium in a balanced system of ongoing adaptive behavior, induced by associated nociception, response to tissue damage, negative subjective feelings, disruption of ongoing activity, negative thoughts, variable response of significant others, and so on. In a systems view, pain experience is always more than affect, but at the same time pain can never exist apart from affect.

Emotions and physiological disruption occasioned by pain stand in intricate interdependence, and are not separate in a mind-body dualism. Therefore, even simple emotional arousal can exacerbate pain states, for example, contributing to musculoskeletal pain. At the same time, the impact of pain on function, the internal representation of the threat involved, and the meaning of pain for the individual can amplify the magnitude of the negative emotional component of pain. Finally, the visceral changes brought on by nociception dynamically contribute to the construction of emotional states, because any sensory feature, generated either externally or internally, is processed in a parallel, distributed manner throughout the central networks constructing the corporal-affective-cognitive matrix involved in pain experience.

Moment-to-Moment Dynamic Neuronal Networks. The dynamical framework helps underscore that pain experience is a product of multiple nervous system components that involve much of the body and brain in a unified construction, where affect, stress, motivation, and cognition are intimately intertwined with tissue damage, nociception, and sensitization. These components do not combine additively but, rather, do so synergistically. Moreover, the neuronal activity derived from sensory information, memory schemas, and ongoing representations of the world at the affective, cognitive, and behavioral levels, which together cohere into pain experience, is not necessarily stable. At any given moment, neuronal activity patterns are subject to reassembly; the currently active pattern competes with secondary, possible patterns, and the predominant pattern can be changed. For example, neuronal networks underlying pain experience may alter to reflect its reduction when an individual stops catastrophizing and engages in a relaxation or distraction technique. Or the networks may dynamically alter in self-organizational response to new system elements. In this regard, increased pain perception may develop in response to information that a short-term, pain-related disability has led to a permanent job loss. These examples demonstrate that the neuronal networks underlying the integrated pain experience are processes undergoing continuous and active reconstruction, modeling, and reformation, depending on changes in sensory information, affect, stress, motivation, cognition, and context. Moreover, the changes may be more orderly, progressive, flexible, and adaptive, or more disordered, regressive, inflexible, and maladaptive, depending on the past history and the present context.

Two Views of Chronic Pain from a Nonlinear Dynamical Systems Perspective

We are now ready to consider how nonlinear dynamical system modeling can account for chronic pain. So far, we have concentrated on the moment-to-moment construction of pain from the confluence of system elements interacting at any one time. However, in the chronic pain patient, the course of pain experience follows a trajectory much like those described by nonlinear dynamical systems models. In the ensuing sections, we consider both the chaotic branch of nonlinear dynamic system modeling and the more recent complexity system view as ways to account for chronic pain. Chronic pain, according to nonlinear dynamical systems theory, appears to stabilize around an attractor of pain but, also, the system appears unstable, or in a runaway process to increased instability. However, there are individual differences to consider, because some pain patients are responsive to therapy and do improve.

Dynamical Attractors in Relation to Chronic Pain

Acute Pain. To review, the processes that produce pain as a subjective experience have physiological concomitants, such as peripheral nerve and central neuronal network activity and, in addition, there are cognitive, emotional, behavioral, and social contributions. However, previous relevant states of the system, its history, exert an influence. Pain, therefore, is never an output of a linear, sequential (first transmission, then brain, then experience) system, which reduces to one pathway. Rather, it is an emergent property of all the components of the system of which it is part.

Chronic Pain. As pain experience continues beyond the acute state, it moves continuously through more global, self-organized, emergent patterns that derive from the interaction of all the system components. No one element of the system is the primary pain-generating mechanism to which all the other components in the system are subservient, in a reductionist process. The emergent system patterns are not prefigured or preordained, but are natural patterned outgrowths, self-organizational states, or outcomes, deriving from the ongoing configuration of elements and the prior states of the system.

Chronic, disabling pain that develops through the prolongation of acute pain appears to be an entrenched, maladaptive state of accommodation to a complex array of physiological, psychological, and social components. In cases such as these, the system "adapts," in the process sense of the word, but the adaptation is to a "maladaptive" state, in the functional sense of the word. Viewed from this point of view of adaptation, at the beginning of the pain process, when one is in acute pain, withdrawal from daily responsibility and the like may be appropriate in light of the physical conditions involved. However, once chronic pain sets in, the relevant system patterns seem to hold the person in a state of illness and disability that is not adaptive in the functional sense. Attempts to change the chronic pain at a simple mechanism level, such as through surgery, typically fail in the long run, because the system as a whole does not respond to such procedures, and it returns to the entrenched state of disability, dysphoria, and hopelessness, despite the intervention. The self-organization properties of the complete system, reflecting cross-system integration and pattern formation dynamics, resist the change and maintain the system in its chronic pain status. Multiple factors play roles in sustaining chronic pain and disability, yet the literature to date has produced piecemeal knowledge about across-system, full-scale change mechanisms that consider the integrated nature of systems.

Chronic Pain Attractors. Francis (1995) referred to chronic pain in his model of health and illness attractors. However, despite mention of chronic pain, Francis did not elaborate on this example of illness. He has left the task to us. That is, chronic pain may be characterized as a dysfunctional attractor state, in what may be called a "chronic pain attractor." Gottman's (1991) research provides an excellent example of how the concept of attractors can apply to psychological systems that become chronically dysfunctional by getting out of control, in the sense of losing capacity to autoregulate toward equilibrium, yet still having the flexibility to achieve adaptive change.

With respect to the concept of chronic pain attractors, then, it appears to us that chronic pain represents a dynamical pain experience system that is "stuck" in certain attractor states. A human being, as a system, can therefore get "stuck" in a state of chronic pain, leading to sickness and dysfunction, even in the absence of a traditional medical explanation for the pain. Moreover, small modifications in the input to the system, such as a minor strain added to ongoing pain, can release a torrent of pain experience, in a runaway system response far out of proportion to the input itself.

To use the language of nonlinear dynamical systems theory, chronic pain indicates the presence of dynamical attractors in neuronal firings and related central and psychological processes, to which the system readily gravitates in the range of its possible states. Although individual cases of chronic pain vary markedly, overall, chronic pain experience has a persistent, pervasive, and consuming character. The patient appears to have settled into a dynamical attractor that is marked by debilitating pain and disability, with sickness behavior predominant.

Moreover, such dynamical pain attractors appear to have lowered thresholds of reassembly to its configuration of elements. For example, individuals may readily experience excruciating pain even though peripheral nociception has been reduced with time because dynamical neuronal network attractors are readily reassembled in the system's state space because of their past sensitization.

Similarly, for many patients, chronic pain appears to be the product of a system governed by attractors with runaway processes involving negative emotions, persistent and pervasive pain experience, instability in mood, less predictability, and increased dysfunctionality, disability, and poor adaptive flexibility.

When acute pain degenerates into chronic pain, attractors may include cognitive-affective schemas, such as, "excruciating suffering," "depressing pain," "I'm anxious because the pain stops me from working," "Therapy is not helping; I can't cope," or "This pain has to be financially compensated." In some patients, schemas may relate to malingering.

Finally, in terms of the classic thermodynamic understanding of disorder in a system as energy dissipation, the concept applies perfectly to chronic pain patients, for they expend much "wasted energy" in running from doctor to doctor, doing everything that they can to avoid further injury and pain, and worrying excessively.

Individual Differences. As discussed already in this chapter, there are many individual variables that negate a dose-response relationship in tissue damage, pain experience, and psychological response, including of affect. Therefore, in modeling chronic pain in terms of dynamical pain attractors, it is cardinal that we build into the model individual differences. Comprehensive models of chronic pain that recognize individual differences should allow for more adaptive responses to the presence of the pain, considering that some chronic pain patients may not experience somatic preoccupation, work stoppage, and so on, and that some chronic pain patients respond to therapy that is correctly matched to their needs. Therefore, with respect to dynamical attractors, for some patients, there may be system behavior patterns marking attractors that are more constructive in daily efforts at adaptation. Chronic pain is a subjective experience unique to the individual, and our models should allow for recovery as much as evolution toward permanence even when the pain is chronic. For some patients, pain does not become entrenched nor resistant to psychotherapy, and they do not deny that the objective evidence at the physical level is showing improvement. For these pain patients, as mentioned, the pain does not become part of a generalized collapse in normal affective-social-cognitive functioning. Moreover, psychotherapy may be the primary factor that helps, and they improve in their pain experience, mood, and functional activity.

This being said, a frequent pattern for chronic pain patients is one of descent into increasingly maladaptive patterns that capture their behavior and lifestyle. The chronic pain patient falls into vicious circles in pain experience, sleep disruption, other neurovegetative effects, mood disturbance, and functional impairments. Pain becomes part of a complex web of disturbance, with multifocal causality, where pain experience both helps maintain and exacerbate the negative cascade, and is increased in a feedback loop.

Complexity Theory and Chronic Pain

We now examine the concept of Complex Adaptive Systems as a model of chronic pain. In terms of complexity theory, in certain chronic pain patients, the system appears to have gravitated toward increasing complexity, but of a maladaptive kind. It is as if the patient is unable to maintain her or his ongoing trajectory toward stability or increased complexity in a positive adaptive sense, and becomes fixated, instead on pain-focused, maladaptive complexity. There is a descent into systemic order of a maladaptive kind, which impedes any movement toward constructive change and healing. Moreover, the entrenchment into chronic pain has become pervasive, persistent, and all encompassing, infiltrating many parts of the daily functioning of the individual. In terms of the metaphor of attractors, there appear to be multiple pain attractors that have become increasingly integrated into a suprasystem of complex adaptivity. In these chronic pain patients manifesting decline toward debilitation and disability, there appears to be "order" in the entrenched nature of the pain and in the resistance to change. The system may appear more entrenched or ordered in terms of system, *qua* system but, at the psychological level, one finds disorder, mismanagement, and disorganization, as if being stuck in two or more attractors marked by dissolution of adaptive patterns, plasticity, and flexibility. In systems terms, the system is ordered and complex; however, at the psychological level, the pain patient appears to exhibit a decline into disorder, at multiple and integrating strata.

Considering dual/multiple attractors in complex nonlinear dynamical systems may help explain lack of progress in pain patients, or sudden reversions or regressions after some progress has been made. In this regard, "repellor" attractors function as regions in a system's state space to which it does not gravitate. It is as if there is an antimagnet keeping the proverbial rolling ball in a ditch out of its bottom location or on the side of a hill from which the ball cannot roll up (Lewis & Granic, 2000). This concept may be important to consider in developing models of illness and pain attractors, because healthy attractors may have once existed, but may transform in the case of chronic pain to regions of avoidance. For a particular patient, aside from the person having developed the equivalent of a pain attractor, the individual may also develop the equivalent of a repellor attractor related to health. For example, the patient's state never gravitates back to the healthy region, it is assiduously avoided, and it is feared. As for repellors in the therapeutically involved and rehabilitating pain patient, they would be regions of avoidance of pain-related and illness-related behaviors and lifestyles to which the patient does not want to return in any way, no matter what the circumstance.

Therapy with Chronic Pain Patients

Change Model of Therapy

Stages of Change. Gatchel (2005) describes the stages of change model, developed by DiClemente and Prochaska (1982) and Prochaska, DiClemente, and Norcross (1992). We also consulted Prochaska, Norcross, and DiClemente (1994) and Maddox (1995) in describing the model. In the stages of change model, patients pass through five stages, but may also relapse. In the phase preceding change, that of precontemplation, the individual is not ready for change. In the last stage of the five that follow precontemplation, the individual achieves problem resolution, confidence, and control. In between lie four stages, three considered transitional stages. The patient goes from the first stage involving change, that of contemplating change, or weighing the pros and cons, to the transitional stage of preparing/deciding/determining. Then, the patient moves to the next stage of undertaking concrete activities that will lead to change, in what is called the action stage. In the last transitional stage, the fourth stage of change, called the maintenance phase, gains are consolidated and preventative steps are instituted. Note that the final stage of the change model, involving resolution, does not appear in

Gatchel's version of the model, given that it does not always appear in the work of Prochaska and colleagues (Maddox, 1995). Nor does it appear in the work of Kerns, Rosenberg, Jamison, Caudill, and Haythornthwaite (1997), who developed a "Pain Stages of Change Questionnaire."

Gatchel's (2005) stage model of chronic pain describes a degenerative process, whereas Prochaska's and DiClemente's general model of change describes a constructive one. However, change processes may follow the same dynamic whether regressive or progressive, so that the transitions in the negative direction may be multiple, and follow several steps rather than just one. We address these issues, in building a general change model equally applicable to both progression and regression, and consisting of five stages, including three intermediate transition ones.

A General Change Model Applied to Pain. Young (1997) described a five-step model of change, seeking a general terminology that can apply across a wide variety of systems, and in either positive or negative directions. He applied the five-step change model to the substages that recycle within a Piagetian stage approach to cognitive development. The stages are called coordination, hierarchization, systematization, multiplication, and integration. Therefore, as systems evolve, at first, they start to coordinate new acquisitions; then, the coupled acquisitions develop a dominant–subordinate relationship, with one as primary; and, then, the two acquisitions coalesce into a single new structure. In the next step, the new structure propagates throughout the system in which it is embedded and, finally, in the step of integration, the full system is characterized by the new structure, ready for renewed coordination.

Young (1997) showed how the Prochaska and DiClemente model of change maps onto his own, providing a more generalized language. In contemplation of change, the individual is coordinating present condition and future possibility. In preparing/deciding/determining, the individual is hierarchically organizing commitment and planning as primary. In deliberate action, systematization is evident. Next, maintenance reflects multiplication or propagation of the gains made in systemization to wider regions of the system and, finally, problem resolution indicates integration.

In terms of therapy for chronic pain, the present model suggests that individuals first show a readiness by coordinating their understanding of their present condition and an appreciation of how much they can improve. Then, they hierarchically organize as primary a will to change. Then, they engage in deliberate action in one or more areas of concern, such as participating better in physiotherapy or psychotherapy; systematization is evident. Next, they multiply or propagate their good attitude and habits into more aspects of their life and, finally, they achieve a healthier lifestyle freer of pain, indicating integration.

Therapy and Nonlinear Dynamical Systems

Research on chronic pain patients in multidisciplinary pain centers is demonstrating that long-term chronic pain patients can benefit from treatment, contrary to past perceptions of the chronic pain patient (Gatchel, 2004, 2005; Turk & Okifuji, 2003). In order to be effective, treatment should be multifactorial and address each patient's individual needs.

Current research indicates that individual patients experience chronic pain in different ways, and that "treatment matching" to these differences is essential (Gatchel, 2005; Turk, Monarch, & Williams, 2004). Research has identified subgroups of pain patients based on behavioral and psychosocial characteristics, including those evident on standardized pain instruments. For example, Turk and Rudy (1988) described subgroups of pain patients as dysfunctional, interpersonally distressed, and adaptive pain copers, with hybrid styles possible. Hadjistavropoulos and Williams (2004) reviewed the literature on the psychological treatment of chronic pain. They concluded that although the evidence supports the efficacy of the cognitive-behavioral treatment approach, more research is needed to determine why patients vary in their response to treatment.

The nonlinear dynamical systems model facilitates an appreciation of individual differences in pain because, at its base, it does not attempt to explain normative data. It provides a strong basis for ipsative characterization of pain. There is no one pain pathway, or pain system, that is applicable to all pain patients. According to the model, pain-related attractors can vary in predominant configuration due to incoming information, alteration of system components, or structural instability. For example, in any one individual, a newly learned psychotherapeutic technique may lead to attractor network reassembly with less pain experience. Or, if pain leads to negative consequences, such as an employer laying off a worker, therapy may lead to enough stabilization processes to generate a new degree of stability in a healthy attractor dynamic, with associated resistance to increased pain and negative affect.

There even may be so-called "butterfly effects," or catastrophic inversions, which happens when the system's ongoing attractor dynamic is unstable and a relatively minor input eventually leads to major attractor assembly transformation. The system moves out of its stable but far-from-equilibrium dynamic to an unstable dynamic. Therapeutically, amelioration of chronic pain may appear rapidly, for example. Such an event would be readily understandable to clinicians familiar with nonlinear dynamical systems concepts. However, the conventional biomedically oriented professional may consider the sudden change in pain experience as anomalous.

In the following, we examine therapy that is effective from the point of view of nonlinear dynamical systems. In terms of its attractor model, nonlinear dynamical systems theory suggests that the best way to weaken the attractor that holds a patient in the sickness and disability state is to intervene at multiple psychological and social levels and not only at the medical level.

Francis (1995) described similar concepts with respect to health and illness, although without mentioning chronic pain. For example, therapy can help "provide sufficient energy to the individual so that he or she can now begin exploring other basins of attraction" (p. 260). This allows new patterns of self-organization possibly to emerge. Therapy allows a larger phase space to be explored, facilitating the establishment of a flexibility, adaptivity, and movement through phase space toward a health attractor from an illness one.

In terms of complexity theory, therapy in the pain patient can be conceived as a process that inhibits the pathway to disorder, and facilitates reorganization or movement toward the cusp of change, balancing between order and disorder. This is the dynamic region that is considered healthy, because it can lead to more ordered, complex states, where attractors related to or representing a return to flexibility, readiness for or openness to constructive change, optimal adaptation, rehabilitation, restoration of function, and healing may capture the patient. When effective, therapy essentially functions as a guide to reorganization, reduction of energy dissipation, and movement toward higher-order, more complex, and more adaptive states. It is as if the patient must cohere, in a balancing point of transition, the positive (order) and the negative (e.g., disorder) so that she or he may better work through the negative, toward more adaptive psychological states.

Therapy as Appropriate Energy Flow

Schore (2000) contends that a central tenet of nonlinear dynamical systems theory is that energy flow helps the components of a self-organizing system to better interconnect, constructing development. For example, in the infant, appropriate stimuli, such as the caregiver's face, elicit catecholamine-mediated arousal, which exerts an enduring effect on neural growth. Therefore, Schore maintains that emotions mark the incorporation of energy into a system. This is an intriguing suggestion, and may help tie in our emphasis on the importance of the relationship between pain and negative affect. It reminds also that therapy with chronic pain patients can be conceptualized as a process of increasing positive affect and reducing the negative in order to ameliorate chronic pain experience.

In terms of complexity theory, then, we suggest tentatively that therapy may help move the chronic pain patient toward the cusp of change by facilitating appropriate marking of energy flow into the system, as indexed by adaptive emotional responses.

Therapy as Activation/Inhibition Coordination

Young (1997; Young & Gagnon, 1990) has proposed that the coordination of activation/inhibition is an essential common process, operating at multiple levels of the neuraxis and also in behavioral organization. For example, neuronal networks in the brain comprise interdependent inhibitory feedback loops as well as excitatory loops and activation commands. Behavior requires control of the multiple interfering effects that can compromise its efficiency. As a person proceeds in adaptation to the world in everyday life, she or he relates the self to others through coordinating appropriate activations and inhibitions. This happens both at the microlevel, second by second, moment to moment, or tonic, and at macrolevels, phasic in terms of integrating self-goals into ongoing societal transactions. It is as if an activation/inhibition coordination fractal propagates throughout the human system at different levels, both within each individual at multiple levels, facilitating the individual's interaction with others, and within larger units or groups. No matter the size of the system, activation/inhibition coordination may be a crucial metric or control parameter that facilitates optimal adaptation.

In terms of the pain system, adaptational activation/inhibition coordination, whether at the behavioral, neuraxial, or any related level, may become disrupted during ongoing nociception, as pain becomes too intense and disabling. Therefore, one approach to therapy would be to construe it as an active attempt to reestablish appropriate activation/inhibition coordination at various levels of the behavior and brain systems involved in the nonlinear dynamical system governing pain experience. We suggest rather tentatively that we can conceptualize therapy for chronic pain as exploring and ameliorating disequilibrium in fractal equivalents in terms of activation/inhibition coordination at various levels of the pain system so as to facilitate constructive energy flow, resulting in improvement in the condition of pain in patients.

Optimization of activation/inhibition coordination dynamics in therapy may function in multiple ways and, fractally, at multiple levels, to assure its effectiveness. In terms of nonlinear dynamical system terminology, it may act to: (a) dampen or de-amplify potentially disorganizing perturbations to the system, (b) optimize energy incorporation, work, and transfer within components and across levels of the system, (c) equilibrate negative and positive affective components of the system as they feed backward and feed forward into emerging, moment-to-moment pain experience in transactional exchange processes, (d) facilitate transition beyond thresholds of change within extant system configurations, or attractors related to pain, to more adaptive configurations, and (e) move the system toward the cusp of change, where more complex and better functioning adaptive systems can coalesce in context. In the following, we add another view of the pain pathway on which an improved activation/inhibition coordination in therapy may act in order to facilitate movement toward an improved pain condition.

Steps in the Development of Chronic Pain: A Nonlinear Dynamical Systems Model

Stage Models in Chronic Pain. We have seen that Gatchel (2005) has formulated a stage model of the development of chronic pain, which is interlinked with emotional factors. To review briefly, in the first phase of acute pain, the patient may experience the emotions of worry, anxiety, and fear. In the second stage, pain increases, and the patient experiences depression, demoralization, learned helplessness, anger, frustration, distrust, and so on. Preexisting issues often influence the degree of exacerbation or are exacerbated, in turn. Somatization and symptom magnification/exaggeration may develop. In stage 3, the pain becomes chronic.

TABLE 8.1. Parallel Five-step Models of Stages of Change in Therapy and in Chronic Pain, with Proposed Nonlinear Dynamical System Transitions

Stages of change in therapy	Stages of change in chronic pain	Nonlinear dynamical system transitions
Contemplation	Coordination	
		Cyclical attractor
Preparation	Hierarchization	
		Chaotic attractor
Action	Systematization	
		Inhabiting cusp of change
Maintenance	Multiplication	
		Complex Adaptive System processes
Resolution	Integration	

Note: The stage model of therapy is presented in Prochaska et al. (1994), Maddox (1995), and Young (1997). The stage model of pain is based on an elaboration of Gatchel (2005), after Young (1997). The transition sequence in nonlinear dynamical systems theory is explained in the text.

This five-step change model developed by Young (1997), and describe a above, can account for the development of chronic pain in the following way (see Table 8.1). In the coordination phase, the negative effects of acute pain are coordinated with the patient's ongoing lifestyle. In the hierarchization stage, chronic pain becomes predominant. In the next phase, a powerful chronic pain lifestyle develops. Next, the chronic pain gradually propagates throughout all aspects of the patient's life. Finally, the individual transforms fully into a chronic pain patient, where the pain is deeply entrenched, resistant to treatment, and impregnated in personal identity.

With respect to the development of chronic pain, the present model, compared to Gatchel's, gives more consideration to the intermediate steps, although Gatchel's transition step is a gradual one. Overall, his model provides the basic framework of how chronic pain evolves, but we have added more steps. However, it is important to note that, with all stage models, sequences described are not universal. For example, in the current case, the course of the development of chronic pain may vary across individuals and, furthermore, some patients do make good progress, recovering instead of continuing descent toward permanent disability.

A Dynamic Model of Stages in Pain. In a further theoretical refinement, we suggest that transition processes described in nonlinear dynamical systems theory may model well the processes that underlie passage through our proposed five-step model of chronic pain, because the five steps reflect chaotic and complex processes at work. Previously in the chapter, we proposed that systems may inherently self-organize to pass through the steps of (a) cyclic attractors, (b) chaotic attractors, (c) gravitating to the region between order and disorder, the cusp of change, and (d) creating Complex Adaptive Systems. There are many possible dynamic schemes, or dynamic transition processes, that facilitate change in systems, and this four-step one being suggested may self-organize especially under optimal conditions. Similar models may involve the insertion of a torus attractor before the chaotic one, and/or not yet integrated dual/multiple attractors after it.

Our proposed five-stage model of the development of chronic pain may be facilitated by such a transition sequence of four dynamical mediatory steps, as shown in the following.

In general, cyclical attractors may mediate the shift from the coordination to the hierarchical stage, where pain begins to predominate in the five-step model of development of chronic pain, and chaotic attractors may mediate the shift to pain systemization, the shift from the second to the third step. Gravitating to the cusp of change between system order and disorder may mediate the shift from the systemization stage of chronic pain to the one of multiplication throughout the life of the patient, and active adaptive complexity processes may mediate the shift to the final stage of pain entrenchment, or integration.

To explain further, a cyclical attractor oscillates between two locations in its state space, and we have presented the example of competing poles in health and illness behavior representing the cyclical alterations in such an attractor. This fits the placement of the first step of our proposed four-step dynamic in system transition, that of emergence of a cyclical attractor dynamic, between the coordination and hierachization stages of the current five-step model of chronic pain.

Chaotic attractors are stable configurations far from equilibrium that can readily jump to new regions in state space, for example, due to minor perturbations. In this sense, in terms of the transition from the second to the third step in our five-step model of chronic pain, the passage from a hierachically arranged coupling of poles, where pain predominates, to a more systematic pain experience fully governing a key aspect in the life of the pain patient, reflects a chaotic attractor transition.

In dynamical transitions, our model suggests that after chaotic attractors emerge in systems, they may gravitate to regions between order and disorder to facilitate increased adaptation. Therefore, in terms of transition from the third to the fourth step in our model of chronic pain, with each new systemic acquisition in the step of diffusion of the pain dynamic throughout the life of the patient, the multiplicative process may be facilitated by the pain system remaining on the cusp of change in the region between order and disorder.

Finally, processes that self-organize complexity in adaptation of systems would appear to facilitate the movement of chronic pain into the fifth stage, from the multiplication to the integration stage. When systems function as Complex Adaptive Systems, they are characterized by an integrated network of multiple attractors. In terms of chronic pain, which becomes pervasive, persistent, and entrenched, the networked multiple attractors permit continual, yet conservative online adjustment to variations, vicissitudes, and vagaries so that a system functioning at this dynamic constantly emerges intact as the same or comparable whole in its moment-to-moment transactions with context, deeply immersed in stability, and quite resistant to change. In this regard, chronic pain may become integrated as a permanent, disabling feature in the life of the patient. Nevertheless therapy may still be useful in addressing issues such as acceptance and eventually reducing amplitude of mood variations.

This tentative model of how dynamical transitions may facilitate passage through the stages of chronic pain seems to fit the patterns in the various proposed change models, but it needs further elaboration and support. At the same time, it allows a relationship between more traditional change models and nonlinear dynamical systems theory, so that practitioners and researchers can collaborate in refining the model.

It would appear to the typical observer that the regressive process apparent in chronic pain development does not fit a pattern toward increasing adaptive complexity. In particular, at the psychological level, it appears that there is increasing maladaptive behavior. However, in terms of the quality of the system being formed, in terms of its networked elements, integration of different levels, inclusion of significant others into the system dynamic, and so on, the increasing domination of chronic pain in the life of the individual suggests an increasingly ordered and complex system, *qua* system, which contrasts with the increasingly disordered state at the psychological level. In this regard, whether there is progressive change in therapy, or regressive change in the development of chronic pain, the pain patient may undergo the same qualitative shifts through the five stages described, with nonlinear dynamic transition mechanisms facilitating stages evolving in certain sequences, as underlying self-organizational mechanisms change.

Conclusions. Finally, the proposed five-step change model in the development of chronic pain, with its underlying activation through different nonlinear dynamic system mechanisms, supports the inclusion of the complexity theory approach to nonlinear dynamical systems into a model of stages in pain development along with the more commonly used attractor/chaos theory. The two approaches have proved complementary in our efforts to clarify the problem of pain, and the proposed five-step chronic pain model, with an underlying four-step dynamical transition mechanism, does suggest different roles for these approaches in the transition from acute to chronic pain, as well.

The two-book series of which this chapter is part (see Young, Kane, and Nicholson, 2006) concerns causality, in particular, and the proposed five-step model of change is couched in a nonlinear dynamical systems model, which is an increasingly important one in understanding causality in psychology, in general and, indeed, across diverse areas of many physical and social sciences. Therefore, the proposed model helps connect the focus of the book, causality for court purposes, with wider approaches to causality across multiple areas of inquiry.

Summary of Nonlinear Dynamical Systems and Prior Models

A nonlinear dynamical systems approach to pain is consistent with the influential biopsychosocial view of pain and other psychological difficulties. The biopsychosocial model emphasizes that sensory, cognitive, affective, and behavioral factors interact in generating pain experience. The social includes influences such as cultural expectations, socioeconomic status, family attitude, loss of employment due to the injury, litigation status, and timely therapeutic availability or withdrawal by the third party payor. In this sense, in terms of nonlinear dynamical systems, the attractors that hold some people in the grip of chronic, disabling pain are never simple but, rather, are multifactorial.

Nonlinear dynamical system thinking reinforces the view of Melzack and Katz (2006) that there is no one pain center in the brain, and no fixed anatomical pain pathways in the brain, just as there is no simple one-to-one transmission of tissue damage signals to the brain and pain experience. Melzack and Wall (1965) posited gating mechanisms in the spinal cord that modulate nociceptive transmission, and these, in turn, respond to descending influences from higher centers, opening the way for multiple psychological influences on pain perception. Moreover, in terms of their other models, Melzack and Katz have proposed a model for somatic awareness that is consistent with nonlinear dynamical systems, in their concepts of the "neuromatrix" and the unified "body-self."

Figure 8.1 provides a historical understanding of classical to contemporary models of pain, going from passive, nociception models at the bottom of the figure to models involving the spinal cord, and then to models involving the brain, including Melzack's conceptions. At the same time, we point out that the nonlinear dynamical approach is a relatively new one that complements and adds to these views. Therefore, the figure represents both a historical depiction of different schools of thought on pain, and our proposed model of pain experience. At present, we understand that pain is emergent and constructed continuously at each moment due to the confluence of all the variables active in the nonlinear dynamical pain experience system. The brain itself is not the end-point of a monotonic process of what is involved in pain because, on the one hand, pain experience is co-constructed, involving the self and the other and, on the other hand, pain experience is a product of a nonlinear dynamical system where the whole emerges from not only tissue damage, transmission signals, brain activity, and so forth but, also, from integrated activity of all the components of the system. Finally, the figure reveals that nonlinear dynamical system theory offers a perspective on chronic pain in terms of attractors and chaos, and also in terms of complexity and adaptive systems.

Yet there are so many interacting parts, subsystems, and levels in the pain system that it is hard to grasp how a coherent pattern can emerge out of it. It is as if the different components are too diverse for the system to achieve functional integrity, even if it is in terms of a chronic pain condition. However, the different

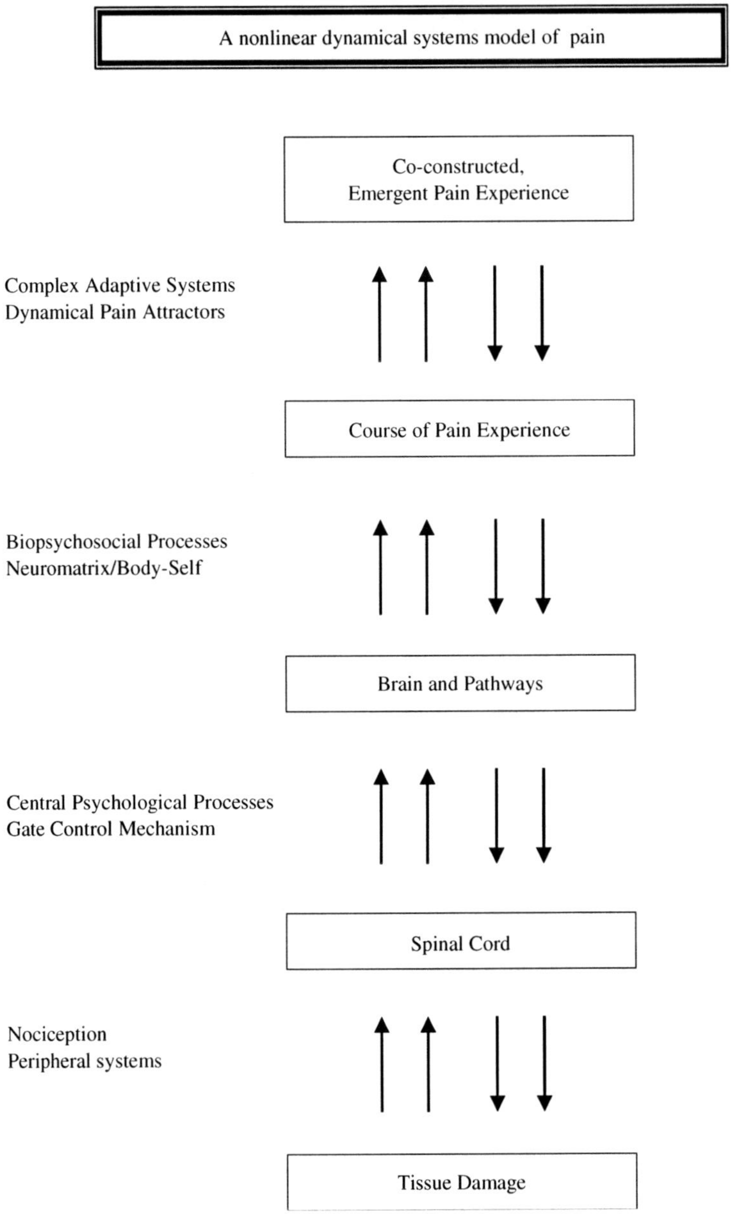

FIGURE 8.1. The figure presents a nonlinear dynamical systems model of pain. The lower level specifies the early reactions of the body to tissue damage. There are transduction, transmission, and modulation processes at work, as peripheral nerves fire after tissue damage. Already at this level, Melzack has shown that descending pathways from the brain can influence pain related processes (nociception), for example, through hypothalamus-mediated opioid mechanisms (see the chapter by Melzack & Katz, 2006).

Gating mechanisms in the spinal cord constitute the next level. Nociceptors transmit information to the dorsal horns, which can act to open or close the gate, depending on the types of fibers activated and whether activation or inhibition processes are set in motion. Opening the gate, for example, through small-fiber stimulation, facilitates the passage of tissue injury signals to the brain. Melzack has shown that central control processes in the brain involving psychological mechanisms can contribute to opening or closing the gate. Psychological or central control processes concern affect (e.g., depression, anxiety, fear, anger), stress (e.g., chronic activation of the hypothalamic-pituitary-adrenocortical axis (HPA), which releases excessive, deletrious cortisol), motivation (e.g., social withdrawal, "crying out for help," keeping financial compensation in mind), and cognitive factors (e.g., catastrophizing, pessimism), as influences on pain experience.

In the next level, multiple, parallel, distributed neuronal networks in different regions of the brain and its pathways are activated, to encompass the multiple central factors involved in pain experience. There is not a pain center in the brain nor one nociceptive pathway. Nevertheless, there are certain regions that typically are involved, for example, the hypothalamus, limbic system, and portions of the cortex. Melzack and Katz refer to the "neuromatrix" in this regard, which has a continuously forming felt unitary "body-self" as its primary output, a backdrop onto which pain experience is integrated. This view is consistent with the biopsychosocial model of pain, in which sensory, biological, psychological, and social factors interact in generating pain experience.

The nonlinear dynamical systems view adds that pain experience is constantly reconstructed, or reconfigured, out of the matrix of components comprising the pain-related system. Components of the pain system include not only sensory information, for example, currently and on its course since the tissue damage but, also, cognitions, emotions, stress, and motivation, in addition to context, treatment, disability, litigation status, and so on. An individual's pain experience constantly emerges *de novo*, or is constantly reassembled according to the pattern of elements comprising the system at any one time. These factors may include preexisting ones, such as prior depression, ongoing ones, such as increased pain-related transmission after a physical activity, and expected ones, such as the anticipated stress of job loss due to the injury. In terms of nonlinear dynamical systems modeling, in chronic pain, patterns of system activation that have emerged after the injury are sensitized. The patient lapses into illness patterns. These may be called "dynamical chronic pain attractors," or areas in the system's state space to which the system may gravitate more readily. In terms of complexity theory, chronic pain patients appear to follow a movement toward an order of integrated, multiple attractors, considered adaptive in term of systems, *qua* systems, but that is entrenched, less flexible, and maladaptive from the psychological point of view. They gravitate away from a region in their state space that lies between order and disorder, as they descend into a state resistant to therapy.

components of the pain system may share common features that facilitate their interaction, and the glue may involve affect.

Depression, Anxiety, and Pain

To return to the particular topic of the chapter, that of pain and affect, we are arguing that pain, sensory information, affect, cognition, and associated behaviors are not separable entities that may come together at times, or cohere at times into fully or partially unified pain experience complexes. Rather, they are component elements of a whole that dynamically and continuously emerges as a coherent, unified subjective experience, what Melzack and Katz (2006) refer to as a unified body-self emanating from the neuromatrix. Pain and related sensory information are not separate from affect, just as affect and cognition are conjoined in the constantly reassembled but unified schemas that they form to help construe and adapt to the world.

The connection between affect and pain is the subject of continued research, and space limitations allow us to review just a few select, recent studies that underscore important points. Vowles, Gross, and Sorrell (2004) examined factors that predict return to work after participation in a 4 to 6 week interdisciplinary program for chronic pain. They employed psychological instruments with acceptable psychometric properties, such as the Beck Depression Inventory (BDI II; Beck, Steer, & Brown, 1987, 1996; Beck, Steer, & Garbin, 1988) and the McGill Pain Questionnaire (MPQ), short form (Melzack & Katz, 2001). Of the multiple demographic, physical, psychological, and treatment factors examined, level of depression proved to be the best predictor of return to work status, along with chronological age. The authors concluded that general emotional distress may be the most important predictor of return to work following chronic pain.

Hadjistavropoulos, Asmundson, and Kowalyk (2004) examined the differential ability of measures of four anxiety-related constructs to predict adjustment to musculoskeletal pain longitudinally over 3 months in patients who had participated in physiotherapy. The anxiety constructs related to health anxiety, trait anxiety, pain-related anxiety, and anxiety sensitivity (also see Asmundson & Taylor, 2006). Psychological instruments included the Multidimensional Pain Inventory (MPI, section 1; Kerns & Jacob, 1992) and the Anxiety Sensitivity Index (ASI, Reiss, Peterson, Gursky, & McNally, 1986). After the appropriate statistical controls, for example, for pain severity, the various anxieties uniquely predicted different psychological outcomes. Health anxiety proved the best predictor of disability, and anxiety sensitivity best predicted negative affect. The findings address the importance of individual differences in pain patients, and indicate that anxiety is a multifaceted construct.

These studies stand as examples of current research providing a more nuanced perspective on the relationship of pain experience, affect, disability, and therapy. The studies show that the constructs need differentiation, as do the measures, in each of the areas of pain, affect, and outcome. Ideally, research along these lines involves longitudinal designs with comprehensive measures, including of any preexisting emotional difficulties, psychopathology, lifetime stresses, and so on, to balance the search for emotional complications that develop after pain is initiated.

Pain needs to be considered from the perspective of all the possible components of the system that generate its experience. It is constructed from the interaction of biological, psychological, and social factors in its biopsychosocial program. These factors evolve over time, not only in terms of the onset of pain but, also, in terms of preexisting vulnerabilities, psychopathologies, and so forth, in a whole person perspective. This approach is crucial in the forensic and medicolegal arenas, because preexisting factors may explain much of or even all of the stresses serving to maintain or exacerbate the pain system.

Is There a Chronic Pain Disorder?

Problems. The psychologist assessing individuals expressing pain needs to undertake a comprehensive assessment because of the multiple factors that contribute to the expression of pain. Affective states serve as important moderating influences in the transition from the acute stage to chronic pain (see Gatchel and Kishino, 2006). Many extraneous variables are at work in litigation cases, so that it is difficult to assess the cause of pain without considering these factors. Melzack and Katz (2006) point out that pain patients diagnosed with chronic Pain Disorder due to psychological factors may be unjustly given a psychiatric diagnosis, especially because there are always physiological underpinnings in cases of pain. They disagree that pain can be constituted by primarily psychological factors (presumably excluding cases of malingering). Moreover, they suggest that when clinicians use the label of chronic Pain Disorder, they may be understood as saying that the pain is fully psychological in origin; that is, that, at its root, pain could be attributed to psychological or emotional disturbance, distress, or psychopathology, without associated physiological processes, in a manner of blaming the patient. The notion that the nervous system of the patient may be trapped in a dysfunctional and dysphoric state that she or he cannot willfully change would seem acceptable to most people for most psychiatric and neurological disorders, but the current climate of opinion tends to resist this for chronic pain.

Typically, professionals work for one side or the other of the adversarial legal process, and are subject to biases that may be hard to avoid (see also the section by Kane, this volume). Therefore, some professionals may give the diagnosis of chronic Pain Disorder to convey that there is "psychological overlay," unexplained pain, symptom "magnification," or even malingering. However, professionals on the other side may become unduly sympathetic to individuals with a diagnosis of chronic Pain Disorder, fostering dependency, and so forth, which may not help patients recover enough to mitigate their losses. Moreover, pain patients may be exaggerating their symptoms either consciously (with awareness), or unconsciously (without awareness), they may be experiencing their pain due to stresses related to secondary gain issues rather than to stresses directly related to the original pain onset and its effects, or they may be partially or even fully malingering. All of these confounds complicate the clinical picture.

Solutions. Problems such as these could be obviated by more precise diagnostic criteria for chronic Pain Disorder in the DSM IV (APA, 1994, TR in 2000). The criteria, as they exist, leave room for ambiguity in interpretation, and, accordingly, the working committee of the DSM V may need to reconsider the disorder, as Melzack and Katz (2006) imply. They show that, at present, the diagnosis of chronic Pain Disorder allows for diagnoses due to medical factors, psychological factors, or both. This division suggests an implicit dualism, a separation of mind and body, and denial of the fact that, in valid pain cases, there is always a concomitant physiological disturbance.

At the same time, it may be possible to salvage the diagnosis of Pain Disorder by ensuring that its multiple causality is understood. In this scenario, only one type of chronic Pain Disorder could be diagnosed; there would be no separate diagnoses involving medical vs. psychological factors. Appreciation of the biopsychosocial model, the neuromatrix and somatic awareness models, nonlinear dynamical systems models of pain experience, and so on, can facilitate acceptance of this approach.

Nevertheless, the various extraneous influences described above that complicate the clinical picture in cases of chronic pain may becloud the assessment and diagnosis of chronic pain, and it may be best not to include the diagnosis of chronic Pain Disorder in the revised DSM. In such a scenario, the pain assessor would list the presence of chronic pain on the DSM axis of medical factors (Axis III), rather than on the clinical axis (Axis I), and document the effects of the pain experience, *per se*, on the individual, rather than using any diagnostic label such as chronic Pain Disorder. If there are psychiatric difficulties arising from the pain experience, most likely they will concern affective conditions such as depression, anxiety, or adjustment disturbances. The assessor would examine carefully the sources of any emotions, stresses, and motivational issues, clarifying to what extent they involve preexisting factors, litigation issues, and so on, relative to injury and post-injury factors of a more straightforward nature.

However, if the working committee of the DSM V insists on keeping the diagnosis of chronic Pain Disorder, either as a unified entity or as several different types, it may want to consider using a category such as "Chronic Pain Complications Disorder." A diagnosis such as this would allow specification of the psychological distress and functional effects of the individual's pain experience without leaving a pejorative connotation, yet still allow the assessor in other cases to list litigation and malingering factors, where warranted. In its criteria, the causality of the disorder would not be addressed, *per se*, but it would be explained in the text of the manual that valid cases of chronic pain always express an interaction of physiological and psychological factors, including social ones.

The ICD-10 (WHO, 1992) is another system of psychiatric diagnosis. On the one hand, it contains a category of "Persistent Somatoform Pain Disorder" that expresses the worst fears of Melzack and Katz, because it is defined as involving persistent, severe, and distressing pain complaints that are mainly caused by emotional conflicts or psychosocial problems, leading to increased personal/medical support/attention. On the other hand, the ICD includes a nonclinical category for chronic pain that can specify auxiliary problems. The DSM V could adopt and expand this sort of approach.

Finally, chronic pain is an essential aspect of the evaluation of permanent impairment, and the AMA has published guidelines on this (Cocchiarella & Andersson, 2001). In explaining chronic pain, the Guides recognize that "anxiety and depression almost always magnify pain, and vice versa" (p. 366), consistent with the centrality given to affect in the current dynamical model. At the same time, the guidelines are imprecise in defining impairment, indicating that, in particular, marked or extreme impairment significantly impedes or precludes useful functioning (in any of the areas of activities of daily living, social functioning, concentration, and adaptation). We recommend that in using these Guides, the psychological or other assessor adopts a comprehensive assessment strategy, including with respect to pain experience and its complications, both in terms of effects of pain on the daily life of the patient and in terms of the confounds that may affect or reduce its legitimacy, including that of malingering.

Conclusions

Summary

We have considered chronic pain from the perspective of nonlinear dynamical systems. Earlier approaches examined how systems evolve patterns out of the ensemble of their components in context, including their history of prior states. Nonlinear systems may change in a discontinuous fashion that is out of proportion to system input. Attractors govern a system when it almost always gravitates over time to certain fixed values, or to an oscillation among several values, considering initial value and perturbations. In cyclical attractors, the system gravitates periodically between two different poles in state space. A chaotic attractor comprises trajectories that do not repeat themselves, giving it an apparently unpredictable characteristic. However, at the mathematical level, differential equations can account for chaotic functions. Complex systems lie at the interface of cyclic and chaotic attractors (Kauffman, 1993), and in our application of complexity theory, Complex Adaptive Systems cohere multiple attractors into integrated structures, being constituted by their networking. Systems may gravitate to the cusp of change between stability and instability, because being in this region facilitates movement toward change.

In terms of pain experience, chronic pain may represent a dynamical pain experience system that is "stuck" in certain states. Pain reflects the ongoing emergence of subjective awareness emanating from the confluence of components involved in tissue damage and its consequences over time at the physiological, psychological, and social levels, and the influence of past states, but it is always constructed anew from moment to moment. The neuronal networks that are part of the pain system undergo continuous and active reconstruction. Affect and the physiological disruption accompanying pain are interdependent, and are not separate in a mind-body dualism. The nonlinear dynamical systems model provides a framework allowing individual differences in pain experience. For example, to use the language of nonlinear dynamical systems theory, for any one individual, a newly learned psychotherapeutic technique may lead to attractor network reassembly with less pain experience. One approach to therapy would be to perceive it as an active attempt to reestablish appropriate activation/inhibition coordination at various levels.

Gatchel (2005) presents a stage model of how acute pain can develop into chronic pain. Gatchel underscores that the development of chronic pain is entwined with emotional factors. Prochaska and DiClemente indicate that patients pass through five stages in change, but may also relapse. Young (1997) describes a five-step model of change, using a more general terminology. This five-step change model can account for the development of chronic pain. It is also used to present a five-step change model for therapy. The passage through these steps may be facilitated by a transition sequence in nonlinear dynamical system self-organization in terms of (a) cyclic attractors, (b) chaotic attractors, (c) gravitating to the cusp of change, or to region between order and disorder, and (d) Complex Adaptive Systems. There are many possible dynamic schemes, and the one suggested may self-organize especially under optimal conditions.

The nonlinear dynamical systems models of pain that we develop is broadly consistent with contemporary models of pain, such as the biopsychosocial model and the gate control and neuromatrix models of pain (Melzack & Katz, 2006). To conclude, we evaluate the suggestion by Melzack and Katz to reconsider the placement of Pain Disorder in psychiatric diagnostic manuals. In this regard, we propose that the category of "Chronic Pain Complications Disorder" may be appropriate. At several points in the chapter, we call for more research.

Limitations and Possibilities

Nonlinear dynamical system modeling brings new perspectives on the subject matter to which it is applied. It has gained widespread currency across multiple disciplines, because it reflects natural phenomena, and helps explain findings that seem incongruous, such as the so-called "butterfly effect" or catastrophic system inversions, where a small input into a system can lead to massive, often surprising, change.

However, mathematical modeling of a system requires extensive data. It is feasible to apply this approach to electroencephalographic (EEG) data from a large multiple electrode array, but it is very hard to characterize human beings at the psychosocial level with this type of modeling.

Moreover, the computational approach to such modeling departs from the work that psychologists normally undertake. For example, one can model and interpret multi-array EEG from a single individual but not across individuals. Variability in the system is not considered to be confounding or "noise," as it is in classical inferential statistics, but part of the data to explain.

Until a clearer understanding of chronic pain, its diagnosis, and its complications develops, it will be difficult to ascertain the nature of impairments that it may generate. Nonlinear dynamical systems models seek predictability in finding overarching patterns but, at the same time, acknowledge the difficulty in making particular predictions about any one data trajectory. Granted, the nonlinear dynamical systems approach emphasizes the unique nature of the individual case. Nevertheless, from an empirical point of view, in individual cases involving psychological injury, pain, and so forth, the nonlinear dynamical systems approach and the data that it may generate would need to be applied prudently to the evaluation of causality. In this sense, it resembles any other approach to the question of addressing psychological injury in court.

However, problems in evaluation of chronic pain always will persist because of the contentious nature of the adversarial system in which pain patients find themselves, and the difficulty in arriving at certain diagnoses even with comprehensive assessments. Improved concepts and more research on chronic pain can reduce the uncertainties in the field and minimize the adversarial influence in assessment, but can never fully resolve these issues.

The danger in using terminology derived from nonlinear dynamical systems models is that the terms can become reified when, in fact, they are merely constructs, and cannot replace the hard empirical data that they are meant to describe. At this point, nonlinear dynamical models primarily serve as metaphors for understanding causality in systems but, as such, they provide powerful conceptual windows that can illuminate understanding despite a lack of hard empirical data.

In this regard, the nonlinear dynamical systems framework provides a powerful theoretical structure and language for characterizing chronic pain and its apparent anomalies. The theoretical model provided in the present chapter may help clarify the nature of chronic pain, and lead to better practical approaches in diagnosis and in establishing functional improvements.

Comorbid PTSD and Chronic Pain, and Nonlinear Dynamical Systems Modeling

The nonlinear dynamical systems model of chronic pain experience presented in this chapter speaks to the relatively new area of research on the interaction of PTSD and chronic pain, which is addressed in several chapters in the companion volume by Young et al. (2006). Briefly, the empirical literature indicates that individuals experiencing either chronic pain or PTSD as primary diagnoses often have the other condition comorbidly.

Sharp and Harvey (2001) have proposed that comorbid pain and PTSD are subject to mutually maintaining and exacerbatory factors, such as attentional biases. Asmundson and Taylor (2006) proposed a shared vulnerability model, especially based on predisposing anxiety sensitivity. Others have proposed a fear avoidance model, which includes catastrophizing. Otis, Pincus, and Keane (2006) present a triple vulnerability model, comprised of (a) a common biological vulnerability, (b) a common early psychological vulnerability of a lessened control over salient events, and (c) a specific psychological vulnerability, for example, to pain and traumatic events. The various models in the field all describe predisposing vulnerabilities common to the two conditions of chronic pain and PTSD, and they all describe triggers, such as pain onset and trauma, which can elicit them together.

The situation of having comorbid chronic pain and PTSD complicates, delays, or even undermines an individual's recovery, making it difficult to arrive at conclusions about causality for any one individual being assessed. Until precise conceptual models on the mutually interacting and cofacilitating nature of chronic pain and PTSD are obtained, these limitations in dealing with causality will continue, and research into effective treatment for the comorbidity of the conditions will be hampered.

In this regard, we propose that the nonlinear dynamical systems approach that we have developed to help explain chronic pain and its relationship to affect, and other pain system components, may help explain the mutual maintenance and exacerbation of comorbid pain and PTSD. We have framed pain and affect as part of a larger system influenced by prior states, but also by ongoing conditions, and subject to possible radical shifts in response to even minor inputs. There is no reason to exclude PTSD from the negative affect that reciprocally interacts with pain in a dynamical way within the pain system, along with other components in the system. Asmundson and Taylor and Otis et al. have shown that pain and PTSD share common vulnerabilities and partially share triggers, which we propose reflect their integrated nature, within what may be a single pain-trauma system. This notion helps explain the difficulty in treating these two conditions when they are comorbid, because both need to be treated simultaneously and in individually tailored ways for treatment to be effective.

To use systems theory language, in cases of comorbid chronic pain and PTSD, dynamical attractors in neuronal firings and related components become tightly integrated across two subsystems, forming an integrated attractor system of subordinate systems. Moreover, the patient's adapting system complex readily gravitates to the integrated attractor system once it is formed. It serves as a magnet in the system's state space, quickly reassembling from its subordinate systems and their components, through sensitization and mutual reciprocity.

Therefore, in cases of comorbid pain and PTSD, in nonlinear dynamical system terms, mutual maintenance and exacerbation takes place because the integrated system reacts by resisting change to interventions addressing only one component of the comorbid pain-PTSD complex. The system accommodates to the treatment input by recreating an equilibrium around the combined chronic pain experience-PTSD dynamical attractor, and the result is negative. Asmundson and Taylor describe ongoing research on interventions targeting simultaneously both pain and PTSD in comorbid cases. Their intervention strategy in these cases of comorbid chronic pain and PTSD is consistent with our nonlinear dynamical systems approach in explaining the development of dynamical, integrated attractors across pain and PTSD.

At the same time, despite examples such as these that help explain difficult areas related to the study of pain, we remind again that the application of nonlinear dynamical system modeling to the study of pain is in its infancy, there are as yet no empirical data deriving from this approach, and continued thought and research are needed.

Appendix 1

Some Basic Mathematics of Nonlinear Dynamical Systems Theory

Nonlinear dynamical systems, at the mathematical level, comprise of a set of coupled differential equations. Differential equations describe changes in the values of a system over time. For example, if a variable's value at time $t+1$ is 10 greater than at t, linear growth is taking place in the system. But growth is nonlinear when a quadratic [squared], or higher-order term, is involved, for example, variable x at time $t_1 = x$ at t multiplied by the constant r $(1 - x$ at $t)$, which gives the formula $x_{(t+1)} = rx_t - rx_t^2$. The behavior of the system defined by this equation depends on whether r can vary and on the initial condition of x, or x_0. For this equation, when r is between 0 and 2, all x values converge over time, but when r is around 2.7, the system's behavior becomes "totally" unpredictable for very small changes in the initial value, so that the final values of x over time vary "wildly and irregularly" (Boom, 2004, p. 81). Even slight perturbations of the system can lead to radical state shifts, so that we can describe the system as becoming "chaotic." (The so-called "butterfly" effect, related to sensitivity to initial conditions in far-from-equilibrium system states, is consistent with this description of chaos by Boom.)

References

Abraham, F. D. (1995). Introduction to dynamics: A basic language; a basic metamodeling strategy. In F. D. Abraham & A. R. Gilgen (Eds.), *Chaos theory in psychology* (pp. 31–49). Westport, CT: Greenwood.

Abraham, F. D., & Gilgen, A. R. (Eds.). (1995). *Chaos theory in psychology*. Westport, CT: Greenwood Press.

American Psychiatric Association. (1994). *Diagnostic and statistical manual of mental disorders* (4th ed.). Washington, DC: Author.

American Psychiatric Association. (2000). *Diagnostic and statistical manual of mental disorders: Text revision* (4th ed.). Washington, DC: Author.

Asmundson, G. J. G., & Taylor, S. (2006). PTSD and chronic pain: Cognitive-behavioral perspectives and practical implications. In G. Young, A. W. Kane, & K. Nicholson (Eds.), *Psychological knowledge in court: PTSD, pain, and TBI* (pp. 225–241). New York: Springer Science+Business Media.

Beck, A. T., Steer, R. A., & Brown, G. K. (1987). *Beck depression inventory: Manual.* San Antonio, TX: Harcourt Brace.

Beck, A. T., Steer, R. A., & Brown, G. K. (1996). *Beck depression inventory: Manual* (2nd ed.). San Antonio, TX: Harcourt Brace.

Beck, A. T., Steer, R. A., & Garbin, M. (1988). Psychometric properties of the Beck Depression Inventory: Twenty-five years of evaluation. *Clinical Psychology Review, 8*, 77–100.

Boom, J. (2004). Individualism and collectivism: A dynamic systems interpretation of Piaget's interactionism. In J. I. M. Carpendale & U. Müller (Eds.), *Social interaction and the development of knowledge* (pp. 67–85). Mahwah, NJ: Erlbaum.

Burns, J. W., Bruehl, S., & Caceres, C. (2004). Anger management style, blood pressure reactivity, and acute pain sensitivity: Evidence for "Trait x Situation" models. *Annals of Behavioral Medicine, 27*, 195–204.

Chapman, C. R. (2004). Pain perception, affective mechanisms, and conscious experience. In T. Hadjistavropoulos & K. D. Craig (Eds.), *Pain: Psychological perspectives* (pp. 59–85). Mahwah, NJ: Erlbaum.

Chapman, C. R., Nakamura, Y., & Flores, L. Y. (1999). Chronic pain and consciousness: A constructivist perspective. In R. J. Gatchel & D. C. Turk (Eds.), *Psychosocial factors in pain: Critical perspectives* (pp. 35–55). New York: Guilford Press.

Cocchiarella, L., & Andersson, G. B. J. (Eds.). (2001). *Guides to the evaluation of permanent impairment* (5th ed.). Chicago, IL: American Medical Association.

Damasio, A. R. (1994). *Descartes' error: Emotion and reason in the human brain.* New York: Grosset/Putman.

DiClemente, C. C., & Prochaska, J. O. (1982). Self-change and therapy change of smoking behavior: A comparison of processes of change in cessation and maintenance. *Addictive Behaviors, 7*, 133–142.

Feeney, S. L. (2004). The relationship between pain and negative affect in older adults: Anxiety as a predictor of pain. *Journal of Anxiety Disorders, 18*, 733–744.

Fishbain, D. A., Turner, D., Rosomoff, H. L., & Rosomoff, R. S. (2001). Millon behavioral health inventory scores of patients with chronic pain associated with myofascial pain syndrome. *Pain Medicine, 2*, 328–335.

Francis, S. E. (1995). Chaotic phenomena in psychophysiological self-regulation. In R. Robertson & A. Combs (Eds.), *Chaos theory in psychology and the life sciences* (253–265). Mahwah, NJ: Erlbaum.

Fredrickson, B. L., & Losada, M. F. (2005). Positive affect and the complex dynamics of human flourishing. *American Psychologist, 60*, 678–686.

Freeman, W. J. (1995a). *Societies of brain: A study in the neuroscience of love and hate.* Hillsdale, NJ: Erlbaum.

Freeman, W. J. (1995b). The kiss of chaos and the sleeping beauty of psychology. In F. D. Abraham & A. R. Gilgen (Eds.), *Chaos theory in psychology* (pp. 19–29). Westport, CT: Greenwood.

Gatchel, R. J. (1991). Early development of physical and mental deconditioning in painful spinal disorders. In T. G. Mayer, V. Mooney, & R. J. Gatchel (Eds.), *Contemporary conservative care for painful spinal disorders* (pp. 278–289). Philadelphia: Lea & Febiger

Gatchel, R. J. (1996). Psychological disorders and chronic pain: Cause and effect relationships. In R. J. Gatchel & D. C. Turk (Eds.), *Psychological approaches to pain management: A practitioner's handbook* (pp. 33–52). New York: Guilford Press.

Gatchel, R. J. (2004). Comorbidity of chronic pain and mental health disorders: The biopsychosocial perspective. *American Psychologist, 59*, 795–805.

Gatchel, R. J. (2005). *Clinical essentials of pain management.* Washington, DC: American Psychological Association.

Gleick, J. (1987). *Chaos.* New York: Viking Penguin.

Gottman, J. M. (1991). Chaos and regulated change in families: A metaphor for the study of transitions. In P. A. Cowen & M. Hetherington (Eds.), *Family transitions* (pp. 247–272). Hillsdale, NJ: Erlbaum.

Granic, I., & Patterson, G. R. (2006). Toward a comprehensive model of antisocial development: A dynamic systems approach. *Psychological Review, 113*, 101–131.

Guastello, S. J. (1995). *Chaos, catastrophe, and human affairs: Application of nonlinear dynamics to work, organizations, and social evolution.* Mahwah, NJ: Erlbaum.

Hadjistavropoulos, H. D., Asmundson, G. J. G., & Kowalyk, K. M. (2004). Measures of anxiety: Is there a difference in their ability to predict functioning at three-month follow-up among pain patients? *European Journal of Pain, 8*, 1–11.

Hadjistavropoulos, H. D., & Williams, A. C. de C. (2004). Psychological interventions and chronic pain. In T. Hadjistravropoulos & K. D. Craig (Eds.), *Pain: Psychological perspectives*. (pp. 271–301). Mahwah, NJ: Erlbaum.

Heath, R. A. (2000). *Nonlinear dynamics: Techniques and applications in psychology.* Mahwah, NJ: Erlbaum.

Howe, M. L., & Lewis, M. D. (2005). The importance of dynamic systems approaches for understanding development. *Developmental Review, 25*, 247–251.

Hufford, M. R., Witkiewitz, K., Shields, A. L., Kodya, S., & Caruso, J. C. (2003). Relapse as a nonlinear dynamic system: Application to patients with alcohol use disorder. *Journal of Abnormal Psychology, 112*, 219–227.

Kauffman, S. (1990). The sciences of complexity and "origins of order". *PSA: Proceedings of the Biennial Meeting of the Philosophy of Science Association, 2*, 299–322.

Kauffman, S. A. (1991). Antichaos and adaptation. *Scientific American, 265*, 78–84.

Kauffman, S. A. (1993). *The origins of order*. New York: Oxford University Press.

Kerns, R. D., & Jacob, M. C. (1992). Assessment of psychosocial context of the experience of chronic pain. In D. C. Turk & R. Melzack (Eds.), *Handbook of pain assessment* (pp. 235–253). New York: Guilford Press.

Kerns, R. D., Rosenberg, R., Jamison, R. N., Caudill, M. A., & Haythorthwaite, J. (1997). Readiness to adopt a self-management approach to chronic pain: The pain stages of change questionnaire. *Pain, 72*, 227–234.

Krueger, R. F., Tackett, J. L., & Markon, K. E. (2004). Structural models of comorbidity among common mental disorders: Connections to chronic pain. *Advances in Psychosomatic Medicine, 25*, 63–77.

Lansing, J. S. (2003). Complex adaptive systems. *Annual Review of Anthropology, 32*, 183–204.

Lewis, M. D., & Granic, I. (2000). Introduction: A new approach to the study of emotional development. In M. D. Lewis & I. Granic (Eds.), *Emotion, development, and self-organization: Dynamic systems approaches to emotional development* (pp. 1–12). Cambridge, UK: Cambridge University Press.

Livneh, H., & Parker, R. M. (2005). Psychological adaptation to disability: Perspectives from chaos and complexity theory. *Rehabilitation Counseling Bulletin, 49*(1), 17–28.

Maddox, J. E. (1995). Yes, people can change, but can psychotherapists? *Contemporary Psychology, 40*, 1047–1048.

Masterpasqua, F., & Perna, P. (Eds.). (1997). *The psychological meaning of chaos: Translating theory into practice*. Washington, DC: American Psychological Association.

McNally, R. J. (2003). *Remembering trauma*. Cambridge, MA: Harvard University Press.

Melzack, R., & Katz, J. (2001). The McGill Pain Questionnaire: Appraisal and current status. In D. C. Turk & R. Melzack (Eds.), *Handbook of pain assessment* (pp. 35–52). New York: Guilford Press.

Melzack, R., & Katz, J. (2006). Pain in the 21st century. The neuromatrix and beyond. In G. Young, A. W. Kane, & K. Nicholson (Eds.), *Psychological knowledge in court: PTSD, pain, and TBI* (pp. 129–148). New York: Springer Science+Business Media.

Melzack, R., & Wall, P. D. (1965). Pain mechanisms: A new theory. *Science, 150*, 971–979.

Otis, J. D., Pincus, D., & Keane, T. M. (2006). Comorbid chronic pain and Posttraumatic Stress Disorder across the lifespan: A review of theoretical models. In G. Young, A. W. Kane, & K. Nicholson (Eds.), *Psychological knowledge in court: PTSD, pain, and TBI* (pp. 242–268). New York: Springer Science+Business Media.

Porro, C. A. (2003). Functional imaging and pain: Behavior, perception, and modulation. *Neuroscientist, 9*, 354–369.

Prochaska, J. O., DiClemente, C. C., & Norcross, J. C. (1992). In search of how people change: Applications to addictive behaviors. *American Psychologist, 47*, 1102–1114.

Prochaska, J. O., Norcross, J. C., & DiClemente, C. C. (1994). *Changing for good: The revolutionary program that explains the six stages of change and teaches you how to free yourself from bad habits*. New York: Morrow.

Reiss, S., Peterson, R. A., Gursky, M., & McNally, R. J. (1986). Anxiety sensitivity, anxiety frequency, and the prediction of fearlessness. *Behaviour Research and Therapy, 24*, 1–8.

Robertson, R., & Combs, A. (Eds.). (1995). *Chaos theory in psychology and the life sciences*. Mahwah, NJ: Erlbaum.

Robinson, M. E., & Riley, J. L., III. (1999). The role of emotion in pain. In R. J. Gatchel & D. C. Turk (Eds.), *Psychosocial factors in pain* (pp. 74–88). New York: Guilford Press.

Schore, A. N. (2000). The self-organization of the right brain and the neurobiology of emotional development. In M. D. Lewis & I. Granic (Eds.), *Emotion, development, and self-organization: Dynamic systems approaches to emotional development* (pp. 155–185). Cambridge, UK: Cambridge University Press.

Sharp, T. J., & Harvey, A. G. (2001). Chronic pain and Posttraumatic Stress Disorder: Mutual maintenance? *Clinical Psychology Review, 24*, 857–877.

Thelen, E., & Smith, L. B. (1994). *A dynamical systems approach to the development of cognition and action*. Cambridge, MA: MIT Press.

Turk, D. C., & Monarch, E. S. (2002). Biopsychosocial perspective on chronic pain. In D. C. Turk & R. J. Gatchel (Eds.), *Psychological approaches to pain management* (pp. 3–29). New York: Guilford Press.

Turk, D. C., Monarch, E. S., & Williams, A. D. (2004). Assessment of chronic pain sufferers. In T. Hadjistravropoulos & K. D. Craig (Eds.), *Pain: Psychological perspectives* (pp. 209–243). Mahwah, NJ: Erlbaum.

Turk, D. C., & Okifuji, A. (2003). Pain management. In I. B. Weiner (Series Ed.), A. M. Nezu, C. M. Nezu, & P. A. Geller (Vol. Eds.), *Handbook of psychology: Vol. 9, Health psychology* (pp. 293–315). Hoboken, NJ: Wiley.

Turk, D. C., & Rudy, T. E. (1988). Toward an empirically-derived taxonomy of chronic pain patients: Integration of psychological assessment data. *Journal of Consulting and Clinical Psychology, 56*, 233–238.

Vallacher, R. R., Read, S. J., & Nowak, A. (2002). The dynamical perspective in personality and social psychology. *Personality and Social Psychology Review, 6*, 264–273.

Vollmer-Conna, U., Fazou, C., Cameron, B., Li, H., Brennan, C., Luck, L., Davenport, T., Wakefield, D., Hickie, I., & Lloyd, A. (2004). Production of pro-inflammatory cytokines correlates with the symptoms of acute sickness behavior in humans. *Psychological Medicine, 34*, 1289–1297.

Von Korff, M., Crane, P., Lane, M., Miglioretti, D. L., Simon, G., Saunders, K., Stang, P., Brandenburg, N., & Kessler, R. (2005).Chronic spinal pain and physical-mental comorbidity in the United States: Results from the national comorbidity survey replication. *Pain, 113*, 331–339.

Vowles, K. E., Gross, R. T., & Sorrell, J. T. (2004). Predicting work status following interdisciplinary treatment for chronic pain. *European Journal of Pain, 8*, 351–358.

Waldrop, M. M. (1992). *Complexity: The emerging science at the edge of order and chaos*. New York: Touchstone.

Ward, L. M. (2002). *Dynamical cognitive science*. Cambridge, MA: MIT Press.

Ward, N. G., Bloom, V. L., & Friedel, R. O. (1979). The effectiveness of tricyclic antidepressants in the treatment of coexisting pain and depression. *Pain, 7*, 331–341

Watkins, L. R., & Maier, S. F. (2005). Immune regulation of central nervous system functions: From sickness responses to pathological pain. *Journal of Internal Medicine, 257*, 139–155.

Wieseler-Frank, J., Maier, S. F., & Watkins, L. R. (2005). Immune-to-brain communication dynamically modulates pain: Physiological and pathological consequences. *Brain Behavior and Immunity, 19*, 104–111.

Witkiewitz, K., & Marlatt, G. A. (2004). Relapse prevention for alcohol and drug problems: That was Zen, this is Tao. *American Psychologist, 59*, 224–235.

Williams, C., & Arrigo, B. (2002). *Law, psychology, and justice: Chaos theory and the new (dis)order*. Albany, NY: State University of New York Press.

World Health Organization. (1992). *International classification of diseases. Mental and behavioral disorders (including disorders of psychological development), clinical descriptions and diagnostic guidelines* (10th rev.). Geneva: WHO.

Young, G. (1997). *Adult development, therapy, and culture: A postmodern synthesis*. New York: Plenum.

Young, G., & Chapman, C. R. (2006). Pain and affect as a nonlinear dynamical system. In G. Young, A. W. Kane, & K. Nicholson (Eds.), *Psychological knowledge in court: PTSD, pain, and TBI* (pp. 181–192). New York: Springer Science+Business Media.

Young, G., & Gagnon, M. (1990). Neonatal laterality, birth stresses, familial sinistrality, and left brain inhibition. *Developmental Neuropsychology, 6*, 127–150.

Young, G., Kane, A. W., & Nicholson, K. (Eds.). (2006). *Psychological knowledge in court: PTSD, pain, and TBI*. New York: Springer Science+Business Media.

Zautra, A. J., Johnson, L. M., & Davis, M. C. (2005). Positive affect as a source of resilience for women in chronic pain. *Journal of Consulting and Clinical Psychology, 73*, 212–220.

9

Considering Course and Treatment in Rehabilitation: Sequential and Dynamic Causality

J. DOUGLAS SALMON, JR., MAREK J. CELINSKI, AND GERALD YOUNG

In this chapter, we expand the chronic pain model presented by Gatchel (Gatchel, 1991; Gatchel & Kishino, 2006) and apply related principles to the general rehabilitation context. Our model is presented in general enough terms to apply not only to chronic pain, but also to traumatic brain injury (TBI), and Posttraumatic Stress Disorder (PTSD), covering the major psychological injury and rehabilitation conditions. The model permits understanding of individual differences in rehabilitation patients relative to the unfolding recovery process, may help guide the course of treatment, and may facilitate maximal treatment adherence. The model is comprehensive and multifactorial, describing interactions between the "precipitating event," which may be a trauma or illness/disease, and the broad range of processes that shape the recovery process.

In addition to considering functional outcome, recovery is viewed as a psychological state cumulatively representing individuals' attitude toward recovery, their strategy for coping, and the manner in which coping is implemented. We term such an outcome the "subjective recovery strategy." We postulate that individuals in rehabilitation are governed by this evolving process. It reflects a complex interplay of emotional, behavioral, and cognitive-perceptual variables in conjunction with the influence of environmental and incidental factors. The model emphasizes that individuals' reactions to a precipitating event, be it injury or illness, are best conceived in terms of sequential and dynamic causality. The former is characterized by a typical stepwise process, or stages through which individuals pass, and the latter by additional synergistic processes associated with internal and external factors over which individuals have various degrees of control, and which varies with the state of their recovery. Such a model provides a conceptual framework whereby corresponding assessment tools can effectively monitor the change in individuals' recovery status over time, and guide intervention accordingly.

Models of Course of Recovery in Pain and Related Clinical Conditions

In this section, we review standard models of the course of chronic pain, TBI, PTSD, the major clinical conditions of psychological injury. By definition, chronic Pain Disorder speaks to the cessation of recovery, or its absence, from a discrete acute pain episode. Gatchel's model (1991; Gatchel & Kishino, 2006) provides a description of the sequentially occurring stages leading from acute to chronic pain. According to Gatchel's model, at the initial stage, which typically extends from 2 to 4 months, there are normal emotional reactions associated with pain, such as fear, anxiety, and worry but, if the pain persists, the second stage develops, which is associated with a broader range of behavioral and psychological reactions. These reactions manifest as learned helplessness, distress, anger, and somatization, which are secondary responses to the newly developing, more chronic nature of pain.

In Gatchel's model, if the pain continues, in the third stage, the person's life begins to be consumed by pain, causing habituation and resignation to the pain, reflected in adopting a "sick role." The chronic pain patient eventually relinquishes normal responsibilities and social obligations and, in the perception of the patient, this role may become a secondary gain of not being healthy.

According to Gatchel's conceptualization, the way in which pain patients respond to their prolonged pain is influenced by their premorbid or preexisting personality/psychological characteristics (which provides a habitual way of responding to stressful situations) as by their current socioeconomic and environmental factors. By acknowledging the importance of preexisting factors, this model is referred to as a diathesis/stress model, whereby the stress of coping with chronic pain exacerbates individuals' preexisting characteristics (diathesis).

In reviewing the diathesis/stress model, Turk (2002) stated that the impact of an initiating event is more likely to contribute to disability in people who interpret symptoms as indicative of serious problems, are preoccupied with bodily processes, respond with fear to the perceived symptoms, and also believe that the way to prevent exacerbation of pain and possibly further physical damage is to avoid activities that increase their pain.

Dersh, Polatin, and Gatchel (2002) concluded that the diathesis-stress model has received the most support for explaining the development of depressive disorder and personality disorder in the context of chronic pain. According to them, less evidence has accumulated for explaining the development of anxiety disorders, substance abuse, and somatoform disorders (other than pain) in relation to chronic pain.

With respect to TBI, Mateo and Glod (2003) also described three stages through which severely brain-traumatized patients pass during the recovery process. In the first stage, TBI patients do not have much insight into their condition and overestimate their abilities. In the second stage, such patients have more insight, but this has a negative consequence in the way of greater levels of depression, anxiety, and low self-esteem. In the third stage, TBI patients exhibit levels of distress that depend on their state of recovery.

Gatchel's (1991) chronic pain model has both interesting differences from and similarities to Mateo and Glod's TBI model. According to Mateo and Glod, in the first stage, lack of awareness in severely brain-traumatized patients prevents them from developing concerns and worries about their physical condition, resulting in an overestimation of their capacities. Increased awareness would make it possible to acknowledge their impaired functioning in the broader context of the impact on the self, on their overall life situation, and on remembered pretraumatic abilities. As a result, severely impacted TBI patients, at first, do not become depressed, anxious, or develop low self-esteem. However, as awareness of their difficulties increase, the reaction of TBI patients, in the second phase of dealing with their injury, is quite similar to the one described by Gatchel for chronic pain.

The final stage in the evolution of TBI patients' response to their injury, as described by Mateo and Glod, is similar to what is described by Gatchel's (1991) model, in that a severely brain-injured person may develop a sense of serious disability, habituation to her or his limitations, and resignation to her or his losses and that recovery to the pretraumatic level is not possible. Eventually, severe TBI patients find that their condition provides at least some sense of comfort, in that they are excused from various social and other responsibilities. Mood fluctuations will occur, depending on whether they act from the perspective of an unacceptable sense of loss or with respect to acceptance of their perceived situation.

Mateo and Glod's (2003) emphasis on regained awareness of psychosocial issues as a source of negative emotional dynamics in TBI cases is congruent with the notion that the nature of a patient's conceptualization of her or his own condition and overall situation (schemas), together with her or his coping abilities, are factors that influence posttraumatic adjustment. In this regard, often in rehabilitation therapy, efforts to modify an individual's schemas and coping abilities become the major objects of intervention.

Mateo and Glod (2003) stipulate that treatment should flexibly respond to the changing cognitive, psychological, and behavioral needs of the patient, and to the changing educational needs of the caregivers. When treatment is appropriately targeted to the patient's and to the caregivers' needs, the recovery process is more rapid and complete.

In the context of PTSD, whereas the most common course is that of relatively immediate onset followed by gradual improvement in symptomotology over time, alternate courses, including delayed onset and a worsening course, have been documented (see Chapter 5 by Young, this book). A worsening PTSD course has been associated with initial bad dreams, physiological responses to reminders of the trauma, panic and avoidance, anger at time of trauma, negative interpretations to recollections, and numbing and dissociative symptoms (e.g., Ehlers, Mayou, & Bryant, 1998). A study by Bryant and Harvey (2002) supported the idea that delayed-onset PTSD may be in some cases due to initial presence of subclinical PTSD features that, with progression of time, further deteriorate to the degree that symptoms meet full diagnostic criteria. As with the case of chronic pain and TBI, the recovery outcomes with regard to PTSD also vary, ranging from full recovery, to less than optimal outcome, to significant disability to even becoming totally disabled.

In all three cases (chronic pain, TBI, PTSD), in order to optimize recovery, the course of intervention must first serve to identify, address, and move beyond barriers that impede the potential recovery from occurring. If the condition stabilizes below the projected optimal level, intervention efforts should turn to addressing barriers, and to the maximization of the individual's coping and functional capacities through the utilization of compensatory strategies, activity/environmental modifications, and accommodative resources, even though the individual still is experiencing lingering symptoms (Mukherjee, Heller, & Alper, 2001).

Adherence to Treatment: Mitigating Losses in the Recovery Process

In presenting evidence to court, forensic psychologists and other mental health professionals need to assess complainants in a comprehensive manner in order to meet evidence requirements demanded by judicial rules and regulations, such as specified in the *Daubert* trilogy. (See the Section 2 by Kane). This refers not only to careful analysis of the index or precipitating event and its consequences in terms of psychological symptoms, disorders, diagnoses, disabilities, and functional impairments, but also in terms of injured patients' adherence to their treatment regime. A related issue is their motivation to return to their preevent psychological status and daily functional activities, whether at home, at work, or at school, and their subsequent efforts in returning to their primary preevent daily functional activities, for example, in terms of utilizing recommended assisted devices, following a preliminary plan of returning to modified duties, and so on.

For our purposes, with respect to the rehabilitation context, forensic assessors need to carefully evaluate the degree of treatment compliance. Did the patient attend all recommended physical and psychological sessions? Did the clinical notes indicate a constructive attitude and full participation? Barriers to or difficulties with treatment compliance may be iatrogenically created when the interventions are not focused upon the client's primary perceived barriers, and treatment does not address the client's primary rehabilitation objectives, including those of functional role fulfillment and independent living priorities (Salmon, 1998).

Antoniazzi, Celinski, and Alcock (2002) observed a similar phenomenon in their survey of rehabilitation staff and patients. They found that whereas patients undergoing rehabilitation for bodily injuries regarded pain as a very high treatment priority, rehabilitation staff did not perceive reduction of pain to be an equally important goal. In a similar vein, Clay and Hopps (2003) emphasized that treatment should be generally congruent with a patient's gender-related lifestyle and with rehabilitation objectives. Patient adherence to treatment is further predicted by social support, motivation, personality, environmental factors, and treatment factors (Chervinsky et al., 1998; Clay & Hopps, 2003; MacMillan, Williams, & Bryant, 2003). According to Chervinsky et al. (1998), motivation and factors that are linked to motivation, such as level of denial, self-awareness, hostility, apathy, expectations, locus of control, values, and knowledge of treatment, all play a role in treatment adherence. Further patient variables that contribute to treatment adherence include: socioeconomic status, support system, health beliefs and behaviors, self-esteem and self-efficacy, level of adjustment, and depression (Clay & Hopps, 2003). McMillan, Williams, and Bryant (2003) also found that severity of cognitive deficits played a major role in patients' ability to reflect on their traumatic experience, thereby making treatment adherence more difficult. Contributing environmental characteristics include social support, transportation needs, and access to treatment facilities (Clay & Hopps, 2003). Facilitative treatment characteristics include: minimal treatment side effects, minimal requirement for patient deviation from regular routine, and treatment simplicity and brevity (Clay & Hopps, 2003).

To summarize, treatment adherence factors explain, in part, the variance of recovery across and within individuals over time. Treatment objectives, strategies, and methods must systematically readjust to patients' emerging or changing needs, and continually reengage them for ongoing maximal treatment compliance to occur.

The next section introduces our interactive model that captures the constructs of both sequential and dynamic causality, viewed as critical factors in the interplay between the evolving clinical course, interventions, and treatment adherence.

Sequential and Dynamic Causality

At any given time, to evaluate patients' stage and style of recovery, assessing professionals need to determine: whether a person has been responsive to therapy, how much recovery has been achieved, and whether ongoing intervention is justified. To this end, one must take into consideration: the normative success rate for the condition when it is treated; the secondary, tertiary, and incidental interactive factors at play; the individual's schemas; and individual's coping style and coping strategies. Consequently, an individual's subjective recovery strategy evolves with the ongoing impact of therapeutic interventions.

However, psychologists need quantitative indices of the scope of recovery after psychological injury, and such measures are noticeably lacking. Typically, psychologists ask patients how they are doing, perhaps using verbal report according to an 11-point subjective distress scale from 0 to 10, where 10 represents the worst possible psychological condition, or no improvement. We propose that psychologists and other mental health professionals would profit from having more quantitative measures with adequate reliability and validity that can chart patients' progress after the onset of psychological injury. When response to recovery is graphed in a quantitative manner, using standardized instruments with known reliability and validity parameters, the recovery of the patient is being monitored by a recovery curve. A recovery curve may provide clues about the variables intervening between the initial impact of the index event and the patient's current psychological state. For instance, a deteriorating course in the face of a minor injury may suggest the potential presence of coexisting physical or emotional pathology, a lack of adherence/effort in therapy, the working of a misinformed illness etiology schema, or malingering or related symptom amplification processes. (See Section II, this book.)

Through accurate identification of such recovery curves, one can better determine whether the individual's recovery trajectory predominantly reflects an expected course after the type of event that had been experienced, given the person's context and other attributes, secondary or tertiary reactions to trauma, or factors unrelated to the event. By understanding that event-triggered causality represents sequentially unfolding mental states and psychophysiological conditions (that may be causal sources of varied symptoms in their own right), we emphasize not only the causal onset of the condition, but also predisposing and preexisting factors, causal maintenance and evolution, resulting in symptom worsening or exacerbation, and confounding factors, such as possible malingering.

Therefore, we argue that the mental health assessor cannot arrive at a comprehensive understanding of the patient presenting with psychological symptoms after an index event without considering the patient's recovery curve in rehabilitation up to the point of the assessment. In our view, the concepts of *sequential and dynamic causality* reflect the recovery process, in which, with the progression of time, the primary reaction to the "precipitating event" may evolve in the context of internal and external factors that, in turn, may become supplementary sources of causation on their own. Our multifactorial model (Figure 9.1) specifies that with the onset of the event, the individual must deal with difficult physical, emotional, and/or cognitive symptoms that alter existing life schemas and interfere with daily functioning. Further changes in initial psychological manifestations may occur as a result of dynamics in secondary and tertiary stages after the initial event. Therefore, the model consists of three phases in the response of patients to

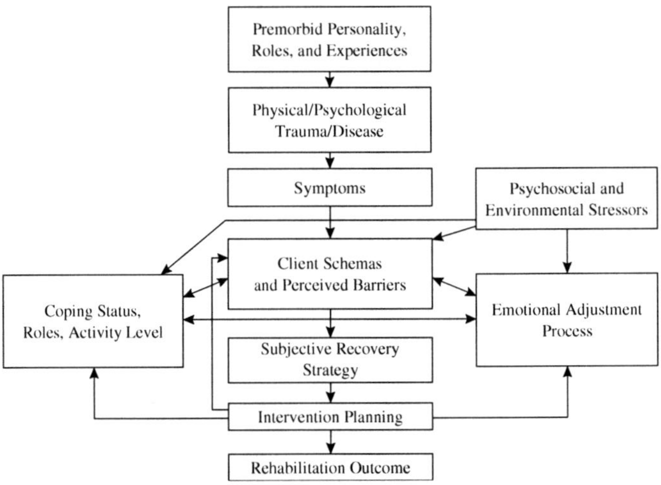

FIGURE 9.1. Rehabilitation assessment and intervention process model

precipitating factors, along with incidental or unrelated factors. We describe these phases in more detail in the following:

I. *Primary Impacts Directly Related to Event.* Primary impacts concern direct reactions to bodily injury/illness (such as acute pain or psychophysiological discomfort) or to the threat of substantial bodily harm or personal loss. Primary impacts are comprised of the initial physical, cognitive, and psychological symptoms. Typically, if psychiatric/psychological diagnoses or related mental states apply, they refer to conditions such as acute pain, TBI or mild concussion, Acute Stress Disorder, phobic and more generalized anxiety reactions, dissociation, and Conversion Disorder (Diagnostic and Statistical Manual of Mental Disorders, *DSM-IV* TR; 1994, 2000). By definition, these conditions would not arise unless the event is *perceived as significantly injurious or psychotraumatic* to the victim. Studies clearly link PTSD with perceived life threat during the trauma (Elklit, 1997; Ozer, Best, Lipsey, & Weiss, 2003). Ozer et al. (2003), and Malt and Olafsen (1992) noted that there is relatively weak association between the real danger of an event, or severity of an injury, and the appraisal of the gravity of the situation. In the emotional realm, the effects of trauma may occasionally be delayed. In delayed onset, psychotraumatic symptoms may develop through subsequent reappraisal of the event as potentially life threatening.

II. *Secondary Impacts/Processes to the Original Event.* Secondary impacts reflect sequentially triggered (mal)adjustment response(s) to the primary impacts of an event that may have been injurious. Secondary and tertiary psychological impacts serve to worsen the individual's condition, by imposing mild to significant affective distress, such as depression, anxiety, and anger/irritability and related symptoms. In the emotional domain, examples of secondary reactions that may be diagnosed include Generalized Anxiety Disorder, Major Depressive Disorder, and the broad category of Adjustment Disorders (in terms of *DSM-IV* classification criteria). These conditions may not be present, at first, but may appear as products of further processing of the original primary impact and the individual's ensuing residual physical, emotional, and cognitive symptoms in her or his context. The latter would include her or his psychosocial and therapeutic environment, and pretraumatic vulnerabilities, supports, and coping abilities, including history of traumas and preexisting physical and psychological conditions. These negative developments can be ameliorated to some degree by intervention, with barriers or complications in recovery largely dependent on the characteristics of the individual and her or his context.

For chronic pain, secondary impacts refer to the continuation of acute pain beyond a normative time frame for an injury in question, given the psychosocial context and other characteristics of the individual involved. In the case of TBI, when a concussion is mild, postconcussive effects may last beyond the expected time frame of a few months at most. Even in the absence of an initial primary physical, emotional, or cognitive impairment that reaches diagnostic levels, secondary adjustment responses may be triggered by the index event, especially in cases of delayed PTSD (or phobia), as mentioned above. Further, if there are initial symptoms as well as delayed ones, it is not uncommon for the secondary effects to form a negative feedback loop by aggravating the primary symptoms, which may, in turn, exacerbate the secondary symptoms in a vicious cycle. An example is that delayed perception of an accident as quite catastrophic will act to increase anxiety and pain sensitivity (Robinson & Riley, 1999), which, in turn, will increase adjustment problems. Melzack (1999) summarized this relation of primary and secondary impacts by stating, "Each kind of stressor can produce physiological effects that are additive with the effects of other stressors" (p. 99).

Moreover, symptom diffusion may occur at this level when a secondary emotional process like Major Depressive Disorder (Dersh et al., 2002) creates altogether new (or additional sources of) physical and/or cognitive symptomotology, such as a sleep disturbance and secondary attentional/ memory disturbance, respectively. Secondary processes/factors that have been recognized as constituting sources of disablement in their own right include anxiety, depression, fear of pain, and fear of reinjury (Turk, 2002), psychological distress and pain-related impairments (Turner, Jensen, & Romano, 2000; Turner, Jensen, Warms, & Cardenas, 2002), and the psychosocial environment when, according to Turk and Flor (1999), it "perhaps unwittingly supports the 'pain patient role' [and] can impede alleviation of pain, successful rehabilitation, reduction of disability, and improvement in adjustment" (p. 25).

III. *Tertiary and More Remote Reactive Impacts.* In the next phase of the sequential model, the patient may experience changes that further worsen or perpetuate her or his physical and psychological condition. Although removed from the *secondary* reactive impacts, *tertiary* impacts remain traceable to the original event. Physically, examples of tertiary impacts include the evolution of obesity, high blood pressure, or physical deconditioning/cardiac problems from injury-related inactivity. Psychologically, tertiary impacts include additional emotional distress due to change in psychosocial status, strained family relations, divorce, loss of social contact, termination of employment, and street drug/alcohol abuse as a way of "self medicating." As complicating stressors, they may trigger adverse emotional consequences not initially present that are associated with a deepening sense of helplessness and further functional limitations.

IV. *Incidental/Unrelated Factors.* There are numerous unrelated events, preexisting or coexisting, which may have an adverse cumulative effect upon the recovery process, including, but not limited to: the death or serious illness of a loved one; unrelated medical conditions; and loss of a job due to employer closure. Their impact often produces an augmentation of disability perception and regression in psychological symptoms (primary or otherwise), particularly by way of increased anxiety and depressive reactions. The difficulty lies in disentangling their effects from ones more directly related to the consequences of the precipitating event, whether primary, secondary, or tertiary. The assessor needs to consider the overall coping ability and resources of the patient, and how the incidental and unrelated factors have weakened them, contributing to any general inability to handle supplementary stresses. The psychologist should consider that postevent developments in the life of the patient, such as the ones described, may have been handled better had the event in question not occurred therefore, rendering even seemingly unrelated stressors to the event quite related to them through the reduced coping skills and resilience caused by the event.

In sum, secondary and tertiary effects, and other exacerbating factors arising from the precipitating event, often form vicious circles that may contribute to the maintenance and worsening of psychological symptoms, impairments, disorders, or disabilities, if they are not closely monitored and dealt with in the rehabilitation context. The greater the degree of influence of secondary, tertiary, and incidental factors, the greater the prognosis will depart from the expected or uncomplicated recovery curve. In other words, as these factors take on greater influence, there is a departure from the expected prognosis of any given injury or illness, given the characteristics of the original injury, the individual involved, and the context, due to the multifactorial and synergistic processes involved in recovery.

The variables described below refer to other factors to consider in assessing an individual's response to a precipitating event and its subsequent effects (see Figure 9.1).

a. *Premorbid psychosocial, health, and personality status.* Relevant medical and psychological history prior to an illness or injury can significantly affect the recovery process, as can certain preexisting personality traits. Factors such as these act as modifying variables on postevent primary and secondary psychological processes. Dersh et al. (2002) unify these under an overall concept of "diathesis," defined as "preexisting semidormant characteristics of the individual before the onset of chronic pain that are then activated and exacerbated by the stress of this chronic condition, eventually resulting in diagnosable psychopathology" (p. 773). An equivalent concept in the legal field is the "Thin Skull Rule" (McInnes, 1997), which specifies that any negligent person must take victims as they find them, including their emotional and/or physical vulnerabilities.
b. *Client schemas.* In rehabilitation, schemas refer to cognitive representations, or perceptual fields of reference of relevant life domains, and to attitudes that act to filter and shape behavior in contexts bearing on them. Relevant psychological schemas in rehabilitation include the "existential," or generalized attitudinal/values schema, and perception of illness schema, concerning the individual's overall context (Dalal & Pande, 1988; Lipowski, 1970, 1981), which research has linked to rehabilitation outcome (Keljtikangas-Jarvinen, 1986). The coping schema reflects, in part, individuals' long-standing characteristics activated postmorbidly. It includes individuals' sense of self-efficacy (Bandura, 1997) and subjective interpretations that individuals may assign to events that require coping strategies (Groomes & Leahy, 2002). The symptom coping schema refers to how patients perceive their capacity to live with their symptoms and to their perception of overall adaptive potential. Studies have

indicated that certain coping strategies used by rehabilitation clients are particularly instrumental in promoting favorable adaptation and outcomes (i.e., Rosentiel & Keefe, 1983), such as finding benefit in adversity by perceiving positive change and personal growth (Tennen & Affleck, 1999), remaining engaged and optimistic rather than passive and pessimistic (Carver & Scheier, 1999), and minimizing or eliminating catastrophizing attitudes that involve a belief that a situation is much worse than it is objectively (Peterson & Moon, 1999). Other schemas include the disability, handicap/participation, and illness schemas, and clients' perception of limiting symptoms/disability, role impacts, and illness etiology.

c. *Specific coping abilities, roles, and activity level.* This aspect of the model pertains to *actual* (as opposed to perceptions or schemas of) specific coping skills available and employed in the context of recovery. Aimed toward maximizing rehabilitation activities and premorbid role continuation, these strategies include activity/role modification abilities, pain and stress management skills, pace and persist strategies, emotional coping skills, problem solving skills, role rehearsal, compensatory strategies, and treatment adherence capacities. These approaches redirect the patient's attention to her or his residual resourcefulness and to the goal of enablement vs. disability. They may, in part, mediate the level of functioning achieved in rehabilitation, even in the presence of interfering symptoms and barriers.

To conclude, our sequential processes model (Figure 9.1), depicting the variety of possible steps and influences in an individual's response to injury in precipitating events, is quite congruent with Gatchel's (1991) model of the transition from acute pain to chronic pain. At the same time, it represents an extension of the model, because it is generalized to rehabilitation of various types of other conditions, such as TBI and PTSD. It is also compatible with the diathesis-stress model describing how predisposing factors interact with reactions to precipitating events, possibly setting in motion a cascade of psychological processes leading to disability (Turk, 2002). However, in addition to these regressive possibilities, our model stresses the possibility of more progressive, adaptive outcomes, such as through appropriate therapy, treatment compliance, good coping strategies, and other factors that would optimize the recovery process, producing positive recovery curves. [See chapter 8 for an expansion of Gatchel's three-stage model into a five-stage one.]

Rehabilitation Processes and the Role of Process-Oriented Outcome Measurements

Attempts to assess dynamic rehabilitation processes should be based on knowledge of the *typical* and *optimal* recovery course as a benchmark, or frame of reference, against which an individual result can be compared. Much research is needed to specify such outcomes, and one goal of this book is to present the current state of the field on this question.

In accordance with such an approach, Salmon (1998) developed a dynamic measurement system to analyze recovery over time on an individualized basis. For example, in neuropsychological assessment of an elderly person who has sustained mild to moderate brain trauma, the initial neurocognitive profile may suggest a differential diagnosis of brain trauma vs. early progressive dementia. In the absence of clarifying neuroradiological evidence, the differential diagnosis may only be possible through serial investigation of the condition over time; a measured deteriorating course (ruling out the impact of coexisting complications) would be supportive of progressive dementia, whereas improvement over time would be supportive of brain trauma-related pathology. Naturally, in confirmed progressive dementia, one cannot necessarily rule out the possibility that brain trauma had also occurred and may have added to the initial (and ongoing) functional decline. The point is that, in the absence of sequential measurement, relying on static (singular) assessment alone for diagnostic determination may be highly restrictive and misleading. Similarly, a pain patient may be doing quite well adhering to treatment regimen, but may suddenly stop improving and move on to a chronic pain state through the interplay of multiple factors (see Figure 9.1), ones that may even include additional stress generated by supplementary physical injury in physiotherapy or by psychological factors such as heeding solicitious behavior by significant others that encourage adopting a sick role. With respect to delayed PTSD, an assessor may find that once serious physical injuries begin healing, the patient focuses on delayed psychotraumatic reactions.

It is important to recognize that in order to more fully address issues of dynamic rehabilitation processes (and, secondarily, dynamic causality), it is insufficient to measure predominantly diagnosis/symptom-derived outcomes. In accordance with the World Health Organization's model, rehabilitation of impairments, disability, and restriction of participation, along with functional outcome and role engagement, have become at least equally important areas of measurement (Heinman, 2005; Mermis, 2005). Moreover, a serial assessment approach that fosters a greater understanding of the underlying cognitive and behavioral processes involved has also been endorsed (Mermis, 2005; Turk & Burwinkle, 2005).

Uomoto and Fann (2004) emphasize that the clinical needs of the patient often change during the recovery process due to his or her cognitive style and manner of interpreting the events that caused the injury. Edwards, McNeil, and Greenwood (2003) carried out a study in which inpatient progress was monitored at different times during treatment. Lower functional independence scores were correlated with longer hospital stay; the treatment course also had to be extended for those with lower levels of impairment but greater behavioral and motivational problems. Thus, to ensure that treatment is properly targeted, the patient's level of motivation, behavioral problems, functional abilities, and levels of impairment/dependency need be continually monitored and reassessed.

Rehabilitation Outcome Management System (ROMS; www.rrees.com), developed by the present authors (Salmon, 1998; Salmon, 2003a, 2003b; Salmon & Celinski, 2002), is a process-oriented outcome measurement system that serves as a graphically-based rehabilitation, differential diagnostic, and treatment planning methodology. It is compatible with the currently presented rehabilitation process and dynamic causality model. Given the validity research to date, as works in progress, it is a promising methodology for assessing constructs discussed in this chapter.

The first instrument developed in the ROMS series, as a distinctly rehabilitation focused measure, is the Rehabilitation Checklist (RCL; Salmon, 1998). As a stand-alone schema-based measure, the RCL may readily supplement a standardized battery of traditional measures. For example, the RCL has the client prioritize her or his rehabilitation barriers. The primary barriers selected will either be consistent or inconsistent with the presenting diagnosis and ensuing limitations, and may reveal adverse schemas. Moreover, the prioritized rehabilitation barriers reflect the most pressing issues for the patient, suggesting that these be addressed therapeutically. After prioritizing the barriers, the patient is next asked to rate her or his perceived limitations across a range of life role domains (participation schema). In subsequent sections of the RCL, the client rates her or his perception of emotional/ physical progress over time, projected into the future. The self-rating of rehabilitation barriers should be repeated over the rehabilitation course, because such perceptions may change during the recovery process. For instance, in the acute phase, cognitive or emotional impairments may be deemphasized, because issues pertaining to physical injury, mobility, self-care, communication, and other basic activities of daily life (ADL) are of the highest priority. At the midpoint, emphasis may be on more pressing cognitive and psychological impairments, whereas vocational issues may still be too distant to consider. Should rehabilitation prove successful, as it moves toward discharge, return to vocational or other functional roles may become a priority. Overall, understanding the client's priorities, and ensuring that treatment aims/modalities are synchronized with them, may enhance treatment compliance. The RCL also allows for the identification of secondary, tertiary, and incidental (including vocational, psychosocial, and secondary gain) factors that may be hindering the rehabilitation course.

Conclusions

In order to understand individuals' reactions to a precipitating event or illness as they unfold over time, we need to consider the multitude of possible interacting variables and processes, consistent with our sequential, dynamic causality and rehabilitation model. Assessment tools need to be developed that allow for the graphing of individuals' recovery curves as they pass through the rehabilitation process. When these graphs are reviewed in the context of clients' physical, emotional, and cognitive symptoms as they evolve in the course of their rehabilitative efforts, and with awareness of any complicating and personal factors, the assessor may obtain a better grasp of the causality underlying individuals' clinical presentation.

These concepts that we are espousing are contrasted with other simplified attempts to predict outcomes, which rely on less dynamic and unfolding perspectives. The concepts of recovery curves, and sequential and dynamic causality, are consistent with contemporary literature describing the complex interactions among premorbid vulnerabilities, event or illness factors, postevent stress, various subjective schemas, and coping abilities that shape rehabilitation outcomes. We emphasize the need for evaluative monitoring over time, of the patient in rehabilitation, along with psychological intervention aimed at preventing or ameliorating any secondary and tertiary impairments, and complications from incidental or unrelated stresses. In mental health assessments for court purposes, the assessor needs to address the patient's recovery progression or regression, to help better grasp her or his sequential and dynamic rehabilitation and causality. Forensically, it is imperative that the plaintiff acts upon her or his obligation to mitigate loss following injury. In order to do so effectively and meaningfully, this necessitates that the patient fully cooperates with, participates in, and adheres to an appropriate treatment regimen. At the same time, clinicians are obliged to facilitate optimal treatment adherence, client motivation, and client-centered treatment goal and modality selection. The use of appropriate measurement tools in rehabilitation that effectively graph recovery curves may help monitor these obligations on the part of patients and treating practitioners, helping to verify whether they are being adequately addressed in the framework of the plaintiff's complaints.

Turk and Okifuji (2002), while proposing process-oriented research with respect to pain conditions, stated that, "Little is known about the evolution and changes that accompany pain conditions over time as well as throughout the process of treatment" (p. 685). They added that, "Process research is important not only for observing the evolution of chronic pain syndromes but, also, for learning about the cooccurrence of physical and psychological factors over time" (p. 685). We echo their concerns, and call for the requisite research leading to psychometrically sound instruments that can gauge individual recovery curves sufficiently well for court purposes in all three areas of psychological injury (PTSD, chronic pain, TBI).

References

American Psychiatric Association. (1994, 2000). *Diagnostic and statistical manual of mental disorders: Text revision* (4th ed.). Washington, DC: Author.

Antoniazzi, M., Celinski, M., & Alcock, J. (2002). Self-responsibility and coping with pain: Disparate attitudes towards psychosocial issues in recovery from work place injury. *Disability and Rehabilitation, 24*, 948–953.

Bandura, A. (1997). Self-efficacy: Towards a unifying theory of behavior change. *Psychological Review, 84*, 1918–1215.

Bryant, R. A., & Harvey, A. G. (2002). Delayed-onset Posttraumatic Stress Disorder: A prospective evaluation. *Australian and New Zealand Journal of Psychiatry, 36*, 205–211.

Carver, C. S., & Scheier, M. F. (1999). Optimism. In C. R. Snyder (Ed.), *Coping* (pp. 182–204). New York: Oxford University Press.

Chervinsky, A. B., Ommaya, A. K., DeJonge, M., Spector, J., Schwab, K., & Salazar, A. M. (1998). Motivation for traumatic brain injury rehabilitation questionnaire (MOT-Q): Reliability, factor analysis, and relationship to MMPI-2 variables. *Archives of Clinical Neuropsychology, 13*, 433–446.

Clay, D. L., & Hopps, J. A. (2003). Treatment adherence in rehabilitation: The role of treatment accommodation. *Rehabilitation Psychology, 48*, 215–219.

Dalal, A. K., & Pande, N. (1988). Psychological recovery of accident victims with temporary and permanent disability. *International Journal of Psychology, 23*, 25–40.

Dersh, J., Polatin, P. B., & Gatchel, R. J. (2002). Chronic pain and psychopathology: Research findings and theoretical considerations. *Psychosomatic Medicine, 64*, 773–786.

Edwards, M., McNeil, J., & Greenwood, R. (2003). Process and outcome during early inpatient rehabilitation after brain injury. *Disability & Rehabilitation, 25*, 405–410.

Ehlers, A., Mayou, R. A., & Bryant, B. (1998). Psychological predictors of chronic Posttraumatic Stress Disorder after motor vehicle accidents. *Journal of Abnormal Psychology, 107*, 508–519.

Elklit, A. (1997). The aftermath of an industrial disaster. *Acta Psychiatric Scandinavica Supplementum, 392*, 1–25.

Gatchel, R. (1991). Early development of physical and mental deconditioning in painful spinal disorders. In T. G. Mayer, V. Mooney, & R. Gatchel (Eds.), *Contemporary conservative care for painful spinal disorders*. Philadelphia, PA: Lea and Febiger.

Gatchel, R., & Kishino, N. (2006). The influence of personality characteristics on pain patients: Implications for causality in pain. In G. Young, A. W. Kane, & K. Nicholson (Eds.), *Psychological knowledge in court: PTSD, pain, and TBI* (pp. 149–162). New York: Springer Science+Business Media.

Groomes, D. A. G., & Leahy, M. J. (2002). The relationship among the stress appraisal process, coping disposition, and level of acceptance of disability. *Rehabilitation Counselling, 46*, 15–24.

Heinemann, A. W. (2005). Putting outcome measurement in context: A rehabilitation psychology perspective. *Rehabilitation Psychology, 50*, 6–14.

Kelitikangas-Jarvinen, L. (1986). Psychological meaning of illness and coping with disease. *Psychotherapy and Psychosomatics, 45*, 84–90.

Lipowsky, Z. (1970). Physical illness: The individual and the coping process. *Psychiatric Medicine, 1*, 91–102.

Lipowsky, Z. (1981). Psychosomatic reactions to physical illness. In K. A. Achte & A. Pakaslahti (Eds.), *Psychosomatic factors in chronic illness: Proceedings of the Signe and Ane Gyllenberg foundation symposium, Espoo, Finland 1980. Psychiatric fennica supplementum*, 11–18. Helsinki, Finland: The Foundation.

Malt, U. F., & Olafsen, O. M. (1992). Psychological appraisal and emotional response to physical injury: A clinical phenomenological study of 109 adults. *Psychiatric Medicine, 10*, 117–134.

Mateo, M. A., & Glod, C. A. (2003). Mild traumatic brain injury and psychiatric disorders. *Journal of the American Psychiatric Nurses Association, 9*, 129–133.

McMillan, T. M., Williams, W. H., & Bryant, R. (2003). Posttraumatic Stress Disorder and traumatic brain injury: A review of causal mechanisms, assessment, and treatment. *Neuropsychological Rehabilitation, 13*, 149–164.

McInnes, M. (1997). Causation in tort law. Back to basics at the Supreme Court of Canada. *Alberta Law Review, 1013*, 1–20.

Melzack, R. (1999). Pain and stress: A new perspective. In R. J. Gatchel & D. C. Turk (Eds.), *Psychosocial factors in pain: Critical perspectives* (pp. 89–106). New York: Guilford Press.

Mermis, B. J. (2005). Developing a taxonomy for rehabilitation outcome measurement. *Rehabilitation Psychology, 50*, 15–23.

Millon, T. (1977). *Millon Clinical Multiaxial Inventory manual.* Minneapolis, MN: NCS Interpretive Scoring Systems.

Mukherjee, D., Heller, W., & Alper, J. (2001). Social and institutional factors in adjustment to traumatic brain injury. *Rehabilitation Psychology, 46*, 82–99.

Ozer, E. J., Best, S. R., Lipsey, T. I., & Weiss, D. S. (2003). Predictors of Posttraumatic Stress Disorder and symptoms in adults: A meta-analysis. *Psychological Bulletin, 129*, 52–73.

Peterson, C., & Moon, C. H. (1999). Coping with catastrophes and catastrophizing. In C.R. Snyder (Ed.), *Coping* (pp. 252–278). New York: Oxford University Press.

Robinson, M. E., & Riley, J. L. III (1999). The role of emotion in pain. In R. J. Gatchel & D. C. Turk (Eds.), *Psychosocial factors in pain: Critical perspectives* (pp. 74–88). New York: Guilford Press.

Rosentiel, A., & Keefe, F. (1983). The use of coping strategies in chronic low back pain clients: Relationship to client characteristics and current adjustment. *Pain, 17*, 33–34.

Salmon. J. D. Jr. (1998). *Rehabilitation Checklist user's manual.* North Tonawanda, NY and Toronto, ON: Multi-Health Systems.

Salmon. J. D. Jr. (2003a). *Rehabilitation Activities of Daily Living manual.* Toronto, ON: Rehabilitation Research, Education and Evaluation Services.

Salmon. J. D. Jr. (2003b). *Rehabilitation Functional Status Markers manual.* Toronto, ON: Rehabilitation Research, Education and Evaluation Services.

Salmon, J. D. Jr., & Celinski, M. J. (2002). *Rehabilitation Survey of Problems and Coping, Technical manual.* North Tonawanda, NY and Toronto, ON: Multi-Health Systems.

Tennen, H., & Affleck, G. (1999). Finding benefits in adversity. In C.R. Snyder (Ed.), *Coping* (pp. 279–304). New York: Oxford University Press.

Turk, D. C. (2002). A diathesis-stress model of chronic pain and disability following traumatic injury. *Pain Research and Management, 7*, 9–19.

Turk, D. C., & Burwinkle, T. M. (2005). Assessment of chronic pain in rehabilitation: Outcomes measures in clinical trials and clinical practice. *Rehabilitation Psychology, 50*, 56–64.

Turk, D. C., & Flor, H. (1999). Chronic pain: A biobehavioral perspective. In R. J. Gatchel & D. C. Turk (Eds.), *Psychosocial factors in pain: Critical perspectives* (pp. 18–34). New York: Guilford Press.

Turk, D. C., & Okifuji, A. (2002). Psychological factors in chronic pain: Evolution and revolution. *Journal of Counselling and Clinical Psychology, 70*, 678–690.

Turner, J. A., Jensen, M. P., & Romano, J. M. (2000). Do beliefs, coping and catastrophizing independently predict functioning in patients with chronic pain? *Pain, 85*, 115–125.

Turner, J. A., Jensen, M. P., Warms, C. A., & Cardenas, D. D. (2002). Catastrophizing is associated with pain intensity, psychological distress, and pain-related disability among individuals with chronic pain after spinal cord injury. *Pain, 98*, 127–134.

Section II

Causality in Court: Psychological Considerations

10

Basic Concepts in Psychology and Law

ANDREW W. KANE

In-depth consideration of causality is central to the determination of responsibility in tort actions. If causality and responsibility are not immediately evident, and if psychological factors play a potentially significant role in the plaintiff's disability, the case may be set for trial. Adequately demonstrating the presence or absence of causality in depositions and in court requires that a psychologist (or other mental health professional) be retained as an expert to do a comprehensive assessment that will provide the court with sufficient information to assist with the determination of liability. That information must be valid, must be obtained using legitimate methods, and must present the information in a manner of value to the trier of fact (judge or jury). The psychologist must be well-acquainted with the requirements of the court, and the attorneys and judge must be sufficiently familiar with psychological concepts, in order for the members of the mental health and legal professions to meaningfully interact. This chapter and the three that follow will address these issues from the perspectives of both the psychologist and the court.

Causality

Until the 1970s, the law did not permit an individual to be compensated for a psychological injury unless there was a physical injury as well. It was not until 1993 that the United States Supreme Court ruled, in *Harris v. Forklift Systems, Inc.*, 114 S.Ct. 367 (1993), that evidence of psychological harm to an individual could be a significant factor in determining whether an employer is liable for sexual harassment. This was the first time that the Supreme Court indicated that evidence of the presence of a diagnosable psychological injury could be presented in the liability phase of a trial to demonstrate that tortious behavior had occurred (Call, 2003). Moreover, mental health experts have demonstrated their value in court. A review of a number of cases involving psychological or psychiatric testimony found that the likelihood of receiving compensatory, rather than only nominal, damages in cases alleging a violation of constitutional rights was substantially greater when there was expert testimony on behalf of the plaintiff (Haney & Smith, 2003).

A problem with the testimony of many experts is that it incompletely addresses psychological or psychiatric issues because a thorough evaluation was not conducted, or it addresses mental health issues that have no obvious relationship to legal issues and is therefore irrelevant to the matter before the court. For example, a detailed description of an individual's psychological state is irrelevant if it is not specifically tied to the individual's ability to work, to care for children, to attend school, or otherwise to maintain a "normal" life. Diagnoses, in particular, have been problematic, since many experts suggest either that all people with a given diagnosis behave in the same manner, or that the presence of a given diagnosis tells a great deal about the functional ability of the individual, neither of which is correct. What is needed is for the expert to "present the logic that links these observations to the specific abilities and capacities with which the law is concerned" (Grisso, 2003, pp. 12–13).

"Relevance" is defined by Federal Rule of Evidence (FRE, 2004) 401 as "having any tendency to make the existence of any fact that is of consequence to the determination of the action more probable or less probable than it would be without the evidence." Relevant evidence may be excluded, however, "if its probative value is substantially outweighed by the danger of unfair prejudice, confusion of the issues, or misleading the jury, or by considerations of undue delay, waste of time, or needless presentation of cumulative evidence" (FRE 403). Relevance is also referred to as "fit." The testimony of an expert must provide a link in the chain of evidence that is relevant to a fact in dispute in order for that testimony to be admitted by the court (Faigman & Monahan, 2005).

It cannot be emphasized too strongly that the expert's responsibility includes consideration of each reasonably possible cause of a given injury or condition, and the conducting of a reasoned analysis of whether that possible cause is, or is not, likely to be *a*, or *the*, cause of the injury or condition. A *post hoc* analysis is never sufficient, nor is an assumption that a close temporal relationship between an alleged cause and the demonstrated effect means that the alleged cause was the actual, and sole, cause. Further, one must identify other factors that may play a significant role (e.g., preexisting disorders or problems) and, similarly, consider their contributions and rule them in or out. Without following this path, the expert cannot legitimately draw conclusions to a reasonable degree of psychological/medical/scientific/etc. certainty (Fleishman, Jackson & Rothschild, 1999). Further,

> a differential diagnosis that fails to take serious account of other potential causes may be so lacking that it cannot provide a reliable basis for an opinion on causation … . Thus, if an expert utterly fails to consider alternative causes or fails to offer an explanation for why the proferred alternative cause was not the sole cause, a district court is justified in excluding the expert's testimony [*Cooper v. Smith & Nephew*, 259 F.3d 194 (4th Cir. 2001)].

In order to accomplish these goals, the expert must have a sound database that includes information of high enough quality, quantity, and relevance to support any conclusions that are made. If an expert in a personal injury case has not thoroughly reviewed pretrauma medical and functional (e.g., school, work, physical activity, hobbies) information, the expert is not likely to have sufficient data on the case in question to draw a valid conclusion regarding causality. Similarly, an expert extrapolating from data on a research study sample, the characteristics of which are significantly different from the plaintiff, may be making an inappropriate inferential leap (Ackerman & Kane, 1998; Grisso, 2003).

The expert should be able to identify the expected influence of a given deficit on the individual's ability to function—both what the individual would be expected to be able to do, and what the individual would not be expected to be able to do. Memory problems, for example, ought to lead to deficits in functions in which memory plays a significant role, especially learning of new information, though the individual may retain good recall of well-learned and practiced historical information. By addressing his or her expectation of the apparent functional deficit on the actual behavior and abilities of the individual, the expert can identify the degree to which the individual's presentation is consistent with expectations that are based on the expert's experience and the research literature. Discrepancies need to be investigated and resolved (Faust & Heard, 2003).

General Causation vs. Specific Causation

Courts commonly distinguish between general and specific causation in medical cases. The former refers to the question of whether a substance, material or event can cause a physical disorder, for example, cancer. The latter refers to whether the alleged causal agent produced a specific disorder in a specific patient. According to Faigman and Monahan (2005), the parallel in psychology would be in terms of "social authority, social facts, and social frameworks." The first would be analogous to a legal precedent, but in the form of previous research. Examples would include psychological research that bears on major social questions presented to the courts, for example, abortion, segregation, or whether juveniles should be subject to the death penalty—all issues on which the United States Supreme Court has ruled, in part based on the social authority of the research. The second, specific, cause would be in the form of facts specifically relevant to a case, for example, the results of a survey commissioned for that case. One area in which this has been relevant is regarding whether the average person would find that a specific work, for example, a book, taken as a whole, appeals to prurient interests, in obscenity cases. Psychologists also address issues of competencies, mental illness, prediction of violence, and so forth. The last, social frameworks, would be a combination of the two, that is, social facts that are alleged to be specific examples of social authorities. Examples include the "battered woman syndrome" or "rape trauma syndrome," which entail both a general (social authority) component and a specific (does an alleged victim fall under the relevant syndrome category) component.

Requirements for Expert Testimony: *Daubert* and Progeny in the U.S., *Mohan* in Canada

Daubert

Prior to 1993, there was conflict among U.S. federal and appellate courts regarding whether general acceptance of a scientific method or technique within the professional community was required in order for expert testimony based on that method or technique to be considered adequately reliable and, therefore, admissible. In 1993, in *Daubert v. Merrell Dow Pharmaceuticals, Inc.* (509 U.S. 579, 113 S.Ct. 2786, 125 L.Ed. 2d 469), the U.S. Supreme Court held that the general acceptance test (*Frye v. United States* (1923), 54 App. D.C. 46, 293 F. 1013, 34 ALR 145) was superseded by the Federal Rules of Evidence (FRE), and that general acceptance was not a necessary prerequisite for admissibility of expert testimony under Federal Rule of Evidence 702:

> We interpret the legislatively-enacted Federal Rules of Evidence as we would any statute … . Rule 402 provides the baseline: "All relevant evidence is admissible. … Evidence which is not relevant is not admissible … ." "Relevant evidence" is defined as that which has "any tendency to make the existence of any fact that is of consequence to the determination of the action more probable or less probable than it would be without the evidence." Rule 401. [P. 479]
>
> Here there is a specific Rule that speaks to the contested issue. Rule 702, governing expert testimony, provides:
>
> If scientific, technical, or other specialized knowledge will assist the trier of fact to understand the evidence or to determine a fact in issue, a witness qualified as an expert by knowledge, skill, experience, training, or education may testify thereto in the form of an opinion or otherwise … .
>
> Nothing in the text of this Rule establishes "general acceptance" as an absolute prerequisite to admissibility … . [A] rigid "general acceptance" requirement would be at odds with the "liberal thrust" of the Federal Rules and their "general approach of relaxing the traditional barriers to 'opinion' testimony … ." That the Frye test was displaced by the Rules of Evidence does not mean, however, that the Rules themselves place no limits on the admissibility of purportedly scientific evidence. Nor is the trial judge disabled from screening such evidence. To the contrary, under the Rules the trial judge must ensure that any and all scientific testimony or evidence admitted is not only relevant, but reliable … .
>
> The subject of an expert's testimony must be "scientific … knowledge." The adjective "scientific" implies a grounding in the methods and procedures of science. Similarly, the word "knowledge" connotes more than subjective belief or unsupported speculation. The term "applies to any body of known facts or to any body of ideas inferred from such facts or accepted as truths on good grounds." Webster's Third New International Dictionary 1252 (1986). Of course, it would be unreasonable to conclude that the subject of scientific testimony must be "known" to a certainty; arguably, there are no certainties in science … . But, in order to qualify as "scientific knowledge," an inference or assertion must be derived by the scientific method. Proposed testimony must be supported by appropriate validation—that is "good grounds," based on what is known. In short the requirement that an expert's testimony pertain to "scientific knowledge" establishes a standard of evidentiary reliability … .

Rule 702 further requires that the evidence or testimony "assist the trier of fact to understand the evidence or to determine a fact in issue." This condition goes primarily to relevance ..., [including] "whether expert testimony proffered in the case is sufficiently tied to the facts of the case that it will aid the jury in resolving a factual dispute" [pp. 480–481].

Unlike an ordinary witness ..., an expert is permitted wide latitude to offer opinions, including those that are not based on first-hand knowledge or observation ... . Presumably, this relaxation of the usual requirement of first-hand knowledge ... is premised on an assumption that the expert's opinion will have a reliable basis in the knowledge and experience of his discipline.

Faced with a proffer of expert scientific testimony, then, the trial judge must determine at the outset ... whether the expert is proposing to testify to (1) scientific knowledge that (2) will assist the trier of fact to understand or determine a fact in issue. This entails a preliminary assessment of whether the reasoning or methodology underlying the testimony is scientifically valid and of whether that reasoning or methodology properly can be applied to the facts in issue ... .

Many factors will bear on the inquiry, and we do not presume to set out a definitive checklist or test. But some general observations are appropriate.

Ordinarily, a key question to be answered in determining whether a theory or technique is scientific knowledge that will assist the trier of fact will be whether it can be (and has been) tested ... . Another pertinent consideration is whether the theory or technique has been subjected to peer review and publication. Publication (which is but one element of peer review) is not a *sine qua non* of admissibility; it does not necessarily correlate with reliability ... and in some instances well-grounded but innovative theories will not have been published ... . But submission to the scrutiny of the scientific community is a component of "good science" in part because it increases the likelihood that substantive flaws in methodology will be detected ... . Additionally, in the case of a particular scientific technique, the court ordinarily should consider the known or potential rate of error ... . Finally, "general acceptance" can yet have a bearing on the inquiry. A "reliability assessment does not require, although it does permit, explicit identification of a relevant scientific community and an express determination of a particular degree of acceptance within that community ...".

The inquiry envisioned by Rule 702 is, we emphasize, a flexible one. Its overarching subject is the scientific validity—and thus the evidentiary relevance and reliability—of the principles that underlie a proposed submission. The focus, of course, must be solely on principles and methodology, not on the conclusions that they generate [pp. 482–484].

[T]here are important differences between the quest for truth in the courtroom and the quest for truth in the laboratory. Scientific conclusions are subject to perpetual revision. Law, on the other hand, must resolve disputes finally and quickly ... . We recognize that in practice, a gatekeeping role for the judge, no matter how flexible, inevitably on occasion will prevent the jury from learning of authentic insights and innovations. That, nevertheless, is the balance that is struck by Rules of Evidence designed not for the exhaustive search for cosmic understanding but for the particularized resolution of legal disputes [p. 485].

In summary, the *Daubert* decision instructed federal trial courts to act as gatekeepers for expert evidence, and to apply the appropriate *Daubert* criteria to the case at bar. According to the Supreme Court in *Kumho Tire Co. v. Carmichael*, the four "*Daubert* factors" are: (1) "whether it can be and has been tested ... [and] can be falsified;" (2) whether the "theory or technique has been subjected to peer review and publication;" (3) that consideration be given to the "known or potential rate of error;" and (4) that there is "general acceptance of the particular technique within the scientific community" (p. 137).

In addition, in *Daubert* the Supreme Court identified other relevant factors that may be applied by the trial court as part of its gatekeeping function: (1) that the expert's testimony "pertain to scientific knowledge," (2) that the "evidence or testimony assist the trier of fact to understand the evidence or to determine a fact in issue" (relevance), (3) "whether that reasoning or methodology properly can be applied to the facts in issue," (4) "the existence and maintenance of standards controlling the technique's operation" (the Court used the example of standards for spectrographic analysis) (*Daubert*, pp. 593–594) and/or (5) that there be "evidentiary reliability" (*Daubert*, p. 590). In footnote 9, the Supreme Court indicated that, while scientists "distinguish between 'validity' ... and 'reliability' ... our reference here is to evidentiary reliability—that is, trustworthiness." It should be noted that some legal scholars list the *Daubert* factors slightly differently, for example, separating testability requirement into "whether it is testable" and "whether it has been," and adding "whether there are standards controlling the technique's operation" as an additional *Daubert* factor (Imwinkelried, 2000, p. 21).

The Supreme Court explicitly indicated that this list is flexible, and these and/or other criteria are to be used by the trial courts to address the scientific validity of the evidence or testimony, emphasizing that it is the "principles and methodology, not ... the conclusions that they generate" that must be addressed by the trial court. "*Daubert*'s ultimate legacy for the law is its insistence that legal policy and legal outcomes be crafted in light of a sophisticated appreciation for the complexity and subtlety of the state of the art of the science" (Faigman, 2000, p. 338).

Daubert also indicated that the goal of a court is to make a definitive decision, not to reach a consensus on an issue as the scientific community may do. As a result, the attorneys on the respective sides of an issue generally seek out experts from the opposing ends of the bell curve who will strengthen the arguments of one side or the other. In spite of this tendency, many experts feel a responsibility to be available as impartial witnesses for testimony in court, believing that the most qualified experts must be available if scientifically valid evidence is to be presented in court (National Academy of Sciences, 2002).

In 1983, the Supreme Court ruled, in *Barefoot v. Estelle*, that the testimony of a psychiatrist, testifying on the basis of his clinical experience, was admissible because "the rules of evidence generally extant at the federal and state levels anticipate that relevant, unprivileged evidence should be admitted and its weight left to the fact finder, who would have the benefit of cross-examination and contrary evidence by the opposing party." (p. 898) This standard is very different from the one dictated by *Daubert*, suggesting that testimony based on clinical experience should be treated differently from testimony based on scientific research. When clinical testimony is based even in part on research, for example on a psychological test or a diagnostic syndrome, however, courts have been more willing to subject the testimony to a rigorous degree of scrutiny (Shuman, 2002a). According to Sales and Shuman (2005), a Texas federal district court decision, *Antoine-Tubbs v. Local 513 Air Transp. Div.* (50 F. Supp. 2d 601), indicates that the following criteria could be used in a *Daubert* analysis of clinical testimony:

(a) personal examination of the plaintiff by the doctor; (b) personally taking a detailed medical history from the plaintiff; (c) using differential diagnosis and etiology; (d) reviewing tests, reports, and opinions of other doctors; (e) reviewing other facts or data reasonably relied on by medical experts in forming opinions or inferences as to medical causation; (f) reference to medical literature; and (g) using the doctor's training and experience. [p. 80]

Sales and Shuman note that there are potential problems with each of these criteria, in large part because they are not specifically based upon scientific criteria and therefore have a potential for error. Because clinical testimony is accepted by nearly all trial courts, however, the paradigm suggested by the court in *Antoine-Tubbs v. Local 513 Air Transp. Div.* is one reasonable way to address testimony that is not based directly on research.

The Supreme Court remanded *Daubert* to the Ninth Circuit Court of Appeals, which indicated, in a ruling often referred to as "*Daubert II*," (*Daubert v. Merrell Dow Pharmaceuticals, Inc.*, 43 F.3d 1311 (9th Cir. 1995)) that:

Under *Daubert*, we must engage in a difficult, two-part analysis. First, we must determine nothing less than whether the expert's testimony reflects "scientific knowledge," whether their findings are "derived by the scientific method," and whether their work product amounts to "good science ... ." Second, we must ensure that the proposed expert testimony is "relevant to the task at hand ...," that is, that it logically advances a material aspect of the proposing party's case. The Supreme Court referred to this second prong of the analysis as the "fit" requirement ... .

The first prong of *Daubert* puts federal judges in an uncomfortable position. The question of admissibility only arises if it is first established that the individuals whose testimony is being proffered are experts in a particular scientific field ... . Yet something doesn't become "scientific knowledge" just because it's uttered by a scientist; nor can an expert's self serving assertion that his conclusions are "derived by the scientific method" be deemed conclusive ... . [T]herefore, though we are largely untrained in science and certainly no match for any of the witnesses whose testimony we are reviewing, it is our responsibility to determine whether these experts' proposed testimony amounts to "scientific knowledge," constitutes "good science," and was "derived by the scientific method ... ."

The [Supreme] Court recognized, however, that knowledge in this context does not mean absolute certainty ... . Rather, the Court said, "in order to qualify as 'scientific knowledge,' an inference or assertion must be derived by the scientific method ... ." Our task, then, is to analyze not what the experts say, but what basis they have for saying it.

Which raises the question: How do we figure out whether scientists have derived their finding through the scientific method or whether their testimony is based on scientifically valid principles ... ? ... [T]he party presenting the expert must show that the expert's findings are based on sound science, and this will require some objective, independent validation of the expert's methodology ... . We read the Supreme Court as instructing us to determine whether the analysis undergirding experts' testimony falls within the range of accepted standards governing how scientists conduct their research and reach their conclusions.

One very significant fact to be considered is whether the experts are proposing to testify about matters growing naturally and directly out of research they have conducted independent of the litigation, or whether they have developed their opinions expressly for purposes of testifying … . That an expert testifies based on research he has conducted independent of the litigation provides important, objective proof that the research comports with the dictates of good science … . [This] provides the most persuasive basis for concluding that the opinions he expresses were "derived by the scientific method … ." If the proffered expert testimony is not based on independent research, the party proffering it must come forward with other objective, verifiable evidence that the testimony is based on "scientifically valid principles."

One means of showing this is by proof that the research and analysis supporting the proffered conclusions have been subjected to normal scientific scrutiny through peer review and publication … . Peer review and publication do not, of course, guarantee that the conclusions reached are correct; much published scientific research is greeted with intense skepticism and is not borne out by further research. But the test under *Daubert* is not the correctness of the expert's conclusions but the soundness of his methodology … . That the research is accepted for publication in a reputable scientific journal after being subjected to the usual rigors of peer review is a significant indication that it is taken seriously by other scientists, that is, it meets at least the criteria of good science.

One criterion for trustworthiness (reliability, validity) of testimony, then, is whether the expert has personally done research in the area of testimony independent of the instant case, or whether he or she is utilizing information published in peer-reviewed journals to support his or her conclusions (Eder, 2007).

Joiner

The U.S. Supreme Court reaffirmed its conclusions in *Daubert* in *General Electric Company v. Joiner*, 118 S.Ct. 512, 522 U.S. 136 (1997), and specified that the standard for reviewing the admission or exclusion of scientific evidence by federal district courts was *abuse of discretion*: "an error of judgment by a trial court in making a ruling that is clearly unreasonable, erroneous, or arbitrary and not justified by the facts or the law applicable in the case" (Merriam-Webster's Dictionary of Law (1996). Available from http://dictionary.lp.findlaw. com/ scripts/, last accessed June 11, 2005).

"Nothing in either *Daubert* or the Federal Rules of Evidence requires a district court to admit opinion evidence which is connected to existing data only by the ipse dixit ['he said it himself'] of the expert." [*General Electric Company v. Joiner*, 118 S.Ct. 512, 520 (1997)] The goal is to "secure the basic objectives of the Federal Rules of Evidence, which are … the ascertainment of truth and the just determination of proceedings." (Justice Breyer, concurring, citing Fed. Rule Evid. 102)

According to Gutheil and Bursztajn (2003), the best way for experts to avoid having conclusions labeled as *ipse dixit* opinions is to address the empirical, theoretical, clinical, rational, and scientific bases for their opinions, and to try to educate attorneys regarding these bases.

Kumho

On March 23, 1999, the U.S. Supreme Court ruled, in *Kumho Tire Co. v. Carmichael*, 526 U.S. 137 (1999) that an individual may be considered an expert if he or she has any type of specialized knowledge or experience that may contribute to the fact finder's understanding of a case:

> This case requires us to decide how *Daubert* applies to the testimony of engineers and other experts who are not scientists. We conclude that *Daubert*'s general holding—setting forth the trial judge's general "gatekeeping" obligation—applies not only to testimony based on "scientific" knowledge, but also to testimony based on "technical" and "other specialized" knowledge. We also conclude that a trial court *may* consider one or more of the more specific factors that *Daubert* mentioned when doing so will help determine that testimony's reliability. But, as the Court stated in *Daubert*, the test of reliability is "flexible," and *Daubert*'s list of specific factors neither necessarily nor exclusively applies to all experts or in every case. Rather, the law grants a district court the same broad latitude when it decides *how* to determine reliability as it enjoys in respect to its ultimate reliability determination … . [pp. 141–142].
>
> Experts of all kinds tie observations to conclusions through the use of what Judge Learned Hand called "general truths derived from specialized experience." [citation omitted] And whether the specific expert testimony focuses upon specialized observations, the specialized translation of those observations into theory, a specialized theory itself, or the application of such a theory in a particular case, the expert's testimony often will rest "upon an experience confessedly foreign in kind to [the jury's] own." … And where such testimony's factual basis, data, principles, methods, or their application are called sufficiently into question … the trial judge must determine whether the testimony has "a reliable basis in the knowledge and experience of [the relevant] discipline" [*Daubert*, p. 592][p. 149].
>
> The objective … is to make certain that an expert, whether basing testimony upon professional studies or personal experience, employs in the courtroom the same level of intellectual rigor that characterizes the practice of an expert in the relevant field … [p. 152].
>
> [T]he question before the trial court was specific, not general. The trial court had to decide whether this particular expert had sufficient specialized knowledge to assist the jurors "in deciding the particular issues in the case" [citation omitted][p. 156].

Imwinkelried (2000, p. 28) indicates that, while little specific guidance was provided to trial courts, "the opinion did seem to underscore … [t]he factor of whether the expert had employed 'the same level of intellectual rigor' customary in practice." While a second major statement in *Kumho* has received substantially less publicity than the above, it is also very important to note that the focus should be on the expert's "particular method of analyzing the data thereby obtained, to draw a conclusion regarding *the particular matter to which the expert testimony was directly relevant* … . The relevant issue was whether the expert could reliably determine the cause of *this* tire's separation" (p. 154, emphasis in original). Thus, the expert need not go to great lengths to demonstrate the validity and reliability of an area of research or practice in general, he or she must only build a base from the general data that will support statements made about "the particular matter" that is the focus of the expert's testimony (Risinger, Saks, Thompson, & Rosenthal, 2002).

Daubert, Joiner, and *Kumho Together*

Taken together, *Daubert, Joiner*, and *Kumho* make it clear that judges have an obligation to exercise their gatekeeping function in all cases involving expert testimony, and that appellate courts are to limit their reviews of admissibility to questions regarding whether the trial judge abused his or her discretion (Parry, 2000). Further, "[a]n expert's qualifications are a necessary but not sufficient condition of the admissibility of the expert's testimony. In the face of appropriate objection, the trial court must assess, as a threshold question, the validity and reliability of the methods and procedures relied on by the expert to reach any proffered opinions" (Shuman, 2002a, pp. 37–38). In addition, "Conclusions cannot stand unless they are rationally supported by the data. And the data cannot stand unless they are generated by sound methodology" (Saks, 2000, p. 236).

It should be noted, however, that trial judges are not obligated to question expert testimony; rather, it is up to the attorneys to identify admissibility issues and bring motions before the court, address the issues during testimony before the jury, or choose to disregard them. The last option is most likely if, for example, experts on both sides face the same criticisms, if the *Daubert* challenge is seen as too costly, or if it is seen as a tactical advantage to present the criticisms to the jury (Shuman & Sales, 2001; Sales & Shuman, 2005).

A 1998 survey of all active U.S. district court judges by the Federal Judicial Center yielded 303 usable surveys, a response rate of 51%. The judges reported on 297 federal civil trials, of which the largest portion, 45%, were tort cases. In 46% of the cases, there was no admissibility issue raised. In the cases in which admissibility was raised as an issue, 72% were addressed in the context of a *motion in limine* ("a motion, petition, or order regarding the admissibility of evidence whose exclusion is sought" (Merriam-Webster's Dictionary of Law (1996), available from http://dictionary.lp.findlaw.com/scripts/, last accessed June 11, 2005), while 64% were in response to an objection raised at trial. In only 3% of cases did the judge raise an issue of admissibility (Johnson, Krafka & Cecil, 2000).

In a later article, Krafka, Dunn, Johnson, Cecil, and Miletich (2002) indicate that 92% of the 299 trials (two more than previously reported) included expert testimony on behalf of plaintiffs, 79% on behalf of defendants, and 73% had experts on both sides. Medical and mental health constituted the primary areas in which experts testified, totaling 43.2% of the experts. The issues most frequently addressed by the experts at trials "were the existence, nature, or extent of injury or damage (68% of 299 trials) and the cause of injury or damage (64%), findings that are consistent with the fact that tort cases represented almost half of all cases reported" (p. 321).

Motions *in limine* more than doubled between surveys in 1991 and 1998, from 32% to 72% of cases in which there was an admissibility challenge. The most frequent reasons indicated for exclusion of testimony were lack of relevance (47%), lack of qualifications of the expert (42%), or because the planned testimony would not be of assistance to the trier of fact (40%). At least part of the increase in the number of challenges post-*Daubert* was due to a 1993 change in Federal

Rule of Civil Procedure 26(a)(2), requiring a written report from any expert who may testify at trial, setting out a complete statement of the expert's opinions, the expert's reasoning, and all information considered by the expert in forming his or her opinions.

Krafka et al. (2002) indicated that both judges and attorneys (who were later surveyed) identified two primary problems with experts: that some became advocates for the side that retained them rather than remaining objective, and that there was a very significant expense associated with retaining experts.

Forensic experts are advised to base their testimony not only on the prevailing clinical standards of their communities but, also, on other, broader bases of validity such as research that is reported in peer-reviewed journals (Youngstrom & Busch, 2000). The Supreme Court noted, however, that "it might not be surprising in a particular case ... that a claim made by a scientific witness has never been the subject of peer review, for the particular application at issue may never previously have interested any scientist" (*Kumho* at 151). Thus, while the expert would best emphasize or exclusively use peer-reviewed articles, other professional literature is by no means excluded. Further, some of the most important data may come from articles refused by peer-reviewed journals because they did not fit with the prevailing theory or research in a given area, yet time and further experimentation or study may demonstrate that the originally rejected article was in fact a better statement of the nature of a phenomenon than were the published peer-reviewed articles. The expert should be familiar with both peer-reviewed and nonpeer-reviewed research and theories, to ensure that all relevant information is considered.

The Supreme Court largely adopted the proposition in an amici brief by the National Academies (National Academy of Sciences, National Academy of Engineering, Institute of Medicine and the National Research Council, collectively abbreviated "NAS"), and the American Association for the Advancement of Science (AAAS) "that scientific evidence should be evaluated by the standards of the scientific community. Justice Blackmun noted that 'there are no certainties in science,' and quoted the AAAS/NAS amici brief: 'Science is not an encyclopedic body of knowledge about the universe. Instead, it represents a *process* for proposing and refining theoretical explanations about the world that are subject to further testing and refinement' " (National Academy of Sciences, 2002).

As a result of the combined influence of *Daubert, Joiner* and *Kumho*, Rule 702 of the Federal Rules of Evidence was amended in 2000 to read:

Rule 702. Testimony by Experts

If scientific, technical, or other specialized knowledge will assist the trier of fact to understand the evidence or to determine a fact in issue, a witness qualified as an expert by knowledge, skill, experience, training, or education, may testify thereto in the form of an opinion or otherwise, <u>if (1) the testimony is based upon sufficient facts or data, (2) the testimony is the product of reliable principles and methods, and (3) the witness has applied the principles and methods reliably to the facts of the case</u>. [Underlined portion was added to the old Rule 702.]

To the factors specified by the Supreme Court in *Daubert*, the Advisory Committee on the Federal Rules of Evidence (2000) added five additional suggested areas of consideration based on court rulings after *Daubert*:

(1) Whether experts are "proposing to testify about matters growing naturally and directly out of research they have conducted independent of the litigation, or whether they have developed their opinions expressly for purposes of testifying." *Daubert v. Merrell Dow Pharmaceuticals, Inc.*, 43 F.3d 1311, 1317 (9th Cir. 1995).
(2) Whether the expert has unjustifiably extrapolated from an accepted premise to an unfounded conclusion.
(3) Whether the expert has adequately accounted for obvious alternative explanations.
(4) Whether the expert "is being as careful as he would be in his regular professional work outside his paid litigation consulting." *Sheehan v. Daily Racing Form, Inc.*, 104 F.3d 940, 942 (7th Cir. 1997).
(5) Whether the field of expertise claimed by the expert is known to reach reliable results for the type of opinion the expert would give.

State Courts

It must be noted that the requirements of *Daubert, Joiner* and *Kumho* are mandatory in federal courts, but are not mandatory in state courts unless a given state has specifically adopted these requirements, either via a decision by its highest court or by action of its legislature (Youngstrom & Busch, 2000). However, the evidence law of most states mirrors the Federal Rules (Saks, 2000; Shuman, 2002a; Sales & Shuman, 2005).

Because many state laws and appellate court decisions leave room for interpretation, lists of states adopting *Daubert* or other standards may differ to some degree. According to Bernstein and Jackson (2004), while a number of states have adopted a standard other than "general acceptance," by the middle of 2003 only 27 states had adopted standards highly consistent with *Daubert*, but only nine states had adopted standards consistent with all three cases, *Daubert, Joiner*, and *Kumho*: Arkansas, Delaware, Louisiana, Massachusetts, Mississippi, Nebraska, Oklahoma, Texas and Wyoming. For Louisiana, this is based upon two appellate court rulings, the Louisiana Supreme Court has not yet ruled on whether *Joiner* applies in that state. Six states have adopted *Daubert* and *Kumho* but not *Joiner*: Kentucky, Ohio, New Hampshire, North Carolina, Rhode Island, and South Dakota. Seven states have adopted *Daubert* but not all parts of *Joiner* or *Kumho*: Alaska, Connecticut, Montana, New Mexico, Oregon, Vermont, and West Virginia. Alabama has adopted *Daubert* solely for cases involving DNA evidence. Five other states (Colorado, Hawaii, Tennessee, Indiana, and Iowa) have adopted selected portions of *Daubert, Joiner*, and/or *Kumho*, but not the entirety of any of them. Maine has not adopted *Daubert* or its progeny but its prerevision version of Federal Rule of Evidence 702 parallels *Daubert*. States that reject both *Daubert* and *Frye* (general acceptance) but selectively use elements of one or both (or similar parallels with Federal Rule of Evidence 702 either before or after the 2000 revision) include: Georgia, Idaho, Nevada, New Jersey, North Dakota, South Dakota, Utah, Virginia, and Wisconsin (Bernstein & Jackson, 2004).

Parry (2004) offers a slightly different breakdown. He indicates that 13 states still essentially follow *Frye*, 20 states have adopted *Daubert*, 12 largely follow Federal Rule of Evidence 702 but have not adopted *Daubert*, and six states have unique rules for admissibility. Parry notes that, while many states have adopted either the criteria in *Daubert* or a rule equivalent to Federal Rule of Evidence 702, courts do not generally apply those requirements for reliability to testimony unless it is considered "scientific" or "highly specialized." Thus, a physician might testify regarding his or her patient based solely on training, experience, and knowledge of the patient.

The Influence of *Daubert* and its Progeny on Actual Court Cases

While novel areas of testimony often lead to rigorous scrutiny by the trial judge, most testimony by experts—particularly testimony by psychologists and psychiatrists—does not. Rather, the initial focus is typically upon the qualifications of the witness, with the expectation being that a strong cross-examination, combined with the testimony of the expert for the opposing side, will lead to adequate scrutiny of the reliability and validity of the expert's testimony and methodology (Shuman, 2002a, 2002b; Slovenko, 2002). In addition, *Daubert*'s influence in cases involving psychology and other behavioral sciences has been relatively small because many of these cases primarily or exclusively involve clinical rather than scientific testimony. For example, there is no way to calculate an error rate or demonstrate falsifiability for child custody, involuntary civil commitment, criminal, and many other types of cases. In these areas, the expert is likely to testify based on his or her clinical experience, rather than basing testimony primarily on a substantial scientific literature. Peer review has relatively little relevance to clinical writings and testimony. Although *Daubert* may be relevant to some of the data collection instruments in these cases, it does not apply to most aspects of these evaluations (Shuman & Sales, 1999).

Gutheil and Bursztajn (2005) note that many of the *Daubert* challenges are attempts by attorneys to have a "dry run" prior to trial, or to supplement the probing of an expert that occurred in a deposition. It may also serve as a means of assessing the trial judge's attitude toward a case. In jurisdictions in which depositions are not held (including Canadian courts—see *Mohan*, below), the challenge provides an advance view of the expert's opinions and of the expert's ability to defend his or her opinions and the data upon which they are based. And, of course, when an attorney believes his case is weak, he or she may attempt to knock the opposing expert out of the case by a *Daubert/Mohan* challenge as a means of trying to obtain summary judgment.

Federal district court judges are not required to become experts in science, technology, or other fields in order to exercise their gatekeeping role. If they have sufficient knowledge to understand and rule on the issues before the court, they may do so. If, however, the judge feels the need for his or her own expert to advise regarding the scientific or other issues before the court, Federal Rule of Evidence 706 permits the judge to appoint an expert for that purpose. The expert may also be called to testify by the court or any party, and is subject to cross-examination by each party. With increasingly complex cases coming before the courts, court-appointed experts are more common now than in the past (Brown & Eder, 1999; Eder & Brown, 2004).

A study by Dixon and Gill (2002) addressed changes in challenges to reliability (trustworthiness) in federal courts between 1980 and 1999. They found that there was an increase in successful challenges to reliability prior to *Daubert*, but that it was also evident that there was a general tightening of reliability standards post-*Daubert*. The percentage of challenged evidence, and the percentage found unreliable, both increased for all categories of evidence, though the percentages rose for physical science prior to rising for the other areas, including social and behavioral sciences. By 1999, however, the percentage of evidence successfully challenged had declined, possibly because experts had responded to *Daubert* by improving the data supporting reliability.

Dixon and Gill also indicate that the criterion of "general acceptance" has increased in importance since *Daubert*. Adding that the "[e]xistence and maintenance of standards controlling use of technique or method," (e.g., "Were samples properly collected? Were instruments properly calibrated?") to the four *Daubert* factors listed above, Dixon and Gill indicate that these five "*Daubert* factors" were addressed significantly more often post-*Daubert* than prior to it (pp. 280–281). By 1999, "general acceptance" had become the most frequent factor considered, "peer review and publication" second, and the other three were substantially lower. In general, "judges and challengers increasingly focused on the clarity and coherence of the expert's explanation of the underlying theory, methods, and procedures" (p. 285). Successful challenges to expert evidence may result in the granting of summary judgment to defendants.

Federal Rule of Civil Procedure 56 addresses "summary judgment." A motion for summary judgment requests that the court look at the evidence proferred via affidavits, statements under oath during depositions or in responses to interrogatories, and admissions of or stipulations to facts by the parties. Only admissible evidence is considered by the judge. The litigant moving for summary judgment must allege "that there is no genuine issue as to any material fact and that the moving party is entitled to a judgment as a matter of law" (FRCP 56(c)). Some possible bases for a summary judgment include proof that the plaintiff signed a legally binding release that prevents the plaintiff from suing the defendant; that a given defendant had nothing to do with the accident that caused the plaintiff's injury; or that the expert evidence proffered by the plaintiff was so seriously in violation of the *Daubert* requirements that the expert would not be permitted to testify in the trial, leaving the plaintiff without admissible expert testimony. *Daubert* itself was decided by the trial court on this last basis, that is, that the evidence offered by eight well-credentialed experts for the plaintiff "did not meet the applicable [*Frye v. United States*] 'general acceptance' standard for the admission of expert testimony" (*Daubert*, p. 509). The Court of Appeals affirmed, and the U.S. Supreme Court took up the case and held that the *Frye* standard was superseded by the Federal Rules of Evidence.

Parry (2004) notes that "[i]n general, an accepted scientific technique also must be validated—capable of duplication and used by different persons at various times. Even if the underlying theory is scientifically sound, the techniques used to test, support, or demonstrate the theory may not be" (p. 137).

Further, Parry (2004) notes, while some people have claimed that psychology and psychiatry are "soft" rather than "hard" sciences, and therefore lack the ability to provide precise, quantifiable, and objective data, even the "hard" sciences, for example, physics, involve theories that cannot be verified when, or even soon after, they are proposed. Some of Einstein's theories have only recently been validated, and some have yet to be validated, because physicists do not yet possess the tools that would permit that validation. (Note: the present author was recently told by a theoretical physicist that his work includes the identification of what a given particle or effect looks like and how it acts under various conditions, *if, in fact, it exists*.)

In addition, psychologists and psychiatrists spend many years in graduate programs, and work under supervision of more senior members of their professions before and/or after receiving their doctoral degrees. Through this education, training, and postdoctoral experience, psychologists and psychiatrists do achieve a substantial degree of expertise regarding normal and abnormal behavior, far more than the average layperson. Courts commonly admit testimony by psychologists and psychiatrists on this basis, since the expertise gained will most likely supplement whatever knowledge the jurors may have (Shuman, 1994a, 2002 supplement).

There is a web site devoted to cases in which the admissibility rates for *Daubert* and its progeny are indicated, www.*Daubert*ontheweb.com. According to this web site, as of April 16, 2006, there had been 761 federal appellate court decisions on *Daubert* issues since January 1, 2000. Of these, the appellate court affirmed the federal trial court decision to admit or exclude expert testimony 661 times, an overall affirmation rate of .869. Of 421 trial court decisions to admit expert testimony, the appellate court affirmed 371 of them, a rate of .881. Of 340 trial court decisions to exclude expert testimony, 290 were affirmed, a rate of .853. The web site notes that other attorneys might have placed a given appellate decision in a different category, that the ratings are based on the raters' reading of how the appellate court perceived the issues, that in mixed decisions the raters assessed the weight of the evidence and categorized the appellate decision accordingly, and that generally the numbers were based on expert-by-expert decisions, not case-by-case decisions. From the data presented, the appellate courts clearly affirmed the vast majority of trial court decisions regarding admissibility of expert testimony.

Eleven of the 12 circuit courts of appeal had at least 10 cases listed. The overall affirmation rates among those 11 appellate courts ranged from .772 in the

Seventh Circuit (based on 79 cases) to 1.00 in the Federal Circuit (based on 14 cases). The Ninth Circuit had the most cases (113), the D.C. Circuit the fewest (4).

Finally, *Daubertontheweb* identifies 60 cases involving psychologists and/or psychiatrists as of April 16, 2006 (7.9% of the 761 cases). Of these, the appellate courts found that 22 were admissible, a rate of .367. Of the 32 professions listed, only 12 have at least 10 appellate cases: accident reconstructionists (30 cases), accountants and economists (82), attorneys (12), chemists (18), criminologists and forensic experts (211), engineers (77), fire experts (23), physicians (87), polygraphers (32), psychologists and psychiatrists (60), statisticians (16), and toxicologists (12). The lowest admissibility rate was for polygraphers (.125), the highest rate was for criminologists and forensic experts (.844). Physicians' admissibility rate was .471.

The most common themes for affirming exclusion of psychological or psychiatric evidence were: the lack of a link between proposed testimony and an issue before the court (lack of relevance); lack of data regarding pretrauma status on which a conclusion about the effect of the trauma might be based; the psychologist did not provide evidence that he or she was qualified to give the proposed opinion; the expert used unreliable methodology; the expert's failure to identify how his or her assertions have been tested or whether publications cited have been peer-reviewed, or the expert did not address a rate of error; the expert based his opinion on a false premise; the experts relied on insufficient facts or data to link their theories to the facts of the case; the expert used a psychological test that has not been standardized for the population of which the individual was a member; and the expert's report did not cite any scientific studies or principles supporting his or her conclusions. These results strongly emphasize the need for psychologists to be very well prepared before testifying, including careful review of the material in this book and in other books on the state of the art in assessing psychological injuries, and review of the most current published articles in order to update the information in this and other books.

Heilbrun (2001) indicates that, of 276 appellate cases that cited *Daubert* between 1993 and 1996, there was a direct or indirect relationship to forensic mental health assessments in only 12 cases (4.3%). This is just over half the rate identified by *Daubertontheweb* for the 2000–2006 period. While the numbers are small, *Daubert* challenges appear to be playing a larger role in appellate cases.

Gatowski et al. (2001) surveyed 400 state trial judges throughout the United States. Regardless of the admissibility standard followed by their states, 91% of the judges favored having a gatekeeping role as defined by *Daubert*. However, few of the judges had the scientific sophistication to address many of the *Daubert* issues, particularly those of falsifiability and error rate. Most of the judges indicated that they would reject information that had not been subjected to peer review. Nearly all of the judges indicated that general acceptance was a useful standard for addressing the value of scientific evidence, and half of the judges would give general acceptance the greatest weight of the *Daubert* criteria. This may be because the judges understood this concept better than most of the other *Daubert* criteria. The primary need, Gatowski et al. indicate, is that "judges need to know … not how to design the best scientific study, but how to evaluate imperfect ones … . [T]hey need to be trained to be critical consumers of the science that comes before them" (p. 455).

In a followup of the Gatowski et al. (2001) study, 325 of the 400 state trial court judges were asked to comment on their gatekeeping function with regard to syndrome and profile evidence. The former includes "battered woman," "rape trauma," "repressed memory," and "posttraumatic stress." The latter includes "battering parent," "battering spouse," and "sexual predator." Judges could also comment on other syndromes and profiles with which they had experience. Of the 213 judges who both had experience with syndrome evidence and gave codable answers, 41% indicated that all syndrome evidence was admitted, 10% indicated that it was admitted at least 90% of the time, and 11% indicated that it was admitted at least 75% of the time. There was a similar pattern for profile evidence. Judges tended to rely primarily on standards for admissibility involving general acceptance and the qualifications of the expert rather than on other *Daubert* criteria. Only three judges mentioned either "falsifiability" or "error rate," though eight mentioned "all *Daubert* criteria." The authors conclude that *Daubert*'s affect on syndrome and profile testimony has been minimal (Dahir et al., 2005). Clearly, the survey indicates that judges were not familiar with two concepts that are essential to science, falsifiability, and error rates (Sales & Shuman, 2005).

According to Shuman and Sales (2001), *Daubert* has not had a major impact upon the type of psychological and other evidence offered in court. *Daubert* challenges are especially unlikely in child custody or visitation cases, or cases involving guardianship or wills, though psychological testimony is frequently part of those cases. "What is perhaps most significant about the *Daubert* challenges to psychological evidence is that they do not appear to result in different outcomes than pre-*Daubert* challenges to this same evidence" (p. 75). There is one significant exception: toxic torts and product liability cases. In these cases, *Daubert* challenges are common, and many experts' testimony is ruled insufficiently reliable for admission (Shuman, 2001).

Shuman and Sales (2001) indicate that *Daubert* is perhaps most important because it reminds mental health professionals of their ethical obligation to be aware of the latest research in the areas about which they testify, and to offer information to the court that is valid and reliable and has been derived with appropriate methodology. The experts must also be prepared to present evidence that their methodology in a given case is also valid and reliable. This is particularly true if the expert is basing testimony on scientific knowledge, since *Daubert* challenges are much more likely in such instances than in testimony based upon clinical experience. In effect, they indicate, "preparation for a *Daubert* challenge is preparation for cross-examination" (p. 76). The psychologist who is prepared to show how his or her methods, data and conclusions are relevant to the instant case, and that they are valid and reliable, should have minimal difficulty with either admissibility or credibility.

There is evidence that some cases that would have gone to trial are not filed now because of the extreme cost of experts in "time, money and energy as the trial itself, challenging the skills of lawyers, the patience of judges and the pocketbooks of litigants … . Unless potential damages top $1 million, some trial lawyers say, the risk of hiring a battery of experts to push the science past a *Daubert* challenge is not worthwhile" (Brickley, 2003).

Mohan

In *R. v. Mohan*, 2 S.C.R. (1994), the Supreme Court of Canada ruled that:

Admission of expert evidence depends on the application of the following criteria: (a) relevance; (b) necessity in assisting the trier of fact; (c) the absence of any exclusionary rule; and (d) a properly qualified expert.

Relevance is a threshold requirement to be decided by the judge as a question of law … . Expert evidence should not be admitted where there is a danger that it will be misused or will distort the fact-finding process, or will confuse the jury … . [E]xpert evidence which advances a novel scientific theory or technique is subjected to special scrutiny to determine whether it meets a basic threshold of reliability and whether it is essential in the sense that the trier of fact will be unable to come to a satisfactory conclusion without the assistance of the expert. The closer the evidence approaches an opinion on an ultimate issue, the stricter the application of this principle … .

Necessity in Assisting the Trier of Fact: With respect to matters calling for special knowledge, an expert in the field may draw inferences and state his opinion. An expert's function is precisely this: to provide the judge and jury with a ready-made inference which the judge and jury, due to the technical nature of the facts, are unable to formulate … . As in the case of relevance …, the need for the evidence is assessed in light of its potential to distort the fact-finding process … . There is also a concern inherent in the application of this criterion that experts not be permitted to usurp the functions of the trier of fact … . [T]he criteria of relevance and necessity are applied strictly, on occasion, to exclude expert evidence as to an ultimate issue … .

The Absence of any Exclusionary Rule: Compliance with criteria (a), (b) and (d) will not ensure the admissibility of expert evidence if it falls afoul of an exclusionary rule of evidence separate and apart from the opinion rule itself … . [For example, in one case that met the three other criteria] expert evidence … was excluded by reason of the rule that prevents the Crown from adducing evidence of the accused's disposition unless the latter has placed his or her character in issue … .

A Properly Qualified Expert: [T]he evidence must be given by a witness who is shown to have acquired special or peculiar knowledge through study or experience in respect of the matters on which he or she undertakes to testify … .

In summary, *Mohan*, like *Daubert, Joiner*, and *Kumho*, requires that the trial judge act as a gatekeeper for expert evidence. Both Supreme Court decisions require relevance and that the expert testimony assist the trier of fact to understand the issues and evidence in order to determine a fact in issue. Both require that the expert testimony pertain to special knowledge that the expert acquired through education or experience, that is, that the expert be qualified to testify in a particular area of inquiry. Although *Mohan* specifies that there must not be any exclusionary rule that would preclude the expert testimony, this is certainly implied by *Daubert* and its progeny and is included in other parts of the Federal Rules of Evidence. The final three *Daubert* criteria are not specifically addressed by *Mohan*, that is, whether there has been peer review and publication, that consideration be given to the known or potential error rate, and/or that there is general acceptance of a particular technique within the scientific community. *Mohan*'s comments on expert testimony regarding the ultimate issue are similar to Federal Rule of Evidence 704, above. In most respects, *Mohan* and *Daubert* and its progeny are comparable decisions by the respective Supreme Courts of Canada and the United States that attempt to identify when expert testimony is and is not appropriate.

Critical Concepts for the Expert Witness

Base Rates

"[B]ase rate refers to … the established probability of events in a population prior to the introduction of any novel procedure" (Urbina, 2004, p. 262). An expert who has not considered relevant base rates will make errors in both diagnosis and prognosis. A base rate of 50% provides no guidance, since a given individual is as likely to have a given condition as to not have it. As the base rate deviates from 50%, however, the value of the base rate information increases. For example, if an individual is struck in the head by an object moving at a rate of one-half mile per hour, the likelihood that the person will suffer a traumatic brain injury is very small—that is, the base rate is at or near zero. Neuropsychological testing is not necessary, since the probability of injury is so low that the time and expense of testing is not worthwhile (Faust, 2003).

Lees-Haley and Brown (1993) identified base rates for a number of complaints common among personal injury claimants. They found that 93% of claimants reported anxiety or nervousness—but so did 54% of the control group. Three other common complaints among personal injury claimants were headaches (88% vs. 62% for controls), concentration problems (78% vs. 26% for controls) and memory problems (53% vs. 20% for controls). In each of these examples, the probative value of the expert's testimony is very limited unless base rates have been considered, and a good case can be made for excluding the expert's testimony if they have not (Fleishman, Jackson & Rothschild, 1999).

According to U.S. Department of Health and Human Services (1999) *Mental Health: A Report of the Surgeon General*, the base rate for mood disorders (Major Depression, Bipolar Disorder, Dysthymia, Cyclothymia) in one year in the United States is 7%. Similarly, the base rate for an anxiety disorder is over 16% for adults 18–54 years of age during one year, with the base rate for a Posttraumatic Stress Disorder being 3.6%. The lifetime prevalence of exposure to significant trauma in the United States is between 40% and 70%, and the lifetime prevalence of PTSD is between 8% and 14% (Frueh, Elhai, & Kalouopek, 2004). The presence of a mood or anxiety disorder, by itself, is not proof that the individual suffered from the trauma claimed in a given legal case.

Error Rates

The critical issue with regard to questions of "error rates" is primarily the mandate to avoid false-positives and false-negatives to the degree possible. Testimony by the expert must address the likelihood that a given result may be a false conclusion, imparting blame or causality when it is not deserved, or indicating a lack of blame or causality when it is in fact present. Other definitions of "error rate" also exist, ensuring confusion (Kraus & Sales, 2003; Youngstrom & Busch, 2000). In science, absolute truth does not exist. An hypothesis may be demonstrated to be false, but can never be considered absolutely true. Science is always evolving, and the evidence in favor of a given proposition may change with the discovery of new information. The goal of research is to test hypotheses to identify those that are likely to be true based on current knowledge. A major purpose of publication is to permit others to replicate experiments or respond to ideas so that the conclusions drawn may be either supported or negated. The fact that there are disagreements about the conclusions drawn from research is a reflection of a strength of scientific inquiry, and always precedes a point at which consensus is achieved (National Academy of Sciences, 2002). It should be noted, of course, that new questions and issues continually arise as the psychological sciences progress, making this an ongoing process.

Further confusing matters, *Daubert* gives no guidance to judges in trial courts regarding what error rate should be considered unacceptable. One judge might use 10%, another 20%, and a third another amount. One judge might allow a substantially larger error rate if the scientific evidence underlying the expert's opinion has been tested and has been published in a peer-reviewed journal, while another might demand a low error rate unless the scientific evidence has been generally accepted within the scientific community, regardless of testability or publication issues. According to Kraus and Sales (2003),

> Under the present conceptualization of the *Daubert* standard, eventual admissibility decisions will be a product of ... what scientific information the forensic expert offers during the testimony, the pragmatic reliability, considerations chosen by the judge to evaluate that testimony, the manner in which the judge weighs the different chosen reliability considerations, and the level at which the judge attempts to fit the science to the legal question [p. 552].

Diagnosis

The primary psychiatric diagnostic system in North America is the *Diagnostic and Statistical Manual of Mental Disorders, Fourth Edition* (*DSM-IV*, American Psychiatric Association, 1994). There is also a "text revision," *DSM-IV-TR* (2000), but none of the diagnoses relevant to this chapter were changed. (Note: The American Psychiatric Association indicates that its timetable for publication of *DSM-V* includes: 2004–2007, "Review of data from ten conferences sponsored by the American Psychiatric Association and the National Institutes on Health on 'the future of psychiatric diagnoses;' " 2007, "Appointment of *DSM-V* Work

Groups;" 2011, "Publication of *DSM-V*." The web site for the *DSM-V* Prelude Project is www.dsm5.org.)

The rest of the world utilizes the *International Classification of Diseases, Injuries, and Causes of Death, Tenth Edition* (*ICD-10*, World Health Organization, 1992). The psychiatric section is titled The *ICD-10* Classification of Mental and Behavioural [sic] Disorders, which is Chapter 5 of *ICD-10*. Because the predecessor to *ICD-10* lacked the specificity desired by hospitals and professionals, a clinical modification, *ICD-9-CM*, was developed in 1979. It remains in use in North America despite a decade of work on a clinical modification of *ICD-10*, *ICD-10-CM*, which has been available since 2003. When testing of *ICD-10-CM* by hospitals and clinicians is completed, it will be adopted in the United States over a 2-year period. No implementation date has yet been set (National Center for Health Statistics, last reviewed April 16, 2006, accessed at www.cdc.gov/nchs/about/otheract.icd9/abticd10.htm).

That the *DSM* is standardized and relatively comprehensive is its strength. Its primary weakness is that psychiatric diagnoses are explanatory fictions or constructs that are primarily meant to permit professionals to communicate with one another, a shorthand that is useful in the clinical context but much less so in other contexts (Ackerman & Kane, 1998). Although a great deal of research was done to refine categories and diagnoses, *DSM-IV* and *ICD-10* (psychiatric section) remain quite imperfect. Each *DSM* has been adopted on the basis of a vote by a group of psychiatrists, after a review of the research evidence, thereby representing to some degree a value judgment rather than a pure scientific endeavor (Shuman, 2002a; State Justice Institute, 1999). Further, while *DSM-IV* diagnoses are frequently used in court, they are not designed to be used in this context according to the authors of *DSM-IV*, who wrote that

> [t]he purpose of *DSM-IV* is to provide clear descriptions of diagnostic categories in order to enable clinicians and investigators to diagnose, communicate about, study, and treat people with various mental disorders. It is to be understood that inclusion here ... of a diagnostic category ... does not imply that the condition meets legal or other nonmedical criteria for what constitutes mental disease, mental disorder, or mental disability ... [*DSM-IV* at xxvii].

Despite this, these diagnoses are used and accepted in court cases involving workers' compensation, torts, criminal infractions, family law, disability regulations, and other areas. Further, the *DSM* has significantly impacted litigation by, for example, identifying PTSD as an entity to which tort claims could be tied. This is consistent with the responsibility of attorneys to identify theories or practices that buttress the claims or defenses of their clients. It also supports the need for courts to act as gatekeepers for the admission of evidence and testimony based on diagnoses, while recognizing that the *DSM* diagnoses were not intended for use in court (Shuman, 2002a).

The most common diagnosis in personal injury litigants is PTSD (Ackerman & Kane, 1998; Koch, Douglas, Nicholls & O'Neill, 2006). The most commonly used diagnostic text in North America is the *Diagnostic and Statistical Manual of*

Mental Disorders, Fourth Edition (*DSM-IV*, 1994). The "Text Revision," *DSM-IV-TR* (2000), criteria for PTSD are identical to those of *DSM-IV*, so the two texts may be used interchangeably for diagnostic purposes. Although PTSD will be used here to exemplify the forensic causality issues, similar discussions could be had regarding a number of other diagnoses.

The diagnostic criteria for PTSD in the *International Classification of Diseases and Related Problems, Classification of Mental and Behavioral Disorders* (*ICD-10* psychiatric section, 1992) are substantially different from those in *DSM-IV*. The *ICD-10* diagnostic code for PTSD is F43.1, which indicates that "Post-traumatic stress disorder" (note slightly different spelling of the first word) arises as a delayed and/or protracted response to a stressful event or situation (either short- or long-lasting) of an exceptionally threatening or catastrophic nature, which is likely to cause pervasive distress in almost anyone (e.g., natural or man-made disaster, combat, serious accident, witnessing the violent death of others, or being the victim of torture, terrorism, rape, or other crime) (*ICD-10* Classification of Mental and Behavioral Disorders, p. 147).

Peters, Slade, and Andrews (1999) compared the *DSM-IV* and *ICD-10* criteria for PTSD in diagnosing a sample of 1,364 individuals using the Composite International Diagnostic Interview (CIDI). They found that the 12-month prevalence for PTSD was 3% when the *DSM-IV* criteria were used and 6.9% when the *ICD-10* criteria were used. The largest group (33 people) that met *ICD-10* but not *DSM-IV* criteria failed to meet the requirements of *DSM-IV* Criterion C, regarding avoidance and numbing. Second largest (9 people) was the group that did not meet Criterion A of *DSM-IV* (actual or threatened death or serious injury, and intense fear, helplessness or horror).

The *ICD-10* definition is closer to that of *DSM-III-R* (1987) than that of *DSM-IV*. It is broader than the initial diagnostic criterion of *DSM-IV*, presented below, because it would permit the diagnosis to be used when the stressful event falls short of being a severe threat to life or limb, for example, crimes such as burglaries or sexual misconduct by professionals (clergy, physicians, mental health professionals, etc.) or sexual harassment. Since it is the primary diagnostic manual in North America, however, this chapter will primarily address *DSM-IV*.

PTSD (and its short-term predecessor, Acute Stress Disorder) is the only diagnosis in the *DSM* that requires that there be a specific traumatic event that initiates the disorder. The initial requirement (Criterion A) that must be met for the *DSM-IV* (1994) diagnosis to be applicable is that "the person experienced, witnessed, or was confronted with an event or events that involved actual or threatened death or serious injury, or a threat to the physical integrity of self or others." In addition, it is required that "the person's response involved intense fear, helplessness, or horror," or, for children, that "this may be expressed instead by disorganized or agitated behavior" (pp. 427–428).

There is then a requirement that the individual re-experienced (Criterion B) the trauma in one or more of five listed ways, persistently avoided "stimuli associated with the trauma and [experienced] numbing of general responsiveness" (Criterion C) in three or more of seven listed ways, exhibited "persistent symptoms of increased arousal" (Criterion D) in two or more of five listed ways, that the symptoms have lasted more than one month, and that the symptoms cause "clinically significant distress or impairment in social, occupational, or other important areas of functioning." It is recognized that onset may be delayed six or more months after the stressor, in which case one specifies "with delayed onset" (*DSM-IV*, pp. 427–429).

While PTSD is often thought of as purely a psychological phenomenon, Wilson (2004) indicates that "PTSD is a normal, biologically hardwired pattern of reactivity to extremely stressful situations" (p. 15). He notes that "[r]eexperiencing phenomena involves cognitive processing, information storage, and retrieval from memory" (p. 19), and potentially involves 16 different forms of reliving the traumatic experience via conscious or unconscious behavior, changes in state of awareness, changes in the senses and perception, and hyperarousal-related bodily symptoms. People protect themselves from the severe impact of the trauma via up to seven symptoms associated with avoidance, and exhibit hyperarousal that may take the form of one or more of: "sleep cycle disturbance … , anger, irritability, and hostility … , impairment in cognitive processing of information … , hypervigilance … , [and/or] hyperarousal and self-monitoring difficulties" (pp. 27–28).

It must also be recognized that PTSD is not a unitary phenomenon with a single manner of presentation. A given individual may evidence different diagnostic indicators at different points in time, and two individuals may be accurately diagnosed with PTSD while sharing few or no symptoms. It has increasingly been recognized that PTSD is often not the transient phenomenon that it was once thought to be. Half of all individuals who develop PTSD recover within a year, while between 30% and 40% continue to have PTSD even 5 years later (Keane, Quoted in Moran, 2003).

It is not unusual for a clinician or forensic expert to indicate a diagnosis of Posttraumatic Stress Disorder when the individual's experience and/or symptoms do not meet the full diagnostic criteria. Particularly problematic is Criterion A. For example, many of the people sexually victimized by clergy exhibit most of the symptoms of PTSD except for Criterion A. They were generally not threatened with death or serious injury, nor a "threat to the physical integrity of self or others," and may not have felt "intense fear, helplessness, or horror." Technically, this precludes use of the PTSD diagnosis. One result has been that many clinicians and experts indicate a "Posttraumatic Stress Syndrome" that meets all the criteria of the *DSM-IV* diagnosis except for Criterion A (see, for example, Moreau and Zisook, 2002). Alternatively, the clinician may simply focus on the symptoms, describing in reports and testimony the specific anxiety and other symptoms that characterize the individual's psychopathology. The key question is whether, in the words of *Daubert*, "the reasoning or methodology properly can be applied to the facts in issue" (*Daubert v. Merrell Dow Pharmaceuticals*, p. 593). Whether utilizing formal *DSM-IV* diagnoses, syndrome evidence, or description of symptoms, the task is to apply them to the facts of the case and to identify their accuracy and relevance.

Much more important than the specific diagnostic criteria, regardless of the cause of the trauma, is the process of comprehensively identifying the individual's specific symptoms, followed by a discussion of those diagnostic categories that may be applicable, and ruling in or out a number of potentially relevant psychiatric disorders in the process of making a *differential diagnosis* (Ackerman & Kane, 1998; Brown & Eder, 1999). While testimony about all of the alternative diagnoses considered would likely bore the court, enough should be presented to make it clear that many diagnoses were considered and why the expert arrived at the final diagnosis or diagnoses (Macartney-Filgate & Snow, 2004).

Among the diagnostic categories that overlap with PTSD to some degree are: Panic Disorder, Social Phobia (Social Anxiety Disorder), Specific Phobia, Generalized Anxiety Disorder, Major Depressive Episode, Somatoform Disorders, Brief Psychotic Disorder, Antisocial Personality Disorder, Substance-Related Disorders, some Organic Mental Disorders, and some Adjustment Disorders (Ackerman & Kane, 1998). One must also consider the possibility of malingering. The careful application of the differential diagnosis process will provide many of the answers needed by the forensic assessor. At the same time, one must avoid the "*post hoc, ergo propter hoc*" ("after this, therefore because of this") logical error. The presence of a PTSD or any other disorder does not prove that the traumatic event in question was the cause of the disorder. The cause may be a different event, or a series of events that included the currently relevant traumatic event. Similarly, the presence of a correlation between an event and a psychological disorder never, by itself, indicates causation. There is a high correlation between height and weight, for example, but no causation (Ackerman & Kane, 1998).

Differences Between Science and Law

A judge at a workshop on science and law identified a number of differences between the two:

> (1) Law is backward-looking and its findings are based on precedent … . Science is forward-looking in assuming that the truth is not yet fully known; (2) propositions to be tested in science are predictive; experiments are designed to be repeatable. Theories to be proved in court arise out of situations that occurred in the past and cannot be repeated; (3) scientists recognize that "truth" is mutable and may evolve over a long period of time. In adjudication, "truth," at least for the limited purpose of resolving disputes, must become final in a relatively short time; (4) scientists are often uncomfortable in the courtroom, especially during cross-examination. The dialogue is controlled by the lawyers and the judge, not by the expert witness; (5) disputes in science are resolved over time by peer review and the scrutiny of the scientific community at large. Legal disputes are resolved by cross-examination. Courts are not designed to determine whether scientific conclusions are correct [National Academy of Sciences, 2002, pp. 22–23].

In addition, a "not demonstrated" conclusion in science indicates that more research needs to be done or an assertion needs to be restated. In court, "not demonstrated" means that a jury was not convinced, and that one of the parties loses the case (National Academy of Sciences, 2002). The standard for "reasonable certainty" in science is typically 95% or 99%, that is, the likelihood of getting the results obtained by chance is statistically estimated to be at most either 5% or 1%. In court, however, the standard is "likelier than not," that is, the party that has more than 50% of the evidence on its side (as determined by the trier of fact) wins the case. Causality need not be demonstrated "beyond a reasonable doubt" or even by "clear and convincing evidence," it must only be demonstrated by a simple preponderance of the evidence. The intent appears to be to permit the expert to make a qualitative statement that he or she is "reasonably certain" that he or she is correct, recognizing that there cannot be absolute certainty in many (and perhaps any) areas of testimony (Bradford, 2001). [See, e.g., *Burke v. Town of Walpole*, Case No. 04–1226 (1st Circuit Court of Appeals, April 26, 2005): "[T]he commonly accepted meaning among lawyers and judges to the term 'reasonable degree of scientific certainty'—'a standard requiring a showing that the injury was more likely than not caused by a particular stimulus, based on the general consensus of recognized [scientific] thought.' Black's Law Dictionary 1294 (8th ed. 2004)."]

It is because of concern that juries may overestimate the ability of an expert to draw accurate conclusions that courts generally require that experts state conclusions to a "reasonable degree of certainty." If the expert indicates that the causal relationship between the trauma and the injury is only "possible," rather than "present to a reasonable degree of psychological (or medical) certainty," a court may conclude that the required degree of certainty is absent, and exclude the testimony (Shuman, 1994a, 2002 Supplement).

Even when the expert states that his or her conclusions are true to a reasonable degree of psychological (or medical) certainty, the actual degree of certainty is unclear, at times appearing to reflect the degree of certainty in making patient care decisions (usually made at a relatively low level of certainty in order to protect patients) while at other times it may appear to parallel "preponderance of the evidence," "clear and convincing," or even "beyond a reasonable doubt" levels of certainty. Further, there is reliance on the honesty and good faith of the expert, while, at the same time, taking a chance that an expert who is too candid about his or her uncertainty will have his or her testimony excluded. While expert testimony tends to be admitted even when substantial uncertainty is indicated by the expert, these issues are generally addressed by giving more or less weight to the evidence (Shuman, 1994a, 2003 supplement).

Bases for Expert Opinions

Federal Rule of Evidence 703 provides the standard regarding bases for expert testimony:

> The facts or data in the particular case upon which an expert bases an opinion or inference may be those perceived by or made known to the expert at or before the hearing. If of a type reasonably relied upon by experts in the particular field in forming opinions or inferences upon the subject, the facts or data need not be admissible in evidence <u>in order for the opinion or inference to be admitted. Facts or data that are otherwise inadmissible shall not be</u>

disclosed to the jury by the proponent of the opinion or inference unless the court determines that their probative value in assisting the jury to evaluate the expert's opinion substantially outweighs their prejudicial effect. [underlined portion was added on December 1, 2000].

There are, thus, three bases for expert testimony: facts or information learned by direct observation or by studying various information, facts or information learned during a trial, and facts or information obtained through reading or through discussions with others. It is further required that the facts or data be of the kind upon which other experts in the same field would rely, and that relying on that information is reasonable. Information learned at a trial includes information from other witnesses. It is also possible for an attorney to pose a hypothetical question that includes relevant facts from the case at hand and to ask the expert to give his or her opinion on the basis of the statements in the hypothetical question (Kirkpatrick & Mueller, 2003). Rule 703 was strengthened by the addition of the requirement that the court determine whether the probative value of the information the expert wants to have admitted exceeds its prejudicial effect, at least in part to prevent experts from easily introducing hearsay evidence upon which they had relied but that could not otherwise be introduced. Experts will now be able to testify regarding hearsay only if the statements are admissible under a hearsay exception or the probative value substantially outweighs the prejudicial effect (Faigman & Monahan, 2005).

Opinion on the Ultimate Issue

Federal Rule of Evidence 704 indicates that

(a) Except as provided in subdivision (b), testimony in the form of an opinion or inference otherwise admissible is not objectionable because it embraces an ultimate issue to be decided by the trier of fact.
(b) No expert witness testifying with respect to the mental state or condition of a defendant in a criminal case may state an opinion or inference as to whether the defendant did or did not have the mental state or condition constituting an element of the crime charged or of a defense thereto. Such ultimate issues are matters for the trier of fact alone.

Thus, in any civil case, expert evidence may include an opinion on the ultimate issue (e.g., what was and what was not the cause of the plaintiff's current condition), so long as the expert provides the reasoning that allowed him or her to reach that opinion, and so long as the information is helpful to the judge or jury. Most states have similar provisions in their rules of evidence (Shuman, 1994, 2003 supplement).

Learned Treatises

Federal Rule of Evidence 803(18) defines "learned treatises" as:

statements contained in published treatises, periodicals, or pamphlets on a subject of history, medicine, or other science or art, established as a reliable authority by the testimony or admission of the witness or by other expert testimony or by judicial notice. If admitted, the statements may be read into evidence but may not be received as exhibits ... .

That is, they may not be given to the jury for consideration in their deliberations. It is believed that learned treatises are likely to be trustworthy because they have been written by professionals with training, knowledge and skills, for the purpose of having others in the same field(s) read them. Because other professionals will criticize inaccurate information, and because it is assumed that authors who are professionals want their writings to be well-accepted in the professional community, it is expected that they will take care to ensure that their writings are accurate and trustworthy (Kirkpatrick & Mueller, 2003). *Daubert* indicates the special value of peer-reviewed treatises, since those have gone through a formal review process by experts in the relevant area prior to publication. Treatises that have not gone through that formal review process may still be of equal or greater value in a particular case, however. It should also be noted that most published professional articles and chapters are informally reviewed by colleagues of the author(s), to try to ensure that the contents are both accurate and readable.

Experts must be very familiar with the professional literature related to the issues in a given case. That familiarity is dictated by codes of ethics and forensic guidelines, as well as by the justifiable expectation of the courts that someone who is retained as an expert *is* an expert, including real familiarity with the professional literature relevant to the case. Finally, it is that literature that provides the nomothetic (population) data with which the expert may compare the idiographic (individual) data that results from the assessment of the plaintiff.

Tort Law and the Role of the Psychological Assessment

The purpose of tort law is to distribute the costs of events in which harm was done to an individual or entity, on the basis of evolved social policies. For the individual who was harmed, "the commonly understood goal of tort compensation is to restore the injured to their pre-accident condition, to make them whole" (Shuman, 1994b). The plaintiff must demonstrate that the defendant owed a duty to the plaintiff, was derelict in that duty, directly caused harm to the plaintiff, and that the harm was significant and the plaintiff should be compensated for the harm done (damages). Both tort law and mental health professionals want to reduce harm, and to restore the functioning of those who are harmed by others. Tort law is meant to do so through deterring unreasonable conduct and compensating injured individuals with money that may be used for treatment or other means of compensation. To achieve that end, "a plaintiff must establish both liability (i.e., that the defendant's conduct was intentionally or negligently unreasonable and should be deterred) and damages (i.e., that the plaintiff has suffered injury and should be compensated" (Shuman & Daley, 1996, pp. 294–295). In order to establish liability, a showing that the defendant's intentional or negligent conduct is below the societal standard for reasonable care must be shown, as well as a direct, causal relationship between the defendant's behavior and the injury—that is, *but for* the defendant's behavior, the injury would not have taken place. The typical standard for negligence is the "reasonable person test," that is, whether a reasonable person would have behaved as did the defendant (Shuman & Daley, 1996; McLearen, Pietz, & Denney, 2004).

When the harm is physical, for example, a broken leg that resulted from an automobile accident, it is often easy to assign responsibility (liability) and assess the degree of disability (damages). When the harm is primarily or exclusively psychological/emotional, however, it is likely to be much more difficult both to assign responsibility for the harm that was done and to assess the degree of disability that is the result of that harmful event. A growing, but difficult, area of claims to assess is the "lost enjoyment of life" as a result of limitations caused by the injury (McLearnen et al., 2004). Most often, it will require the assistance of an expert, often a psychologist, who will do an assessment to try to provide the trier of fact with the essential information. A great deal rides on the quality of the psychological assessment, which may substantially determine whether the injured party receives a damage award to address the pain, suffering, loss of income, and other areas in which harm occurred—or, conversely, whether the defendant is absolved of responsibility for harm for which he or she was not responsible.

A primary purpose of the assessment is to identify whether the alleged cause of harm to the individual was, in fact, the primary or exclusive cause of that harm. To this end, the forensic expert considers data regarding whether the plaintiff was functioning well until the alleged harmful event occurred, the degree of harm, if any, of the alleged event, other possible or likely causes of harm to the plaintiff that may explain part or all of the harm alleged, whether the alleged harmful event is merely correlated with (rather than causative of) the alleged harm or appears to in fact to be the cause of that harm, whether other possible causes can be ruled out, and so forth (Sella, 1997). Numerous formats exist for such assessments. One common format is in the chapters on "Mental and Behavioral Disorders" and "Pain" in the American Medical Association's *Guides to the Evaluation of Permanent Impairment, Fifth Edition* (Cocchiarella & Andersson, 2001). Another is Wilson and Moran's (2004) "Matrix Model." No model is necessarily better than any other, so long as it facilitates the integration of data to indicate whether the traumatic event in question appears to be the proximate cause of the plaintiff's injury.

Another purpose of the assessment is to try to address the likelihood that the plaintiff would be helped by psychotherapy or other services. If the individual has previously been in psychotherapy or has received other psychological or psychosocial services, prediction can reasonably be based in part on the person's past experience. If not, an attempt at prediction may be based on a combination of verbal skills, awareness of him- or herself, and the assessed level of suffering experienced by the individual (Greenberg, Otto, & Long, 2003).

The forensic psychologist or other professional must have the requisite knowledge, skill and experience to conduct an appropriate evaluation, and must know enough about the legal arena to be able to make appropriate decisions regarding the nature and extent of the assessment, what kind of data must be gathered and what should be avoided. In most cases, a clinical psychologist with specialized knowledge and/or training in forensic work will be appropriate. If there is a significant question regarding traumatic brain injury, however, the expert should generally be a forensic neuropsychologist, though a forensic psychologist and a neuropsychologist who does not normally do forensic work might work together.

Wettstein (2005) indicates that the most significant problem area indicated in empirical research on forensic reports is the failure of the evaluator to identify the reasoning by which he or she reached the opinions stated in the report. Further, it is common for evaluators to fail to connect identified psychopathology, results from psychological tests, diagnosis, and relevant functional impairments. An evaluator who fails to present his or her reasoning and to connect these essential parts of the report is inviting a *Daubert/Mohan* hearing. Conversely, presentation of this information in the report makes a *Daubert/Mohan* hearing less likely.

References

Ackerman, M. J., & Kane, A. W. (1998). *Psychological experts in personal injury actions* (3rd ed.). New York: Aspen Law and Business.

Advisory Committee on the Federal Rules of Evidence. (2000). Notes of Advisory Committee on Proposed Rules. Washington, DC: Judicial Conference of the United States. Retrieved July 26, 2006 from http://www.access.gpo.gov/uscode/title28a/ 28a_5_7_.html.

American Psychiatric Association. (1994). *Diagnostic and statistical manual of mental disorders* (4th ed.). Washington, DC: Author.

Antoine-Tubbs v. Local 513 Air Transp. Div., 50 F. Supp. 2d 601 (N.D. Tex. 1998).

Barefoot v. Estelle, 463 U.S. 880 (1983).

Bernstein, D. E., & Jackson, J. D. (2004). The *Daubert* trilogy in the states. *Jurimetrics, 44*. Retrieved April 6, 2004, from Social Science Research Network Electronic Paper collection, http://ssrn.com/abstract=498786.

Bradford, G. E. (2001). Dissecting Missouri's requirement of "reasonable medical certainty." *Journal of the Missouri Bar, 57*. (January 1, 2004); retrieved August 12, 2004, from www.mobar.org.

Brickley, P. (2003). Science v. law. *Scientific American, 289*, 30–31.

Brown, J. J. (ed.) (1999). *Scientific evidence and experts handbook*. New York: Aspen Law and Business.

Brown, J. J., & Eder, E. (1999). The standards of admissibility of scientific and technical evidence. In J. J. Brown (Ed.), *Scientific evidence and experts handbook* (pp. 1–42). New York: Aspen Law & Business.

Burke v. Town of Walpole, 405 F.3d 66 (1st Cir. 2005).

Call, J. A. (2003). Liability for psychological injury: Yesterday and today. In I. Z. Schultz & D. O. Brady (Eds.), *Psychological injuries at trial* (pp. 40–64). Chicago: American Bar Association.

Cocchiarella, L., & Andersson, G. B. J. (2001). *Guides to the evaluation of permanent impairment* 5th ed. Chicago: American Medical Association.

Cooper v. Smith & Nephew, 259 F.3d 194 (4th Cir. 2001).

Dahir, V. B., Richardson, J. F., Ginsburg, G. P., Gatowski, S. I., Dobbin, S. A., & Merlino, M. L. (2005). Judicial application of *Daubert* to psychological syndrome and profile evidence. *Psychology, Public Policy and Law, 11*, 62–82.

Daubert v. Merrell Dow Pharmaceuticals, Inc. 509 U.S. 579, 113 S.Ct. 2786, 125 L.Ed. 2d 469 (1993).

Daubert v. Merrell Dow Pharmaceuticals, Inc., 43 F.3d 1311 (1995).

Daubertontheweb.com, Retrieved April 16, 2006, from http://www.daubertontheweb.com/.

Dixon, L., & Gill, B. (2002). Changes in the standards for admitting expert evidence in federal civil cases since the *Daubert* decision. *Psychology, Public Policy, and Law, 8*, 251–308.

Eder, E. (2007). The standards of admissibility of scientific and technical evidence. In J. J. Brown (Ed.), *Scientific evidence and experts handbook* (2007 cumulative supplement). New York: Aspen Law and Business. Retrieved November 9, 2006 from Loislaw.com.

Faigman, D. L. (2000). The gatekeepers: Scientific expert testimony in the trial process. *The Trial Lawyer, 23*, 335–346.

Faigman, D. L., & Monahan, J. (2005). Psychological evidence at the dawn of the law's scientific age. *Annual Review of Psychology, 56*, 631–659.

Faust, D. (2003). Holistic thinking is not the whole story: Alternative or adjunct approaches for increasing the accuracy of legal evaluations. *Assessment, 10*, 428–441.

Faust, D., & Heard, K. V. (2003). Objectifying subjective injury claims. In I. Z. Schulze & D. O. Brady (Eds.), *Psychological injuries at trial* (pp. 1686–1705). Chicago: American Bar Association.

Federal Rules of Civil Procedure, retrieved July 18, 2004, from www.loislaw.com.

Federal Rules of Evidence (2004). Retrieved February 20, 2005, from http://judiciary. house. gov/media/pdfs/printers/108th/evid2004.pdf.

Fleishman, W., Jackson, J. R., & Rothschild, M. (1999). Defensive litigation strategy in scientific evidence cases. In J. J. Brown (Ed.), *Scientific evidence and experts handbook* (pp. 305–385). New York: Aspen Law and Business.

Frueh, B. C., Elhai, J. D., & Kaloupek, D. G. (2004). Unresolved issues in the assessment of trauma exposure and posttraumatic reactions. In G. M. Rosen (Ed.), *Posttraumatic Stress Disorder: Issues and controversies*. West Sussex, England: Wiley.

Frye v. United States, 293 F. 1013, 34 ALR 145 (D. C. Cir. 1923).

Gatowski, S. I., Dobbin, S. A., Richardson, J. T., Ginsburg, G. P., Merlino, M. L., & Dahir, V. (2001). Asking the gatekeepers: A national survey of judges on judging expert evidence in a post-*Daubert* world. *Law & Human Behavior, 25*, 433–458.

General Electric Co. v. Joiner, 522 U.S. 136, 118 S.Ct. 512 (1997).

Greenberg, S. A., Otto, R. K., & Long, A. C. (2003). The utility of psychological testing in assessing emotional damages in personal injury litigation. *Assessment, 10*, 411–419.

Grisso, T. (2003). *Evaluating Competencies* (2nd ed.). New York: Kluwer/Plenum.

Gutheil, T. G., & Bursztajn, H. (2003). Avoiding ipse dixit mislabeling: Post-*Daubert* approaches to expert clinical opinions. *Journal of the American Academy of Psychiatry and the Law, 31*, 205–210.

Gutheil, T. G., & Bursztajn, H. (2005). Attorney abuses of *Daubert* hearings: Junk science, junk law, or just plain obstruction? *Journal of the American Academy of Psychiatry and Law, 33*, 150–152.

Haney, C., & Smith, A. (2003). Science, law, and psychological injury: The *Daubert* standards and beyond. In I. Z. Schulze & D. O. Brady (Eds.), *Psychological injuries at trial* (pp. 184–201). Chicago: American Bar Association.

Harris v. Forklift Systems, Inc., 114 S.Ct. 367 (1993).

Heilbrun, K. (2001). *Principles of forensic mental health assessment*. New York: Kluwer/ Plenum.

Imwinkelried, E. J. (2000). Evaluating the reliability of nonscientific expert testimony: A partial answer to the questions left unresolved by *Kumho Tire Co. v. Carmichael. Maine Law Review, 52*, 20–41.

Johnson, M. T., Krafka, C., & Cecil, J. S. (2000). Expert testimony in federal civil trials, a preliminary analysis. Retrieved May 2, 2004, from the Federal Judicial Center, http://www.fjc.gov/newweb/jnetweb.nsf/autoframe?openform&url_r=pages/556&url_l=index.

Kirkpatrick, L. C., & Mueller, C. B. (2003). *Evidence: Practice under the rules*. New York: Aspen Law and Business.

Koch, W. J., Douglas, K. S., Nicholls, T. L. & O'Neill, M. L. (2006). *Psychological injuries: Forensic assessment, treatment, and law*. Oxford: Oxford.

Krafka, C., Dunn, M. A., Johnson, M. T., Cecil, J. S., & Miletich, D. (2002). Judge and attorney experiences, practices, and concerns regarding expert testimony in federal civil trials. *Psychology, Public Policy, and Law, 8*, 309–332.

Kraus, D. A., & Sales, B. D. (2003). Forensic psychology, public policy, and the law. In I. B. Weiner (Series Ed.) & A. M. Goldstein (Vol. Ed.), *Handbook of psychology: Vol. 11, Forensic psychology* (pp. 543–560). Hoboken, NJ: Wiley.

Kumho Tire Co. v. Carmichael, 526 U.S. 137, 119 S.Ct. 1167 (1999).

Lees-Haley, P. and Brown, R. S. (1993). Neuropsychological complaint base rates of 170 personal injury claimants. *Archives of Clinical Neuropsychology, 8*, 203–209.

Macartney-Filgate, M. S., & Snow, G. W. (2004). The practitioner as expert witness. In D. R. Evans (Ed.), *The law, standards, and ethics in the practice of psychology* (2nd ed., pp. 287–309). Toronto: Edmond Montgomery Publications.

McLearen, A. M., Pietz, C. A., & Denney, R. L. (2004). Evaluation of psychological damages. In W. T. O'Donohue & E. R. Levensky (Eds.), *Handbook of forensic psychology* (pp. 267–299). Amsterdam: Elsevier.

Merriam-Webster's Dictionary of Law (1996). Retrieved June 11, 2005, from http://dictionary.lp.findlaw.com/scripts/.

Moran, M. (2003). Trauma-response strategies still missing in action. *Psychiatric News, 38*, 42.

Moreau, C., & Zisook, S. (2002) Rationale for a posttraumatic stress spectrum disorder. *Psychiatric Clinics of North America, 25*, 775–790.

National Academy of Sciences (2002). The age of expert testimony: Science in the courtroom, report of a workshop. Washington, DC. Retrieved February 22, 2004, from http://www.nap.edu/openbook/0309083109/html/.

National Center for Health Statistics, Retrieved October 13, 2005, from www.cdc.gov/nchs/about/otheract.icd9/abticd10.htm

Parry, J. W. (2000). Admissibility of expert evidence. *Mental and Physical Disability Law Reporter, 24*, 10.

Parry, J. W. (2004). Expert evidence and testimony: *Daubert* versus *Frye. Mental and Physical Disability Law Reporter, 28*, 136–140.

Peters, L., Slade, T., & Andrews, G. (1999). A comparison of ICD-10 and DSM-IV criteria for Posttraumatic Stress Disorder. *Journal of Traumatic Stress, 12*, 335–343.

R. v. Mohan [1994] 2 S.C.R. 9, 1994 CanLII 80 (S.C.C.).

Risinger, D. M., Saks, M. J., Thompson, W. C., & Rosenthal, R. (2002). The *Daubert/Kumho* implications of observer effects in forensic science: Hidden problems of expectation and suggestion. *California Law Review, 90*, 1–56.

Saks, M. J. (2000). The aftermath of *Daubert*: An evolving jurisprudence of expert evidence. *Jurimetrics, 40*, 229–241.

Sales, B. D., & Shuman, D. W. (2005). *Experts in court: Reconciling law, science, and professional knowledge*. Washington, DC: American Psychological Association.

Sella, G. (1997). Causation. *Forensic Examiner, 32*, 32.

Sheehan v. Daily Racing Form, Inc., 104 F.3d 940 (7th Cir. 1997).

Shuman, D. W. (1994a). *Psychiatric and psychological evidence* (2nd ed.). Deerfield, IL: Clark, Boardman, Callaghan. (Supplemented 2002, 2003, 2004).

Shuman, D. W. (1994b). The psychology of compensation in tort law. *Kansas Law Review, 43*. Retrieved April 6, 2003, from www.lexis.com.

Shuman, D. W. (2001). Expertise in law, medicine and health care. *Journal of Health Politics, Policy and Law, 26*, 267–290.

Shuman, D. W. (2002a). Retrospective assessment of mental states and the law. In R. I. Simon & D. W. Shuman (Eds.), *Retrospective assessment of mental states in litigation* (pp. 21–45). Washington, DC: American Psychiatric.

Shuman, D. W. (2002b). Softened science in the courtroom: Forensic implications of a value-laden classification. In J. Z. Sadler (Ed.), *Descriptions and prescriptions* (pp. 217–228). Baltimore: Johns Hopkins University Press.

Shuman, D. W., & Daley, C. E. (1996). Compensation for mental and emotional distress. In D. B. Sales & D. W. Shuman (Eds.), *Law, mental health, and mental disorder*. Pacific Grove: Brooks/Cole.

Shuman, D. W., & Sales, B. D. (1999). The impact of *Daubert* and its progeny on the admissibility of behavioral and social science evidence. *Psychology, Public Policy, and Law, 5*, 3–15.

Shuman, D. W., & Sales, B. D. (2001). *Daubert*'s wager. *Journal of Forensic Psychology Practice, 1*, 69–77.

Slovenko, R. (2002). From *Frye* to *Daubert* and beyond. In R. Slovenko, *Psychiatry in law* (pp. 43–64). New York: Routledge.

State Justice Institute. (1999). The bench: Companion to a judge's deskbook on the basic philosophies and methods of science. Retrieved November 6, 2004, from www.unr.edu/bench/.

Urbina, A. (2004). *Essentials of psychological testing*. Hoboken, NJ: Wiley.

U.S. Department of Health and Human Services. (1999). *Mental health: A report of the Surgeon General*. Rockville, MD: Author.

Wettstein, R. M. (2005). Quality and quality improvement in forensic mental health evaluations. *Journal of the American Academy of Psychiatry and Law, 33*, 158–175.

Wilson, J. P. (2004). PTSD and complex PTSD. In J. P. Wilson & T. M. Keane (Eds.), *Assessing psychological trauma and PTSD* (2nd ed., pp. 7–44). New York: Guilford Press.

Wilson, J. P., & Moran, T. A. (2004). Forensic/clinical assessment of psychological trauma and PTSD in legal settings. In J. P. Wilson, & T. M. Keane (Eds.), *Assessing psychological trauma and PTSD* (2nd ed., pp. 603–636). New York: Guilford Press.

World Health Organization. (1992). *International classification of diseases, injuries, and causes of death, 10th edition* (ICD-10). Geneva: Author.

Youngstrom, E. A., & Busch, C. P. (2000) Expert testimony in psychology: Ramifications of Supreme Court decision in *Kumho Tire Co., Ltd. v. Carmichael*. *Ethics & Behavior, 10*, 185–193.

11

Conducting a Psychological Assessment

ANDREW W. KANE

The Goals of an Assessment

A primary goal, and an ethical requirement, for an evaluator is to be impartial, regardless of who retained him or her, acknowledging the strengths and weaknesses of the data while advocating for the conclusions he or she has drawn from the data, not for a given side in a case. Among the means of maintaining impartiality for the evaluator are (1) set and maintain professional boundaries regarding the retaining attorney; (2) avoid becoming invested in a particular outcome of a case; the evaluator is to advocate for his or her data and conclusions, not to try to "win;" (3) communicate the results of the evaluation clearly and in simple language, avoiding superlatives (e.g., "absolutely" or "completely"), in both the report and testimony (Heilbrun, Marczyk, & DeMatteo, 2002; Macartney- Filgate & Snow, 2004; Greenberg, 2003; see also the *Specialty Guidelines for Forensic Psychologists*, Guidelines VII.B, C, and D). According to Murphy (2000), the American Bar Association has indicated that expert witnesses must be independent, rather than loyal to or an advocate for his or her client, the attorney. "In essence, an expert must analyze, explain, and offer an accurate opinion of the relevant issue before the court, not strive to advocate and persuade the fact-finder of a certain point of view. The expert's main duty to provide truthful and accurate information comes from the court and the ethical guidelines of his professional organization, if any" (Murphy, p. 6 of document retrieved April 4, 2003 from www.law-forensics.com/ethic and experts.htm.)

The case-related goal of the assessment is to identify whether, and if so to what degree, the traumatic event caused the plaintiff to suffer a psychological injury. The options include (1) the traumatic event was the sole cause of the individual's assessed psychopathology—a rare event. (2) The traumatic event was the major cause of the individual's assessed psychopathology. *But for* the traumatic event, the individual would not have the degree of psychopathology assessed. (3) The traumatic event was a significant contributing factor ("material contribution" or "substantial contribution") to the degree of assessed psychopathology, but not the major factor. The assessed disorder was identifiably worse because the traumatic event occurred, however. (4) The traumatic event had little affect on the assessed psychopathology of the individual, but may have exacerbated an existing psychopathology to some degree. (5) No significant relationship was identified between the traumatic event and any psychopathology that was found by the assessment (Ackerman & Kane, 1998; Melton, Petrila, Poythress, & Slobogin, 1997; see also the discussion by Young, Chapter 3 in this volume). There is no gold standard for the conduct of an evaluation. Each evaluator must design an evaluation that properly, adequately, and comprehensively addresses the legal questions at issue in each individual case. A number of authors have suggested models that may be used for an evaluation (see, e.g., Greenberg, 2003; Grisso, 2003; Heilbrun, 2001; Wilson & Moran, 2004). It should also be noted that psychopathology is not a black-and-white issue, it is a continuum. It is through the comprehensive evaluation process, including review of the pertinent scientific literature, that the expert identifies where on the continuum an individual's psychopathology falls, and avoids basing testimony on his or her *ipse dixit* ["he said it himself"], as required by *Daubert* (Gutheil & Bursztajn, 2003).

Psychologists and other evaluators must determine the degree to which an index event has contributed to an individual's condition, if at all. The means of identifying which of the above five conclusions is most applicable is scientific reasoning, based on the data obtained in a comprehensive evaluation. Hypotheses having been formulated, each is subjected to analysis leading (in most instances) to either confirmation or falsification by the idiographic data of the case. The interpretation of the data should be parsimonious: the best conclusion is generally the one that accounts for the most data with the simplest, most direct explanation (Greenberg, Otto, & Long, 2003; Heilbrun, 2001). Because the evaluator does not know until near the end of the evaluation what data will ultimately be relevant, everything that may be relevant should be noted, because relevance is the legal standard for discovery. Information that appears relevant but proves to be either irrelevant or immaterial will be in the evaluator's notes, but is left out of the report (Greenberg, 2003). At the time of trial, if there is not a settlement, the judge will decide what information will be admitted under the standards for admissibility of evidence in the relevant jurisdiction.

According to Rogers (2002), four established methods of retrospective analysis may be used to address issues: (1) the corroborative model, involving collection of independent sources to support or counter the accounts of people being evaluated; (2) the analogue model, offering information regarding ways in which various factors may affect remembering or reporting of clinical data; (3) the time-lapse model, in which an attempt is made to reproduce a given condition, and (4) the biological marker model, in which the individual's report is confirmed by an established biological marker. Shuman (2002) notes that the corroborative model is most broadly applicable, but that the forensic expert must take care to use standardized measures to assess constructs in a systematic manner.

If a relationship is found between the traumatic event and the individual's psychological condition, recommendations should be made for treatment, and a prognosis stated regarding the likelihood of a return to his or her prior level of functioning. *Rehabilitation* means that the individual can return to a previous, higher level of functioning. If the injury is sufficiently severe that a more or less complete recovery is not likely, then the expert addresses *habilitation*, the highest level of functioning that the individual is likely to achieve, which is expected to be lower than the pretrauma level of functioning. Prognosis is, in effect, "future damages" (Greenberg, 2003, p. 245). The evaluator is to make a statement regarding the likelihood the plaintiff can be treated, the likelihood (if there is data to so indicate) that the plaintiff will be a survivor, and an estimate of the period of time required for optimal or maximal recovery to occur if the individual actively participates in treatment. A cost estimate, based on community rates, is usually of value as well.

Conducting the Evaluation

It is essential that multiple methods and sources be utilized in the assessment, to try to ensure that all important factors are considered and that the data from each factor can be compared with those from the other factors, looking for convergent validity. The issue is not, *per se*, how damaged the individual may now be, but, rather, how different the individual is from the way he or she was prior to the traumatic incident. Significant inconsistencies must also be addressed (Ackerman & Kane, 1998; Greenberg et al., 2003; Heilbrun, 2001; Heilbrun et al., 2002; McLearen, Pietz, & Denney, 2004; Walker & Shapiro, 2003; Weiner, 2002). In most cases, this will involve three areas of investigation: review of records, psychological testing, and clinical interviews.

Review of Records

The forensic expert needs to review the complaint and all records that are reasonably likely to shed light upon the status of the individual, both pretrauma and posttrauma. The pretrauma information identifies a baseline, what the individual was like prior to the traumatic event. The posttrauma data indicates the changes the individual went through as a result of the trauma *or other events in his or her life*. In general, the records reviewed should go back at least 5 years, and a minimum of 3 years, prior to the allegedly traumatic event, to try to ensure that nothing important is missed, and to form a substantial baseline of pretrauma functioning. The records reviewed should include all medical records (including psychotherapy records), arrest records, school records, employment records, military records, personnel records, and any other records that may shed light on the individual's functional abilities prior to and following the traumatic event. Important information regarding whether the individual's lifestyle has changed since the accident may be available via checkbook registers and credit card statements (Greenberg, 2003). Medication records should identify any direct or side effects that may contribute to the clinical picture. For example, an individual who appears depressed may be heavily medicated (to the degree required by his or her condition), or overmedicated. While these data do not stand alone as unequivocal evidence of changes caused by the traumatic event, without a strong database (preferably going back at least 5 years) it will be difficult to clearly identify the pretraumatic status and posttraumatic changes for the individual. Although there is strong evidence that Posttraumatic Stress Disorder (PTSD) is likely to cause a work-related disability, other factors (social support, perceived employment support, satisfaction with work and life) may affect the level of disability, and therefore need to be carefully assessed (Koch, O'Neill, & Douglas, 2005). Without a strong database it will also be difficult, if not impossible, for an expert to testify to a "reasonable degree of psychological (or medical or social work, etc.) certainty," and the record review should be considered to be below the standard of practice (Ackerman & Kane, 1998; Heilbrun, 2001).

According to Sageman (2003),

> It is of the utmost importance to gather the most comprehensive information on the litigant, including past medical and mental health records, previous neuropsychological testing, occupational history, depositions, all legal testimonies, diaries (if available), and contemporary pictures and/or videos. The standard for a mental health expert is to review all the available evidence before seeing the subject of a forensic examination, especially if retained by the opposite side. ... The more thorough the review of the evidence, the greater is the credibility of the expert. ... Failure to consider all the evidence may also be a cause of action to sue an expert witness for malpractice. In most jurisdictions, experts have immunity for their testimony. However, if the method to reach their opinion falls below the usual standards of practice, which include relying on all the available evidence, and this faulty method costs the retaining party a case that might have been won or reduces the compensation, then the psychologist is at strong risk of being successfully sued for malpractice [p. 324].

It should also be noted that, in *Deatherage v. Washington Examining Board of Psychology* (1997), the Washington Supreme Court ruled that a psychologist did not have immunity from discipline by the state's psychology licensing board for failing to qualify statements made in child custody evaluations, mischaracterizing information, failing to verify information, and misinterpreting test data (Cohen, 2004; Ewing, 2003). Further, although witness and/or quasi-judicial immunity prevents civil lawsuits against experts by nearly anyone, a few courts have permitted litigants to sue their own experts for malpractice, alleging that the expert was negligent and/or practiced below the minimum standard for his or her profession (Cohen; Ewing).

The records reviewed are likely to generate numerous questions and hypotheses about the individual and his or her adjustment and functioning prior to and following the traumatic event. These questions and hypotheses can be addressed in part through psychological testing and, especially, during the clinical interview.

Informed Consent

Prior to beginning the assessment, the psychologist is ethically bound to obtain the informed consent of the individual being assessed, absent a good reason (e.g., court order, age of the individual) not to (Ethical Standard 9.03, *Ethical Principles of Psychologists and Code of Conduct*, 2002). This includes telling the person the nature and purpose of the evaluation (including who retained the psychologist), the fact that the evaluation is not confidential (though the number of people with access to the information may be small), and who may have access to the results of the evaluation (*Specialty Guidelines for Forensic Psychologists*, 1991, Guideline IV.E.). If there is any reason to question the individual's understanding of the explanation given, the person should be questioned regarding his or her understanding, and he or she should be asked to paraphrase the information given to him or her. If the individual does not understand and cannot therefore give informed consent, this should be discussed with the retaining attorney, who should contact the individual's attorney prior to proceeding with the evaluation, unless the evaluation is court-ordered or otherwise not voluntary. When the evaluation is not voluntary, or the examinee cannot understand a full explanation, the examiner gives a simple explanation and seeks assent rather than consent. The psychologist's report should indicate the questionable understanding, and discuss the apparent reason(s) for it and any impact that it may have on the results of the evaluation (Heilbrun, 2001).

Psychological Testing

Testing Process

Experts can use psychological tests and other sources of information to reliably describe individuals' emotional, motivational, intellectual, neuropsychological, and social characteristics, as well as their daily behavior. In addition, there is empirical research that connects these types of information with past, present, and future behavior and outcomes. Further, there are theories of both normal and abnormal behavior that use constructs and assumptions to connect behavior with its causes. A behavioral theory is a reasoned construct or a "convenient fiction that is useful for generating hypotheses about how various events, behaviors, and human characteristics interrelate" (Grisso, 2003, p. 31).

According to the *Standards for Educational and Psychological Testing*,

> [a] test is an evaluative device or procedure in which a sample of an examinee's behavior in a specified domain is obtained and subsequently evaluated and scored using a standardized process. While the label *test* is ordinarily reserved for instruments on which responses are evaluated for their correctness or quality and the terms *scale* or *inventory* are used for measures of attitudes, interest, and dispositions, the *Standards* uses the single term *test* to refer to all such evaluative devices [American Educational Research Association, 1999, p. 3].

Further, tests and other instruments used in an evaluation must be addressed both in terms of what they have been empirically demonstrated to do and the limits of what they can do in light of research on their validity and reliability and the purposes for which they were constructed. Tests and other instruments are valid for a specific purpose, and not valid for other purposes. The evaluator must be prepared to demonstrate that the instruments he or she uses in an evaluation are valid for the specific evaluation for which they are being utilized, including having appropriate standardization and research support for use with the plaintiff in the tort action (Grisso & Vincent, 2005).

Clinical vs. Actuarial Assessment

There has been debate among psychologists for many years regarding the relative merits of actuarial (statistical) vs. clinical assessment. The former emphasizes use of extensively researched instruments like the Minnesota Multiphasic Personality Inventory, Second Edition (MMPI-2) rather than clinical methods (e.g., interviews, some projective techniques). When structured interviews are available, the actuarial approach would be to use them, rather than the relatively free-form clinical interview. Research comparing these two methods indicates that about half of the time the actuarial method is better, while the other half of the time there is no difference. "While these results provide no evidence for the superiority of clinical over actuarial approaches for any predictive task, they also do not provide a compelling consistent advantage for actuarial approaches" (Heilbrun, 2001, p. 126). When there is a valid and reliable actuarial instrument available that is appropriate for use in a specific assessment, it should generally be used, given this research. However, clinical assessment clearly has a major role to play in assessments as well.

Forensic Assessment Instruments and Norms

Grisso (1986, 2003) emphasized a need for the development of "forensic assessment instruments" (FAIs), psychological instruments that would directly address both legal and clinical issues, minimizing the need to extrapolate from clinical instruments in order to address legal issues. Much of the development of these instruments has focused on the criminal arena, for example, the competency to stand trial. There are few instruments that directly address tort issues. Instead, most research has focused on the development of forensic norms for instruments that are also used for other purposes, for example, the MMPI-2. Research on the MMPI-2 to date has established response patterns associated with defensiveness, malingering, and other factors that may be germane to a given psychological injury assessment. Although test profiles in psychological injury cases differ greatly depending on the type of injury, whether the individual is exaggerating or feigning symptoms, the amount of time since the injury occurred, and other factors, the MMPI-2 validity scales generally provide a great deal of information about response style, and clinical scales often provide significant information regarding specific clinical patterns (Butcher, 1995).

Perhaps the closest instrument to an FAI in the psychological injury realm is the MacArthur Competence Assessment Tool—Treatment (MacCAT-T) (Grisso & Appelbaum, 1998). In *Zinermon v. Burch*, the U.S. Supreme Court indicated that an individual must be assessed to be competent prior to allowing that person to consent to a voluntary psychiatric hospitalization. The same applies, of course, to informed consent for a medical hospitalization, for surgery, and so forth. By using the MacCAT-T, a physician or medical or psychiatric facility should be able to identify an individual who is not competent to consent, and to document the ability of an individual who is competent to consent to treatment. This documentation makes a future lawsuit much less likely.

Correct Administration is Essential

To be valid and reliable, a psychological instrument must be correctly administered. When developed, psychological instruments are standardized with a specific population under specific testing conditions. The further one deviates from the standardized conditions, the less likely one is to have test results that are valid. Among the considerations indicated by Ackerman and Kane (1998):

(1) Tests and other assessment instruments, and interviews, should be administered in a relatively quiet area that is free of distractions. When this is not possible, decide whether the conditions are acceptable (noise level not excessive, relative privacy, and so forth) and proceed with the assessment if the conditions are satisfactory. Include in the report any environmental factors believed to have affected the results (See also Heilbrun, 2001).

(2) The individual being assessed should be alone with the examiner, since assessment instruments are standardized under this condition and there is no research literature indicating whether, and to what degree, the results of a nonstandardized administration may change the results of a particular instrument. This is also true with regard to audio- or video-recording. There is some research indicating that there is an adverse impact on the validity of an assessment when a third party is present or the assessment is recorded. There is *no* research indicating that the assessment is as valid when a third party is present or the assessment is recorded as when it is not. (See also Constantinou, Ashendorf, & McCaffrey, 2002; Constantinou & McCaffrey, 2003; Greiffenstein, 2005; Kehrer, Sanchez, Habif, Rosenbaum, & Townes, 2000; Lees-Haley, 2005; Lezak, Howieson, & Loring, 2004.) Further, the U.S. Supreme Court, in *Estelle v. Smith* (451 U.S. 454, 470, n. 14, 1981) indicated that the physical presence of an attorney during an evaluation "could contribute little and might seriously disrupt the examination."

   A number of lower court cases have also ruled that the presence of a third party, including audio- or video-taping of a psychological evaluation, is not appropriate. For example, in *Shirsat v. Mutual Pharmaceutical Co.* (169 F.R.D. 68, p. 70, E.D. Pa. 1996), the court found that "an observer, court reporter, or recording device, would constitute a distraction during the examination and work to diminish the accuracy of the process." In *Tomlin v. Holocek* (150 F.R.D. 628, D. Minn. 1993), the court ruled that "to require a recording of Dr. Aletsky's interview would potentiate toward invalidating her evaluatory technique" (p. 631), and that "the presence of third parties would lend a degree of artificiality to the interview technique which would be inconsistent with applicable, professional standards" (p. 632). In *Hertenstein v. Kimberly Home Health Care, Inc.* (189 F.R.D. 620, Kan. 1999), the court indicated that the "plaintiff has no right to have her attorney present. … [T]he court also finds that she has no right to the presence of any third person or mechanical recording device at the examination" (p. 629). Quoting from *Ragge v. MCA/ Universal Studios* (165 F.R.D. 605, 609–10; C.D. Cal. 1995), the court indicated that "[t]hird parties may, regardless of their good intentions, contaminate a mental examination." In *In re air crash at Tapei, Taiwan,* the United States District Court for the Central District of California (2003) indicated that

> [T]he majority of federal courts have rejected the notion that a third party should be allowed, even indirectly through a recording device, to observe a Rule 35 examination. Holland v. United States, 182 F.R.D. 493, 495 (D.S.C. 1998). "Several factors militate against allowing any third person or recording device at the mental [or physical] examination of [a] plaintiff." Hertenstein, 189 F.R.D. at 630; Holland, 182 F.R.D. at 495–96; Tomlin, 150 F.R.D. at 631–33. These factors include:
>
> First, … the presence of a third party during the examination under Rule 35 "would lend a degree of artificiality to the interview technique which would be inconsistent with applicable professional standards." Second, … one of the purposes of Rule 35 is "to provide a 'level playing field' between the parties in their respective efforts to appraise" the plaintiff's condition. Therefore, the party requesting the examination should be free from oversight by the opposing party. … [B]oth the plaintiff's and defendants' experts were "bound by the methodologies of their discipline and by the same formal or informal principles of professional integrity." Third, … [such an intrusion would] promote "the infusion of the adversary process into the … examining room[.]" Holland, 182 F.R.D. at 495–96 (citations omitted); Hertenstein, 189 F.R.D. at 630–31; Tomlin, 150 F.R.D. at 631–34. Additionally, "the presence of a[n audiotape] could influence [plaintiff], even unconsciously, to exaggerate or diminish his reactions to [the examiner's] physical examination." Holland, 182 F.R.D. at 496; see Sreenivasan Decl., 4–5. Finally, the infusion of the adversary process into the examining room by a recording device is "inconsistent with the just, speedy and inexpensive resolution of civil disputes [under Rule 1], and with the dictates of Rule 35." Hertenstein, 189 F.R.D. at 631 (quoting Tomlin, 150 F.R.D. at 634).
>
> The Court finds the above reasoning to be persuasive. "Weighing the concerns of the parties and the physicians, the court finds the presence of a mechanical recording device inappropriate under the facts of this case. Plaintiff[s] ha[ve] demonstrated no need for it. Its presence may invalidate the results of the examination[s], as it may consciously or unconsciously influence plaintiff[s] 'to exaggerate or diminish [their] reactions' to the examination[s]." Hertenstein, 189 F.R.D. at 631 (quoting Holland, 182 F.R.D. at 496).

Ethical standards also suggest that there may be serious problems with validity if there is a third party present or if other nonstandard conditions are present. Ethical Standard 9.02 of the *Ethical Principles of Psychologists and Code of Conduct* (2002) indicates that "(a) Psychologists administer, score, interpret, or use assessment techniques, interviews, tests, or instruments in a manner and for purposes that are appropriate in application of the techniques." Ethical Standard 9.06 indicates that "When interpreting assessment results ... , psychologists take into account ... various test factors. ... They indicate any significant limitations of their interpretations." Ethical Standard 9.11 indicates that "Psychologists make reasonable efforts to maintain the integrity and security of test materials and other assessment techniques consistent with law and contractual obligations, and in a manner that permits adherence to this Ethics Code."

Similarly, Standard 1.4 of the *Standards for Educational and Psychological Testing* (1999) indicates that "if a test is used in a way that has not been validated, it is incumbent on the user to justify the new use, collecting new evidence if necessary." Standard 5.4 refers to a need for "minimal distraction." Standard 12.19 indicates that the examiner "should take cognizance of the many factors that may influence a particular testing outcome."

There are only two circumstances, to my knowledge, in which there is a benefit to the presence of a third party and/or audio- or videotaping. One is when a child is interviewed as part of the investigation of alleged sexual or other abuse. A given child may not speak without a parent or other significant adult present. When that is the case, it is much better to have the third party present than to lose access to the information from the child. Children should also have the fewest number of interviews possible; therefore, an interview by a skilled interviewer or interviewers should be taped (preferably videotaped) so that the interview data is available to all parties. The videotape may also make it unnecessary for the child to testify in person in some jurisdictions. For these and other reasons, the American Academy of Child and Adolescent Psychiatry (1990) endorsed videotaping of interviews of children when sexual abuse is alleged.

The second circumstance in which the presence of a third party may be beneficial is when any individual refuses an interview without that third party, whether it is a family member, a therapist, an attorney, or someone else. If the evaluator believes that it is better to permit the third party's presence than to request a court order, he or she may proceed with the interview after admonishing the third party to be as inconspicuous as possible. While the data from the interview may be open to some question regarding its validity, it is generally better to have an interview with the individual rather than have information only from secondary sources or under the duress of a court order.

Finally, according to Dean (2004), "[I]n theory, a medical examination itself is not part of the adversarial proceedings, so generally, federal courts do not permit a party's attorney to be present at a Rule [of Civil Procedure] 35 physical examination unless there is some compelling reason to do so" (p. 141).

(3) The psychologist should personally administer all tests and other formal instruments, if possible, to ensure that standard testing conditions were in place and to record extra-test behavior (e.g., reactions, expressions, side comments) as well. If absolutely necessary, testing may be done by the psychologist's well-trained staff, under the psychologist's direct supervision.
(4) *No standardized test should ever be taken home by or left with the individual being assessed.* If the administration is not directly observed, the psychologist cannot guarantee that the test or other instrument was in fact answered by the individual being assessed, nor that the individual was sober while taking the test, nor that other people did not influence the individual's responses to the test (Ethics Committee, American Psychological Association, 1993).
(5) Tests and other assessment instruments must be appropriate for the individual being assessed. If reading level is a concern, it must be assessed (e.g., with the Wide Range Achievement Test, Third (or the recently published Fourth) Edition (WRAT3/4)) prior to administering a test or other instrument that will be read by the individual being assessed. The MMPI-2, for example, has a minimum of a sixth-grade reading level (Butcher et al., 2001), though some questions have been found to require a high-school graduate or even college reading level. A test or other instrument that is available only in English should generally not be administered to an individual who is not fluent in English. Although a translator could be used in an interview, a translator could not administer the test items because there is no research indicating that a translator can correctly translate each item or would not otherwise influence the examinee's responses.
(6) If standardized conditions and administration are not followed, if the test or other instrument is not personally administered by the psychologist (or, sometimes, a well-trained assistant), if the administration is not observed by the psychologist or a well-trained assistant, and so forth, the burden is on the psychologist to demonstrate that the test or other instrument remains valid and reliable in spite of the changes from the standardized procedures. If the psychologist cannot ensure that the changes did not have an adverse effect, he or she also cannot testify to a reasonable degree of psychological/scientific certainty that the results are valid (Ackerman and Kane, 1998).

Response Style

A key factor in any evaluation is to address the response style of the individual. When tests and related instruments are involved, this may also be referred to as "test-taking attitude." According to Heilbrun (2001, pp. 165–166),

> Response style has been defined to include four particular styles: (1) reliable/honest (a genuine attempt is made to be accurate; factual inaccuracies result from poor understanding or misperception), (2) malingering (conscious fabrication or gross exaggeration of psychological and/or physical symptoms, understandable in light of the individual's circumstances and not attributable merely to the desire to assume the patient role, as in

Factitious Disorder), (3) defensive (conscious denial or gross minimization of psychological and/or physical symptoms, as distinguished from ego defenses, which involve intrapsychic processes that distort perception), and (4) irrelevant (failure to become engaged in the evaluation; responses are not necessarily relevant to questions and may be random). It is useful to broaden the fourth response style to include instances in which the individual refuses to respond, or responds minimally, and call this uncooperative rather than irrelevant. (See also Rogers & Bender, 2003; Rogers, 1997).

Heilbrun, Warren, and Picarello (2003, p. 71) add two additional categories: "uncooperative, in which the individual responds minimally or not at all to assessment questions," and "impaired: it involves experiencing communication deficits resulting from young age, thought and speech disorganization, intellectual deficits, and/or memory problems."

Psychological tests that are both valid and reliable should be utilized to address relevant issues in the instant (i.e., at hand) case. The instrument that is nearly universally used by forensic psychologists for assessment of adults in psychological injury cases, if response style and/or psychopathology are relevant, is the MMPI-2, which is among the few instruments to offer significant information regarding both the plaintiff's test-taking attitude (response style) and the nature of any psychopathology present (Boccaccini & Brodsky, 1999; Greenberg et al., 2003; Lees-Haley, 1992; Otto, 2002; Posthuma, Podrouzek, & Crisp, 2002; Rabin, Barr, & Burton, 2005; Shuman, 1994, 2002 supplement). The MMPI-2 is particularly well-suited for addressing whether an individual is malingering or otherwise not answering questions in an open, forthright manner (Rogers, 2003; Rogers, Sewell, Martin, & Vitacco, 2003; Rogers & Shuman, 2005), although the results may be ambiguous, and interpretations must be carefully considered.

Further, the MMPI-2 should have no difficulty meeting the requirements of the Federal Rules of Evidence (or their state equivalents), including the requirements for relevance, reliability, falsifiability, peer review and publication, and general acceptance with the scientific community. A search of case law found 19 cases in which the admissibility of expert testimony on the basis of MMPI/MMPI-2 results was challenged. No appellate cases were found in which such testimony was excluded based on any of the standards in *Daubert* or its primary predecessor, *Frye v. United States*, in which "general acceptability" within the scientific community was the standard (Otto, 2002).

In contrast, evaluators who rely on computer-based *interpretations* of the MMPI-2 or other tests/instruments could face a number of problems (Otto, 2002). For many tests, the computer program will generate a report that suggests how the test data could be interpreted. While the computer printout normally specifies that the statements made are hypotheses subject to verification by other data, some evaluators use the computerized interpretation as if it were a set of facts, or even quote the printed interpretation in the evaluator's report as if it constituted the evaluator's own product rather than that of a computer-generated test report. The evaluator would virtually never know the algorithm utilized by the test's author, and the suggested interpretation is likely to be based on a common interpretation of the most significant results, while giving little or no information about some test results that may be highly germane to a given case.

Factitious Disorders do not clearly fit within the categories suggested by Heilbrun and colleagues, above, but are potentially relevant in psychological injury cases. These disorders involve consciously producing symptoms in order to be able to assume (or benefit from) the patient role, based on unconscious motivation. If the motivation is also conscious, and if the goal is to obtain money, drugs, or other specific benefit other than the patient role, the label is likely to be malingering rather than Factitious Disorder. Eisendrath and McNiel (2002, pp. 392–393) offer guidelines for identifying the presence of a Factitious Disorder:

I. Factitious disorder diagnosis … .
  A. The person intentionally produces or feigns physical signs or symptoms.
  B. The motivation for the behavior is to assume the role of a sick person.
  C. External incentives for the behavior are absent.
II. Data that are supportive of a diagnosis of Factitious Disorder:
  A. Indicators of factitious origin of symptoms [including] … :
    1. Direct observation: a record existed of personal observation of the patient's factitiously producing illness.
    2. Nonphysiologic physical signs [were reported] that contradicted typical pathological findings or were nonphysiologic (e.g., elevated temperature … without increased pulse) and that appeared to require conscious production.
    3. Physical evidence … of a factitious cause of symptoms (e.g., a syringe or surreptitious medication was discovered … .)
    4. Atypical course of illness … that did not follow the natural history of the presumed biomedical disease process … .
  B. Associated [but not diagnostic] features:
    1. Patient predicts worsening: the individual made accurate and repeated predictions of worsening of his or her condition.
    2. Invites invasive procedures … such as surgery.
    3. Previous diagnosis of Factitious Disorder … .
    4. Numerous prior poor outcomes … (more than five) … .
    5. Worked in a health-related occupation … .
III. Other factors associated with abnormal illness-affirming behavior … .
  A. Symptom model: the individual [had] a close friend or relative who had previously had similar symptoms … .
  B. Recent loss: the individual reported an event involving significant psychological loss and associated it with the onset of illness.
  C. Multiple somatic complaints … that appeared to be unexplained or were out of proportion to any biomedical disease that may have been present.
  D. History of childhood loss … (e.g., of a parent) … .
  E. Psychiatric illness … history. There is often comorbidity between somatic symptoms and a psychiatric disorder.

F. History of secondary gain: The patient had received "rewards" for illness (secondary gain), such as disability income, a successful litigation that produced a financial award, or relief from a noxious situation … .
G. History of childhood illness … that required hospitalization or surgery … .

Rogers and Shuman (2005, p. 24) note that we have no method for accurately ascertaining the conscious or unconscious motivations of an individual to portray himself or herself as having more, or more serious, psychological or physical problems than are really present. They therefore recommend using the term "feigning," indicating "deliberate fabrication or gross exaggeration of psychological or physical symptoms," rather than attempting to discriminate between malingering and a Factitious Disorder. Rogers and Shuman also recommend avoiding imprecise terms such as "overreporting," "secondary gain," and "suboptimal effort," because the terms may imply motivation that cannot be measured or known with any certainty. (See the sections by Young and by Nicholson and Martelli, this volume, for further discussion of these issues.)

Specific Tests and Other Instruments

Tests are primarily used in forensic evaluations to help formulate hypotheses that may be validated or unsubstantiated by multiple measures, and/or to address various hypotheses that have been formed on other bases. Either way, the goal is to use hypotheses that can be supported or falsified in order to draw conclusions regarding individuals (Heilbrun, 2001; Greenberg et al., 2003).

Frequency of Test Use

The most widely used test in forensic or clinical evaluations is the MMPI-2, which surveys indicate was used by 85–94% of evaluators (Boccaccini & Brodsky, 1999; Camara, Nathan, & Puente, 2000; Watkins, Campbell, Nieberding, & Hallmark, 1995; Camara, Nathan, & Puente, 2000; Boccaccini & Brodsky, 1999). By assessing the plaintiff's test-taking attitude (response style) with the MMPI-2 validity scales, the evaluator obtains data that identify whether (and to what degree) the individual was consistent, defensive, exaggerated symptoms, and so forth. This test-taking attitude can generally be extended, cautiously, to the whole evaluation. The person who produces a valid MMPI-2 is relatively likely to also produce valid results from other tests and various means of gathering information (Boccaccini & Brodsky, 1999; Graham, 2006; Pope, personal communication, May 14, 2006; Pope, Butcher, & Seelen, 2000).

While not used nearly as often as the MMPI-2, the second most utilized test in forensic evaluations is the Wechsler Adult Intelligence Scale, the current edition of which is the third (WAIS-III). Surveys indicated use by 50–94% of evaluators (Boccaccini & Brodsky, 1999; Camara et al., 2000; Watkins et al., 1995). The WAIS would generally be used when a measure of intellectual ability is required.

Third, according to recent studies, is the Millon Clinical Multiaxial Inventory, Second or Third Edition (MCMI-II or III), used by 33–49% of forensic evaluators (Boccaccini & Brodsky, 1999; Camara et al., 2000; Watkins et al., 1995).

The frequency of forensic use of the MCMI is a matter for some concern, since it is well-documented that the MCMI exaggerates an individual's psychopathology (Ackerman & Kane, 2005; Craig, 1999; Groth-Marnat, 2003; Hess, 1998; Hynan, 2004; Rogers, Salekin, & Sewell, 1999, 2000; Schutte, 2000). The test was standardized only on clinical samples, that is, there is no "normal" reference group with which to compare the responses of a given individual. In clinical work, this is not a problem, as the test magnifies any psychopathology present so that the therapist can be certain to address the identified area of concern. In forensic work, in contrast, the exaggeration can make a "normal" individual appear psychologically pathological. It is therefore extremely difficult to defend the use of this instrument in a forensic test battery (Ackerman & Kane, 2005; Faust & Heard, 2003). One article in a forensic journal went so far as to label the research on the MCMI-III as "fatally flawed" (Rogers et al., 2000). Further, the MCMI-III scales have a minimal degree of construct validity, and test results are not accurate in most attempts to diagnose *DSM-IV* personality disorders (Rogers, 2003).

Tests used less frequently (but not infrequently) by clinical or forensic psychologists are the Rorschach Inkblot Technique 28–82% (Boccaccini & Brodsky, 1999; Camara et al., 2000; Watkins et al., 1995); the Beck Depression Inventory (BDI) 18–71% (Boccaccini & Brodsky, 1999; Camara et al., 2000; Watkins et al., 1995); the Trauma Symptom Inventory (TSI) 15% (Boccaccini & Brodsky, 1999); Structured Inventory of Reported Symptoms (SIRS) 11% (Boccaccini & Brodsky, 1999); the Halstead Reitan battery, 7–29% (Boccaccini & Brodsky, 1999; Camara et al., 2000; Watkins et al., 1995); the Thematic Apperception Test (TAT), 3–82% (Boccaccini & Brodsky, 1999; Camara et al., 2000; Watkins et al., 1995); and the Symptom Check List 90-Revised (SCL-90-R), 14–26% (Boccaccini & Brodsky, 1999; Watkins et al., 1995).

The wide ranges for some instruments very likely relate to the specific samples of respondents chosen by the authors. Only Boccaccini and Brodsky (1999) limited their sample to forensic psychologists, but their sample was small, consisting of 80 psychologists. The tests utilized in a given case will depend upon the nature of the case.

The three tests most often used by neuropsychologists, according to Lees-Haley, Smith, Williams, and Dunn (1995) are, in order, the Wechsler Adult Intelligence Scale, the current edition being the third (WAIS-III), 76%; the Minnesota Multiphasic Personality Inventory, Second Edition (MMPI-2), 68%; and the Wechsler Memory Scale, the current edition of which is the third (WMS-III), 51%. Other commonly used tests included the BDI (25%), the Rorschach (14%), the MCMI (various forms) (9%), the TAT (6%), and the SCL-90-R (5%). A larger, more-recent study indicates that the most frequently used neuropsychological assessment instruments are the WAIS-R or WAIS-III, 63.1%; the WMS-R or WMS-III, 42.7%; the Trail Making Test, 17.6%; California Verbal Learning Test (1st or 2nd edition), 17.3%; the Wechsler Intelligence Scale for Children (WISC-III),

15.9%; and the Halstead-Reitan Neuropsychological Battery (HRNB), 15.5%. When assessing "return to work," these neuropsychologists primarily utilize the MMPI-2 (39.9%), with other instruments utilized including the WAIS-R/WAIS-III (15.9%), a driving evaluation (13.5%), the Beck Depression Inventory (BDI, first or second edition, 12.5%), a clinical interview (12%), the Finger Tapping Test (10.3%). The rank order also differed depending on whether the assessment was primarily addressing memory, attention, or executive function (Rabin et al., 2005). Standard texts on neuropsychology, for example, *Neuropsychological Assessment* by Lezak et al. (2004) provide further information on available tests, including information regarding the reliability and validity of the tests.

PTSD Instruments

If the plaintiff is indicating symptoms consistent with PTSD, the areas of symptoms to address are those involving three components: reexperiencing, avoidance, and hyperarousal (Briere, 2004, p. 102). While few instruments address all three of these areas, three that do are the TSI, the Detailed Assessment of Posttraumatic Stress (DAPS), and the Clinician-Administered PTSD Scale (CAPS). The TSI addresses 10 types of posttraumatic responses, as well as having three validity scales (Briere, 2004; Briere, Elliott, Harris, & Cotman, 1995; Demare' & Briere, 1996; Edens, Otto, & Dwyer, 1998). An alternative for the expert who wishes to use an instrument with a documented correlation with the criteria for PTSD in *DSM-IV-TR* is the DAPS (Briere; McLearen et al., 2004; Greenberg et al., 2003). The DAPS also includes two validity scales and assesses comorbid conditions often found with PTSD: dissociation, substance abuse, and suicidality (Briere; see also Chapters 6–8 in Briere). The CAPS is a structured clinical interview that assesses all 17 criterion-related symptoms of PTSD and many of its associated features, and is frequently cited as the "gold standard" for evaluation of PTSD (Keane, Buckley, & Miller, 2003; Koch et al., 2005; Weathers, Keane, & Davidson, 2001). All three of these instruments have a high degree of both validity and reliability.

Malingering and Exaggerated Responding

There are a number of instruments that are designed to identify whether the individual is malingering. In a psychological injury case, at least one such instrument should be utilized. The validity scales of the MMPI-2 are the most frequently used scales for this purpose (Fishbain, Cutler, Rosomoff, & Rosomoff, 2003; Kane, 1999; Pope et al., 2006; Rogers, 1997; Rogers et al., 2003). The individual who is forthright and consistent on the MMPI-2's validity scales is relatively likely to be forthright and consistent throughout the evaluation. Conversely, the individual who significantly exaggerates, is extremely defensive, is inconsistent, or otherwise obfuscates raises a question about the veracity of the balance of the evaluation. Significantly elevated validity scales may be indications of malingering, of a "cry for help," or of severe psychopathology. Individuals who have been stigmatized or rejected due to posttraumatic changes may respond in a manner that draws attention to their felt pain and injury, so that their problems and psychological pain do not get overlooked (Briere, 2004).

Scales on the MMPI-2 are measured in standardized scores called "T Scores." The MMPI-2 has a number of validity scales and one additional factor, the number of items to which no response was given or for which both "true" and "false" were marked, the "Cannot Say" or "?" Scale. Samuel, DeGirolamo, Michaels, and O'Brien (1995) indicate that significantly more blanks are left by people involved in personal injury litigation than among people who are not so involved. They also indicate that the closer the evaluation is to the date of the injury, the more likely it is that the individual will leave more than 30 items blank, producing a profile that is likely to be invalid, or, at the least, questionable. Among other reasons, this may be due to the individual's emotional reaction to an item, especially one that evokes a memory of the traumatic event. It is often possible to address this problem by asking the person to answer the questions left blank, either by reading from the test booklet or by reading the items to the individual. This small variation in the standardized procedure should be noted in the report, but would not be expected to adversely affect the validity of the test. Next, the consistency of responding is addressed with two scales. The Variable Response Inconsistency Scale (VRIN) consists of 67 paired items, with the two items in each pair being either similar or opposite in meaning. An individual who responds too inconsistently (above a T Score of 79) has invalidated the MMPI-2. Since either random responding or a fixed response set could cause an elevation on other validity scales and the F – K Index, both VRIN and TRIN should be examined prior to concluding that psychopathology is being overreported (Butcher et al., 2001).

The True Response Inconsistency Scale (TRIN) consists entirely of paired items that have opposite content. T Scores above 79 indicate a significant tendency to have answered either "true" or "false" without regard to the content of the items, invalidating the test (Butcher et al., 2001).

The L Scale addresses the degree to which the individual tries to appear "perfect" or especially "virtuous," that is, to present him- or herself in an unrealistically positive light. T Scores of 65–69 suggest accentuation of the positive. T Scores of 70 or more suggest blatant exaggeration of positive qualities (Pope et al., 2006). MMPI-2 profiles are generally invalidated by T Scores of 80 or more (Butcher et al., 2001).

The F (Infrequency) Scale consists of items among the first 361 on the MMPI-2 that were endorsed by 10% or fewer of the normative population. T Scores below 79 are likely to indicate a valid protocol. T Scores from 80 to 89 generally indicate that exaggerating is likely. T Scores of 90 or greater indicate that a protocol may be invalid (Butcher et al., 2001). T Scores of 110 or more signify a profile that is not interpretable due to extreme responses (Pope et al., 2006). The causes of an invalid score may include malingering, exaggeration of problems (including a cry for help), extreme defensiveness, random responding, and/or significant psychopathology (Groth-Marnat, 2003). Importantly, research indicates that high F Scale scores correlate with histories of trauma, depression, dissociation, PTSD, and traumatic environments in an individual's family of origin (Elhai et al., 2004).

Thus, the F Scale is much less useful in assessing malingering among trauma victims than among other populations.

The F_B (F Back) Scale consists of items numbered 281 or higher, primarily addressing infrequent responses in the second half of the MMPI-2. High scores may result from fatigue or from any of the factors listed, above, for the F Scale. The same cutoff scores as for the F Scale may be used (Butcher et al., 2001; Pope et al., 2006). Rogers et al.'s (2003) meta-analysis suggested a cutoff score for F_B that is 12 points higher than the score on the F Scale, to reduce false-positives.

The K Scale addresses a more subtle and sophisticated defensiveness than does the L Scale. A high score does not imply psychopathology. T Scores from 65 to 74 suggest substantial defensiveness, whereas T Scores of 75 or higher suggest "faking good," that is, the individual is presenting an unrealistically positive impression of self or of life due to conscious or unconscious exaggeration. High K Scale T Scores make it much less likely that psychopathology will be indicated on the clinical scales (Butcher et al., 2001). On the original MMPI, individuals with advanced education and/or high socioeconomic status were relatively likely to produce elevations on the K Scale regardless of whether they were intentionally being defensive. The K Scale on the MMPI-2 is normed on a population with a higher educational level, making it unnecessary to interpret the scale differently for those individuals with substantial education. It should be noted, however, that K may be lower for individuals who have less education than high school (Pope et al., 2006; Graham, 2006).

The S (Superlative Self-Presentation) Scale is similar to the K Scale, but includes items from throughout the test, rather than only the first 370 items. Individuals with high scores may be claiming one or more positive qualities, for example, a belief in human goodness, a feeling of serenity, feeling content with life, denial of negative feelings, and/or denial of moral flaws. T Scores of 69 or less suggest a valid test protocol, 70–74 moderate defensiveness, and 75 or more that the protocol may be invalid due to "faking good," that is, the individual is presenting an unrealistically positive impression of self or of life due to conscious or unconscious exaggeration. When this is the case, interpretation of the clinical scales may need to be modified to adjust for the unrealistic presentation. If the T Score is 65 or more, the five subscales of the S Scale may be interpreted (Butcher et al., 2001; Pope et al., 2006).

The F_P (Infrequency-Psychopathology) Scale consists of items that were answered in the scored direction by no more than 20% of either the normative sample or a sample of psychiatric inpatients. When the F Scale is elevated and random responding has been ruled out, a T Score of 100 or more on F_P suggests significantly excessive reporting of psychopathology, that is, "faking bad," conscious or unconscious exaggeration of psychopathology. In contrast, if F_P is below 70, it is relatively likely that any severe psychopathology reported is real. T Scores between 70 and 99 suggest either exaggeration of symptoms or a "cry for help" (Butcher et al., 2001; Nichols, 2001). Scores of 100 or more strongly suggest malingering (Graham, 2006). The F_P Scale is the most specific, and most sensitive, measure of overreporting on the MMPI-2 (Nichols, 2001; Polusny & Arbisi, 2006; Pope, Butcher, & Seelen, 2000). Rogers et al. (2003) specify that "F_P appears to be the most effective scale in the assessment of feigning," in part because "these cut scores appear to be effective across disorders and even moderately useful with the problematic diagnosis of PTSD" (p. 173). Even so, automatic application of cutting scores to differentiate groups is seldom appropriate. Numerous variables must be considered in this process. Briere (2004) and Elhai et al. (2004) indicate that F_P appears to be more sensitive than the F Scale in determining whether a PTSD protocol is valid.

Elhai et al. (2004) also developed an F_{PTSD} Scale designed to improve upon both F and F_P in the detection of malingering of PTSD. They found that F_{PTSD} was better than F, but not as good as F_P, at the detection of malingering in civilian PTSD, but F_{PTSD} did prove to be a better detector for male veterans alleging combat-related PTSD.

The F – K (F minus K) Index, also known as the Dissimulation Index, suggests "faking bad" if the *raw* score for the F Scale is 15 or more points greater than the *raw* score for the K Scale (Butcher et al., 2001). Scores of 25 or more strongly suggest exaggeration of psychopathology (Nichols, 2001; Rogers, Sewell & Salekin, 1994). If F – K is equal to or less than –8, it is very unlikely that the person was feigning (Rogers et al.). The F – K Index has been found to be especially good at identifying "motivated faking" (Briere, 2004).

The ODecp (Other Deception) Scale was developed by Nichols and Greene (1997) as a means of identifying highly defensive individuals. A cutoff score of 20 identified 95% of those individuals in the authors' research. This scale (with slightly different content) was known as the Positive Malingering (M_P) Scale on the MMPI.

The Wiggins Social Desirability (Wsd) Scale has been identified by some authors as the best indicator of "impression management," that is, a conscious or unconscious attempt by an individual to be seen positively by an evaluator (Nichols, 2001; Rogers & Bender, 2003). While Odecp (or M_P) involves denial of negative characteristics, Wsd involves asserting positive characteristics. A T Score of 60 suggests an overly positive self-presentation, whereas a T Score of 65 suggests a high degree of impression management, that is, the individual presents as a model citizen, free of self-doubt, assertive, having good self-control, friendly, and highly virtuous.

The Gough Dissimulation Scale (Ds, modified as the Dsr for the MMPI-2) was designed to indicate psychopathology, but used items that psychiatric patients did not usually endorse (Graham, 2006). It was found by Rogers et al. (2003) to be nearly as good as the F and F_p Scales at identifying malingering. Rogers et al. recommended utilizing F_p, along with either F or Dsr, based on their meta-analysis of 65 feigning and 11 diagnostic studies.

The Fake Bad Scale (FBS) (Lees-Haley, English, & Glenn, 1991) was designed to try to identify individuals who were dissimulating or malingering on the MMPI-2 in personal injury cases. Research published on the FBS has been mixed, some studies finding that it worked well, others that it was among the worst MMPI-2 scales for addressing the possibility of malingering (Pope et al., 2006). Iverson and Lange (2006) concluded that "the literature, as a whole, supports the use of the FBS as an indicator of exaggeration in personal injury cases" (p.102). Crawford, Greene, Dupart, Bongar, and Childs (2006) compared graduate student simulators with inpatients diagnosed with Major Depressive Disorders, using a mixed-group validation design to better assess true-positive and false-positive rates when evaluating real or simulated physical injuries. They found that the FBS was the only MMPI-2 validity scale that produced adequate true- and false-positive rates, as well as being the only validity scale that correlated significantly with malingering status. Given the mixed nature of the research, my recommendation is that the psychologist study the existing research, review continuing research as it is published, and make a decision regarding use of this instrument that can be defended in court if the Fake Bad Scale is utilized.

Other commonly used instruments that have been demonstrated to be both valid and reliable measures of malingering include the Structured Interview of Reported Symptoms (SIRS), the Personality Assessment Inventory (PAI), the Test of Memory Malingering (TOMM), and the Validity Indicator Profile (VIP) (Ackerman & Kane, 1998; Briere, 2004; Rogers, 1997; Rogers & Bender, 2003; Rogers & Shuman, 2005).

Neuropsychologists assessing malingering are also likely to use the MMPI-2, with one of the others above as an alternative or addition, or they may use a forced-choice test (e.g., the Portland Digit Recognition Test (PDRT) (Lally, 2003) or the TOMM (Tombaugh, 1996)). With these and/or other instruments designed to detect malingering, it is usually possible to at least raise a significant question about malingering, and sometimes possible to make a statement with a substantial degree of certainty.

To further assess malingering, Wilson and Moran (2004, p. 628) have developed a list of "critical cues to malingering":

- Noncooperation with psychological and medical assessment requests and procedures (e.g., psychological testing, medical evaluations, etc.).
- Evasiveness, vagueness, and inability to produce details about the trauma.
- Incorrect details of the stressors or providing improbable or implausible information about the trauma experience.
- Manifestation of behaviors inconsistent with known scientific/medical/clinical patterns of PTSD.
- A general tendency to focus blame for all problems on symptoms of the trauma.
- Falsification or alteration of documents, certificates, reports, or other forms of "evidence … ."
- An overemphasis on PTSD-related "flashback" experiences relative to other PTSD symptom clusters.
- Psychometric testing shows a pattern of inconsistency, defensiveness, malingering …, or lying but *does not* indicate probable PTSD (e.g., low scores on measures of PTSD on MMPI, TSI …, etc.).
- A history of antisocial personality or behaviors or previous claims for compensation or lawsuits (i.e., litigation proneness) that preceded the traumatic event.

As indicated elsewhere in this chapter, no single method of identifying malingering or exaggeration will be the best under all circumstances. Because an accusation of malingering can have dire consequences, the assessment must be comprehensive. Ideally, all measures will suggest the same conclusion. In practice, the evaluator is likely to have to address both convergent and divergent results, and to come to a valid conclusion regarding the likelihood that malingering or exaggeration is a significant factor in the evaluation (Rogers & Bender, 2003). Evaluators should specify in their reports and in testimony that psychological tests are one means of generating or testing hypotheses that may be compared with various forms of data generated by the evaluation. This avoids overstatements about the validity of any given piece of data and reminds the reader or listener that discordant test results are hypotheses to be addressed, not results that are contradictory (Greenberg, 2003).

The reader who is interested in an extensive review of the published literature on malingering should consult Section III, Chapters 14–19 by Nicholson and Martelli in this volume.

Other Factors

Any test or other standardized instrument utilized should have an identified level of *sensitivity* and *specificity*. The former refers to the ability of the instrument to correctly detect pathology that is present (correct positives). The latter refers to the ability to identify when the pathology is not present (correct negatives). No instrument is perfect; therefore, there are likely to be some false-positives, people whom the instrument indicates have psychopathology but who do not. Similarly, there will be some false-negatives, people whom a given instrument indicates do not have psychopathology, but who do have psychopathology according to other evidence. The goal is to minimize both false-positives and false-negatives (Gouvier, Hayes, & Smiroldo, 2003).

Part of the evaluation of malingering or secondary gain consists of the assessment of secondary cost. The sick role involves a variety of limitations on behavior, travel, and general functioning. If the potential gain from a lawsuit is relatively small, for example, a few thousand dollars, there is little reason to suspect that the individual is consciously (malingering) or unconsciously (secondary gain) demonstrating the degree of dysfunction associated with the injury (Miller, 2003).

Gathering Information

A great deal of information must be gathered in the course of an assessment. Some may be gathered using psychological tests, some by using standardized or nonstandardized questionnaires, and some through formal interviews of the plaintiff and third parties. The goal is to assess the complete symptomatology of the plaintiff both through his or her own eyes and through those of people who observe the plaintiff: the examiner, family, friends, coworkers, neighbors, and so forth. This includes the individual's pretrauma status, the impact of the trauma, and the posttraumatic adjustment (Ackerman & Kane, 1998; Briere, 2004; Wilson & Moran, 2004).

Standardized and Nonstandardized Questionnaires

Self-report questionnaires can provide important information for the evaluation and understanding of an individual's beliefs, attitudes, and behavior (Heilbrun, 2001). There are a number of instruments commercially available or easily constructed that are not meant to be formal evaluation instruments in the same sense as those cited above. Most are face-valid, that is, it is not difficult to figure out what the assessor is looking for by simply looking at the items included in the instrument. Most also have no, or minimal, validity scales, and could be falsified by an individual who is so inclined. The forensic expert may also design questionnaires that are meant to gather relevant information without tying up the limited time of the assessor, who would otherwise have to gather the information through interviews. All of these instruments may be considered to be "information-gathering instruments" or "interview extensions," rather than tests with established validity and reliability. Although most are not standardized in the sense that there are formal research studies that assess their validity, reliability, and so forth, if they are a standard part of an evaluator's assessments, they will generally be accepted as part of the body of information that forms the basis for the expert's opinion. Some examples:

Behavior Change Inventory: 68 adjectives, from "absentminded" to "optimistic" to "worrisome," with separate columns for "before" and "after" the traumatic event.

Posttraumatic Cognitions Inventory (PTCI): The individual is asked to rate, on a seven-point scale from "totally disagree" to "totally agree," thirty-six items such as "The event happened because of the way I acted," "I feel dead inside," and "My life has been destroyed by the trauma." The individual's ratings can be divided into "negative cognitions about self," "negative cognitions about the world," and "self-blame" (Foa, Ehlers, Clark, Tolin, & Orsillo, 1999).

A personal history form may be utilized to ask numerous background questions, including history of psychological/psychiatric/alcohol or other drug abuse treatment; family history of such treatment or other evidence of dysfunction; work satisfaction; depressing times in the individual's life; questions about present and past suicidal ideation/attempts; developmental history problems; history of experience of traumas including accidents, sexual or other assaults, victimization; history of problems with the law; the current major stressors in the individual's life; and so forth, to try to ensure that nothing important is left out.

A *medical history form* that includes information regarding his or her current medical status and medical history. This form is also a convenient means of asking the individual to rate his or her score, on a scale from 0 to 10 for each category, regarding the levels of depression, anxiety, irritability, hopelessness, helplessness, suicidal thoughts or urges, guilt, happiness, and difficulty concentrating, in addition to the specific medical items addressed.

A major life events questionnaire is an important part of an evaluation. The individual should be asked to identify, for each 5-year period of his/her life (0–4, 5–9, etc.), what major life events (both positive and negative) occurred. Examples offered include a death in the family, parental or personal divorce, a birth in the family, being arrested, being jailed, getting married, being hired for a job, being fired, becoming pregnant, winning an award, and so forth. *This is usually the only form I permit the individual to take home to fill out*, since it is advantageous to give the person time to think about his/her life history and, if available, to get input from other family members regarding incidents that he/she may not recall, especially those from early in life.

A "differences questionnaire": Because the key issue is how the individual has changed as a result of the traumatic incident, he or she should be asked to fill out an open-ended questionnaire that asks the individual to specify "*how are you different as a result of the accident or incident*." Sub-questions include "how did you change ..., what is the current impact of those changes ..., how does the event(s) ... affect your ability to function normally ..., compare the way you were *before* with the way you are *now*." There need to be two columns, one headed "BEFORE" and one headed "NOW," with at least a half dozen pages divided into those two columns given to the individual to make it clear that the person should put down as much relevant information as possible.

A PTSD diagnostic questionnaire: The individual who alleges symptoms of a Posttraumatic Stress Disorder (PTSD) should be asked questions that will elicit data that support or contradict the diagnostic criteria in the *Diagnostic and Statistical Manual of Mental Disorders, Fourth Edition (DSM-IV)*. One may use a standardized interviewing instrument or one written by the evaluator. I do both: I use the CAPS, a structured interview, but have also devised my own instrument because I want to ask questions regarding *past* as well as *present* symptoms, to identify whether some symptoms were present but have remitted by the time of the evaluation. This provides information regarding the history of the disorder that might otherwise not be assessed.

A work history questionnaire is important, asking the name of each employer, the years the individual held the job, the nature of the job, the specific duties associated with the job, when and why the individual left the job, and anything else he/she wants to add. The period of time should extend back at least several years prior to an alleged accident or injury.

For the individual who alleges pain, one or more *pain questionnaires* is very important. Again, it may be a standardized measure or one devised by the psychologist. If I utilize only one, I prefer the latter, because I want to know how the pain has affected and changed the individual's life. The form that I use first asks "what does the pain make more difficult—but you do it in spite of the pain." Second, it asks, "what does the pain keep you from doing at all." The first question addresses the degree to which the individual fights his or her pain symptoms, the second addresses the point at which he or she feels so much pain that the activity is no longer attempted. For a discussion of pain assessment instruments, see Gatchel and Kishino (2006) and Sherman and Orbach (2006) in the companion text to this volume.

Norris and Hamblen (2004, pp. 66–98) describe a number of other instruments, with varying degrees of standardization, that address PTSD symptoms. They note that many of the trauma-specific and more general (e.g., the MMPI-2) psychological instruments do not tie the individual's responses to a particular trauma. Further, a response that could be due to a trauma could also, in many cases (e.g., irritability, sleep problems), be due to some other factor. This is another reason for the forensic expert to use multiple measures and techniques to try to ascertain whether a given symptom picture meets the diagnostic criteria for PTSD or another disorder.

All of these information-gathering forms address *the key question: how has the individual changed as a result of the incident/accident?* What objective evidence is there that the claimed changes are real/valid, and are interfering with the individual's life in some way?

A related question is that of motivation. Does it appear that the individual did his or her best in responding to the tests and other instruments? Does it appear that the individual wants to get better, or is there evidence that he or she is comfortable in the "sick role?" Some of this data will come from the above instruments, and some from the clinical and collateral interviews. (See the section of this volume by Nicholson and Martelli for an extensive discussion of the difficulties in assessing motivation.)

Interviews

A personal interview of the plaintiff is extremely important in any evaluation. Without it, there is a marked limitation to the conclusions that may be drawn about the individual and the impact of the traumatic event on that individual, even if the expert has access to psychological testing of and other information regarding the plaintiff and his or her description of the traumatic event (Greenberg, 2003; Heilbrun, 2001; O'Donnell, Creamer, Bryant, Schnyder, & Shalev, 2006; Shuman, 1994, 2003 supplement). The *Specialty Guidelines for Forensic Psychologists* (1991) indicate that forensic psychologists must attempt to have an "examination of the individual adequate to the scope of the statements, opinions, or conclusions to be issued … . When it is not possible or feasible to do so, they make clear the impact of such limitations on the reliability and validity of their professional products, evidence, or testimony" (Committee on Ethical Guidelines for Forensic Psychologists, 1991). Without an interview, the expert lacks a key source of data concerning the connection between historical, test, and other information and the legal question at issue. Even if there is an interview, the clinician may not have an adequate basis for an opinion if the interview had been too short, if essential areas were not covered, if there was not sufficient privacy during the interview, and so forth. Courts generally admit testimony under these conditions (Shuman, 1994,

2002 supplement). However, "standard psychiatric and psychological diagnostic techniques include an examination of the patient … . Thus, an in-court opinion not based on a personal examination of the patient, when it is possible to do so, violates accepted practice. This failure should bear on the weight given the resulting opinions" as well (Shuman, 1994, 2003 supplement, chapter 9, p. 7).

In the United States, Rule 35(a) of the Federal Rules of Civil Procedure (and their state equivalents) permits a party to the litigation to have an evaluation of the plaintiff by an independent expert in nearly every case:

> (a) Order for examination. When the mental or physical condition … of a party … is in controversy, the court in which the action is pending may order the party to submit to a physical or mental examination by a suitably licensed or certified examiner … . The order may be made only on motion for good cause shown … and shall specify the time, place, manner, conditions, and scope of the examination and the person or persons by whom it is to be made.

The party requesting the examination must make the report of the examination available to the opposing party if so requested. If the report is not given to the requesting party, the expert's testimony may be excluded by the judge. If the attorney requesting the examination does not like the contents or conclusions of the verbal report offered by the expert, however, he or she will most likely not request a written report, thereby eliminating the unfavorable testimony by the expert (Greenberg, 2003). States generally have similar provisions in their statutes.

Although some psychologists prefer a structured interview, others prefer to use formal and informal instruments such as those listed above to address most, if not all, of the areas that must be considered, and to spend several hours interviewing the individual regarding his or her experience and the responses to the tests and questionnaires. Asking about specific test responses is often very important, especially when the individual achieves a significant score on a test scale, to identify why the person responded as he or she did (Greenberg et al., 2003).

The goal is to not only formally evaluate the individual but, also, to understand *what the trauma means to the individual*, since no two people have exactly the same response to a given event (Ackerman & Kane, 1998; Weiss & Ozer, 2006; Wilson & Moran, 2004). Of three randomly chosen people who experience the same traumatic event, it would not be exceptional for one to be largely back to normal within a week, the second to be largely back to normal in 2 or 3 months, but the third to still evidence significant traumatization a year or more later. It is essential that the evaluator understand the meaning of the stressor for the individual being evaluated. This is in many ways the primary purpose of the interview.

Another aspect of identifying the meaning of the trauma for the individual is the assessment of whether the person has a psychological need to identify a physical or other traumatic cause for his or her symptoms. Without clear evidence to the contrary, the individual who does present in this manner is not malingering, the pain and suffering are real. It should also be noted that there is a high degree of comorbidity among chronic pain, PTSD, TBI, and other factors. Because there is evidence that having social support following traumatic events is associated with an improved prognosis, it is important to assess the individual's perceived and actual levels of social support (Briere, 2004). If the person's family and friends accept the fact that emotional injuries are as real as physical injuries, the injured person is relatively likely to discuss his or her symptoms in a straightforward manner. For many people, however, nonphysical injuries are not "real" injuries, and any suffering claimed by the individual may be attributed to malingering, secondary gain, or otherwise be considered illegitimate. When this is the case, it is relatively likely that the injured person will assert that his or her injury is organic, for example, a mild traumatic brain injury, a soft tissue injury, or another form of injury not readily detectable (to rule in or rule out) on the basis of formal diagnostic tests (e.g., X-ray or MRI). These individuals are generally not primarily seeking financial gain, they are trying to have their suffering acknowledged by family and friends—and, in the legal context, by having the jury independently confirm that the individual has really been hurt, and that it is not his or her fault (Miller, 2003). Some plaintiffs have such goals as trying to prevent the defendant from hurting someone else, punishing the defendant, or other "social justice" goals (Ackerman & Kane, 1998).

Number and Length of Assessment Sessions

Although legal requirements often limit an evaluation to a single session, for many reasons a complete evaluation nearly always requires at least two meetings with the plaintiff (Ackerman & Kane, 1998; Wilson & Moran, 2004). In some circumstances, even longer evaluations/observations provide quite significant information and, therefore, benefit to the forensic opinions and legal process. Some pain patients, for example, may be brought into the hospital for several days in order to more fully assess behavioral/psychological aspects of the patient's condition (Nicholson, personal communication, January 31, 2006). It is simply not possible to do a complete evaluation in a single session; the story of the traumatic experience requires ample time if it is to be fully told (Wilson & Moran). Although the needed tasks might be accomplished in one eight-hour day, there will be a real question about whether fatigue is an increasing factor as the day wears on, making conclusions potentially less valid. It is also very difficult to get a complete picture of an individual in a single day. Further, scheduling a second session a week or so later permits the tests and other instruments from the first day to be scored and interpreted, and some, if not all, collateral calls to be made, so that the value of the clinical interview (at session two) is greater. My usual practice is to schedule two four-hour sessions about a week apart, and to reserve the possibility of an additional session of one to four hours if needed to complete the evaluation. If the plaintiff or his/her attorney refuses to permit sufficient time for a complete evaluation as I define the term, it becomes necessary to discuss with the retaining attorney what, if anything, might be left out without a severe reduction in the validity of the evaluation—and whether it may be necessary to request that the court order that the plaintiff be available for two or three evaluation sessions of up to four hours each in order to permit the complete evaluation to occur. If the time restriction for the evaluation is too severe, the psychologist has an ethical responsibility to withdraw from the case, since he or she will not be able to testify to a reasonable degree of psychological certainty as to the status of the plaintiff or the cause(s) of the plaintiff's disability.

References

Ackerman, M. J., & Kane, A. W. (1998). *Psychological experts in personal injury actions* (3rd ed.). New York: Aspen Law and Business.

Ackerman, M. J., & Kane, A. W. (2005). *Psychological experts in divorce actions* (4th ed.). New York: Aspen Law and Business.

American Academy of Child and Adolescent Psychiatry. (1990). *Guidelines for the clinical evaluation of child and adolescent sexual abuse.* Retrieved April 16, 2006 from http://www.aacap.org/publications/policy/Ps22.htm.

American Educational Research Association (1999). *Standards for educational and psychological testing.* Washington, DC: Author.

American Psychiatric Association. (1994). *Diagnostic and statistical manual of mental disorders* (4th ed.). Washington, DC: Author.

American Psychological Association. (2002). Ethical principles of psychologists and code of conduct. *American Psychologist, 57*, 1060–1073.

American Psychological Association Ethics Committee. (1993, April 18). *Policy statement of the APA Ethics Committee regarding "take home" tests. Washington, DC:* Author.

American Psychological Association Ethics Committee. (1994). "Take home" tests. *American Psychologist, 49*, 665–666.

Boccaccini, M. T., & Brodsky, S. L. (1999). Diagnostic test usage by forensic psychologists in emotional injury cases. *Professional Psychology: Research and Practice, 30*, 253–259.

Briere, J. (2004). *Psychological assessment of adult posttraumatic states* (2nd ed.). Washington, DC: American Psychological Association.

Briere, J., Elliott, D. M., Harris, K., & Cotman, A. (1995). Trauma Symptom Inventory: Psychometrics and association with childhood and adult victimization in clinical samples. *Journal of Interpersonal Violence, 10*, 387–401.

Butcher, J. N. (1995). Personality patterns of personal injury litigants: The role of computer-based MMPI-2 evaluations. In Y. S. Ben-Porath, J. R. Graham, G. C. N. Hall, R. D. Hirschman, & M. S. Zaragoza (Eds.), *Forensic applications of the MMPI-2*. Thousand Oaks, CA: Sage.

Butcher, J. N., Graham, J. R., Ben-Porath, Y. S., Tellegen, A., Dahlstrom, W. G., & Kaemmer, B. (2001). *MMPI-2 Manual for administration, scoring, and interpretation* (Rev. ed.). Minneapolis: University of Minnesota Press.

Camara, W. J., Nathan, J. S., & Puente, A. E. (2000). Psychological test usage: Implications in professional psychology. *Professional Psychology: Research & Practice, 31*, 141–154.

Cohen, F. L. (2004). The expert medical witness in legal perspective. *The Journal of Legal Medicine, 25*, 185–209.

Committee on Ethical Guidelines for Forensic Psychologists. (1991). Specialty guidelines for forensic psychologists. *Law and Human Behavior, 15*, 655–665.

Constantinou, M., Ashendorf, L., & McCafFrey, R. J. (2002). When the 3rd party observer of a neuropsychological evaluation is an audio-recorder. *The Clinical Neuropsychologist, 16*, 407–412.

Constantinou, M., & McCafFrey, R. J. (2003). The effects of 3rd party observation: When the observer is a video camera. *Archives of Clinical Neuropsychology, 18*, 788–789.

Craig, Robert J. (1999). Testimony based on the Millon Clinical Multiaxial Inventory: Review, commentary, and guidelines. *Journal of Personality Assessment, 73*, 290–304.

Crawford, E. F., Greene, R. L., Dupart, T. M., Bongar, B., & Childs, H. (2006). MMPI-2 assessment of malingered emotional distress related to a workplace injury: A mixed group validation. *Journal of Personality Assessment, 86*, 217–221.

Dean, B. P. (2004). Discovery in scientific evidence cases. In J. J. Brown (Ed.), *Scientific evidence and experts handbook* (2004 cumulative supplement) (pp. 137–229). New York: Aspen Law and Business.

Deatherage v. Board of Psychology, 134 Wn.2d 131, 948 P.2d 828 (Wn. Sup. Ct. 1997).

Demare' D., & Briere, J. (1996, August). *Validation of the Trauma Symptom Inventory with Abused and Nonabused University Students*. Paper presented at the 104th Annual Convention of the American Psychological Association, Toronto, Canada.

Edens, J. F., Otto, R. K., & Dwyer, T. J. (1998). Susceptibility of the Trauma Symptom Inventory to malingering. *Journal of Personality Assessment, 71*, 379–392.

Eisendrath, S. J., & McNiel, D. E. (2002). Factitious disorders in civil litigation: Twenty cases illustrating the spectrum of abnormal illness-affirming behavior. *Journal of the American Academy of Psychiatry and Law, 30*, 391–399.

Elhai, J. D., Naifeh, J. A., Zucker, I. S., Gold, S. N., Deitsch, S. E., & Frueh, B. C. (2004). Discriminating malingered from genuine civilian Posttraumatic Stress Disorder: A validation of three MMPI-2 infrequency scales (F, F_P, and F_{PTSD}). *Assessment 11*, 139–144.

Estelle v. Smith, 451 U.S. 454, 101 S.Ct. 1866 (1981).

Ewing, C. P. (2003). Expert testimony: Law and practice. In I. B. Weiner (Series Ed.) & A. M. Goldstein (Vol. Ed.), *Handbook of psychology: Vol. 11, Forensic psychology* (pp. 55–66). Hoboken, NJ: Wiley.

Faust, D., & Heard, K. V. (2003). Biased experts: Some practical suggestions for identifying and demonstrating unfair practices. In I. Z. Schulze & D. O. Brady (Eds.), *Psychological injuries at trial* (pp. 1706–1739). Chicago: American Bar Association.

Fishbain, D. A., Cutler, R., Rosomoff, H. L., & Rosomoff, R. S. (2003). Chronic pain disability exaggeration/malingering and submaximal effort research. In I. Z. Schultz & D. O. Brady (Eds.), *Psychological injuries at trial* (pp. 1064–1122). Chicago: American Bar Association.

Foa, E. B., Ehlers, A., Clark, D. M., Tolin, D. F., & Orsillo, S. M. (1999). The Posttraumatic Cognitions Inventory (PCTI): Development and validation. *Psychological Assessment, 11*, 303–314.

Frye v. United States, 293 F. 1013, 34 ALR 145 (D. C. Cir. 1923).

Gatchel, R.J., & Kishing, N. (2006). Influence of personality characteristics of pain patients: Implications for causality in pain. In G. Young, A. W. Kane, & K. Nicholson (Eds.), *Psychological knowledge in court: PTSD, pain and TBI*. New York: Springer Science+Business Media.

Gouvier, W. D., Hayes, J. S., & Smiroldo, B. B. (2003). The significance of base rates, test sensitivity, test specificity, and subjects' knowledge of symptoms in assessing TBI sequelae and malingering. In I. Z. Schulze & D. O. Brady (Eds.), *Psychological injuries at trial* (pp. 641–671). Chicago: American Bar Association.

Graham, J. R. (2006). *MMPI-2: Assessing personality and psychopathology* (4th ed.). New York: Oxford University Press.

Greenberg, S. (2003). Personal injury examinations in torts for emotional distress. In I. B. Weiner (Series Ed.) & A. M. Goldstein (Vol. Ed.), *Handbook of psychology: Vol. 11, Forensic psychology* (pp. 233–258). Hoboken, NJ: Wiley.

Greenberg, S. A., Otto, R. K., & Long, A. C. (2003). The utility of psychological testing in assessing emotional damages in personal injury litigation. *Assessment, 10*, 411–419.

Greiffenstein, M. F. (2005). Quoted in Heilbronner, R. L. (Ed.), *Forensic neuropsychology casebook* (p. 349). New York: Guilford Press.

Grisso, T. (1986). *Evaluating competencies*. New York: Kluwer/Plenum.

Grisso, T. (2003). *Evaluating competencies* (2nd ed.). New York: Kluwer/Plenum.

Grisso, T., & Appelbaum, P. S. (1998). *Assessing competence to consent to treatment*. New York: Oxford University Press.

Grisso, T., & Vincent, G. M. (2005). The empirical limits of forensic mental health assessment. *Law and Human Behavior, 29*, 1–5.

Groth-Marnat, G. (2003). *Handbook of psychological assessment*. Hoboken, NJ: Wiley.

Gutheil, T. G., & Bursztajn, H. (2003). Avoiding *ipse dixit* mislabeling: Post-*Daubert* approaches to expert clinical opinions. *Journal of the American Academy of Psychiatry and the Law, 31*, 205–210.

Heilbrun, K. (2001). *Principles of forensic mental health assessment*. New York: Kluwer/Plenum.

Heilbrun, K., Marczyk, G. R., & DeMatteo, D. (2002). *Forensic mental health assessment: A casebook*. Oxford: Oxford University Press.

Heilbrun, K., Warren, J., & Picarello, K. (2003). Third party information in forensic assessment. In I. B. Weiner (Series Ed.) & A. M. Goldstein (Vol. Ed.), *Handbook of psychology: Vol. 11, Forensic psychology* (pp. 69–86). Hoboken, NJ: Wiley.

Hertenstein v. Kimberly Home Health Care, Inc. 189 F.R.D. 620 (Kan. 1999).

Hess, A. (1998). Millon Clinical Multiaxial Inventory-III. In James C. Impara & Barbara S. Plake (Eds.), *The thirteenth mental measurements yearbook* (pp. 665–667). Lincoln: University of Nebraska-Lincoln.

Hynan, D. J. (2004). Unsupported general differences on some personality disorder scales of the Millon Clinical Multiaxial Inventory-III. *Professional Psychology: Research and Practice, 35*, 105–110.

In re: Air Crash at Tapei, Taiwan on October 31, 2000 (C.D. Cal. 2003).

Iverson, G. L., & Lange, R. T. (2006). Detecting exaggeration and malingering in psychological injury claims. In W. J. Koch, K. S. Douglas, T. L. Nicholls, & M. L. O'Neill (Eds.), *Psychological injuries: Forensic assessment, treatment, and law*. (pp. 76–112). Oxford: Oxford University Press.

Kane, A. W. (1999). Essentials of malingering assessment. In M. J. Ackerman (Ed.), *Essentials of forensic psychological assessment* (pp. 78–99). New York: Wiley.

Keane, T. M., Buckley, T. C., & Miller, M. W. (2003). Forensic psychological assessment in PTSD. In R. Simon (Ed.), *Posttraumatic Stress Disorder in litigation* (2nd ed.). Washington, DC: American Psychiatric Association.

Kehrer, C. A., Sanchez, P. N., Habif, U., Rosenbaum, J. G., & Townes, B. D. (2000). Effects of a significant-other observer on neuropsychological test performance. *The Clinical Neuropsychologist, 14*, 67–71.

Koch, W. J., O'Neill, M., & Douglas, K. S. (2005). Empirical limits for the forensic assessment of PTSD litigants. *Law and Human Behavior, 29*, 121–149.

Lally, S. J. (2003). What tests are acceptable for use in forensic evaluations? A survey of experts. *Professional Psychology: Research and Practice, 34*, 491–498.

Lees-Haley, P. R. (1992). Psychodiagnostic test usage by forensic psychologists. *American Journal of Forensic Psychology, 10*, 25–30.

Lees-Haley, P. R. (2005). Quoted in Heilbronner, R. L. (Ed.), *Forensic neuropsychology casebook*. New York: Guilford Press, p. 359.

Lees-Haley, P. R., English, L. T., & Glenn, W. J. (1991). A fake bad scale on the MMPI-2 for personal injury claimants. *Psychological Reports, 68*, 203–210.

Lees-Haley, P. R., Smith, H. H., Williams, C. W., & Dunn, J. T. (1995). Forensic neuropsychological test usage: An empirical survey. *Archives of Clinical Neuropsychology, 11*, 45–51.

Lezak, M. D., Howieson, D. B., & Loring, D. W. (2004). *Neuropsychological assessment* (4th ed.). Oxford: Oxford University Press.

Macartney-Filgate, M. S., & Snow, G. W. (2004). The practitioner as expert witness. In D. R. Evans (Ed.), *The law, standards, and ethics in the practice of psychology* (2nd ed., pp. 287–309). Toronto: Edmond Montgomery.

McLearen, A. M., Pietz, C. A., & Denney, R. L. (2004). Evaluation of psychological damages. In W. T. O'Donohue & E. R. Levensky (Eds.), *Handbook of forensic psychology* (pp. 267–299). Amsterdam: Elsevier.

Melton, G. B., Petrila, J., Poythress, N. G., & Slobogin, C. (1997). *Psychological evaluations for the courts* (2nd ed.). New York: Guilford.

Miller, W. (2003). Evidentiary issues in the psychological injury case. In I. Z. Schulze & D. O. Brady (Eds.), *Psychological injuries at trial* (pp. 202–235). Chicago: American Bar Association.

Murphy, J. P. (2000). Expert witnesses at trial: Where are the ethics? *Georgetown Journal of Legal Ethics, 14*. Retrieved April 4, 2003 from www.law-forensics.com/ethic_and_experts.htm

Nichols, D. S. (2001). *Essentials of MMPI-2 assessment*. New York: Wiley.

Nichols, D. S., & Greene, R. L. (1997). Dimensions of deception in personality assessment: The example of the MMPI-2. *Journal of Personality Assessment, 68*, 251–266.

Norris, F. N., & Hamblen, J. L. (2004). Standardized self-report measures of civilian trauma and PTSD. In J. P. Wilson & T. M. Keane (Eds.), *Assessing psychological trauma and PTSD* (2nd ed., pp. 63–102). New York: Guilford Press.

O'Donnell, M. L., Creamer, M., Bryant, R. A., Schnyder, U., & Shalev, A. (2006). Posttraumatic disorders following injury: Assessment and other methodological considerations. In G. Young, A. W. Kane, & K. Nicholson (Eds.), *Psychological knowledge in court: PTSD, pain and TBI*. New York: Springer Science+Business Media.

Otto, R. K. (2002). Use of the MMPI-2 in forensic settings. *Journal of Forensic Psychology Practice, 2*, 71–91.

Polusny, M. A., & Arbisi, P. A. (2006). Assessment of psychological distress and disability after sexual assault in adults. In G. Young, A. W. Kane, & K. Nicholson (Eds.), *Psychological knowledge in court: PTSD, pain and TBI*. New York: Springer Science+Business Media.

Pope, K. S., Butcher, J. N., & Seelen, J. (2000). *The MMPI, MMPI-2 & MMPI-A in court* (2nd ed.). Washington, DC: American Psychological Association.

Pope, K. S., Butcher, J. N., & Seelen, J. (2006). *The MMPI, MMPI-2 & MMPI-A in court* (3rd ed.). Washington, DC: American Psychological Association.

Posthuma, A., Podrouzek, W., & Crisp, D. (2002). The implications of *Daubert* on neuropsychological evidence in the assessment of remote mild traumatic brain injury. *American Journal of Forensic Psychology, 20*, 21–37.

Rabin, L. A., Barr, W. B., & Burton, L. A. (2005). Assessment practices of clinical neuropsychologists in the United States and Canada: A survey of INS, NAN, and APA Division 40 members. *Archives of Clinical Neuropsychology, 20*, 33–65.

Ragge v. MCA/Universal Studios, 165 F.R.D. 605 (C.D. Cal. 1995).

Rogers, R. (1997). Structured interviews and dissimulation. In R. Rogers (Ed.), *Clinical assessment of malingering and deception* (2nd ed., pp. 301–327). New York: Guilford.

Rogers, R. (2002). Validating retrospective assessments: An overview of research models. In R. Simon & D. W. Shuman (Eds.), *Retrospective assessment of mental states in litigation: Predicting the past* (pp. 287–306). Washington, DC: American Psychiatric Publishing.

Rogers, R. (2003). Forensic use and abuse of psychological tests: Multiscale inventories. *Journal of Psychiatric Practice, 9*, 316–320.

Rogers, R., & Bender, S. D. (2003). Evaluation of malingering and deception. In I. B. Weiner (Series Ed.) & A. M. Goldstein (Vol. Ed.), *Handbook of psychology: Vol. 11, Forensic psychology* (pp. 109–129). Hoboken, NJ: Wiley.

Rogers, R., Salekin, R. T., & Sewell, K. W. (1999). Validation of the Millon Clinical Multiaxial Inventory for axis II disorders: Does it meet The *Daubert* standard? *Law and Human Behavior, 23*, 425–443.

Rogers, R., Salekin, R. T., & Sewell, K. W. (2000). The MCMI-III and The *Daubert* standard: Separating rhetoric from reality. *Law and Human Behavior, 24*, 501–506.

Rogers, R., Sewell, K.W., & Salekin, R.T. (1994). A meta-analysis of malingering on the MMPI-2. *Assessment, 1*, 227–237.

Rogers, R., Sewell, K. W., Martin, M. A., & Vitacco, M. J. (2003). Detection of feigned mental disorders: A meta-analysis of the MMPI-2 and malingering. *Assessment, 10*, 160–177.

Rogers, R., & Shuman, D. W. (2005). *Fundamentals of forensic practice*. New York: Springer Science+Business Media.

Sageman, M. (2003). Three types of skills for effective forensic psychological assessments. *Assessment, 10*, 321–328.

Samuel, S. E., DeGirolamo, J., Michaels, T. J., & O'Brien, J. (1995). Preliminary findings on the MMPI "Cannot Say" responses with personal injury litigants. *American Journal of Forensic Psychiatry, 16*, 59–72.

Schutte, James W. (2000). Using the MCMI-III in forensic evaluations. *American Journal of Forensic Psychology, 19*, 5–20.

Sherman, J. J., & Ohrbach, R. (2006). Objective and subjective measurement of pain: Current approaches for forensic applications. In G. Young, A. W. Kane, & K. Nicholson (Eds.), *Psychological knowledge in court: PTSD, pain and TBI*. New York: Springer Science+Business Media.

Shirsat v. Mutual Pharmaceuticals Co., 169 F.R.D. 68 (E.D. Pa. 1996).

Shuman, D. W. (1994, 2002 supplement). *Psychiatric and psychological evidence* (2nd ed.). Deerfield, IL: Clark, Boardman, Callaghan.

Shuman, D. W. (2002). Retrospective assessment of mental states and the law. In R. I. Simon & D. W. Shuman (Eds.), *Retrospective assessment of mental states in litigation* (pp. 21–45). Washington, DC: American Psychiatric.

Tombaugh, T. N. (1996). *TOMM: The Test of Memory Malingering*. North Tonawanda, New York: MultiHealth Systems.

Tomlin v. Holocek, 150 F.R.D. 628 (D. Minn. 1993).

Walker, L. E. A., & Shapiro, D. L. (2003). *Introduction to forensic psychology*. New York: Kluwer/Plenum.

Watkins, C. E., Campbell, V. L., Nieberding, R., & Hallmark, R. (1995). Contemporary practice of psychological assessment by clinical psychologists. *Professional Psychology: Research and Practice, 26*, 54–60.

Weathers, F. W., Keane, T. M., & Davidson, J. R. T. (2001). Clinician-Administered PTSD Scale: A review of the first ten years of research. *Depression and Anxiety, 13*, 132–156.

Weiner, I. B. (2002). Psychodiagnostic testing in forensic psychology: A commentary. *Journal of Forensic Psychology Practice, 2*, 113–119.

Weiss, D. S., & Ozer, E. J. (2006). Predicting who will develop Posttraumatic Stress Disorder. In G. Young, A. W. Kane, & K. Nicholson (Eds.), *Psychological knowledge in court: PTSD, pain and TBI* (pp. 85–96). New York: Springer Science+Business Media.

Wilson, J. P., & Moran, T. A. (2004). Forensic/clinical assessment of psychological trauma and PTSD in legal settings. In J. P. Wilson, & T. M. Keane (Eds.), *Assessing psychological trauma and PTSD* (2nd ed., pp. 603–636). New York: Guilford Press.

Zinermon v. Burch, 494 U.S. 113, 110 S.Ct. 975 (1990).

12

Other Psycho-Legal Issues

ANDREW W. KANE

There are numerous issues that must be addressed if an assessment is to be both valid and reliable. In addition, the evaluator must be aware of relevant research, professional and ethical issues, the limits of what an evaluation can accomplish, the importance of maintaining a consistent and appropriate role, the need for independence and impartiality, and problems associated with biases. If the evaluator is not licensed/certified in the jurisdiction in which the evaluation and/or testimony will occur, there could be severe consequences for the evaluator and the personal injury case itself. By paying attention to these issues, the evaluator can adequately address them in an appropriate manner.

Review of Relevant Research

There is a large body of research addressing aspects of causality and the assessment of psychological status, disability, and related factors. The research addresses samples of people with various characteristics (e.g., age, education, gender, trauma history, education) who have been assessed using specified instruments under various conditions. This is referred to as *nomothetic* data. Nomothetic data are group- or population-based, and are especially useful for establishing the validity and reliability of instruments (tests, information forms, etc.) used for forensic assessments, and for prediction related to the course of psychological disorders and impairments. Nomothetic data also tell us what is statistically "normal," and what is significantly different from normal. In addition, base rates are established by nomothetic data. Hypotheses may be generated on the basis of research regarding the typical behavior (including test results) of individuals who have experienced one or more specific types of traumatic events, and/or the absence of behavior or other characteristics *not* typical of individuals who have experienced a traumatic event (Heilbrun, 2001). Experts must be able to identify relevant professional journals or other learned treatises that support their methodology, if asked, and it may be appropriate for the expert to include that information in his or her report (Baer & Neal, 2000).

Idiographic data are those pertaining to the individual who is being assessed. Through psychological testing, use of information-gathering forms, and interviews, and review of documents related to the case, the psychologist identifies relevant characteristics of the individual, the nature of the alleged traumatic incident and its meaning for the individual, and the impact of the alleged traumatic incident on the individual (Ackerman & Kane, 1998a; Wilson & Moran, 2004). In the course of doing so, the psychologist develops a number of hypotheses, each of which may be tested against further data that becomes available from some source. The greater the consistency among sources (e.g., tests, life history information, interviews of the individual and collaterals), the greater the likelihood that a given piece of data is accurate. Through the analysis of idiographic data, in the context of nomothetic information, the psychologist identifies causal links between changes in the condition of the individual and the alleged traumatic incident (Greenberg, Otto, & Long, 2003; Heilbrun, 2001).

The primary difficulty that may arise is if the individual (ideographic) data does not closely enough match the parameters of the group (nomothetic) data, so that hypotheses about the individual cannot be adequately tested, nor, therefore, firm conclusions drawn. If all research in a particular area of inquiry has been conducted on men, for example, it may not be possible to accurately generalize to women. If the normative group consists solely of psychiatric patients, it may not be possible to accurately generalize to individuals who are not psychiatric patients (see the discussion of the MCMI, in Chapter 11). Further, some information is available based on controlled experiments, whereas other information is based on naturalistic groups. For example, while research is done with an acute pain challenge in "normals," many of whom rate such pain as severe, acute and chronic pain are quite different, and there is limited generalizability from experiments involving acute vs. chronic pain. Therefore, to more validly study pain we have to conduct research with people who have already been injured, and who already feel severe pain, to try to better understand their pain experience. There is also inter-individual variability in the presentation of the conditions that are the focus of this book and its companion volume, and individual idiosyncracies and unique characteristics that prevent individuals from perfectly matching many qualities identified in research on groups of individuals (nomothetic data).

Even so, it is the task of the expert to accurately identify the ways the individual is similar to and different from both the controlled and naturalistic research populations, and to carefully draw conclusions from that data (Haney & Smith, 2003). The expert must also be at all times cognizant of the fact that "trial courts are usually concerned with specific effects on specific individuals. While science attempts to discover the universals hiding among the particulars, trial courts attempt to discover the particulars hiding among the universals" (Faigman, 2000, p. 340).

Every Evaluation has Some Limits

Every evaluation leaves some questions unanswered, or only marginally answered. Exhausting every possible avenue of inquiry and administration of every psychological test or other instrument that might have utility would take so much time, and be so expensive, that it could not be justified. In addition, limits imposed by the parties or the court (e.g., number of hours permitted for the assessment) could also hinder the ability of an evaluator to provide a strong statement regarding some of his or her conclusions. There may also be inconsistencies among the results of different parts of the evaluation, including between two tests, between a test and an interview, and so forth. Further, information considered important or essential may not be available, for example, school records, medical records, or other objective information. It is incumbent on the evaluator to identify any significant limits of the evaluation and to indicate them in his or her report, together with a statement regarding the impact of those limits on the validity of his or her conclusions. The expert also has an obligation to indicate any significant findings that are not consistent with his or her conclusions (Heilbrun, 2001).

Because every evaluation has some limits, experts are expected to testify not to absolute certainty but, instead, to a "reasonable degree" of medical/psychological/scientific/professional/ etc. certainty (whichever applies for a given expert in a given jurisdiction). Experts and courts generally define "reasonable certainty" as "more likely than not," rather than a more stringent standard. See "Differences Between Science and Law," in Chapter 10 (this section), and the discussion of the concept of "reasonable certainty," below.

Ecological Validity

"Ecological validity" refers to the degree to which an instrument or procedure yields information applicable not only to the standardization sample or theoretical model but, also, to an individual's real-world functioning. A given injury may cause one individual to spend much of each day in bed, while another person with a seemingly identical injury is much more active, goes to work, and so forth. Further, a "normal" psychological or neuropsychological test does not mean that the individual does not have a valid problem and a real inability to function in certain areas (Miller, 2003).

The ecological validity of the individual's complaints may also be addressed by interviewing people familiar with the plaintiff's daily functioning. Both the plaintiff and the collaterals may be asked questions regarding exactly what the individual is able or unable to do, how the individual has changed since the trauma or other index event, what the individual complains about, and so forth. If the individual shows significant deficits in areas of motor skills, reaction time, coordination, and attention when tested, for example, it may be important to know whether the individual regularly drives a car or uses potentially dangerous equipment without evident difficulty (Faust & Heard, 2003; Koch, O'Neill, & Douglas, 2005).

Information from collaterals also increases the *face* (apparent) *validity* of the evaluation, and can help identify whether an apparent or claimed deficit is a problem in the individual's daily life (Heilbrun, 2001; Heilbrun, Marczyk, & DeMatteo, 2002). There is research indicating that collateral interviews conducted over the telephone are equivalent to face-to-face interviews regarding the quality of the information obtained from the client, suggesting that telephone collateral interviews regarding the plaintiff may also be equivalent to face-to-face interviews (Heilbrun, 2001). The possibility of biased responding by a collateral can be addressed by gathering information from multiple sources, developing conclusions based on trends in the data collected rather than any single response, as well as utilization of those measures completed by collaterals that have validity scales. The evaluator wants to know what the collateral source saw and heard, not any conclusions drawn by the collateral source. The potential problem with a collateral being influenced by the evaluator (suggestibility) may be addressed by avoiding leading questions, and by starting with very general questions and moving to more specific questions, thereby getting the collateral to volunteer more information. Lack of memory of specific events may be addressed also by beginning with very general questions and moving toward increasingly specific ones, as well as by giving the collateral some details that were offered by the plaintiff or another observer (Greenberg, 2003; Heilbrun, 2001).

To identify collaterals who might be interviewed, the evaluator might request that the plaintiff provide the names and telephone numbers of individuals who have knowledge about his or her functioning, using an informed consent form that has room to list each individual, his or her telephone number, and the relationship with the plaintiff for each of several people. If the plaintiff refuses, the evaluator has still done his or her job properly by making the request (Greenberg, 2003). The form should contain a statement like:

> The undersigned hereby requests that each of the people listed above fully and unconditionally release any and all information about me to Dr. ___________, for the purpose of helping him (or her) to evaluate and understand me and my day-to-day functioning. This release holds for privileged information as well as any knowledge you have about me regardless of how it was obtained. That information may be discussed with Dr. ___________ at whatever length he wishes.

The plaintiff signs and dates that release. If possible, the list should include some people who are not personal friends, in addition to the usual friends and family. Coworkers may be especially important sources. Health care providers in the United States may require that the plaintiff sign the release of information form used by their offices, to ensure that the form signed is compliant with the Health Insurance Portability and Accountability Act (HIPAA).

If the plaintiff is part of a couple, there is often value in having the partner come to the first evaluation session but sit in a different room and fill out questionnaires that address his or her perception of the plaintiff. For example, the partner could list "things my husband/wife/partner used to do alone, but which I now have to help with or do for him or her." The partner could describe an average day for the plaintiff, could describe the plaintiff before and after the traumatic event (with an open-ended question and/or using an instrument like the Behavior Change Inventory) (Hartlage, 1989). It is important that this information be gathered at the first evaluation session, as the couple is likely to discuss the nature of the testing and interviewing of the plaintiff after the first session, and the partner's responses might be different after hearing what the plaintiff indicated to the evaluator. Although there cannot be a guarantee of the veracity of the information offered by either the plaintiff or the partner without other corroboration, the more consistent the two data sources are with one another, the more likely it is that the information received is accurate.

Incremental Validity

Each source of data in a forensic evaluation adds some amount of *information*, but it does not necessarily add *new* or *useful* information. The concept of "incremental validity" includes the notion that a substantial amount of data should be acquired in the course of making judgments regarding an individual or a legal question, but that more data does not always mean better data. There is also a question of relative cost: while more data could always be acquired, at some point the cost of acquiring the data exceeds the likely contribution of the data to the questions or issues being addressed.

The goal, then, is to investigate all of the relevant and important issues to the degree necessary to formulate and test hypotheses and draw conclusions, and then stop, unless there is a reason to believe that there is another source that has a significant likelihood of producing data that will add to the validity of the data already gathered should the assessment continue (Hunsley, 2003; Hunsley & Meyer, 2003; Faust, 2003). It should be kept in mind that an evaluator cannot know what a given test, interview, or review of records will produce until he or she has the data available from the procedure. However, when there has been a substantial amount of data collected, there is a clear direction to the data collected, and little or no contrary data, under most circumstances the evaluator should stop data collection.

With regard to assessment of adults, Garb (2003) indicates that personality inventories for example, the MMPI-2 (Butcher, Graham, Ben-Porath, Tellegen, Dahlstrom, & Kaemmer, 1989), interviews, and brief self-rating instruments, generally add incremental validity in both diagnosis and the assessment of psychopathology and personality. Projective tests may add predictive validity as well, but generally less than the previously cited methods. However, projective tests often prove to be a rich source of hypotheses that may be addressed in the evaluation (Ackerman & Kane, 1998a).

Current Controversy Regarding the Comprehensive System for the Rorschach

The Rorschach Inkblot Method is the most widely used projective test. Projective tests are unstructured, in order to force the individual to project some aspects of his or her personality and psychodynamics into his or her responses. Because the average individual has no way to know what is a "normal" or "abnormal" response, these tests can sometimes identify psychopathology that is missed by objective tests and other instruments and by interviews.

A 1999 study by Shaffer, Erdberg, and Haroian had an impact far beyond the intent of the researchers. The authors set out to provide data on how nonpatients respond to the Rorschach, the Wechsler Adult Intelligence Scale-Revised (WAIS-R), and the Minnesota Multiphasic Personality Inventory, Second Edition (MMPI-2). The results of administration of these three tests to 123 nonpatient adults were very similar to the standardization samples for the WAIS-R and the MMPI-2, but not to those of the most frequently used scoring and interpretive system for the Rorschach, the "Comprehensive System" (CS) developed by John Exner (2005). The Comprehensive System identified these adults as having significant psychopathology, despite all the contrary indicators from other sources. Because of the degree of controversy generated, and the substantial number of psychologists who use the Comprehensive System, this will be discussed at some length.

Numerous articles addressing the Shaffer et al. (1999) results and other issues have been published in the past several years. Much of the criticism of the Comprehensive System has come from psychologists James M. Wood, M. Teresa Nezworski, Howard N. Garb, and Scott O. Lilienfeld. In articles and a book published in 2000–2005, they indicated that many of the norms for the Comprehensive System are not accurate, and that using those norms makes an individual appear to have more psychopathology than he or she actually has. All 14 variables they studied were found to differ significantly for nonpatients in the Comprehensive System's normative groups and nonpatients tested by other researchers. They also found that the reliability of some Comprehensive System scores is far below acceptable levels. As a result, these authors recommend that psychologists avoid use of the present Comprehensive System norms in either clinical or forensic work, because inaccurate results could potentially harm a client, constituting an ethical violation. Any psychologists who continue to use the Comprehensive System norms, they indicate, have at the least an ethical obligation to describe the controversy and the possible limitations of those norms (Lilienfeld, Fowler, & Lohr, 2003; Lilienfeld, Lynn, & Lohr, 2003; Lilienfeld, Wood, & Garb, 2000; Wood, Lilienfeld, Nezworski, & Garb, 2001; Wood, Nezworski, Garb, & Lilienfeld, 2001).

Hunsley and Bailey (2001) caution that many authors confuse criticisms of the CS with criticisms of the Rorschach Inkblot Test (or Method) itself. Although some researchers criticize aspects of the Rorschach, it is the CS that is the object of most concerns. They note that many psychologists do not attempt interpretations utilizing the CS norms, preferring other systems or using idiographic (case specific) interpretations. They also suggest that the reputation of the Rorschach for identifying psychopathology may be based to a substantial degree on the apparent tendency of the CS to overpathologize.

Several CS proponents have responded to the above articles. Weiner (2001) wrote that the CS calls for a standardized administration and scoring, and that the test can be reliably scored. Further, the CS does have reasonable norms, even if some of those about which questions have been raised are included, and the CS scoring of the Rorschach remains valid for most scoring purposes. Further, he writes, the CS adds incremental validity in situations in which decisions must be made, including forensic evaluations. It must also be noted, he indicates, that many psychologists use the CS recommendations for administration of the Rorschach, but use different interpretive strategies from those recommended by Exner, the primary author of the CS. Even if all the criticisms of the CS norms were valid, use of these other interpretive strategies would not be affected. Further, Meyer and Archer (2001) indicate that the Rorschach has well-demonstrated validity and reliability in many clinical and forensic evaluations, and often adds incremental validity to an assessment. They acknowledge that the CS may appear to overpathologize, because the reference group is made up of people who are both relatively healthy and functioning well, and recommend that further research should be conducted, with a sample representative of the U.S. population being collected.

Masling (2002) indicates that six scoring systems other than the CS have been demonstrated by research to be both valid and reliable means of assessing personality dynamics. He praises projective tests for being resistant to conscious manipulation, unlike many objective tests.

Hibbard (2003) directly addresses the criticisms of Lilienfeld, Wood, Garb and their coauthors. He indicates that some of the research cited by these authors was not legitimately usable for the purpose for which it was cited, that the authors misstated the nature of some of the variables studied, and that the CS is more than adequately reliable.

Gronnerod (2003) addresses the stability (test-retest reliability) of the Rorschach in a meta-analytic review. He found that, over an average test-retest period of three years, the reliability of the test was high, and that the CS produced higher levels of stability than did other scoring methods.

Widiger (2001, 2002), sought a middle ground. While noting that the CS was a major advance over other, less concrete systems, he acknowledges that the problems identified must be rectified. The Rorschach itself, he indicates, "does provide useful and valid information and, as a projective test, it is a very intriguing instrument that might be helpful in the assessment of dispositions, needs, or conflicts that the person is unable or reluctant to acknowledge." He suggests that the Rorschach remains both useful and effective as a source of hypotheses that may then be explored and validated by data from other sources.

The latest salvo was fired by Garb, Wood, Lilienfeld, and Nezworski (2005). They indicate that, while they endorse the use of CS scores that are valid, reliable, and adequately normed, they also strongly endorse a moratorium on use of all other scale scores until research has established the validity and reliability of those scales. They address, and dismiss, most arguments by "pro-CS" authors. Foremost among their criticisms is that most "pro-CS" authors endorse (1) "informal validation" of scores, that is, because they have found the Rorschach/CS to be useful and helpful, it must be valid, and (2) the notion that a very good Rorschach interpreter could intuitively extract all essential information from the test. The former, the authors suggest, is akin to astrology, and that popularity of an assessment or treatment does not indicate validity, using lobotomies as an example. They also indicate that research has long demonstrated that intuitive interpretation does not lead to accurate interpretations. The only acceptable solution, Garb et al. (2005) indicate, is to scientifically validate every CS score prior to using it in clinical or forensic evaluations.

The present author believes that the Rorschach Inkblot Method has much to offer in forensic evaluations. It has often yielded hypotheses about an individual that led to areas of inquiry that might have been missed without the input from this test. As indicated above, the Rorschach, like any single instrument, should not be used in isolation. There is strong evidence for its validity and reliability, and it can be a critical part of a complete evaluation. Its primary purpose should be to generate hypotheses regarding the individual taking the test, so that other sources of information (other tests, parent/child interviews, collateral interviews, historical information, and so forth) may be used to confirm or deny the hypotheses formed. Given the difficulty with accurate scoring of the CS, it is recommended that all Rorschach protocols scored with the CS be scored using the computer program designed for that purpose: the Rorschach Interpretation Assistance Program: Version 5 FE (forensic edition)(RIAP5 FE) (Weiner, 2004). There is evidence that indicates that the computer program is more accurate than the vast majority of clinicians at scoring the test. Psychologists should avoid making strong statements, including predictions, predicated on CS-based interpretive criteria until the ongoing research has established new guidelines.

Sources of Bias

It is extremely difficult to completely avoid biases when doing an assessment. Even the most dedicated evaluator is likely to feel some pull to slant the results in the direction of his or her preconceived notions, or toward the view favored by whomever retained the expert, or in some other way. In pure research, this is addressed through double-blind protocols in which neither the researcher nor the recipient knows, for example, which is the real drug and which is the placebo. In forensic work, it is addressed by the expert's ensuring that he or she carefully considers the potential effect of each type of potential bias. Significant areas of potential bias include:

"*Anchoring bias*," which refers to research indicating that information received early in the diagnostic process is remembered better and is used more than information received later in the process. If the clinician begins the evaluation by getting information about the traumatic event and the individual's response to it, this may bias the whole evaluation (Bowman, 2003; Risinger, Saks, Thompson, & Rosenthal, 2002).

"*Attribution bias*" involves "discounting contextual factors accounting for behavior and imputing it instead to a permanent characteristic of an individual"

(Sageman, 2003, p. 325). For example, an individual may be aggressive in a situation in which he or she has been attacked, or passive in a situation in which he or she is fearful. In the other 99% of his or her life, however, neither is a common characteristic.

"*Confirmation bias*" refers to evaluators giving more weight to information that is consistent with their own beliefs. For example, a clinician who believed that no one could go psychologically unscathed through a serious motor vehicle accident, or being a soldier in active combat, or enduring some other major traumatic event, may selectively hear information confirming that bias, and disregard contrary information. Because evaluators, like everyone else, have hypotheses and expectations, they must take great care not to let them color the results of an evaluation (Bowman, 2003; Risinger et al., 2002).

"*Conformity effects*" refer to "our tendency to conform to the perceptions, beliefs, and behavior of others" (Risinger et al., 2002, p. 20). The evaluator may have difficulty arguing against the theory of the attorney who has retained the expert, or against the findings of another expert whom the evaluator respects, regardless of the actual findings of the evaluator.

"*Halo effect*" refers to "when an examiner's evaluation of an individual's symptomatology is influenced by the nature of the traumatic event reported by the individual" (Polusny & Arbisi, 2006, p. 103). This is especially true when the examiner has an emotional reaction to the event, for example, to the death of a loved one, or a sexual assault, or another severe event.

"*Hindsight bias*" occurs when people who are aware of how an incident turns out believe that that outcome was more likely than objective prediction would indicate. Since both experts and juries generally know how an incident turned out, their attempt to objectively judge foreseeability may be compromised (Shuman, 1995; Wayte, Samra, Robbennolt, Heuer, & Koch, 2002).

"*Observer effects*" refer to the fact that the thoughts, feelings, experiences, and expectations of people, including scientists, influence their perceptions and conclusions. It is well-documented that scientists make errors of various kinds, including simple counting errors, when they have a conscious or unconscious reason to skew the data in a given direction (or even when there is no evident motivation for skewing the data). This is why double-blind research is important in any area of science in which observer effects may bias the results—provided it is possible in the given research project. It is essential in research on medications, but is often difficult or impossible in psychological research (Risinger et al., 2002).

"*Overconfidence bias*" results when the clinician feels certain of his or her conclusions and therefore assumes they are valid. Research, however, has found that confidence in and validity of conclusions are not well-correlated. Regardless of his or her level of confidence, the clinician must keep an open mind while examining all of the relevant data (Bowman, 2003).

In addition, there are a number of other types of error that may be made. According to Risinger et al. (2002), these include errors when a person or situation is initially perceived, errors when information is recorded, errors in memory (especially when the actual memory conflicts with the conscious or unconscious wish or expectation of the evaluator for the evaluation to have a certain result), errors in transforming data into conclusory statements, and errors when interpreting the data about which conclusions have been drawn.

Although there is no unequivocal solution to these problems of possible bias, awareness is a significant part of the answer. The expert must be aware of these natural tendencies to bias the data, and guard against them. He or she might keep a log of hypotheses generated by various pieces of data, some leading toward one conclusion and some toward other conclusions. Together with a commitment to impartiality, this should at the least reduce the influences of these biases on the expert's conclusions.

Treating Expert vs. Expert Witness

A psychologist, psychiatrist, or other mental health professional who treats someone who has been traumatized may have a great deal of information that would be of value to the trier of fact, but he or she is not, and cannot be, an independent expert. A treating psychologist who attempted to conduct a formal evaluation for the purpose of court testimony as an "independent expert" would likely violate the provisions of the *Ethical Principles of Psychologists and Code of Conduct* of the American Psychological Association regarding multiple relationships, avoiding harm, and conflicts of interest, and similar provisions of the *Canadian Code of Ethics for Psychologists*. Further, therapists have a legal duty to maintain the confidentiality of the information received from their patients, with exceptions generally made only when the information must be released in order to protect the patient or someone else. There would also be a danger of appearing to feather his or her own nest if additional psychotherapy were recommended. The mandatory consideration of malingering could permanently damage the therapeutic relationship if any such evidence is identified. Thus, for many reasons, the roles of treatment professional and expert witness are incompatible, and should be avoided if at all possible (Ackerman & Kane, 1998a; Greenberg & Shuman, 1997; Heilbrun, 2001; Shuman, 1994a, 2002 supplement; Simon & Wettstein, 1997; Strassburger, Gutheil, & Brodsky, 1997). This in no way limits the treating professional from being interviewed by the evaluator or offering testimony as a fact witness, testifying about his or her knowledge of the plaintiff, the nature of treatment, and so forth. It should be noted that courts may accept a treating professional as an expert witness (Greenberg & Shuman, 1997), and may permit or request the expert to state opinions as if he or she were an independent expert under Federal Rule of Evidence 701 or an equivalent rule at the state or provincial level (Goodman-Delahunty, 1997). If this occurs, the therapist must proceed cautiously, minimizing any harm that may result from the testimony by, for example, discussing embarrassing and potentially harmful information with the patient prior to testifying and getting the patient's informed, written consent to discuss that information with his or her attorney prior to court testimony (Greenberg & Shuman, 1997).

Expert Consultant vs. Expert Witness

Experts are sometimes retained to advise an attorney regarding the psychological issues in a case, review documents, help the attorney formulate questions for the expert on the other side, and so forth. These nontestifying experts are bound by the attorney's work product privilege.

They may not ordinarily be deposed or called to testify at trial, nor does the retaining attorney have to tell the opposing attorney that the expert has been retained. Only if the consulting expert has information that the opponent in the case cannot reasonably get from any other source will the consulting expert potentially be called upon to release that information.

For Whom Does the Expert Witness Advocate?

While they may have been retained by one side or the other, experts are bound by the ethical codes of their professions and the statutes and administrative codes governing their licenses. For psychologists, this means an obligation to be beneficent and nonmaleficent, to understand and utilize scientific methodology and data, and to advocate for their positions once they have formulated those positions on the basis of a reasoned, scientific analysis of the data. Many authorities indicate that experts should consider themselves friends of the court (*amici*) rather than advocates for one side or the other. This principal will not produce agreement among experts, since experts come to any given case with beliefs based on both theory and experience, and in each area may differ substantially from other experts. The principal also does not prevent experts from pointing out what they believe are weaknesses in or limits of the data and conclusions of the opposing expert (Heilbrun, 2001).

The *Specialty Guidelines for Forensic Psychologists* (Committee on Ethical Guidelines for Forensic Psychologists, 1991, p. 665) indicate that the psychologist's "essential role [is] as expert to the court ... to assist the trier of fact to understand the evidence or to determine a fact in issue." The psychologist can do so only by being objective, by advocating for his or her data but not for either side, and by undertaking a professional, competent, comprehensive, scientifically supported and reasoned, impartial evaluation.

Peer Review: A Flawed Assumption of Trustworthiness

According to Kassirer and Cecil (2002), "just because a study has been published in a prestigious peer-reviewed journal is no assurance that its results or conclusions are correct." Further, they indicate, there remain many areas of practice in which objective data are difficult to find, with most of the literature consisting of case studies (Kassirer & Cecil, p. 1383).

In 2003, the Cochrane Collaboration, a prestigious reviewer of research and publication quality, published a report indicating that, "at present there is little empirical evidence to support the use of editorial peer review as a mechanism to ensure quality of biomedical research" (quoted in Hagan, 2003a). The same year, the Royal Society, Britain's leading academic and scientific institution, announced that it would investigate the peer review process, due to concern that the current system was undermining the confidence of the public in science (Hagan, 2003b).

That publication in a peer-reviewed publication as a relative guarantee of reliability (validity, trustworthiness) should be questioned was supported by a study by Garcia-Berthou and Alcaraz (2004). The authors examined the statistical results in two highly distinguished journals, including every paper in volumes 409–412 of *Nature* and 12 randomly selected articles in *BMJ*, the *British Medical Journal*. They found that 11.6% (21 of 181) of the computations presented in *Nature* were incorrect, as were 11.7% (7 of 63) in *BMJ*. Further, 38% (12 of 32) of *Nature* articles and 25% (3 of 12) of the *BMJ* articles contained at least one computational error. The authors suggest that the real error total may be higher, since they did not include errors that may be due to rounding. Their data provide evidence that peer review is not a guarantee of accuracy, even in two of the most prestigious journals.

Peer review has also been called into question by a study that examined "all original research studies published in three major general clinical journals or high-impact factor specialty journals in 1990–2003 and cited more than 1,000 times in the literature" (Ioannidis, 2005, p. 218). Forty-nine studies were identified. Of these, 45 claimed a high rate of effectiveness, and many physicians accepted the information as factual and changed their recommendations to patients accordingly. However, 16% were contradicted by later research, another 16% found stronger results than did the original studies, only 44% had been replicated, and 24% had not yet been seriously challenged. Randomized studies fared better than did nonrandomized studies, with 30 out of 39 of the former holding up (as of the date of acceptance for publication), whereas only one nonrandomized study had not either been contradicted or had stronger effects identified. A third of the most-often-cited studies had problems with attempts to replicate the research. Ioannidis concludes that "positive" studies are more readily published than negative ones, and that peer review is clearly no guarantee of the quality of the research published.

Kaplan (2005, p. 321) goes so far as to indicate that "peer review is known to engender bias, incompetence, excessive expense, ineffectiveness, and corruption," and that "investigation of the peer-review system has failed to provide validation for its use." He indicates that the problem is so serious that four international congresses had been held to address how peer review could be improved. A Fifth International Congress on Peer Review and Biomedical Publication was held in Chicago in September, 2005. Among the papers presented was one indicating that manuscripts submitted to journals are more likely to be accepted for publication if the manuscripts cite the work of likely reviewers (Egger et al., 2005). Another paper reported that, of medical/scientific journals ranked 1st or 2nd by impact factor, only 54% had conflict of interest policies for authors, reviewers, and/or editors, while 25% of those ranked 3rd–7th had such policies (Ancker & Flanagin, 2005). A third paper evaluated the level of agreement among reviewers and editors for one medical journal. For 964 manuscripts, the rate of agreement for expert reviewers was 37.1%. Agreement between decisions by expert reviewers and editors was 47% (Scott, Martin, & Burmeister, 2005).

Further, not all articles in "peer-reviewed" journals are, in fact, peer reviewed. Some are included because the editor wants to make a point. Some receive a single review, others a number of reviews. There is also evidence of peer-reviewed articles that have been proven to be wrong. Finally, "peer review" is also used to describe papers presented at conference, workshops, and other forums rather than being published in a scholarly journal. The ideas and conclusions presented by the professional are generally not subject to significant criticism in these forums (Sales & Shuman, 2005).

Thus, there is no guarantee that publication in a peer-reviewed journal will produce higher-quality information. Many articles in peer-reviewed journals are subject to valid criticisms, contain data that cannot be replicated, or are demonstrated to be invalid by later research (Faigman & Monahan, 2005). Conversely, many articles that are not peer reviewed contain reliable, valid, and useful information. Although peer review is an essential part of the advancement of science, it does not guarantee any particular degree of excellence. With continuing criticisms and self-regulation, however, it has the potential to become adequately valid and reliable.

Licensing/Certification across Jurisdictions

There are a variety of circumstances that may lead to a psychologist or other expert to travel to a "foreign jurisdiction," that is, a place where the expert is not licensed or certified. Among them, a plaintiff could be hospitalized, could be incarcerated, or could be afraid to fly or drive. It may also be easier for an expert to go to the jurisdiction in which the case has been or will be filed rather than having the plaintiff and, if relevant, the plaintiff's spouse or significant other go to the office of the expert. Triers of fact may also give more credence to interviews of collaterals that take place face-to-face rather than over the telephone.

Every state and province has specific statutes and rules regarding licensing of psychologists and other professionals. Many permit psychologists from other jurisdictions to temporarily practice in order to conduct a forensic evaluation and/or for testimony—but a number do not, and the penalty for "unlicensed practice" can range from a civil forfeiture ($100–$50,000 per day) to a felony conviction. Further, if the expert does not meet licensing requirements in the given jurisdiction, he or she may not be permitted to do an evaluation and/or testify. In Wisconsin, for example, psychologists from other jurisdictions may practice for up to 60 days per year, but must report the nature and extent of that practice if it is more than 20 days in one year. In nine states or provinces, however, interjurisdictional practice is expressly forbidden according to the latest research by the present author (see Table 12.1) (see also McLearen, Pietz, & Denney, 2004; Tucillo, DeFilippis, Denney, & Dsurney, 2002; Simon & Shuman, 1999).

It is *essential* that a psychologist who is entering another jurisdiction in order to conduct a forensic evaluation or to testify be aware of the requirements for temporary practice in that jurisdiction. While the retaining attorney is one source of information, the psychologist would be wise to check for him- or herself rather than depending on anyone else, given the gravity of making an error. Contact information for all of the provincial and state licensing boards is available from the Association of State and Provincial Psychology Boards at www.asppb.org. If a court requests that a psychologist do an evaluation, unless statutes and administrative code are very clear regarding the legality of going to that state or province, the psychologist should request a ruling regarding his or her freedom to do the evaluation and testify regarding conclusions without concern for a licensing/certifying board action (Ackerman & Kane, 1998b, 2004 supplement, 2005; McLearen, 2004; Simon & Shuman, 1999; Shuman, Cunningham, Connell, & Reed, 2003).

A solution to the problem is advocated by Shuman et al. (2003). They discuss the problems associated with the high degree of variability across jurisdictions, including the difficulty a psychologist from a different jurisdiction has in trying to comply with the requirements outside of his or her own state or province. The authors recommend a model rule that would offer uniformity, protection of the public and the profession, and a practical solution to the present situation if adopted by all jurisdictions:

1. The evaluation, diagnosis, or expert testimony regarding the mental condition or characteristics of a person to assist a party or the court in assessing the validity of a claim or defense or to provide other assistance to the parties or the court (including but not limited to litigation or reasonably anticipated litigation involving personal injury, child custody, bail, juvenile waiver, various competencies, mental state at time of offense, and sentencing determinations) constitutes the practice of psychology for which a valid and current license to practice in this state is required.
2. A psychologist who holds a valid and current license to practice psychology in another state may engage in the temporary practice of psychology in this state for up to 30 days (consecutive or dispersed) in that calendar year, as an expert consultant or witness to assist a party or the court in assessing the validity of a claim or defense, or provide other assistance to the parties or the court … . [pp. 236–237]

The authors of the present text endorse this model rule. Until it or another rule is enacted, however, psychologists must be careful when practicing outside of their home states or provinces. The following table specifies the existing law and practice in all of the states and provinces at the time this book was published, to the best of my knowledge. ***Warning:*** *statutes and administrative code* *change frequently. While carefully researched, this table is a guide, not a definitive statement regarding statutes, administrative code, or other documents. Contact the licensing, registering, or certifying board in the state or province in which you wish to temporarily practice for up-to-date information (contact information may be found at http://asppb.org/about/boardContactStatic.aspx).*

TABLE 12.1. Temporary Psychological Practice in the United States and Canada©[1]

State or province	National register accepted?[2]	CPQ accepted?[3]	Temporary practice
Alabama	No	No	No[4]
Alaska	No	In process	Yes, 30 days in one year, once in a lifetime. 30 days' notice required[5]
Alberta	Yes	Yes	Yes, maximum of one year[a]
Arizona	Yes (but separate EPPP score verification is necessary)	Yes	Yes, may testify as an expert witness or consult for up to 20 days/year[6]
Arkansas	Yes	Yes	Permits consultation on one case, including evaluation and testimony, with *prior* Board approval "if possible." No time limit[7]
British Columbia	Yes	Yes	Yes, may practice for up to 15 consecutive days per calendar year. May apply for temporary registration twice in any calendar year. Applies to expert witnesses[8]
California	Yes	Yes	Yes, may practice in California for up to 30 days per calendar year[9]
Colorado	Yes	In process	Yes, may practice for up to 20 days/calendar year. Must inform any client in Colorado that he/she is not licensed in Colorado[10]
Connecticut	No	Yes	Yes[a]
Delaware	In process	In process	Yes, if doctoral level, may practice up to 6 days per calendar year[11]
District of Columbia	Yes	Yes	Yes, may practice as an expert witness for up to 30 days[a]
Florida	No	No	Yes, may practice psychology up to 5 days in any month or 15 days in any calendar year[12]
Georgia	No	Yes	Yes, may practice psychology for up to 30 days/calendar year[13]

Continued

TABLE 12.1. (Continued)

State or province	National register accepted?[2]	CPQ accepted?[3]	Temporary practice
Hawaii	Yes	Yes	Yes, for up to 90 days in a calendar year[14]
Idaho	No	Yes	No, may only testify as an expert witness[15]
Illinois	No	No	No[16]
Indiana	Board has approved, awaiting legislative approval	No	Yes. Statute effective July 1, 2006, permitting 30 days' practice every 2 years. There may be a delay while administrative code is approved to implement the new law[17]
Iowa	Yes (but separate EPPP score verification is necessary)	In process	Yes, valid 10 consecutive business days or 15 days in any 90-day period[18]
Kansas	No	No	Yes, up to 10 calendar days per year. If longer is needed, a temporary license permitting up to 90 days' practice may be requested[19]
Kentucky	No	Yes	Yes, to testify as an expert witness; for maximum of 30 days in a period of 2 years. If practicing by electronic means or telephone into Kentucky, must register with the board and get board approval[20]
Louisiana	No	Yes	Yes, up to 30 days per year. Must be associated with a Louisiana psychologist[21]
Maine	No	In process	Under discussion[22]
Manitoba	Yes	Yes	Yes, if testifying as an expert witness[23]
Maryland	Yes (but separate EPPP score verification is necessary)	In process	Yes. Requires a letter to the Board and other submissions. prior to the temporary practice[24]
Massachusetts	Yes (251 CMR 3.09(3))	Yes (251 CMR 3.09(2)(b))	Yes, for up to 1 year. Must register with the Board. May be required to consult with or be supervised by a Mass. psychologist[25]
Michigan	No	Yes	No, unless the psychologist is licensed in a contiguous state[26]

State or province	National register accepted?[2]	CPQ accepted?[3]	Temporary practice
Minnesota	Yes (but separate EPPP score verification is necessary)	In process	Yes, if licensed at the doctoral level in another jurisdiction; up to 7 calendar days if serving as an expert witness, or longer with "guest licensure"[27]
Mississippi	No	Yes	Yes, may practice for up to 10 days during any 12-month period; must report intent to practice *prior to* working in the state[28]
Missouri	Yes	Yes	Yes, for testimony as an expert witness or for a limited consultation, up to 10 consecutive days in a 90-day period or 15 in a nine-month period[29]
Montana	Yes	No	Yes. No notice is necessary if If 10 days/year or fewer. Up to 60 days is permitted with notice to the Board[30]
Nebraska	Yes	Yes	Yes, up to 30 days/year of practice or consultation. Must register with Board[31]
Nevada	Yes	Yes	Yes, if testifying as an expert witness or doing a limited consultation; up to 30 days/year; requires invitation by Nevada-licensed psychologist[32]
New Brunswick	Yes	In process	Yes, if under supervision of a N.B licensed psychologist[33]
New Hampshire	No	Yes	Testimony is permitted but treatment is not. Testimony containing treatment recommendations is considered the practice of psychology and is forbidden without a NH license[34]
New Jersey	No	Yes	Yes, 10 consecutive business days or 15 business days in a 90-day period[35]
New Mexico	Yes (but separate EPPP score verification is necessary)	Yes	Yes, but the evaluation must be court-ordered and the psychologist must agree to a number of conditions[36]
New York	No	No	Yes, may testify as an expert witness or consult up to 10 consecutive days or 15 intermittent days in any 90-day period[37]

Continued

TABLE 12.1. (Continued)

State or province	National register accepted?[2]	CPQ accepted?[3]	Temporary practice
Newfoundland/ Labrador	Yes	In process	Under discussion; may be possible under some circumstances[38]
North Carolina	Board has approved, awaiting Legislative approval	In process	Yes, for up to 5 days per calendar year, or 30 days/year under some circumstances[39]
North Dakota	In process	In process	Yes, up to 30 days per year[40]
Nova Scotia	Yes, but may only apply to residents of Canada	Yes	Yes, up to 21 days per calendar year[41]
Ohio	No	Yes	Yes, up to 30 days/year; should get approval of board[42]
Oklahoma	No	Yes	Yes, up to 5 days/calendar year. Must inform board prior to providing services[43]
Ontario	Yes, but may only apply to residents of Canada	Yes	No[44]
Oregon	Yes	Yes	Yes, may practice for up to 120 days[45]
Pennsylvania	Yes	Yes	Yes, if "on assignment" in PA 14 days or less, notice is not necessary; may give notice of practice to board and practice up to six months[46]
Prince Edward Island	Yes	In process	Yes, special certificate available if registered in another jurisdiction and briefly visiting Prince Edward Island[47]
Quebec	Yes	Yes	Yes[48]
Rhode Island	Yes	Yes	Yes, up to one year[49]
Saskatchewan	Yes	In process	Only via a fast-track licensing process that may take up to three months[50]
South Carolina	Yes, accepts NR listing as primary source documentation	No	Temporary license available for up to 60 days/year[51]
South Dakota	No	In process	Yes, up to 30 days without applying for a license[52]
Tennessee	Yes	Yes	Yes, up to 12 days in one year; requires written request, and name of and letter from a supervising Tennessee psychologist. Board must approve application[53]

State or province	National register accepted?[2]	CPQ accepted?[3]	Temporary practice
Texas	Yes	No	Yes, for up to 30 days in a calendar year. Must submit a request in writing to the board at least 30 days prior to working in Texas[54]
Utah	No	Yes	Yes, as an expert witness or to consult on a limited basis with a Utah professional[55]
Vermont	No	Yes	Yes, for up to 10 days or 80 hours in any 12-month period; must obtain a temporary Vermont license[56]
Virginia	Yes	Yes	Yes. No time limit specified[57]
Washington	Yes	Yes	Yes, but must obtain a temporary permit; maximum of 90 days per year[58]
West Virginia	Yes	Yes	Yes, up to 10 days per calendar year[59]
Wisconsin	No	Yes	Yes, may practice up to 20 working days without notifying the board; may practice up to 40 additional working days with board notification[60]
Wyoming	In process	Yes	Yes[61]

All information was obtained from statutes and/or administrative code and/or direct contact with the licensing board *unless* there is a superscript "a" for ASPPB, the Association of State and Provincial Psychology Boards (which may be accessed at www.asppb.org), indicating that ASPPB was the source of the information. The National Register of Health Service Providers in Psychology may be accessed at www.nationalregister.org. The Canadian Register of Health Service Providers in Psychology applies in Canada. It may be accessed at www.crhspp.com.ca.

It was assumed that the information on the ASPPB Web site was correct for acceptance of the CPQ, and that the information on the National Register Web site was correct for acceptance of the National Register listing. Psychologists should find that National Register listing or CPQ certification will ease the approval process for both temporary practice (where permitted) and, if one wishes to obtain it, a license or registration in a state or province.

[1] Virtually all jurisdictions that permit temporary practice specify that the psychologist must have a valid license from a state or province that has requirements for licensing/registration/certification that are at least as stringent as are those of the jurisdiction in which the psychologist wishes to temporarily practice. *The inclusion of the National Register and CPQ columns in this table is in part because a state may use one or both to help validate equivalence of requirements.* For psychologists seeking a license in a state in which he/she is not currently licensed, NR and/or CPQ should speed the process of obtaining that license. However, there is no guarantee that consent will be given. Many jurisdictions require payment of a fee and/or a period of advance notice to the Board of one's intent to temporarily practice psychology in that jurisdiction. Some require a jurisprudence or other special examination.

[2] The CPQ is the Certificate of Professional Qualification in Psychology issued by the ASPPB to indicate that the individual is currently licensed for the independent practice of psychology for at least five

years, and has not been disciplined by a licensing board in any jurisdiction. The psychologist must also have a Ph.D. or Psy.D. or equivalent, have passed the national examination, and have had appropriate supervision. The last two provisions may be waived if the individual was licensed/certified prior to 1981.

[3] Most jurisdictions that honor the National Register listing "waive documentation of doctoral degree, internship and postdoctoral year, and EPPP [national psychology licensing test] score" (National Register Web site, accessed August 30, 2006). Exceptions are noted in the table.

[4] Confirmed by personal communication with the **Alabama** Board, July 21, 2004. A psychologist may testify without an Alabama license, but may not conduct an evaluation within the state without an Alabama license. Consistent with ASPPB listing as of August 30, 2006. A certificate may be granted to psychologists licensed in other jurisdictions "if in the public interest to do so" (§34-26-45).

[5] **Alaska** §12 AAC 60.035. "COURTESY LICENSE. (a) A courtesy license authorizes the licensee to practice psychology for no more than 30 days in a 12-month period. An applicant will only be issued one courtesy license in that person's lifetime. A courtesy licensee shall submit a report to the board each month during the period of courtesy licensure indicating the number of days practiced under the courtesy license during the month." Must apply at least 30 days prior to beginning to practice unless "the applicant has shown reasonable cause or excusable neglect."

[6] **Arizona** Board Web site, accessed May 27, 2005: "Pursuant to A.R.S. §32-2075(A)(4), you may practice for up to 20 days per year if the activities and services conducted in Arizona are within your customary area of practice and are not otherwise in violation of Board statutes and rules and the client, public and the consumer is notified of the limited nature of these activities and services and that you are not licensed in Arizona."

[7] **Arkansas** §17-97-103(2). "Nothing in this chapter prevents the provision of expert testimony by psychologists who are exempted by this chapter." Board Rules & Regulations §5.6.D and E: "It is not considered to be practicing if the licensed individual from another jurisdiction is involved in … [o]ne-time case consultation, with prior Board approval … . The one-time licensed individual from another jurisdiction must notify the Board at the time, or in advance if possible, of any such consultation."

[8] Bylaws, **British Columbia** Board, §46: "(1) A person who satisfies the requirements for registration under section 45 or 45.1, other than the requirement in section 45(2)(d) or 45.1(2)(e), as applicable, may apply for temporary registration to practice psychology for a period of 15 consecutive days in a calendar year. (2) An applicant … may only hold a temporary registration twice in any calendar year."

[9] **California** Business and Professional Code §2912: "Nothing in this chapter shall be construed to restrict or prevent a person who is licensed or certified as a psychologist in another state or territory of the United States or in a foreign country from offering psychological services in this state for a period not to exceed 30 days in any calendar year."

[10] **Colorado** Mental Health Statute §12-43-215(9): "The provisions of this article shall not apply to a person who resides in another state and who is currently licensed or certified as a psychologist … in that state to the extent that the licensed or certified person performs activities or services in this state, if the activities and services … (b) Do not exceed twenty days per year in this state; … [and it is] (d) Disclosed to the public that the person is not licensed or certified in this state."

[11] **Delaware** Statutes, Title 24, Chapter 35, Subchapter II, §3510(c): "Nothing in this chapter shall be construed to prohibit the practice of psychology in this State by a person holding an earned doctoral degree in psychology from an institution of higher education, who is licensed or certified as a psychologist under the laws of another jurisdiction; provided, that the aggregate of 6 days of professional services as a psychologist, per calendar year, under the provision of this subsection is not exceeded."

[12] §490.014 **Florida** statutes: "(2) No person shall be required to be licensed or provisionally licensed under this chapter who … (e) Is not a resident of the state but offers services in this state, provided: 1. Such services are performed for no more than 5 days in any month and no more than 15 days in any calendar year; and 2. Such nonresident is licensed or certified by a state or territory of the United States, or by a foreign country or province."

[13] **Georgia** Code Chapter 43-39.7(8): "An individual licensed to practice psychology in another jurisdiction may practice psychology in Georgia without applying for a license, so long as the requirements

for a license in the other jurisdiction are equal to or exceed the requirements for licensure in Georgia, and the psychologist limits that person's practice in Georgia to no more than 30 days per year."

[14] **Hawaii** statutes, §465-9: "A person not licensed in the State who wishes to engage in the practice of psychology for a period not to exceed ninety days within a calendar year shall petition the board for a temporary permit."

[15] §24.12.01(300) of the **Idaho** Administrative Code indicates that "[n]o temporary licensed to practice psychology will be issued by the board." The Idaho Board of Psychological Examiners has begun discussion of temporary licensure, but, even if approved, it will take some time to change the Code. (Personal communication with the Board, January 30, 2006).

[16] Confirmed by personal communication from the **Illinois** Board, July 27, 2004. Consistent with statute and administrative code as of October, 2005. Penalty for unlicensed practice: civil fine up to $5,000 for each offense (225 ILCS 15/16.5), and/or a Class B misdemeanor for the first offense and a Class 4 felony for subsequent violations (ILCL 15/26).

[17] "SECTION 69. IC 25-33-1-4.5 IS ADDED TO THE **INDIANA** CODE AS A NEW SECTION TO READ AS FOLLOWS [EFFECTIVE JULY 1, 2006]: Sec. 4.5. (a) A person who: (1) is licensed to practice psychology by any board or licensing agency of another state or jurisdiction; and (2) meets the requirements established by the board; may be issued a temporary psychology permit limited by terms and conditions considered appropriate by the board. A limited scope temporary psychology permit issued under this subsection is valid for a nonrenewable period of not more than thirty (30) days. A psychologist may practice under a limited scope psychology permit not more than thirty (30) days every two (2) years. (b) The board may adopt rules under section 3 of this chapter establishing requirements for limited scope temporary psychology permits. (c) An individual who holds a limited scope temporary psychology permit under this section may be disciplined by the board under IC 25-1-9." Retrieved June 29, 2006 from http://www.kse50.com/billdatabase/billTexts.php?show=IN+SB+0333.

[18] **Iowa** Chapter 240.8 (154(b). "Exemption to licensure. Psychologists residing outside the state of Iowa and intending to practice in Iowa under the provisions of Iowa Code section 154B.3(5) shall file a summary of intent to practice and provide verification of the license from the other jurisdiction. The summary shall be submitted to and approved by the board prior to practice in Iowa. The exemption shall be valid for 10 consecutive business days or not to exceed 15 business days in any 90-day period. The summary and supporting documentation shall be accompanied by a check or money order."

[19] **Kansas** K.S.A. §74-5345: "A psychologist who is not a resident of this state and offers professional services in this state for not more than ten (10) days in any calendar year is exempt from the provisions of this act." K.S.A. 74-5316: "The Board may grant a temporary license without examination, valid for a period not to exceed 90 days in one calendar year, to a nonresident psychologist who could be licensed in this state and who is temporarily employed to come into the state to render psychological services, the fee for which shall be $15."

[20] **Kentucky** §319.015(8). The practice of psychology does not include "[a]ny nonresident temporarily employed in this state from rendering psychological services for not more than thirty (30) days every two (2) years, if he or she holds a valid current license or certificate as a psychologist in his or her home state or country and registers with the board prior to commencing practice in the Commonwealth." Note also that §201 KAR 26:215 requires a written notice to the Board giving the dates of intended practice and other information. The visiting psychologist is also required to "submit a written report to the board of each date on which psychological services were rendered in this state, and the location of the site of those services."

[21] **Louisiana** R.S. 37-2365.D. "Any nonresident duly licensed or certified for independent practice as a psychologist in the state of his residence, and which state will permit residents of this State a like and similar privilege as provided herein may, if associated with a psychologist who is a resident of the State of Louisiana and licensed under this Chapter, practice as a psychologist for a period not to exceed thirty days in any calendar year to the same extent and manner as if licensed in this state."

[22] Personal communication with the **Maine** licensing board, July 21, 2004. Still under discussion as of June 22, 2006 (personal communication with the Maine licensing board).

[23] Personal communication with the **Manitoba** Board, July 21, 2004.
[24] Personal communication with the **Maryland** Board, July 21, 2004. Also, the Board of Psychologists' Web site (www.dhmh.state.md.us/psych/faq.html, accessed April 16, 2006) indicates that "If you are licensed in another state and want to work temporarily in Maryland you may petition the Board for a temporary exception … . Please put your request in writing to the Board and include a copy of your license and curriculum vitae. Please mention in your letter the nature of your work, when it will occur, and how long you will be working temporarily in Maryland."
[25] **Massachusetts** "Chapter 112: Section 124. Temporary licenses. The board may grant a temporary license for a period not to exceed one year to a psychologist with legal residence outside the commonwealth to practice within the commonwealth provided he registers with the board and practices in consultation with, or under the supervision of, a licensed psychologist or possesses qualifications acceptable to the board."
[26] §333.16171(h) of the **Michigan** Public Health Code: "License for practice of health profession; exemptions. An individual residing adjacent to the land border between this state and an adjoining state who is authorized under the laws of that state to practice a health profession and whose practice may extend into this state, but who does not maintain an office or designate a place to meet patients or receive calls in this state."
[27] §148.916. A psychologist licensed, certified, or registered in another jurisdiction at the doctoral level may practice psychology in **Minnesota** for up to seven days per year as a "psychological consultant." If that is not enough time, the psychologist may "apply to the board for guest licensure [to permit practice for up to] 30 days per calendar year. Application [for guest licensure] shall be made no less than 30 days prior to the expected date of practice in Minnesota and shall be subject to approval by the board or its designee."
[28] Personal communication with the **Mississippi** Board, October 24, 2005: "Temporary practice: … Such practice must be limited in scope and duration, not exceeding ten (10) days during a consecutive twelve (12) month period. The psychologist shall report the nature of such practice to the Board prior to providing such service and shall make available to the Board a current copy of his/her license or verification of a valid licensed in said jurisdiction."
[29] §337.045 "Nothing in sections 337.010 to 337.090 shall in any way limit … : (5) The practice of psychology in the state of **Missouri** for a temporary period by a person who resides outside the state of Missouri, and who is licensed or certified to practice psychology in another state and conducts the major part of his or her practice outside the state. The temporary period shall not exceed ten consecutive business days in any period of ninety days, nor in the aggregate exceed fifteen business days in any nine-month period; or (6) The provision of expert testimony by psychologists or other persons who are otherwise exempted by sections 337.010 to 337.090."
[30] **Montana** §37-17-104. "This chapter does not prevent … : (4) the activities and services of a person who is not a resident of this state in rendering consulting psychological services in this state when these services are rendered for a period which does not exceed, in the aggregate, 60 days during a calendar year if the person is authorized under the laws of the state or country of that person's residence to perform these activities and services; however, these persons shall report to the department the nature and extent of the services in this state prior to providing those services if the services are to exceed 10 days in a calendar year."
[31] **Nebraska** §155-004.03 "THIRTY DAYS PRACTICE WITHIN A ONE YEAR PERIOD: A person holding a doctoral degree in psychology … who is licensed as a psychologist under the laws of another jurisdiction and who provides no more than an aggregate of 30 days of professional services as a psychologist during the 12 month period beginning with the first date of issuance may be issued a letter to practice." The person must submit an application indicating the planned nature of the practice. §155-004.03F "Board Recommendation: The Board will act within 150 days upon all completed applications for temporary practice."
[32] **Nevada:** §NRS 641.410 "Practice by nonresident as consultant. A psychologist, not a resident of Nevada and not licensed in Nevada, who is certified or licensed in another state whose requirements for certification or licensure are equivalent to the requirements of this chapter is not subject to the provisions of this chapter if he does not practice psychology in the State of Nevada for over 30 days in any 1 calendar year, and if he is invited as a consultant by a psychologist licensed in Nevada."

[33] The **New Brunswick** Board is working on a mechanism to permit nonprovince-licensed psychologists to do evaluations. Until enacted, a psychologist could work under the supervision of a N.B. licensed psychologist. The psychologist must also tell the client, the court, and any other relevant individual or body that he/she is licensed in [jurisdiction] but is not licensed in **New Brunswick**, and the specific purpose for being in the Province. Prior notification of the Board of the purpose, dates, and location of the evaluation and testimony is requested. (Personal communications with New Brunswick Board, November 1 and November 4, 2004.)

[34] **New Hampshire:** "The Board considers expert testimony permissible as long as you are not doing treatment, your opinion is based on your knowledge and your role as an expert is for litigation purposes only. The Board would consider expressing to the Court any expert opinions about recommendations for treatment options to be conducted by someone else as practicing without a license." This policy became effective July 16, 2004. (Personal communication with the New Hampshire board, July 31, 2004).

[35] §45:14B-6(d): "As a practicing psychologist for a period not to exceed 10 consecutive business days or 15 business days in any 90 day period, if he resides outside, and his major practice is outside, of the State of **New Jersey** and gives the board a summary of his qualifications and a minimum of 10 days' written notice of his intention to practice in the State of New Jersey ... provided he ... is certified or licensed in another State."

[36] **New Mexico:** §16.22.3.8(G)(2): "The out-of-state psychologist shall file with the Board in writing a request for permission to conduct a court-ordered independent examination at least thirty (30) days in advance ... and shall identify a New Mexico licensed psychologist ... who agrees to sponsor the out-of-state psychologist .... (3) The Board will grant limited permission to conduct a court-ordered independent examination only if the out-of-state psychologist acknowledges and agrees to the following limitations and conditions: ... (b) The psychologist shall agree that the psychological services shall be limited to only services reasonable and necessary to satisfy the requirements of a specific court-ordered examination in an individual cause of action." Treatment is absolutely prohibited. "(c) The psychologist shall agree to perform the services in New Mexico within the number of days specified by the Board .... (6) The sponsoring psychologist shall agree in writing to sponsor an out-of-state psychologist."

[37] Psychology licensing board Web site FAQs: Exceptions: "The representation as a psychologist and the rendering of services in **New York** State by a person who resides outside of this State provided the person has filed with the Department evidence that he or she has been licensed or certified in another State .... Such temporary period shall not exceed ten consecutive business days in one consecutive 90-day period or in the aggregate exceed more than fifteen business days in one 90-day period." (Accessed October 21, 2005 at www.op.nysed.gov/psych-licques.htm.)

[38] "Under the Psychologists Act, only a person registered by the NBEP [**Newfoundland/Labrador**] Board of Examiners in Psychology] may use the designation, psychologist .... The Psychologists Act does not currently provide for temporary registration. Psychologists, registered in other jurisdictions, who wish to practice in Newfoundland and Labrador, however briefly, must be registered with the NBEP. Visiting psychologists are advised to consider the time needed to process applications, and contact the Registrar for more information." Accessed October 25, 2005 at http://nbep.info/.

[39] §90-270.4(a). "Nothing in this Article shall prevent the provision of expert testimony by psychologists who are otherwise exempted by this act." §90-270.4(f): "Nothing in this Article is to be construed as prohibiting a psychologist who is not a resident of **North Carolina** who holds an earned doctoral, masters, or specialist degree in psychology ... from engaging in the practice of psychology, including the provision of health services, in this State for up to five days in any calendar year. All such psychologists shall comply with the supervision requirements established by the Board, and shall notify the Board in writing of their intent to practice in North Carolina, prior to the provision of any services in this State." §90-270.5(f): "A nonresident psychologist who is either licensed or certified by a similar Board in another jurisdiction ... may be issued a temporary licensed by the Board for the practice of psychology in the State for a period not to exceed the aggregate of 30 days in any calendar year."

[40] **North Dakota** §43-32-30. Persons exempt from this chapter. (3). "A nonresident licensed or certified in the state of the person's residence who does not practice psychology in this state for a period of more than thirty days in any calendar year."

[41] According to the **Nova Scotia** Web site, "NSBEP extends temporary registration to colleagues from other jurisdictions as a courtesy. Psychologists registered and in good standing in other jurisdictions may apply for temporary registration in Nova Scotia. Temporary registration is available to psychologists: (a) once per calendar year (b) for a maximum of 45 working days. All placements on the Courtesy Registrar must be approved by the Registrar." The applicant must submit proof of registration/licensure and a list of planned work dates and the nature of the work, and wait for approval. The procedure is detailed at http://www.nsbep.org/pages/requirements.html. Last accessed August 31, 2006.
[42] **Ohio** §4732.22 "Exceptions … . B) Any nonresident temporarily employed in this state to render psychological services for not more than thirty days a year, who, in the opinion of the board, meets the standards … of the Revised Code, and who holds whatever license or certificate, if any, is required for such practice in his home state or home country."
[43] **Oklahoma** §59-1353. "Activities exempt … . 9. The activities and services of a nonresident of this state who renders consulting or other psychological services if such activities and services are rendered for a period which does not exceed in the aggregate more than five (5) days during any year … . Such person shall inform the Board prior to initiation of the services."
[44] "**Ontario** does not have temporary licenses for psychologists. The only way a person can practice psychology in Ontario as a psychologist is to register with the College through the usual application process" (Personal communication with the Ontario board, November 7, 2005).
[45] **Oregon** §675.063. "Limited permit to practice as psychologist … . [T]he State Board of Psychologist Examiners may issue a limited permit to practice as a psychologist to an applicant holding a certificate or licensed to practice psychology issued by another state … The limited period shall be valid for a period of not more than 180 calendar days in any 24-month period." "OAR 858-101-0055 is the administrative rule regarding Limited Permits." Requires an advance application, proof of licensure, a specific description of planned work, payment of a fee, and a notarized statement that one has reviewed and understands Oregon laws regarding psychological practice and will follow those laws.
[46] **Pennsylvania** §41.52(c) "[A] psychologist licensed for independent practice by a statutory board of psychologist examiners or another state or a province of Canada … may practice psychology on temporary assignment in this Commonwealth for up to 6 months, after written notification to the Board and receipt from the Board, in writing, of temporary permission to practice … . A psychologist on temporary assignment in this Commonwealth for an aggregate of no more than 14 days is exempted from the notification requirement."
[47] **Prince Edward Island** §P-27.1. "10. [special certificate] (1) Pursuant to section 11 of the Act, the Board may, without the applicant's having to fully provide all of the materials required by section 2, grant a special certificate of registration to a person who pays the prescribed fee and who is comparably registered in another jurisdiction recognized by the Board, for the purpose of visiting the province for a brief period of practice or under such other unusual circumstances as the Board may determine."
[48] "**Québec** Psychological Order does not have any provision in its bylaws regarding temporary practice other than for French language. In Québec there are yet no reserved act in the field of psychology, only the title of "psychologist" is reserved. It would not be against the law for an American psychologist to come to Québec to evaluate a client and testify in court … . That psychologist would not be able to advertise himself as "a psychologist registered in Québec" and ethics would require that the client being evaluated and the judge be clearly informed of that reality." (Personal communication from the Secrétaire général of the Ordre des psychologues du Québec, November 8, 2005.)
[49] **Rhode Island** §5-44-11(b). "A psychologist licensed or certified under the laws of another jurisdiction may be authorized by the board to practice psychology for a maximum of one year; provided, that the psychologist has applied to the board of licensure and has met the educational and experience requirements for licensure in this state."
[50] **Saskatchewan:** There is no courtesy register permitting temporary practice. However, the College of Psychologists has a fast-track procedure, especially if one holds a CPQ or is listed in the National Register. An oral examination requirement will be waived. If the psychologist has a clean record and there are no complications, the process would take up to three months. "Expert witness testimony is

acceptable, but any seeing of the patient, for assessment or service, requires registration." (Personal communications with David Randall, Ph.D., R.D. Psych., Registrar, Saskatchewan College of Psychologists, October 20, 2004 and November 2, 2005.)

[51] **South Carolina** §40-55-110. "A person or firm of consultants not licensed in this State and nonresidents of this State who wishes [sic] to perform practices under the provisions of this chapter for a period not to exceed sixty days within a calendar year, must petition the Board for a temporary permit to perform such practices. If the petitioner is licensed or certified in another state … , a permit will be issued for a fee." §40-55-170. "A person who practices or offers to practice psychology without being licensed as required by this chapter is guilty of a felony and, upon conviction, must be fined not more than fifty thousand dollars or imprisoned for more than one year."

[52] **South Dakota** §36-27A-11. "A psychologist licensed by another state may practice within this state for a maximum of six months, during which time his credentials must be reviewed and his application for licensing accepted or denied. With 30 calendar days after the commencement of his practice in this state, he shall apply to the Board of Examiners of Psychologists for licensing." In other words, temporary practice is permitted for up to 30 days without applying for a license.

[53] **Tennessee** §1180-2.05(f). "A psychologist licensed in another jurisdiction can apply to the Board for authorization to perform functions [of a psychologist] for a period not to exceed twelve (12) days within a one (1) year period. A written request for authorization must include the reason for the authorization, the dates of these activities, and the name of [and a letter from] the supervising Tennessee psychologist."

[54] **Texas** Administrative Code §463.27. "A person licensed as a psychologist and in good standing in another state, may perform psychological services … for a period of time not to exceed 30 days within a calendar year. Persons applying for temporary privileges must apply in writing to the Board at least 30 days prior to the expected working days in Texas. The petition for temporary privileges must include but shall not be limited to psychological services to be performed; the specific dates of the psychological services; and documentation of credentials."

[55] **Utah** §58-1-307. "Exemptions from licensure. (1) Except as otherwise provided by statute or rule, the following persons may engage in the practice of their occupation or profession, subject to the stated circumstances and limitations, without being licensed under this title … . (d) an individual residing in another state and licensed to practice a regulated occupation or profession in that state, who is called in for a consultation by an individual licensed in this state, and the services provided are limited to that consultation … . 58-61-307. Exemptions from licensure. (4) an individual who is offering expert testimony in any proceeding before a court, administrative hearing, deposition upon the order of any court or other body having power to order the deposition, or proceedings before any master, referee, or alternative dispute resolution provider."

[56] **Vermont** §2.12 "Temporary License. A person licensed and in good standing to practice psychology in another jurisdiction may apply to the Board for a temporary license to practice in Vermont for no more than 10 days or 80 hours in any 12-month period. Information about temporary licenses and associated fees may be obtained from the Office."

[57] **Virginia** §54.1-3601(10). "Exemption from requirements of licensure. … Any person duly licensed as a psychologist in another state or the District of Columbia who testifies as a treating psychologist or who is employed as an expert for the purpose of possibly testifying as an expert witness." "There is nothing in statute or regulations that address[es] a time period." (Personal communication with the Board of Psychology, November 3, 2005.)

[58] **Washington** RCW §18.83.082 "Temporary permit. A person, not licensed in this state, who wishes to perform practices under the provisions of this chapter for a period not to exceed ninety days within a calendar year, must petition the board for a temporary permit to perform such practices. If the person is licensed or certified in another state deemed by the board to have standards equivalent to this chapter … a permit may be issued. No fee shall be charged for such temporary permit."

[59] **West Virginia** §30-21-3. "License required. … Provided … That no such license or temporary permit shall be required for a psychologist who is not a resident of this state, who is the holder of a license or certificate to engage in the practice of psychology issued by a state with licensing or certification requirements determined by the board to be at least as great as those provided in this article, who has no regular place of practice in this state and who engages in the practice of psychology in this state for a period of not more than ten days in any calendar year."

[60] **Wisconsin** §455.03 "Temporary practice. A psychologist who is licensed or certified by a similar examining board of another state or territory of the United States or of a foreign country or province … may offer services as a psychologist in this state for not more than 60 working days in any year without holding a license issued under §455.04 (1). The psychologist shall report to the examining board the nature and extent of his or her practice in this state if it exceeds 20 working days within a year."
[61] **Wyoming** §33-27-114. Exemptions. "(d) … Nothing in this act shall prevent the provision of expert testimony by psychologists who are exempted by this act. Persons holding an earned doctoral degree in psychology from an institution of higher education may use the title "psychologist" in conjunction with the activities permitted in this subsection."

Thin Skulls, Eggshell Personalities, and Crumbling Skulls

The law of torts indicates that the tortfeasor is liable whether the stressor/trauma caused the injury or aggravated a preexisting condition. In most cases, there will be some combination of the two: a direct psychological/emotional injury and a degree to which preexisting problems are exacerbated by the traumatic event. The U.S. Department of Health and Human Services (1999) "Mental Health: A Report of the Surgeon General" indicates that, during any year, 28% of the population has a diagnosable mental or substance abuse disorder. The Population and Public Health Branch (PPHB) of Health Canada estimates the annual prevalence in Canada to be 20% (Health Canada, 2004). Since most disorders are relatively time-limited, the lifetime prevalence of diagnosable mental disorders is much larger than these figures. In practice, then, the likelihood that a traumatized individual has a diagnosable mental or substance abuse disorder is about 20–28%, whereas the likelihood that the individual has had a disorder at some prior point in his or her life is substantially greater.

The fact that a given plaintiff may have a preexisting or prior diagnosable mental disorder led to the concept of the "thin-skulled man" or "eggshell personality" or variations on those terms. A common example is when an elderly individual is injured. There is a relatively high base rate for symptoms of, or similar to, Posttraumatic Stress Disorder (PTSD) in these individuals, for example, cognitive impairment, difficulty sleeping, and mood disorders, and/or the individual had experienced a major trauma prior to the one in question in a current case. As in any case, the psychologist must evaluate, to the degree possible, the preinjury status of the individual, the additional problems associated with the current trauma index event, and the affect of the current trauma on the individual's ability to function. However, this is made more difficult by the high base rate of certain symptoms and, possibly, by the lower level of daily activity of the elderly individual. Given that most elderly individuals do not hold regular jobs, lost income is often not an issue, but loss of the quality of life and treatment for the psychological and physical injuries caused by the traumatic incident may be significant, including the possibility of long-term nursing home care (Miller, 2001).

Importantly, a traumatic event means different things to different people, based on the individual's history of experience with trauma and other factors. Thus, *it is the individual's appraisal of the event, rather than the event itself, that is generally responsible for the specific affect of a trauma on a specific individual.* Some combination of the meaning of a stressful event for an individual and the resilience of that individual, together with such factors as temperament and personality, determines the actual affect of the stressor on a given individual. (Levy & Rosenberg, 2003). The resilient individual may experience no significant loss of functioning, and the trauma may quickly change from a stressor to an opportunity for growth (Maddi, 2005; Linley & Joseph, 2005).

The Supreme Court of Canada discussed a variation, the "crumbling skull," in *Athey v. Leonati*, (1996) 3 S.C.R. 458. The case involved an individual who was in two motor vehicle accidents in 1991, one in February and one in April. In the fall of that year his physician permitted him to resume his regular exercise routine. Athey herniated a disk. The Supreme Court indicated that

> [t]he so-called "crumbling skull" rule simply recognizes that the pre-existing condition was inherent in the plaintiff's "original position." The defendant need not put the plaintiff in a position *better* than his or her original position. The defendant is liable for the injuries caused, even if they are extreme, but need not compensate the plaintiff for any debilitating effects of the pre-existing condition *which the plaintiff would have experienced anyway*. The defendant is liable for the additional damage but not the pre-existing damage [citations omitted]. Likewise, if there is a measurable risk that the pre-existing condition would have detrimentally affected the plaintiff in the future, regardless of the defendant's negligence, then this can be taken into account in reducing the overall award [citations omitted]. This is consistent with the general rule that the plaintiff must be returned to the position he would have been in, with all of its attendant risks and shortcomings, and not a better position [emphasis added].

In a crumbling skull case, then, if there had been a preexisting condition that would, without the traumatic event, still proceed to follow its course, the defendant need not compensate the plaintiff for that degree of damage attributable to the progression of that condition. In *Athey*, the Canadian Supreme Court ruled that the herniated disk would not have occurred but for the motor vehicle accidents, making the crumbling skull irrelevant, and there was accordingly no reduction in the monetary award to the plaintiff on this basis. Rather, the "thin-skulled man" principle was more appropriate to the circumstances of this case and the award was justified on that basis. These same principles have been recommended for application in workers' compensation cases by the Royal Commission on Workers' Compensation in British Columbia (Royal Commission on Workers' Compensation in British Columbia, 1999).

Searches of Loislaw and Findlaw identified no U.S. cases in which the term "crumbling skull" was used. However, a Louisiana case (*Miramon v. Bradley*, 701 So.2d 475 (La. App. 1 Cir., 9/23/97)) contains the same principle. A woman had been in car accidents in 1988 and 1990. She had serious symptoms after the first accident, and was still in treatment at the time of the second accident. "All of her treating physicians and therapists agreed that the second accident exacerbated Ms. Miramon's problems" (p. 477). Because the experts could not specify a single factor that caused the exacerbation, the trial court denied Ms. Miramon any recovery. The appellate court reversed and ordered that both medical expenses and compensation for pain and suffering be paid to Ms. Miramon on the basis that, "if a defendant's tortious conduct aggravates a pre-existing condition, the defendant is liable to the extent of the aggravation. ... This is true even though the tortious conduct is not the sole factor in the aggravation, but is a significant contributing factor" (p. 478).

The Other Major Pretestimony Task of the Expert: Educating the Attorney

Relatively few attorneys are well versed in the evaluation, diagnosis, and treatment of psychological disorders. Accordingly, they retain an expert in part because they need to know whether the expert believes that there *is* a clinical case to be made, and that it is possible to identify a causal link between the traumatic incident and the symptoms of the plaintiff. At the beginning of most cases, the primary function of the expert is to assess the plaintiff and the degree to which a causal nexus can be identified and, when evidence has been accumulated and reviewed, whether it adequately supports the presence of that causal nexus. Thus, well before testimony at deposition or trial, the expert's task is likely to be educating the retaining attorney regarding the clinical issues in the case. Whether the case moves forward is generally based upon the belief of both the expert and the attorney that a causal nexus exists in both clinical and legal areas (Gutheil & Bursztajn, 2003).

It should be noted that, although experts are commonly deposed in tort cases in the United States, experts in Canada are not deposed prior to trial. Rather, the expert's report is normally given to the other side well (e.g., 90 days) before the scheduled trial, and entered into evidence at the trial (Macartney-Filgate & Snow, 2004).

Expert Testimony

When the expert testifies, he or she has the task of teaching the judge and/or jury regarding the methods used in the evaluation, the data derived from the evaluation, the conclusions derived from the data, and the opinions formed on the basis of the conclusions. At the same time, the expert needs to keep from boring the trier of fact by presenting too much detail, without leaving out any essential details. It is strongly recommended that visual aids (e.g., flip charts, PowerPoint, etc.) be utilized, as they help the judge and jury learn and understand the information presented (Rogers & Shuman, 2005). Many attorneys prefer experts who regularly teach graduate or undergraduate courses, since they have practiced getting information across to students on many occasions, honing their skill at presentation.

Expert Ethics

American Psychological Association Ethical Principles of Psychologists and Code of Conduct and related codes

The American Psychological Association adopted a revised code of ethics in 2002, which became effective on June 1, 2003. Many of the changes are in direct response to *Daubert* and its progeny. Psychologists have unequivocal ethical responsibility to practice only within areas in which they are competent on the basis of "their education, training, supervised experience, consultation, study, or professional experience" (*Ethical Principles of Psychologists and Code of Conduct* (EPPCC), Std. 2.01(a), 2002). They are also responsible for becoming reasonably familiar with legal rules that govern their conduct when they are functioning in forensic roles (EPPCC, Std. 2.01(f), 2002). Their work is to be based upon "established scientific and professional knowledge" (EPPCC, Std. 2.04, 2002). Their opinions are to be based "on information and techniques sufficient to substantiate their findings" (EPPCC, Std. 9.01(a), 2002). In all cases except those in which only a records review is deemed sufficient for a given purpose, "psychologists provide opinions of the psychological characteristics of individuals only after they have conducted an examination of the individuals adequate to support their statements or conclusions" (EPPCC, Std. 9.01(b), 2002). If a personal examination is not possible, the psychologist must indicate the "probable impact of their limited information on the reliability and validity of their opinions, and appropriate limit the nature and extent of their conclusions or recommendations" (EPPCC, Std. 9.01(b), 2002). Similarly, assessment instruments and methods are to be used only for populations upon which they have been standardized and for which validity and reliability have been established. If the psychologist utilizes instruments and methods that do not meet this requirement, the psychologist is required to indicate how that may impact the validity and reliability of his or her findings and interpretations (EPPCC, Std. 9.02(b), 2003).

Similarly, the Association of State and Provincial Psychology Boards' (ASPPB) *Code of Conduct* indicates that "[a] psychologist rendering a formal professional opinion about a person … shall not do so without direct and substantial professional contact with or a formal assessment of that person" (Section III.A.6, Association of State and Provincial Psychology Boards, 2005).

Psychologists also indicate any significant limitations on their interpretations due to the characteristics of the person being evaluated, for example, language or cultural differences (EPPCC, Std. 9.06, 2002). The *Canadian Code of Ethics for Psychologists* covers essentially the same points as well, though in less detail. Because certain behavior may be considered normal in one culture but aberrant in another, cultural factors must be carefully considered by the evaluator (Briere, 2004).

The above requirements fit well with *Daubert* and its progeny. The ethical psychologist will base his or her reports and testimony on reliable and valid scientific and professional knowledge, to the degree possible, will make it clear when he or she strays from that base, and will indicate why he or she could not strictly adhere to the standard.

Raw Data

An area of contention for many years is the conflicting responsibilities of psychologists and attorneys regarding raw test data. The psychologist has an ethical and legal duty to maintain the integrity of the testing materials, while an attorney wants to obtain all information upon which a psychologist bases his or her opinion. This battle may be eased somewhat by an attempt to differentiate test data from test materials. Thus, test data refers to raw and scaled scores, client/patient responses to test questions or stimuli, and psychologists' notes and recordings concerning client/patient statements and behavior during an examination. Those portions of test materials that include client/patient responses are included in the definition of test data (EPPCC, Std. 9.04(a), 2002).

If the psychologist has a signed release, he or she may provide test data to the client/patient or other persons who are identified in the release. However,

> Psychologists may refrain from releasing test data to protect a client/patient or others from substantial harm or misuse or misrepresentation of the data or the test, recognizing that in many instances release of confidential information under these circumstances is regulated by law (EPPCC, Std. 9.04(a), 2002).

This section is generally taken to indicate that the raw (test) data must be released only to someone who is able to interpret it, that is, another licensed or certified psychologist, to prevent the harm that may occur if the data are misinterpreted or misrepresented.

This Ethical Standard must be considered along with Ethical Standard 9.11, Maintaining Test Security:

> The term *test materials* refers to manuals, instruments, protocols, and test questions or stimuli, which do not include test data as defined in Standard 9.04, Release of Test Data. Psychologists make reasonable efforts to maintain the integrity and security of test materials and other assessment techniques consistent with law and contractual obligations, and in a manner that permits adherence to this Ethics Code [EPPCC, Std. 9.11, 2002].

Thus, test data refer to a specific client/patient and to the responses of that particular individual, while test materials refer to the instrument or test to which the client/patient was responding. Test material, therefore, contains nothing that is unique to a given individual. Taken together, these two Ethical Standards indicate that

(1) Psychologists may provide test data, as defined, to attorneys, provided that the client/patient has given informed consent, in writing, to that release.

(2) However, the psychologist may withhold test data from the client/patient, from the attorney, and/or from others if the psychologist believes that release of the test data may cause substantial harm to the client/patient or others, or if the psychologist believes that the test data that are released may be misused or misrepresented. Release of raw test data to someone who is not trained in its interpretation may, in and of itself, constitute the creation of a potential for misunderstanding, misuse, and/or misrepresentation.
(3) Psychologists are required to follow statutory law related to release of information. Thus, if a state or provincial law prohibits release under conditions or circumstances that exist in a given case, the law would take precedence, and the psychologist would not release the test data. The same would be true if release of the test data was believed by the psychologist to violate the U.S. HIPAA regulations. It is also important to note that "HIPAA does not require release of [records] in situations in which information is compiled in reasonable anticipation of, or for use in, civil, criminal, or administrative actions or proceedings" (Fisher, 2003, p. 195).
(4) If the client/patient has not provided a written, informed consent for release, the psychologist is not permitted to release the test data without specific statutory authority or a court order. A subpoena from an attorney is not a sufficient basis for the release of test data. Attorneys are not trained to understand or evaluate most of the raw data from an evaluation. Therefore, intentional or not, it is likely that they will be unable to validly use or present the data without the assistance of a psychologist retained for that purpose. A psychologist who releases test data with neither a signed, informed consent from the client/patient nor a court order is likely to be in violation of Standard 9.04, as well the statutes and/or administrative code of many jurisdictions.
(5) "Test materials" are defined as the test instruments themselves. If the client/patient responds by writing on the test materials, or if the psychologist writes the individual's responses on the test materials, the test materials become test data, because of the presence of those client/patient responses. If, however, the responses are recorded on a separate document or paper, it is only the responses, not the test questions or stimuli, that may be released.
(6) If the psychologist has been retained by an attorney, appointed by a court, or otherwise retained by an organization rather than by the individual who is being evaluated, the test data does not have to be released to that individual because he or she is not the client.
(7) Whenever possible, psychologists have a responsibility to avoid releasing test materials, due to the need to maintain the integrity and security of those test materials, the contractual agreements between the psychologist and the test publisher, and the need to minimize entry of the test materials into the public domain.
(8) Ethical Standard 9.04 specifies that "test data" includes "psychologists' notes and recordings concerning client/patient statements and behavior during an examination. ... The term 'notes' in this standard is limited to the assessment

or test and does not include psychotherapy notes documenting or analyzing the contents of conversation during a private counseling session."

Adding to the above, the ASPPB *Code of Conduct* (2005) indicates that the "psychologist shall not reproduce or describe in popular publications, lectures, or public presentations psychological tests or other assessment devices in ways that might invalidate them" (III. I. 4).

Kaufmann (2005) adds a psycho-legal perspective, noting that attorneys and their clients could manipulate test results if they had knowledge about test construction, test items, and specific answers, "thereby undermining the conclusions and expert opinions based on those results." Further, since release of this information could reduce the value of the psychological tests, the court's search for truth would be impeded. "The primary rationale for the psychologist nondisclosure privilege is to promote justice" (p. 100). "Court appointed independent evaluators, who protect the objectivity, fairness, and integrity of the testing process, perform a valuable truth-seeking function for the court" (p. 118). "Limiting access to psychological test materials improves the early detection of exaggerated or frivolous claims. ... Seeking truth in courtrooms is a vital interest that outweighs the overly zealous need to discover information in a single case. Justice for all outweighs the needs of a single case. ... Handing test answers to test takers or their attorneys violates the court's rational means of ascertaining the truth" (pp. 125–126). "Reason, experience, and past practice require limiting administration and scoring of psychometric tests to licensed psychologists or those under direct supervision by licensed psychologists" (p. 127). Finally, Kaufmann proposes that both statutes and case law should affirm a privilege that shields psychological test materials and data from public disclosure. "Recognizing a psychologist privilege not to disclose psychological test materials promotes the truth-seeking function of the judiciary and serves public policy" (p. 131).

Specialty Guidelines for Forensic Psychologists

There are also *Specialty Guidelines for Forensic Psychologists* (Committee on Ethical Guidelines for Forensic Psychologists, 1991). The Specialty Guidelines are aspirational, not binding, but many courts and licensing boards have considered them when addressing the conduct of forensic psychologists.

Psychologists, as do most people, tend to support their own opinions and avoid undermining their own conclusions. Statements may therefore be made more strongly than is warranted by the data, and disconfirming data may be left out of the report or testimony. The best reports are generally those that state the hypotheses that were investigated, identifying those that were supported and those that were not, and why. The psychologist who is candid regarding his or her findings is generally able to present a strong case during a direct examination, and to avoid surprises during cross-examination. These psychologists strive for objectivity, whether retained by the plaintiff, the defendant, or the court. Their work is consistent with the forensic specialty guideline requiring that "forensic psychologists are aware that their essential role as expert to the court is to assist the trier of fact to understand the evidence or to determine a fact in issue" (Specialty Guideline VII.F, p. 665).

In contrast, the expert who uses psychological tests or other instruments that have not been validated for the purpose for which they are being used, avoids including disconfirming information in his or her report, and becomes doctrinaire regarding his or her conclusions, is in violation of both ethical principles and standards and of the Specialty Guidelines. The cross-examining attorney, particularly one who has retained a psychologist to review the data, is often able to point out many areas in which these experts fail both the *Daubert* requirements and those of the psychologist's ethical code and forensic guidelines.

Finally, the expert who is testifying will be most likely to come across well to the jury if he or she (1) has credentials that support his/her experience and knowledge base; (2) appears trustworthy; (3) explains technical terms and processes well in lay terms; (4) addresses the pros and cons of each significant interpretation of the data; (5) summarizes his or her conclusions; and (6) is consistent and concise (McGaughey & Walker, 2002).

The *Specialty Guidelines* are undergoing revision as this chapter is being written. The revised *Guidelines* are expected to be adopted in 2007.

The Expert in Danger: Laws, Ethics, and Malpractice

Shuman and Greenberg (2003) indicate that experts frequently report that they are subject to pressure by attorneys to conclude, and state during testimony, that the data reviewed by the expert and the conclusions he or she has reached support the attorney's theory of the case. Thus, while professional ethics dictate that the psychologist is to be impartial and to advocate for his or her data but not for either side in a case, psychologists may feel pressured to abrogate their ethical duty. Further, if the psychologist cites his or her ethical duty during testimony, and is permitted or ordered by the judge to testify on a given point in spite of that duty, the psychologist could be open to discipline by an ethics committee or a state or provincial licensing/certifying board as a result. Psychologists are not immune to either ethics or licensing/certifying actions in any state or province, regardless of their witness, quasi-judicial, or judicial immunity in court. It is also possible that the psychologist will be sued for malpractice by a party that feels harmed by the psychologist's testimony. The legal question generally involves immunity and duty (Shuman, 1994a, 2003 supplement). The North Carolina Medical Board, for example, suspended the license of neurosurgeon Gary Lustgarten in 2002 because of testimony in a medical malpractice case. The Board indicated that Dr. Lustgarten misstated facts and the appropriate standard of care, thereby engaging in unprofessional conduct (North Carolina Medical Board Web site, http://glsuite.ncmedboard.org/DataTier/Documents/Repository/LegacyImages/00/01/07/00010779.tif, last accessed October 13, 2005).

Part of the problem is that each state and province has its own definition of professional practice for each profession. Although all of these practice acts are likely to specify that conducting a psychological assessment falls under the definition of the "practice of psychology," few statutes or administrative codes indicate whether the offering of expert testimony is included in the practice definition (Cohen, 2004). It would behoove every forensic psychologist to try to determine whether his or her state or provincial licensing or certifying board considers the offering of expert testimony to be part of the practice of psychology.

The best (and perhaps only) defense against attacks on one's testimony, Shuman and Greenberg indicate, is to be impartial. They suggest that this impartiality has five components: competence (do not accept a case if one is not competent to give an expert opinion regarding that specific case, and ensure that one has an adequate scientific foundation in the subject area prior to agreeing to serve as an expert); relevance (disclose all information relevant to one's report and planned testimony, including any changes that occur over time or at trial, but not information that is not relevant to one's report or planned testimony); perspective (be familiar with the pleadings by both sides, identify evidence in favor of or adverse to one's own conclusions and the conclusions of any other experts, be prepared to address competing perspectives); balance (weigh each hypothesis fairly, do not allow biases to interfere with one's conclusions, do not testify as an expert for one's own patient); candor (freely give requested relevant information, be candid about the weight given to each hypothesis, do not shade testimony in the direction of the retaining attorney, remember that one will be judged on the basis of the professional standard of care or practice if a complaint is made to an ethics committee or licensing board). Following these recommendations makes an expert's testimony more persuasive, reduces the risk of ethics or malpractice actions, and helps ensure that the testimony of the expert is trustworthy.

According to Sales and Shuman (2005), the competence of an expert may be in issue in another context as well. First, some individuals who are highly expert in one or more areas may agree to testify as an expert in an area of practice in which he or she is not an expert. It is essential that an expert have expertise in the specific area under consideration. Second, an expert may function at a level lower than his or her actual level of expertise due to a failure to adequately prepare for an evaluation and/or testimony. This includes a need for the expert to remain abreast of the professional literature on the topic at issue, because the expert who is not aware of the most recently published research may make errors when testifying. Third, the expert may not adequately understand evidentiary issues in a case, and may as a result make errors that lead to part or all of his or her testimony being struck. The psychologist has an ethical responsibility to ensure that these factors do not interfere with participation in a case. Attorneys need to ask questions regarding these factors to ensure that the case is not jeopardized because of these types of ethical breaches by an expert.

Common Errors in Evaluating Impairment and Disability

Schultz (2003) identifies eight common misconceptions or problems regarding psychological impairment and disability.

(1) "Impairment" and "disability" are often confused. "Impairment" refers to the presence of a diagnosable disorder that makes it more difficult for an individual to function at his or her full capacity. Impairment is determined by clinicians who carefully evaluate the individual and who can, therefore, discuss the individual's difficulty with normal functioning. In contrast, "disability" refers to the relationship of that impairment to the actual work situation, including both psychological and physical demands of a given job, the skills, education, work history, flexibility, and other factors affecting an individual's ability to adequately perform a specific form of work. Clinical and forensic psychologists normally address only impairment, whereas vocational experts (including Industrial/Occupational psychologists) address disability.

(2) It is often assumed that the greater the psychological impairment, the greater the vocational disability. Research does not support a simple linear relationship. If the work environment is in some way similar to the traumatic event, a relatively minor impairment could lead to a substantial vocational disability (e.g., a fireman who acquires a phobia related to fires, or a construction worker who acquires a fear of heights). In contrast, if the work environment has essentially no relationship to the traumatic event, vocational impairment may be minimal.

(3) Standardized tests and clinical assessments often provide minimal data regarding actual or potential work performance ability. The amount of predictive validity possible depends on the assessment instruments used and their ability to forecast relevant vocational disabilities.

(4) The attorney and the expert need to identify the relevant occupational disability questions. Among the possibilities are loss of capacity to work at the former job or occupation, loss of ability to earn as much as was previously earned, the anticipated duration of the disability (and, if different, when it is possible to return to work), whether the person is employable at all, whether the person requires accommodations in order to be able to return to his or her former job or to work at a new job, whether the person needs to change jobs, whether he or she is capable of working at a new job, and whether the person is employable at all.

(5) Further, it is necessary to determine the degree of disability preceding the traumatic event, if any, to contrast with the its degree following the traumatic event.

(6) The individual's perception of his or her disability must be differentiated from the objectively assessed disability.

(7) There must be an assessment of the role of pain in the impairment and disability determinations, if pain has been an issue, while also being aware that pain, depression, and anxiety are often intertwined.
(8) Motivation plays a significant role in recovery, in ability to return to work, and in other areas of recovery of vocational functioning. Unfortunately, it can only be assessed indirectly.

There is an additional consideration in the forensic context. If the expert primarily or exclusively rules out potential causes and results, without clearly ruling in one or more specific causes to a "reasonable degree of certainty," his or her testimony may not be admissible:

> Experts must do something more than just "rule out" other possible causes. They must explain how they were able to "rule in" the product [in a product liability case] in question. If all the expert does is rule out other possible causes, he or she may fail to account for other potential (and sometimes unknown or unthought of) causes. When an expert only rules out causes, the trier of fact knows only what did not cause the harm. This does not necessarily aid the trier of fact in determining what did cause the harm—and that is what the law requires in tort cases, especially those that involve allegedly toxic products. [*Siharath v. Sandoz Pharmaceuticals Corp*, 131 F. Supp.2d 1347 (N.D.Ga. 2001), p. 1371–1372.]

Psychological Harm Resulting from Tort Cases and/or Unnecessary Delays in Resolving Tort Cases

Every tort case involves some degree of interference with the lives of the litigants, including the search for evidence of harm to the litigants, and each step in the process of filing a complaint, undergoing evaluations and depositions, and, in some cases, going through a court trial. Particularly in litigants with significant emotional complaints or other problems with resilience, the iatrogenic effect of this process on the litigant may be a significant part of the trauma with which the plaintiff is dealing (Wayte et al., 2002). People who have PTSD tend to relive the trauma, and to experience the psychological and (if relevant) physical disabilities caused by the traumatic incident, slowing the healing process. By its nature, tort cases force the individual to recall the trauma, preventing to some degree the person's ability to resolve the PTSD (Samra & Connolly, 2004; Samra & Koch, 2002; Scrignar, 1996; Simon & Wettstein, 1997). Plaintiffs discuss the trauma and its consequences with their attorneys until they arrive at a cogent statement that includes all of the material facts. If there is not an early settlement, the trauma and its consequences are likely to be discussed with experts for the plaintiff and defense. There will be further reminders while preparing for and testifying at a deposition, and again in trial. The plaintiff is reminded, overtly and by implication, that nothing important is to be forgotten, since the details may need to be presented to a jury. Bills for treatment, and unpaid bills for other expenses, become conditioned stimuli that evoke reminders of the original trauma. The stress of the litigation is added to the stress from the traumatic event, adding to the suffering of the plaintiff and reducing the potential for psychotherapy to ameliorate symptoms (Strasburger, 1999; Wayte et al., 2002). The potential to resolve the PTSD relatively quickly diminishes, and, with time, a chronic PTSD becomes increasingly likely.

Not surprisingly, research indicates that the shorter the interval between the trauma and the settlement, the less the psychological impairment that is found (Binder, Trimble, & McNeil, 1991). It is important to understand that the settlement does not cause remission. Rather, it removes some anxiety associated with the trauma and the litigation process, permitting the healing process to more fully take hold, something that often cannot take place as long as the litigation continues.

In addition, the lengthier the litigation process, the more likely that the plaintiff will be diagnosed with a chronic PTSD and possibly other anxiety-related disorders. The likelihood that time will heal the individual decreases. Further, since the plaintiff has identifiable PTSD-related anxiety on a daily basis, new stressors are likely to have a greater affect on the person than they would have had if the PTSD were in remission. Even *positive* stressful events, such as marriage or a birth, can exacerbate the PTSD. At the time of trial, the plaintiff may have more PTSD-related psychological problems than when the case was originally filed, due to the addition of stress-related conditions resulting from the posttrauma period. It may be possible to argue that an unnecessarily drawn-out case is, itself, a cause of an exacerbation of the prior psychological/emotional injury, prompting a tort claim or a claim for punitive damages (Ackerman & Kane, 1998a). Further,

> [d]elay exacerbates both the acute and chronic loss that the claimant experiences, and the cost to the injurer and society which they must ultimately pay either directly through tort judgments and disability program payments by means of taxes and insurance premiums, or indirectly because of decreased productivity. [U]necessary delay ... may also exacerbate harm to defendants for whom allegations of fault become the dominant disturbing focus of their lives [Shuman, 2000a, pp. 882–883].

In addition, traumatic stress cases are usually about more than just money. Plaintiffs who feel demeaned or otherwise harmed by the litigation process may fight harder for what they perceive as justice. Several authors have indicated that apologies facilitate settlements prior to trial in civil cases, and that plaintiffs have frequently indicated that "a sincere apology" might have prevented a lawsuit (Shuman, 1994b, 2000a, 2000b; Wayte et al., 2002). Plaintiffs may also feel dignified and empowered by the process of pursuing justice (including having the judge and/or jury indicate that the defendant was in fact at fault) and the perception that the defendant may be prevented from harming others by virtue of the litigation (Ackerman & Kane, 1998a; Shuman, 1994b, 2000a; Shuman & Daley, 1996).

Hundreds of research articles document that stress increases the likelihood that an individual will be susceptible to physical illness, will make errors that cause physical injuries, and will be less productive in his or her occupational/ professional and personal lives. An individual who is a party to a lawsuit will nearly always experience significant stress, particularly at times when he or she must prepare for and appear at a court hearing or a deposition.

Although there continue to be occasional claims that plaintiffs tend to suffer from "compensation neuroses," that is, they continue to show problems as long as the litigation continues but cease to have these problems once the case is settled or won, there is strong evidence that this claim is not correct (Ackerman & Kane, 1998a; Binder & Willis, 1991; Binder & Rohling, 1996; Binder et al., 1991; Bryant & Harvey, 2003; Call, 2003; Samra & Koch, 2002; Shuman, 2000a; Wilson & Moran, 2004). Some people largely recover the ability to function somewhat normally early in the litigation process, whereas many continue to be plagued with serious problems for years postlitigation. Of those who recover only at the end of litigation, some may be responding to no longer having to repeatedly talk about the trauma, no longer having to review documents, the long-awaited absence of having to deal with the litigation process, or no longer having to fear the stressful process of offering testimony, while others may be responding to whatever positive benefits they derived from the litigation (e.g., money, justice, the conclusion that the plaintiff was not at fault) (Shuman, 1994b; Wilson & Moran, 2004).

References

Ackerman, M. J., & Kane, A. W. (1998a). *Psychological experts in personal injury actions* (3rd ed.). New York: Aspen Law and Business.

Ackerman, M. J., & Kane, A. W. (1998b, 2004 supplement). *Psychological experts in divorce actions* (3rd. ed.). New York: Aspen Law and Business.

Ackerman, M. J., & Kane, A. W. (2005). *Psychological experts in divorce actions* (4th ed.). New York: Aspen Law & Business.

American Psychological Association. (2002). Ethical principles of psychologists and code of conduct. *American Psychologist, 57*, 1060–1073.

Ancker, J. S., & Flanagin, A. (2005). *Conflict of interest policies at scientific journals: A cross-disciplinary comparison*. Paper presented at the Fifth International Congress on Peer Review and Biomedical Education, Chicago, September 17, 2005.

Association of State and Provincial Psychology Boards. (2005). *ASPPB code of conduct*. Accessed January 31, 2006 at www.asppb.org.

Athey v. Leonati [1996] 3 S.C.R. 458.

Baer, L. G., & Neal, J. K. (2000). Admissibility of medical causation expert opinions in federal courts, part I: The current state of the law. *The Trial Lawyer, 23*, 323–334.

Binder, L., & Rohling, M. L. (1996). Money matters: A meta-analytic review of the effects of financial incentives on recovery after closed-head injury. *American Journal of Psychiatry, 153*, 7–10.

Binder, R. L., Trimble, M. R., & McNeil, D. E. (1991). The course of psychological symptoms after resolution of lawsuits. *American Journal of Psychiatry, 148*, 1073–1075.

Binder, L., & Willis, S. C. (1991). Assessment of motivation after financially compensable minor head trauma. *Psychological Assessment, 3*, 175–181.

Bowman, M. L. (2003). Problems inherent to the diagnosis of Posttraumatic Stress Disorder. In I. Z. Schulze & D. O. Brady (Eds.), *Psychological injuries at trial* (pp. 820–849). Chicago: American Bar Association.

Briere, J. (2004). *Psychological assessment of adult posttraumatic states* (2nd ed.). Washington, DC: American Psychological Association.

Bryant, R. A., & Harvey, A. G. (2003). The influence of litigation on maintenance of Posttraumatic Stress Disorder. *Journal of Nervous and Mental Disease, 191*, 191–193.

Call, J. A. (2003). Liability for psychological injury: Yesterday and today. In I. Z. Schultz & D. O. Brady (Eds.), *Psychological injuries at trial* (pp. 40–64). Chicago: American Bar Association.

Canadian Psychological Association. (2000). *Canadian code of ethics for psychologists* (3rd ed.). Accessed April 20, 2006 at http://www.cpa.ca/cpasite/userfiles/Documents/Canadian%20Code%20of%20Ethics%20for%20Psycho.pdf.

Cohen, F. L. (2004). The expert medical witness in legal perspective. *The Journal of Legal Medicine, 25*, 185–209.

Committee on Ethical Guidelines for Forensic Psychologists. (1991). Specialty guidelines for forensic psychologists. *Law and Human Behavior, 15*, 655–665.

Egger, M., Wood, L. von Elm, E., Wood, A., Ben Shlomo, Y., & May, M. (2005). *Are reviewers influenced by citations of their own work? Evidence from the International Journal of Epidemiology*. Paper presented at the Fifth International Congress on Peer Review and Biomedical Education, Chicago, September 17, 2005.

Exner, J. E., & Erdberg, P. (2005) *The Rorschach: A comprehensive system* (3rd ed.). New York: John Wiley & Sons, Inc.

Faigman, D. L. (2000). The gatekeepers: Scientific expert testimony in the trial process. *The Trial Lawyer, 23*, 335–346.

Faigman, D. L., & Monahan, J. (2005). Psychological evidence at the dawn of the law's scientific age. *Annual Review of Psychology, 56*, 631–659.

Faust, D. (2003). Holistic thinking is not the whole story: Alternative or adjunct approaches for increasing the accuracy of legal evaluations. *Assessment, 10*, 428–441.

Faust D., & Heard, K. V. (2003). Biased experts: Some practical suggestions for identifying and demonstrating unfair practices. In I. Z. Schulze & D. O. Brady (Eds.). *Psychological injuries at trial* (pp. 1706–1739). Chicago: American Bar Association.

Fisher, C. (2003). *Decoding the ethics code: A practical guide for psychologists*. Thousand Oaks: Sage.

Garb, H. N. (2003). Incremental validity and the assessment of psychopathology in adults. *Psychological Assessment, 15*, 508–520.

Garb, H. N., Wood, J. M., Lilienfeld, S. O., & Nezworski, M. T. (2005). Roots of the Rorschach controversy. *Clinical Psychology Review, 25*, 97–118.

Garcia-Berthou, E., & Alcaraz, C. (2004). Incongruence between test statistics and p values in medical papers. *BMC Medical Research Methodology, 4*, retrieved August 12, 2004 from www.biomedcentral.com/1471-2288/4/13.

Goodman-Delahunty, J. (1997). Forensic psychological expertise in the wake of *Daubert. Law & Human Behavior, 21*, 121–140.

Greenberg, S. (2003). Personal injury examinations in torts for emotional distress. In I. B. Weiner (Series Ed.) & A. M. Goldstein (Vol. Ed.), *Handbook of psychology: Vol. 11, Forensic psychology* (pp. 233–258). Hoboken, NJ: Wiley.

Greenberg, S. A., Otto, R. K., & Long, A. C. (2003). The utility of psychological testing in assessing emotional damages in personal injury litigation. *Assessment, 10*, 411–419.

Greenberg, S. A., & Shuman, D. W. (1997). Irreconcilable conflict between therapeutic and forensic roles. *Professional Psychology: Research and Practice, 28*, 50–57.

Gronnerod, C. (2003). Temporal stability in the Rorschach Method: A meta-analytic review. *Journal of Personality Assessment, 80*, 272–293.

Gutheil, T. G., & Bursztajn, H. (2003). Avoiding ipse dixit mislabeling: Post-*Daubert* approaches to expert clinical opinions. *Journal of the American Academy of Psychiatry and the Law, 31*, 205–210.

Hagan, P. (2003a). Review queries usefulness of peer review. *The Scientist*, retrieved October 19, 2005 from www.the-scientist.com/news/20030128/05/.

Hagan, P. (2003b). Peer review under scrutiny. *The Scientist*, retrieved October 19, 2005 from www.the-scientist.com/news/20030203/04/.

Haney, C., & Smith, A. (2003). Science, law, and psychological injury: the *Daubert* standards and beyond. In I. Z. Schulze & D. O. Brady (Eds.), *Psychological injuries at trial* (pp. 184–201). Chicago: American Bar Association.

Hartlage, L. C. (1989). *Behavior Change Inventory*. Clinical Psychology Publishing Co.

Health Canada, retrieved January 25, 2004 from http://www.hc-sc.gc.ca/english/.

Heilbrun, K. (2001). *Principles of forensic mental health assessment*. New York: Kluwer/ Plenum.

Heilbrun, K., Marczyk, G. R., & DeMatteo, D. (2002). *Forensic mental health assessment: A casebook*. Oxford: Oxford University Press.

Hibbard, S. (2003). A critique of Lilienfeld et al.'s (2000) The scientific status of projective techniques. *Journal of Personality Assessment, 80*, 260–271.

Hunsley, J. (2003). Introduction to the special section on incremental validity and utility in clinical assessment. *Psychological Assessment, 15*, 443–445.

Hunsley, J., & Bailey, J. M. (2001). Whither the Rorschach? An Analysis of the Evidence. *Psychological Assessment, 13*, 472–485.

Hunsley, J., & Meyer, G. J. (2003). The incremental validity of psychological testing and assessment: conceptual, methodological, and statistical issues. *Psychological Assessment, 15*, 446–455.

Ioannidis, J. P. A. (2005). Contradicted and initially stronger effects in highly cited clinical research. *Journal of the American Medical Association, 294*, 218–228.

Kaplan, D. (2005). How to fix peer review: Separating its two functions—improving manuscripts and judging their scientific merit—would help. *Journal of Child and Family Studies, 14*, 321–323.

Kassirer, J. P., & Cecil, J. S. (2002). Inconsistency in evidentiary standards for medical testimony. *Journal of the American Medical Association, 288*, 1382–1387.

Kaufmann, P. M. (2005). Protecting the objectivity, fairness, and integrity of neuropsychological evaluations in litigation. *Journal of Legal Medicine, 26*, 95–131.

Koch, W. J., O'Neill, M., & Douglas, K. S. (2005). Empirical limits for the forensic assessment of PTSD litigants. *Law and Human Behavior, 29*, 121–149.

Levy, M. I., & Rosenberg, S. E. (2003). The "eggshell plaintiff" revisited: Causation of mental damages in civil litigation. Retrieved from www.apanet.org/disability/reporter/feature.html on 4/22/03.

Lilienfeld, S. O., Fowler, K. A., & Lohr, J. M. (2003). And the band played on: Science, pseudoscience, and the Rorschach Inkblot Method. *The Clinical Psychologist, 56*, 6–7.

Lilienfeld, S. O., Lynn, S. J., & Lohr, J. M. (2003). *Science and pseudoscience in clinical psychology*. New York: Guilford.

Lilienfeld, S. O., Wood, J. M., & Garb, H. N. (2000). The scientific status of projective techniques. *Psychological Science in the Public Interest, 1*, 27–66.

Linley, P. A., & Joseph, S. (2005). The human capacity for growth through adversity. *American Psychologist, 60*, 262–264.

Macartney-Filgate, M. S., & Snow, G. W. (2004). The practitioner as expert witness. In D. R. Evans (Ed.), *The law, standards, and ethics in the practice of psychology* (2nd ed., pp. 287–309). Toronto: Edmond Montgomery Publications.

Maddi, S. R. (2005). On hardiness and other pathways to resilience. *American Psychologist, 60*, 261–262.

Masling, J. (2002). How do I score thee? Let me count the ways. Or some different methods of categorizing Rorschach responses. *Journal of Personality Assessment, 79*, 399–421.

McGaughey, B. D. & Walker, J. D. (2004). The scientific expert's approaches to litigation testimony. In J. J. Brown (Ed.), *Scientific evidence and expert's handbook* (1999, 2004 cumulative supplement, pp. 43–67). New York: Aspen Law and business.

McLearen, A. M., Pietz, C. A., & Denney, R. L. (2004). Evaluation of psychological damages. In W. T. O'Donohue & E. R. Levensky (Eds.), *Handbook of forensic psychology* (pp. 267–299). Amsterdam: Elsevier.

Meyer, G. J., & Archer, R. P. (2001). The hard science of Rorschach research: What do we know and where do we go? *Psychological Assessment, 13*, 486–502.

Miller, L. (2001). Crime victim trauma and psychological injury: Clinical and forensic guidelines. In E. Pierson (Ed.), *2001 expert witness update* (pp. 173–207). New York: Aspen Law and Business.

Miller, W. (2003). Evidentiary issues in the psychological injury case. In I. Z. Schulze & D. O. Brady (Eds.) *Psychological injuries at trial* (pp. 202–235). Chicago: American Bar Association.

Miramon v. Bradley, 701 So.2d 475 (La. App. 1 Cir. 1997).

Risinger, D. M., Saks, M. J., Thompson, W. C., & Rosenthal, R. (2002). The *Daubert/Kumho* implications of observer effects in forensic science: Hidden problems of expectation and suggestion. *California Law Review, 90*, 1–56.

Rogers, R. & Shuman, D. W. (2005). *Fundamentals of forensic practice*. New York: Springer Science+Business Media.

Royal Commission on Workers' Compensation in British Columbia. (1999). *Final Report, Volume II*, Chapter 4. British Columbia: Author.

Sageman, M. (2003). Three types of skills for effective forensic psychological assessments. *Assessment, 10*, 321–328.

Sales, D. B., & Shuman, D. W. (2005). *Experts in court: Reconciling law, science, and professional knowledge*. Washington, DC: American Psychological Association.

Samra, J., & Connolly, D. A. (2004). Legal compensability of symptoms associated with Posttraumatic Stress Disorder: A Canadian perspective. *International Journal of Forensic Mental Health, 3*, 55–66.

Samra, J., & Koch, W. J. (2002). The monetary worth of psychological injury: What are litigants suing for? In J. R. P. Ogloff (Ed.), *Taking psychology and law into the twenty-first century* (pp. 285–321). New York: Kluwer/Plenum.

Scrignar, C. B. (1996). Post-traumatic stress disorder: Diagnosis, treatment, and legal issues (3rd ed.). New Orleans: Bruno Press.

Schultz, I. Z. (2003). The relationship between psychological impairment and occupational disability. In I. Z. Schulze & D. O. Brady (Eds.), *Psychological injuries at trial* (pp. 65–101). Chicago: American Bar Association.

Scott, J.R., Martin, S., & Burmeister, L. (2005). *Consistency between reviewers and editors about which papers should be published*. Paper presented at the Fifth International Congress on Peer Review and Biomedical Education, Chicago, September 17, 2005.

Shaffer, T. W., Erdberg, P., & Haroian, J. (1999). Current nonpatient data for the Rorschach, WAIS-R, and MMPI-2. *Journal of Psychological Assessment, 73*, 305–316.

Shuman, D. W. (1994a). *Psychiatric and psychological evidence* (2nd ed.). Deerfield, IL: Clark, Boardman, Callaghan. (Supplemented 2002, 2003, 2004)

Shuman, D. W. (1994b). The psychology of compensation in tort law. *Kansas Law Review, 43*. Retrieved April 6, 2003 from www.lexis.com.

Shuman, D. W. (1995). Persistent reexperiences in psychiatry and law. In R. I. Simon (Ed.), *Posttraumatic Stress Disorder in litigation*. Washington, DC: American Psychiatric Press.

Shuman, D. W. (2000a). When time does not heal: Understanding the importance of avoiding unnecessary delay in the resolution of tort cases. *Psychology, Public Policy and Law, 6*, 880–897.

Shuman, D. W. (2000b). The role of apology in tort law. *Judicature, 83*, 180–189.

Shuman, D. W., Cunningham, M. D., Connell, M. A., & Reid, W. H. (2003). Interstate forensic psychology consultations: A call for reform and proposal of a model rule. *Professional Psychology: Research and Practice, 34*, 233–239.

Shuman, D. W., & Daley, C. E. (1996). Compensation for mental and emotional distress. In D. B. Sales & D. W. Shuman (Eds.), *Law, mental health, and mental disorder*. Pacific Grove: Brooks/Cole.

Shuman, D. W., & Greenberg, S. A. (2003). The expert witness, the adversary system, and the voice of reason: Reconciling impartiality and advocacy. *Professional Psychology: Research and Practice, 34*, 219–224.

Siharath v. Sandoz Pharmaceuticals Corp., 113 F.Supp.2d 1347 (N.D. Ga. 2001).

Simon, R. I., & Shuman, D. W. (1999). Conducting forensic examinations on the road: Are you practicing your profession without a license? *Journal of the American Academy of Psychiatry and Law, 27*, 75–82.

Simon, R. I., & Wettstein, R. M. (1997). Toward the development of guidelines for the conduct of forensic psychiatric examinations. *Journal of the American Academy of Psychiatry and Law, 25*, 17–30.

Strasburger, L. H. (1999). The litigant-patient: Mental health consequences of civil litigation. *Journal of the American Academy of Psychiatry and Law, 27*, 203–211.

Strassburger, L., Gutheil, T., & Brodsky, A. (1997). On wearing two hats: Role conflict in service as both psychotherapist and expert witness. *American Journal of Psychiatry, 154*, 448–450.

Tucillo, J. A., DeFilippis, N. A., Denney, R. L., & Dsurney, J. (2002). Licensure requirements for interjurisdictional forensic evaluations. *Professional Psychology: Research and Practice, 33*, 377–383.

U.S. Department of Health and Human Services. (1999). *Mental health: A report of the Surgeon General*. Rockville, MD: Author.

Wayte, T., Samra, J., Robbennolt, J. K., Heuer, L., & Koch, W. J. (2002). Psychological issues in civil law. In Ogloff, J. R. P. (Ed.), *Taking psychology and law into the twenty-first century* (pp. 323–369). New York: Kluwer/Plenum.

Weiner, I. B. (2001). Advancing the science of psychological assessment: The Rorschach Inkblot Method as exemplar. *Psychological Assessment, 13*, 423–432.

Weiner, I. B. (2004). *Rorschach Interpretation Assistance Program: Version 5 Forensic Edition* (RIAP5 FE). Lutz, FL: Psychological Assessment Resources.

Widiger, T. A. (2001). The best and worst of us? *Clinical Psychology: Science and Practice, 8*, 374–377.

Widiger, T. A. (2002). *Training implications of empirically supported assessments*. Paper presented at the 110th Annual Convention of the American Psychological Association, Chicago, August 25, 2002.

Wilson, J. P., & Moran, T. A. (2004). Forensic/clinical assessment of psychological trauma and PTSD in legal settings. In J. P. Wilson, J. P. & T. M. Keane (Eds.), *Assessing psychological trauma and PTSD* (2nd ed., pp. 603–636). New York: Guilford Press.

Wood, J. M., Lilienfeld, S. O., Nezworski, M. T., & Garb, H. N. (2001). Coming to grips with negative evidence for the Comprehensive System for the Rorschach: A comment on Gacono, Loving, and Bodholdt; Ganellen; and Bornstein. *Journal of Personality Assessment, 77*, 48–70.

Wood, J. M., Nezworski, M. T., Garb, H. N., & Lilienfeld, S. O. (2001a). The Misperception of psychopathology: Problems with the norms of the Comprehensive System for the Rorschach. *Clinical Psychology: Science and Practice, 8*, 350–373.

Wood, J. M., Nezworski, M. T., Garb, H. N., & Lilienfeld, S. O. (2001b). Problems with the norms of the Comprehensive System for the Rorschach: Methodological and conceptual considerations. *Clinical Psychology: Science and Practice, 8*, 397–402.

13

Summary and Conclusions

ANDREW W. KANE

Causality is at issue throughout psychological injury cases. The Supreme Courts of the United States (*Daubert v. Merrell Dow Pharmaceuticals*, 1993) and Canada (*R. v. Mohan*, 1994) have provided a framework within which evidence may be presented in federal courts, subject to the gatekeeping of the judge in the trial court. In most cases, expert testimony will be accepted if it is both relevant to the case and helpful to the trier of fact. In both countries, however, expert testimony may be limited or excluded if it has neither a strong clinical basis nor a strong foundation in the research literature, especially literature that is peer-reviewed. In nearly all cases, appellate courts have found that the trial court did not abuse its discretion in accepting, limiting, or excluding expert testimony. Most state and provincial courts follow rules similar to those of the federal courts, though data regarding admissibility in state and provincial courts are not readily available.

Experts need to be aware of a number of concepts if they are to provide evidence that is relevant to the case and helpful to the trier of fact. They must be familiar with the differences between law and science, and be able to adequately translate from each area into the other. They must understand informed consent, and ensure that it is addressed appropriately in the evaluation process. Ecological and incremental validity must be evident. Actual and potential biases must be carefully assessed and monitored, so that they will have little or no impact upon the outcome of the assessment. The expert must be familiar with legal terminology and with the relevant case law in his or her jurisdiction and in any other jurisdiction in which he or she conducts an evaluation, and adhere to the requirements of that case law. The expert must understand the meaning and potential relevance of "thin" and "crumbling" skulls, so that the data collected and interpreted address these factors if relevant to a given case.

A well-structured comprehensive evaluation, utilizing appropriate instruments, will produce data that are relevant to the legal process. An impartial evaluator, assessing the nature and extent of the impairment resulting from an incident or accident, and, especially, what the trauma means to the individual, will be able to form opinions that are valid and reliable. By doing so, the forensic expert will be helpful to the fact finder in its deliberations.

Multiple methods must be used to assess an individual for the presence of a psychological injury as the result of an accident or incident. In a given case, this may include psychological testing, interviews of the plaintiff and collaterals, review of all relevant medical, work, arrest/conviction, school, military, and other records, and consultation with the retaining attorney. If no psychological injury is identified, the evaluation process may need to be terminated, because there may be no cause of action for which the psychologist's evaluation is appropriate. If a psychological injury *is* identified, multiple methods should be used to identify whether, and to what degree, the incident or accident was the proximate cause of the identified injury.

Most (if not all) of the methodology of an assessment should utilize instruments and methods widely accepted in the professional community, with well-established reliability and validity. (Note that psychological "reliability" differs from the way the term was used by the U.S. Supreme Court in *Daubert*, in which it was defined as "trustworthiness.") These instruments and methods should also be used according to the standardization and validation procedures of the instruments' originators, as well as other uses that have been validated by the research literature.

If the expert utilizes methods or instruments that are not widely used or accepted in the professional community, he or she should be prepared to defend the use of these procedures, including providing evidence that the procedures are valid and reliable for use as tests or as another form of assessment instrument. Various information gathering forms, however, may be addressed as "written interviews" in which the questions are presented in writing to obtain the response in the individual's own words, and to save some time (and expense) in the assessment process. These information gathering forms may be standardized forms or forms devised by the psychologist to facilitate the gathering of information.

Experts must be familiar with base rates for the types of impairments, disorders and other consequences at issue in a given case, if such data are available. They must understand error rates, and be able to address the concept with regard to impairments, disorders, and their consequences at issue. Diagnosis must be carefully made, understanding that diagnosis may be difficult to ascertain with current diagnostic manuals due to the marginal research underpinnings of many diagnoses.

The expert must understand how to conduct an assessment. He or she must be impartial, allowing the data to determine the conclusions regardless of who appointed or retained the expert. Appropriate instruments must be utilized and correctly administered, and interpretations must be grounded in the research for those instruments. The individual's response style must be assessed, as well as using the best available methods to address whether malingering is a factor in the individual's presentation in the evaluation. The expert must not go substantially beyond the data amassed in the evaluation when drawing conclusions. The shortcomings of the peer review process should be understood, especially if the expert is relying on learned treatises other than those published in peer-reviewed journals, so that they may be discussed if relevant to a *Daubert/Mohan* challenge.

The expert must adhere to the best practices of his or her profession, because this will help ensure that the expert's testimony will be admitted by the court. This includes being aware of the latest scientific evidence (learned treatises, including nomothetic data) concerning the assessment of individuals (i.e., the ideographic level) who have allegedly received a psychological/emotional injury. Testimony by an expert who does not follow this requirement might not be admitted by the court.

Psychologists and other mental health experts must adhere to the ethical codes and practice standards of their professions when conducting forensic evaluations. This includes a requirement that the psychologist or other professional be impartial, advocating for his or her data but not for any side in the litigation. Treating professionals should avoid being expert witnesses, because the two roles are incompatible. The expert must do his or her job on a timely basis, because there is evidence that unnecessarily prolonging a case may be harmful to a complainant.

Experts may be requested to provide consultation or do an assessment in a jurisdiction different from the one(s) in which the expert is licensed or certified. It is essential that the expert be aware of the requirements of the "foreign" jurisdiction, so that the expert does not violate its statutes or administrative code in the course of consulting or providing an assessment and testimony. It is not sufficient to have the retaining attorney verify that the psychologist may conduct an evaluation. Because the consequences for the psychologist and a given case could be severe if an error is made, the psychologist must personally identify and adhere to the requirements for the nonlicensed jurisdiction.

Psychologists' training, experience, ethics code, and specialty guidelines make psychologists well-equipped to meet the requirements of *Daubert, Mohan*, and their progeny. In establishing the consequences of legitimate causality by using comprehensive, impartial, and state-of-the-art assessments buttressed by knowledge of the current and foundational science in the area of psychological injury and its assessment, psychologists and other forensic mental health professionals will be well-prepared for court.

References

Daubert v. Merrell Dow Pharmaceuticals, Inc. 509 U.S. 579, 113 S.Ct. 2786, 125 L.Ed. 2d 469 (1993).

R. v. Mohan [1994] 2 S.C.R. 9, 1994 CanLII 80 (S.C.C.).

Section III

Malingering in Psychological Injury: TBI, Chronic Pain, and PTSD

14

Malingering: Overview and Basic Concepts

KEITH NICHOLSON AND MICHAEL F. MARTELLI

This section critically reviews issues associated with malingering, focusing on these in the context of traumatic brain injury (TBI), chronic pain, and Posttraumatic Stress Disorder (PTSD), or other psychoemotional problems such as depression that are often the subject of medicolegal proceedings. There will be very little discussion of malingering and related issues in the context of criminal or other forensic settings, although some such material will be presented given that many pertinent findings or contributions have been made in these other fields. The primary focus of this section will be on the differential diagnosis of malingering. There is an emphasis on TBI and chronic pain, reflecting the interests of the authors but, also, as there has been more research conducted in these areas than in PTSD, depression, or other psychoemotional problems. There is notably considerable overlap in the chapters of this section, which reflects both the commonality of issues, for example, the comorbidity between the disorders of interest or the use of multiscale self-report inventories to assess malingering, exaggeration, or other accentuation of symptomatology in all of the clinical conditions that are a focus of the chapter.

Deception, Deceit, and Lie-Catching

Lying or other deceptive behavior is common in everyday social interactions (Vrij, 2000). Such behavior is not always bad or negative, but is often beneficial, serving to facilitate individual and social functions in a number of ways. Despite a number of popular or stereotypical beliefs about verbal or nonverbal cues that are thought to be associated with lying, there are no strong behavioral markers that indicate when a person may be lying. DePaulo et al. (2003) reviewed over 110 studies and found that, unlike Pinocchio's growing nose, typical verbal or nonverbal behaviors associated with lying do not exist. Although some behaviors may provide some clues that the person is lying, there is very little evidence for consistent, generalizable indicators of deception, and different people display different behaviors at different times when lying (Vrij & Mann, 2003). It is therefore perhaps not surprising that most people (including professional lie catchers such as police officers, customs officers or judges, or mental health professionals such as psychologists or psychiatrists) are poor at detecting lying or other deception (Grubin & Madsen, 2005). In experimental settings, the ability of the average person to catch a liar is seldom above 60% (Vrij, 2000), that is, only slightly better than would be expected on the basis of simply guessing or chance. When accuracy at detecting lies vs. detecting the truth is analyzed separately, it is apparent that there is often a truth bias, that is, people tend to believe that a person is telling the truth more often than that they are lying. However, some professionals (e.g., Secret Service) may be better at detecting deception than others, and some individuals, lay or professional, are much better than others at detecting deception. Unfortunately, it is not possible to simply ask people how good they are at catching liars as a person's confidence in their ability to detect lying is unrelated to their actual ability to do so (DePaulo, Charlton, Cooper, Lindsay, & Muhlenbruck, 1997). However, specific training may enhance a person's capacity at detecting deception. Several authors caution that much of the research about lying and lie detection must be viewed cautiously given that most of this involves simulation studies or experimental situations in which subjects are instructed to lie but who may not behave as they would in a real-life setting (Grubin & Madsen, 2005; Vrij & Mann, 2003).

Byrne and Stokes (2003) studied whether nonhuman primates can malinger. They present observations indicating that many nonhuman primates simulate illness or suffering in order to obtain a reward or avoid some punishment. Such behavior, which sometimes appears to be a "cry for help," is thought to be common in these species. However, with the exception of the great apes (e.g., chimpanzee, gorilla, orangutan), there is no indication that the animals have a conscious awareness of such behavior or intent to deceive. Rather, such behavior is more typically "unintentional malingering" and the animals could not therefore be labeled "morally guilty." It is noted that both human and nonhuman infants or children are capable of instrumental learning whereby a number of tactics may be learned to be useful and, as with nonhuman primates, most human children begin illness deception with their mother as the primary target audience, for example, "I'm sick or hurt so I need your attention," or "I can't go do something I don't want to do." Byrne and Stokes (2003) also note that, among primates, the size of the neocortex, which is involved in higher cognitive functions, varies more than other parts of the brain and is related to evolutionary development. Using an index of deception in a number of long-running field studies in several primate species, it was found that there was a strong positive correlation between the frequency of deception and the size of the neocortex, the latter accounting for 60% of the variance in deceptive behaviors. It was also noted that, for primates, the potential gains for malingering are not so big, in contrast with situations often encountered by humans.

Spence et al. (2003) also note that lying or deception increases with the complexity of the animal's nervous system, and suggest that lying represents a higher "executive" cognitive function mediated by frontal system brain processes. In addition, it is noted that such behavior follows a predictable and normal developmental course in human infants/children, and that humans with specific neurodevelopmental disorders are impaired at lying or other deception. Spence et al. report on a study in which the functional activity of the brain was analyzed utilizing functional magnetic resonance imaging (fMRI) while subjects were telling lies or the truth. It was found that lying was associated with longer response times and greater brain activity in bilateral ventrolateral cortices, with less significant changes in functional activity in other dorsal and medial prefrontal regions. There have been several other studies of lying utilizing fMRI technology (Davatzikos et al., 2005; Ganis, Kosslyn, Stose, Thompson, & Yurgelun-Todd, 2003; Kozel, Padgett, & George, 2004; Kozel, Revell et al., 2004; Langleben et al., 2002, 2005; Lee et al., 2002; Nunez, Casey, Egner, Hare, & Hirsch, 2005; Phan et al., 2005). Overall, results indicate a variable pattern of findings which likely, in part, reflects the somewhat different study designs.

Kozel et al. (2005) summarized the common areas of fMRI activation across various studies as involving the anterior cingulate cortex and the prefrontal cortex. However, almost any behavioral challenge will activate the anterior cingulate cortex, and the prefrontal cortex involves a large portion of the brain involved in a multitude of psychological processes. Kozel et al. (2005) reported on a study in which subjects participated in a mock crime and then lied about doing so. Following development of a model of brain activation when lying, the model was then tested in another sample of subjects (i.e., cross-validated) and it was found that 90% accuracy could be obtained. In contrast to previous studies, this methodology could be used to assess an individual's responses rather than only providing data on groups of subjects. Langleben et al. (2005), noting that the value of fMRI studies of deception will be determined by the accuracy of the discrimination between single deceptive and truthful responses in individual subjects, obtained a 78% accuracy rate in classifying individual lies or truthful responses in individual subjects utilizing a carefully controlled query procedure. Davatzikos et al. (2005) obtained 99% accuracy in classifying true and false responses in a forced-choice paradigm with 22 participants utilizing high-dimensional nonlinear pattern classification methods. Cross validation with subjects not involved in the initial training resulted in 88% accuracy. Whereas paradigms utilizing fMRI technology may eventually be very useful in detecting deception in real-life cases, Kozel et al. (2005) noted that the cooperation of the subject is required and that further work is needed to determine how this technology will work in different settings and with different populations.

There has long been an interest in biomedical or psychophysiological indicators of deception. The polygraph has been the most widely used technique. Greenberg (2002) summarizes a review of the National Academy of Sciences (The Polygraph and Lie Detection, see http://www.nap.edu) evaluating the extensive use of the polygraph to detect potential or actual security risks. It was concluded that polygraph screening was "equivalent to voodooism" and "scientifically unsubstantiated, easily foiled, and of no proven value for detecting or even deterring security lapses" (p. 1309). However, it was suggested that the polygraph may be useful, succeeding well above chance, in detecting deception about specific events such as theft with examinees who are untrained in easily learned and readily available countermeasures. It was noted that polygraphy would often falsely conclude that an innocent person was guilty while failing to detect the guilty (false positive and false negative findings, respectively). The Academy report also suggests that the polygraph is "wielded by a benighted priesthood that has beguiled politics and the public into believing that it possesses a magic instrument for detecting falsehood" (Greenberg, 2002, p. 1309). It was noted that polygraph evidence is not admissible in most state courts and, with minor exceptions, is excluded from federal courts. Nonetheless, it continues to be widely used for both governmental and nongovernmental purposes.

Oksol and O'Donohue (2003) provided another review of the polygraph concluding that the theoretical and empirical foundations for its techniques are weak and that "it is virtually impossible to determine the validity, or accuracy of conclusions using the polygraph because of the lack of standardization" (p. 631) of techniques. However, it was also noted that the polygraph may be useful given that many subjects will confess to some behavior when undergoing such testing. Other biomedical or psychophysiological indices of deception involving TBI, chronic pain, PTSD, or other psychoemotional problems will be discussed throughout this section. Whereas these indices have as yet not been demonstrated to provide good evidence about malingering or related behaviors, they are of potential value and interested readers should be aware of developments in these areas.

Malingering: A Brief History

Historically, interest in the concept of malingering has waxed and waned. Wessely (2003) notes that there are many instances of deliberate deception by feigning illness from biblical and classical times. Mendelson and Mendelson (2004) suggest that the term malingering was formally introduced in 1785 in a publication entitled "Groves Dictionary of the Vulgar Tongue." By the seventeenth century, writers on medical jurisprudence had begun to become preoccupied with the issue of malingering or feigning illness. With the advent of worker's compensation, social insurance, or other plans in many western industrialized countries that provided for financial compensation in cases of injury or disability from the middle to latter part of the nineteenth century, there was a fear that there would be a dramatic increase in claims due to malingering. Wessely (2003) suggests that some members of the medical profession then took it upon themselves to act as gatekeepers for the state in order to curtail a feared flood of unprincipled workers from taking advantage of such plans. In response, some workers began to hold the medical profession in contempt, viewing doctors as "hired guns" of the employers. However, the flood of claims did not materialize and fears subsided until World

War I, when there was again increased concern about the possibility of persons malingering to escape from combat or other military duties. Doctors then began to see many soldiers with signs and symptoms that could not be explained by obvious physical injury. Concerns about war neurosis, shell shock, psychiatric problems, and functional nervous system disorders came to the fore. It was often undecided whether doctors should be treating such problems or if they should be acting as agents of military discipline, identifying malingerers or shirkers, and returning them to active duty (Eckart, 2000). Of course, whether or not people are malingering, or whether they have some actual difficulty, if they are forced to adapt to some adverse circumstance they usually will, although perhaps with reduced capacity.

Palmer (2003) suggests that the term "malingering" originated in the military. A distinction is made between "scrimshanking" or "shirking" vs. malingering. The former are considered "normal" testing of boundaries and avoidance of unpleasant duties or situations, whereas the latter is considered more abnormal or contrary to military ethic. It is also noted that malingering can be a good thing, such as when attempting to escape from the enemy. Palmer notes that charges of malingering may be difficult to substantiate and suggests that the touchstone is to catch the soldier "in flagrante delicto." It is further suggested that it is the responsibility of the officer in charge to know his men well enough to identify who may be malingering. Whereas it had long been suspected that malingering was associated with the "quality of the recruits," it was subsequently realized that the quality of leadership and the morale of the military unit was equally, if not more, important. Palmer suggests that, prior to World War I, soldiers were unlikely to feign mental illness, as they might run the risk of ending their days in an asylum. Shell shock created problems in World War I, as it did not fit the existing dichotomies of the time, that is, behavior or problems could not easily be declared as either organic/social, mad/bad, guilty/not guilty, or honest/deceitful. Doctors were subsequently criticized for encouraging malingering by invoking such terms as battle fatigue "as an excuse for cowardice" (p. 49).

Wessely (2003) suggests that concern about malingering continued after World War I with such problems as "railway spine" or back pain. Although it had begun to be hoped that the science of psychology or other endeavor would provide objective and quantifiable indices or measures of malingering, the focus subsequently shifted from attempts to detect malingering to explaining it. Malingering then increasingly began to be medicalized or seen as a form of mental disorder (e.g., a weak mental stamina) or psychopathology. This was attacked by writers such as Szasz (1956), who provided sociological explanations for concepts of malingering or mental illness. There appears to have then been some shift in the conceptualization of malingering. Halligan et al. (2003) suggest that, for much of the twentieth century, malingering had been regarded as a pejorative term best avoided in clinical practice. Indeed, malingering has often been referred to as the "M word," reflecting the social censure about even uttering this. Nonetheless, interest in such behavior continued and, in 1985, Pilowsky coined the term "malingerophobia" to describe the "irrational and maladaptive fear of being tricked into providing health care to individuals who masquerade as sick, but either have no illness at all, or have a much less severe one than they claim" (p. 571). With the advent of large financial settlements or compensation for TBI, chronic pain, PTSD, or other conditions, there has again been increased interest in detecting and understanding what may or may not be malingering, or other behaviors that may be related to or confused with malingering.

Malingering: Definitions, Criteria, and Controversies

Palmer (2003) cites Webster (1890) as defining malingering as "from the French [malinger—sickly, weakly, prob. from mal, ill + OF heingre, haingre-thin, lean, infirm from L. aeger] and describes a soldier who feigns himself as sick, or who induces or protracts an illness, in order to avoid doing his duty; hence in general, one who shirks duty by pretending illness or inability" (Palmer, 2003, pp. 42–43). Lipman (1962) distinguished between four types of malingering: (1) fabrication of nonexistent symptoms, (2) exaggeration of actual symptoms, (3) extension of symptoms that have actually improved or resolved, and (4) misattribution or fraudulent attribution of symptoms to an injury/accident when they actually preceded or are otherwise unrelated to the accident/injury. Exaggeration of actual symptoms was considered much more frequent than fabrication, and it is currently thought that exaggeration of existing symptoms may be more frequent than fabrication or purposeful misattribution of symptoms (Halligan et al., 2003). It will be argued throughout this section that the distinction between exaggeration as a conscious act purposefully committed to obtain some secondary gain or benefits vs. exaggeration or accentuation of symptomatology due to other psychological or biological factors is critical.

Currently, the most frequently cited definition or criteria for malingering is that of the *Diagnostic and Statistical Manual of Mental Disorders* (*DSM*). The *DSM* Fourth Edition Text Revision (*DSM-IV-TR*; American Psychiatric Association, 2000) defines the essential feature of malingering as "the intentional production of false or grossly exaggerated physical or psychological symptoms, motivated by external incentives such as avoiding military duty, avoiding work, obtaining financial compensation, evading criminal prosecution, or obtaining drugs" (p. 739). It is suggested that malingering should be "strongly suspected" if the assessment is within a medicolegal context, there is marked discrepancy between the person's claimed stress or disability and the objective findings, there is lack of cooperation during the evaluation or complying with treatment recommendations, and/or there is an Antisocial Personality Disorder. Discussion of the differential diagnosis includes mention of Factitious Disorder and Conversion or other Somatoform Disorders. It is suggested that there are not external incentives in Factitious Disorder where there is evidence of an intrapsychic need to maintain the sick role. The production of symptoms in Conversion or other Somatoform Disorders is not considered intentional and not associated with obvious external incentives.

Finally, it is suggested that, in contrast to Conversion Disorder, symptom relief is not obtained in malingering with either suggestion or hypnosis. In contrast with Factitious or Somatoform Disorders, malingering is not considered a mental disorder in the *DSM* but, instead, is a condition that may be the focus of clinical attention (code V65.2). *The Diagnostic and Statistical Manual of Mental Disorders*, Fourth Edition (*DSM-IV*; American Psychiatric Association, 1994) criteria for malingering are identical to those of the *DSM-IV-TR*. The International Classification of Diseases and Related Health Problems (*ICD-10*; World Health Organization, 2006) also does not consider malingering to be a diagnosable disorder but as a factor that may influence presentation. For purposes of exposition, the remainder of this section will focus upon the *DSM* criteria.

There have been many criticisms of the *DSM* formulation (Gerson, 2002; Halligan et al., 2003; Rogers, 1990, 1997a; Rogers & Shuman, 2005; Sweet, 1999). Gerson (2002), following a review of 1,040 malingering studies utilizing *DSM* criteria, concluded that these criteria are far too limited to be considered as a reliable method for detecting malingering, and that reliance on the criteria would result in many false positives, that is, identification of malingering when this was not actually the case. Rogers (1990), following perhaps the only empirical study of the utility of the *DSM* criteria, concluded that relying on these would result in an 80% false positive rate. Thus, not all persons presenting for a medicolegal examination would be expected to be malingering, and it is clearly erroneous that malingering should be "strongly suspected" in such cases. Similarly, not all persons with a concurrent or past Antisocial Disorder are malingering, and it is again doubtful whether malingering should be "strongly suspected" in such cases. There are many reasons why there may be a discrepancy between degree of distress or perceived disability and objective findings, and the underlying biological or psychophysiological processes in many disorders are poorly understood (Stone, Carson, & Sharpe, 2005). There is often poor correspondence between evidence of peripheral tissue damage or injury and subjective complaints or disability that may be due to sensitization effects of the central nervous or other systems (Eriksen & Ursin, 2004; Miller, 2000; Nicholson, 2000), and because catastrophizing or other psychological factors that are commonly associated with pain, depression, or other disorder may be serving to accentuate problems independent of malingering (Nicholson & Martelli, 2006). There are many reasons why there may be lack of compliance with evaluation or treatment recommendations independent from malingering, for example, the person perceives the examination as adversarial, or there are adverse side effects from pharmacological or other recommended treatments. Problems with treatment compliance are common in many psychiatric or other medical conditions, completely independent from any considerations of malingering (Bogduk, 2004) and many patients with *DSM* Axis I disorders (i.e., the primary diagnostic categories) are unreliable or inconsistent in their clinical presentations (Cunnien, 1997).

As the *DSM* defines malingering as the intentional production of false or "grossly exaggerated" physical or psychological symptoms, it might be suspected that moderately or less than grossly exaggerated symptoms should not be considered malingering. Of course, this would not generally be accepted. If a person with a TBI has a 5% decrease in efficiency of memory, speed of processing, or other neuropsychological function, he or she may be awarded much higher compensation if he or she could successfully malinger to indicate a 15–20% reduction in capacity. As will be seen, it is much harder to detect what might be a moderate or less than grossly exaggerated deficit than a gross deficit and, as suggested above, there is often significant exaggeration or accentuation of difficulty independent of malingering but associated with other psychosocial factors. On the other hand, if a person actually has some symptom (e.g., memory problems, pain, psychoemotional distress), but these were preexisting (present before the injury or accident that is the subject of a medicolegal proceeding) and this is consciously misattributed to be a result of the accident or injury in question for the purpose of obtaining some external incentive, then most would also consider such behavior to be malingering. Similarly, it would also be considered to be malingering if the person continues to report having symptoms that have resolved and this behavior is motivated by external incentives.

As most might agree, in accord with the *DSM* criteria, there must be some intention to malinger in order for such behavior to be judged as malingering. However, many consider malingering to fall along a continuum that varies according to the extent of conscious awareness (Nies & Sweet, 1994), and it has long been known that there may be both conscious and unconscious determinants of symptom exaggeration (Clayer, Bookless, & Ross, 1984). As indicated above, Byrne and Stokes (2003) have documented that illness deception in nonhuman primates does not usually involve the conscious intent to deceive. They caution that this may often be the case in humans, or that it may be difficult to determine conscious intent. Slick, Sherman, and Iverson (1999) and Backhaus, Fichtenberg, and Hanks (2004) have similarly suggested that dichotomous diagnostic criteria such as whether some behavior (e.g., malingering, poor effort) is present, conscious and volitional or not may be difficult to assess or may be misleading. Halligan et al. (2003) suggest that inferring the level of consciously mediated intention, usually within the confines of a clinical interview or examination, is "seemingly impossible," and that "there are no reliable or valid methods for objectively determining consciously motivated intention" (p. 4).

Malle (2003), however, suggests that most people, including those intending to malinger as well as examiners who try to detect malingering, rely on a folk concept of intentionality that has evolved over the millennia as people have developed the capacity to infer how others think, feel, or intend. The perception of intentionality is something that develops rapidly in the early years of childhood, and is something that adults do automatically and with ease. Research demonstrates that people can be very good at inferring the intentions of others, although a number of factors either increase or decrease accuracy. It appears that we may generally be well able to evaluate intentionality, but there are few, if any, well-validated formal techniques for documenting this.

As noted above, the *DSM* does not consider malingering to be a mental disorder. In contrast, such behavior may be adaptive, such as when a prisoner of war malingers in an attempt to escape or a person malingers in order to avoid some activity that is generally considered wrong. However, Halligan et al. (2003) suggest that malingering is often at least implicitly medicalized in current practice, and that reliance on the biomedical model obscures the malingerer's capacity for responsibility and free will. They suggest that malingering be thought of, not as an illness, but as a form of social deviance, a willful choice made for personal advantage. They argue that "a belief in the attenuation of free will undermines the notions of moral and legal responsibility and encourages the acceptance of medical/ psychiatric or other biological explanations for all illness behaviors" (p. 23).

Rogers and associates (Rogers, 1990; Rogers & Bender, 2003; Rogers, Sewell, & Salekin, 1994) have proposed a number of models of malingering that were developed primarily in the context of criminal forensic work. One is the pathogenic model, that is, the person is "mad" or mentally ill, which "assumes that the underlying motivation is an ineffective attempt to control the symptoms and clinical presentation of a chronic and progressive mental disorder. With increased impairment, intentionally produced symptoms become gradually less deliberate, until they are involuntary and unintended" (Rogers & Bender, 2003; p. 111). Another proposed model is the criminological model (i.e., the person is bad), which assumes that the primary motivation is characterological, malingering being another antisocial act. However, several studies indicate that sociopaths are not particularly good at feigning mental illness (Rogers, 1990). Finally, the adaptational model assumes that the malingerer perceives circumstances as adversarial and that malingering is a feasible alternative in a cost-benefit analysis of this difficult situation. Of course, all three types or determinants of behavior may be evident in a malingerer, that is, they may have mental health problems, they may be "bad", socially irresponsible, or antisocial, and they may engage in a cost-benefit analysis of the prospective situation, concluding that it is worthwhile to malinger. It also seems unnecessary to assume that there is a progressive disorder with a deteriorating course for a psychopathological explanation of malingering. Rogers and Neumann (2003) later reported that reanalysis of data initially used to develop the models did not confirm previous findings but did indicate that individuals with psychopathic characteristics may use cost-benefit analysis in deciding to malinger. Of note, the data used to develop and test these models did not come from actual malingerers but was data that mental health professionals provided about their opinion of malingerers.

There is some difference of opinion about who should provide a diagnosis, conclusion, or ruling that a person is malingering. Halligan et al. (2003) suggest that doctors may be able to establish whether illness behaviors are consistent with or could be explained by established medical or psychiatric disorders but, noting the many studies indicating that medical or other practitioners are not well able to identify malingering, suggest that this is a legal problem and so responsibility should rest with the courts. Several others have suggested that it should be up to the courts rather than the clinicians to decide if a person is malingering (Mendelson & Mendelson, 2004; Wessley, 2003). Iverson and Binder (2000) suggests that clinicians may be unwilling to diagnose malingering, even if there is strong evidence, as they may be afraid of mislabeling someone, or of being threatened or sued. In this context, it is notable that courts have also been reluctant to label or stigmatize individuals as malingerers (Jones, 2003; Knoll & Resnik, 1999). However, given the complexity of behavioral issues involved, and that the presentation of the person being assessed or treated should be correctly identified one way or the other, we suggest that it is within the mandate of the clinical professional to diagnose or identify whether a person may or may not be malingering. Of course, this may often not be possible, and available information may only raise the possibility rather than provide conclusive evidence that this is actually the case. Indeed, as will be argued throughout this section, there is usually no conclusive evidence to determine whether a person is malingering. As such, any statement about malingering should be carefully considered.

Differential Diagnosis: Factitious, Conversion, and Other Disorders or Conditions

The *DSM-IV-TR* (American Psychiatric Association, 2000) indicates that the differential diagnosis of malingering include consideration of Factitious as well as Conversion or other Somatoform Disorders. The *DSM-IV-TR* defines Factitious Disorder as the intentional production or feigning of physical or psychological symptoms with the motivation to assume the sick role, in the absence of external incentives (e.g., economic gain) for the behavior. There may be fabrication of subjective complaints, falsification of objective signs, self-inflicted conditions, and/or exaggeration or exacerbation of an actual medical condition. The more chronic and severe variant of Factitious Disorder is referred to as Munchausen Syndrome. Although physical or psychological symptoms are intentionally produced in Factitious Disorder, the person is not usually aware of the motivation behind the factitious behavior. Persons with Factitious Disorder may utilize immense medical resources (Pankratz, 2003).

Estimates of the incidence or prevalence of Factitious Disorder vary widely. Feldman, Hamilton, and Deemer (2001) report that there have been more than 2,000 published case reports of Factitious Disorder, but that there is very little empirical evidence related to the epidemiology. Krahn, Li, and O'Connor (2003) suggest that the incidence and prevalence is unknown due to the inherently secretive nature of persons presenting with this disorder. Whereas there have been many clear-cut cases of Factitious Disorder, with well-documented self-injurious or feigned behavior, most cases are not confirmed and the diagnosis is made inferentially or on the suspicion that there is intentional production of symptoms for the purpose of assuming the sick role. However, again, there are many unexplained medical conditions and self-destructive or self-injurious behavior is common in many psychopathological conditions (Brown, 2004). There has been very poor inter-rater reliability found in limited study of this diagnosis (Ziskin & Faust, 1988).

Despite an abundance of related literature, there is no clear operational definition of what the sick role may be for the purpose of making a *DSM* diagnosis. Parsons

(1951), in an early and influential work, explicated the concept of the sick role. Mechanic and Volkart (1960) later coined the term "illness behavior" and Pilowsky (1993) has subsequently written extensively about "abnormal illness behavior". Although these or related concepts are multifaceted, it is generally agreed that adoption of the sick role may relieve the person of various obligations (occupational, familial, etc.) with potential for a number of secondary gains (psychosocial, monetary, or other). There is, however, limited understanding of what the underlying psychological processes may be in adopting a sick role, especially in the case of Factitious Disorder, when the person may endure multiple invasive surgical or other medical procedures.

Feldman et al. (2001) note that there has been almost no empirical evidence related to the etiology of Factitious Disorder, largely because confirmed cases are infrequent or, if confirmed, subjects are unwilling to participate in systematic study. However, a number of behavioral, cognitive, or psychodynamic explanations have been suggested. These include (1) an abnormal focus upon somatic sensations, (2) a history of childhood illness or having a close relative who was seriously ill during childhood that provides a model for the sick role behavior, (3) other past social learning, or present positive and negative reinforcement of illness behavior (e.g., the attention one receives as a patient), and (4) control of intrapsychic conflicts involving dependency, libidinal, or aggressive themes. It may often be unclear to what extent the abnormal illness behavior is associated with reinforcement by psychosocial factors other than specific "external incentives" (i.e., avoiding military duty, avoiding work, obtaining financial compensation, evading criminal prosecution, or obtaining drugs) as specified in the *DSM* criteria. Notably, conscious deception related to illness/illness behavior is often seen in several other mental disorders including eating disorders, substance use disorders, and certain personality disorders (Rogers, 1990).

Although the *DSM-IV-TR* criteria for Factitious Disorder preclude external incentives as a cause for the behavior, Eisendrath and McNiel (2002) have noted that persons with Factitious Disorder may pursue medicolegal avenues where financial or other external incentives are involved. They present a series of 20 cases that were identified from the authors' records of plaintiff evaluations that had been conducted in the previous 15 years. The cases were characterized as having long-standing and multiple medical problems, the persons then becoming involved in civil litigation associated with one or another of their many somatic complaints. It was suggested that the patients had a long history of using somatic complaints as a way of getting their emotional needs met. Aside from the direct positive reinforcement a monetary award may provide, it was suggested that becoming involved in litigation served to validate the individuals' illness behavior. Of note, of the criteria used to make the diagnosis of Factitious Disorder in this series of cases, there was some record of there having been direct personal observation of the patient's factitiously producing illness in 40% of the cases and, in 29% of the cases, there was some physical evidence of a factitious cause of symptoms (e.g., the person being in the possession of a syringe or surreptitious medicine). All or most all of the cases met the other two criteria, that is, nonphysiological physical signs (e.g., an elevated temperature without increased pulse) or a course of illness that did not follow the natural history of the presumed biomedical disease process. We would question whether all such cases were bona fide Factitious Disorder patients or whether some other abnormal illness behavior or somatoform process may have been involved.

The *DSM-IV-TR* notes that the differential diagnosis of malingering also includes consideration of Conversion Disorder or other Somatoform Disorders in which symptoms are not intentionally produced. Conversion Disorder involves one or more symptoms that are not intentionally produced or feigned and that affect voluntary motor or sensory function (e.g., paralysis or loss of sensation in some part of the body) suggestive of a neurological or other general medical condition. However, the symptom(s) cannot be accounted for by a medical condition or by the direct effects of a substance, and psychological factors are judged to be important because the initiation or exacerbation of the symptom(s) is preceded by conflicts or by other stressors. Notably, anxiety may be associated with a number of symptoms suggested to represent conversion symptoms (e.g., difficulty swallowing or the sensation of a lump in the throat, impaired balance, or coordination) but the *DSM-IV-TR* criteria specify that symptoms should not be better accounted for by another mental disorder. A number of other criteria and associated features are outlined in the *DSM-IV-TR* manual.

Again, many medical conditions are poorly understood and there may be a biomedical or psychophysiological explanation for some of the symptoms often thought to represent a conversion of psychological conflicts into physical symptoms (Reuber, Mitchell, Howlett, Crimlisk, & Grunewald, 2005). One example is the presence of nondermatomal sensory deficits (NDSDs). Such sensory deficits do not correspond to any peripheral dermatomal organization as may be apparent with some peripheral nerve injuries. In contrast, they are often hemisensory, involving much (often an entire side) of the body. They vary in how dense they are, for example, whether there is only mildly diminished or complete loss of sensation in the affected body parts. An underlying neurobiological substrate for NDSDs has been demonstrated with functional imaging, but this is also thought to be associated with certain psychological factors (Mailis-Gagnon et al., 2003). Further discussion of such sensory abnormalities will be presented in the chapter devoted to chronic pain (Chapter 17).

Somatization Disorder is another of the Somatoform Disorders that may be especially relevant for the differential diagnosis of malingering, Factitious or Conversion Disorder. The *DSM-IV-TR* criteria for Somatization Disorder include a history of many physical complaints beginning before 30 years of age. The symptoms cannot be fully explained by a known medical condition or the direct effects of a substance or, where there is a related medical condition, the physical complaints, or related disability is in excess of what would normally be expected. There must be at least four pain symptoms, two gastrointestinal symptoms, one sexual symptom, and one pseudoneurological symptom. It has been suggested that Somatization Disorder be construed as a spectrum disorder or, in other words, a matter of degree, rather than representing an either-or/present-absent diagnostic category. It has been found that in 25–50% of all primary care visits (i.e., visits to the family physician or internist), no serious medical cause is found to explain the patient's symptoms, and that up to 85% of all the symptoms patients present to their family physician remain medically unexplained after adequate evaluation (Barsky, Ettner, Horsky, & Bates, 2001). As such, it is apparent that concern with somatic symptoms that are not clearly associated with specific organic pathology is very common. However, it is widely agreed that there is poor understanding of the nature of somatoform or somatization processes, current conceptualizations serving to perpetuate problems associated with mind–body dualism (Janca, 2005). It has also often been noted that Factitious, Conversion, and Somatization Disorders and malingering often overlap, or that a person may present with all of these concurrently (Feldman et al., 2001; Mailis-Gagnon & Nicholson, in preparation, a).

Reid (2000) provides a convenient summary of what distinguishes the various conditions being discussed here. These may be conceptualized in terms of whether the person is conscious of the purpose or nature of the goal of the behavior, and whether the execution or actual production of the behavior is conscious and voluntarily. Thus, the malingerer is consciously aware of the purpose of the behavior (e.g., to obtain some monetary benefit) and voluntarily acts (e.g., feigning paralysis) to obtain the goal. The person with a Factitious Disorder may be unaware of the purpose of their behavior (or could likely poorly formulate or verbalize this), but consciously and voluntarily acts (e.g., claims to have a nonexistent problem as paralysis or engages in some self-injurious behavior) in order to fulfill this goal. A person with a Conversion or other Somatoform or psychosomatic disorder is neither aware of the purpose of the behavior nor do they consciously or voluntarily produce the behavior (e.g., paralysis). However, as has been discussed, these distinctions are usually not so simple or clear-cut.

Related Concepts and Terminology

There are many terms or concepts that may be associated with, similar to, or confused with malingering. Just as it is important to differentiate between such conditions as malingering and Factitious or various Somatoform Disorders, it is important to differentiate between malingering and several other concepts or conditions. Unfortunately, there appears to be a tendency on the part of many practitioners to interpret one or another of these other concepts or conditions as malingering, or to use other such terms to represent thinly veiled euphemisms for malingering.

One most basic concept is that of *response bias*. Simply, response bias denotes a ubiquitous tendency to respond in some manner that differs from a "true" state, for example, to over- or under-report the frequency, intensity, or other characteristic of some stimuli or phenomena (Green & Swets, 1966). There is notably no suggestion about whether any such over- or under-reporting is good or bad or why it may be. Indeed, studies have demonstrated that many, many factors may have an affect on response bias, one way or another, and a response bias can be demonstrated for anyone in one situation or another. Although response bias is a neutral term with respect to the motivation of the person, it has come to be used in a somewhat pejorative sense to imply that the person is exaggerating complaints (e.g., Bush et al., 2005). In accord with generally accepted criteria of malingering, a response bias to report problems (or to not report problems as preexisting that were present before an injury) would be considered malingering if the person intentionally does so for the purpose of obtaining financial compensation or other external incentive. It should also be noted that the definition of deviance from a true state implies that there is a true state that can be ascertained, but this assumption may often be questionable, for example, what is the true degree of pain, or what is the true degree of psychoemotional distress. Many such states are psychological constructs dependent upon subjective experience and, at least currently, there is no methodology to define what these true states may be, although there may be a number of objective correlates of the subjective experience, for example, the common signs and symptoms of a disorder or the presence of a pathological process known to be associated with a neuropsychological disorder or pain. Martelli and associates (Martelli, 2000; Martelli, Nicholson, Zasler, & Bender, 2006; Martelli, Zasler, Mancini, & MacMillan, 1999; Martelli, Zasler, Nicholson, Pickett, & May, 2002) have provided extensive discussion of factors affecting response bias, some of which are associated with malingering and some of which are not. These will be discussed throughout this section. Further discussion of specific techniques utilizing signal detection theory to quantify response bias will be presented in the chapter on chronic pain (Chapter 17).

Feigning is a more specific but still very general concept. The *Webster's Seventh New Collegiate Dictionary* (C & C Merriam Co, 1965) defines "feign" as "1 a: to represent by a false appearance of; sham b: to assert as if true; pretend 2 archaic a; invent, imagine b: to give fictional representation to 3 obs; disguise, conceal" (p. 306). Thus, a malingerer may feign some problem for the purposes of financial compensation or other external incentive, or the person with a Factitious Disorder may feign some problem for the purpose of assuming the sick role. However, one may feign for many other reasons, for example, a person may feign not recalling a social appointment as he or she did not want to see the others involved. As such, feigning is a common everyday occurrence for most people.

The term *dissimulation* is similar to feigning. The *Webster's Seventh New Collegiate Dictionary* (C & C Merriam Co., 1965) defines dissimulate as "to hide under a false appearance" (p. 242). Again, this is a common occurrence in everyday life. A similar or related term that is sometimes used is *dissemble*, which also means to disguise or conceal behind a false appearance, or to feign. However, terms such as feigning or dissimulation are commonly used to mean the intentional production or exaggeration of symptoms for the purposes of malingering/external incentive or factitious behavior.

Response set and *response style* are general terms that have been popularized with the development of several self-report inventories, notably the Minnesota Multiphasic Personality Inventory (MMPI; Hathaway & McKinley, 1967) and its successor, the MMPI-2 (Butcher, Dahlstrom, Graham, Tellegen, & Kaemmer,

1989). Anastasi and Urbina (1997) discuss several of the more common response sets or response styles. An early response set that was identified was that of *acquiescence*. Acquiescence is the tendency to answer "true" or "yes" to questions or questionnaire items. Acquiescence is thought to be a continuous variable with the yeasayers at one end of the continuum and naysayers, who tend to respond "no" or "not true", at the other. Other response sets that were identified early on were *random responding* and *careless responding*, both of which could invalidate results. Another important response set is that of *deviation*, or the tendency to give unusual or uncommon responses. A related response style or set is the tendency to give *extreme choices* on scales, for example, 1s or 7s on a 7-point Likert Scale.

Anastasi and Urbina (1997) note that most self-report inventory test items have one answer that is clearly the more socially desirable or acceptable compared to other(s). As such, one may "fake good" or choose answers that create a favorable impression, or "fake bad" and choose items that would make oneself appear more psychologically disturbed or disabled. There is extensive evidence that respondents, typically college students or other persons instructed to simulate some particular response set, can dissemble on personality inventories. However, the tendency to choose socially desirable responses, or the converse, may not reflect deliberate deception. *Social desirability*, as a more general personality characteristic, has been considered to be the tendency to put up a good front of which the respondent is largely unaware. This tendency may represent lack of insight, self-deception, an unwillingness to face up to one's limitations, or the need for self-protection, avoidance of criticism, social conformity, and/or social approval. Another term that is often used interchangeably with social desirability is that of *defensiveness*, that is, the person is defensive about disclosing or endorsing negative, pathological, or socially undesirable material. Social desirability is a construct or trait that has been found to be related to many health problems (Leclerc, Rahn, & Linden, 2006). There will be further discussion of this issue in the chapter on chronic pain (Chapter 17). On the other hand, individuals who tend to endorse questionnaire items that reflect an unfavorable or negative self-impression (i.e., not socially desirable) may be motivated by a need for attention, sympathy, or help in addressing personal problems; they tend to be critical both of themselves and others, ineffective in dealing with problems of daily life, cynical, and skeptical (Graham, 2006; Millon, 1997).

Another term that is often encountered is that of *impression management*. Anastasi and Urbina (1997) suggest that impression management is conscious dissembling designed to create a specific effect desired by the respondent. On the other hand, *self-deception* is considered to involve more complex intrapsychic processes. However, many response styles may be partly conscious and partly unconscious, involving elements of both conscious impression management and unconscious self, or other, deception.

Anastasi and Urbina (1997) note that response sets or response styles had early on been suggested to account for much of the variance in personality tests or other measures. There then followed much debate and research into what extent responses on personality or other questionnaires reflect general response styles vs.

specific content, for example, specific measures of psychopathology, achievement motivation, and so forth. Anastasi and Urbina suggest that this controversy of content vs. style in personality assessment has never been resolved. It is generally agreed that personality inventory scores are likely to reflect a combination of self-deception, impression management, and realistic self-portrayal, but the weight of these or other factors will vary depending upon the individual and the content being assessed, as well as the particular situation in which the individual is being assessed. There will be further discussion of specific measures of response set or style in subsequent chapters on malingering in TBI, chronic pain, and PTSD or other psychoemotional problems.

Many writers refer to *primary* or *secondary gain*, constructs initially developed in the psychoanalytic literature. Primary gain refers to the intrapsychic benefit associated with the successful psychological defense against an unacceptable impulse, affect, idea, or conflict whereas secondary gain refers to the interpersonal or environmental advantage or benefit of some symptom (Freud, 1959). An example of primary gain is that of a person who finds that aggressive or destructive impulses, thoughts, or wishes are unacceptable (perhaps because they both want to hurt, but also do not want to hurt, someone they love), and then represses such impulses or fantasies, excluding them from consciousness, or denies that something a loved one does is hurtful. Examples of secondary gain are the increased attention one receives when hurt, or not having to go to work or school when injured or ill. There has been very little empirical research concerning primary gain or intrapsychic dynamics in cases involving personal injury.

Rogers and Vitacco (2002) suggest that forensic psychology, in contrast to the psychodynamic and behavioral traditions, "has utilized the concept of secondary gain as a convenient but simplistic explanation for a patient's continued impairment" (p. 88). Rogers and Vitacco also suggest that there has been confusion between the potential for secondary gain with the determination of secondary gain, and erroneous equation of higher levels of reward (e.g., a larger settlement) with higher likelihood of secondary gain. Rogers and Shuman (2005) suggest that this term not be used. In contrast, Fishbain, Rosomoff, Cutler, and Rosomoff (1995) conducted a review of the scientific evidence for the concept of secondary gain within any medical treatment setting with any type of patient, including those suffering from chronic pain. It was suggested that, overall, the results supported the potential importance of this concept in understanding illness behavior, but further research was recommended. Fishbain et al. (1995) noted that one interpretation of the secondary gain concept is in terms of operant conditioning, that is, an environmental event serves to increase or decrease a behavior (e.g., solicitous attention to a pain problem serves to reinforce pain behavior eliciting such solicitous attention). Operant conditioning is a prominent determinant of human behavior in general. Fishbain et al. (1995) suggested that most patients may have some secondary gain associated with an illness, but that there are also often secondary losses, for example, not being able to engage in various activities, often including work, that had previously been enjoyed. Gatchel (2004), also noting the utility of the secondary gain construct in chronic pain, cautions against simplistic interpretations, for example, that because there is some potential secondary gain that this is what is maintaining the pain problem.

It should be noted that the patient or client is not necessarily alone in misrepresenting him- or her-self or acting to potentiate medicolegal processes. Bokan, Ries, and Katon (1981) discuss the concept of *tertiary gain*, that is, when someone other than the patient (doctors, lawyers, rehabilitation workers, etc.) obtains gain from the patient's illness, either conspicuous monetary gain (employment, fees, etc.) or more subtle tertiary gains. Waddell (2002) concluded that many health professionals or Social Security employees derive "much secondary gain" from back pain, perhaps more than most patients. Indeed, there is now a large industry of workers (clinicians, lawyers, etc.) whose livelihood depends upon the management of personal injury and related claims. Several studies have concluded that many doctors collude with patients so that they may obtain benefits that may otherwise not be available. For example, many medical practitioners admit to signing disability certificates where medical evidence does not justify it (Wynia, 2003). Clinicians sensitized to the signs and symptoms of their particular specialty may misdiagnose or over-diagnose problems, with inadequate attention to competing explanations. Chapman and Elstein (2000) have discussed how biases can occur in the face of uncertainty in medical decision-making. Examiners may also display response bias by the tendency to doubt the sincerity of patient complaints or by disregarding their veracity (Lees-Haley, 1997; McBeath, 2000).

There is increasing realization of bias in arbitrators' case perceptions and award recommendations (Eylon, Giacalone, & Pollard, 2000). Martelli, Zasler, and Babin (2004) have reported preliminary data regarding the common suspicion that *examiner bias* is influenced by compensation issues. Compelling evidence of perceived expert witness bias comes from the Federal Judiciary Committee sanctioned study involving a large sample of active Federal judges and the lead plaintiff and defense attorneys who presented the docket cases before them (Johnson, Krafka, & Cecil, 2000). Findings indicate that the primary problem with expert testimony is experts who "abandon objectivity and become advocates for the side that hired them (p. 5)." On a 1 (very infrequent) to 5 (very frequent) Likert Scale measuring this problem, the mean response was 3.69 for judges and 3.72 for attorneys.

Rogers and Vitacco (2002), commenting on the problem of examiner bias, note that a common criticism of forensic examiners is that they are not impartial (Colbach, 1997). Rogers and Vitacco suggest that there is the tendency to either not diagnose malingering at all or only very rarely, vs. the opposite tendency of diagnosing malingering too frequently. They note that some examiners may make an *ad hominem* fallacy, generalizing from some negative attribute (e.g., a manipulative patient) to a diagnosis of malingering. Sweet, Moberg, and Suchy (2000) have noted that the majority of clinical neuropsychologists in the United States are engaged in private practice and that the primary source of referrals in private practice is from attorneys or for medicolegal assessments. As such, it is apparent that there may be major tertiary gains for consulting neuropsychologists acting either for the plaintiff or for the defense, rather than, as ethically required, gathering data to present an impartial determination of the presence or absence of disability.

Faust and Heard (2003) provide a detailed discussion of biased experts, with practical suggestions for attorneys in identifying unfair practices. They note that biased experts tend to misrepresent things as more positive or more negative than is warranted. The defense expert may try to make it appear that there is no pathology or psychopathology, reduce its severity and significance, or disconnect it from the accident/injury in question, whereas the plaintiff expert strives to make the pathology appear, stand out, or to direct blame toward the accident/injury. In terms of intentionality, such bias is thought to be completely inadvertent at one end of the spectrum and fully intentional at the other. Rogers and Shuman (2005) provide a practical guide offering specific suggestions about lines of questioning that may be taken to challenge biased experts.

Symptom magnification and *symptom amplification* are other terms that are encountered in the literature. Rogers and Vitacco (2002) suggest that symptom magnification is sometimes used in forensic cases to "circumvent the classification of malingering" and that "the implied meaning of symptom magnification largely parallels malingering, but lacks its explicit definition" (p. 89). These authors note that specifying levels of exaggeration may be difficult, or that mild to moderate levels of exaggeration may be difficult to operationalize. They therefore suggest that the term symptom magnification not be used in forensic assessments. However, whereas use of the term symptom magnification may sometimes represent conscious exaggeration of symptom severity for the purposes of obtaining an external incentive (i.e., malingering), we maintain that there are other important meanings and that dispensing with terms such as symptom magnification is not useful. The importance of symptom magnification in persons presenting with TBI, chronic pain, PTSD, and other psychoemotional problems has been discussed by several researchers (Ferrari, 2003; Gatchel, 2004; Miller & Donders, 2001). As will be discussed further in subsequent chapters, there is an extensive literature documenting that, in many disorders involving pain or psychological distress, some symptom magnification with exacerbation of complaint or related disability is apparent, which may be related to a number of psychological processes including catastrophizing, pain-related fear, rumination, neuroticism, negative expectations, or other constructs (Goubert, Crombez, & Van Damme, 2004; Ray et al., 2005; Ward, Lyubomirsky, Sousa, & Nolen-Hoeksema, 2003; Watkins & Moulds, 2005). We will return to this issue throughout this section.

Halligan et al. (2003) discuss the general concept of *illness deception* as "a conscious voluntary act or set of actions where the intention is to obtain personal advantage by securing benefits and/or lack of responsibilities that society and the legal system have bestowed upon the sick role" (p. 13). As such, this definition appears to apply to both malingering and Factitious Disorder. Again, it is imperative to distinguish between such intentional acts and either preoccupation with health or somatic concern, or accentuation or exaggeration or illness behavior for the purpose of secondary gain, when there may not be conscious intent to deceive. As documented by Byrne and Stokes (2003) and others, much or most illness deception may only partially be under conscious, volitional control.

Symptom validity, a term that is often used in the context of symptom validity testing, is another general term that refers to whether patient symptoms or test performance are valid. As this term is commonly used, it often at least implicitly implies malingering, that is, if the test results are not valid it means the person is malingering. However, there are many reasons why assessment results may be invalid, for example, (a) poor reading comprehension and inability to respond appropriately to questionnaire items, (b) culturally inappropriate measures, (c) disinterest or more active resistance during the assessment protocol due to a variety of reasons, (d) the examinee has a headache or other condition during the assessment that interferes with performance, (e) examiner error in administration of tests, or even (f) that the results obtained do not measure the construct of interest. With respect to actual symptoms (e.g., back pain, memory problems, psychoemotional problems) that may be reported by the patient/client or inferred from behavioral observation, symptom validity often refers to whether or not the patient is truthfully or accurately representing the nature or degree of problems. As such, this is similar to response bias. Again, it is often suggested that if the self-report is not accurate or if behavioral presentation is unexpected (usually involving symptoms that appear more severe than would normally be expected in the context of the presumed cause), and if the situation involves compensation, then the "invalid" symptoms are being produced purposefully to obtain compensation.

However, there is great variability in the presentation of persons with most diagnoses that are discussed in the present chapter and throughout this book and its companion volume (Young, Kane, & Nicholson, 2006). The signs or symptoms as well as the course, response to treatment, or underlying pathological processes for all these conditions continue to be investigated. Symptoms that may be considered "invalid", that is, as being unexpected in association with some causal event, may be quite valid in association with another event. Thus, a person may have had a minor head injury involving trauma to the head but with little, if any, TBI, but be having significant difficulty due to posttraumatic headache, posttraumatic stress reaction, or other causes. These issues, and the more general question of what is meant by symptom validity or how to assess symptom validity, will be addressed further throughout this section. A related but more subtle term that is sometimes used is whether the data from an assessment are *reliable*, that is, whether they follow expected patterns (e.g., whether recognition memory is relatively better than free recall as is usually observed in neuropsychological assessments). However, this is not how the term reliable is usually used in the psychological literature. Again, there may be other explanations for such observations and the conclusion that this means the assessment results are invalid or the person is malingering may not be justified.

Another term or phrase that has entered the lexicon and is being increasingly utilized is that of *suboptimal effort* (incomplete effort, poor effort, etc.). Such terms suggest that the person did not put forth good effort during an examination, typically on measures of cognitive capacity during neuropsychological assessments. This construct has been criticized by other researchers, because it is erroneously equated with malingering; however, effort may be affected by many genuine disorders (Rogers and Shuman, 2005). This construct will be critically reviewed more fully below in discussion of specific measures purported to measure effort. A final related phrase or term that will be mentioned is that of *suboptimal performance*. This term, often used in the context of neuropsychological assessment but also with some motor performance measures in chronic pain, correctly suggests that there may be an optimal level of performance. Enormous quantities of research with a vast literature have been devoted to determination of factors that influence human performance. Such factors include aspects of the physical environment (e.g., effects of temperature or lighting), the interpersonal or social environment (e.g., the effects of a supportive or punitive social environment), plus intraindividual factors (e.g., the effect of anxiety, achievement motivation, fatigue). Although optimal performance is clearly the ideal, some research reports suggest that suboptimal performance is to be equated with suboptimal effort, symptom validity, malingering, or related constructs (Merten, Green, Henry, Blaskewitz, & Brockhaus, 2005).

Methodology and the Validity of Studies of Malingering

As will be argued throughout this section, even with advances in developing measures or indices of malingering, there is usually no simple nor even more complex or sophisticated way to clearly and unambiguously determine whether a person is malingering or not. Perhaps the most telling indication that a person is malingering is that he or she admits to doing so. However, this very seldom happens and, when it does, it might even be questioned whether such confession is not part of a factitious or other disorder. A strategy that is commonly employed is to have the individual put under surveillance in order to detect whether he or she is able to do things that are widely discrepant with what has otherwise been reported, for example, that the person is able to walk when he or she claims to have been paralyzed and completely unable to walk at all under any circumstance. Whereas information collected from surveillance may be useful, this is likely more often of limited value given that there are not usually such dramatic differences between claimed disability and observed behaviors, and any apparent discrepancies may be due to a number of different reasons, for example, that the person is able to walk and do things to some degree when feeling better but that pain usually prohibits or interferes with such activity. It is often suggested that other inconsistencies in presentation (e.g., between aspects of the reported history and what has otherwise been documented, or between reported and observed behavior) may be indicative of a less than honest presentation, but patients are often poor historians (Cunnien, 1997) and there are many reasons why self-report may not be accurate (Stone, 2000).

Faust and Ackerly (1998) reported on several plaintiffs who were caught on videotape engaging in physical activities that they had denied being able to do whatsoever, although these same persons obtained unremarkable scores on symptom validity testing. Faust and Ackerly discuss the questionable relationship between various signs or indicators of malingering, noting that poor performance on measures claiming to assess malingering or poor effort may not be related to other measures and behaviors. It was noted that there are multiple possible sources of "noise" or error in assessment data, and that there are several different conditions that can lead to nonrepresentative or lowered test performance, and to misreporting symptoms or history.

With respect to specific measures of malingering, there are three primary designs or approaches that have been used to identify indicators and develop or validate measures (Guriel & Fremouw, 2003; Rogers & Bender, 2003). These are commonly known as simulation (or analog) designs, known-groups comparison designs, and differential prevalence comparison designs. A simple and typical simulation design would be to have healthy volunteers (often college students) simulate how they think someone with TBI, chronic pain, PTSD, or other problems would respond to the test materials, that is, the specific measure of malingering or response bias or measure that is actually intended to assess the condition in question, and to then compare their responses with those of healthy control subjects responding genuinely, or with persons with TBI, chronic pain, PTSD, or other problems who are responding genuinely. A refinement of this approach is to have patients (e.g., persons with TBI, chronic pain, etc.) attempt to malinger or simulate having greater difficulty than they actually are having and to then compare responses with similar patients who are responding genuinely. In most such studies, the performance of persons who are simulating is found to be different and usually much worse than that of the healthy control subjects or, in some cases, actual patients responding genuinely. Simulation designs are usually convenient, easy to undertake, and allow manipulation of one variable of interest or another.

Guriel and Fremouw (2003) note that coaching, or providing simulators with information about the disorder/problem to be feigned and/or providing strategies to avoid detection on psychological tests, has become an important component of malingering research. It had earlier been assumed that malingerers were naive to testing procedures, that is, that they were not aware of what different tests were or how specific measures of malingering may work. However, there is now widespread belief that many persons who undergo medicolegal assessments may have been provided with information about testing procedures or symptom presentations either from their attorneys, clinicians with whom they have been involved, other patients, their own research, or from other means (Elhai, Gold, Sellers, & Dorfman, 2001; Hall & Porier, 2001; Lees-Haley, 1997; Wetter & Corrigan, 1995; Youngjohn, 1995). Wetter and Corrigan (1995) surveyed 70 attorneys and found that 79% believed that they should talk with their clients about what psychological testing may involve and 47% thought that the attorney should usually or always inform the client about the nature of validity scales. Essig, Mittenberg, Peterson, Stranman, and Cooper (2001) surveyed 473 attorneys and found that 65% spent up to 2 hours preparing their clients for neuropsychological assessment and 19% discussed issues related to detection of malingering. Aronson, Rosenwald, and Rosen (2001), noting the problem of attorney or clinician coaching of symptoms with persons presenting a claim for PTSD, have proposed that there be some limited modification of attorney-client privilege in order that it could be determined whether such coaching had taken place. This was thought to be consistent with the exception to the physician–patient privilege in the context of litigation. Many malingering simulation studies have begun to provide study participants with specific information about how to best simulate problems, although some studies have found that coaching does not result in any difference in test performance in comparison with persons who have not been coached (Borckardt et al., 2003).

Simulation designs allow one to manipulate one or another experimental variable, allowing for increased internal validity, or confidence that it is the experimental variable in question that is responsible for the observed results (e.g., what effect different types of coaching or other factors have on the capacity to avoid detection when participants are administered a measure of malingering). However, simulation designs have limited external validity, that is, limited degree to which results may generalize to real-life situations. In other words, it is unknown whether such studies are relevant to real-life malingering. Some evidence suggests that the results of simulation studies may not be directly applicable to real-life situations (e.g., the contrast between the incidence of below chance performance on forced-choice techniques with simulators vs. the apparent incidence in real life—see below). Hilsabeck and LeCompte (1997) suggest that instructing simulators in how to fake believable deficits or by providing monetary incentives to produce believable deficits may help with this design. However, another most important problem with simulator/analog designs is that there has been limited investigation in the analog/experimental situations of the impact upon the performance on measures of malingering or symptom validity by factors such as the effects of pain, psychoemotional distress, sleep disturbance, thought or other psychiatric disorder, and so forth (Nicholson & Martelli, 2006). Whereas these or other factors are beginning to be investigated (see below), such work is in very preliminary stages and, given the great heterogeneity or variability in how these or many other factors may impact upon performance, it will likely take considerable further study to determine to what extent they may impact upon performance on measures of malingering or symptom validity.

The known-groups comparison design has generally referred to the comparison of how persons who have already been independently (perhaps more or less correctly) identified as malingering perform on various measures or indicators with actual patient groups responding genuinely (Rogers & Bender, 2003). Such design provides for external validity or generalizability to real-life situations involving real-life malingerers, that is, if performance on a specific measure or indicator is found to discriminate actual malingerers from (relevant) patient groups, then this provides some confidence that such indicator or measure may be used to identify other malingerers in future studies. However, as has been indicated, there are very few such studies because there are very few samples of persons who are clearly or reasonably identified as malingerers. Studies purporting to have identified actual malingerers will be examined more closely in subsequent chapters. Unfortunately, the known groups comparison design has also sometimes been used to refer to how any other patient group (e.g., persons with more significant TBI, persons with chronic pain, persons with well documented PTSD) perform on a measure or indicator of interest, but this does not provide information that is directly applicable to malingering.

Faust and Ackerly (1998) suggested that malingering studies utilizing a simulation design are probably best viewed within the context of discovery relative to the types of discriminations clinicians really need to make. Faust (2003) suggests that it is not necessary to have a "gold standard" or unambiguous criteria to identify someone who is malingering in order to make progress in research about malingering. Rather, at this stage, scientific progress may be a matter of more closely approximating or "getting at" the truth about malingering and related behaviors, something that is true in most scientific endeavors. Faust (2003) also suggests that more rather than fewer indicators of some phenomena, for example, malingering, may not be useful in correctly identifying the phenomena. For example, if there are several indicators of malingering, but if these are all limited in how useful they are, or if they overlap and are correlated with each other, then having more such indicators may actually reduce overall accuracy, especially if some of the indicators are relatively weak or invalid predictors. It is suggested that, in making a diagnosis in psychology or distinguishing one condition from another, or judging the severity of a disorder, about three to five of the most valid and nonredundant variables, if combined properly, will be the most useful. However, as will be discussed further below, there are as yet few, if any, good markers of malingering or related constructs.

Most researchers recommend that multiple sources of information should be used in the detection of malingering or other response styles (Backhaus et al., 2004; Guriel & Fremouw, 2003; Iverson, 2003; Lee et al., 2000; Martelli et al., 2002; Millis & Volinsky, 2001; Rogers & Bender, 2003; Slick et al., 1999; Sweet, 1999; Willison & Tombaugh, 2006). As Hilsabeck and Gouvier (2005) have noted, this is consistent with the multitrait-multimethod strategy to investigate any psychological construct, as advocated by Campbell and Fiske (1959). Such multitrait-multimethod approaches help to prevent a myopic focus upon a singular aspect or interpretation of some phenomena or construct, research then being marshalled to confirm the validity of this singular perspective.

Martelli et al. (2002) have suggested an approach termed "motivation assessment profiling" (MAP), in which behavioral observation, interview, collaborative, historical, personality, and contextual data, along with neuropsychological or other performance data including measures of effort or response bias, are integrated as an optimal method for estimating the degree to which test results are reliable and valid and reflect actual abilities. It is recommended that information from a variety of sources be utilized, including: (1) school records; (2) medical records; (3) driver records; (4) service and criminal records; (5) employment records; (6) psychological/psychiatric records and reports; (7) interviews with family members, friends, teachers, and employers, and so on; and (8) any other available materials (e.g., from attorneys through formal discovery).

Finally, differential prevalence designs utilize groups that are assumed to be different in their response styles, for example, compensation-seeking persons claiming some disability associated with TBI, chronic pain, PTSD, depression, or other psychoemotional problems are compared with similar persons who are not seeking compensation. It is assumed that those seeking or receiving compensation may have greater motivation to exaggerate or fabricate problems related to their claims. Guriel and Fremouw (2003) suggest that differential prevalence designs are the weakest in being able to identify a malingerer or someone who may be exaggerating problems. However, differential prevalence designs have been used extensively, they apply to real-life situations, and there is an apparent conflict of results or interpretation between studies, so we will more closely examine the effect of compensation status below, in Chapter 15.

Incidence, Prevalence, and Base Rates of Malingering

Estimates of the incidence (number of new cases) or prevalence (total number of cases) of malingering in TBI, chronic pain, PTSD, or other psychoemotional disorders have varied widely. This reflects the problem of accurate identification of such behavior and the confusion that this construct or class of behaviors has with other behaviors. Again, there are very few instances of confirmed malingering, and most estimates are based upon questionable criteria that will be critically examined throughout this section, as well as anecdotal evidence, or the opinion/impression of clinicians.

Many studies in which a sample of suspected malingerers are presented would suggest a low prevalence rate, given that relatively few malingerers are identified. For example, Miller's (1961) famous study (see Chapter 15) would indicate a prevalence rate of 1.25% (Fishbain, Cutler, Rosomoff, & Rosomoff, 1999). Craig, Hill, and McMurtry (1999), citing several other studies, concluded that the base rates for malingering were believed to be quite low. Citing estimates of 1% and 5% provided by Kieser (1968) and Waddell (2002), Halligan et al. (2003) suggested that it has commonly been believed that the prevalence rate of illness deception is small, but the difficulty in establishing reliable base rates precludes any such assumptions. Halligan et al. note that there is some tendency to reserve terms such as malingering for the most extreme or obvious cases involving frank deception, and lesser cases of exaggeration would not be registered as malingering. Schretlen (1988) suggested that the prevalence of malingered mental disorders was 2–7%. Boden (1996) estimated that, at most, 3% of injured workers in the United States could be classified as engaging in fraudulent behavior. Binder and Rohling (1996) suggested that, before the development of systematic procedures for the assessment of poor motivation in neuropsychological examinations, anecdotal experience suggested that outright malingering was rare.

Leavitt and Sweet (1986), in a postal survey of orthopedic surgeons and neurosurgeons treating low back pain patients, found that 60% of respondents thought malingering was relatively infrequent, occurring in less than 5% of patients. However, 10% of respondents thought that malingering occurred in more than

25% of cases. One surgeon thought that malingering occurred in 75% of cases! Leavitt (1991) concluded that uncertainty concerning the prevalence of malingering, either deliberate exaggeration of symptomatology or fabrication of nonexisting symptoms, was due to the fact that objective criteria for identifying cases was lacking. Awerbuch (1992), noting that there are many well-publicized reports of staged automobile accidents and other fraudulent claims, suggested that malingering represented less than 5% of claims for whiplash injury in Australia. Fishbain et al. (1999), citing several studies including that of the Institute of Medicine Committee on Pain (Osterwels, Kleinman, & Mechanic, 1987), noted that it had previously been thought that pure malingering (i.e., fabrication of nonexistent symptoms) in personal injury settings was relatively rare, and that malingering in pain settings or clinics was rare, although there appeared to be no data on the frequency of malingering within the chronic pain population to support such opinions. Fishbain et al. (1999), in a systematic review of the literature, concluded that there was extremely weak evidence that malingering may be present from 1.25% to 10.4% of chronic pain patients but, because of poor study quality or methodological problems, such prevalence rates were unreliable and no conclusions concerning prevalence were actually warranted. More recently, Mendelson and Mendelson (2004) concluded that the frequency with which pain is simulated in the medical setting is not known, the claimed frequency varying with the zealousness of the examining clinician.

Rogers, Sewell, and Goldstein (1994), in an opinion-based survey of forensic evaluators, most of whom were psychologists, found that these practitioners thought that the prevalence of malingering was 15.7% in forensic settings and 7.4% in nonforensic settings. Rogers (1997b) later concluded that prevalence rates for malingering were poorly established. Rogers, Salekin, Sewell, Goldstein, and Leonard (1998), in another survey of forensic examiners, found that the mean percentage of forensic cases that were thought to be malingering was 17.44%, whereas the mean percentage of nonforensic cases thought to involve malingering was 7.16%. There was large variability in the estimates of both, the standard deviations being 14.44 and 7.09, respectively. For the forensic cases, this means that most prevalence rates could be expected to fall between 0.0% and 46.2%. In this sample (Rogers et al., 1998), the majority (53.4%) of cases believed to involve malingering were of feigned mental disorders, 19.5% were cognitive disorders, 15.8% were medical disorders, and 11.2% involved multiple problems. It is unknown to what extent the subjects seen involved criminal, child custody, or other cases rather than those presenting specifically with TBI, chronic pain, PTSD, or other psychoemotional disorders that are the focus of this section.

Guriel and Fremouw (2003) note that prevalence rates vary considerably, with estimates of malingering psychological symptoms following personal injury, ranging from 1% to over 50%. With respect to PTSD, Guriel and Fremouw (2003) concluded that exact prevalence rates for malingering were nonexistent. It was suggested that, in part, this was because practitioners believe whatever their clients tell them and so do not formally assess for malingering, but, also, because there is no "gold standard" to identify malingering.

Several studies suggest that the incidence of malingering may be high. Heaton, Smith, Lehman, and Vogt (1978) had early on suggested the prevalence of malingered neuropsychological disorders may be as high as 78%! Griffin, Normingtom, May, and Glassmire (1996), using a composite malingering measure derived from several other scales (which was acknowledged to be not yet validated), suggested that 19% of disability claimants in the United States were malingering "to some degree." Resnick (1997) cited a study in which 40% of those considered totally disabled in association with PTSD and receiving benefits showed "absolutely no disability." Palmer (2003), citing Carroll (2001) and Pankratz (2003), suggests that malingering of PTSD in the U.S. Veterans Administration system is now extremely common. Lees-Haley (1997b) concluded that as many as 20–30% of personal injury claimants may have been feigning posttraumatic disturbances. Larrabee (2003) concluded that the base rate for possible malingering from 11 studies involving a total of 1,363 mild head injury compensation-seeking cases was 40%. Notably, within the domain of health insurance fraud, one study found that the largest group of suspected fraudulent claims were made by medical professionals as claimants and the next largest group of suspected fraudulent claims were made by insurance professionals (LoPiccolo, Goodkin, & Baldewicz, 1999).

Mittenberg, Patton, Vanyock, and Condit (2002) sampled 131 members of the American Board of Clinical Neuropsychology, who reported on 33,531 cases. The reported or suspected base rates of probable malingering or exaggeration were 29% for personal injury, 30% for cases of disability or worker's compensation, 19% for criminal cases, and 8% for psychiatric cases. In terms of diagnosis, the base rates were 39% for mild head injury, 35% for fibromyalgia and chronic fatigue, 31% for chronic pain, 27% for neurotoxic cases, 22% for electrical injury, 15% for depressive disorders, and 11% for dissociative disorders. The diagnosis of malingering was based upon the severity (65% of respondents) or pattern (64% of respondents) of cognitive impairment that was considered to be inconsistent with the presumed cause of the difficulties; scores below recommended cutoffs on forced choice symptom validity testing (see below, 57% of respondents); discrepancies among records, self-report, and observed behavior (56% of respondents); implausible self-reported symptoms during interviews (46% of respondents); implausible changes in test scores across repeated examinations (45% of respondents); and elevated validity scales on objective personality tests (38% of respondents). These and other indices of "malingering" will be reviewed in subsequent chapters of this section.

Boone and Lu (2003) cited several studies of mild TBI, concluding that the high base rates of "noncredible" test performance in this population have been measured at 50% or higher. Finally, Binder, Kelly, Villaneuva, and Winslow (2003), citing numerous studies of mild head injury with chronic symptoms in a medicolegal context that employed specific measures to assess "invalid responding and motivation" during neuropsychological assessment, suggested that the base rates for probable malingering or invalid responding are as high as 32–60% in this population. It was thought that the base rates are likely much lower in other nonmedicolegal settings or with moderate-to-severe TBI subjects.

Whereas it is important to know the base rates of various phenomena to determine the utility or most appropriate cutting scores of any diagnostic sign or test result, Rogers and Neumann (2003) suggest that the instability of base rates concerning malingering mitigates against their use. Malingering base rates are so poorly defined and imprecise that it makes further decision making on the basis of these misleading. For example, the result obtained from a malingering test using some cutting score (i.e., the level or score on the test at which it is concluded that the person is malingering) will yield far too many false positives if used in a situation where there are fewer malingerers than is assumed to be the case (Faust & Ackley, 1998; Gouvier, Hayes, & Smiroldo, 1998). Furthermore, the application of base rates to the interpretation of the relevance or utility of any diagnostic sign assumes that the diagnostic sign is valid, something that cannot be assumed with most current measures of malingering. It should also be realized that the relevance of base rates is dependent upon how serious a problem a false positive or false negative error is considered to be. With respect to malingering, this can simply be rephrased as "what are the implications of falsely identifying someone as malingering" vs. "what are the implications of falsely identifying a person as not malingering."

Gouvier et al. (1998), noting that the base rates of many symptoms (e.g., anxiety or nervousness, problems sleeping, depression, headaches, back pain, concentration, or memory problems) in personal injury claimants without documentation of TBI, or even in the general population, may be very high (Lees-Haley & Brown, 1993), suggests that "the whole field of malingering research is moving toward refining our ability to tell normalcy against a background of pseudo-neuropsychopathology" (p. 661). Throughout the remaining chapters of this section we will return to the problem of differentiating between problems that many persons in the normal population may have, various "pseudo-neuropsychopathological" or other poorly defined problems that may be associated with an injury, formal nosological categories such as TBI or PTSD, and malingering or other reasons for symptom exaggeration/feigning.

References

American Psychiatric Association (1994). *Diagnostic and statistical manual of mental disorders* (4th ed.). Washington, DC: Author.

American Psychiatric Association (2000). *Diagnostic and statistical manual of mental disorders* (4th ed., Text Revision). Washington, DC: Author.

Anastasi, A., & Urbina, S. (1997). *Psychological testing*. Upper Saddle River, NJ: Prentice Hall.

Aronson, R. H., Rosenwald, L., & Rosen, G. M. (2001). Attorney-client confidentiality and the assessment of claimants who allege posttraumatic stress disorder. *Washington Law Review, 76*, 313–347.

Awerbuch, M.S. (1992). Whiplash in Australia: Illness or injury? *Medical Journal of Australia, 157*, 193–196.

Backhaus, S. L., Fichtenberg, N. L., & Hanks, R. A. (2004). Detection of sub-optimal performance using a floor effect strategy in patients with traumatic brain injury. *The Clinical Neuropsychologist, 18*, 591–603.

Barsky, A. J., Ettner, S. L., Horsky, J., & Bates, D. W. (2001). Resource utilization of patients with hypochondriacal health anxiety and somatization. *Medical Care, 39*, 705–715.

Binder, L. M., Kelly, M. P., Villaneuva, M. R., & Winslow, M. M. (2003). Motivation and neuropsychological test performance following mild head injury. *Journal of Clinical and Experimental Neuropsychology, 25*, 420–430.

Binder, L. M., & Rohling, M. L. (1996). Money matters: A meta-analytic review of the effects of financial incentives on recovery after closed-head injury. *American Journal of Psychiatry, 153*, 7–10.

Boden, L. I. (1996). Work disability in an economic context. In S. Moon & S. L. Sauter (Eds.), *Psychosocial aspects of musculoskeletal disorders in office work*. London: Taylor & Francis.

Bogduk, N. (2004). Diagnostic blocks: A truth serum for malingering. *Clinical Journal of Pain, 20*, 409–414.

Bokan, J. A., Ries, R. K., & Katon, W. J. (1981). Tertiary gain and chronic pain. *Pain, 10*, 331–335.

Boone, K. B., & Lu, P. (2003). Noncredible cognitive performance in the context of severe brain injury. *The Clinical Neuropsychologist, 17*, 244–254.

Borckardt, J. J., Engum, E. S., Lambert, E. W., Nash, M., Bracy, O. L., & Ray, E. C. (2003). Use of the CBDI to detect malingering when malingerers do their "homework". *Archives of Clinical Neuropsychology, 18*, 57–69.

Brown, R. J. (2004). Psychological mechanisms of medically unexplained symptoms: An integrative conceptual model. *Psychological Bulletin, 130*, 793–812.

Bush, S. S., Ruff, R. M., Troster, A. I., Barth, J. T., Koffler, S. P., Pliskin, N. H. et al. (2005). Symptom validity assessment: Practical issues and medical necessity. NAN Policy and Planning Committee. *Archives of Clinical Neuropsychology, 20*, 419–426.

Butcher, J. N., Dahlstrom, W. G., Graham, J. R., Tellegen, A., & Kaemmer, B. (1989). *Minnesota Multiphasic Personality Inventory (MMPI-2). Manual for administration and scoring*. Minneapolis: University of Minnesota Press.

Byrne, R. W., & Stokes, E. (2003). Can monkeys malinger? In P. W. Halligan, C. Bass, & D. A. Oakley (Eds.), *Malingering and illness deception* (pp. 54–67). New York: Oxford University Press.

C & C Merriam Co. (1965). *Webster's seventh new collegiate dictionary*. Toronto, Ontario: Thomas Allen & Son Limited.

Campbell, D. T., & Fiske, D. W. (1959). Convergent and discriminant validation by the multitrait–multimethod matrix. *Psychological Bulletin, 56*, 81–105.

Chapman, G. B., & Elstein, A. S. (2000). Cognitive processes and biases in medical decision-making, In G. B. Chapman, B. Gretchen, F. A. Sonnenberg et al. (Eds.), *Decision making in health care: Theory, psychology, and applications. Cambridge series on judgment and decision making* (pp. 183–210). New York: Cambridge University Press.

Clayer, J. R., Bookless, C., & Ross, M.W. (1984). The evaluation of illness behavior and exaggeration of disability. *British Journal of Psychiatry, 148*, 296–299.

Colbach, E. M. (1997). The trouble with American forensic psychiatry. *International Journal of Offender Therapy and Comparative Criminology, 41*, 160–167.

Craig, K. D., Hill, M. L., & McMurtry, B. (1999). *Detecting deception and malingering*. In A. R. Block, E. F. Kremer, & E. Fernandez (Eds.), *Handbook of pain syndromes* (pp. 41–58). Hillsdale, NJ: Lawrence Erlbaum Associates.

Cunnien, A. J. (1997). Psychiatric and medical syndromes associated with deception. In R. Rogers (Ed.), *Clinical assessment of malingering and deception* (2nd ed., pp. 23–46). New York: Guilford.

Davatzikos, C., Ruparel, K., Fan, Y., Shen, D. G., Acharyya, M., Loughead, J. W. et al. (2005). Classifying spatial patterns of brain activity with machine learning methods: application to lie detection. *Neuroimage, 28*, 663–668. Epub 2005 Oct 5.

DePaulo, B. M., Charlton, K., Cooper, H., Lindsay, J. J., & Muhlenbruck, L. (1997). The accuracy-confidence correlation in the detecting of deception. *Personality and Social Psychology Review, 4*, 346–357.

DePaulo, B. M., Lindsay, J. L., Malone, B. E., Muhlenbruck, L., Charlton, K., & Cooper, H. (2003). Cues to deception. *Psychological Bulletin, 129*, 74–118.

Eckart, W. (2000). War, emotional stress, and German medicine. In R. Chickering & S. Forster (Eds.), *Great war, total war: Combat and mobilization on the Western Front, 1914–1918* (pp. 133–149). Cambridge: Cambridge University Press.

Eisendrath, S. J., & McNiel, D. E. (2002). Factitious disorders in civil litigation: Twenty cases illustrating the spectrum of abnormal illness—Affirming behavior. *Journal of the American Academy of Psychiatry and the Law, 30*, 391–392.

Elhai, J. D., Gold, P. B., Sellers, A. H., & Dorfman, W. I. (2001). The detection of malingered posttraumatic stress disorder with MMPI-2 Fake Bad indices. *Assessment, 8*, 221–236.

Eriksen, H. R., & Ursin, H. (2004). Subjective health complaints, sensitization, and sustained cognitive activation (stress). *Journal of Psychosomatic Research, 56*, 445–448.

Essig, S., Mittenberg, W., Peterson, R., Stranman, S., & Cooper, J. (2001). Practices in forensic neuropsychology: Perspectives of neuropsychologists and trial attorney. *Archives of Clinical Neuropsychology, 16*, 271–291.

Eylon, D., Giacalone, R. A., & Pollard, H. G. (2000). Beyond contractual interpretation: Bias in arbitrators' case perceptions and award recommendations. *Journal of Organizational Behavior 21*, 513–524.

Faust, D. (2003). Alternatives to four clinical and research traditions in malingering detection. In P. W. Halligan, C. Bass, & D. A. Oakley (Eds.), *Malingering and Illness Deception* (pp. 107–121). New York: Oxford University Press.

Faust, D., & Ackerly, M. A. (1998). Did you think it was going to be easy: Some methodological suggestions for the investigation and development of malingering detection techniques. In Reynolds (Ed.), *Detection of malingering during head injury litigation* (pp. 261–286). New York: Plenum Press.

Faust, D., & Heard, K. V. (2003). Biased experts: Some practical suggestions for identifying and demonstrating unfair practices. In I. Z. Schultz & D. O. Brady (Eds.), *Psychological injuries at trial* (pp. 1706–1739). Chicago, IL: American Bar Association.

Feldman, M. D., Hamilton, J. C., & Deemer, H. N. (2001). Factitious disorder. In K. A. Philips (Ed.), *Somatoform and factitious disorders*. Washington, DC: American Psychiatric Publishing.

Ferrari, R. (2003). The clinical relevance of symptom amplification. *Pain, 107*, 276–277.

Fishbain, D. A., Cutler, R., Rosomoff, H. L., & Rosomoff, R. S. (1999). Chronic pain disability exaggeration/malingering and submaximal effort research. *Clinical Journal of Pain, 15*, 244–274.

Fishbain, D. A., Rosomoff, H. L., Cutler, R. B., & Rosomoff, R. S. (1995). Secondary gain concept: A review of the scientific evidence. *The Clinical Journal of Pain*, 11, 6–21.

Freud, S. (1959). *Introductory lectures on psychoanalysis*. London: Hogarth.

Ganis, G., Kosslyn, S. M., Stose, S., Thompson, W. L., & Yurgelun-Todd, D. A. (2003). Neural correlates of different types of deception: An fMRI investigation. *Cerebral Cortex, 13*, 830–836.

Gatchel, R. J. (2004). Psychosocial factors that can influence the self-assessment of function. *Journal of Occupational Rehabilitation, 14*, 197–206.

Gerson, A. (2002). Beyond DSM-IV: A meta-review of the literature on malingering. *American Journal of Forensic Psychology, 20*, 57–69.

Goubert, L., Crombez, G., & Van Damme, S. (2004). The role of neuroticism, pain catastrophizing and pain-related fear in vigilance to pain: a structural equations approach. *Pain, 107*, 234–241.

Gouvier, W. D., Hayes, J. S., & Smiroldo, B. B. (1998). The significance of base rates, test sensitivity, test specificity, and subjects' knowledge of symptoms in assessing TBI sequelae and malingering. In C. R. Reynolds (Ed.), *The detection of malingering during head injury litigation. Critical issues in neuropsychology* (pp. 55–79). New York: Plenum.

Graham, J. R. (2006). MMPI-2: Assessing personality and psychopathology (4th ed.). New York: Oxford University Press.

Green, D. M., & Swets, J. A. (1966). *Signal detection theory and psychophysics*. New York: Wiley.

Greenberg, D. S. (2002). Polygraph fails scientific review in the USA. *Lancet, 26, 360*(9342): 1309.

Griffin, G. A., Normington, J., May, R., & Glassmire, D. (1996). Assessing dissimulation among social security disability income claimants. *Journal of Consulting and Clinical Psychology, 64*, 1425–1430.

Grubin, D., & Madsen, L. (2005). Lie detection and the polygraph: A historical review. *The Journal of Forensic Psychiatry & Psychology, 16*, 357–369.

Guriel, J. & Fremouw, W. (2003). Assessing malingered posttraumatic stress disorder: A critical review. *Clinical Psychology Review, 23*, 881–904.

Hall, H. V., & Poirier, J. G. (2001). *Detecting malingering and deception* (2nd ed.). New York: CRC Press.

Halligan, P. W., Bass, C., & Oakley, D. A. (2003). Willful deception as illness behavior. In P. W. Halligan, C. Bass, & D. A. Oakley (Eds.), *Malingering and illness deception* (pp. 3–28). New York: Oxford University Press.

Hathaway, S. R., & McKinley, J. C. (1967). *Minnesota Multiphasic Personality Inventory manual*. New York: Psychological Corporation.

Heaton, R. K., Smith, H. H. Jr., Lehman, R. A., & Vogt, A. T. (1978). Prospects for faking believable deficits on neuropsychological testing. *Journal of Consulting and Clinical Psychology, 46*, 892–900.

Hilsabeck, R. C., & Gouvier, W. D. (2005). Detecting simulated memory impairment: Further validation of the Word Completion Memory Test (WCMT). *Archives of Clinical Neuropsychology, 20*, 1025–1041.

Hilsabeck, R. C., & LeCompte, D. C. (1997). *Word Completion Memory Test (WCMT)*. Durham, NC: CogniSyst.

Iverson, G. L. (2003). Detecting malingering in civil forensic evaluations. In A. M. Horton & L. C. Hartlage (Eds.), *Handbook of forensic neuropsychology* (pp. 137–177). New York: Springer Science+Business Media.

Iverson, G. L., & Binder, L. M. (2000). Detecting exaggeration and malingering in neuropsychological assessment. *Journal of Head Trauma Rehabilitation, 15*, 829–858.

Janca, A. (2005). Rethinking somatoform disorders. *Current Opinion in Psychiatry, 18*, 65–71.

Johnson, M. T., Krafka, C., & Cecil, J. S. (2000). *Expert testimony in federal civil trials: A preliminary analysis*. Federal Judicial Center.

Jones, M. A. (2003). Law, lies, and videotape: malingering as a legal phenomenon. In P. W. Halligan, C. Bass, & D. A. Oakley (Eds.), *Malingering and illness deception* (pp. 209–219). New York: Oxford University Press.

Kieser, L. (1968). *The transgenic neurosis*. Philadelphia, PA: Lippincott.

Knoll, J. L., & Resnick, P. J. (1999). U.S. v. Greer: longer sentences for malingerers. *Journal of the American Academy of Psychiatry and Law, 27*, 621–625.

Kozel, F. A., Johnson, K. A., Mu, Q., Grenesko, E. L., Laken, S. J., & George, M. S. (2005). Detecting deception using functional magnetic resonance imaging. *Biological Psychiatry, 58*, 605–613.

Kozel, F. A., Padgett, T. M., & George, M. S. (2004). A replication study of the neural correlates of deception. *Behavioral Neuroscience, 118*, 852–856.

Kozel, F. A., Revell, L. J., Lorberbaum, J. P., Shastri, A., Elhai, J. D., Horner, M. D. et al. (2004). A pilot study of functional magnetic resonance imaging brain correlates of deception in healthy young men. *Journal of Neuropsychiatry and Clinical Neuroscience, 16*, 295–305.

Krahn, L. E., Li, H., & O'Connor, M. K. (2003). Patients who strive to be ill: Factitious disorder with physical symptoms. *American Journal of Psychiatry, 160*, 1163–1168.

Langleben, D. D., Loughead, J. W., Bilker, W. B., Ruparel, K., Childress, A. R., Busch, S. I. et al. (2005). Telling truth from lie in individual subjects with fast event-related fMRI. *Human Brain Mapping, 26*, 262–272.

Langleben, D. D., Schroeder, L., Maldjian, J. A., Gur, R. C., McDonald, S., Ragland, J. D. et al. (2002). Brain activity during simulated deception: an event-related functional magnetic resonance study. *Neuroimage, 15*, 727–732.

Larrabee, G. (2003). Detection of malingering using atypical performance patterns on standard neuropsychological tests. *The Clinical Neuropsychologist, 17*, 410–425.

Leavitt, F. (1991). Predicting disability time using formal low back pain measurement: the Low Back Pain Simulation Scale. *Journal of Psychosomatic Research, 35*, 599–607.

Leavitt, F., & Sweet, J. J. (1986). Characteristics and frequency of malingering among patients with low back pain. *Pain, 25*, 357–364.

Leclerc, J., Rahn, M., & Linden, W. (2006). Does personality predict blood pressure over a 10-year period? *Personality and Individual Differences, 40*, 1313–1321.

Lee, A., Boone, K. B., Lesser, I., Wohl, M., Wilkins, S., & Parks, C. (2000). Performance of older depressed patients on two cognitive malingering tests: False positive rates for the Rey 15-Item Memorization and Dot Counting Tests. *The Clinical Neuropsychologist, 14*, 303–308.

Lee, T. M., Liu, H. L., Tan, L. H., Chan, C. C., Mahankali, S., Feng, C. M. et al. (2002). Lie detection by functional magnetic resonance imaging. *Human Brain Mapping, 15*, 157–164.

Lees-Haley, P. R. (1997a). *Challenges to validity and reliability in neurotoxic assessment of mass injuries*. Presentation at the National Academy of Neuropsychology Annual Meeting, Las Vegas.

Lees-Haley, P. R. (1997b). MMPI-2 base rates for 492 personal injury plaintiffs: Implications and challenges for forensic assessment. *Journal of Clinical Psychology, 53*, 745–755.

Lees-Haley, P. R. & Brown, R. (1993). Neuropsychological complaint base rates of 170 personal injury claimants. *Archives of Clinical Neuropsychology, 8*, 203–209.

Lipman, F. D. (1962). Malingering in personal injury cases. *Temple Law Quarterly, 35*, 141.

LoPiccolo, C. J., Goodkin, K., & Baldewicz, T. T. (1999). Current issues in the diagnosis and management of malingering. *Annals of Medicine, 31*, 166–174.

Mailis-Gagnon, A., Giannoylis, I., Downar, J., Kwan, C., Mikulis, D., Crawley, A. et al. (2003). Altered central somatosensory processing in chronic pain patients with "hysterical" anaesthesia. *Neurology, 60*, 1501–1507.

Mailis-Gagnon, A., & Nicholson, K. (in preparation). *Factitious, conversion and malingering: A case study.*

Malle, B. F. (2003). The social cognition of intentional action. In P. W. Halligan, C. Bass, & D. A. Oakley (Eds.), *Malingering and illness deception* (pp. 83–92). New York: Oxford University Press.

Martelli, M. F. (2000). Psychological assessment of response bias in impairment and disability ratings. Presentation as part of Symposium #2301 (The Psychologist's Role in the Social Security Disability Process) at the American Psychological Association 2000 Convention, Washington, D.C.

Martelli, M. F., Nicholson, K., Zasler, N. D., & Bender, M. C. (2006). Assessment of response bias in clinical and forensic evaluations of impairment following brain injury. In N. D. Zasler, D.I. Katz, & R. D. Zafonte (Eds.), *Brain injury medicine: Principles and practice.* New York: Demos Medical.

Martelli, M. F., Zasler, N. D., & Babin, P. R. (2004). Preliminary consumer guidelines for choosing a neuropsychologist for evaluation and treatment after acquired brain injury. *Brain Injury Professional*, 1(2), 24–27.

Martelli, M. F., Zasler, N. D., Mancini, A. M., & MacMillan, P. (1999). Psychological assessment and application in impairment and disability evaluations. In R. V. May & M. F. Martelli (Eds.), *Guide to functional capacity evaluation with impairment rating applications* (pp. 1–84). Richmond: NADEP.

Martelli, M. F., Zasler, N. D., Nicholson, K., Pickett, T. C., & May, V. R. (2002). Assessing the veracity of pain complaints and associated disability. In R. B. Weiner (Ed.), *Pain management: A practical guide for clinicians* (6th ed.) (pp. 789–805). Boca Ratan, FL: St. Lucie Press.

McBeath, J. G. (2000). Labelling of postconcussion patients as malingering and litigious: a common practice in need of criticism. *Headache, 40*, 609–610.

Mechanic, D., & Volkart, E. H. (1960). Illness behavior and medical diagnoses. *Journal of Health and Human Behavior, 1*, 86–94.

Mendelson, G., & Mendelson, D. (2004). Malingering pain in the medicolegal context. *Clinical Journal of Pain, 20*, 423–432.

Merten, T., Green, P., Henry, M., Blaskewitz, N., & Brockhaus, R. (2005). Analog validation of German-language symptom validity tests and the influence of coaching. *Archives of Clinical Neuropsychology, 20*, 719–726.

Miller, H. (1961). Accident neurosis. *British Medical Journal, 1*, 919–925.

Miller, L. (2000). Neurosensitization: A model for persistent disability in chronic pain, depression, and posttraumatic stress disorder following injury. *Neurorehabilitation, 14*, 25–32.

Miller, L. J., & Donders, J. (2001). Subjective symptomatology after traumatic head injury. *Brain Injury, 15*, 297–304.

Millis, S. R., & Volinsky, C. T. (2001). Assessment of response bias in mild head injury: Beyond malingering tests. *Journal of Clinical and Experimental Neuropsychology, 23*, 809–828.

Millon, T. (1997). *Millon Clinical Multiaxial Inventory-III Manual.* 3rd ed. Minneapolis, MN: NCS Pearson.

Mittenberg, W., Patton, C., Vanyock, E. M., & Condit, D. C. (2002). Base rates of malingering and symptom exaggeration. *Journal of Clinical and Experimental Neuropsychology, 24*, 1094–1102.

Nicholson, K. (2000). At the crossroads: Pain in the 21st Century. *NeuroRehabilitation, 14*, 57–67.

Nicholson, K., & Martelli, M. (2006). The confounding effects of pain, psychoemotional problems or psychiatric disorder, premorbid ability structure, and motivational or other factors on neuropsychological test performance. In G. Young, A. W. Kane, & K. Nicholson (Eds.), *Psychological knowledge in court: PTSD, pain and TBI* (pp. 335–351). New York: Springer Science+Business Media.

Nies, K. J., & Sweet, J. J. (1994). Neuropsychological assessment and malingering: A critical review of past and present strategies. *Archives of Clinical Neuropsychology, 9*, 501–552.

Nunez, J. M., Casey, B. J., Egner, T., Hare, T., & Hirsch, J. (2005). Intentional false responding shares neural substrates with response conflict and cognitive control. *Neuroimage, 25*, 267–277.

Oksol, E. M. & O'Donohue, W. T. (2003). A critical analysis of the polygraph. In W. T. O'Donohue & E. R. Levensky (Eds.), *Handbook of Forensic Psychology* (pp. 601–634). Elsevier, New York.

Osterwels, R., Kleinman, A., & Mechanic, D. (Eds.). (1987). *Institute of medicine committee on pain, disability and chronic illness behavior: pain and disability, clinical behavioral and public policy perspectives*. Washington, DC: National Academy Press.

Palmer, I. P. (2003). Malingering, shirking, and self-inflicted injuries in the military. In P. W. Halligan, C. Bass, & D. A. Oakley (Eds.), *Malingering and illness deception* (pp. 42–53). New York: Oxford University Press.

Pankratz, L. (2003). The misadventures of wanderers and victims of trauma. In P. W. Halligan, C. Bass, & D. A. Oakley (Eds.), *Malingering and illness deception* (pp. 184–196). New York: Oxford University Press.

Parsons, T. (1951). *The social system*. Free Press: New York.

Phan, K. L., Magalhaes, A., Ziemlewicz, T. J., Fitzgerald, D.A., Green, C., & Smith, W. (2005). Neural correlates of telling lies: A functional magnetic resonance imaging study at 4 Tesla. *Academic Radiology, 12*, 164–172.

Pilowsky, I. (1985). Malingerphobia. *Medical Journal of Australia, 143*, 571–572.

Pilowsky, I. (1993). Aspects of abnormal illness behaviour. *Psychotherapy and Psychosomatics, 60*, 62–74.

Ray, R. D., Ochsner, K. N., Cooper, J. C., Robertson, E. R., Gabrieli, J. D., & Gross, J. J. (2005). Individual differences in trait rumination and the neural systems supporting cognitive reappraisal. *Cognition, Affect, Behavior and Neuroscience, 5*, 156–168.

Reid, W. H. (2000) Malingering. *Journal of Psychiatric Practice, 6*, 226–228.

Resnick, P. J. (1997). Malingering of posttraumatic disorders. In R. Rogers (Ed.), *Clinical assessment of malingering and deception* (2nd ed., pp. 130–152). New York: Guilford.

Reuber, M., Mitchell, A. J., Howlett, S. J., Crimlisk, H. L., & Grunewald, R. A. (2005). Functional symptoms in neurology: questions and answers. *Journal of Neurology Neurosurgery and Psychiatry, 76*, 307–314.

Rogers, R. (1990). Models of feigned mental illness. *Professional Psychology: Research and Practice, 21*, 182–188.

Rogers, R. (Ed.). (1997a). *Clinical assessment of malingering and deception* (2nd ed.). New York: Guilford.

Rogers, R. (1997b). Introduction. In R. Rogers (Ed.), *Clinical assessment of malingering and deception* (2nd ed., pp. 1–19). New York: Guilford.

Rogers, R. & Bender, S. D. (2003). Evaluation of malingering and deception. In A. M. Goldstein (Ed.), *Comprehensive handbook of psychology: Forensic psychology* (Vol. 11, pp. 109–129). New York: Wiley.

Rogers, R., & Neumann, C. S. (2003). Conceptual issues and explanatory models of malingering. In P. W. Halligan, C. Bass, & D. A. Oakley (Eds.), *Malingering and illness deception* (pp. 71–82). New York: Oxford University Press.

Rogers, R., Salekin, R. T., Sewell, K. W., Goldstein, A. & Leonard, K. (1998). A comparison of forensic and nonforensic malingerers: A prototypical analysis of explanatory models. *Law and Human Behavior, 22*, 353–367.

Rogers, R., Sewell, K. W., & Goldstein, A. (1994). Explanatory models of malingering: A prototypical analysis. *Law and Human Behavior, 18*, 543–552.

Rogers, R., Sewell, K. W., & Salekin, R. T. (1994). A meta-analysis of malingering on the MMPI-2. *Assessment, 1*, 227–237.

Rogers, R., & Shuman, D. W. (2005). *Fundamentals of forensic practice: Mental health and criminal law*. New York: Springer Science+Business Media.

Rogers, R., & Vitacco, M. J. (2002). Forensic assessment of malingering and related response styles. In B. Van Dorsten (Ed.), *Forensic psychology: From classroom to courtroom* (pp. 83–104). Boston: Kluwer Academic/Plenum.

Schretlen, D. (1988). The use of psychological tests to identify malingered symptoms of mental disorder. *Clinical Psychology Review, 8*, 451–476.

Slick, D. J., Sherman, E. M., & Iverson, G. L. (1999). Diagnostic criteria for malingered neurocognitive dysfunction: Proposed standards for clinical practice and research. *The Clinical Neuropsychologist, 13*, 545–561.

Spence, S., Farrow, T., Leung, D., Shah, S., Reilly, B., Rahman, A. et al. (2003). Lying as an executive function. In P. W. Halligan, C. Bass, & D. A. Oakley (Eds.), *Malingering and illness deception* (pp. 255–256). New York: Oxford University Press.

Stone, S., Carson, A., & Sharpe. M., (2005). Functional symptoms and signs in neurology: assessment and diagnosis. *Journal of Neurology, Neurosurgery and Psychiatry, 76*, 2–12.

Stone, A. A. (2000). *The science of self-report: implications for research and practice*. New York: Erlbaum.

Sweet, J. J. (1999). Malingering: Differential diagnosis. In J. J. Sweet (Ed.), *Forensic neuropsychology: Fundamentals and practice* (pp. 255–285). Exton, PA: Swets & Zeitlinger.

Sweet, J. J., Moberg, P. J., & Suchy, Y. (2000). Ten-year follow-up survey of clinical neuropsychologist: Part II. Private practice and economics. *The Clinical Neuropsychologist, 14*, 479–495.

Szasz, T. (1956). Malingering: Diagnosis or social condemnation. *Archives of Neurology and Psychiatry, 76*, 432–443.

Vrij, A. (2000). Detecting lies and deceit: the psychology of lying and the implications for professional practice. Chichester, U.K.: Wiley.

Vrij, A., & Mann, S. (2003). Deceptive responses and detecting deceit. In P. W. Halligan, C. Bass, & D. A. Oakley (Eds.), *Malingering and Illness Deception* (pp. 348–362). New York: Oxford University Press.

Waddell, G. (2002). *Models of disability: Using low back pain as an example*. London: Royal Society of Medicine Press.

Ward, A., Lyubomirsky, S., Sousa, L., & Nolen-Hoeksema, S. (2003). Can't quite commit: rumination and uncertainty. *Personality, Social Psychology Bulletin, 29*, 96–107.

Watkins, E., & Moulds, M. (2005). Distinct modes of ruminative self-focus: Impact of abstract versus concrete rumination on problem solving in depression. *Emotion, 5*, 319–328.

Wessely, S. (2003). Malingering: Historical perspectives. In P. W. Halligan, C. Bass, & D. A. Oakley (Eds.), *Malingering and illness deception* (pp. 31–41). New York: Oxford University Press.

Wetter, M., & Corrigan, S. (1995). Providing information to clients about psychological tests: A survey of attorneys' and law students' attitudes. *Professional Psychology: Research and Practice, 26*, 474–477.

Willison, J., & Tombaugh, T. N., (2006). Detecting simulation of attention deficits using reaction time tests. *Archives of Clinical Neuropsychology, 21*, 41–52.

World Health Organization (2006). *Manual of the international statistical classification of diseases and related health problems* (10th Revision). Geneva: Author.

Wynia, M. K. (2003). When the quantity of mercy is strained: US physicians' deception of insurers for patients. In P. W. Halligan, C. Bass, & D. A. Oakley (Eds.), *Malingering and illness deception* (pp. 197–208). New York: Oxford University Press.

Young, G., Kane, A. W., & Nicholson, K. (Eds.). (2006). *Psychological knowledge in court: PTSD, pain and TBI.* New York: Springer Science+Business Media.

Youngjohn, J. R. (1995). Confirmed attorney coaching prior to neuropsychological evaluation. *Assessment, 2*, 279–283.

Ziskin, J., & Faust, D. (1988). *Coping with psychiatric and psychological testimony* (4th ed.). Los Angeles: Law and Psychology Press.

15

The Effect of Compensation Status

KEITH NICHOLSON AND MICHAEL F. MARTELLI

As discussed in Chapter 14, there had been increased concern about the possibility of malingering or related behaviors following the advent of various compensation plans from the mid-late 1800s. The relationship between compensation status, that is, whether the person is receiving compensation benefits or has the prospects of receiving compensation, and various aspects of response to injury or disability, has subsequently been extensively investigated. Of note, there are many different possible methods for procuring compensation with different types of injuries or disabilities in different jurisdictions, for example, various worker's compensation, Social Security, and disability schemes, automobile insurance involving either tort liability or no-fault compensation, various private insurance plans, the U.S. Veterans Administration, and others.

Weintraub (1995) suggested that the notion of "compensation neurosis," introduced in the mid-late 1800s, was meant to indicate some mix of outright malingering or fraud and a host of other factors that might influence presentation when compensation is involved. Kennedy (1946), in an early and influential study, reported that only 5% of Danes, for whom a lump sum payment was made with no further ongoing benefits, continued to have a "neurosis" following an accident, but that 95% of Germans, living 30 miles away and for whom a stipend was paid while disabled, remained ill. It was suggested that "a compensation neurosis is a state of mind, born out of fear, kept alive by avarice, stimulated by lawyers, and cured by a verdict" (p. 20). In another early and influential study, Miller (1961) suggested that accident or compensation neuroses were characterized by an inverse relationship between symptom severity and the provoking injury, a conviction by the persons affected that they were unable to work despite no overt disability, and a failure to respond to therapy until the compensation issue was settled, after which nearly all of the individuals described recovered completely without treatment. However, noting that exaggeration is a part of both accident neuroses and conscious symptom simulation, Miller did not think it was possible to distinguish between conscious and unconscious purpose.

An increasing number of studies have subsequently examined the role of compensation and related factors in the presentation of persons following an accident or injury. In an early review of the literature, Weighill (1983) suggested that limited conclusions could be drawn from research findings to date. It was suggested that there was general agreement that problems associated with accident neurosis involve a variety of secondary gains, not just financial, as well as an array of interacting physical, employment, psychological, social, and cultural factors. The author noted that "blaming" others for an accident was of poor prognostic value, and that becoming involved with a lawyer may be iatrogenic. There was little support for the generally held view that problems resolve on settlement of a case, most studies indicating that problems then continued, at least to some extent.

Mendelson (1995), in a more current review of the literature, concluded that the overwhelming majority of follow-up studies of personal injury litigants indicate that individuals continued to have problems subsequent to settlement of their case. A number of possible factors that may be associated with compensation status were reviewed, including adoption of a "victim" role, iatrogenic factors associated with diagnosis or treatment, regression, object loss, personality traits, workplace and economic variables, and changes in marital or other social relationships.

Several studies have found a relationship between availability of compensation and the number or nature of claims. Robertson and Keeve (1983) found that changes in injury claim rates were largely explained by increases in worker's compensation rates over the course of 8 years in three U.S. states. Further review of the literature has suggested that a 10% increase in worker's compensation benefits results in a 1–11% increase in the number of claims, and a 2–11% increase in the duration of claims (Loeser, Henderlite, & Conrad, 1995; Loeser & Sullivan, 1995). Several researchers have noted that there have been dramatic increases or expansion in benefits for psychological or medical impairments or illness in the past few decades, despite improvement on most objective measures of health and reduced work-related risks (Halligan, Bass, & Oakley, 2003; Waddell, 2002).

There have been extensive efforts made to delineate the role that compensation has on presentation of persons with traumatic brain injury (TBI), chronic pain, Posttraumatic Stress Disorder (PTSD) or various other psychoemotional problems. Greiffenstein, Baker, and Gola (1994) reviewed the available literature in which litigation status was evaluated as a possible factor associated with poor performance, concluding that results were mixed, several studies finding that mild TBI subjects presented with impairment independent of litigation status. Binder and Rohling (1996) conducted a meta-analytic review of the effects of financial incentives on recovery after closed-head injury. Briefly, meta-analysis is a technique that enables the pooling of results from many different studies and yields a measure of how strong a given variable is. Binder and Rohling's meta-analysis included 18 studies, with 673 patients receiving compensation and 1,680 patients not receiving compensation. The weighted mean effect size (i.e., the overall difference between compensation and noncompensation groups on the measures assessed) was .47, suggesting that, if compensation status was causally related and all financial compensation was eliminated, the abnormal findings and complaints associated with closed-head injury would decrease by some 23%. Several of the studies reviewed were considered to shed light on the causal relationship between compensation status and variables of interest. Patients seeking compensation had greater disability or abnormal findings despite having less severe injuries. Those on compensation also performed more poorly on measures of "effort" or related measures (see below) even if head injury severity was more severe in the noncompensation groups. It was eventually suggested that consideration should be given to the possibility of secondary gain in every case of closed-head injury, particularly milder injuries. However, as will be discussed further below, there is a problem with the interpretation of such studies or findings because many factors other than head/brain injury severity or compensation status may contribute to presentation, for example, chronic pain, PTSD, or other psychoemotional distress, sleep disturbance, and so forth (Nicholson, 2000a; Nicholson & Martelli, 2006; Nicholson, Martelli, & Zasler, 2001).

Many studies subsequent to Binder and Rohling's (1996) study have examined the relationship between compensation or litigation status and some aspect of (especially mild) TBI. Carroll et al. (2004) reviewed 120 studies considered to be of acceptable scientific quality (out of a possible 428 studies), concluding that there was consistent and methodologically sound evidence that children's prognosis after mild TBI is good, with quick resolution of symptoms and little evidence of residual cognitive, behavioral, or academic deficits. The majority of studies indicated recovery for most adults with mild TBI within 3–12 months. Compensation/litigation status was found to be associated with persisting symptoms. It was noted that there was consistent evidence that adults experience various symptoms, especially headache, in the acute post–head injury stage. However, headache was not considered as a predictor variable for persisting effects. It was also noted that few studies had adequately assessed for psychological distress or depression after injury, medication side effects, or pain from associated injuries. In addition, it was noted that studies were of varying quality, and that causal inferences were often mistakenly drawn from cross-sectional studies. As such, the causal relationship between compensation and symptomatology was thought to be unclear, and that various other factors may account for persisting problems that lead an individual to seek compensation.

Cassidy, Carroll, Cote, Holm, and Nygren (2004) studied cases of mild TBI resulting from motor vehicle accidents in the province of Saskatchewan, Canada, before and after the transition from a tort to a no-fault insurance system. There was a 25% decrease in claims following the change and the median time to claim closure also decreased with adoption of the no-fault system. A number of other factors were found to be associated with time to claim closure, for example, there was a longer time to claim closure for those who had more than 20% of their body in pain, although no-fault payments were not made for "pain and suffering". The authors concluded that they could not be sure why there were fewer claims after no-fault was adopted, but suggested that this was unrelated to medical care given that this was not affected by the change in systems.

There has been extensive study of the relationship between compensation status and chronic pain perhaps, in part, because there have been dramatic increases in compensation for chronic pain problems. Fordyce (1985) reported a

2,680% increase in the rate of compensation for low back pain from 1960 to 1980 with no corresponding evidence of any change in the incidence of actual problems. This was the fastest growing rate of compensation for any disorder or disease during this period, lung disease being the second at 400%. Others have described the growth in compensation claims for chronic pain as an "epidemic" (Chapman & Brena, 1989), threatening to bankrupt national economies (Nachemson, 1994). As has previously been noted (Nicholson, 2000b), such increases may reflect a number of factors including societal response to pain problems, with more effective treatment programs and more liberal compensation policies leading to increased reporting of pain, such pain problems then coming "out of the closet."

Rohling, Binder, and Langhinrichsen-Rohling (1995) conducted a meta-analytic review of the association between financial compensation and the experience and treatment of chronic pain. Of the 157 relevant studies that were identified, only 32 were considered to be of acceptable scientific quality and containing quantifiable data that could be included in the meta-analysis. The majority of studies included were with low back pain patients. Liberal statistical procedures yielded a mean effect size of .60 and conservative procedures yielded an effect size of .48 indicating that compensation is related to increased reports of pain and decreased treatment efficacy. However, it was noted that the meaning of such findings was dependent upon the causal relationship between variables. If compensation in some way causes increased pain problems or complaints then, simply, the obtained effect size conservatively suggests that there would be a decrease of 24% in chronic pain problems if compensation were eliminated.

Rohling et al. (1995) concluded that the results did suggest that compensation results in increased pain perception and a reduction in the ability to benefit from medical and psychological treatment rather than the converse, that is, that increased pain and related problems resulted in persons seeking or obtaining compensation, or that some other factor(s) were mediating the obtained association. In particular, it was noted that comparison of treatment effectiveness utilized matched group designs in which a compensated and a noncompensated sample of pain patients were matched for such variables as organic pathology or pain severity. If, therefore, persons on compensation had poorer outcomes, it could not be attributed to these variables. It was suggested that a behavioral model (e.g., Fordyce, 1985), in which various operant reinforcements may maintain or exacerbate a pain problem, best accounted for the association between compensation and increased pain problems. It was noted that this model does not require a person to be conscious of the relationship between pain and compensation for compensation to reinforce pain experience.

Rohling et al. (1995) were unable to substantiate that other factors (e.g., employment status) accounted for differences between compensated and noncompensated groups, although it was acknowledged that there may not have been sufficient power to detect the effect of other such variables. It was also noted that there were too few studies to determine whether a number of other possible mediating factors (e.g., psychiatric history, depression, or anxiety) would better account for the observed relationships. Caution concerning their causal inference of compensation "causing" pain and disability was recommended, and it was acknowledged that patients who experience greater pain and have a more difficult time in treatment may be the same patients who are more likely to seek and obtain compensation.

Hadjistavropoulos (1999) reviewed the literature concerning the influence of litigation and compensation on chronic pain syndromes and concluded that effects continued to be controversial, but that compensation factors may contribute to delay in recovery and reinforcement of the sick role. Teasell (2001) more systematically reviewed the literature relevant to chronic pain of varied etiology and worker's compensation, concluding that there was no definitive evidence that compensation affects the incidence of injury or the development of chronic pain because there were insufficient good quality studies addressing this issue. Consistent with studies cited above, there was moderate evidence that, as the ratio of compensation to preinjury wages increases, the duration of claims also increases. There was moderate evidence that compensation influences chronic pain disability. There was limited evidence that worker compensation status, particularly when combined with higher pain intensities, is associated with a poorer prognosis for treatment of patients with chronic musculoskeletal pain; that retaining a lawyer is associated with a longer claim duration; that filing a compensation claim is not by itself associated with either length of time out of work or regaining of physical function; that compensation had the least impact on the lower and higher income groups; and that the middle income group was the least likely to go back to work if replacement wages through compensation were available.

Whereas it had early on been suggested that recovery rates dramatically improve following the settlement of claims, and some studies have supported this proposition (e.g., Burke, 1978; Kay & Morris-Jones, 1998; Miller, 1961; Miller & Cartlidge, 1972), many studies have found that this does not happen (e.g., Greenough & Fraser, 1989; Kelly & Smith, 1981; Kolbinson, Epstein, & Burgess, 1996; Mendelson, 1992, 1995; Norris & Watt, 1983; Rainville, Sobel, Hartigan, & Wright, 1997; Tarsh & Royston, 1985). Thomas (2002) suggested that differences in the results or conclusions of various studies concerning outcome in compensation cases might be due to the orientation of referral sources or attitude of the researcher conducting the study. Subjects assessed by authors who concluded that high levels of exaggeration were involved, or that there was resolution of symptomatology on resolution of the legal case, were usually referred by the defendant's solicitor (attorney) or insurance companies, whereas litigants in the studies who were reported to have persisting difficulties postlitigation, were seen on behalf of the claimants' solicitors.

Several other more recent studies have examined the relationship between compensation status and various aspects of chronic pain. Most of these have found that compensation or litigation are associated with increased problems or adverse outcomes. McNaughton, Sims, and Taylor (2000) conducted a retrospective review of 100 back pain patients and found that the variable most strongly associated with continued problems was whether the claimant was receiving earnings-related compensation, although it was acknowledged that many variables of possible interest were not able to be measured given the nature of the study. Blyth, March, Nicholas, and Cousins (2003), utilizing a community sample, found that past or present litigation for chronic pain was the strongest of several predictors of pain-related disability. This relationship remained even after taking into account certain other factors associated with poor functional outcomes. Osti et al. (2005) compared factors related to early (within 9 months) or late (more than 24 months) settlement of a compensation claim for whiplash following motor vehicle accidents. Consulting a solicitor was associated with a highly significant, four-fold increase of late settlement of the claim, whereas having a concurrent workers' compensation claim, prior neck disability, and undergoing physiotherapy or chiropractic treatment were weakly associated with late settlement. The degree of damage to the vehicle was not a significant predictor of late settlement.

Tait (2004) reviewed the literature examining the relationship of compensation and chronic pain, concluding that "the data generally show that compensation patients present with more severe and disabling symptoms and respond more poorly to treatment (unless the treatment explicitly targets functional and psychosocial factors)" (p. 560). However, it was also concluded that the incidence of malingering was generally thought to be low, and that various psychosocial factors interact with compensation status to influence symptom presentation and treatment response, for example, employment status, depression, and fear or pain avoidance behaviors.

Rodriguez et al. (2004) reviewed the literature relevant to the pathophysiology, diagnosis, treatment, and prognosis of whiplash-associated disorder, concluding that there was great variability in outcome which, in part, depended upon the receipt of financial compensation for injury. Pobereskin (2005), in a large sample of persons involved in rear-end collisions, found that the most important predictors of neck or other pain at one year postaccident were the initial neck pain severity ratings and the presence of a compensation claim. There was only weak evidence that measures of the severity of the impact were associated with outcomes. Importantly, several studies have found that initial pain severity is predictive of development of many chronic pain problems, suggesting that sensitization effects at onset may account for ongoing problems (Nicholson, 2000b). Busse, Dufton, Kilian, and Bhandari (2004) reviewed a total of 1,101 consecutive files of patients presenting to a single chiropractor's practice with whiplash-associated disorder and found that, among the many variables studied, higher self-reported disability on initial assessment was associated with being female and, in particular, with retaining a lawyer. Of note, female gender is associated with a greater incidence or severity of most chronic pain problems (Nicholson, 2000b).

Balk, Hagberg, Buterbaugh, and Imbriglia (2005) found very little difference in the outcome of surgical intervention for tennis elbow between those receiving worker's compensation and those who did not. However, although a majority of patients in both groups returned to work, a significantly higher percentage of patients in the worker compensation group changed jobs because of persistent symptoms. Several other studies have also found that compensation or litigation is associated with increased problems or adverse outcomes in chronic back pain patients (Pearce, 2000; Suter, 2002), spinal disorder patients (Hee, Whitecloud, Myers, Roesch, & Ricciardi, 2002), patients receiving acromioplasty (i.e., shoulder surgery; Lopez, Ernst, & Wright, 2000), patients receiving physiotherapeutic McKenzie treatment for cervical nerve root compression (Rasmussen, Rechter, Schmidt, Hansen, & Therkelsen, 2000), and subjective complaints but not objective findings following anterior cruciate ligament reconstruction for knee problems (Barrett, Rook, Nash, & Coggin, 2001).

There have been several studies examining outcomes and prognostic factors for several pain problems before and after the transition from a tort to a no-fault system in Saskatchewan, Canada, in which compensation for pain and suffering was eliminated. Cassidy et al. (2000) found that there was a 28% reduction in the incidence of whiplash claims following introduction of the no-fault system, and median time to claim closure was reduced 54%. Those individuals who were involved in an accident before the change in systems reported more intense and widespread pain than did those injured after. Under the tort insurance system, those who were not at fault for the collision had slower recovery than those who were at fault. Regardless of the insurance system, strong and independent associations were found between the retention of a lawyer shortly after the collision and delayed recovery. Cassidy et al. noted that several studies in the United States have shown that claims in which a lawyer is involved take longer to close and cost more than those that do not involve a lawyer, for both workers' compensation and litigation for motor vehicle accident injuries (Butterfield, Spencer, Redmond, Feldstein, & Perrin, 1998; Insurance Research Council, 1994). However, again, effects may be bidirectional, that is, those with more significant problems may seek and obtain legal counsel, or, the presentation of those who may be malingering or who are more vulnerable to the effects of operant reinforcement for prolonged pain and disability may be adversely influenced by involvement in litigation or compensation factors.

In another study of the transition from a tort to a no-fault system in Saskatchewan, Cassidy, Carroll, Cote, Berglund, and Nygren (2003) examined the incidence and prognosis for collision-related low back pain. Although this was a common problem in both systems, the incidence decreased by 31% after the introduction of no-fault insurance and the median time to claim closure dropped by 58%. However, measures of bodily pain, physical functioning, and depressive symptoms showed a strong and consistent temporal relation to the rate of claim closure for both tort and no-fault claimants. Prognosis was found to be worse for females, those with intense pain, and those represented by lawyers.

In yet another study of the transition from the tort to no-fault systems in Saskatchewan, Cote, Hogg-Johnson, Cassidy, Carroll, and Frank (2001) found that lower pain, better function, and the absence of depressive symptoms were strongly associated with faster time to claim closure and recovery after whiplash, independent of the insurance system, indicating that these factors, rather than compensation or litigation, were relevant. Similarly, Scholten-Peeters et al. (2003), in a more recent systematic review of prospective cohort studies to assess prognostic factors associated with functional recovery of patients with whiplash injuries, concluded that there was strong evidence for high initial pain intensity being an adverse prognostic factor but that other factors that have often been found to be associated with poor outcome, for example, age, gender, and compensation, did not seem to be of prognostic value.

Of note, there have been several critiques of the studies examining changes after the transition from the tort to no-fault system in Saskatchewan, perhaps the most important being that, as compensation for pain and suffering was eliminated, persons with pain and suffering would not apply for benefits, were denied benefits, or claims were closed prematurely on the basis of this legislative change. With regard to the Cassidy et al. (2000) study, we also note that the authors' conclusions minimized or neglected the combination of two important considerations. Data presented on anxiety levels prior to injury demonstrated that higher preinjury anxiety was associated with delayed claims closure only in the tort system. Further, under the no-fault system, in addition to eliminating most court actions and associated delays and obstacles to treatment, income replacement and medical benefits were increased. These observations suggest that removal of medicolegal associated treatment barriers, especially in persons with higher than average levels of anxiety that may be heightened by difficulties inherent in the tort system, is an important ingredient for preventing delayed postinjury recovery. This conclusion is consistent with the findings of Evans (1994) who conducted a longitudinal study of personal injury litigants in automobile accidents. Evans found that the strongest predictors of successful outcome were the inclusion of psychological services in the treatment plan and receipt of immediate intervention with treatment focused toward return to work, including return at reduced status or modified duties. In contrast, by 6 months and every point thereafter, uncooperativeness and delayed bill paying of medical insurance carriers (vs. medical symptoms) were the most frequently reported stressors. Of patients whose insurance carriers paid bills promptly (i.e., ≤30 days), 97% had returned to work. In contrast, for patients whose insurance carriers delayed payments (i.e., >90 days), only 4% had returned to work.

In commenting on the Cassidy et al. (2000) study, Deyo (2000) suggested that, whereas the vast majority of whiplash claimants may initially present with "real" symptoms, further medicalization prolongs problems. It was noted that merely assigning a diagnostic label may increase illness-related behavior (Haynes, Sackett, Taylor, Gibson, & Johnson, 1978) and that excessive testing or medical investigation may lead to the conviction that one has a disease, as well as to anxiety and overreaction (Colledge, 1993). Again, it was noted that adversarial systems, in which any improvement threatens the patient's credibility and financial well-being, may impede the patient's recovery (Hadler, 1996). Finally, Deyo suggested that the "myths" of either (1) that malingering with no actual symptoms accounts for most litigation and compensation claims, versus (2) that illness-related behavior after injuries such as whiplash is a consequence of purely biologic processes, are diametrically opposed and needed to be dispelled. Rather, it was suggested that disability and compensation claims are the result of complex interactions among biologic factors, psychosocial factors, legal influences, and economic incentives.

Several other studies suggest that cultural, ethnic, or political factors may be important in determining the presentation of various pain or other problems including response to injury and disability. Carron, DeGood, and Tait (1985) studied back pain sufferers with comparable initial levels of pain frequency and intensity in the United States and New Zealand, the latter having a no fault compensation system that automatically reimburses to the patient the costs of patient care and basic income losses for any accident, irrespective of fault or how the injury occurred. Participants were taking part in an outpatient treatment program and were surveyed at the start of the program and one year later. The U.S. patients consistently used more medication, experienced more dysphoric mood states, and were more hampered in social-sexual, recreational, and vocational functioning. It was suggested that the adversarial system in the United States, where claims are processed much more slowly and often require a claimant to "prove" their disability, may promote poor functioning. In contrast, there is more assured provision of income replacement and rehabilitation services in New Zealand. In addition, if an injured person in New Zealand who has not been able to return to his or her preinjury occupation is eventually found able to do some work after rehabilitation or reassessment, then the person must do so or have benefits decreased. It was concluded that, compared to the United States, the New Zealand compensation-disability system is used less, or for shorter durations of time. Volinn, Nishikitani, Volinn, Nakamura, and Yano (2005) found that, although back pain is common among workers in both the United States and Japan, there is a dramatic disparity in worker's compensation claims, rates being some 60 times greater in the United States. Several studies have concluded that recovery from whiplash tends to be much faster in jurisdictions operating under a system that does not compensate for pain and suffering, or in countries where litigation is less common (Awerbuch, 1992; Borchgrevink, Lereim, Royneland, Bjorndal, & Haraldseth, 1996; Harder, Veilleux, & Suissa, 1998; Malleson, 2002; Partheni et al., 2000).

Schrader et al. (1996), in a frequently cited study of 202 people involved in rear-end accidents in Lithuania, where few drivers have personal injury insurance and there is no legal system that encourages personal injury lawsuits or the expectation of financial gain, found that there was no significant difference between accident victims surveyed 1–3 years after the accident and uninjured matched controls with respect to headache, neck, or back pain problems. Approximately one-third of both groups reported neck pain, and half of both groups reported chronic headaches. About 12% of the accident victims had chronic back pain compared with 15% of the control group. Mickeviciene et al. (2002) studied 200 persons in Lithuania who had sustained a minor head injury and 200 matched control subjects who had not. Whereas all of the head injury subjects reported having headaches in the acute stage after trauma, headaches had fully resolved in 96% of cases within a month whereupon there was no significant difference in prevalence compared to the control subjects. Of note, this study suggests a much different incidence of headache in the general population than the study of Schrader et al. (1996), giving rise to some conflict of interpretation.

Davis et al. (2002) analyzed compensation claims for medical injury under the no-fault system in New Zealand, concluding that, although the New Zealand system is generally free of financial and legal barriers, a change in legal doctrine alone has not in itself been sufficient to remove completely the claims traditionally associated with patient compensation under tort. Aceves-Avila, Ferrari, and Ramos-Remus (2004) suggest that many illnesses that lack objective features of pathology (e.g., fibromyalgia, chronic fatigue syndrome, Gulf War syndrome, chronic whiplash, chronic low back pain) are culture-driven, with a number of underlying factors, including disability and compensation systems, serving to shape clinical presentation.

There has also been considerable research into the association of compensation status and PTSD or other psychiatric or psychoemotional disorders. Rosen (1995) reported on an unusually high incidence (86%) of claimed PTSD among crew members following a boating accident. The extraordinary incidence rate appeared to be explained, at least in part, by crew members' reports of attorney advice and symptom sharing. Citing the work of Burkett (e.g., Burkett & Whitley, 1998) and others, Pankratz (2003) argued that much of the PTSD research has been based upon veterans' dubious self-reported experiences. In particular, Pankratz critiques the National Vietnam Veteran Readjustment Study (NVVRS; Kulka et al., 1988) in which it was concluded that 50% of Vietnam veterans had experienced PTSD, although only 15% were involved in combat. Data collection for the study involved having interviewers repeatedly ask the same question from different angles until they got the responses that they expected, persisting in their questioning in the belief that Vietnam veterans would be unwilling to talk about their experiences. It was suggested that both patients and clinicians may have wrongfully attributed various problems or experiences to either an actual or nonexistent traumatic event. Pankratz concluded that a large industry has erroneously been constructed, suggesting that, in many instances, Veterans Affairs (VA) programs do not cure PTSD but that they teach it.

Frueh et al. (2003) reviewed evidence suggesting that the presentation of veterans seeking compensation through the Department of Veterans Affairs system in the United States for PTSD may be influenced by financial incentives. Note was made that studies consistently demonstrate that the combat veterans who are evaluated for PTSD in the VA system exhibit extreme and diffuse levels of psychopathology on several instruments, with elevations on validity scales suggesting an over-reporting of symptomatology. This issue will be discussed further below, but Frueh et al. noted that there may be a number of possible explanations for such findings, including the co-occurrence of other disorders and symptomatology, a "cry for help," a sociological phenomenon known as "Vietnam syndrome," the influence of systemic variables within the VA, as well as financial incentives.

Kimbrell and Freeman (2003), expressing concern about the increase in claims and possible exaggeration of symptomatology, note that after a claim for a service-connected disability is filed, the Department of Veterans Affairs gives claimants a detailed list of the psychiatric symptoms that correspond to each level of monetary compensation. If a claimant is denied 100% disability with maximal benefits, they may report further symptoms on subsequent visits in an attempt to procure further benefits. Kimbrell and Freeman note that the problem of possible exaggerated symptomatology in an attempt to procure benefits is not limited to the VA system, citing studies that document a surge in claims for Social Security Disability Income for psychiatric disorders.

Bryant and Harvey (2003) cite several studies that challenge the notion that compensation issues significantly influence PTSD status. For example, Blanchard et al. (1998), in a longitudinal study of 132 motor vehicle accident victims, found no difference in PTSD over time between those who did and did not settle their compensation claims. However, it was noted that compensation status is associated with symptom severity in both veterans and civilian trauma survivors seeking compensation. It was suggested that increased symptom reporting in people who are involved in compensation may happen because more severe trauma reactions lead to seeking compensation, although disentangling the factors associated with litigation from factors associated with trauma response is a difficult task that has often limited the inferences that can be drawn from studies of the relationship between litigation and PTSD.

In summary, despite numerous studies over the course of several decades, many or most of which document at least some relationship between compensation status and aspects of presentation or disability in persons with TBI, chronic pain, PTSD, or other problems, the nature of the causal relationship remains poorly understood. It seems likely that this relationship, generally found to be quite moderate, is multifactorial. In particular, it remains unclear to what extent such findings reflect the greater difficulty (either associated with biomedical indices of impairment, various psychological injuries/disorder, or greater psychological difficulty coping with injury) persons who seek and obtain compensation may have vs. to what extent difficulties are presented as more serious or maintained due to the prospects of obtaining or remaining on compensation. Several studies have indicated that, as compensation increases proportional to preinjury wages, the incidence and/or duration of claims increase. Of course, this correlation may reflect economic realities that workers face when they are injured and have to decide whether to remain at or return to work despite ongoing problems in order to better support themselves or their families, vs. not working and having a lower standard of living. It may also be that some workers who have little, if any, injury-related problems decide that they would rather not be working and receiving a percentage of their regular take-home pay.

Whereas some of the persons seeking or receiving compensation may be malingering (either outright fabrication or exaggeration, misattribution, etc., of actual symptoms), we suspect that this accounts for relatively little of the variance in the relationship between presentation and compensation status. Rather, there are a host of other possible factors that may mediate such relationship. These include operant reinforcement of illness behavior independent of any conscious dissimulation. Several studies have documented that more severe pain, psychoemotional distress, and related problems lead to compensation seeking. As has been discussed above and will be discussed further below, this may be of particular relevance for those studies of the relationship between compensation status and mild TBI. Numerous other studies involving differential prevalence designs will be presented below in the context of discussing malingering and TBI, chronic pain, PTSD, or other psychoemotional disorders that may be a focus of medicolegal proceedings.

References

Aceves-Avila, F. J., Ferrari, R., & Ramos-Remus, C. (2004). New insights into culture driven disorders. *Best Practice and Research Clinical Rheumatology, 18*, 155–171.

Awerbuch, M. S. (1992). Whiplash in Australia: Illness or injury? *Medical Journal of Australia, 157*, 193–196.

Balk, M. L., Hagberg, W. C., Buterbaugh, G. A., & Imbriglia, J. E. (2005). Outcome of surgery for lateral epicondylitis (tennis elbow): Effect of worker's compensation. *American Journal of Orthopedics, 34*, 122–126.

Barrett, G. R., Rook, R. T., Nash, C. R., & Coggin, M. R. (2001). The effect of Workers' Compensation on clinical outcomes of arthroscopic-assisted autogenous patellar tendon anterior cruciate ligament reconstruction in an acute population. *Arthroscopy, 17*, 132–137.

Binder, L. M., & Rohling, M. L. (1996). Money matters: A meta-analytic review of the effects of financial incentives on recovery after closed-head injury. *American Journal of Psychiatry, 153*, 7–10.

Blanchard, E. B., Hickling, E. J., Taylor, A. E., Buckley, T. C., Loos, W. R., & Walsh, J. (1998). Effects of litigation settlements on posttraumatic stress symptoms in motor vehicle accident victims. *Journal of Traumatic Stress, 11*(2), 337–354.

Blyth, F. M., March, L. M., Nicholas, M. K., & Cousins, M. J. (2003). Chronic pain, work performance and litigation. *Pain, 103*, 41–47.

Borchgrevink, G. E., Lereim, I., Royneland, L., Bjorndal, A., & Haraldseth, O. (1996). National health insurance consumption and chronic symptoms following mild neck sprain injuries in car collisions. *Scandinavian Journal of Social Medicine, 24*, 264–271.

Bryant, R. A., & Harvey, A. G. (2003). The influence of litigation on maintenance of posttraumatic stress disorder. *Journal of Nervous and Mental Disease, 191*, 191–193.

Burke, F. D. (1978). Lumbar disc surgery: A review of a series of patients. *British Journal of Clinical Practice, 30*, 29–31.

Burkett, B. G., & Whitley, G. (1998). *Stolen Valor*. Dallas, TX: Verity Press.

Busse, J. W., Dufton, J. A., Kilian, B. C., & Bhandari, M. (2004). The impact of non-injury-related factors on disability secondary to whiplash associated disorder type II: A retrospective file review. *Journal of Manipulative Physiological Therapy, 27*, 79–83.

Butterfield, P. G., Spencer, P. S., Redmond, N., Feldstein, A., & Perrin, N. (1998). Low back pain: Predictors of absenteeism, residual symptoms, functional impairment, and medical costs in Oregon workers' compensation recipients. *American Journal of Industrial Medicine, 34*, 559–567.

Carroll, L. J., Cassidy, J. D., Peloso, P. M., Borg, J., Von Holst, H., & Holm, L. (2004). WHO collaborating centre task force on mild traumatic brain injury. Prognosis for mild traumatic brain injury: Results of the WHO collaborating centre task force on mild traumatic brain injury. *Journal of Rehabilitation Medicine, 43* (Suppl.), 84–105.

Carron, H., DeGood, D. E., & Tait, R. R. (1985). A comparison of low back pain patients in the United States and New Zealand: Psychosocial and economic factors affecting severity of disability. *Pain, 21*, 77–89.

Cassidy, J. D., Carroll, L., Cote, P., Berglund, A., & Nygren, A. (2003). Low back pain after traffic collisions: A population-based cohort study. *Spine, 28*, 1002–1009.

Cassidy, J. D., Carroll, L. J., Cote, P., Holm, L., & Nygren, A. (2004). Mild traumatic brain injury after traffic collisions: A population-based cohort study. *Journal of Rehabilitation Medicine, 43* (Suppl.), 15–21.

Cassidy, J. D., Carroll, L. J., Cote, P., Lemstra, M., Berglund, A., & Nygren, A. (2000). Effect of eliminating compensation for pain and suffering on the outcome of insurance claims for whiplash injury. *New England Journal of Medicine, 342*, 1179–1186.

Chapman, S. L., & Brena, S. F. (1989). Pain and litigation. In P. D. Wall & R. Melzack (Eds.), *Textbook of pain* (pp. 1032–1041). Edinburgh, Scotland: Churchill Livingstone.

Colledge, A. (1993). A model for the prevention of iatrogenic disease associated with work-related low back pain. *Journal of Occupational Rehabilitation, 3*, 223–232.

Cote, P., Hogg-Johnson, S., Cassidy, J. D., Carroll, L., & Frank, J. W. (2001). The association between neck pain intensity, physical functioning, depressive symptomatology and time-to-claim-closure after whiplash. *Journal of Clinical Epidemiology, 54*, 275–286.

Davis, P., Lay-Yee, R., Fitzjohn, J., Hider, P., Briant, R., & Schug, S. (2002). Compensation for medical injury in New Zealand: Does "no-fault" increase the level of claims making and reduce social and clinical selectivity? *Journal of Health Politics, Policy and Law, 27*, 833–854.

Deyo, R. A. (2000). Pain and public policy. *New England Journal of Medicine, 342*, 1211–1213.

Evans, R.W. (1994). The effects of litigation on treatment outcome with personal injury patients. *American Journal of Forensic Psychology, 12*(4), 19–34.

Fordyce, W. E. (1985). Back pain, compensation, and public policy. In J. C. Rosen & L. J. Solomon (Eds.), *Prevention in health psychology* (pp. 390–400). Hanover, NH: University Press of New England.

Frueh, B. C., Elhai, J. D., Gold, P. B., Monnier, J., Magruder, K. M., Keane, T. M. et al. (2003). Disability compensation seeking among veterans evaluated for posttraumatic stress disorder. *Psychiatric Services, 54*, 84–91.

Greenough, C. G., & Fraser, R. D. (1989). The effects of compensation on recovery from low back injury. *Spine, 14*, 947–955.

Greiffenstein, M. F., Baker, W. J., & Gola, T. (1994). Validation of malingered amnesia measures with a large clinical sample. *Psychological Assessment, 6*, 218–224.

Hadler, N. M. (1996). If you have to prove you are ill, you can't get well: The object lesson of fibromyalgia. *Spine, 21*, 2397–2400.

Hadjistavropoulos, T. (1999). Chronic pain on trial—The influence of litigation and compensation on chronic pain syndromes. In A. R. Block, E. F. Kremer, & E. Fernandez (Eds.), *Handbook of pain syndromes: Biopsychosocial perspectives* (pp. 59–76). Mahwah, New Jersey: Lawrence Erlbaum Associates.

Halligan, P. W., Bass, C., & Oakley, D. A. (2003). Willful deception as illness behavior. In P. W. Halligan, C. Bass, & D. A. Oakley (Eds.), *Malingering and illness deception* (pp. 3–28). New York: Oxford University Press.

Harder, S., Veilleux, M., & Suissa, S. (1998). The effect of socio-demographic and crash-related factors on the prognosis of whiplash. *Journal of Clinical Epidemiology, 51*, 377–384.

Haynes, R. B., Sackett, D. L., Taylor, D. W., Gibson, E. S., & Johnson, A. L. (1978). Increased absenteeism from work after detection and labeling of hypertensive patients. *New England Journal of Medicine, 299*, 741–744.

Hee, H. T., Whitecloud, T. S., Myers, L., Roesch, W., & Ricciardi, J. E. (2002). Do worker's compensation patients with neck pain have lower SF-36 scores? *European Spine Journal, 1*, 375–381.

Insurance Research Council. (1994). *Auto injuries: Claiming behavior and its impact on insurance costs.* Oak Brook, IL: Author.

Kay, N. R., & Morris-Jones, H. (1998). Pain clinic management of medico-legal litigants. *Injury, 29*, 305–308.

Kelly, R., & Smith, B. N. (1981). Posttraumatic syndrome: Another myth discredited. *Journal of the Royal Society of Medicine, 74*, 275–277.

Kennedy, F. (1946). The mind of the injured worker: Its effect on disability periods. *Compensation Medicine, 1*, 19–21.

Kimbrell, T. A., & Freeman, T.W. (2003). Clinical care of veterans seeking compensation. *Psychiatric Services, 54*, 910–911.

Kolbinson, D. A., Epstein, J. B., & Burgess, J. A. (1996). Temporomandibular disorders, headaches, and neck pain following motor vehicle accidents and the effect of litigation: Review of the literature. *Journal of Orofacial Pain, 10*, 101–125.

Kulka, R. A., Schlenger, W. E., Fairbank, J. A., Hough, M., Jordon, B. K., Marmar, C. R. et al. (1988). *Trauma and the Vietnam war generation.* New York: Brunner/Mazel.

Loeser, J. D., Henderlite, S. E., & Conrad, D. A. (1995). Incentive effect of workers' compensation benefits: A literature synthesis. *Medical Care Research Review, 52*, 34–59.

Loeser, J. D. & Sullivan, M. (1995). Disability in the chronic low back pain patient. *Pain Forum, 4*, 114–121.

Lopez, J. G., Ernst, M. D., & Wright, T. W. (2000). Acromioplasty: Comparison of outcome in patients with and without workers' compensation. *Journal of the Southern Orthopedic Association, 9*, 262–266.

Malleson, A. (2002). *Whiplash and other useful illnesses.* Montreal: McGill-Queen's University Press.

McNaughton, H. K., Sims, A., & Taylor, W. J. (2000). Prognosis for people with back pain under a no-fault 24-hour-cover compensation scheme. *Spine, 25*, 1254–1258.

Mendelson, G. (1992). Compensation and chronic pain. *Pain, 48*, 121–123.

Mendelson, G. (1995). Compensation neurosis revisited: Outcome studies of the effects of litigation. *Journal of Psychosomatic Research, 39*, 695–706.

Mickeviciene, D., Schrader, H., Nestvold, K., Surkiene, D., Kunickas, R., Stovner, L. J. et al. (2002). A controlled historical cohort study on the post-concussion syndrome. *European Journal of Neurology, 9*, 581–587.

Miller, H. (1961). Accident neurosis. *British Medical Journal, 1*, 919–925.

Miller, H., & Cartlidge, N. (1972). Simulation and malingering after injuries to the brain and spinal cord. *Lancet, 1*, 580–585.

Nachemson, A. (1994). Chronic pain—the end of the welfare state? *Quality of Life Research, 3*, S11–S17.

Nicholson, K. (2000a). Pain, cognition and traumatic brain injury. *NeuroRehabilitation, 14*, 95–103.

Nicholson, K. (2000b). At the crossroads: Pain in the 21st century. *NeuroRehabilitation, 14*, 57–67.

Nicholson, K., & Martelli, M. (2006). The confounding effects of pain, psychoemotional problems or psychiatric disorder, premorbid ability structure, and motivational or other factors on neuropsychological test performance. In G. Young, A. W. Kane, & K. Nicholson (Eds.), *Psychological knowledge in court: PTSD, pain and TBI* (pp. 335–351). New York: Springer Science+Business Media.

Nicholson, K., Martelli, M. F., & Zasler, N. D. (2001). Does pain confound interpretation of neuropsychological test results. *NeuroRehabilitation, 16*, 225–230.

Norris, S. H., & Watt, I. (1983). The prognosis of neck injuries resulting from rear-end collisions. *Journal of Bone and Joint Surgery Britain, 65*, 608–611.

Osti, O. L., Gun, R. T., Abraham, G., Pratt, N. L., Eckerwall, G., & Nakamura, H. (2005). Potential risk factors for prolonged recovery following whiplash injury. *European Spine Journal, 14*, 90–94.

Pankratz (2003). The misadventures of wanderers and victims of trauma. In P. W. Halligan, C. Bass, & D. A. Oakley (Eds.), *Malingering and illness deception* (pp. 184–196). New York: Oxford University Press.

Partheni, M., Constantoyannis, C., Ferrari, R., Nikiforidis, G., Voulgaris, S., & Papadakis, N. (2000). A prospective cohort study of the outcome of acute whiplash injury in Greece. *Clinical and Experimental Rheumatology, 18*, 67–70.

Pearce, J. M. (2000). Aspects of the failed back syndrome: Role of litigation. *Spinal Cord, 38*, 63–70.

Pobereskin, L. H. (2005). Whiplash following rear end collisions: A prospective cohort study. *Journal of Neurology, Neurosurgery and Psychiatry, 76*, 1146–1151.

Rainville, J., Sobel, J., Hartigan, C., & Wright, A. (1997). The effect of compensation involvement of the reporting of pain and disability by patients referred for rehabilitation of chronic low back pain. *Spine, 22*, 2016–2024.

Rasmussen, C., Rechter, L., Schmidt, I., Hansen, V. K., & Therkelsen, K. (2000) [Significance of unresolved financial compensation for the course of cervical root compression]. *Ugeskr Laeger, 162*, 4931–4934.

Robertson, L. S., & Keeve, J. P. (1983). Worker injuries: The effect of workers' compensation and OSHA inspections. *Journal of Health Politics and Policy Law, 8*, 581–597.

Rodriguez, A. A., Barr, K. P., & Burns, S. P. (2004). Whiplash: Pathophysiology, diagnosis, treatment, and prognosis. *Muscle Nerve, 29*, 768–781.

Rohling, M. L., Binder, L. M., & Langhinrichsen-Rohling, J. (1995). Money matters: A meta-analytic review of the association between financial compensation and the experience and treatment of chronic pain. *Health Psychology, 14*, 537–547.

Rosen, G. M. (1995). The Aleutian Enterprise sinking and posttraumatic stress disorder: Misdiagnosis in clinical and forensic settings. *Professional Psychology: Research & Practice, 26*, 82–87.

Scholten-Peeters, G. G., Verhagen, A. P., Bekkering, G. E., van der Windt, D. A., Barnsley, L., Oostendorp, R. A. et al. (2003). Prognostic factors of whiplash-associated disorders: A systematic review of prospective cohort studies. *Pain, 104*, 303–322.

Schrader, H., Obelieniene, D., Bovim, G., Surkiene, D., Mickeviciene, D., Miseviciene, L., et al. (1996). Natural evolution of late whiplash syndrome outside the medicolegal context. *Lancet, 347*, 1207–1211.

Suter, P. B. (2002). Employment and litigation: Improved by work, assisted by verdict. *Pain, 100*, 249–257.

Tait, R. C. (2004). Compensation claims for chronic pain: Effects on valuation and treatment. In R. H. Dworkin & W. S. Breitbart (Eds.), *Psychosocial Aspects of Pain: A Handbook for Health Care Provider. Progress in Pain Research and Management*, (Vol. 27, pp. 547–569). Seattle: IASP Press.

Tarsh, M. J., & Royston, C. (1985). A follow-up study of accident neurosis. *British Journal of Psychiatry, 146*, 18–25.

Teasell, R. W. (2001). Compensation and chronic pain. *Clinical Journal of Pain, 17*, 46–64.

Thomas, C. S. (2002). Psychological consequences of traumatic brain injury. *British Journal of Psychiatry, 180*, 392–393.

Volinn, E., Nishikitani, M., Volinn, W., Nakamura, Y., & Yano, E. (2005). Back pain claim rates in Japan and the United States: Framing the puzzle. *Spine, 30*, 697–704.

Waddell, G. (2002). *Models of disability: Using low back pain as an example.* London: Royal Society of Medicine Press.

Weighill, V. E. (1983). "Compensation neurosis": A review of the literature. *Journal of Psychosomatic Research, 27*, 97–104.

Weintraub, M. I. (1995). Chronic pain in litigation: What is the relationship? *Neurologic Clinics, 13*, 341–349.

16

Malingering: Traumatic Brain Injury

KEITH NICHOLSON AND MICHAEL F. MARTELLI

Heaton, Smith, Lehman, and Vogt (1978), using a simulation design, provided the first evidence that it was possible to purposefully do poorly on neuropsychological measures derived from the Halstead-Reitan Neuropsychological Battery and the Minnesota Multiphasic Personality Inventory (MMPI). It was also early on documented that neuropsychologists, even if highly experienced, were very poor at detecting malingering if relying solely upon subjective impression or clinical experience and not specific, empirically-validated techniques (Faust, Hart, & Guilmette, 1988a; Faust, Hart, Guilmette, & Arkes, 1988b; Frederick, Sarfaty, Johnson, & Powell, 1994; Heaton et al., 1978). This is consistent with the more general finding that empirically based, systematic, formally validated, statistical and objective decision making procedures are superior to subjective or impressionistic clinical decision-making, reflecting the longstanding clinical vs. actuarial debate (Grove & Meehl, 1996). This distinction holds for most other domains of human experience and scientific investigation, for example, use of a ruler with a formal rating system will result in more accurate assessment of the length of a room than would "eyeballing" it or other less objective procedure. However, the superior predictive capacity of formal empirical and statistical techniques rests upon those techniques being valid. If an objective measure does not actually measure the construct of interest, no matter what the supporting statistical or other evidence may be, then it will not be useful and may well not be better than clinical or other personal judgment. In contrast, clinicians can make reliable and valid observations and inferences, which may then become the basis for actuarial or statistical decision making rules (Westen & Weinberger, 2005).

This chapter will present a critical overview of the major current strategies of detecting malingering in traumatic brain injury (TBI) or other neuropsychological assessment. As previously indicated, there have been many reports of attorneys or others coaching their clients about the nature of neuropsychological or other psychological tests and how to "beat" these or circumvent detection of malingering. Given the increasing concern about test security and coaching of examinees

(Bauer & McCaffrey, 2006; Essig, Mittenberg, Peterson, Stranman, & Cooper, 2001; Hilsabeck & Gouvier, 2005; Kaufmann, 2005), and because space prohibits detailed discussion, this section will not describe in detail the techniques that have been utilized, nor will it exhaustively present the many hundreds of studies that have been conducted with the numerous different measures. Interested readers are referred to several other good reviews of this literature, for example, Bianchini, Mathias, Greve, Houston, & Crouch, 2001; Iverson & Binder, 2000; Lezak, Howieson, & Loring, 2004; Lynch, 2004; Meyers & Volbrecht, 2003; Nelson et al. 2003; Reynolds, 1998; Sweet, 1999; Tan, Slick, Strauss, and Hultsch, 2002.

There have been a number of psychophysiological studies of malingering cognitive deficit. Rosenfeld and Ellwanger (1999) reviewed a series of studies, some of which involved psychophysiological assessment using a modification of forced choice techniques with simulators feigning memory deficit, and found that the P300 event related potentials (ERPs) may be helpful in identifying simulators. Several other studies have explored this or other psychophysiological indices (Miller, Rosenfeld, Soskins, & Jhee, 2002; Rosenfeld, 2002; Rosenfeld et al., 1999; Tardif, Barry, Fox, & Johnstone, 2000; Tardif, Barry, & Johnstone, 2002). Whereas such techniques may become useful, especially as they are relatively easy and inexpensive to administer in comparison with other functional imaging techniques (e.g., fMRI), these should still be considered experimental, and further research with clinical populations is necessary. Again, however, the problem of procuring samples of persons who are actually malingering may be a problem, as would the possible confounding effects of pain, psychoemotional disturbance/psychiatric disorder or other factors, all of which may have pronounced effects on brain activity (Nicholson, Martelli, & Zasler, 2001).

The psychometric detection of malingering, symptom validity, response bias, poor effort, noncredible performance, or related constructs in neuropsychological assessment has primarily relied upon: (1) the use of specific measures of malingering, symptom validity, effort, or other constructs that were developed for this purpose, (2) aberrant patterns of performance on actual neuropsychological measures that were developed and are commonly used to assess the status of neuropsychological function, and (3) scores on the validity scales of self-report inventories. We will critically review the literature in these areas and present discussion of possible confounding effects of pain, psychoemotional distress/psychiatric disorder, intelligence, age, neurological disease, or other factors on measures of malingering/symptom validity. Finally, we will critically review what have been termed possible, probable, or definite malingering, illustrating these with several examples from the literature.

Measures of Malingering or Symptom Validity

With respect to specific measures of malingering or symptom validity, the French Psychologist Andre Rey had early on introduced measures (i.e., the 15 Item Test, the Dot Counting Test, the Word Recognition Test) that were quickly adopted and became widely used (Lezak, 1983, 1995; Rey, 1964; Rey & Osterrieth, 1993). These measures, which are actually quite simple and performed very well by most healthy individuals or many neurologic patients but poorly by those with suspect motivation or who are malingering, are still widely used despite debate about sensitivity (i.e., how well they identify malingerers) or specificity (i.e., how well they do not mistakenly identify others) (Boone et al., 2002; Davidson, Suffield, Orenczuk, Nantau, & Mandel, 1991; Frederick, 2002b; Lynch, 2004). The methodological basis for establishing sensitivity and specificity will be discussed further below.

Another approach or strategy that was developed early on relied upon forced choice techniques, such procedures eventually becoming known as symptom validity testing (Pankratz, 1983). This strategy had initially been applied to suspicious perceptual deficits (Brady & Lind, 1961; Grosz & Zimmerman, 1965; Pankratz, Fausti, & Peed, 1975). Several symptom validity measures based upon the forced choice methodology that have more recently been developed focus on memory, attention, or related cognitive processes. The more commonly used procedures include the Digit Memory Test (DMT; Hiscock & Hiscock, 1989), the Portland Digit Recognition Test (PDRT; Binder, 1990, 1993), the 21-Item Test (Iverson, Franzen, & McCracken, 1991; Iverson, Franzen, & McCracken, 1994), the Test of Memory Malingering (TOMM; Rees, Tombaugh, Gansler, & Moczynski, 1998; Tombaugh, 1996), the Word Memory Test (WMT; Green, Allen, & Astner, 1996; Green, 2003), the Medical Symptom Validity Test (MSVT; Green, 2004), the Letter Memory Test (LMT; Inman et al., 1998), the Victoria Symptom Validity Test (VSVT; Slick, Hopp, Strauss, & Thompson, 1997; Slick et al., 2003), the Computerized Assessment of Response Bias (CARB; Allen, Conder, Green, & Cox, 1997; Conder, Allen, & Cox, 1992), the 48 Pictures Test (Chouinard & Rouleau, 1997), and the Amsterdam Short Term Memory Test (ASTM; Schagen, Schmand, de Sterke, & Lindeboom, 1997; Schmand et al., 1998).

There are many variations upon the theme but, simply, forced choice methodologies involve presentation of some sensory, cognitive, or other stimuli/test material whereupon the person is subsequently asked to provide a response. Possible responses are limited, usually to an either-or decision, with one response being correct and one wrong. If the person chooses more wrong responses than could be expected on the basis of chance responding, it may be concluded that he or she was intentionally performing below his or her true capacity or deliberately choosing wrong responses in an effort to appear more impaired than he or she actually is. For example, in assessing a purported sensory deficit such as impaired sense of smell, the person may be presented with either a test tube containing a lemon odor or a test tube containing a peppermint odor. On each trial, the person is simply asked to indicate whether the lemon or peppermint odor had been presented and, if unsure, to guess. Different intensities of the odor may be presented to sample possible subthreshold (i.e., below the intensity to normally detect) and suprathreshold (i.e., above the threshold to normally detect) responses. If the person responds incorrectly more often than would be expected on the basis of chance or random responding, then it may be concluded that he or she knew the correct response and was intentionally answering incorrectly. In the cognitive domain, the person may be presented with a picture, a number, a word, or other such stimulus and asked to remember that stimulus. He or she is later presented with two stimuli, one of which was the one that had earlier been presented (the target) and another which is a foil and usually similar to but different from the target stimulus. If there are 50 trials, then it might be expected that a person would obtain about 25 correct and 25 wrong just by guessing. If the person were to only obtain 15 correct, this would be quite unusual and would only be expected to occur by chance about 3 times in 1,000. Thus, for the person to do so poorly, it is typically inferred that he or she must have known what the right and wrong answers were in order to respond so frequently with the wrong answer.

It is generally accepted that statistically significant below-chance levels of performance on forced choice techniques represents the strictest, strongest, or clearest psychometric evidence of malingering there is. However, relying upon the most frequently used probability level for a single statistical test (i.e., $p < .05$), it could be expected that 1 out of 20 times when a person was indeed just responding by guessing, there would be a false positive simply due to chance. In some forced choice paradigms, especially those involving more effortful processing, and with patients who have severe migraine headaches, affective distress or psychiatric disorders, or other conditions that markedly interfere with capacity to attend, process information and respond appropriately, they may legitimately be performing at chance. Bierley et al. (2001), citing Cohen's (1994) admonition, also notes that a statistically significant below-chance level of performance does not provide a probability that malingering has occurred. Rather, it provides a probability that that this may have happened by chance alone (usually $p < .05$ or 5% or 1 in 20). This is not the same as saying that the probability of malingering has a 95% chance of being true. It is cautioned that one must interpret statistically improbable events carefully (e.g., the symptoms associated with a rare tumor) in conjunction with multiple data sources (Denney, 1996). In this context, it should also be noted that some researchers cite below-chance levels of performance as indicative of malingering even though levels are not specified as *significantly* below chance.

It is also generally accepted that many or most malingerers do not perform so poorly as to score significantly below chance on forced choice techniques (Bianchini et al., 2001; Vickery, Berry, Inman, Harris, & Orey, 2001). Indeed, there are very few studies documenting significantly below-chance levels of performance in clinical populations and, where this does occur, frequency of below-chance levels of performance is far less than has been demonstrated to occur in many simulation studies. Guilmette, Hart, and Giuliano (1993) and Martin, Bolter, Todd, Gouvier, and Niccolls (1993) found that 34% and 28%, respectively, of healthy individuals asked to feign memory impairment on the DMT produced significantly below-chance performances. Iverson et al. (1991) found that 60% of those simulating malingering scored below chance. Binder and Willis (1991) found that 77% of healthy simulators scored "at chance" and 15% significantly below chance on the PDRT. Several other studies reviewed below document that simulators often perform at chance, significantly below chance, or well below cut-off levels (see below) that are typically used for various symptom validity measures. Such rates of simulators scoring significantly below chance or otherwise very poorly appear far greater than is evident in studies with actual patients in which it is concluded there is suspected or probable or definite malingering. The criteria for these "grades" of malingering will be discussed further below. Whereas it may be that examinees have become more sophisticated as coaching or other sources of information about testing procedures have become more readily available, we are not aware of any studies where such a rate of significantly below-chance performance had been documented in a clinical sample even well before the relevant information about testing procedures became more publicly known. Such discrepancy raises questions about the applicability of simulation studies to real-life behavior.

As Inman and Berry (2002) have noted, tests designed for the detection of malingering usually have a low true difficulty level for most people, but may appear difficult such that malingerers are enticed into performing poorly. In contrast, on most symptom validity measures, healthy individuals usually do very well, often scoring perfectly or near perfectly, for example, above the 90th percentile on the measure administered (Bianchini et al., 2001). Different measures have somewhat different cutting scores, that is, the score below which the examinee is considered to have "failed" the test, or to be malingering or putting forth poor effort, and above which they have "passed" and are putting forth good effort. Such cutting scores are typically decided upon by choosing a particular score for which all or most all healthy people trying to do well score above, and all or most all persons simulating score below. In most paradigms, this will result in perfect or almost perfect hit rates, that is, correct identification of persons who are feigning and those who are not. In addition, cutting scores are usually also determined by what level of performance discriminates well between persons with documented brain injury responding genuinely and without apparent motivation to perform poorly, vs. those suspected of not putting forth good effort. The latter has most often involved persons with mild TBI seeking compensation, or in litigation and performing more poorly than would be expected (Boone & Lu, 2003). The reasoning is that if persons with a less severe brain injury (or perhaps with no clear evidence of brain injury at all but only some possible head trauma) do much more poorly than those with clear evidence of brain injury, then the former must be malingering, putting forth poor effort, producing invalid test results or other such explanation. This logic is explicitly stated by Green and Flaro (2003) as "the WMT effort scores were actually significantly higher in the definite brain injury group than in the mild head injury group. Such results could not be explained on the basis of differences in ability because more severe brain injuries should cause greater impairment than less severe injuries. The only reasonable explanation was in terms of lower effort or greater exaggeration of difficulty in the least severely injured patients" (p. 191). Of course, this is not the only possible or reasonable explanation.

Many factors other than brain injury may contribute to the presentation of persons who have sustained a brain, head, or other injuries. These include premorbid level of ability, the presence of acute or chronic pain, psychoemotional disturbance or psychiatric disorder, sleep disturbance, general level of intellectual ability, as well as motivational or other factors. Pain, in particular posttraumatic headache but also neck or other pain, may be most pertinent given the high comorbidity with head injury or mild TBI. There are often very large effect sizes associated with such factors, and some persons so affected may have marked difficulty on neuropsychological tasks and even very simple activities of daily living. However, there is considerable variability in what effect such factors may have and the variability in presentation is only partially understood. In almost any diagnostic category, for example, in any psychiatric or neurological diagnostic category, there is immense variability in how severely affected the person may be or what the particular symptom complex may be. Thus, one may be mildly affected in the early stages of Alzheimer's disease, but profound impairment and death are characteristic of the final stages. The variability in *DSM* categories is further compounded by the requirement of clinician rating of the severity or clinical significance of symptoms, and the variable treatment recommendations. It is likely that a combination of factors (e.g., chronic pain and especially more severe headache, psychoemotional distress, sleep disturbance, medication side effects, etc.) may be most potent in causing difficulty in many patient populations such as those with persistent postconcussive syndrome or a mild TBI that does not resolve as would normally be expected. These issues have been reviewed in detail in several recent publications (Hart, Martelli, & Zasler, 2000; Hart, Wade, & Martelli, 2003; Nicholson, 2000; Nicholson et al., 2001; Nicholson & Martelli, 2004, 2006). Numerous studies continue to document that such factors may interfere with aspects of performance. Conversely, it should also be noted that many persons with more significant moderate-to-severe TBI do not show evidence of impairment or disability on neuropsychological assessment (Lannoo, Colardyn, Jannes, & de Soete, 2001).

Most cognitive symptom validity tests utilize a memory paradigm in which the task may appear difficult, but which is performed well by healthy individuals and various patient groups including those with a documented impairment of memory function, for example, persons with Alzheimer's disease or an encephalopathy in which lesions of bilateral medial temporal structures interfere with the transformation of information to what is often referred to as long term memory. There are several different components of memory function, and many such patients with marked anterograde memory impairment have preserved capacity for immediate or short term memory and are thus able to perform quite well on tasks such as most of the symptom validity tests. Conversely, many things may interfere with attention to and registration of the material to be learned, for example, pain, anxiety, and so on. As such, it is not surprising that persons with bilateral medial temporal anterograde memory impairment may do well on symptom validity tests, but this does not inform very well what the validity of these symptom validity measures may be with regard to many other populations that may be of greater relevance for the differential diagnosis of malingering, poor effort, or related behaviors. It has also been suggested that, because children (Green & Flaro, 2003) or mentally retarded persons (Brockhaus & Merten, 2004) may do well on symptom validity tests, this adds to the validity of these measures. However, again, most children and many mentally retarded persons are likely well able to attend to and respond to such simple tasks, and comparison with such populations may not be relevant to understanding what actually interferes with performance in many clinical cases. Moreover, as will be discussed further below, not all children or mentally retarded persons do well on symptom validity testing.

Performance on neuropsychological tests is considered vulnerable to malingering as this endeavor requires that the patient is cooperative and motivated to do well (Greve, Bianchini, Mathias, Houston, & Crouch, 2003). However, most authors caution that "failing" symptom validity tests may not mean malingering, and that there may be a number of other possible explanations (Bush et al., 2005; Green, 2003; Iverson & Binder, 2000; Slick, Sherman, & Iverson, 1999). As indicated above, the most common meaning of "symptom validity" is that persons with lesser severity of TBI do more poorly on standard neuropsychological tests or symptom validity tests than persons with more severe TBI (as determined by such biomedical indices such as depth and duration of coma, loss of consciousness or posttraumatic amnesia, identification of lesions on neuroimaging studies, etc.), which is counter-intuitive to what may be expected, and so it is thought that their symptoms are not valid or not due to brain injury associated with trauma. However, again, there may be many reasons for someone to do poorly on neuropsychological assessment.

Failure on symptom validity testing has increasingly been interpreted as due to "poor effort" in the last several years (Green, Rohling, Lees-Halley, & Allen, 2001; Green, Lees-Haley, & Allen, 2002; Green & Flaro, 2003). Whereas this interpretation avoids the problems and pitfalls of labeling one as "malingering," it affords the opportunity to disregard the person's difficulties on formal assessment, and therefore their actual symptoms or complaints, as merely due to poor effort, as if they could have done better if they had only tried. Similarly, or as a corollary, it is often suggested that persons "failing" symptom validity testing are exaggerating their difficulties, even if they are not fabricating them. However, there is very little evidence to support such interpretations.

There have been a few reports of individuals who have acknowledged that they were not performing with full effort when they failed symptom validity tests. Green and Flaro (2003) reported that 14% of 135 children (between 7 and 18 years of age who were referred for neuropsychological assessment for a variety of neurologic or psychiatric reasons) failed the WMT. The researchers "gently" questioned the children who had failed, suggesting to them that they had not done their best. In this context it was reported that all the children freely admitted that they had made a poor effort. Five of six children were then readministered the WMT during the same testing session, with an incentive of a small prize if they were able to pass. The one child who did not then pass the WMT had been diagnosed with oppositional-defiant behavior. It was noted that the 14% failure rate in this sample was not motivated by financial incentives.

Whereas some persons who do not pass symptom validity tests may very well fail because they were not putting forth good effort, it remains questionable, and we believe unlikely, that many or most who fail do so simply because of poor effort. Other than citing poor performance on symptom validity testing as evidence of poor effort, or a very few case reports of persons admitting to not putting forth good effort, there has been no support offered for such an interpretation. There has been no operational definition of this construct and little, if any, experimental manipulation of what this construct may actually entail. Bowden, Shores, & Mathias (2006) suggest that the WMT has an appreciable false-positive rate, and that studies of the WMT (and this applies to other symptom validity tests) are conducted under the assumption that the WMT is measuring effort, results then offered as validation of the construct.

There are numerous neurological (e.g., frontal system disorders such as Parkinson's disease) or other medical disorders (e.g., hypothyroidism) in addition to drug-induced or socioenvironmental causes that may be associated with motivational problems and, in particular, disorders of diminished motivation (Marin & Chakravorty, 2005). With most such disorders, individuals may do better when presented with a "stimulating" stimulus array that engages them and activates arousal, or when they are encouraged to try for one reason or another.

Martelli and associates (Martelli, Nicholson, Zasler, & Bender, 2006; Martelli, Zasler, Mancini, & MacMillan, 1999) have previously presented discussion of factors that are associated with poor postinjury adaptation and possible motivational problems during examination. These include anger, resentment or perceived mistreatment; loss of self-confidence and self-efficacy associated with residual impairments; fear of failure or rejection (e.g., as being "damaged goods" subsequent to an injury); fear of reinjury or exacerbation of pain including conditioned avoidance pain-related disability with either phobic reactions associated with gross motor activity (kinesiophobia) or cognitive exertion (cogniphobia); external (health, pain) locus of control; poor residual coping resources and skills; psychological decompensation; discrepancies between personality/coping style and injury consequences (e.g., highly physically active person with few intellectual resources who has a back injury); passive, aggressive, impatient, or rebellious personality traits; greater reinforcement for "illness" vs. "wellness" behavior; cultural differences, and others. Of particular importance for the medicolegal examination is whether the examinee feels that the examiner is trying to understand and, at least to some significant degree, does understand his or her situation. On review of symptom validity assessment practices, Bush et al. (2005) have recently also noted that there should be consideration of cultural factors, and that such factors "may lead to either exaggeration of symptoms or denial of symptoms without any conscious or unconscious motivation to deceive" (p. 425).

Importantly, there are several studies claiming very high rates of malingering, poor effort, or invalid results on the basis of below cut-off levels of performance on symptom validity testing. Schmand et al. (1998) reported that 43% of 108 late post-whiplash syndrome patients failed the Amsterdam Short Term Memory Test. Rohling, Green, Allen, and Iverson (2002) reported that 41.6% of 719 consecutive compensation related evaluations, most of which involved chronic pain, were found to have "suboptimal" performance on either the CARB or the WMT.

Van Hout, Schmand, Wekking, Hageman, and Deelman (2003) reported that 46% of subjects presenting with toxic exposure to solvents failed one or more measures from the Amsterdam Short Term Memory Test or the TOMM. Green et al. (2001) suggested that half of the variance of neuropsychological assessment is due to poor effort. We suspect that the interpretation of such high failure rates as poor effort, suboptimal performance, and so forth, is misleading, and that these "failures" may in many or most cases represent actual difficulty. Several studies have found that performance on various symptom validity measures correlates well with performance on many or most other neuropsychological measures (Constantinou, Bauer, Ashendorf, Fisher, & McCaffrey, 2005; Loring, Lee, & Meador, 2005).

The sensitivity (i.e., how sensitive or how well a measure identifies a person it is supposed to identify) and the specificity (i.e., how well the measure identifies only the persons it is supposed to identify and not other persons) of measures of malingering or symptom validity are typically calculated using research paradigms in which the performance of healthy simulators or "suspect" groups, such as those with persistent postconcussive symptoms, are compared to healthy persons trying to do well or certain patient groups trying to do well. However, these statistics should not be construed, as they often are, as the sensitivity and specificity of measures of malingering. In terms of sensitivity, as has been suggested, many simulators may perform more poorly than many malingerers or those "exaggerating" difficulty for whatever reason. Conversely, in terms of specificity, if the most relevant patient groups are not used, then estimates of specificity are meaningless. For example, if more severe TBI patients generally do well on symptom validity tests, then this is taken as an indication of good specificity. However, if the relevant discrimination should really concern those mild TBI patients having evidence of a persistent postconcussive syndrome including headaches and sleep disturbance, highly anxious patients who may have a PTSD, or other patients having problems that actually interfere with performance, then these patients should constitute the comparison groups upon which specificity is assessed.

Although some variant of forced choice testing, with simple tabulation of the number correct and number incorrect interpreted in terms of various cutting scores, is the most common form of symptom validity testing, these approaches may be vulnerable to the effects of coaching. Most of the forced choice symptom validity testing procedures are quite transparent, especially when the examinee has been provided with even minimal information (Suhr & Gunstad, 2000). In a survey of 473 attorneys, Essig et al. (2001) found that most spent some time preparing their clients for neuropsychological assessment, most often with discussion about the content of neuropsychological measures, and with 19% of such attorney briefings specifically involving discussion about detection of malingering and some involving discussion about specific symptom validity tests. Bauer and McCaffrey (2006), noting the problem of test information being made available on the internet, have provided a review of the literature on coaching, concluding that some studies document that coaching does help simulators to evade detection whereas other studies do not. Several studies using symptom validity testing procedures have found that coached simulators may do better than uncoached simulators, but still perform below generally accepted cut-offs. However, if a person is provided with explicit information about the nature of the "malingering" test and instructed to perform as well as possible on such measures, it is unlikely that they would fail if there were not other factors interfering with performance (Forrest, Allen, & Goldstein, 2004; Hilsabeck & Gouvier, 2005). In contrast with the general concern about the possibility of attorney coaching, we have become aware of attorneys advising their clients to put forth their best effort throughout the examination, perhaps because there has been such an increase in procedures to detect poor effort or malingering.

Whereas many symptom validity measures may be readily identified and perhaps "beat" if an examinee is provided with explicit information about the nature of the tests, there are a number of measures that may be more difficult for potential malingerers to detect or "beat" even with coaching. Hilsabeck, LeCompte and colleagues developed the Word Completion Memory Test (WCMT; Hilsabeck & LeCompte, 1997), which relies upon a priming phenomena that allows for dissociation of automatic and intentional processing of test materials. Given that intentional but not automatic processing is normally under conscious control, differences in performance may allow distinction between those trying to do well and those trying to do poorly. Several studies have demonstrated the utility of this technique in distinguishing between healthy individuals trying to do well, well-coached simulators, and actual memory impaired patients (Hilsabeck, LeCompte, Marks, & Grafman, 2001; Hilsabeck & Gouvier, 2005; Merten, Henry, & Hilsabeck, 2004). However, there is as yet no information on whether various other factors such as pain or psychoemotional problems may affect results, and the generalizability of these analogue studies is unknown.

Another approach that may be resistant to coaching is analysis of performance curves, as has been utilized with the Forced Choice Test of Nonverbal Ability (Frederick & Foster, 1991) and the Validity Indicator Profile (VIP; Frederick, 1997, 2002a). The latter utilizes both verbal and nonverbal material with items of varying difficulty. Interpretation is based upon analysis of performance curves (i.e., the pattern of responding to easy and harder items) and results are classified as valid or not valid, the latter being further differentiated as either (1) poor effort but motivated to do well (careless), (2) inconsistent and intentional poor responding (irrelevant), and (3) consistent and intentional poor responding (malingering). Bender and Rogers (2004) have more recently developed the Test of Cognitive Abilities (TOCA), which provides multiple detection strategies including statistically below-chance level of responding, the floor effect (i.e., performance is uniformly or almost uniformly poor on all measures, easy or difficult), magnitude of error (i.e., errors are unusually extreme or aberrant), performance curves, and reaction time measures. In the initial validation study, magnitude of error appeared to be the most promising measure. There was little effect of coaching simulators on the magnitude of error, reaction time, or floor effect measures. Strategies such as have been utilized in development of the WCMT, VIP, and TOCA may well become more important in the future, but these measures have as yet received relatively little attention in the literature.

Response or reaction times (in particular, slower than normal reaction times) have often been suggested to be a useful indicator of malingering/feigning, in part, because it is thought that it takes time to purposively formulate a wrong response (Allen et al., 1997; Bianchini et al., 2001; Dunn, Shear, Howe, & Ris, 2003; Leark, Dixon, Hoffman, & Huynh, 2002). However, Bender and Rogers (2004) suggest that results utilizing such measures have been mixed. Whereas reaction time measures may be somewhat sensitive in detecting malingering/feigning, they may have poor specificity, because many clinical populations have aberrant reaction times to test materials. In this regard, the preliminary report of Anger et al. (1999) and the subsequent report of Storzbach, Rohlman, Anger, Binder, and Campbell (2001) are of particular interest. Storzbach et al. reported results of testing conducted with 239 cases of medically unexplained "Gulf War" syndrome (with symptoms such as fatigue, muscle pain, memory problems), finding that objective assessment in most cases did not provide documentation of neurobehavioral or neuropsychological difficulty despite subjective complaints. However, a minority (n = 30, or 12.5%), initially identified on the basis of slowed reaction times, did have much more significant difficulty on neuropsychological measures. All of these cases had evidence of significant psychological distress but none showed evidence of poor motivation on a computerized version of the PDRT. Willison and Tombaugh (2006), also noting that response or reaction time measures have been inconsistent in their capacity to detect malingering, have recently developed a series of reaction time tests, the Computerized Tests of Information Processing, and found that measures derived from these (i.e., reaction time measures as well as incorrect responses and increased variability in levels of performance) discriminated between those simulating the effects of TBI and actual mild or severe TBI patients. It remains to be seen whether this technique will be resistant to interference effects, as was evident in the Storzbach et al. (2001) study.

Performance on Tests of Neuropsychological Function

Several researchers have proposed that performance on tests that had been developed for and are commonly used to assess the integrity of neuropsychological functions may also "double" as measures of malingering, effort, or symptom validity. There are a number of advantages to utilizing such "internal validity indicators." Several studies have documented that not all malingerers malinger in the same way, that is, some may chose one or another function on which to malinger, or they may malinger impairment in one or more functions (e.g., sensory, motor) but not others (e.g., memory, problem solving) (Meyers & Volbrecht, 2003; Forrest et al., 2004). As such, it would be useful to have indicators of response validity "built in" to all neuropsychological measures, allowing for direct evidence of invalid performance on all measures administered rather than relying only on one or more specific symptom validity measures. Such an approach may also help to circumvent possible adverse effects of coaching. It would be very difficult for an examinee to be familiar with all possible malingering or related measures, especially as interpretation of symptom validity on standard neuropsychological tests involves pattern analyses that would be difficult to circumvent. One further advantage in using such an approach is that time devoted to administration of specialized symptom validity measures could be saved.

Numerous measures from standard neuropsychological tasks have been developed as indicators of poor effort, validity, malingering, or related constructs. These include the Finger Tapping Test (Arnold et al., 2005), the Rey Auditory Verbal Learning Test (Boone, Lu, & Wen, 2005; Sullivan, Deffenti, & Keane, 2002), the Halstead Category Test (Forrest et al., 2004), the Wechsler Adult Intelligence Scales (Greve et al., 2003), the Halstead-Reitan (Reitan & Wolfson, 2002) and Luria-Nebraska (Golden & Grier, 1996) neuropsychological batteries, the Test of Variables of Attention (Henry, 2005), the Stroop Test (Lu, Boone, Jimenez, & Razani, 2004), the Trail Making Test (Iverson, Henrichs, Barton, & Allen, 2002), the Wisconsin Card Sorting Test (King, Sweet, Sherer, Curtiss, & Vanderploeg, 2002), the Rey-Osterrieth Complex Figure Test (Lu, Boone, Cozolino, & Mitchell, 2003), the Wechsler Memory Scale—Third Edition (Langeluddecke & Lucas, 2003), the Memory Assessment Scales (Ross, Krukowski, Putnam, & Adams, 2003), and the Recognition Memory Test (RMT) (Millis & Putnam, 1994). Of note, this list is far from exhaustive and is only meant to illustrate the range of tests in which scores are currently being interpreted as measures of malingering/poor effort, and so forth. Inman and Berry (2002) have provided a summary of many additional studies using a variety of standard neuropsychological measures in which internal validity indices are assessed.

There have been somewhat mixed reviews of the utility of using such internal validity indicators. Strauss et al. (2002) concluded that, "attempts to develop malingering indices from conventional neuropsychological tests have met with varying degrees of success, and the consensus is that they may not be sufficiently effective in identifying malingering" (p. 424). Inman and Berry (2002) concluded that, "although there have been many studies examining these indicators, the indicators are rarely cross-validated, they lack consistent cutting scores, and they are rarely directly compared with other methods of assessing motivation" (p. 2). Inman and Berry (2002) also suggest that these indicators are prone to false positive diagnoses, falsely attributing malingering to sincere assesses. Iverson (2003) also cautions that several of the measures derived from neuropsychological tests that have been proposed as indicators of malingering or poor effort may result in many false positives and, conversely, that others have poor sensitivity.

However, some measures have been well studied with good replication of recommended cutting scores. For example, the Reliable Digit Span (RDS) and other measures derived from the digit span test have been well studied (Greiffenstein, Baker, & Gola, 1994; Greiffenstein, Gola, & Baker, 1995; Inman & Berry, 2002; Iverson & Binder, 2000; Larrabee, 2003a; Mathias, Greve, Bianchini, Houston, & Crouch, 2002; Merten, Green, Henry, Blaskewitz, & Brockhaus, 2005; Meyers & Volbrecht, 1998; Nelson et al., 2003; Strauss et al., 2002). The RDS is calculated by summing the longest forward and backward digit strings for which two trials are successfully completed. Etherton, Bianchini, Greve, and Heinly (2005c) suggest that there has been some variability in the results of different studies, but that a score of 7 or less is generally associated with specificity of greater than 90% in comparing brain injured and healthy populations with simulators. Meyers and Volbrecht (2003) suggested that a score of 7 should be considered suspicious, and that a score of 6 or less has a false positive rate of zero. More recently, Babikian, Boone, Lu, and Arnold (2006) studied the performance of "real-world suspect effort patients" compared to clinic patients with no motive to feign and controls. The suspect effort patients were considered to have met the criteria for probable malingering (see below) on the basis of below-cut-off performance on two of six possible measures. It was noted that Somatoform or Conversion disorders could not be ruled out as is required for a diagnosis of probable malingering. Indeed, we would question whether this sample of patients was not adversely affected by their medical (e.g., pain) or psychiatric problems and, therefore, whether the logic of validating one measure by reference to another of questionable criteria is not circular. This issue will be examined further below. In any case, it was found that using the often recommended RDS cutoff of 7 resulted in a sensitivity of 62% but with an unacceptably high false positive rate (23%). Dropping the cutoff to 6 raised the specificity to 93% but sensitivity fell to 45%.

Very poor performance on measures such as the RDS in which malingering or poor effort may be suspected is an example of what is considered the "floor effect," that is, performance is so poor it is "on the floor" and is far less than what would be expected on the basis of known brain injury. Backhaus, Fichtenberg, and Hanks (2004) recently investigated the utility of assessing the floor effect with 14 measures assessing a broad range of neuropsychological functions. This was an archival study of moderate-to-severe traumatic brain injured patients, litigating mild TBI patients who were considered to be putting forth good effort during assessment, and litigating patients with a history of mild head trauma who were thought to be malingering. Cases in the suspected malingering group had obtained a score indicative of suboptimal effort on either the RMT or the TOMM. It was found that using a cut-off of 50% of the mean moderate-severe TBI patients' scores best discriminated between groups and, specifically, that the overall classification for correctly identifying both malingerers and mild TBI cases was approximately 90% when more than one third of an individual's scores were positive (i.e., below the 50th percentile of the moderate-severe TBI cases). It was suggested that when more stringent criteria were used (i.e., scores below the 25th or 10th percentile of the moderate-severe TBI cases), positive findings were pathognomic of malingering (i.e., unambiguous markers of malingering or poor effort). However, it was not reported whether the suspected malingerers had psychoemotional or psychiatric problems, pain, sleep disturbance, or other problems that may have interfered with optimal performance and, in particular, resulted in failure on either the RMT or the TOMM. Of note, several other researchers have suggested that identification of very unusual or improbable symptoms (such as forgetting one's name or uncontrollable laughter as a symptom of minor head trauma) may be markers of malingering (Rogers & Bender, 2003; Slick et al., 1999) although these are not usually considered pathognomic.

Another indicator of possible malingering or feigning that has been suggested is that of greater than expected variability in level of performance during neuropsychological assessment (Strauss et al., 2002). However, there is considerable intraindividual variability in the protocols of most subjects undergoing neuropsychological examination (Heaton, Grant, & Matthews, 1991; Ingraham & Aikken, 1996; Overall, 1996; Schretlen, Munro, Anthony, & Pearlson, 2003). There is also considerable change in performance on repeated testing for most neuropsychological measures (Salinsky, Storzbach, Dodrill, & Binder, 2001). Various confounding factors such as pain, psychiatric or psychoemotional problems, sleep disturbance, or other factors may also produce unusual variability in results (Nicholson & Martelli, 2006).

More specific indicators of malingering, suboptimal effort, or related behaviors involve use of a pattern analysis of neuropsychological test results. Again, studies utilizing such an approach have mostly involved comparison of healthy normal controls simulating with those responding honestly or selected patient groups. Examples include unusual patterns of serial position effects in list learning or other memory tasks, poor recognition memory relative to free recall, and relatively poor performance on measures of memory relative to performance on measures of attention and concentration (Meyers & Volbrecht, 2003). Performance on such measures may be difficult to successfully coach or feign. It is likely that further work will reveal more clearly how these or other such measures may successfully discriminate between those who are actively malingering, putting forth poor effort for various other reasons, performing poorly due to actual interference effects associated with psychoemotional problems or other causes, and various clinical groups or normal controls.

Some batteries of malingering tests involve a combination of standard neuropsychological tests and other measures, for example, the Cognitive Behavioral Driver's Inventory (Borckardt et al., 2003; Ray et al., 1997). With the proliferation of measures that may be used at one time or another and, especially when there are many possible measures administered to one individual during the course of an assessment that may be interpreted as indicative of malingering if performed poorly, it should be realized that there is then a problem with multiple comparisons and, again, it may be that some poor results could be expected simply due to chance. Normative studies of healthy individuals indicate that in a typical battery of neuropsychological tests the majority of individuals will have some "impaired" scores (Posthuma, Podrouzek, & Crisp, 2002). In contrast, Boone and Lu (2003), in discussing the problem of false positive rates, suggest that multiplying the false positive rates of individual tests together may produce an overall false positive rate. For example, if the false positive rate for three independent measures is 1/10 then, considering their combination, (1/10)(1/10)(1/10) would produce an overall false positive rate of 1/1000. However, it is questionable whether many such measures are actually independent.

Comparison of Methods for Detecting Malingering or Poor Effort

There have been a number of studies comparing the relative effectiveness of commonly used symptom validity tests or actual neuropsychological measures in the detection of malingering, feigning, suboptimal effort, or related behaviors. Rose, Hall, Szalda-Petree, and Bach (1998) administered the computerized Portland Digit Recognition Test (PDRT-C), the Dot Counting Test, the Nonverbal Forced-Choice Test, and the 21-Item Test to college students, head-injured patients, and community volunteers, and found that only the PDRT-C was effective in identifying simulators. Tombaugh (1997) found that the TOMM and an abbreviated version of the Hiscock and Hiscock task were equally effective in identifying simulators. Bolan, Foster, Schmand, and Bolan (2002) found that the Amsterdam Short Term Memory test and the TOMM were comparable in identifying community volunteers simulating amnesia, and that they were both better than the Digit Recognition Test.

Vickery et al. (2001) presented a meta-analytic review of selected procedures utilized to detect malingering or inadequate effort on neuropsychological testing. Vickery et al found that, overall, studies using the DMT, the PDRT, the 15-Item Test, the 21-Item Test, and the Dot Counting Test had average effect sizes, indicating that dissimulators obtain scores that are approximately 1.1 standard deviations below those of honest responders. In order of effectiveness in discriminating between honest and dissimulating responders, the DMT was the best, followed by the 21-Item Test, the PDRT, the 15-Item Test, and the Dot Counting Test. All measures demonstrated high specificity rates in the samples studied. The DMT had the highest sensitivity and overall hit-rate.

Inman and Berry (2002), noting that scores on standard neuropsychological tests or specific measures of malingering are seldom cross-validated and that there has been little direct comparison between various measures of malingering, studied university students who either had a history of (mostly mild) head injury or no such history, and who were either instructed to respond honestly or to feign difficulty. They provided data cross-validating several specific measures of malingering as well as several indicators of malingering derived from nine neuropsychological measures. The specificity of the LMT and the DMT were both 100%, and their respective sensitivity ratings were 73% and 64%. Use of the 21-Item Test and the 15-Item Test contributed nothing to the overall hit rate. Previously published cutting scores and discriminant functions for several of the neuropsychological tests (Digit Span, Seashore Rhythm Test, Digit Symbol Test, Grooved Pegboard Test, Wisconsin Card Sorting Test, and Auditory Verbal Learning Test) were cross-validated and indicated good specificity (100%), but poor to moderate sensitivity (2–27%). There was no difference between the simulating and non-simulating groups on the Grip Strength, Information, and Verbal Fluency tests. It was noted that over 50% of the healthy university students responding honestly had at least one impaired score on the neuropsychological tests that were administered.

Tan et al. (2002) compared the performance of university students instructed to feign believable impairment following a brain injury or to perform like they had recovered from such an injury on the WMT, the TOMM and the Victoria Symptom Validity test (VSVT). Using conventional cut-scores, the WMT proved most efficient in discriminating between groups. However, the VSVT was most successful in yielding significantly below chance levels of performance, with 32% of participants performing so poorly on this measure. Specificity of both the WMT and the VSVT was 100%, whereas the TOMM misclassified 4% of controls as suspect. All simulators were correctly identified by the WMT, but the VSVT did not identify 12% and the TOMM did not identify 20% of the simulators.

Nelson et al. (2003) studied the relationship between eight measures utilized in the assessment of "effort," several of which were measures derived from standard neuropsychological tests (i.e., the 15 Item Test, the Dot Counting Test, the Word Recognition Test, the RAVLT recognition trial, the Rey-Osterrieth Complex Figure Test, the Digit Span test, the RMT-Words, and the "b" Test) in a sample of 105 patients in litigation or attempting to obtain/maintain disability compensation and who were suspected of noncredible presentation on the basis of other psychometric performance and behavioral criteria. There was only modest to moderate correlation between these measures, with only two measures sharing more than 50% score variance. It was suggested that the use of these various tests generally provides non-redundant data regarding patient credibility in neuropsychological evaluations. It was concluded that concurrent use of several such measures is appropriate because they do not appear to be highly correlated with one another. However, it might also be asked what these various different measures are assessing if they do provide such discrepant results.

Gervais, Rohling, Green, and Ford (2004) reported on the relative failure rates on the WMT, the TOMM, and the CARB in a sample of 519 claimants referred for disability or personal injury related assessments. Of note, these were not patients with TBI but, rather, were mostly those with orthopedic injuries, fibromyalgia, chronic fatigue, or other problems. It was found that more than twice as many subjects failed the WMT than the TOMM. The CARB failure rates were intermediate. However, as will be discussed further below, failure rate was significantly related to pain, and we suspect that results are an artifact of pain and related problems. There were notably few instances of below chance levels of performance.

In another well-designed study, Vickery et al. (2004) studied the effectiveness of three measures, the TOMM, the LMT, and the DMT. They investigated whether persons who had sustained moderate–severe TBI, but were no longer involved in any litigation or compensation, would be able to feign deficits any better than community controls instructed to feign believable sequelae. The community controls and head injured patients who were instructed to malinger were given detailed information about head injury as well as general strategies to avoid detection. It was found that persons who had experienced an actual moderate–severe TBI with the accompanying clinical or legal attention, but who were no longer involved in litigation/compensation, were no better than community controls at faking believable deficits. Head injured patients did poorly on actual neuropsychological tests whether they were simulating difficulty or responding genuinely, but only those head injured patients simulating difficulty did poorly on measures of motivation or malingering. Again, the DMT appeared to be more effective than the TOMM or LMT, which were approximately equivalent in distinguishing between groups. Given that each of the measures had varying sensitivity and specificity, it was suggested that, in individual assessments, more than one usually be administered.

In summary, although there is evidence that some measures of malingering, motivation, or symptom validity may be better than others, we consider such comparisons to be somewhat premature at present, given that there is no "gold standard" of malingering with which to compare the utility of different measures, and the varying criteria by which measures are currently compared. One criterion that may currently be considered the closest psychometric evidence to a gold standard of malingering is whether a measure elicits significantly below chance levels of performance by simulators or suspected malingering/poor effort groups. However, such measures tend to be the more difficult tasks, which may result in poor specificity when used as the basis of establishing other cut-off scores. The relative utility of different symptom validity tests will generally depend upon a number of factors, several of which involve a trade-off of risks or benefits. If a test is very sensitive, there may be relatively poor specificity. If a test is highly specific and sensitive in simulation studies, it may be more readily identifiable and vulnerable to the effects of coaching. We suspect that the most serious problem in evaluating the relative value of a symptom validity measure is whether it is vulnerable to interference effects associated with a host of psychosocial or neurobiologic factors independent of deliberate dissimulation or (simply) poor effort. Those measures that are currently deemed more effective in identifying dissimulation or poor effort utilizing cutting scores, as discussed above, may be the measures that are more vulnerable to actual interference effects.

Self-Report Questionnaires

It is usual to ask a person what problems he or she may be having following some accident, injury or trauma. In addition to what the person reports spontaneously, any number of other questions may be asked or issues raised in order to clarify the nature of their problems. Questionnaires are commonly administered to provide information concerning an injured person's problems. These generally require less clinician time and may provide more standardized information. However, Lees-Haley and Dunn (1994) showed that uncoached student simulators are well able to endorse symptoms and satisfy criteria of major depression, Generalized Anxiety Disorder (GAD), mild TBI, or PTSD when presented with a list of symptoms in a checklist format. It was suggested that checklists should not be used in forensic settings. Many questionnaires that are routinely used to assess anxiety or mood disorders, the effects of trauma, or various other problems are essentially quite transparent checklists on which statements about symptomatology may readily be endorsed and which may, therefore, also be vulnerable to malingering or other response sets.

Several self-report inventories or questionnaires include validity scales that provide information concerning response bias or response style that may affect response to the inventory items. Some of these include the MMPI (Hathaway & McKinley, 1967) and the more recent MMPI-2 (Butcher, Dahlstrom, Graham, Tellegen, & Kaemmer, 1989), the Personality Assessment Inventory (PAI; Morey, 1991), and the Millon Clinical Multiaxial Inventory-III (MCMI-III; Millon, 1997). Table 16.1 presents a brief description of such validity indicators for these inventories. The best studied and, indeed, the best studied of any psychological test, is the MMPI/MMPI-2. This review will focus primarily upon this inventory. There were several validity scales built into the original MMPI, several more were developed for the publication of the MMPI-2, and several more have been developed with independent research. In addition to the validity scales listed in the table, there are several others assessing whether a respondent has responded carelessly, randomly or inconsistently. Interested readers are referred to the more detailed description of the MMPI-2 validity scales provided by Kane in Chapter 11 (Conducting a Psychological Assessment) of this volume, as well as standard texts, for further information about MMPI-2 validity and clinical scales (e.g., Butcher, 2006; Graham, 2006). As will be stressed throughout this section, there are multiple interpretations of validity scale elevations, and these do not provide unambiguous differentiation of different response styles nor distinguish unambiguously between response style and specific response content or psychopathology (Faust & Ackerly, 1998).

There have been three meta-analytic reviews of the MMPI or MMPI-2 and malingering or simulation (Berry, Baer, & Harris, 1991; Rogers et al., 1994b; Rogers, Sewell, Martin, & Vitacco, 2003). Again, most of the studies in these reviews involve comparison of healthy normal controls instructed to feign in some manner (often global impairment, generalized problems following trauma, or some specific psychiatric condition) with either normal controls responding honestly or various patient groups responding honestly. Several have involved comparison of patients in litigation/seeking compensation with patients who were not. There have been very few such studies of independently identified malingerers. Although relatively few of these studies have focused upon TBI, we will present this material at this time as it is relevant for all of the remaining chapters of this section. Rogers et al. (2003) summarize the results of the Berry et al. (1991) meta-analytic review as difficult to interpret because there was such a broad array of clinical and nonclinical samples, and as there was such wide variability in the cutting scores utilized across studies. However, the largest effect sizes that discriminated between groups (usually healthy normal controls instructed to feign vs. healthy normal controls or mentally disordered patients responding honestly) were for the F, Ds, and F − K (F minus K) indices. Rogers et al. (1994), in a review of 14 MMPI-2 feigning studies, again noted that there was wide variability in the values of cutting scores across studies. Similar to the results of the Berry et al. study, there were large effect sizes for the F, Ds,

TABLE 16.1. Multiscale Self-Report Inventory Validity Scales

MMPI validity scale	Description of scale
L (Original name: Lie)	Elevation may represent relatively unsophisticated attempts to portray oneself favorably.
F (Infrequency)	Items that are infrequently endorsed, with an emphasis on psychoticism. Elevation may indicate severe psychopathology/ distress, a psychotic process, gross eccentricity, low reading ability/ comprehension, careless or random responding, a "cry for help," symptom exaggeration, or malingering.
K (Correction)	This scale is similar to L but with more subtle items. Elevation may reflect defensiveness or denial of symptomatology but may also be related to education or socioeconomic status.
F – K	Difference between F and K raw scores; high scores are correlated with overreporting, excessive frankness and self-criticism or a deliberate attempt to fake bad. Low (especially negative) scores suggest underreporting, defensiveness or an attempt to fake good.
FBS (Fake-Bad Scale)	Designed specifically to assess overreporting of psychological distress/symptoms in personal injury claimants.
O-S (Obvious-Subtle)	Based on the premise that obvious items are easier to fake than those that are subtle; large differences between the two scales are associated with overreporting.
Ds or Ds2 (Gough Dissimulation Scale)	Items reflect stereotypical views of neuroticism.
Fb (F back)	MMPI scale derived from the latter part of the test, intended to serve the same function as F scale derived from items in the first part of the test. Elevation of the Fb scale may reflect severe affective disturbance more than psychoticism. A normal F Scale but high Fb may indicate fatigue or carelessness.
Fp (Infrequency psychopathology)	MMPI-2 items endorsed fewer than 20% of the time by psychiatric inpatients or the normative sample.
MCMI validity scale	Description of scale.
X—Disclosure	Measure of frankness or openness; elevation suggests overly frank responding.
Y—Social desirability	Similar to the MMPI-2 L scale.
Z—Debasement	Elevation may indicate symptom exaggeration and unfavorable view of self.
PAI validity scale	Description of scale.
NIM—Negative impression management	Measures atypical responses; elevation is associated with exaggeration/ malingering.
Positive impression management	Similar to the MMPI-2 L and MCMI-III Y validity scales.
MI—Malingering index	Designed to complement the NIM to increase specificity in the detection of malingering.

and F − K as well as the O-S (T score difference) validity scales. In other words, several MMPI/MMPI-2 validity scales were well able to distinguish between those who were simulating and those who were not, but the values of the cutting scores by which these validity scales distinguished between groups was not consistent across studies.

In the most recent meta-analysis, Rogers et al. (2003) studied 62 MMPI-2 simulation studies, known groups comparison studies, or studies utilizing a differential prevalence design, plus 11 MMPI-2 diagnostic studies, the latter included to provide further information about how psychiatric patients score on the validity scales of this inventory for comparison with the simulation, known groups comparison, and differential prevalence design studies. Results from the 18 differential prevalence design studies were not included in calculation of validity scale effect sizes. A distinction was made between several possible detection strategies: (1) a rare symptoms strategy, that is, symptoms rarely endorsed by healthy individuals or psychiatric patients and assessed with the F, Fb, and Fp scales, (2) a symptom severity strategy based upon review of "critical" items representing problems such as suicidal ideation or aggression, (3) comparison of the pattern of endorsement of obvious and subtle items on the rationale that those who are feigning may not endorse the subtle items as frequently, (4) an erroneous stereotypes strategy, which presupposes that persons feigning may tend to endorse items that are associated with common misperceptions about psychopathology or maladjustment, that is, the Ds and FBS scales, (5) absence of defensiveness based on the rationale that most people have some defensiveness and those who are malingering will not endorse items on the L or K scales, and (6) symptom selectivity based on the possibility that some malingerers will endorse psychopathology indiscriminately resulting in extreme clinical scale elevations. The latter two strategies were noted to have received little prior attention in the literature.

Rogers et al. (2003) found that comparison of persons instructed to feign impairment and healthy normal controls resulted in very large effect sizes on most of the MMPI-2 validity indices, those who were feigning having much higher elevations. The only exception was the modest effect size for the Subtle (S) scale. There were extremely large effect sizes for the F, Obvious (O), and Fb scales. However, there were only very modest differences on the MMPI-2 validity scales between those in litigation and those who were not. Furthermore, the validity scale elevations of those in litigation were substantially lower than those of the actual psychiatric patients. Indeed, the psychiatric patients with legitimate disorders responding genuinely had marked elevation on many of the validity indices. It was concluded that genuine patients with schizophrenia may have extreme elevations on the F scale and marked elevations on Fp. Patients with genuine depression may have extreme elevations on F and Fb, whereas patients with genuine PTSD may have very extreme elevations on Fb and extreme elevations on F with slightly higher elevations on other scales. It was eventually cautioned that feigning vs. healthy control comparisons may provide highly inflated effect sizes when the task involves discrimination of real from feigned psychopathology. Nonetheless, across all diagnostic categories, several validity scales discriminated well between those simulating psychopathology and actual psychiatric groups. In particular, in descending order of effectiveness, the F, Obvious, F − K, Fp, Ds, Fb, O-S, and the Lachar-Wrobel critical items measures were found to be useful.

Rogers et al. (2003) found that cutting scores, constructed to ensure that few genuine patients were misclassified as feigning, generally resulted in scores being useful only with very extreme elevations. They again noted the problem that different studies had concluded that different cutting scores were most appropriate, that is, that there was inconsistency in what values were determined to differentiate well between simulators and either genuine patients or healthy persons responding genuinely. There was noted to be better consistency for recommended cutting scores of the Ds scale, and this consistency in findings was thought to outweigh its somewhat lower classification accuracy rate.

Contrary to expectation, Rogers et al. (2003) found that the F scale was better at distinguishing between simulators and genuine psychiatric patients than was the Fp scale. The Fp scale had been designed "to detect infrequent responding in settings characterized by relatively high base rates of psychopathology and psychological distress" (Arbisi & Ben-Porath, 1995, p. 424) and was thought to more specifically discriminate between those who are faking bad and genuine psychiatric patients compared to the F scale. The Fp scale has been reviewed in greater length recently by Arbisi, Ben-Porath, and McNulty (2003). Rogers et al. (2003), noting that several studies have indicated good consistency for the Fp cutting scores, also recommended use of this scale.

Rogers et al. (2003) provided a table of normative cut scores based upon the distribution of scores for the entire patient group, that is, the validity scale values that distinguished those simulating/feigning and most all (98%) of the patient group as a whole. Whereas these cut scores may be considered as quite conservative (apparently misclassifying only 2% of the patients), they may be quite misleading given that there were several patient samples that did not have highly elevated validity scales (in contrast to those with Schizophrenia, depression or PTSD). As such, use of these cutting scores could result in substantial number of false positive cases suggested to be malingering if used with genuine patient populations that have higher validity scale elevations. For example, on the basis of the reported mean and standard deviation of all PTSD patients, approximately 20% of genuine patients would be misclassified as malingering if the F scale cut-off were used. The number of patients misclassified in many forensic settings may actually be higher, given that it is often the more symptomatic that become involved in litigation or other medicolegal proceedings. This issue will be addressed further in chapter 18 (Malingering: PTSD and Depression).

Whereas the primary focus of the Rogers et al. (2003) meta-analysis was the discrimination of persons simulating disorder with those who had an actual psychiatric disorder, several of the studies examined the association of cognitive impairment or TBI with validity indices. It was concluded that TBI status had relatively little effect, that is, that validity scale elevations were not typical across studies involving TBI or cognitive impairment. It was also found that the Fake Bad Scale (FBS; Lees-Haley, English, & Glenn, 1991) was poor at discriminating between simulators and genuine psychiatric patients. However, the FBS was developed for use in personal injury settings in which feigning of some psychiatric disorders, especially Schizophrenia, is unusual, although feigning symptoms associated with PTSD, depression, TBI, pain or related problems may not be uncommon (Larrabee, 1998, 2003b; Lees-Haley et al., 1991).

The remainder of this section will examine studies of the MMPI or MMPI-2 in detecting dissimulation in cases of TBI/head injury, as well as the FBS, as this scale is most pertinent to assessment of "faking bad" the problems that are the focus of this section. We will reserve further discussion of studies that specifically address chronic pain, PTSD, depression, or other psychoemotional disorders for subsequent chapters.

Several MMPI/MMPI-2 studies involving simulation of the effects of TBI/closed head injury (CHI) or the relationship of TBI and compensation/litigation status have been conducted. Several have found that simulators produce elevations of validity as well as clinical scales. Heaton et al. (1978) found that head injury simulators produced elevations on the MMPI F, 1, 3, 6, 7, and 8 scales. Although full discussion of what these scales may measure is beyond the scope of this chapter, a very brief summary is presented as follows: F-infrequently endorsed items; 1—somatic concerns; 2—depression; 3—hysteria; 6—paranoia; 7—anxiety related problems; 8—thought disorder or other schizophreniform symptomatology. Berry et al. (1995) subsequently reviewed several studies that had utilized the MMPI or MMPI-2 to investigate the validity of CHI presentations, concluding that results had been heterogeneous and sometimes conflicting but that CHI patients tend to produce relatively higher scores on the neurotic triad (i.e., scales 1, 2, and 3) as well as on scales 7 and 8. Berry et al. (1995) studied the MMPI-2 profiles of normal controls responding either genuinely or simulating and CHI patients who were either compensation-seeking or not. It was found that healthy experimental simulators tended to have elevated validity scales (F, Fb, Fp, and Ds) relative to all other groups and that those CHI patients who were seeking compensation tended to have such elevations relative to those who were not seeking compensation. Simulators had the highest clinical scale elevations followed by those seeking compensation whom, again, had relatively high elevations on scales 1, 2, 3, 7, and 8 in comparison with those not seeking compensation.

Youngjohn, Davis, and Wolf (1997) found that litigating mild head injured patients produced significantly greater elevations on scales 1, 2, 3, and 7 than did either litigating or nonlitigating moderate–severe head injured patients, and that they also had greater elevations on scale 8 and a measure of Health Concerns in comparison with nonlitigating moderate–severe patients. It was noted that few persons having a mild head trauma or mild TBI go on to complain of persisting symptomatology, and it was suggested that a parsimonious explanation for the results was that the clinical scale elevations reflected emotional difficulties, psychopathology, or personality disturbances. Youngjohn et al. (1997) cited Putnam and Millis (1994) as similarly concluding that such presentations were associated with a Somatoform Disorder, that is, one in which psychological factors are associated with physical complaints. Whereas it may be that psychological factors associated with a Somatoform Disorder do contribute in such cases, it may also be that there are actual pain and related problems in such cases, possibly associated with a sensitization effect as discussed above. Of note, the reported validity scale indices (L, F, and K) were no different for the different groups in the Youngjohn et al. (1997) study, all being within normal limits.

Larrabee (1998) suggested that malingering during neuropsychological examinations can occur in two ways, that is, with either deliberately poor performance on neuropsychological tests (cognitive malingering) and/or exaggeration and distortion of somatic complaints. The latter was considered to be primarily represented by elevations on scales 1 and 3 of the MMPI/MMPI-2, which assess complaints such as pain, paresthesias, and malaise. Larrabee (1998) studied 12 cases who had failed cognitive symptom validity testing, six with significantly below chance levels of performance on one of several measures. Cases had been selected from a file review if they had failed symptom validity testing and if they had elevations on scales 1 and 3 of either the MMPI or MMPI-2. Most presented with complaints of chronic pain. It was found that the MMPI/MMPI-2 traditional validity indices were relatively insensitive to detecting abnormal response bias or malingering, but that the Fake Bad Scale (FBS; Lees-Haley et al., 1991) identified 11 of 12 such individuals using the cut-off initially proposed by Lees-Haley et al. (1991). The cases also had marked elevations of clinical scales 1, 2, 3, 7, and 8. Larrabee (1998) suggested that a distinction be made between somatic malingering and actual somatoform disorders, the former identified by elevations of the FBS scale as well as elevations of scales 1 and 3 exceeding a *T* score of 80.

Lees-Haley et al. (1991) reported that the FBS was developed on a rational basis to detect malingerers in personal injury claims. It was composed of 43 MMPI-2 items, many of which overlap with scales 1 or 3, and most reflecting either somatic complaints or high social desirability. As will be discussed below in the chapter on malingering and chronic pain (Chapter 17), high social desirability has been found to be associated with chronic pain, a relationship known to be mediated by a neurobiological substrate. In contrast, the interpretation suggested by Lees-Haley et al. and others has been that endorsement of such items reflects an attempt at impression management in the direction of appearing good and virtuous but as having unusually severe problems due to a compensable injury.

Lees-Haley et al. (1991) administered the MMPI-2 to personal injury claimants considered to either be responding honestly or malingering, as well as medical outpatients simulating emotional distress caused by motor vehicle accidents, industrial stress or toxic exposure. Simulators were instructed to fake believable problems that could undergo scrutiny in personal injury court proceedings. A score on the FBS of 20 or more was recommended as a useful cutting score, as this resulted in 93% accurate classification of suspected malingerer and nonmalingerer claimants. The malingerers mean score of 27.6 (SD = 4.7) was similar to the simulating outpatients mean score of 25 (SD = 8.5). An estimate of the mean score for a sample of 540 psychiatric patients (whose data were reported in the MMPI-2 manual) was 19.1 for women and 16.9 for men. The mean score of the nonmalingerer claimants was 15.7 (SD = 4.1) whereas the estimate of the normal control group from the MMPI-2 was 13.8 for women and 11.7 for men. Subsequent studies have suggested a number of different cutting scores, usually higher, depending on the subjects studied.

There have been several studies investigating the utility of the FBS in discriminating between simulating, malingering, litigating and nonlitigating, mild vs. more severe TBI, normal, psychiatric, or other populations. Slick, Hopp, Strauss, and Spellacy (1996) found that the FBS correlated better with measures from the Victoria Symptom Validity Test and the PDRT than did several other MMPI-2 validity scales. Tsushima and Tsushima (2001) studied 120 personal injury litigating patients, 208 clinical nonlitigating patients, and 43 normal participants. Of several MMPI-2 validity indices, including the FBS, F, Fb, Fp, and Ds2 scales, only the FBS significantly differentiated the litigating and clinical patients, whereas both of these groups scored significantly higher than the normal participants on the FBS, F, Fb, and Ds2 scales.

Similar to the findings of Youngjohn et al. (1997), Miller and Donders (2001) also found that individuals with mild traumatic head injuries, whether or not they were litigating, had paradoxically greater symptomatology on MMPI-2 clinical scales (especially scales 1, 2, 3, 6, 7, and 8) than did nonlitigating moderate–severe TBI patients. The litigating mild traumatic head injured patients had higher elevations than did the nonlitigating mild head injured patients, especially on scales 1, 2, 3, and 8. The same pattern of results was true for the FBS scores, that is, both mild injured groups had much higher scores than did the moderate–severe injured patients (4% surpassing the cut-off) and the litigating mild injured had higher scores (50% surpassing the cut-off) than the non-litigating mild injured (30% passing the cut-off). It was concluded that elevations on the FBS scale may not reflect conscious or intentional exaggeration or fabrication of symptoms for personal gain. It was suggested that the name of the FBS scale should be changed, as elevations may not be due to faking, and elevation of this scale may serve as an indicator of possible premorbid or comorbid difficulties that can contribute to maintenance of symptoms. It was also suggested that elevation of the first three clinical scales, with an unusual emphasis on physical complaints, may be associated with headaches that could be exacerbated by psychosocial stress, and that the relative elevation of scale 8 may relate to cognitive inefficiencies, emotional despair, and being misunderstood, features possibly associated with a passive-dependent coping style.

Greiffenstein, Baker, Gola, Donders, and Miller (2002) studied cases of atypical litigating mild head injury (considered to be equivalent to the persistent post-concussive syndrome) and litigating moderate–severe TBI patients, the latter considered to be presenting legitimately. The former had significantly higher FBS scores than the latter, but there were no differences on the F and F – K validity indices. Whereas there was reasonable sensitivity in identifying the former (83%), there was a high false positive rate (47%) in identifying the latter using the FBS cut-off initially recommended by Lees-Haley et al. (1991). It was concluded that endorsement of FBS items overlap with objective neurological abnormalities. Of note, Greiffenstein et al. (2002) cited Grillo, Brown, Hilsabeck, and Price (1994) as reporting that the FBS correlated with "MMPI derived personality disorder measures suggesting that FBS may be related to longstanding personality styles unrelated to personal injury" (Greiffenstein et al., 2002, p. 1592). Iverson et al. (2002) found that the cut-off initially proposed by Lees-Haley et al. (1991) resulted in an unacceptably high false positive rate of classification of medical or psychiatric patients.

Larrabee (2003c) found that the FBS was more sensitive than F, Fb, or F(p) in detecting exaggeration in a retrospective sample of litigants meeting criteria for either definite or probable malingered neurocognitive dysfunction (MND). Depending on the cut-off employed, the FBS identified anywhere from 94% (FBS > 19) to 54% (FBS > 23 for males, and >25 for females) of the litigants as probable or definite MNDs. It was again found that those with MND had MMPI-2 clinical scale elevations on 1, 2, 3, 7, and 8.

Butcher, Arbisi, Atlis, and McNulty (2003) examined the construct validity of the FBS with six different groups (personal injury litigants, chronic pain patients, general medical and psychiatric inpatients, Veteran's Administration patients, and correctional/criminal cases) involving over 20,000 cases. A content analysis of the 43 FBS items resulted in five item groupings: (1) somatic symptoms including pain (14 items); (2) sleep disturbance (2 items); (3) tension or stress (4 items); (4) low energy/anhedonia (8 items); and (5) denial of deviant attitudes or behaviors, that is, items reflecting high social desirability (15 items). It was eventually concluded that the FBS is not a psychometrically sound measure of somatic malingering. Rather, it was suggested that this scale more likely measures general maladjustment, psychopathology, and somatic complaints rather than malingering. When used as a measure of malingering, the rate of false positives, especially in psychiatric settings, was considered unacceptably high. If used in this capacity, an unacceptably large number of individuals experiencing genuine distress would be classified as malingerers. It was also noted that the scale has a bias toward classifying women as malingerers.

Ross, Millis, Krukowski, Putnam, and Adams (2004), on review of the literature, also concluded that investigation into the utility of traditional MMPI/MMPI-2 validity indices in the detection of malingering in forensic neuropsychological settings, particularly in the evaluation of mild TBI or head injury, had produced mixed findings. Ross et al. compared a sample of compensation-seeking mild head injured cases, all of whom scored within the chance range of responding on the RMT, with subjects considered to be bona fide head injured cases, although 7 of 59 of the latter also scored within the chance range on the RMT. The FBS, using a cut-off of 21, distinguished between groups with a sensitivity of 90% and specificity of 90%, whereas the traditional MMPI-2 validity indices did not distinguish between groups as well. However, as with several other studies reporting such findings, it is suspected that the mild head injured cases were actually suffering greater somatic or other psychological distress, leading to poor performance on symptom validity testing as well as elevated FBS scores.

Dearth et al. (2005), on review of the literature, concluded that the use of the FBS for detecting malingered somatic complaints during forensic neuropsychological examinations for TBI was generally positive, although there were some concerns especially regarding its specificity for psychiatric disorder. Dearth et al. (2005) studied moderate-severe head injured patients and community volunteers instructed to either feign difficulty or respond honestly. Most of the MMPI-2 validity scales (i.e., F, Fb, Fp, and Ds2) had perfect specificity and were well able to discriminate those who had not been instructed to feign difficulty, but had low to modest sensitivity (the capacity to detect those who had been instructed to feign). The FBS had both moderate sensitivity and specificity, with a false positive rate of 24%. Overall, the F scale best discriminated between groups even in comparison with several symptom validity measures (DMT, LMT, TOMM) that had been administered.

Nelson, Sweet, and Demakis (2006) have very recently conducted a meta-analysis of the FBS, concluding that "the FBS performs as well as, if not superior to, other validity scales in discriminating overreporting and comparison groups; the preponderance of the present literature supports the scale's use within forensic settings" (p. 39). The between-group weighted effect size of the FBS was 0.96, that is, close to one standard deviation difference between groups. The "overreporting" groups were primarily those involved in litigation or compensation claims, or simulators. Note was made of the Butcher et al. (2003) analysis, including the subsequent response by Lees-Haley and Fox (2004) and rejoinder by Arbisi and Butcher (2004). Our opinion of this debate is that, consistent with the opinion expressed by Butcher et al. (2003), elevations on the FBS scale may represent actual somatic and related complaints or psychological predisposition/distress that, although possibly accentuated on the basis of psychological factors, may not represent any conscious or deliberate attempt to deceive or exaggerate for the purposes of secondary gain. Whereas in some cases elevation may represent deception, we suspect that, as has been found for many of the MMPI validity indices, there is a problem distinguishing between accentuation or exaggeration associated with various psychosocial factors independent from financial or other incentives that may be related to malingering, and conscious malingering. This will be discussed more fully below in the chapters on chronic pain and PTSD/depression (Chapters 17 and 18). Of note, Nelson et al. (2006) did caution about conclusions based on the FBS being made with chronic pain or PTSD patients, given the few studies that had examined the effect of such conditions.

Confounding Effects of Pain, Psychoemotional Distress/Psychiatric Disorder, Neurologic Disease, or other Factors

As has been noted, performance on neuropsychological tests may be adversely affected by many factors secondary to accident or injury. Several researchers have cautioned that such factors need to be taken into account when interpreting performance on neuropsychological measures, including measures of symptom validity (Bush et al., 2005; Iverson & Binder, 2000; Slick et al., 1999; Sweet,

1999). Several studies indicate that poor performance on symptom validity tests may be associated with pain, psychoemotional distress, or other confounding factors. Post (1975) had early on found that depression was associated with a "no-saying" bias on recognition memory tests. Thus, if unsure, someone who is depressed may have a bias to respond "no," which could by itself lower a score to below symptom validity test cut-offs. Gorman (1982) suggested that psychiatric disorders and personality factors might interact with brain injury to produce behavior that is mistaken for malingering. Pankratz (1988) also cautioned that depressed patients may perform similarly to malingerers because they do not properly attend to stimuli. Notably, the *DSM* diagnostic criteria (American Psychiatric Association, 2000) for depression include attentional or mnemonic problems, and numerous studies have documented that depression is associated with various cognitive problems in addition to interpersonal or other difficulties (Iverson & Binder, 2000; Nicholson & Martelli, 2006).

Several studies have begun to systematically assess the effect of various confounding factors on measures of malingering or symptom validity. Using the Rey 15-Item test, Davidson et al. (1991) contrasted the performance of 40 normal volunteers feigning brain injury with 40 normal controls, 52 brain injured patients, 25 spinal cord injury patients, and 50 chronic pain patients. Whereas 90% of the controls were correctly classified, 40% of brain injured, 24% of spinal cord injured, and 30% of chronic pain patients fell into the suspected feigner category. Schretlen, Brandt, Krafft, and van Gorp (1991) found that 27% of 148 patients with amnesia, dementia, severe mental illness, or other neuropsychiatric disorder scored in the "malingering" range on the Rey 15-Item test. Performance on the 15-Item test was found to correlate highly with measures of intelligence and performance on the Mini-Mental State Examination. Lee et al. (2000) studied the performance of community dwelling middle-aged and elderly adults (who were not taking medication) on the Rey 15-Item and Dot Counting Tests. Scores on the Hamilton Depression Scale indicated that 22 were mildly depressed, 31 were moderately depressed, and 11 were severely depressed. There were a number of false positives from measures derived from the 15-Item Test (e.g., 4.7% obtained fewer than 9 items, 10.9% fell below the cut-off of <8 adjusted score, 4.7% produced within row errors, 23% produced perseverative errors, and 28% produced fewer than 3 rows correctly placed on the page). No patient failed the Dot Counting Test. Although it was reported that there was no significant effect of level of depression, there was a trend for poorer performance with increasing level of depression, which future research may find significant using a larger sample size.

Binder and Willis (1991) studied the performance of six groups on the PDRT. These included: (1) mild TBI patients seeking financial compensation (mTBI-Comp), (2) well documented brain injured patients seeking financial compensation (BD-Comp), (3) well documented brain injured patients not seeking financial compensation (BD-NoComp), (4) affective disorder patients not seeking compensation (AD-NoComp), (5) nonpatients instructed to simulate the effects of mild TBI in order to obtain financial compensation (NP-Comp), and (6) nonpatients instructed to respond honestly or to do their best (NP-NoComp). The AD-NoComp performed more poorly than either the NP-NoComp or the BD-NoComp but better than any of the compensation groups. The NP-Comp group performed the poorest. As such, affective disorders clearly impacted performance on this symptom validity test and, as is typical, the simulators performed the poorest. It was noted that the mTBI-Comp group was composed of those who did relatively well and those who did relatively poorly. The mild TBI group, which did relatively poorly, also reported greater affective distress on the SCL-90-R. It was also reported that some of the mTBI-Comp subjects who performed poorly had carpal tunnel syndrome and/or "cervical" problems. It was suggested that these problems might have "conceivably" resulted in some "mild" sensorimotor deficits. However, these problems could have been associated with very significant pain and manual motor function problems. It was not reported whether subjects had headache or other problems often seen in the persistent postconcussive syndrome.

Boone and Lu (1999) conducted a retrospective chart review and found that 13 of 19 litigating/compensation seeking cases considered to be presenting with a somatoform disorder, and with peak elevations on the MMPI or MMPI-2 scales 1 and 3, also had noncredible performance on a variety of cognitive measures, both specific measures of symptom validity and standard neuropsychological tests. Only one subject had an elevation of the F validity scale. It was suggested that results indicated that "symptom fabrication associated with somatization/conversion personality orientations can extend to noncredible cognitive symptomatology, and not just the oft-described physical complaints of pain, seizures, paralysis/weakness, impaired coordination and balance, headache, dizziness, and visual disturbances (e.g., double vision, blindness)" (pp. 416–417). Although it was suggested that such symptom fabrication was not conscious, there was no indication that symptoms may have represented an actual psychophysiological disturbance, as has been documented with many such disorders.

Bierley et al. (2001) reported a case series of four patients with mild TBI who did poorly on the difficult but not the easier items of the Sternberg Recognition Memory Task (SMRT), on which even well documented TBI patients usually perform well. Poor performance was correlated with level of depression and, particularly, the degree of somatization or somatic preoccupation as indicated by items on the Hamilton Rating Scale for Depression. Whereas performance had been fully intact soon after injury, it then deteriorated to approximately chance level of responding when assessed at 6 and 12 months, but had largely recovered when tested at 24 months. The recognition hit scores from the recognition trial of the CVLT followed the same general pattern as for the SMRT, although it was not as dramatic. None of the participants were involved in litigation or claims for compensation that could account for the pattern of results. It was noted that Flor-Henry et al. (1981) had previously reported that 90% of patients with Somatization Disorder were classified as having neuropsychological abnormalities. It was suggested that performance was not consciously or intentionally produced but, in accord with the terminology of Reitan and Wolfson (1996), there was non-deliberate production of invalid performance. However, although "invalid" here may mean not typical of TBI, results may be quite valid in the sense that this level of performance was ecologically valid, that is, difficulties likely represented real interference effects that would also be evident in the patients' everyday lives. It was noted that it may not have been an impairment of memory but an impairment of attention or effortful processing that interfered with performance. In this context, it is notable that Eccleston, Crombez, Aldrich, and Stannard (1997) found that somatic preoccupation accounted for attentional deficits in chronic pain patients.

Loring et al. (2005) studied the performance of an unselected clinical sample of nonlitigating epilepsy surgery patients who were administered the Victoria Symptom Validity Test (VSVT) in addition to several neuropsychological measures. In this sample of 97 patients, no patient scored significantly below chance on the 24 hard items of the VSVT. However, 14 patients (12%) had scores of 17/24 or below on the hard VSVT measure indicating "invalid" responding. Another 10 patients had "questionable" scores of 18–20/24 on the hard items. Older patients were more likely to have "invalid" results. Whereas it was also suggested that these subjects (24/97 or 24.7% of the entire sample) were performing in the "sub-optimal" range or "not to the best of their ability," no consideration was given to the possibility that they were actually performing at their usual level of ability, giving full effort, or that poor performance was actually associated with a variety of interference effects. However, it was acknowledged that, "with the exception of less than chance scores, it cannot be determined precisely what the effects of lowered IQ from lifelong disease may exert on VSVT performance" (p. 615). It was noted that VSVT scores were systematically related to neuropsychological measures and, in particular, that persons scoring poorly on the VSVT scored low on most of the other cognitive measures, including general intellectual ability. There was no mention of performance on the easy items of the VSVT so, presumably, all did well on this part of the VSVT. The hard items involve discrimination between targets and foils with some identical digits, whereas the easy items involve completely different digits for the target and foils. It was also noted that the VSVT failure rates in this study were similar to those of Doss, Chelune, and Naugle (1999) who studied VSVT performance in a mixed clinical sample that included epilepsy, neurodegenerative disease, stroke, tumor, and other etiologies. Martelli et al. (in preparation) have studied moderate–severe residential TBI patients with no external incentives to malinger, many of whom fail symptom validity tests including the WMT. Several other studies have found that persons with dementia, other neurological problems, or mental retardation may perform poorly on symptom validity testing (Hurley & Deal, 2006; Meyers & Volbrecht, 2003; Teichner & Wagner, 2004; Weinborn, Orr, Woods, Conover, & Feix, 2003).

Duncan (2005) studied psychiatric patients' (both criminal and civil forensic cases) performance on the TOMM, noting that several previous studies with forensic (criminal) psychiatric groups had demonstrated that such patients may produce below cut-off scores on this technique, although it was unclear whether poor performance may have been due to conscious dissimulation, effects of psychiatric disorder, or various other factors. Duncan excluded patients if there had been a history of head injury, mental retardation, or various other factors, including if suboptimal effort had been suggested from performance on the CVLT-II forced choice recognition memory subtest. Seven of the initial 62 patients evaluated for the study were also excluded, two because of stress and five as they were unable to complete all tests. Of the 50 patients who eventually completed the study, 29 were deemed to have concentration problems from their performance on a continuous performance task. Analyses were conducted on the concentration impaired and concentration not impaired subjects. The former scored lower on trials 1 and 2 of the TOMM, but scores of the two groups were equivalent on the retention trial and, overall, patients in both groups did quite well. However, 8% of the patients would have been considered to be false positives, that is, performing below recommended cut-offs on the TOMM, which was noted to be lower than the 27% and 9.6% false positive rates of the dementia and cognitive impairment groups of the TOMM normative sample. It was suggested that either concentration problems secondary to psychiatric disorders or generalized distress may have led to difficulties in the study. Given the various exclusionary criteria in this study, such false positive rates may be low for many psychiatric populations.

Of note, two of the patients in the Duncan (2005) study who had been approached to participate were considered unable to provide informed consent and were also excluded. It should be noted that many persons with more disabling psychoemotional or psychiatric disorders may not agree to participate in such studies or may not be able to provide informed consent, so there may be a selection bias of studying individuals who are relatively intact. Again, there is great heterogeneity in the presentation of persons with psychiatric disorder, some being much more disabled but some being quite high functioning.

Yanez, Fremouw, Tennant, Strunk, and Coker (2006) found that 3 of 20 participants (i.e., 15%) with high levels of depression, as measured by the Beck Depression Inventory, 2nd Edition (BDI-II), and with current diagnoses of Major Depressive Disorder, “failed” either Trial 2 or the retention trial of the TOMM, although there was not a significant difference between the depressed and control groups mean test scores. It was suggested that the results indicated that the TOMM can be used even with severely depressed participants, but a 15% false positive rate is of significant concern.

As previously mentioned, Gervais et al. (2004) reported on the failure rates of the WMT, the TOMM, and the CARB in a sample of 519 claimants referred for disability or personal injury related assessments. These were mostly patients with orthopedic injuries in addition to fibromyalgia, chronic fatigue, PTSD or other anxiety disorder, repetitive strain, or depression. All were involved in workers’ compensation, long-term disability, or personal injury claims. However, 63% of the sample (the Psychological group) were being assessed to determine their eligibility for long-term disability benefits, or to evaluate the extent of pain or other psychological damages in the context of personal injury litigation. The other 193 claimants (37% of the total sample; the Vocational group) had been deemed medically fit to return to work and were being assessed to determine their suitability for vocational retraining. If they were to demonstrate competence during the assessment, there was the possibility that they could receive funding for further education or training and extended disability benefits during the retraining period. As such, it was assumed that the Psychological group would be motivated to perform poorly and that the Vocational group would be motivated to perform well. There was an overall high (35%) failure rate on symptom validity testing, mostly due to performance falling below previously established cut-off scores on one of three symptom validity tests administered. More of the Psychological cases failed symptom validity testing than did the Vocational group; but there were still substantial failure rates in the latter (i.e., 12% of the Vocational group failed the WMT, 4% failed the CARB, but only 1% failed the TOMM). The mean pain ratings of subjects who failed any of the symptom validity measures were significantly higher than those not failing any, irrespective of group. Claimants who failed any one of the symptom validity tests (termed the "exaggerators") were twice as likely to report having pain at the high end of the scale, whereas those who passed all such tests (termed the "genuine" claimants) were 1.8 times more likely to report their pain at the low end of the scale. There were, unfortunately, no other measures of pain-related problems such as sleep disturbance or psychoemotional problems.

Whereas we would interpret the results of the Gervais et al. (2004) study to indicate that pain and related problems likely had an adverse effect on performance, it was suggested by the authors that the higher pain ratings in the "exaggerating" claimants group were due to exaggeration of their pain report. The reasoning for this interpretation appears circular. The authors did present some further "highly selected" analyses to support their view that high pain report and poor performance on symptom validity test were both associated with exaggerating. Patients in the exaggerator and genuine groups who both had high pain severity ratings were compared, and it was found that those in the exaggerating group did poorer on neuropsychological testing. However, we would expect that if pain and related difficulties had an adverse effect on performance, this would include an adverse effect on both symptom validity and standard neuropsychological testing. As such, those subjects would have been selected as exaggerators on the basis of poor performance on symptom validity testing, and it would be expected that they would also do poorly on standard neuropsychological testing. Conversely, it would not be expected that the "genuine" patients would have difficulty on neuropsychological testing, having already been preselected as those who did not have difficulty on symptom validity testing. It should be noted that there is not a simple linear relationship between pain and cognitive or other pain-related interference effects (Hart et al., 2000, 2003; Nicholson & Martelli, 2004). Gervais et al. (2004) also reported that both genuine patients who had low pain severity ratings and those who had high pain severity ratings did equally well on neuropsychological testing. Again, if these subjects have been selected on the basis of there being no adverse effect of pain and related problems on cognitive performance, then it would be expected that there would not be a difference on neuropsychological testing. The same problem of circular reasoning may apply to other studies, such as that of Rohling et al. (2002), in which it was noted that those depressed patients who had failed symptom validity testing also did poorly on neuropsychological testing, whereas those depressed patients who had passed symptom validity testing did not.

Etherton, Bianchini, Greve, and Ciota (2005b) studied healthy subjects who were administered the TOMM under either standard instructions, having been instructed to simulate pain-related memory deficit, or while experiencing cold-induced pain. Whereas both the abstract and the body of the article state that the TOMM was unaffected by this acute pain challenge, it was also reported that those experiencing experimentally induced pain did poorer on the first of the two TOMM trials, that is, 7 of 20 (35%) failed the first trial, whereas none of the controls did. It was noted that most participants were able to leave their hand in the cold water, only briefly taking it out, indicating generally good tolerance or that pain was not intolerable. However, one subject declined to participate following disclosure that one condition involved moderate cold-induced pain, one subject withdrew from the study after undergoing several minutes of the cold-pain procedure, and the data from a third were discarded because of failure to attend to the test stimuli because he was repeatedly looking at his hand (this being the painful body part) and talking with the experimenter rather than attending to the test stimuli. Of note, most of the simulators performed very poorly, that is, nearly 50% who failed scored at a level consistent with guessing or "at chance," and the remainder, also nearly 50%, scoring statistically significantly below chance (i.e., at a level worse than guessing). It was eventually suggested that the presentation of pain patients may vary considerably, some having more significant problems with sleep disturbance, medication side effects, psychoemotional distress, or other factors and that, in clinical practice, TOMM performance below empirically established cutoffs (but not worse than chance) could potentially be due to factors other than deliberate misrepresentation.

Etherton et al. (2006) found that several nonmalingering chronic pain patients performed poorly on the Working Memory Index (WMI) derived from the Wechsler Adult Intelligence Scale-3 (Wechsler, 1997), 14% being impaired with scores of 75 or less. This and other studies will be discussed more fully in the chapter on pain and malingering (Chapter 17).

The first author of this chapter has recently seen a case in which a person was seen for serial neuropsychological assessment as part of medicolegal proceedings (Nicholson, in preparation). The person failed the WMT on more than one examination, but passed several other symptom validity tests (e.g., TOMM, PDRT) and also performed within expectation on most measures of neuropsychological function, including several measures of memory function (e.g., WMS-III Logical Memory), but did very poorly on the Denman Paired Associative Learning task in which one has to learn a set of pairs of words, similar to that required on the WMT. The Denman Paired Associative Learning task and the WMT both stress conditional associative learning, a function that is especially vulnerable to the integrity of frontal system function (Saint-Cyr, Taylor, & Nicholson, 1995).

Several reports suggest that psychoemotional distress, pain or other factors may not have an effect on various symptom validity tests. Rees, Tombaugh, and Boulay (2001) studied the performance of 26 consecutive inpatients from an affective disorders unit. However, over half of the subjects were only minimally or mildly depressed as assessed with the Beck Depression Inventory. There was no effect of level of depression on performance on the TOMM, the performance of all patients falling within normal limits. It was noted that depression has a greater effect on effortful processing and less of an effect on recognition memory, which is what the TOMM assesses. Ashendorf, Constantinou, and McCaffrey (2004) studied archival data from 197 community dwelling elders on the TOMM, attempting to assess the effects of both anxiety and depression on level of performance. However, again, there was relatively little depression or anxiety. Only 18 of the subjects' scores on a measure of anxiety (State-Trait Anxiety Inventory) fell above the cut-off indicating a significant degree of anxiety. The remaining 179 subjects' scores were within the normal range. There was also little depression in this sample, with 166 of the subjects' scores falling within the normal range on the Beck Depression Inventory and the mean score of the remaining 31 subjects indicating a minimal degree of depression. All subjects performed within normal limits on the TOMM.

Etherton, Bianchini, Ciota, and Greve (2005a) compared the performance of healthy subjects who were assigned to one of three groups, either (1) a control group who were administered the RDS under standard conditions, (2) those subjected to an acute cold pain challenge while being administered the RDS, and (3) those administered the RDS and asked to simulate pain-related memory impairment. The acute pain challenge did not adversely affect performance on the RDS despite 18 of the 20 subjects reporting severe pain ratings. The pain group performed no worse than the control group, all members of both groups scoring 8 or higher. In contrast, 65% of the simulators earned a score of 7 or less. It was noted that there were a number of differences between how healthy volunteers may respond to an acute pain challenge that is under their control (i.e., they were able to withdraw from the pain if it became too severe) and the responses of actual chronic pain patients, in part, because there may be other adverse effects associated with a chronic pain condition such as psychological distress, sleep disturbance, or medication side effects.

Etherton, Bianchini, Greve, and Heinly (2005c) also studied pain patients who were identified as definite malingerers from their statistically below-chance performance on a forced-choice symptom validity test (the PDRT, TOMM or a tactile symptom validity test). These patients were contrasted with non-malingering pain patients who had some objective clinical abnormalities of the spine and non-malingering patients who had sustained moderate–severe TBI. Participants were excluded from the non-malingering groups if there was any evidence of symptom exaggeration or response bias, including elevations of $T > 85$ on the MMPI-2 F or Fb scales, suggesting that these were not patients with high psychoemotional distress. The clinical non-malingering and malingering pain groups did not differ in their mean pain ratings. The malingering pain group scored significantly lower on the RDS than both the non-malingering pain group and the TBI group, which did not differ from each other. The mean RDS scores for the two non-malingering clinical groups in this study were almost identical to those of the control and cold acute pain challenge groups reported by Etherton et al. (2005a), whereas the malingering pain group scored almost identically to Etherton et al.'s (2005a) simulator group.

In summary, several studies indicate that performance on symptom validity testing may be adversely affected by pain, somatic preoccupation, psychoemotional problems, neurologic disorder, or various other factors aside from malingering, poor effort, or compensation status that are commonly offered as interpretation of poor performance on these measures. The effect of a number of possible factors that may interfere with performance, for example, sleep disturbance, has not yet been tested, although sleep disturbance and other factors may have a marked effect on performance (Nicholson & Martelli, 2006; Paradee, Rapport, Hanks, & Levy, 2005; Philibert, 2005). There has been no study to date of how a combination of factors (e.g., pain, sleep disturbance, psychoemotional problems) may interfere with performance on symptom validity tests. Interindividual variability is known to be a prominent factor in the expression of most problems, including sleep disturbance (Van Dongen, Vitellaro, & Dinges, 2005). Not all persons experiencing pain, psychoemotional distress, sleep disturbance, or other such problems have difficulty on symptom validity or other measures. It is expected that future research will clarify what confounding factors or combination of factors in which individuals may result in poor performance on symptom validity testing, for example, what premorbid personality characteristics or aspects of the premorbid ability structure may interact with injury-related factors, including situational factors at time of injury and subsequent problems, to produce difficulties in performance on symptom validity testing. Further work will be required to determine how malingering, poor effort, or exaggeration of difficulties for the purposes of secondary gain/external incentives may be distinguished from actual difficulties due to interference effects associated with various confounding factors, vs. cases in which there may be exaggeration or accentuation of difficulty associated with a variety of other psychosocial factors.

Possible, Probable, Definite Malingering?

Slick et al. (1999) proposed criteria for possible, probable, and definite malingering of neurocognitive dysfunction that are still widely accepted and utilized. The criteria for *definite* malingering of neurocognitive dysfunction involve: (a) presence of a substantial external incentive, (b) definite negative response bias, that is, below chance performance ($p < .05$) on one or more forced choice measures of cognitive function, and (c) behaviors meeting the second criterion are not fully accounted for by psychiatric, neurological, or developmental factors. The criteria for *probable* malingering of neurocognitive dysfunction involve: (a) the presence of substantial external incentive, (b) two or more types of evidence from neuropsychological testing (excluding definite negative response bias) or one type of evidence from neuropsychological testing and one or more types of evidence from self-report, and (c) behaviors meeting the second criterion are not fully accounted for by psychiatric, neurological, or developmental factors. The criteria for *possible* malingering of neurocognitive dysfunction involve: (a) presence of a substantial external incentive, (b) evidence from self-report (see below), and (c) behaviors that are taken as evidence of the second criterion are not fully accounted for by psychiatric, neurological, or developmental factors, or criteria for definite or probable malingering are met but primary psychiatric, neurological, or developmental etiologies cannot be ruled out.

As has been discussed above, it is widely accepted that significantly below chance performance on symptom validity testing is the strongest psychometric evidence of conscious and deliberate feigning/malingering there is. However, if a person is actually performing "at chance," it would be expected that approximately one out of every 20 such times that there would be a significantly (i.e., $p < .05$) below chance level of performance on forced-choice techniques. Given the large number of symptom validity tests that are being administered on a daily basis, some of which may be with patients who are responding essentially "at chance" as they are not able to attend well to the test stimuli, there may be many that are scoring "significantly" below chance simply on the basis of chance.

Importantly, the Slick et al. (1999) criteria for possible, probable, or definite malingering all involve consideration of other factors (e.g., psychiatric, neurological, or developmental) that may account for difficulties on symptom validity testing. Unfortunately, the criteria do not consider the possible effects of pain, sleep disturbance, or other psychological factors that may not be characterized as psychiatric, neurological, or developmental. When other such factors are prominent (e.g., a person having a migraine headache, with very fragmented sleep, and with intense psychoemotional disturbance involving anxiety, depression, or anger, and/or who may have some subclinical thought disorder, etc.) there may be marked interference effects on neuropsychological assessment, and performance may actually be at or below chance on many forced-choice techniques or, at the least, below usual cutting scores. Whereas it might be expected that any reasonable clinician could appreciate that a person with a severe headache or other problems as described above may not be performing optimally for these reasons, such factors are often neglected.

The Slick et al. (1999) criteria for "evidence from self-report" involve discrepancy between patient self-report and documented history, known patterns of brain functioning, behavioral observations, or information provided by collateral informants. In addition, elevations on "well-validated" validity scales or indices on self-report measures of psychological adjustment (e.g., MMPI-2) that are "strongly suggestive of exaggerated or fabricated distress or dysfunction" (p. 554) may be utilized. As discussed above, some such discrepancies between self-report and other sources of information may be associated with fabrication or exaggeration with the intent to deceive to obtain some financial or other goal. For example, the person who claims to have been involved in an accident and to have suffered some related injury and associated disability is discovered to not have been involved in the accident at all, or complaints, if actually real, had been evident prior to the supposed accident/injury; in another example, a person claiming complete disability who could not possibly work or perform many basic activities of daily living is discovered to be working at a job and actively engaged in various other activities; or, the person who claims paralysis and inability to walk at all, who attends to the assessment in a wheelchair with his or her spouse, is observed to get out of the wheelchair in the parking lot at lunch time, put the wheelchair in the car, and walk off to have lunch, returning after the lunch break again wheelchair bound.

However, many or likely most instances of apparent discrepancy between self-report and other information may be explained by multiple other factors and should not be taken as evidence to meet this criterion. For example, complaints of memory or other cognitive problems following a mild TBI may be considered discrepant with known patterns of brain functioning because most persons recover quickly and completely from such brain injury, but there may be other factors such as posttraumatic headache and related problems serving to interfere with cognitive function; or, there may be a discrepancy between a person's self-reported history in the current assessment that is at odds with what had been reported by another clinician, but there are commonly differences in information obtained between clinicians on clinical interview that likely reflect clinician skill more than any patient-related factors. As has been discussed above and as will be discussed further below, it is often questionable whether elevation on self-report inventory validity scales are associated with exaggeration or reflect actual symptomatology associated with a disorder in question and, furthermore, whether any actual exaggeration is associated with conscious dissimulation vs. other psychosocial causes.

As has been noted, there are very few cases of confirmed malingering reported in the literature. This is in marked contrast to the large numbers that are being considered to be putting forth suboptimal effort or otherwise producing invalid test results, which is often at least implied to involve malingering. Whereas some of the studies reported in the literature do present strong evidence of malingering, or at least active feigning, the presentation of cases in many other studies is questionable. We will review just a few to illustrate the range of findings that are being interpreted as indicating malingering.

A number of studies have reported significantly below chance levels of performance on symptom validity testing. Binder (1993) found that 12% of minor head trauma and 3% of more serious brain injury patients seeking compensation scored significantly below chance on the PDRT. Bianchini, Greve, and Love (2003) reported three cases of moderate–severe TBI in which the psychometric evidence appears quite convincing that these persons were consciously and deliberately malingering. Each performed significantly below chance on at least one forced-choice symptom validity test. Boone and Lu (2003) also presented two severe TBI cases who subsequently became involved in litigation and were then documented to display "noncredible" cognitive symptoms as demonstrated by (1) failed performance on cognitive effort tests, that is, scoring below suggested cut-offs although not significantly below chance on forced-choice paradigms, (2) noncredible performance on standard neuropsychological instruments, (3) questionable validity of personality inventory profiles, and (4) marked inconsistency in test performance across assessments or marked inconsistency between test scores and activities of daily living documented through surveillance videotapes. We agree that the data from these cases strongly suggest that the complainants were malingering or purposefully presenting themselves as having greater problems than they actually had for the purposes of secondary gain (presumably financial compensation). Notably, however, the evidence appeared much stronger in the first case and was less striking in the second case, this person having performed well on a number of measures of effort and many neuropsychological tests.

One of the very few studies in which there were sizeable numbers of (likely) definite malingerers/feigners was that of Etherton et al. (2005c), in which the records of approximately 200 pain patients seen for psychological evaluation of pain and related problems were reviewed, and it was determined that 35 (approximately 17.5%) had significantly below chance levels of performance on the TOMM, PDRT, or a tactile symptom validity test. There are some caveats about this study that we discuss below in the chapter on chronic pain and malingering (Chapter 17). In addition, it should be realized that there may be differences between persons who have clearly been injured, with evidence of TBI, pain, PTSD or other problems, who may purposely do poorly on symptom validity or other testing as compared with persons with no such history of significant injury or problems who do poorly on testing. The former may not be malingering for the purpose of obtaining some external (e.g., financial) incentive. They may also not be feigning for the purposes of assuming a sick role (i.e., Factitious Disorder), but they may be feigning in an ill-guided attempt to prove that they are actually having problems that have been contested in the medicolegal proceedings.

One of the very few neuropsychological studies in which a sizeable sample of "definite" malingerers were reported was that of Larrabee (2003b), in which 26 "definite" malingerers were identified on the basis of significantly worse than chance performance on any one of the easy, hard, total, or any individual trial of the PDRT. There was no indication of what probability level was used to assess "significantly" below chance level of performance but, given the multiple measures utilized (i.e., seven), there should have been a corresponding reduction of the usual probability level (i.e., $p < .05$). In any case, the reported mean PDRT easy, difficult, and total scores (i.e., 17.58, 12.23, and 29.81, respectively) suggests that many of the persons identified as definite maligners actually did not consistently perform significantly below chance, even using the $p < .05$ probability level. Furthermore, whereas it was reported that the participants did not have neurologic, psychiatric, or developmental problems that may have accounted for poor performance, as the Slick et al. (1999) criteria require, there was no indication of whether pain may have been a problem, and there were no objective measures of distress or psychopathology reported.

Borckardt et al. (2003) identified five "malingerers" on the basis of "some combination" of an extensive list of possible indices, several of which contained multiple measures. None of these involved significantly below chance performance on symptom validity testing. There were reported to be elevations on several of the MMPI-2 or MCMI-III validity indices, but there was no information presented on clinical scale elevations and no other information concerning pain, psychoemotional distress, or other factors that may have been affecting performance, although medical or neurological cause for their presentation was apparently ruled out. We would question whether these participants were actually malingerers.

Bianchini et al. (2001) reported on the results of a "probable" group of malingering TBI patients seeking compensation. Following the strategy of Greiffenstein et al. (1994), five collateral markers for identification of probable malingering were utilized. These included: (1) an improbable symptom history that was contradicted by records, (2) total disability in work or a major social role for 1 year or more after mild TBI, (3) claims of remote memory loss, (4) elevated ($T > 80$) score on the MMPI-2 F scale, and (5) a score below the recommended cut-off of any one of six formal malingering measures (e.g., Rey 15-Item Test, the TOMM, RDS). Of the 38 TBI patients who were not seeking compensation, that is, the control group, 15 were positive on one or more of the collateral markers. Of the "probable" malingering group, 20 of 26 were positive on two markers, five were positive on three, and one was positive on four. Eighteen of the "probable" malingerers were positive on the MMPI-2 F scale. There was no information provided on pain, psychoemotional distress, or other factors. We strongly suspect that many of these "probable" malingerers were not malingering.

In summary, although we have presented only a very few of the many possible studies for illustrative purposes, we conclude that there is much variability in what is being offered as psychometric evidence of malingering. As has been indicated above, the majority of studies in which it is suspected that results are invalid due to poor effort, conscious dissimulation, or related behaviors rest upon below cut-off criteria on various symptom validity or actual neuropsychological tests. We suspect that many, if not most, of those scoring below such cut-offs are not malingering, nor are they simply putting forth poor effort. Of note, there have been very few follow-up studies of those initially identified as malingering. Rutherford, Merrett, and McDonald (1982) did follow patients for one year after they had sustained concussion and onset of posttraumatic headache. Of the total sample of patients ($n = 128$), 11.7% were initially suspected as malingerers. However, 60% of these were symptom free at 1 year and 88.5% of the patients not thought to be malingering were asymptomatic at 1 year. It was concluded that the initial diagnosis of malingering was erroneous in most cases.

References

Allen, L. M., Conder, R. L., Green, P., & Cox, D. R. (1997). *CARB '97 Manual for the computerized assessment of response bias*. Durham, NC: CogniSyst.

American Psychiatric Association (2000). *The diagnostic and statistical manual of mental disorders, 4th* edition, text revision. Washington, DC: Author.

Anger, W. K., Storzbach, D., Binder, L. M., Campbell, K., Rohlman, D., & McCauley, L. (1999). Evidence of cognitive deficits in Persian Gulf War veterans: Interim report from a population-based study. *Journal of the International Neuropsychological Society, 5*, 203–212.

Arbisi, P. A., & Ben-Porath, Y. S. (1995). An MMPI-2 infrequent response scale for use with psychopathological populations: The Infrequency-Psychopathology Scale, F(p). *Psychological Assessment, 7*, 424–431.

Arbisi, P. A., Ben-Porath, Y. S., & McNulty, J. (2003). Refinement of the MMPI-2 F(p) scale is not necessary. *Assessment, 10*, 123–128.

Arbisi, P. A., & Butcher, J. N. (2004). Failure of the FBS to predict malingering of somatic symptoms: Response to critiques by Greve and Bianchini and Lees-Haley and Fox. *Archives of Clinical Neuropsychology, 19*, 341–345.

Arnold, G., Boone, K. B., Lu, P., Dean, A., Wen, J., Nitch, S., & McPherson, S. (2005). Sensitivity and specificity of finger tapping scores for the detection of suspect effort. *The Clinical Neuropsychologist, 19*, 105–120.

Ashendorf, L., Constantinou, M., & McCaffrey, R. J. (2004). The effect of depression and anxiety on the TOMM in community-dwelling older adults. *Archives of Clinical Neuropsychology, 19*, 125–130.

Babikian, T., Boone, K. B., Lu. P., & Arnold, G. (2006). Sensitivity and specificity of various digit span scores in the detection of suspect effort. *The Clinical Neuropsychologist, 20*, 145–159.

Backhaus, S. L., Fichtenberg, N. L., & Hanks, R. A. (2004). Detection of sub-optimal performance using a floor effect strategy in patients with traumatic brain injury. *The Clinical Neuropsychologist, 18*, 591–603.

Bauer, L., & McCaffrey, R. J. (2006). Coverage of the Test of Memory Malingering, Victoria Symptom Validity Test, and Word Memory Test on the internet: is test security threatened? *Archives of Clinical Neuropsychology, 21*, 121–126.

Bender, S. D., & Rogers, R. (2004). Detection of neurocognitive feigning: Development of a multi-strategy assessment. *Archives of Clinical Neuropsychology, 19*, 49–60.

Berry, D. T. R., Baer, R. A., & Harris, M. J. (1991). Detection of malingering on the MMPI: A meta-analytic review. *Clinical Psychology Review, 11*, 585–598.

Berry, D. T. R., Wetter, M. W., Baer, R. A., Youngjohn, J. R., Gass, C. S., Lamb, D. G. et al. (1995). Overreporting of closed-head injury symptoms on the MMPI-2. *Psychological Assessment, 7*, 517–523.

Bianchini, K. J., Greve, K. W., & Love, J. M. (2003). Definite malingered neurocognitive dysfunction in moderate/severe traumatic brain injury. *The Clinical Neuropsychologist, 17*, 574–580.

Bianchini, K. J., Mathias, C. W., Greve, K. W, Houston, R. J., & Crouch, J. A. (2001). Classification accuracy of the Portland Digit Recognition Test in traumatic brain injury. *The Clinical Neuropsychologist, 15*, 461–470.

Bierley, R. A., Drake, A. I., Ahmed, S., Date, E. S., Rosner, M., Warden, D., Salazar, A. M., & the Defense and Veterans Head Injury Program (DVHIP) Study Group. (2001). Biased responding: A case series demonstrating a relationship between somatic symptoms and impaired recognition memory performance for traumatic brain injured individuals. *Brain Injury, 15*, 697–714.

Binder, L. (1993). Assessment of malingering after mild head trauma with the Portland Digit Recognition Test. *Journal of Clinical and Experimental Neuropsychology, 15*, 170–182.

Binder, L. M. (1990). Malingering following minor head trauma. *The Clinical Neuropsychologist, 4*, 25–36.

Binder, L. M., & Willis, S. C. (1991). Assessment of motivation after financially compensable minor head trauma. *Psychological Assessment: A Journal of Consulting and Clinical Psychology, 3*, 175–181.

Bolan, B., Foster, J. K., Schmand, B., & Bolan, S. (2002). A comparison of three tests to detect feigned amnesia: The effects of feedback and the measurement of response latency. *Journal of Clinical and Experimental Neuropsychology, 24*, 154–167.

Boone, K. B., & Lu, P. (2003). Noncredible cognitive performance in the context of severe brain injury. *The Clinical Neuropsychologist, 17*, 244–254.

Boone, K. B., Lu, P., Back, C., King, C., Lee, E., Philpott, P. et al. (2002). Sensitivity and specificity of the Rey Dot Counting Test in patients with suspect effort and various clinical samples. *Archives of Clinical Neuropsychology, 17*, 625–642.

Boone, K. B., & Lu, P. H. (1999). Impact of somatoform symptomatology on credibility of cognitive performance. *The Clinical Neuropsychologist, 13*, 414–419.

Boone, K. B., Lu, P., & Wen, J. (2005). Comparison of various RAVLT scores in the detection of noncredible memory performance. *Archives of Clinical Neuropsychology, 20*, 301–319.

Borckardt, J. J., Engum, E. S., Lambert, E. W., Nash, M., Bracy, O. L., & Ray, E. C. (2003). Use of the CBDI to detect malingering when malingerers do their "homework." *Archives of Clinical Neuropsychology, 18*, 57–69.

Bowden, S. C., Shores, E. A., & Mathias, J. L. (2006). Does effort suppress cognition after traumatic brain injury? A re-examination of the evidence for the Word Memory Test. *The Clinical Neuropsychologist, 20*, 858–872.

Brady, J. P., & Lind, D. L. (1961). Experimental analysis of hysterical blindness. *Archives of General Psychiatry, 4*, 331–339.

Brockhaus, R., & Merten, T. (2004). Neuropsychologische Diagnostik suboptimalen Leistungsverhaltens mit dem Word Memory Test [Neuropsychological assessment of suboptimal performance: The Word Memory Test]. *Nervenarzt, 75*, 882–887.

Bush, S. S., Ruff, R. M., Troster, A. I., Barth, J. T., Koffler, S. P., Pliskin, N. H. et al. (2005). Symptom validity assessment: Practical issues and medical necessity. NAN Policy and Planning Committee. *Archives of Clinical Neuropsychology, 20*, 419–426.

Butcher, J. N. (2006). *MMPI-2: A Practitioners Guide.* Washington, DC: American Psychological Association.

Butcher, J. N., Arbisi, P. A., Atlis, M., & McNulty, J. L. (2003). The construct validity of the Lees-Haley Fake Bad Scale: Does this scale measure somatic malingering and feigned emotional distress? *Archives of Clinical Neuropsychology, 18*, 473–485.

Butcher, J. N., Dahlstrom, W. G., Graham, J. R., Tellegen, A., & Kaemmer, B. (1989). *Minnesota Multiphasic Personality Inventory (MMPI-2). Manual for administration and scoring*. Minneapolis: University of Minnesota Press.

Chouinard, M. J., & Rouleau, I. (1997). The 48-Pictures test: A two-alternative forced-choice recognition test for the detection of malingering. *Journal of the International Neuropsychological Society, 3*, 545–552.

Cohen, J. (1994). The earth is round … $p < 0.05$. *American Psychologist, 49*, 997–1003.

Conder, R., Allen, L., & Cox, D. (1992). *Manual for the computerized assessment of response bias*. Durham, NC: CogniSyst.

Constantinou, M., Bauer, L., Ashendorf, L., Fisher, J. M., & McCaffrey, R. J. (2005). Is poor performance on recognition memory effort measures indicative of generalized poor performance on neuropsychological tests? *Archives of Clinical Neuropsychology, 20*, 191–198.

Davidson, H., Suffield, B., Orenczuk, S., Nantau, K., & Mandel, A. (1991). *Screening for malingering using The Memory for Fifteen Items Test (MFIT)*. Poster presented at the annual meeting of the International Neuropsychological Society Meeting.

Dearth, C., Berry, D., Vickery, C., Vagnini, V., Baser, R., Orey, S. et al. (2005). Detection of feigned head injury symptoms on the MMPI-2 in head injured patients and community controls. *Archives of Clinical Neuropsychology, 20*, 95–110.

Denney, R. L. (1996). Symptom validity testing of remote memory in a criminal forensic setting. *Archives of Clinical Neuropsychology, 11*, 589–603.

Doss, R. C., Chelune, G. J., & Naugle, R. I. (1999). Victoria Symptom Validity Test: Compensation seeking vs. non-compensation-seeking patients in a general clinical setting. *Journal of Forensic Neuropsychology, 1*, 5–20.

Duncan, A. (2005). The impact of cognitive and psychiatric impairment of psychotic disorders on the Test of Memory Malingering (TOMM). *Assessment, 12*, 123–129.

Dunn, T. M., Shear, P. K., Howe, S., & Ris, M. D. (2003). Detecting neuropsychological malingering: Effects of coaching and information. *Archives of Clinical Neuropsychology, 18*, 121–134.

Eccleston, C., Crombez, G., Aldrich, D., & Stannard, C. (1997). Attention and somatic awareness in chronic pain. *Pain, 72*, 209–215.

Essig, S., Mittenberg, W., Peterson, R., Stranman, S., & Cooper, J. (2001). Practices in forensic neuropsychology: Perspectives of neuropsychologists and trial attorney. *Archives of Clinical Neuropsychology, 16*, 271–291.

Etherton, J. L., Bianchini, K. J., Ciota, M. A., & Greve, K. W. (2005a). Reliable Digit Span is unaffected by laboratory-induced pain: Implications for clinical use. *Assessment, 12*, 101–106.

Etherton, J. L., Bianchini, K. J., Ciota, M. A., Heinly, M. T., & Greve, K. W., (2006). Pain, malingering and the WAIS-III Working Memory Index. *The Spine Journal, 6*, 61–71.

Etherton, J. L., Bianchini, K. J., Greve, K. W., & Ciota, M. A. (2005b). Test of Memory Malingering performance is unaffected by laboratory-induced pain: implications for clinical use. *Archives of Clinical Neuropsychology, 20*, 375–384.

Etherton, J. L., Bianchini, K. J., Greve, K. W., & Heinly, M. T. (2005c). Sensitivity and specificity of Reliable Digit Span in malingered pain-related disability. *Assessment, 12*, 130–136.

Faust, D., & Ackerly, M. A. (1998). Did you think it was going to be easy: Some methodological suggestions for the investigation and development of malingering detection techniques. In C. R. Reynolds, (Ed.), *Detection of malingering during head injury litigation* (pp. 261–286). New York: Plenum Press.

Faust, D., Hart, K., & Guilmette, T. J. (1988a). Pediatric malingering: The capacity of children to fake believable deficits on neuropsychological testing. *Journal of Consulting and Clinical Psychology, 56*, 578–582.

Faust, D., Hart, K., Guilmette, T. J., & Arkes, H. R. (1988b). Neuropsychologists' capacity to detect adolescent malingerers. *Professional Psychology: Research and Practice, 19*, 508–515.

Flor-Henry, P., Fromm-Auch, D., Tapper, M., & Schopflocher, D. (1981). A neuropsychological study of the stable syndrome of hysteria. *Biological Psychiatry, 16*, 731–742.

Forrest, T. J., Allen, D. N., & Goldstein, G. (2004). Malingering indexes for the Halstead Category Test. *The Clinical Neuropsychologist, 18*, 334–347.

Frederick, R. (1997). *The Validity Indicator Profile manual.* Minneapolis, MN: NCS-Pearson.

Frederick, R. (2002a). Review of the Validity Indicator Profile. *Journal of Forensic Neuropsychology, 2*, 125–145.

Frederick, R. (2002b). A review of Rey's strategies for detecting malingered neuropsychological impairment. *Journal of Forensic Neuropsychology, 2*, 1–25.

Frederick, R. I., & Foster, H. G. (1991). Multiple measures of malingering on a forced-choice test of cognitive ability. *Psychological Assessment: A Journal of Consulting and Clinical Psychology, 3*, 596–602.

Frederick, R. I., Sarfaty, S. D., Johnson, J. D., & Powell, J. (1994). Validation of a detector of response bias on a forced choice test of nonverbal ability. *Neuropsychology, 8*, 118–125.

Gervais, R. O., Rohling, M. L., Green, P., & Ford, W. (2004). A comparison of WMT, CARB, and TOMM failure rates in non-head injury disability claimants. *Archives of Clinical Neuropsychology, 19*, 475–487.

Golden, C., & Grier, C. (1996). Detecting malingering on the Luria-Nebraska Neuropsychological Battery. In C. Reynolds (Ed.), *Detection of malingering in head injury litigation*. New York: Plenum.

Gorman, E. (1982). Defining malingering. *Journal of Forensic Science, 27*, 401–407.

Graham, J. R. (2006). *MMPI-2: Assessing personality and psychopathology (4th edition)*. New York: Oxford University Press.

Green, P. (2003). *Green's Word Memory Test. User's manual*. Edmonton, Canada: Green's Publishing.

Green, P. (2004). *Green's Medical Symptom Validity Test (MSVT) for MicrosoftWindows. User's manual*. Edmonton, Canada: Green's Publishing.

Green, P., Allen, L., & Astner, K. (1996). *The Word Memory Test: A users guide to the oral and computer-administered forms, US version 1.1*. Durham, NC: Cognisyst.

Green, P., & Flaro, L., (2003). Word Memory Test performance in children. *Child Neuropsychology, 3*, 189–207.

Green, P., & Iverson, G. L. (2001). Validation of the computerized assessment of response bias and litigating patients with head injuries. *The Clinical Neuropsychologist, 15*, 492–497.

Green, P., Lees-Haley, P. R., & Allen, L. M. (2002). The Word Memory Test and the validity of neuropsychological test scores. *Journal of Forensic Neuropsychology, 3–4*, 97–124.

Green, P., Rohling, M. L., Lees-Halley, P. R., & Allen, L. (2001). Effort has a greater effect on test scores than severe brain injury in compensation claims. *Brain Injury, 15*, 1045–1060.

Greiffenstein, M., Gola, T., & Baker, J. (1995). MMPI-2 validity scales vs. domain specific measures in detection of factitious traumatic brain injury. *The Clinical Neuropsychologist, 9*, 230–240.

Greiffenstein, M. F., Baker, W. J., & Gola, T. (1994). Validation of malingered amnesia measures with a large clinical sample. *Psychological Assessment, 6*, 218–224.

Greiffenstein, M. F., Baker, W. J., Gola, T., Donders, J., & Miller, L. (2002). The Fake Bad Scale in atypical and severe closed head injury litigants. *Journal of Clinical Psychology, 58*, 1591–1600.

Greve, K. W., Bianchini, K. J., Mathias, C. W., Houston, R. J., & Crouch, J. A. (2003). Detecting malingered performance on the Wechsler Adult Intelligence Scale: Validation of Mittenberg's approach in traumatic brain injury. *Archives of Clinical Neuropsychology, 18*, 245–260.

Grillo, J. B., Brown, R. S., Hilsabeck, R., & Price, J. R. (1994). Raising doubts about claims of malingering: Implications of relationships between MCMI-II and MMPI-2 performances. *Journal of Clinical Psychology, 50*, 651–655.

Grosz, H. J., & Zimmerman, J. (1965). Experimental analysis of hysterical blindness. *Archives of General Psychiatry, 13*, 255–260.

Grove, W. M., & Meehl, P. E. (1996). Comparative efficiency of informal (subjective, impressionistic) and formal (mechanical, algorithmic) prediction procedures: The clinical-statistical controversy. *Psychology, Public Policy, and Law, 2*, 293–323.

Guilmette, T., Hart, K., & Giuliano, A. (1993). Malingering detection: The use of a forced choice method in identifying organic vs. simulated memory impairment. *The Clinical Neuropsychologist, 7*, 59–69.

Hart, R. P., Martelli, M. F., & Zasler, N. D. (2000). Chronic pain and neuropsychological functioning. *Neuropsychology Review, 10*, 131–149.

Hart, R. P., Wade, J. B., & Martelli, M. F. (2003). Cognitive impairment in patients with chronic pain: The significance of stress. *Current Pain and Headache Reports, 7*, 1–12.

Hathaway, S. R., & McKinley, J. C. (1967). *Minnesota multiphasic personality inventory manual*. New York: Psychological Corporation.

Heaton, R. K., Grant, I., & Matthews, C. G. (1991). *Comprehensive norms for an expanded Halstead–Reitan Battery: Demographic corrections, research findings, and clinical applications*. Odessa, FL: Psychological Assessment Resources.

Heaton, R. K., Smith, H. H. Jr., Lehman, R. A., & Vogt, A. T. (1978). Prospects for faking believable deficits on neuropsychological testing. *Journal of Consulting and Clinical Psychology, 46*, 892–900.

Henry, G. K. (2005). Probable malingering and performance on the test of variables of attention. *The Clinical Neuropsychologist, 19*, 121–129.

Hilsabeck, R. C., & Gouvier, W. D. (2005). Detecting simulated memory impairment: Further validation of the Word Completion Memory Test (WCMT). *Archives of Clinical Neuropsychology, 20*, 1025–1041.

Hilsabeck, R. C., & LeCompte, D. C. (1997). *Word Completion Memory Test (WCMT)*. Durham, NC: CogniSyst.

Hilsabeck, R. C., LeCompte, D. C., Marks, A. R., & Grafman, J. (2001). The Word Completion Memory Test (WCMT): A new test to detect malingered memory deficits. *Archives of Clinical Neuropsychology, 16*, 669–677.

Hiscock, M., & Hiscock, C. (1989). Refining the forced-choice method for the detection of malingering. *Journal of Clinical and Experimental Neuropsychology, 11*, 967– 974.

Hurley, K. E., & Deal, W. P. (2006). Assessment instruments measuring malingering used with individuals who have mental retardation: potential problems and issues. *Mental Retardation, 44*, 112–119.

Ingraham, L. J., & Aikken, C. B. (1996). An empirical approach to determining criteria for abnormality in test batteries with multiple measures. *Neuropsychology, 10*, 120–124.

Inman, T., Vickery, C., Berry, D., Lamb, D., Edwards, C., & Smith, G. (1998). Development and initial validation of a new procedure evaluating adequacy of effort given during neuropsychological testing: The Letter Memory Test. *Psychological Assessment, 10*, 128–139.

Inman, T. H., & Berry, D. T. R. (2002). Cross-validation of indicators of malingering. A comparison of nine neuropsychological tests, four tests of malingering, and behavioral observations. *Archives of Clinical Neuropsychology, 17*, 1–23.

Iverson, G., Franzen, M., & McCracken, L. (1991). Evaluation of an objective assessment technique for the detection of malingered memory deficits. *Law and Human Behavior, 15*, 667–676.

Iverson, G., Franzen, M., & McCracken, L. (1994). Application of a forced-choice memory procedure designed to detect experimental malingering. *Archives of Clinical Neuropsychology, 9*, 437–450.

Iverson, G. L. (2003). Detecting malingering in civil forensic evaluations. In A. M. Horton & L. C. Hartlage (Eds.), *Handbook of forensic neuropsychology* (pp. 137– 177). New York: Springer Science+Business Media.

Iverson, G. L., & Binder, L. M. (2000). Detecting exaggeration and malingering in neuropsychological assessment. *Journal of Head Trauma Rehabilitation, 15*, 829– 858.

Iverson, G. L., Henrichs, T. F., Barton, E. A., & Allen, S. (2002). Specificity of the MMPI-2 Fake Bad Scale as a marker for personal injury malingering. *Psychological Reports, 90*, 131–136.

Kaufmann, P. M. (2005). Protecting the objectivity, fairness, and integrity of neuropsychological evaluations in litigation: A privilege second to none? *The Journal of Legal Medicine, 26*, 95–131.

King, J. H., Sweet, J. J., Sherer, M., Curtiss, G., & Vanderploeg, R. D. (2002). Validity indicators within the Wisconsin Card Sorting Test: Application of new and previously researched multivariate procedures in multiple traumatic brain injury samples. *The Clinical Neuropsychologist, 16*, 506–523.

Langeluddecke, P. M., & Lucas, S. K. (2003). Quantitative measures of memory malingering on the Wechsler Memory Scale—Third Edition in mild head injury litigants. *Archives of Clinical Neuropsychology, 18*, 181–197.

Lannoo, E., Colardyn, F., Jannes, C., & de Soete, G. (2001). Course of neuropsychological recovery from moderate-to-severe head injury: A 2-year follow-up. *Brain Injury, 15*, 1–13.

Larrabee, G. (1998). Somatic malingering on the MMPI and MMPI-2 in personal injury litigants. *The Clinical Neuropsychologist, 12*, 179–188

Larrabee, G. (2003a). Detection of malingering using atypical performance patterns on standard neuropsychological tests. *The Clinical Neuropsychologist, 17*, 410–425.

Larrabee, G. (2003b). Detection of symptom exaggeration with the MMPI-2 in litigants with malingered neurocognitive dysfunction. *The Clinical Neuropsychologist, 17*, 54–68.

Larrabee, G. J. (2003c). Exaggerated MMPI-2 symptom report in personal injury litigants with malingered neurocognitive deficit. *Archives of Clinical Neuropsychology, 18*, 673–686.

Leark, R. A., Dixon, D., Hoffman, T., & Huynh, D. (2002). Fake bad test response bias effects on the Test of Variables of Attention. *Archives of Clinical Neuropsychology, 17*, 335–342.

Lee, A., Boone, K. B., Lesser, I., Wohl, M., Wilkins, S., & Parks, C. (2000). Performance of older depressed patients on two cognitive malingering tests: False positive rates for the Rey 15-Item memorization and dot counting tests. *The Clinical Neuropsychologist, 14*, 303–308.

Lees-Haley, P. R., English, L. T., & Glenn, W. J. (1991). A Fake Bad Scale on the MMPI-2 for personal injury claimants. *Psychological Report, 68*, 203–210.

Lees-Haley, P. R., & Dunn, J. T. (1994). The ability of naive subjects to report symptoms of mild brain injury, post-traumatic stress disorder, major depression, and generalized anxiety disorder. *Journal of Clinical Psychology, 50*, 252–256.

Lees-Haley, P. R., & Fox, D. D. (2004). Commentary on Butcher, Arbisi, Atlis, and McNulty (2003) on the Fake Bad Scale. *Archives of Clinical Neuropsychology, 19*, 333–336.

Lezak, M. D. (1983). *Neuropsychological assessment* (2nd ed.). New York: Oxford University Press.

Lezak, M. D. (1995). *Neuropsychological assessment* (3rd ed.). New York: Oxford University Press.

Lezak, M. D., Howieson, D. B., & Loring, D. W. (2004). *Neuropsychological assessment* (4th ed.). New York: Oxford University Press.

Loring, D. W., Lee, G. P., & Meador, K. J. (2005). Victoria Symptom Validity Test performance in non-litigating epilepsy surgery candidates. *Journal of Clinical and Experimental Neuropsychology, 27*, 610–617.

Lu, P. H., Boone, K. B., Cozolino, L., & Mitchell, C. (2003). Effectiveness of the Rey– Osterrieth Complex Figure Test and the Meyers and Meyers recognition trial in the detection of suspect effort. *The Clinical Neuropsychologist, 17*, 426–440.

Lu, P. H., Boone, K. B., Jimenez, N., & Razani, J. (2004). Failure to inhibit the reading response on the Stroop Test: A pathognomonic indicator of suspect effort. *Journal of Clinical and Experimental Neuropsychology, 26*, 180–189.

Lynch, W. J. (2004). Determination of effort level, exaggeration, and malingering in neurocognitive assessment. *Journal of Head Trauma Rehabilitation, 19*, 277–283.

Marin, R. S., & Chakravorty, S. (2005). Disorders of diminished motivation. In J. M. Silver, T. W. McAllister, & S. C. Yudofsky (Eds.), *Textbook of traumatic brain injury* (pp. 419–436). Washington, DC: American Psychiatric Press.

Martelli, M. F., Nicholson, K., Zasler, N. D., & Bender, M. C. (2006). Assessment of response bias in clinical and forensic evaluations of impairment following brain injury. In N. D. Zasler, D. I. Katz, & R. D. Zafonte (Eds.), *Brain injury medicine: Principles and practice*. New York: Demos Medical Publishing.

Martelli, M. F., Zasler, N. D., Mancini, A. M., & MacMillan, P. (1999). Psychological assessment and application in impairment and disability evaluations. In R. V. May & M. F. Martelli (Eds.), *Guide to functional capacity evaluation with impairment rating applications* (pp. 1–84). Richmond, VA: NADEP Publications.

Martin, R., Bolter, J., Todd, M., Gouvier, W., & Niccolls, R. (1993). Effects of sophistication and motivation on the detection of malingered memory performance using a computerized forced-choice task. *Journal of Clinical and Experimental Neuropsychology, 15*, 867–880.

Mathias, C. W., Greve, K. W., Bianchini, K. J., Houston, R. J., & Crouch, J. A. (2002). Detecting malingered neurocognitive dysfunction using the Reliable Digit Span in traumatic brain injury. *Assessment, 9*, 301–308.

Merten, T., Green, P., Henry, M., Blaskewitz, N., & Brockhaus, R. (2005). Analog validation of German-language symptom validity tests and the influence of coaching. *Archives of Clinical Neuropsychology, 20*, 719–726.

Merten, T., Henry, M., & Hilsabeck, R. C. (2004). The use of symptom validity tests in neuropsychological assessment: An analogue study. *Zeitschrift fuer Neuropsychologie, 15*, 81–90.

Meyers, J. E., & Volbrecht, M. (1998). Validation of reliable digits for detection of malingering. *Assessment, 5*, 303–307.

Meyers, J. E., & Volbrecht, M. E. (2003). A validation of multiple malingering detection methods in a large clinical sample. *Archives of Clinical Neuropsychology, 18*, 261–276.

Miller, A. R., Rosenfeld, J. P., Soskins, M., & Jhee, M. (2002). P300 amplitude and topography in an autobiographical oddball paradigm involving simulated amnesia. *Journal of Psychophysiology, 16*, 1–11.

Miller, L. J., & Donders, J. (2001). Subjective symptomatology after traumatic head injury. *Brain Injury, 15*, 297–304.

Millis, S., & Putnam, S. (1994). The Recognition Memory Test in the assessment of memory impairment after financially compensable mild head injury: A replication. *Perceptual and Motor Skills, 79*, 384–386.

Millon, T. (1997). *Millon Clinical Multiaxial Inventory-III manual* (2nd ed.). Minneapolis, MN: NCS Pearson.

Morey, L. C. (1991). *Personality Assessment Inventory: Professional manual*. Odessa, FL: Psychological Assessment Resources.

Nelson, N. W., Boone, K., Dueck, A., Wagener, L., Lu, P., & Grills, C. (2003). Relationships between eight measures of suspect effort. *The Clinical Neuropsychologist, 17*, 263–272.

Nelson, N. W., Sweet, J. J., & Demakis, G. J. (2006). Meta-analysis of the MMPI-2 Fake Bad Scale: Utility in forensic practice. *The Clinical Neuropsychologist, 20*, 39–58.

Nicholson, K. (2000). Pain, cognition and traumatic brain injury. *NeuroRehabilitation, 14*, 95–103.

Nicholson, K., & Martelli, M. (2004). The problem of pain. *Journal of Head Trauma Rehabilitation, 19*, 2–9.

Nicholson, K., & Martelli, M. (2006). The confounding effects of pain, psychoemotional problems or psychiatric disorder, premorbid ability structure, and motivational or other factors on neuropsychological test performance. In G. Young, A. W. Kane, & K. Nicholson (Eds.), *Psychological knowledge in court: PTSD, pain and TBI*, (pp. 335–351). New York: Springer Science+Business Media.

Nicholson, K., Martelli, M. F., & Zasler, N. D. (2001). Does pain confound interpretation of neuropsychological test results. *NeuroRehabilitation, 16*, 225–230.

Overall, J. E. (1996). How many repeated measurements are useful? *Journal of Clinical Psychology, 52*, 243–252.

Pankratz, L. (1983). A new technique for the assessment and modification of feigned memory deficit. *Perceptual and Motor Skills, 57*, 367–372.

Pankratz, L. (1988). Malingering on intellectual and neuropsychological measures. In R. Rogers (Ed.), *Clinical assessment of malingering and deception* (pp. 169–192). New York: Guilford Press.

Pankratz, L., Fausti, S. A., & Peed, S. (1975). Case study: A forced-choice technique to evaluate deafness in the hysterical or malingering patient. *Journal of Consulting and Clinical Psychology, 43*, 421–422.

Paradee, C. V., Rapport, L. J., Hanks, R. A., & Levy, J. A. (2005). Circadian preference and cognitive functioning among rehabilitation inpatients. *The Clinical Neuropsychologist, 19*, 55–72.

Philibert, I. (2005). Sleep loss and performance in residents and nonphysicians: A meta- analytic examination. *Sleep, 28*, 1392–1402.

Post, F. (1975). Dementia, depression, and pseudodementia. In D. F. Benson & D. Blumer (Eds.), *Psychiatric aspects of neurologic disease* (pp. 99–120). New York: Grune and Stratton.

Posthuma, A., Podrouzek, W., & Crisp, D. (2002). The implications of Daubert on neuropsychological evidence in the assessment of remote mild traumatic brain injury. *American Journal of Forensic Psychology, 20*, 21–23.

Ray, E. C., Engum, E. S., Lambert, E. W., Bane, G. F., Nash, M. R., & Bracy, O. L. (1997). Ability of the Cognitive Behavioral Driver's Inventory to distinguish malingerers from brain-damaged subjects. *Archives of Clinical Neuropsychology, 12*, 491–503.

Rees, L. M., Tombaugh, T. N., & Boulay, L. (2001). Depression and the Test of Memory Malingering. *Archives of Clinical Neuropsychology, 16*, 501–506.

Rees, L. M., Tombaugh, T. N., Gansler, D. A., & Moczynski, N. P. (1998). Five validation experiments of the Test of Memory Malingering (TOMM). *Psychological Assessment, 10*, 10–20.

Reitan, H., & Wolfson, D. (1996). The question of validity of neuropsychological test scores among head-injured litigants: Development of a dissimulation index. *Archives of Clinical Neuropsychology, 11*, 573–580.

Reitan, R. M., & Wolfson, D. (2002). Detection of malingering and invalid test results using the Halstead-Reitan Battery. *Journal of Forensic Neuropsychology, 3*, 275–314.

Rey, A. (1964). *L'examen clinique en psychologie*. Paris: Presses Universitaires de France (The clinical examination in psychology).

Rey, A., & Osterrieth, P. A. (1993). Translations of excerpts from Andre Rey's Psychological examination of traumatic encephalopathy and P. A Osterrieth's The Complex Figure Copy Test. *The Clinical Neuropsychologist, 7*, 4–21.

Reynolds, C. R. (1998). *Detection of malingering during head injury litigation*. New York: Plenum Press.

Rogers, R., & Bender, S. D. (2003). Evaluation of malingering and deception. In A. M. Goldstein (Ed.), *Comprehensive handbook of psychology: Forensic psychology* (Vol. 11, pp. 109–129). New York: Wiley.

Rogers, R., Sewell, K. W., & Goldstein, A. (1994a). Explanatory models of malingering: A prototypical analysis. *Law and Human Behavior, 18*, 543–552.

Rogers, R., Sewell, K. W., Martin, M. A., & Vitacco, M. (2003). Detection of feigned mental disorders: A meta-analysis of the MMPI-2 and malingering. *Assessment, 10*, 160–177.

Rogers, R., Sewell, K. W., & Salekin, R. T. (1994b). A meta-analysis of malingering on the MMPI-2. *Assessment, 1*, 227–237.

Rohling, M. L., Green, P., Allen, L. M., & Iverson, G. L. (2002). Depressive symptoms and neurocognitive test scores in patients passing symptom validity tests. *Archives of Clinical Neuropsychology, 17*, 205–222.

Rose, F. E., Hall, S., Szalda-Petree, A. D., & Bach, P. J. (1998). A comparison of four tests of malingering and the effects of coaching. *Archives of Clinical Neuropsychology, 13*, 349–364.

Rosenfeld, J. P. (2002). Event-related potentials in the detection of deception, malingering, and false memories. In M. Kleiner (Ed.), *Handbook of polygraph testing* (pp. 265–286). San Diego, CA: Academic Press.

Rosenfeld, J. P., & Ellwanger, J. W. (1999). Cognitive psychophysiology in detection of malingered cognitive deficit. In J. J. Sweet (Ed.), *Forensic neuropsychology: Fundamentals and practice* (pp. 287–311). Lisse, Netherlands: Swets & Zeitlinger.

Rosenfeld, J. P., Ellwanger, J. W., Nolan, K., Wu, S., Bermann, R. G., & Sweet, J. (1999). P300 scalp amplitude distribution as an index of deception in a simulated cognitive deficit model. *International Journal of Psychophysiology, 33*, 3–19.

Ross, S. R., Krukowski, R. A., Putnam, S. H., & Adams, K. M. (2003). The Memory Assessment Scales in the detection of incomplete effort in mild head injury. *The Clinical Neuropsychologist, 17*, 581–591.

Ross, S. R., Millis, S. R., Krukowski, R. A., Putnam, S. H., & Adams, K. M. (2004). Detecting incomplete effort on the MMPI-2: An examination of the Fake-Bad Scale in mild head injury. *Journal of Clinical and Experimental Neuropsychology, 26*, 115–124.

Rutherford, W. H., Merrett, J. D., & McDonald, J. R. (1982). Symptoms at one year following concussion from minor head injuries. *Injury, 10*, 225–230.

Saint-Cyr, J. A., Taylor, A. E., & Nicholson, K. (1995). Behavior and the basal ganglia. In W. J. Weiner & A. E. Lang (Eds.), *Advances in neurology: Behavioral neurology of movement disorders* (Vol. 65, pp. 1–28). New York: Raven Press.

Salinsky, M. C., Storzbach, D., Dodrill, C. B., & Binder, L. M. (2001). Test-retest bias, reliability, and regression equations for neuropsychological measures repeated over a 12–16-week period. *Journal of the International Neuropsychological Society, 7*, 597–605.

Schagen, S., Schmand, B., de Sterke, S., & Lindeboom, J. (1997). Amsterdam Short-term Memory Test: A new procedure for the detection of feigned memory deficits. *Journal of Clinical and Experimental Neuropsychology, 19*, 43–51.

Schmand, B., Lindeboom, J., Schagen, S., Heijt, R., Koene, T., & Hamburger, H. L. (1998). Cognitive complaints in patients after whiplash injury: The impact of malingering. *Journal of Neurology, Neurosurgery, and Psychiatry, 64*, 339–343.

Schretlen, D., Brandt, J., Krafft, L., & van Gorp, W. (1991). Some caveats in using the Rey 15-item Memory Test to detect malingered amnesia. *Psychological Assessment, 3*, 667–672.

Schretlen, D. J., Munro, C. A., Anthony, J. C., & Pearlson, G. D. (2003). Examining the range of normal intraindividual variability in neuropsychological test performance. *Journal of the International Neuropsychological Society, 9*, 864–870.

Slick, D., Hopp, G., Strauss, E., & Thompson, G. (1997). *The Victoria Symptom Validity Test*. Odessa, FL: PAR.

Slick, D. J., Hopp, G., Strauss, E., & Spellacy, F. J. (1996). Victoria Symptom Validity Test: Efficiency for detecting feigned memory impairment and relationship to neuropsychological tests and MMPI-2 validity scales. *Journal of Clinical and Experimental Neuropsychology, 18*, 911–922.

Slick, D. J., Sherman, E. M., & Iverson, G. L. (1999). Diagnostic criteria for malingered neurocognitive dysfunction: Proposed standards for clinical practice and research. *The Clinical Neuropsychologist, 13*, 545–561.

Slick, D. J., Tan, J. E., Strauss, E., Mateer, C. A., Harnadek, M., & Sherman, E. M. S. (2003). Victoria Symptom Validity Test scores of patients with profound memory impairment: Nonlitigant case studies. *The Clinical Neuropsychologist, 17*, 390–394.

Storzbach, D., Rohlman, D. S., Anger, W. K., Binder, L. M., & Campbell, K. A. (2001). Neurobehavioral deficits in Persian Gulf veterans: Additional evidence from a population-based study. *Environmental Research, 85*, 1–13.

Strauss, E., Slick, D. L., Levy-Bencheton, J., Hunter, M., MacDonald, S. W. S., & Hultsch, D. F. (2002). Intraindividual variability as an indicator of malingering in head injury. *Archives of Clinical Neuropsychology, 17*, 423–444.

Suhr, J. A., & Gunstad, J. (2000). The effect of coaching on the sensitivity and specificity of malingering measures. *Archives of Clinical Neuropsychology, 15*, 415–424.

Sullivan, K., Deffenti, C., & Keane, B. (2002). Malingering on the RAVLT Part II: Detection strategies. *Archives of Clinical Neuropsychology, 17*, 223–233.

Sweet, J. J. (1999). Malingering: Differential diagnosis. In J. J. Sweet (Ed.), *Forensic neuropsychology: Fundamentals and practice* (pp. 255–285). Exton, PA: Swets & Zeitlinger.

Tan, J. E., Slick, D. J., Strauss, E., & Hultsch, D. F. (2002). How'd they do it? Malingering strategies on symptom validity tests. *The Clinical Neuropsychologist, 16*, 495–505.

Tardif, H. P., Barry, R. J., Fox, A. M., & Johnstone, S. J. (2000). Detection of feigned recognition memory impairment using the old/new effect of the event-related potential. *International Journal of Psychophysiology, 36*, 1–9.

Tardif, H. P., Barry, R. J., & Johnstone, S. J. (2002). Event-related potentials reveal processing differences in honest vs. malingered memory performance. *International Journal of Psychophysiology, 46*, 147–158.

Teichner, G., & Wagner, M. T. (2004). The Test of Memory Malingering (TOMM): Normative data from cognitively intact, cognitively impaired, and elderly patients with dementia. *Archives of Clinical Neuropsychology, 19*, 455–464.

Tombaugh, T. N. (1996). *Test of Memory Malingering*. North Tonawonda, NY: Multi-Health Systems.

Tombaugh, T. N. (1997). The Test of Memory Malingering (TOMM): Normative data from cognitively intact and cognitively impaired individuals. *Psychological Assessment, 9*, 260–268.

Tsushima, W. T., & Tsushima, V. G. (2001). Comparison of the Fake Bad Scale and other MMPI-2 validity scales with personal injury litigants. *Assessment, 8*, 205– 212.

Van Dongen H. P., Vitellaro K. M., & Dinges D. F. (2005). Individual differences in adult human sleep and wakefulness: Leitmotif for a research agenda. *Sleep, 28*, 479–496.

Van Hout, M. S. E., Schmand, B., Wekking, E. M., Hageman, G., & Deelman, B. G. (2003). Suboptimal performance on neuropsychological tests in patients with suspected chronic toxic encephalopathy. *NeuroToxicology, 24*, 547–551.

Vickery, C. D., Berry, D. T. R., Dearth, C. S., Vagnini, V. L., Baser, R. E., Cragar, D. E. et al. (2004). Head injury and the ability to feign neuropsychological deficits. *Archives of Clinical Neuropsychology, 19*, 37–48.

Vickery, C. D., Berry, D. T. R., Inman, T. H., Harris, M. J., & Orey, S. A. (2001). Detection of inadequate effort on neuropsychological testing: A meta-analytic review of selected procedures. *Archives of Clinical Neuropsychology, 16*, 45–73.

Wechsler D. A. (1997). *Wechsler Adult Intelligence Scale-III*. New York: Psychological Corporation.

Weinborn, M., Orr, T., Woods, S. P., Conover, E., & Feix, J. (2003). A validation of the Test of Memory Malingering in a forensic psychiatric setting. *Journal of Clinical and Experimental Neuropsychology, 25*, 979–990.

Westen, D., & Weinberger, J. (2005). Clinical judgment in science. *American Psychologist, 60*, 659–661.

Willison, J., & Tombaugh, T. N. (2006). Detecting simulation of attention deficits using reaction time tests. *Archives of Clinical Neuropsychology, 21*, 41–52.

Yanez, Y. T., Fremouw, W., Tennant, J., Strunk, J., & Coker, K. (2006). Effects of severe depression on TOMM performance among disability-seeking outpatients. *Archives of Clinical Neuropsychology, 21*, 161–165.

Youngjohn, J. R., Davis, D., & Wolf, I. (1997). Head injury and the MMPI-2: Paradoxical severity effects and the influence of litigation. *Psychological Assessment, 9*, 177–184.

17

Malingering: Chronic Pain

KEITH NICHOLSON AND MICHAEL F. MARTELLI

Mendelson and Mendelson (2004) suggest that medical examiners most often suspect malingering in the context of assessing chronic pain. There has long been concern about whether pain may be "real" or feigned. Thomas (1923) thought headache was the most frequent clinical pain problem and the most difficult to detect if feigned. A number of techniques to identify malingerers were suggested, extended observation being considered to be the most reliable. Collie (1932), in an influential work entitled "*Fraud in Medico-Legal Practice*," thought that back pain was the most common complaint in cases where compensation was being claimed. However, such pain was thought to be usually mental rather than physical, reflecting the problem of mind-body dualism (Nicholson, Martelli, & Zasler, 2002).

Pain is currently defined by the International Association for the Study of Pain (IASP) as a "psychological state" characterized by "an unpleasant sensory and emotional experience associated with actual or potential tissue damage, or described in terms of such damage" (Merskey & Bogduk, 1994). In other words, pain is a perception in some ways similar to other sensory modalities such as vision. There is a shared intersubjective experience of many sensory phenomena such as seeing a red apple or acute pain resulting from a minor burn, cut, or bruise, and most people would readily identify with such experiences. Emotional, evaluative, or other psychological processes may have an important effect on the perception of visual stimuli or, vice-versa, visual stimuli may have an important effect on emotional and other psychological processes. However, such effects may be more pronounced with respect to the experience of pain (Nicholson, 2000). The experience of pain is mediated by complex and widespread peripheral and central nervous system mechanisms. There are two principal pain systems, the lateral and medial pain systems, which are thought to mediate the sensory-discriminative and emotional-evaluative aspects of pain (Vogt, Sikes, & Vogt, 1993). The cortical projections of the former are centered on the somatosensory cortex, whereas the latter involve the limbic system and prefrontal cortex that subserve emotional and higher cognitive processes. Although these pain systems are separate, they are highly interdependent, indicating strong bidirectional effects.

Although there is still much to be learned about acute pain (i.e., pain that is experienced immediately upon stimulation of peripheral nociceptors or tissue damage and that generally resolves when the nociceptive stimulus is withdrawn or the tissue heals), there is much more to be learned about chronic pain (i.e., simply, pain that persists for more than 6 months). There is often poor correlation between peripheral pathology and chronic pain (Turk & Melzack, 1993). It has been suggested that persistent pain may be considered a disease state of the nervous system rather than merely a symptom of some other medical condition (Basbaum, 1999).

There is an important distinction made between nociceptive and neuropathic pain, the former representing the normal and the latter the abnormal operation of the nervous system. The *DSM* psychiatric disorders of Pain Disorder Associated with Psychological Factors and a General Medical Condition as well as Pain Disorder Associated with Psychological Factors may both be considered to represent a form of neuropathic pain (Nicholson, 2000). In this regard, it is again noted that there has been increasing attention paid to the role of central sensitization, that is, how the central nervous system becomes sensitized to the effects of chronic pain and other problems (Miller, 2000; Nicholson, 2000; Nicholson & Martelli, 2004).

It is sometimes suggested that a patient's pain is "all in the head" or the "mind" or that they are just "making it up." Whereas it may be trite to note that pain is indeed "all in the head," given that the brain is where pain or other sensory phenomena are perceived, or that pain may never just be "in the mind" (as there is no mind without a biological substrate), it should be realized that there may be a response bias to report pain. As has been suggested above (Chapter 14), the term response bias is neutral with regard to possible underlying motivation or causal mechanisms. It is perhaps not uncommon to think of someone with some pain problem who "exaggerates" the severity of his or her pain, typically in accord with the individual's operant reinforcement history (Fordyce, 1976). For example, a child may report that his or her stomach hurts, thus obtaining sympathy from the mother or being excused from going to school; a person with back pain may accentuate pain behaviors to facilitate the loving attention from a significant other. In this regard, it is important to note that such solicitous or operant reinforcement from a significant other is associated with actual changes in the brain reflecting increased activation of those parts of the brain that have been found to be involved in pain perception (Flor, 2002). It should also be noted that the anticipation of pain may result in activation of parts of the brain that are activated with an actual painful stimulus (Wager et al., 2004). These and other lines of evidence indicate that there is an important interaction of psychological and biological factors in the experience of pain. It has previously been suggested that there is an interaction between nociceptive or neuropathic pain and psychological factors, and that the importance of psychological factors is likely normally distributed, that is, that a minority of individuals may be highly resistant to adverse psychological effects, a minority will have pronounced associated adverse psychological effects involved in their presentation, and most people will lie on a continuum between these extremes (Nicholson, 2000).

With respect to malingering, Thimineur, Kaliszewski, and Sood (2000) suggested that valid criteria to identify individuals who are malingering pain do not exist. A case was presented in which the patient had been labeled as malingering by six different physicians, but who was subsequently found to have a lesion that explained all of her subjective complaints. It was recommended that physicians exercise caution in labeling patients suffering intractable pain as malingerers.

Fishbain, Cutler, Rosomoff, and Rosomoff (1999) conducted a systematic review of exaggeration and malingering or submaximal effort in chronic pain, concluding that there was only extremely weak evidence that malingering may be present in from 1.25% to 10.4% of chronic pain patients but, as studies were of poor quality, such prevalence rates were considered unreliable. Fishbain et al. also concluded that there was, as yet, no reliable method for detecting malingering within chronic pain populations. In particular, it was found that malingering could not be reliably identified by facial expression, questionnaire, sensory testing, or clinical examination; that there was no acceptable scientific information on symptom magnification syndrome; that hand grip testing using the Jamar dynamometer and other types of isometric strength testing did not reliably discriminate between a submaximal/malingering effort and a maximal/best effort; and that repetitive testing with the coefficient of variation was not a reliable method for discriminating a real/best effort from a malingered effort.

Mendelson and Mendelson (2004), in a more recent review, similarly concluded that there were still no valid clinical methods for assessment of malingering. However, there has been considerable research, and several approaches to the assessment of malingering, exaggeration, response bias, or related behaviors in chronic pain. This review will focus upon pain behavior, self-report questionnaires, clinical examination, biomedical investigations, signal detection theory (SDT) measures of response bias, and neuropsychological or other cognitive measures of malingering.

Pain Behavior

Pain behavior involves both verbal and nonverbal behavior. Verbal pain behavior involves both utterances (e.g., grunts, shrieks) that are a more primitive verbal response to pain, as well as more complex verbal responses involving use of language. Nonverbal behavior includes facial expressions, limping, guarding, or other behavior that is partly dependant upon what the particular pain problem is. In the case of acute pain associated with some injury, for example, a burn or cut or other trauma, there is typically some obvious verbal or nonverbal pain behavior. The person may say "ouch" or wince and withdraw the affected body part from the noxious stimulus or source of tissue damage. He or she may then angrily complain of having been hurt, or describe the pain and injury. In the case of chronic pain, the relationship between self-report of pain severity and other behavior may become less apparent, in part because there is then no external stimulus or source of tissue damage to withdraw from or react to. In addition, most persons adapt to most adverse stimuli, their behavior then normalizing to some degree. Although verbal and nonverbal pain behavior typically coexist, Hill and Craig (2004) suggest that nonverbal pain behavior is more believable, as this may be less contrived. However, it should again be noted that pain is an admixture of cognitive, emotional, motivational, sensory, and behavioral indices and, therefore, it may be misleading to focus primarily on nonverbal behavior. In some cases there is a striking discrepancy between the self-reported pain severity and pain behavior that is most apparent in those presenting with "la belle indifference," that is, patients who may describe pain as extremely severe (e.g., 9–10/10 on a numerical analogue scale where "0" = "no pain" and "10" = "the worst that pain could ever be") but who appear entirely comfortable and quite happy. This part of the chapter will present the research concerning nonverbal pain behaviors that may be associated with malingering or simulation (verbal pain behavior is discussed in greater detail in the questionnaires section below), with particular emphasis on facial expressions of pain as these have been studied in greatest detail.

Using detailed coding systems, facial expressions associated with either acute pain or acute exacerbation of a chronic pain problem have been identified. These include a lowered brow, raised cheeks, tightened eye lids, a raised upper lip or opened mouth, and closed eyes (Prkachin, 1992). Facial pain behavior correlates well with the intensity of noxious stimulation as well as self-report of pain severity and unpleasantness, but is unrelated to measures of anxiety and depression despite the correlation between anxiety, depression, and verbal pain reports (Hill & Craig, 2004). Utilizing detailed coding systems, Craig, Hyde, and Patrick (1991) found that chronic pain patients had considerable voluntary control over their facial expressions when asked to either exaggerate or suppress facial pain behavior. However, faked/exaggerated expressions of pain were more of an intensified caricature of the genuine expression. Attempts to suppress facial grimacing were not entirely successful, as residual pain-related facial activity was evident. Hadjistavropoulos and Craig (1994) found that both acute and chronic low back pain patients displayed a relatively stereotyped facial expression of pain when responding to painful movements during a physical examination. Patients were able to conceal or mask facial pain expressions when asked to do so, although some trace elements of facial pain behavior were still evident. When asked to exaggerate facial pain behavior, displays were similar to that of genuine or unexaggerated behavior but more extreme, and also included a number of other facial behaviors (e.g., horizontal pulling of the lip corners, raising of the chin), and the display was again characterized as a caricature of the genuine behavior.

Poole and Craig (1992) noted that genuine vs. simulated facial expressions that do not involve pain may also be discriminated with detailed analysis of specific facial features, but that persons whose work involves detecting dissimulation (e.g., police officers) are poor at using facial cues to distinguish between those who are lying and those who are telling the truth. Poole and Craig (1992) studied how well untrained judges were at discriminating between genuine, faked, and suppressed facial pain behavior of chronic pain patients. Relative to genuine facial expressions, judges attributed more pain to faked expressions and less to suppressed expressions, indicating that dissimulation is possible. It did not help the judges to know that some of the displays were genuine or simulated. Prkachin (1992) studied healthy volunteers who were exposed to different levels of an acute pain challenge or who were instructed to feign pain comparable to different intensity levels of pain. Untrained observers were able to tell the difference between deliberate (faked) and spontaneous (real) expressions of pain to only a modest degree. The observers rated the intensity of faked pain as greater in comparison with the genuine displays when the pain was not of a strong intensity, that is, when simulators were trying to fake moderate pain, or subjects were administered electric shocks that produced moderate pain. However, when pain was more severe, the observer intensity ratings were equivalent for the simulated and genuine pain.

Hadjistavropoulos, Craig, Hadjistavropoulos, and Poole (1996) studied the ability of untrained judges, who had been informed that some of the subjects were simulating while others were genuine, to discriminate between facial expressions associated with no pain, genuine pain, masked (concealed) pain, and exaggerated pain displays. It was found that the judges' performance was better than would be expected by chance or guessing, but that they made many errors. Analysis of specific facial cues using standardized facial coding systems indicated that judges consistently used certain rules of thumb, suggesting that training may be helpful. Hill and Craig (2004) showed videotaped facial expressions of neutral expressions, genuine pain instigated by physiotherapy range of motion assessment, masked pain, and faked pain to judges who were asked to rate the displays (e.g., for pain severity and for which of the four displays were represented) and who were provided with corrective feedback concerning their judgments, training in deception detection or deception training plus feedback, or no training/information. There were significant individual differences in accuracy, with females more accurate than males. Whereas judges were able to rate pain severity and unpleasantness reasonably accurately, they were unsuccessful in categorizing displays as neutral, genuine, faked, or masked. Immediate corrective feedback improved judges' accuracy, but training in deception detection was not helpful.

The studies cited above involve simulation with either deliberate exaggeration or fabrication of pain behavior. None of these studies involve the investigation of actual pain patients who may be exaggerating their behavior, consciously or otherwise, as part of a display that may be independent of external incentives such as monetary gain. There are certainly many pain patients who display exuberant pain behavior, usually with extremely high pain severity ratings and often in the presence of little if any peripheral pathology to account for such behavior. Such exaggerated pain behavior may be related to their operant reinforcement history, sensitization effects, catastrophizing, or other factors (Nicholson, 2000). The distinction between exaggeration/fabrication that is for the purpose of obtaining some financial or other such goal and exaggeration that may be associated with a variety of other psychosocial causes is critical, but there has as yet been little research that informs how these may be distinguished in clinical practice. Sullivan (2004) cautions that the standards upon which pain behavior is judged to be exaggerated have been primarily moral rather than scientific. Sullivan notes that there is huge variability in the nature of the pain response or pain behavior and that, whereas the validation of pain complaint through correlation with tissue damage remains common in clinical and medicolegal settings (Rondinelli & Katz, 2000), this is inconsistent with current conceptualizations of pain (e.g., Basbaum, 1999). Sullivan suggested that judgments about exaggerating or faking pain are made on the basis of socially established criteria of what is considered appropriate behavior. As human societies have become more complex, so have the accommodations made for sick and disabled members of the society, and social and psychological conflicts have become more intertwined in how persons present with illness behavior and how others respond. Similar to the ethological descriptions provided by Byrne and Stokes (2003; see Chapter 14), Sullivan cites Wittgenstein (1980) as illustrating how operant reinforcement of a child's pain behavior results in behavior that may not have the intention to deceive or to create a false appearance. Sullivan notes that from one-third to two-thirds of new symptoms presented to primary care physicians (a large percentage of which involve pain) will never be given a pathophysiological explanation or linked to a known disease process, and that many such complaints may be associated with a psychosomatic or somatization process (Epstein, Quill, & McWhinney, 1999; Kirmayer & Robbins, 1996; Kroenke & Mangelsdorff, 1989). Sullivan makes the distinction between the issue of discovering causes (biomedical or psychosocial) for distress and the assignment of responsibility for such distress. It is suggested that pain behavior usually represents a request for relief of suffering, and that "addressing or dismissing the suffering of another is among the foremost ethical challenges facing us in a civilized society" (p. 437).

Clinical Examination and Biomedical Investigations

There are many signs that may be evident on clinical examination or further biomedical investigations that have been associated with possible response bias to report pain, exaggeration of actual pain, malingering, or related behaviors, although these should all be considered carefully because there are important caveats to all (Martelli, Nicholson, Zasler & Bender, 2006; Martelli, Zasler, Nicholson, Pickett, & May, 2002). This review will focus on a selected few such signs or investigations including the Waddell signs and especially nondermatomal sensory deficits (NDSDs), muscle testing or related measures of effort, diagnostic blocks and the use of sodium amytal interviews, and electrophysiological techniques.

Waddell and associates identified eight "nonorganic" physical signs, grouped into five categories, that had long been associated with either malingering or hysteria, suggesting that if the patient demonstrated signs in three or more categories they should be evaluated for psychological problems, or that these may indicate some magnification of pain and related problems or some abnormal illness behavior (Waddell, Main, & Morris, 1984; Waddell, McCulloch, & Kimmel, 1980). The five categories with their respective signs are: (1) tenderness (skin tender to light touch; "nonanatomic" deep tenderness not localized to one area), (2) simulation (axial loading pressure on the skull of a standing patient induces low back pain; shoulders and pelvis rotated in the same plane produces pain), (3) distraction (difference in straight leg raising in supine and sitting positions), (4) regional (give-away weakness suggesting that the patient does not give full effort on minor muscle testing; or nondermatomal sensory loss in a stocking or glove distribution), and (5) overreaction (disproportionate facial or verbal pain behavior). Of note, continued misinterpretation of the Waddell signs (e.g., as indicating malingering) and criticism of such interpretations prompted Main and Waddell (1998) to provide a re-appraisal of what these might mean, then suggesting that they should be considered as psychological "yellow-flags," multiple signs suggesting that the patient does not have a straightforward physical problem, and that psychological factors also need to be considered.

Fishbain et al. (1999) critically reviewed the Waddell signs, later providing a more thorough structured evidence-based review of these (Fishbain, Cole et al., 2003), and then assessing the relationship between these signs and secondary gain/malingering (Fishbain, Cutler, Rosomoff, & Rosomoff, 2004). On systematic review of 57 studies, Fishbain, Cole et al. (2003) concluded that: (1) there was consistent evidence for Waddell signs being associated with decreased functional performance, poor nonsurgical treatment outcome, and greater levels of pain; (2) there was generally consistent evidence for Waddell signs not being associated with psychological distress, abnormal illness behavior, or secondary gain; (3) there was also generally consistent evidence that Waddell signs are an organic phenomenon and that they cannot be used to discriminate organic from nonorganic problems; (4) there was inconsistent evidence that the Waddell signs demonstrate adequate inter-rater reliability, do not correlate with the "neurotic triad" of the MMPI (Hathaway & McKinley, 1967) or MMPI-2 (Butcher, Dahlstrom, Graham, Tellegen, & Kaemmer, 1989), are associated with poorer surgical treatment outcome, and are associated with nonreturn to work; (5) there was little or no evidence that the Waddell signs have demonstrated test-retest reliability, that they consist of reliable factors, nor that they are associated with self-esteem problems, catastrophizing, or the nonorganic pain drawing of distribution of pain sites.

Fishbain et al. (2004) then conducted a systematic review of 16 studies relating the Waddell signs and secondary gain or malingering. It was found that: (1) there was inconsistent evidence that Waddell signs were not associated with worker's compensation or medicolegal status; (2) there was consistent evidence that Waddell signs improved with treatment; (3) there was consistent evidence that Waddell signs were not correlated with invalid paper-pencil test findings such as on the MMPI-2 validity scales; and (4) there was inconsistent evidence that Waddell signs were not associated with physician perception of effort or exaggeration. It was concluded that there was little evidence for the claims of an association between Waddell signs and secondary gain or malingering, and that the preponderance of the evidence indicated the opposite, that is, no association.

One of the Waddell signs, nondermatomal sensory loss often in a stocking or glove distribution, is of particular interest and will be discussed at greater length.

This has often been interpreted as a symptom of a conversion disorder (Fishbain, Cutler et al., 2003), and therefore associated with psychological causes. Fishbain, Goldberg, Meagher, Steele, and Rosomoff (1986) found that 37.8% of a consecutive series of chronic pain patients demonstrated this finding. Mailis et al. (2001) found that unexplainable nondermatomal somatosensory deficits (NDSDs), involving hemisensory or quadrotomal deficits to pinprick and other cutaneous stimuli, were a prevalent problem associated with chronic pain. In a series of 194 subjects seen for the purpose of an independent medical examination, 25.3% had NDSDs. Fishbain, Cutler et al. (2003) later reported that, of 283 consecutive chronic pain patients, 74 were found to have NDSDs and that the location of the NDSD was associated with perceived pain location.

Mailis et al. (2003) studied four patients with chronic pain and NDSDs using functional magnetic resonance imaging (fMRI). It was found that diminished perception of innocuous and noxious stimuli was associated with altered activity in many parts of the somatosensory pathway or other supraspinal areas. Unperceived stimuli failed to activate areas that were activated with perceived touch and pain, that is, the thalamus, posterior region of the anterior cingulate cortex (ACC), and Brodmann area 44/45. Furthermore, unperceived stimuli were associated with deactivations in primary and secondary somatosensory cortex (S1, S2), posterior parietal cortex, and prefrontal cortex. Finally, unperceived (but not perceived) stimuli activated the rostral ACC. It was suggested that the brain may attempt to "shut down" associated somatosensory circuits involved in an intolerable pain problem, the poor tolerance to pain associated with psychosocial factors.

Many pain problems are associated with a loss of functional capacity, for example, being able to walk, perform simple activities of daily living, work, etc. Such disability is sometimes suspect. For many years the veracity of such complaints has been tested with functional ability testing and, in particular, various forms of muscle testing. Failure on such testing has been interpreted as suboptimal, insincere, or inconsistency of effort, such terms often a euphemism for malingering or that the person could do better if he or she only chose to. As noted above, Fishbain et al. (1999) provided an early review of such procedures concluding that, with the possible exception of isokinetic strength testing, the empirical literature did not support their reliability or validity. Robinson and Dannecker (2004) have recently conducted another systematic review utilizing 29 studies not included in the earlier Fishbain et al. (1999) study. Robinson and Dannecker examined a variety of indices including weakness and decreased range and velocity of motion, variability in performance or force output, force output curves, strength ratios and difference scores, electromyography, and motion analyses. It was concluded that "the current 'state of the art,' though promising in some instances, does not warrant the clinical application of muscle testing as a means of determining sincerity of effort" (p. 397). It was noted that fear of pain or pain avoidance behaviors had been neglected as a possible interpretation of such findings.

Bogduk (2004) suggested that nerve blocks may help to rule out malingering by providing some evidence that there is a peripheral pathological process accounting for complaints when other diagnostic procedures have not been informative. Such nerve blocks involve injecting local anesthetic onto a structure that is suspected as being the source of pain or onto the nerves that supply the suspected source. The patient then either obtains pain relief in the expected manner, in which case there is confirmation of peripheral pathological process, or the patient does not obtain relief, in which case it remains unclear what may be the source of the pain. Bogduk has referred to such blocks as a "truth serum" for the determination of whether pain is "real," but this may only be true if a test is positive (i.e., providing pain relief), and no such determination could be made if the test is negative. However, there is very often a placebo response to most interventions and, therefore, a positive response may not provide unambiguous evidence that the pain is "real" (Nicholson, 2000).

Sodium amytal and related substances have also been considered to represent a truth serum for a variety of functional disorders, and use of such medication has been suggested to be useful in the determination of whether a pain patient is malingering (Shoichet, 1978). However, review of the literature has not supported such claims (Mailis & Nicholson, 2002), but several studies reviewed by Mailis and Nicholson did indicate that sodium amytal testing may be helpful in distinguishing between pain that is secondary to central sensitization effects from that which has an origin in peripheral pathology.

There have been increasing attempts to identify biomedical indices of pain using functional imaging. Salamy, Wolk, and Shucard (1983) had early on noted that chronic pain patients had a differential electrophysiological response to statements about pain, other emotional statements, or neutral statements. It was suggested that such methodology might be helpful in identifying the validity of pain report or malingered pain. Chapman et al. (2002), noting that self-report of pain is a construction with multiple internal or external social or private referents, modeled the accuracy of acute pain reports using electrophysiological data. Flor (2002) and others have begun mapping cortical changes in response to pain and the influence of psychosocial factors in such changes or electrophysiological responses. Although there has been extensive study of the pain system and how the brain processes pain with fMRI (Apkarian, Bushnell, Treede, & Zubieta, 2005; Nicholson, 2000), there is as yet no such biomedical index of the validity of pain report or possible malingering of pain utilizing fMRI technology. However, such techniques have documented the role of psychological factors, such as catastrophizing, in the magnification of the experience of pain and what the underlying neurobiological substrate of such response may be (Gracely et al., 2004). Given that anticipation of pain will activate the same or similar parts of the brain as does an actual painful stimulus (Wager et al., 2004), and that informed or sophisticated subjects may therefore be able to simulate the experience of pain, it is questionable how soon such techniques may usefully be applied to the detection of malingered pain.

Questionnaires

As indicated in the first chapter of this section (Chapter 14), most people are very poor at detecting lies, and there is no evidence that malingering of pain can reliably be detected on the basis of only verbal self-report. There is some evidence that actuarial analysis of self-report questionnaires may be more useful.

Several self-report questionnaires have been utilized to detect malingering, dissimulation, exaggeration, or related constructs in chronic pain. Again, most of these have used simulation designs and/or compensation status to define groups. Clayer, Bookless, and Ross (1984) developed the Conscious Exaggeration Scale using items from the Illness Behavior Questionnaire (Pilowsky & Spence, 1975) that differentiated those instructed to feign a serious injury (not specifically pain) and normal controls or pain patients whose pain was considered to be "neurotically" determined. Clayer, Bookless, and Ross (1986) later found that scores on the Conscious Exaggeration Scale were positively related to independent assessment of conscious malingering by psychiatric interview. However, subsequent studies have not found that this scale is useful in distinguishing between those pain patients in litigation or on compensation vs. those who were not (Mendelson, 1987; Fishbain, Cutler, Rosomoff, & Steele-Rosomoff, 2002).

Melzack, Katz, and Jeans (1985) found that pain scores and pain descriptor patterns on the McGill Pain Questionnaire (MPQ; Melzack, 1975) were virtually identical for chronic low back and musculoskeletal chronic pain patients whether receiving compensation or not. There were, however, significantly lower affective or evaluative MPQ scores and fewer visits to health professionals by compensation patients. It was suggested that the financial security provided by compensation decreases anxiety, which is reflected in the lower affective or evaluative ratings but not the sensory or total MPQ scores.

Leavitt (1985) compared the responses of volunteers instructed to simulate low back pain and actual low back pain patients instructed to choose which of a possible 103 "pain words" described their pain. It was found that choosing 18 or more words distinguished between the two groups, the simulators choosing more words. Findings were replicated in a second study. However, using such a cutting score, more than one-third of the subjects simulating pain in these studies would be erroneously classified as pain patients and almost one in five of the pain patients would be falsely classified as simulating pain. Previous research had suggested that patients with known organic disease used an average of 16 pain words, but patients without organic findings, possibly containing some malingerers or those exaggerating/magnifying complaint for other reasons, used an average of 21 words (Leavitt, Garron, D'angelo, & McNeill, 1979). In a study with back pain patients instructed to either respond honestly or to exaggerate difficulties, this scale also effectively but not perfectly differentiated between groups (Leavitt, 1987). In another study, administration of this scale to a large sample of low back pain patients who were injured at work found that 10.4% of the sample scored above the cut-off indicating possible simulation or exaggeration of complaint (Leavitt, 1991). The identified patients reported greater pain and were disabled longer. Leavitt also found that treating physicians, blind to the patient classification on the Low Back Simulation Scale, rated those patients scoring above the cut-off as having less physical pathology and greater symptom exaggeration. Note was made of several previous studies that have found that patients with less documented physical pathology tend to report high pain severity levels. The distinction between simulation of nonexistent problems and exaggeration of actual problems was stressed. It was concluded that the objective evaluation of malingering low back pain was still not possible.

McGuire, Harvey, and Shores (2001) administered the Pain Patient Profile (Tollison & Langley, 1995) to chronic pain patients with no special instructions, to chronic pain patients instructed to exaggerate their difficulties, and to nonpain patients told to simulate. Both the simulation and exaggeration groups scored higher on the anxiety, depression, and somatization scales when compared to the control pain group. Similar results were obtained when pain patients responding honestly were compared with students instructed to feign pain but to try to avoid detection (McGuire & Shores, 2001a). In another study, McGuire and Shores (2001b) compared the responses of chronic pain patients and student simulators instructed to feign a pain disorder to obtain compensation, but to attempt to avoid detection on the Symptom Checklist 90-Revised (SCL-90-R; Derogatis, 1983). Pain patients obtained generalized elevations, with the highest scores on Depression, Obsessive-Compulsive, and Somatization. However, all clinical scale elevations of the simulators exceeded those of the pain patients. Simulators tended to greatly overestimate the degree of psychological distress in pain patients. Wallis and Bogduk (1996) also found that student volunteer simulators scored significantly higher than whiplash patients on all subscales of the SCL-90-R as well as the visual analogue scale for pain, whereas scores on the McGill Pain Questionnaire were similar. It was concluded that it would be very difficult to fake a psychologic profile typical of a whiplash patient. Sartori, Forti, Birbaumer, and Flor (2003) have recently developed a unique technique whereby self-ratings of functional capacity (i.e., how subjects would deal with a variety of everyday situations) has been shown to effectively distinguish between whiplash patients responding honestly vs. whiplash patients asked to exaggerate symptoms, as well as healthy individuals responding honestly and healthy individuals asked to simulate symptoms.

Fishbain et al. (1999) noted that there were few, if any, MMPI/MMPI-2 studies pertaining to the detection of malingering in chronic pain. It was suggested that a likely explanation for this was that this technique is essentially a measure of psychiatric difficulties and would not be appropriate for the identification of malingering in pain. On review of the literature, it was noted that some MMPI/MMPI-2 studies involving a differential prevalence design had found that those who are litigating or involved in a compensation claim have higher clinical and/or validity scale elevations (e.g., Dush et al., 1994; Harness & Chase, 1994), whereas others have not found such differences (e.g., Melzack et al., 1985; Trabin, Rader, & Cummings, 1987). Fishbain et al. (1999) suggested that compensation patients are clinically similar to noncompensation patients in the relative frequency of cases of psychological disturbance or in which there has been potentiation of psychophysiological reactivity.

It should be noted that there has been extensive study of the MMPI or MMPI-2 with chronic pain patients in attempts to better understand the nature of psychosocial factors, for example, whether these represent premorbid characteristics, postinjury response to injury, or an interaction of premorbid, injury and postinjury factors. Four major subtypes of chronic pain patients have been identified and cross-validated from responses on the MMPI/MMPI-2, although these four groups may only comprise some 50% of all patients (Keller & Butcher, 1991; Slesinger, Archer, & Duane, 2002; Vendrig, 2000). One of these subtypes involves elevations on most scales and has been characterized as a psychopathological subtype; a second involves a "conversion" profile with particular elevations on scales 1 and 3; a third involves elevation on all of the neurotic triad scales, that is, scales 1, 2 and 3; and the last is generally within normal limits. These different subtypes should be kept in mind when evaluating any study purporting to assess malingering or other response bias in chronic pain.

Meyers, Millis, and Volert (2002) compared the responses of nonlitigating and litigating chronic pain patients on the MMPI-2. Whereas all the usual validity scales distinguished between groups, the litigating groups always scoring higher, there were many false positives using individual scales. However, a weighted validity index (which included the F – K, F, Fp, Ds-r, Es, sum of the obvious minus subtle *T* score differences, and the FBS) utilizing cutting scores based upon past research had 100% specificity and 86% sensitivity. It was suggested that score distribution on the weighted index represented a continuum with most chronic pain patients' scores falling at the low end and, with increasing elevations, that exaggeration of response or, with even higher scores, that malingering would be indicated. Although promising, further work is required to validate this new index and, in particular, to distinguish between exaggeration associated with a variety of psychosocial factors independent from malingering vs. malingering.

Arbisi and Butcher (2004) concluded that there did not appear to be a particular profile type associated with compensation seeking in chronic pain populations. Although the MMPI-2 infrequency scales (F, Fb, Fp) may be sensitive to malingering of psychiatric illness, elevation on these scales was thought to be relatively infrequent in chronic pain populations, and studies comparing groups of patients with chronic pain with regard to inferred level of secondary gain (e.g., litigating vs. nonlitigating) have indicated that standard MMPI validity scales are of limited utility. However, it was also suggested that, in the absence of clear independent evidence of compromised cognition or confusion, the production of an invalid MMPI-2 profile based on elevations on the Variable Response Inconsistency Scale (VRIN) or True Response Inconsistency Scale (TRIN) should raise the question of a deliberate attempt to appear confused or, simply, a lack of cooperation. It was suggested that elevation on scale 3 may "tap" into certain aspects of the individual's response to injury that prevents a swift recovery. As will be discussed further below, it was also noted that it is more common for chronic pain patients to have significant elevations on scales associated with positive and extremely virtuous self-presentation and general defensiveness, and that such profiles are associated with poor recovery. However, in contrast to the interpretation presented below, Arbisi and Butcher suggested that elevations on scales indicating high social desirability, accompanied by elevations on scales 1 or 3, suggest that the individual is selectively tailoring his or her presentation to maximize the impact of somatic problems and minimize psychological or psychiatric factors.

Signal Detection Theory and Response Bias

There have been considerable efforts to assess response bias to report pain using the techniques of signal detection theory (SDT). SDT allows response bias as well as the person's ability to detect or discriminate between stimuli to be quantified (Green & Swets, 1966). Depending upon variations in the technique or applications of the technique, different terms have been used for this methodology (Clark, 1994). An example of a simple SDT study would be the detection of auditory thresholds in which auditory signals are presented, or not presented, on each trial at different intensity levels (subthreshold and suprathreshold, or presenting a stimulus below the person's capacity to detect it and, by increasing the intensity level of the stimulus, to above the person's threshold of detection). On each trial the subject must indicate whether he or she heard or did not hear an auditory stimulus. The subject may then correctly report hearing a signal when presented (a hit), fail to report such a signal (a miss), report that no signal occurred when no signal was presented (a correct rejection), or report hearing a signal when none was presented (a false alarm). A measure of sensitivity (how sensitive the person is to correctly identifying the presence of a stimulus) or discriminability (how well the subject could discriminate between a louder or softer stimulus) is calculated from the difference between the hit and false alarm rates. A measure of response bias (or response criterion) is provided by the sum of the hit and false alarm rates. If the subject has a bias to report hearing a signal, he or she will have both a high hit rate but also a high false alarm rate. Conversely, if there is a bias to not report hearing the signal, there would be a low hit rate as well as a low false alarm rate. Sensitivity, discriminability and response bias may vary independently of each other. Various manipulations (e.g., informing the person that there will be some adverse consequence of not identifying a stimulus, increased background noise, fatigue, medications, etc.) may have an effect on the sensitivity, discriminability, and/or response bias.

Whereas SDT has successfully been applied to basic sensory processes, some suggest that it is problematic to do so with pain given that pain is a complex subjective perception and there is no external objective criterion for the definition of pain as there is with sound (e.g., decibel level) or other sensory stimuli with which to compare the report of pain and presentation of a painful stimulus. In the case of other sensory stimuli, one can clearly state that either an auditory stimulus was or was not presented, or that a louder or softer auditory stimulus was presented in order to assess the person's report. However, many proponents of the technique argue that it is not necessary to know whether the person is right or wrong in their response, only that the person may reliably discriminate between stimuli that lie along some continuum (Clark, 1994). Many studies have utilized SDT techniques in the study of pain, again finding that different manipulations or study conditions have an effect on sensitivity, discriminability, and/or response bias to report pain.

Clark (1994) and Fernandez and Turk (1992) reviewed SDT studies in which the effect of biomedical manipulations (e.g., administration of medications), psychological manipulations (e.g., administration of a placebo), or organismic variables (e.g., age, gender, trait anxiety) on SDT indices were assessed. For example, several studies have found that administration of a placebo has an effect on the response bias to report pain (i.e., subjects then increasing their response criterion/bias to report pain) but without having an effect on sensitivity/discriminability. Trait or experimentally induced anxiety has often been found to decrease response bias to report pain. Differences in the response bias to report pain, but not sensitivity or discriminability, have been demonstrated in various demographic groups (e.g., Nepalese workers vs. Westerners, blue collar workers vs. college students, older vs. younger healthy volunteers). Other studies demonstrate that analgesics have an effect on sensitivity/discriminability but not response bias.

Many researchers suggest that various manipulations that have a differential effect on sensitivity/discriminability vs. response bias to report pain reflect the sensory-discriminative vs. the motivational-emotional and/or cognitive-evaluative aspects of pain perception, respectively (Clark, 1994). The sensory-discriminative dimension of pain is suggested by some to correspond to "true" pain or nociceptive input from the periphery associated with tissue damage. This has been questioned, in part, given that pain is a unified perceptual experience (Rollman, 1979) involving multiple levels of the neuroaxis and with both ascending and descending neurobiological/psychobiological modulating influences on the experience of pain. Another problem with SDT methodology, as with many other techniques, is that they typically utilize acute pain challenges and do not directly manipulate or investigate chronic pain. Nonetheless, this methodology may be useful in further exploration of motivational or other factors on the experience of pain.

Importantly, although it may be contrary to common expectation, there is evidence that the response style of social desirability is associated with increased pain related problems as well as several other medical problems. Social desirability, considered a personality trait, was early on defined as "the need of subjects to obtain approval by responding in a culturally appropriate and acceptable manner" (Crowne & Marlow, 1960, p. 353). This is notably distinct from what may be expected from one with an Antisocial Personality Disorder or a malingerer. Deshields, Tait, Gfeller, and Chibnall (1995) found that greater social desirability was associated with less depression and anxiety but higher levels of pain severity in a sample of chronic pain patients. It was suggested that patients with greater social desirability responded in a manner that emphasized physical complaints and minimized any psychological component.

There is a much broader formulation of the role of social desirability that has been linked, together with low trait anxiety, to a construct termed *repressive coping*, which, in turn, has been associated with many medical problems suggesting some form of psychophysiological reactivity (Denollet, 1991; Tomaka, Blascovich, and Kelsey, 1992; Weinberger & Schwartz, 1979; Wickramasekera, 1995). Jamner and Leigh (1999) found that social desirability and repressive/ defensive coping styles were related to dysregulation of the endogenous opioid system and abnormal pain processing. Nicholson and Mailis (in preparation, a), in a large series of chronic pain patients, have found that many present with marked social desirability as well as a characteristic corresponding profile on the Millon Clinical Multiaxial Inventory-III (Millon, 1997). Nicholson and Mailis (in preparation, b) studied the response of a sample of chronic pain patients, all of whom were suspected of having an important psychological component contributing to presentation, to an acute pain challenge. There was a bimodal distribution, with some patients demonstrating a marked response bias to report pain (with very low pain thresholds), and others being very stoical (with very high pain thresholds). The former were characterized by greater distress, sensitivity, and psychoemotional reactivity, whereas the latter had higher social desirability ratings and were less distressed, consistent with the sensitization-repression distinction reported for many other patient groups (Weinberger & Schwartz, 1979).

Cognitive or other Symptom Validity Testing Measures of "Effort" and Malingering

There has been increasing interest in the use of cognitive measures of effort, symptom validity, malingering or related constructs in the assessment of chronic pain patients (Bianchini, Greve, & Glynn, 2005; Waddell, 2004). As has been noted in the presentation of malingering in traumatic brain injury (TBI; Chapter 16), several studies have applied such measures to various chronic pain patient populations. However, there is considerable evidence that pain and related problems (e.g., psychoemotional distress, sleep disturbance) may produce interference effects resulting in poor performance and "failure" on such measures, with false positive identification of malingering or poor effort. This section will further critically review such practice. Readers are referred to Chapter 16 for more detailed discussion of terminology and some of the issues presented in this chapter.

Schmand et al. (1998) administered the Amsterdam Short Term Memory (ASTM) test to a select group of 108 late post-whiplash syndrome patients, 36 of whom were litigating and, of the remaining 72 patients, only 12 were not involved in a compensation claim. Patients were seen on referral from a neurology service for neuropsychological assessment and were therefore also administered several neuropsychological tests. The frequency of "abnormal" scores (i.e., <86 correct) on the ASTM test in the total sample was 43%. These subjects were labeled malingerers. Of the litigating sample, the frequency of failure on the ASTM test was 61% and, in the remaining subjects, was 29%. Failure rate was 33% (i.e., 20 of 60) in the nonlitigating sample who were involved in compensation but only 8% (1 of 12) in those who were not. Of note, in contrast with the results of many simulation studies, there were no instances of below chance levels of performance. Indeed, even in the "malingering" group, scores were well above chance. The "malingerers" also performed more poorly on neuropsychological tests. Unfortunately, there was no information provided concerning pain or associated problems that may have interfered with performance on either the ASTM test or the neuropsychological tests, and we strongly suspect that results may have been an artifact of such interference effects.

Gervais, Green, Allen, and Iverson (2001) compared fibromyalgia patients who were either receiving or applying for disability benefits (the Disability group) with fibromyalgia patients who were not receiving or applying for any such benefits (the No Disability group) and with rheumatoid arthritis patients (the RA group). The Word Memory Test (WMT) and the Computerized Assessment of Response Bias (CARB) were administered in addition to several other psychological tests. Pain severity ratings of the two fibromyalgia groups were similar and higher than the RA group. None of the No Disability fibromyalgia patients and none of the RA patients scored below the cut-off indicating poor effort, malingering, or other such explanation on the CARB, whereas 24% of the Disability fibromyalgia patients did. No one in the RA group failed the WMT, but 4% of the No Disability group failed either of the two WMT "effort" measures, in comparison with 16% of the Disability group. There was a trend toward greater rates of CARB or WMT failure in the patients with fibromyalgia who were seeking disability compared with those patients already receiving disability, but this difference was not statistically significant. The actual scores of the subjects failing either the CARB or WMT were not presented, but it was reported that these were, on average, several standard deviations below those obtained by other reference groups. It is unknown what the distributions of the failure scores were, but, given the reported means and standard deviations, it may have been that there were no instances of below chance performance, and the level of performance of most of those failing either the CARB or the WMT was likely well above chance. The subjects who failed either (or both) the CARB or WMT had higher pain severity ratings and psychoemotional distress. It was suggested that such ratings were also due to exaggeration of pain and psychoemotional distress, but no consideration was given to whether such pain, psychoemotional distress, or other possible problems may have interfered with performance, resulting in the relatively poor levels of performance on symptom validity testing.

As previously discussed in the TBI malingering chapter (Chapter 16), one of the very few studies in which there were sizeable numbers of "definite" malingerers was that of Etherton, Bianchini, Greve, and Heinly (2005), where the records of approximately 200 patients seen for psychological evaluation of pain and related problems were reviewed and it was determined that 35 (approximately 17.5%) had significantly below chance levels of performance on the TOMM, PDRT, or a tactile symptom validity test. Although we would agree that many or most of these 35 subjects were likely malingering, caution should still be exercised concerning any definitive conclusion. It is unknown what probability levels of significantly-below-chance performance were utilized in the Etherton et al. (2005) study, as this information was not provided. If, as is usual, the probability level was $p < .05$, and subjects were just guessing, then there could be expected to be 10 false positives in a sample of 200 cases. If subjects had severe headache or other pain, marked psychoemotional distress, marked sleep disturbance or other problems, they may have been poorly able to attend and may have actually been guessing when responding. Symptom validity testing with sensory deficits may be especially vulnerable to false positives. If there is a dense sensory deficit (i.e., with no feeling in the affected body part, the body part is "dead numb," and the person is unable to perceive any tactile stimulation although there may still be spontaneous pain), the person would actually be guessing whether or not there had been any tactile stimulation. In such cases, we would recommend that a more stringent statistical criterion than is usual be required before it is concluded that there is conscious dissimulation. In other words, rather than a $p < .05$ (i.e., a one in 20 chance of there being a false positive), there should perhaps be at least a $p < .01$ (i.e., a one in a 100 chance of a false positive) level of confidence. It should also be noted that an incidence of 17.5% (suspected) malingerers in a sample of 200 could not be generalized to the entire population of such cases given that this was a selected sample.

Etherton, Bianchini, Ciota, Heinly, and Greve (2006) reported further on the performance of the "definite" malingerers as described above (Etherton et al., 2005). In this study, the performance of definite malingerers on the Working Memory Index (WMI) derived from the Wechsler Adult Intelligence Scale-III (Wechsler, 1997) was compared with that of (1) college students who were administered the tasks with standard administration instructions, or with instructions to feign impairment due to pain, or while concurrently being administered an acute pain challenge, (2) nonmalingering chronic pain patients, and (3) nonmalingering moderate to severe TBI and memory disorder patients. The students feigning impairment and the definite pain malingerers performed very similarly and below the level of the other nonmalingering groups, about half scoring worse than 95% of the nonmalingering clinical patients. Whereas there were no overall significant group differences between the nonmalingering clinical groups, many individual clinical patients, with either brain injury or clinical pain, performed poorly. It was eventually suggested that intentionally poor performance should be suspected in chronic pain patients who score less than 70 on the WMI.

Bianchini et al. (2005) have recently proposed criteria for the malingering of pain-related disability (MPRD) that are modeled after the Slick, Sherman, and Iverson (1999) criteria for malingered cognitive deficit (see Chapter 16) and which utilize results from cognitive or other symptom validity testing. Similar to Slick et al. (1999), Bianchini et al. (2005) also propose making distinctions between definite, probable, and possible MPRD. In addition to the presence of an external incentive (criterion A), these criteria involve evidence from physical evaluation (criterion B), evidence from cognitive/perceptual (neuropsychological) testing (criterion C), evidence from self-report (criterion D), and that behavior meeting necessary criteria from groups B, C, and D are not fully accounted for by psychiatric, neurologic, or developmental factors (criterion E). However, many (or most) of the individual criteria are clearly questionable, and it is likely that such a system will erroneously result in labeling many individuals as malingerers, or raising the suspicion, when this is inappropriate. We have already critiqued many of these individual criteria in this chapter or Chapter 16 (i.e., measures of physical effort or muscle testing, Waddell signs, symptom validity testing and especially below cut-off levels of performance on various symptom validity or neuropsychological measures, discrepancy between cognitive/neuropsychological test data and known patterns of brain functioning, inconsistency between aspects of patient self-report and other sources of information) and so will here only address the other criteria suggested for this proposed classification system. Most of the criteria suggested by Bianchini et al. (2005) that we have not already critiqued are also questionable. Whereas these may sometimes be associated with conscious dissimulation and malingering, it is likely that they more often are not.

Bianchini et al. (2005) suggested that discrepancy between the patient's physical presentation during formal evaluation and their physical capacities, documented when they are not aware of being observed, may be a sign of conscious dissimulation and malingering. Although we would agree that this may be a useful sign, it should be realized that there is considerable variability in the behavior of pain patients (as well as all other individuals), who will all behave differently in different situations. As is true of many disorders, behavior often improves when the person is relaxed or distracted. Similarly, Bianchini et al. suggested that self-reported symptoms discrepant with observations of behavior may be a sign of conscious dissimulation and malingering. However, some such discrepancies are also common with most, if not all, persons. Importantly, this criterion is qualified to involve "marked" discrepancies. Whereas we would agree that such "marked" discrepancies may be a valid sign, discrepancies are not usually so marked, and there may be other possible explanations. Many persons have a marked discrepancy between what they report being able to do and what they are actually able to do. We do agree with the criterion of what is termed "compelling" discrepancies between examination results and other behavior, "such that it is not reasonable to believe the patient is not purposely controlling the difference" (p. 412) if this is clearly associated with malingering for the purposes of obtaining external incentive rather than with factitious behavior or other causes.

Bianchini et al. (2005) suggested that a discrepancy between the subjective report of pain and physiological reactivity (e.g., heart-rate increase with significant change in subjective pain report) may be a sign of conscious dissimulation and malingering. Although some such relationship may generally be true within an experimental acute pain challenge, it is not likely true with most chronic pain patients whose sensitivity to pain and possible response bias to report pain (see above) may be evident independent of conscious dissimulation.

Bianchini et al. (2005) suggest that a discrepancy between neuropsychological test data and observed behavior may be a sign associated with malingering. However, neuropsychological tests have generally, at best, moderate ecological validity (Chaytor & Schmitter-Edgecombe, 2003) and so may not correspond well with everyday behavior. Again, this and other criteria are a matter of degree or kind. In certain cases we would agree that this could be a valid sign but, in other cases, it would not. Thus, a person may perform very poorly on neuropsychological testing (i.e., more poorly than might be expected on the basis of significant TBI or even some dementias) because he or she has a bad headache, has slept very poorly the night before, is anxious or distrusting of the testing situation, or for other reasons, but often perform at a higher level in his or her everyday life when feeling better and involved in some valued activity. On the other hand, some discrepancies would not be explainable on the basis of these or other reasons and would more likely be a possible sign of malingering. Bianchini et al. (2005) suggested that discrepancy between self-reported symptoms and known patterns of physiological or neurological functioning may be a sign of conscious dissimulation or malingering. However, although much is known about the neurobiology and psychophysiology of chronic pain, this is generally agreed to still be poorly understood. An example they give for this sign is that there may be whole body pain with little evidence of peripheral pathology. It has previously been noted that there is a poor relationship between peripheral pathology and chronic pain, and it should be realized that there are neurons in the brain that code for whole body pain, which may provide one possible physiological explanation for such cases. Finally, Bianchini et al. (2005) suggest that evidence from formal psychological evaluation that the person has significantly misrepresented his or her current status may be an associated sign. Elevation on MMPI-2 validity scales is given as an example of data that may be utilized to fulfill this criterion. However, as has been discussed in this and other chapters, and as will be discussed further below, there is controversy about the use of such indices and, in particular, whether these can actually distinguish between elevations that are due to actual distress and problems associated with the disorder, possible exaggeration of distress for reasons other than malingering, or malingering.

References

Apkarian, A. V., Bushnell, M. C., Treede, R. D., & Zubieta, J. K. (2005). Human brain mechanisms of pain perception and regulation in health and disease. *European Journal of Pain, 9*, 463–484. Epub.

Arbisi, P. A., & Butcher, J. N. (2004). Psychometric perspectives on detection of malingering of pain: Use of the Minnesota Multiphasic Personality Inventory-2. *Clinical Journal of Pain, 20*, 383–391.

Basbaum, A. I. (1999). Spinal mechanisms of acute and persistent pain. *Regional Anesthesia and Pain Medicine, 24*, 59–67.

Bianchini, K. J., Greve, K. W., & Glynn, G. (2005). On the diagnosis of malingered pain-related disability: Lessons from cognitive malingering research. *The Spine Journal, 5*, 404–417.

Bogduk, N. (2004). Diagnostic blocks: A truth serum for malingering. *Clinical Journal of Pain, 20*, 409–414.

Butcher, J. N., Dahlstrom, W. G., Graham, J. R., Tellegen, A., & Kaemmer, B. (1989). *Minnesota Multiphasic Personality Inventory (MMPI-2): Manual for administration and scoring*. Minneapolis: University of Minnesota Press.

Byrne, R. W., & Stokes, E. (2003). Can monkeys malinger? In P. W. Halligan, C. Bass, & D. A. Oakley (Eds.), *Malingering and illness deception* (pp. 54–67). New York: Oxford University Press.

Chapman, C. R., Donaldson, G. W., Nakamura, Y., Jacobson, R. C., Bradshaw, D. H., & Gavrin, J. (2002). A psychophysiological causal model of pain report validity. *The Journal of Pain, 3*, 143–155.

Chaytor, N., & Schmitter-Edgecombe, M. (2003). The ecological validity of neuropsychological tests: A review of the literature on everyday cognitive skills. *Neuropsychology Review, 4*, 181–197.

Clark, W. C. (1994). The psyche in the psychophysics of pain: An introduction to sensory decision theory. In J. Boivie, P. Hansson, & U. Lindblom (Eds.), *Touch, temperature and pain in health and disease: Mechanisms and assessments. Progress in Pain Research and Management, Vol 3*. Seattle: IASP Press.

Clayer, J. R., Bookless, C., & Ross, M.W. (1984). Neurosis and conscious symptom exaggeration: Its differentiation by the Illness Behavior Questionnaire. *Journal of Psychosomatic Research, 28*, 237–241.

Clayer, J. R., Bookless, C., & Ross, M. W. (1986). The evaluation of illness behavior and exaggeration of disability. *British Journal of Psychiatry, 148*, 296–299.

Collie, J. (1932). *Fraud in medico-legal practice*. London: Edward Arnold & Co.

Craig, K. D., Hyde, S. A., & Patrick, C. J. (1991). Genuine, suppressed and faked facial behavior during exacerbation of chronic low back pain. *Pain, 46*, 161–71.

Crowne, D., & Marlow, D. (1960). A new scale of social desirability, independent of psychopathology. *Journal of Consulting Psychology, 24*, 349–354.

Denollet, J. (1991). Negative affectivity and repressive coping: Pervasive influence on self-reported mood, health, and coronary-prone behavior. *Psychosomatic Medicine, 53*, 538–556.

Deshields, T. L., Tait, R. C., Gfeller, J. D., & Chibnall, J. T. (1995). Relationship between social desirability and self-report in chronic pain patients. *The Clinical Journal of Pain, 11*, 189–193.

Derogatis, L. R. (1983). *SCL-90-R: Administration, scoring and procedures manual-II.* Towson: Clinical Psychometric Research.

Dush, D. M., Simons, L. E., Platt, M. et al. (1994). Psychological profiles distinguishing litigating and nonlitigating pain patients: Subtle, and not so subtle. *Journal of Personality Assessment, 62*, 299–313.

Epstein, R. M., Quill, T. E., & McWhinney, I. R. (1999). Somatization reconsidered: Incorporating the patient's experience of illness. *Annals of Internal Medicine, 159*, 215–222.

Etherton, J. L., Bianchini, K. J., Ciota, M. A., Heinly, M. T., & Greve, K. W. (2006). Pain, malingering and the WAIS-III Working Memory Index. *The Spine Journal, 6*, 61–71.

Etherton, J. L., Bianchini, K. J., Greve, K. W., & Heinly, M. T. (2005). Sensitivity and specificity of Reliable Digit Span in malingered pain-related disability. *Assessment, 12*, 130–136.

Fernandez, E., & Turk, D. C. (1992). Sensory and affective components of pain: Separation and synthesis. *Psychological Bulletin, 112*, 205–217.

Fishbain, D. A., Cole, B., Cutler, R. B., Lewis, J., Rosomoff, H. L., & Rosomoff, R. S. (2003). A structured evidence based review on the meaning of non-organic physical signs: Waddell signs. *Pain Medicine, 4*, 141–181.

Fishbain, D. A., Cutler, R. B., Lewis, J., Cole, B., Steele-Rosomoff, R., & Rosomoff, H. L. (2003). Is the location of nondermatomal sensory abnormalities (NDSAs) related to pain location? *Pain Medicine, 4*, 248–253.

Fishbain, D. A., Cutler, R., Rosomoff, H. L., & Rosomoff, R. S. (1999). Chronic pain disability exaggeration/malingering and submaximal effort research. *Clinical Journal of Pain, 15*, 244–274.

Fishbain, D. A., Cutler, R. B., Rosomoff, H. L., & Steele-Rosomoff, R. (2002). Does the conscious exaggeration scale detect deception within patients with chronic pain alleged to have secondary gain? *Pain Medicine, 3*, 39–46.

Fishbain, D A., Cutler, R. B., Rosomoff, H. L., & Rosomoff, R. S. (2004). Is there a relationship between nonorganic physical findings (Waddell Signs) and secondary gain/malingering? *Clinical Journal of Pain, 20*, 399–408.

Fishbain, D. A., Goldberg, M., Meagher, R. B., Steele, R., & Rosomoff, H. (1986). Male and female chronic pain patients categorized by DSM-III psychiatric diagnostic criteria. *Pain, 26*, 181–97.

Flor, H. (2002). The modification of cortical reorganization and chronic pain by sensory feedback. *Applied Psychophysiology and Biofeedback, 27*, 215–227.

Fordyce, W. E. (1976). Behavioral methods for chronic pain and illness. St. Louis, MO: Mosby.

Gervais, R., Green, P., Allen, M., & Iverson, G. (2001). Effects of coaching on symptom validity testing in chronic pain patients presenting for disability assessments. *Journal of Forensic Neuropsychology, 2*, 1–19.

Gracely, R. H., Geisser, M. E., Giesecke, T., Grant, M. A. B., Petzke, F., Williams, D. A. et al. (2004). Pain catastrophizing and neural responses to pain among persons with Fibromyalgia. *Brain, 127*, 835–843.

Green, D. M., & Swets, J. A. (1966). *Signal detection theory and psychophysics*. New York: Wiley.

Greve, K. W., Bianchini, K. J., & Ameduri, C. J. (2003a). Use of a forced-choice test of tactile discrimination in the evaluation of functional sensory loss: A report of 3 cases. *Archives of Physical Medicine and Rehabilitation, 84*, 1233–1236.

Hadjistavropoulos, H. D., & Craig, K. D. (1994). Acute and chronic low back pain: Cognitive, affective and behavioral dimensions. *Journal of Consulting and Clinical Psychology, 62*, 341–349.

Hadjistavropoulos, H. D., Craig, K. D., Hadjistavropoulos, T., & Poole, G.D. (1996). Subjective judgments of deception in pain expression: Accuracy and errors. *Pain, 65*, 251–258.

Harness, D. M., & Chase, P. F. (1994). Litigation and chronic facial pain. *Journal of Orofacial Pain, 8*, 289–292.

Hathaway, S. R., & McKinley, J. C. (1967). *Minnesota Multiphasic Personality Inventory manual*. New York: Psychological Corporation.

Hill, M. L., & Craig, K. D. (2004). Detecting deception in facial expressions of pain: Accuracy and training. *Clinical Journal of Pain, 20*, 415–422.

Jamner, L. D., & Leigh, H. (1999). Repressive/defensive coping, endogenous opioids and health: How a life so perfect can make you sick. *Psychiatry Research, 85*, 17–31.

Keller, L. S., & Butcher, J. N. (1991). *Assessment of Chronic Pain Patients with the MMPI-2. MMPI-2 Monographs*. Minneapolis: University of Minnesota Press.

Kirmayer, L. J., & Robbins, J. M. (1996). Patients who somatize in primary care: a longitudinal study of cognitive and social characteristics. *Psychological Medicine, 26*, 937–951.

Kroenke, K., & Mangelsdorff, A. D. (1989). Common symptoms in ambulatory care: Incidence, evaluation, therapy, and outcome. *American Journal of Medicine, 86*, 262–266.

Leavitt, F. (1985). Pain and deception: Use of verbal pain measurement as a diagnostic aid in differentiating between clinical and simulated low-back pain. *Journal of Psychosomatic Research, 29*, 495–505.

Leavitt, F. (1987). Detection of simulation among persons instructed to exaggerate symptoms of low back pain. *Journal of Occupational Medicine, 29*, 229–233.

Leavitt, F. (1991). Predicting disability time using formal low back pain measurement: The Low Back Pain Simulation Scale. *Journal of Psychosomatic Research, 35*, 599–607.

Leavitt, F., Garron, D. C., D'angelo, C. M., & MCneill, T. W. (1979). Low back pain in patients with and without demonstrable organic disease. *Pain, 6*, 191–200.

Mailis, A., Giannoylis, I., Downar, J., Kwan, C., Mikulis, D., Crawley, A. et al. (2003). Altered central somatosensory processing in chronic pain patients with "hysterical" anaesthesia. *Neurology, 60*, 1501–1507.

Mailis, A., & Nicholson, K. (2002). The use of sodium amytal in the assessment and treatment of functional or other disorders. In N. D. Zasler, & M. F. Martelli (Eds.), *Functional medical disorders, state of the art reviews in physical medicine and rehabilitation* (pp. 131–146). Philadelphia: Hanley & Belfus.

Mailis, A., Papagapiou, M., Umana, M., Cohodarevic, T., Nowak, J., & Nicholson, K. (2001). Unexplainable nondermatomal somatosensory deficits in patients with chronic nonmalignant pain in the context of litigation/compensation: a role for involvement of central factors? *Journal of Rheumatology, 28*, 1385–1393.

Main, C. J., & Waddell, G. (1998). Behavioral responses to examination. A reappraisal of the interpretation of "nonorganic signs." *Spine, 23*, 2367–2371.

Martelli, M. F., Nicholson, K., Zasler, N. D., & Bender, M. C. (2006). Assessment of response bias in clinical and forensic evaluations of impairment following brain injury. In N. D. Zasler, D. I. Katz, & R. D. Zafonte (Eds.), *Brain injury medicine: Principles and practice*. New York: Demos Medical.

Martelli, M. F., Zasler, N. D., Nicholson, K., Pickett, T. C., & May, V. R. (2002). Assessing the veracity of pain complaints and associated disability. In R. B. Weiner (Ed.), *Pain management: A practical guide for clinicians* (6th ed.) (pp. 789–805). Boca Ratan, FL: St. Lucie Press.

McGuire, B. E., Harvey, A. G., & Shores, E. A. (2001). Simulated malingering in pain patients: A study with the Pain Patient Profile. *British Journal of Clinical Psychology, 40*, 71–79.

McGuire, B. E., & Shores, E.A. (2001a). Pain Patient Profile and the assessment of malingered pain. *Journal of Clinical Psychology, 57*, 401–409.

McGuire, B. E., & Shores, E.A. (2001b). Simulated pain on the Symptom Checklist 90-Revised. *Journal of Clinical Psychology, 57*, 1589–1596.

Melzack, R. (1975). The McGill Pain Questionnaire: Major properties and scoring methods. *Pain, 1*, 277–279.

Melzack, R., Katz, J., & Jeans, M. E. (1985). The role of compensation in chronic pain: Analysis using a new method of scoring the McGill Pain Questionnaire. *Pain, 23*, 101–112.

Mendelson, G. (1987). Measurement of conscious symptom exaggeration by questionnaire: a clinical study. *Journal of Psychosomatic Research, 31*, 703–711.

Mendelson, G., & Mendelson, D. (2004). Malingering pain in the medicolegal context. *Clinical Journal of Pain, 20*, 423–432.

Meyers, J. E., Millis, S. R., & Volkert, K. (2002). A validity index for the MMPI-2. *Archives of Clinical Neuropsychology, 17*, 157–169.

Merskey, H., & Bogduk, N. (Eds.). (1994). *Classification of chronic pain* (2nd ed.). Seattle: IASP Press.

Miller, L. (2000). Neurosensitization: A model for persistent disability in chronic pain, depression, and Posttraumatic Stress Disorder following injury. *Neurorehabilitation, 14*, 25–32.

Millon, T. (1997). *Millon clinical multiaxial inventory-III manual* (2nd ed.). Minneapolis, MN: NCS Pearson.

Nicholson, K. (2000). At the crossroads: Pain in the 21st Century. *NeuroRehabilitation, 14*, 57–67.

Nicholson, K., & Mailis, A. (in preparation, a). MCMI profiles in a chronic pain population.

Nicholson, K., & Mailis, A. (in preparation, b). Repression and sensitization in chronic pain patients.

Nicholson, K., & Martelli, M. (2004). The problem of pain. *Journal of Head Trauma Rehabilitation, 19*, 2–9.

Nicholson, K., Martelli, M. F., & Zasler, N. D. (2002). Myths and misconceptions about chronic pain: The problem of mind body dualism. In R. B. Weiner (Ed.), *Pain management: A practical guide for clinicians* (6th ed., pp. 465–474). Boca Raton, FL: St. Lucie Press.

Pilowsky, I., & Spence, N. D. (1975). Patterns of illness behavior in patients with intractable pain. *Journal of Psychosomatic Research, 19*, 279–287.

Poole, G. D., & Craig, K. D. (1992). Judgments of genuine, suppressed and faked facial expressions of pain. *Journal of Personality and Social Psychology, 63*, 797–805.

Prkachin, K. M. (1992). The consistency of facial expressions of pain: A comparison across modalities. *Pain, 51*, 297–306.

Robinson, M. E., & Dannecker, E. A. (2004). Critical issues in the use of muscle testing for the determination of sincerity of effort. *Clinical Journal of Pain*, 20, 392–398.

Rollman, G. B. (1977). Signal detection theory measurement of pain: A review and critique. *Pain, 3*, 187–211.

Rollman, G. B. (1979). Signal detection theory measures: Empirical validation studies and adaptation-level effects. *Pain, 6*, 9–21.

Rondinelli, R. D., & Katz, R. T. (Eds.). (2000). *Impairment rating and disability evaluation*. Philadelphia, PA: W. B. Saunders.

Salamy, J. G., Wolk, D. J., & Shucard, D. W. (1983). Psychophysiological assessment of statements about pain. *Psychophysiology, 20*, 579–584.

Sartori, G., Forti, S., Birbaumer, N., & Flor, H. (2003). A brief and unobtrusive instrument to detect simulation and exaggeration in patients with whiplash syndrome. *Neuroscience Letters, 342*, 53–56.

Schmand, B., Lindeboom, J., Schagen, S., Heijt, R., Koene, T., & Hamburger, H. L. (1998). Cognitive complaints in patients after whiplash injury: The impact of malingering. *Journal of Neurology, Neurosurgery, and Psychiatry, 64*, 339–343.

Shoichet, R. P. (1978). Sodium amytal in the diagnosis of chronic pain. *Canadian Psychiatric Association Journal, 23*, 219–228.

Slesinger, D., Archer, R. P., & Duane, W. (2002). MMPI-2 characteristics in a chronic pain population. *Assessment, 9*, 406–414.

Slick, D. J., Sherman, E. M., & Iverson, G. L. (1999). Diagnostic criteria for malingered neurocognitive dysfunction: Proposed standards for clinical practice and research. *The Clinical Neuropsychologist, 13*, 545–561.

Sullivan, M. (2004). Exaggerated pain behavior: By what standard? *Clinical Journal of Pain, 20*, 433–439.

Thimineur, M., Kaliszewski, T., & Sood, P. (2000). Malingering and symptom magnification: A case report illustrating the limitations of clinical judgment. *Connecticut Medicine, 64*, 399–401.

Thomas, J. J. (1923). Malingering and the feigned disorders. In F. Peterson, W. S. Haines, & R. W. Webster (Eds.), *Legal medicine and toxicology* (2nd ed., pp. 696–717). Philadelphia, PA: W. B. Saunders.

Tollison, D. C., & Langley, J. C. (1995). *Pain patient profile manual.* Minneapolis, MN: National Computer Services.

Tomaka, J., Blascovich, J., & Kelsey, R. M. (1992). Effects of self-deception, social desirability, and repressive coping on psychophysiological reactivity to stress. *Personality and Social Psychology Bulletin, 18*, 616–624.

Trabin, T., Rader, C., & Cummings, C. (1987). A comparison of pain management outcomes for disability compensation and non-compensation patients. *Psychology and Health, 1*, 341–351.

Turk, D. C., & Melzack, R. (1993). The measurement of pain and the assessment of people experiencing pain. In D. C. Turk & R. Melzack (Eds.), *Handbook of pain assessment* (pp. 3–14). New York: Guilford Press.

Vendrig, A. A. (2000). The Minnesota Multiphasic Personality Inventory and chronic pain: A conceptual analysis of a long-standing but complicated relationship. *Clinical Psychology Review, 20*, 533–559.

Vogt, B. A., Sikes, R. W., & Vogt, L. J. (1993). Anterior cingulate cortex and the medial pain system. In B. A. Vogt & M. Gabriel (Eds.), *Neurobiology of cingulate cortex and limbic thalamus: A comprehensive handbook* (pp. 313–344). Boston: Birkhauser.

Waddell, G. (2004). *The back pain revolution* (2nd ed.). Edinburgh: Churchill Livingstone.

Waddell, G., McCulloch, J. A., & Kimmel, E. (1980). Non-organic physical signs in low back pain. *Spine, 5*, 117–125.

Waddell, G., Main, C. J., & Morris, E. W. (1984). Chronic low back pain, psychologic distress and illness behavior. *Spine*, 9, 209–213. Library Holdings Bibliographic Links.

Wager, T. D., Rilling, J. K., Smith, E. E., Sokolik, A., Casey, K. L., Davidson, R. J. et al. (2004). Placebo-induced changes in FMRI in the anticipation and experience of pain. *Science, 303*, 1162–1167.

Wallis, B. J., & Bogduk, N. (1996). Faking a profile: Can naive subjects simulate whiplash responses? *Pain, 66*, 223–227.

Wechsler, D. A. (1997). *Wechsler adult intelligence scale-III.* New York: Psychological Corporation.

Weinberger, D. A., & Schwartz, G. E. (1979). Low-anxious, high-anxious, and repressive coping styles: Psychometric patterns and behavioral and physiological response to stress. *Journal of Abnormal Psychology, 88*, 369–380.

Wickramasekera, I. E. (1995). Somatization: Concepts, data, and predictions from the high risk model of threat perception. *The Journal of Nervous and Mental Disease, 83*, 15–23.

Wittgenstein, L. (1980). *Remarks on the philosophy of psychology*. Chicago, IL: University of Chicago Press.

18

Malingering: Posttraumatic Stress Disorder and Depression

KEITH NICHOLSON AND MICHAEL F. MARTELLI

It has long been known that it is possible to feign mental or other disorders and not be detected. Barrows (1971) showed that a wide range of psychiatric, neurologic, pain, fatigue, or other problems, in which there are usually few physical findings, could be readily simulated in the context of teaching or examining medical students. Psychiatric symptoms or syndromes that were readily simulated included depression, agitation, psychosis, neurotic reactions, and thought disorder. Neurologic symptoms that could easily be feigned included paralysis, sensory loss, reflex changes, extensor plantar responses, gait abnormalities, cranial nerve palsy, altered levels of consciousness, coma, seizures, and hyperkinesias. Even after being warned that there were simulators among the examinees, experienced clinicians found it difficult to detect them. Rosenhan (1973) reported that 12 people posing as "pseudopatients" and presenting with some psychiatric symptoms were able to gain admission to psychiatric hospitals in five different states. All but one of the 12 were diagnosed with Schizophrenia and none of the pseudopatients were detected despite hospital stays of from 7 to 52 days.

Posttraumatic Stress Disorder (PTSD) and depression are common in the general population, and are also common sequelae following various accidents or injuries that may be an object of medicolegal proceedings (Nicholson & Martelli, 2006). These disorders are heterogeneous, with marked variability in presentation. There is an immense literature concerning their phenomenology, etiology, genetics, neurobiology, course, treatment, and other pertinent factors. The remainder of this section will focus on the differential diagnosis of malingering in the presentation of these psychoemotional problems.

Sparr and Pankratz (1983) were the first to document persons simulating PTSD following introduction of this diagnosis into the *DSM* nomenclature. They described five men who claimed to have been traumatized by the Vietnam War, although four had never been in Vietnam and two had never been in the military. However, it was concluded that these were cases of Factitious Disorder rather than malingering.

Guriel and Fremouw (2003) reviewed the empirical literature pertaining to the assessment of malingered PTSD. They noted that there is widespread concern about the possibility of malingered PTSD, and that PTSD may be one of several disorders that are vulnerable to malingering, as symptoms are subjective and there are often substantial financial or other associated benefits. They suggest that the possibility of malingering, including verification of the traumatic event if possible, be part of all clinical assessments. However, they note that there is no "gold standard" for the assessment of malingered PTSD and, in contrast, suggest that the empirical investigation into malingered PTSD is only in its infancy. Several MMPI (Hathaway & McKinley, 1967) and MMPI-2 (Butcher, Dahlstrom, Graham, Tellegen, & Kaemmer, 1989) studies, mostly involving simulators but some with differential prevalence designs and some with purported known group designs, were reviewed. It was concluded that results from studies using the earlier MMPI were mixed. Those using the MMPI-2 were suggested to be helpful but not flawless in identifying simulated or malingered PTSD. The MMPI-2 validity scales F, F−K, O-S, F-Fb, and Ds2 were considered particularly useful in detecting simulated response styles (see Chapter 16, Malingering: Traumatic Brain Injury, and Chapter 11, Conducting a Psychological Assessment by Andrew Kane, both in this volume, for a description of MMPI and other validity scales).

As was discussed in Chapter 16 (Malingering: Traumatic Brain Injury), Rogers et al. (2003) conducted a meta-analysis of the MMPI-2 in the detection of malingering. It was concluded that genuine PTSD patients presumed to be responding honestly produced very extreme elevations on the MMPI-2 Fb validity scale (M = 92, SD = 25), extreme elevations on F (M = 86, SD = 22), with slightly higher elevations on other validity scales (i.e., Fp, M = 69, SD = 21; O-S, M = 182, SD = 72; DS, M = 68, SD = 15; F−K, M = 9, SD = 11). As such, there is considerable overlap between the validity scale scores of genuine patients and the scores of those who are feigning (mostly simulators).

Guriel and Fremouw (2003) also reviewed the Personality Assessment Inventory (PAI; Morey, 1991), another multiscale self-report inventory, which had only been used in two empirical studies. Results appeared similar to that of the MMPI-2, that is, possibly helpful but not flawless.

Guriel and Fremouw (2003) summarized the results of several other techniques to detect malingering or other response sets in PTSD. They noted that although there has been a proliferation of scales to measure PTSD, only the Trauma Symptom Inventory (TSI; Briere, 1995) includes validity scales (Atypical Responses, Inconsistency, Response Level). Although cut-off scores to detect fake-bad response styles in PTSD claimants using this instrument have been developed (Edens et al., 1989), it was suggested that these need to be replicated [and see the study of Elhai et al. (2005) discussed below]. Another technique that has demonstrated capacity in distinguishing suspected PTSD simulators from others is a facial emotion identification task (Morel, 1998), although this also needs further study. The Structured Interview of Reported Symptoms (SIRS; Rogers, 1992, 1997), used extensively in criminal forensic work, is another technique that has some promise but limited study with detection of malingering in PTSD, the only study utilizing this technique not having any patients with PTSD in the comparison group (Rogers et al., 1992). Guriel and Fremouw (2003) reported that there have been mixed results utilizing the Rorschach projective technique to detect simulated PTSD. Finally, although psychophysiological assessment may accurately identify PTSD symptomatology, there has been limited study in detecting malingerers, and the utility of such measures in separating malingered from genuine responses remains controversial.

Guriel and Fremouw (2003) eventually concluded that it is difficult to differentiate between malingered and genuine PTSD because an apparent "over-reporting" of symptoms is typical of many actual or legitimate PTSD cases. It was noted that there is a high comorbidity of PTSD with several other clinical or personality disorders, and that PTSD, like other severe pathologies, may include a myriad of symptoms resulting in elevated scales on various measures.

There have been conflicting results on the effect of compensation status on presentation in PTSD. For example, Frueh et al. (2003), utilizing archival data from assessment of 320 adult male combat veterans, concluded that compensation-seeking veterans reported significantly more distress and that they were much more likely to overreport or exaggerate their symptoms than were noncompensation-seeking veterans. In contrast, DeViva and Bloem (2003), in an archival study of 141 combat veterans, found that compensation seeking was not related to psychometric assessment scores or indices of exaggeration. Neither compensation seeking nor indices of exaggeration were related to treatment outcome. However, it was noted that combat veterans seeking treatment for PTSD tend to report high levels of psychopathology on self-report instruments.

On review of the literature, Elhai et al. (2004) also concluded that elevations on the MMPI-2 F scale were confounded with the effects of psychopathology and distress among psychiatric patients generally, and that F scale elevations in PTSD may be misleading as, rather than suggesting malingering, these have been associated with severe trauma exposure history, depression, dissociation, actual PTSD, increased somatic complaints as well as chaotic family-of-origin environments. It was noted that the Fp scale had been used in few studies with conflicting results. Elhai et al. (2004) reported on the utility of the newly created Infrequency-Posttraumatic Stress Disorder scale (Fptsd), which had previously been shown to demonstrate incremental validity over other MMPI-2 scales in detection of malingered PTSD with combat-exposed PTSD patients (Elhai et al., 2002). Elhai et al. (2004) studied the effectiveness of the Fptsd scale in addition to F and Fp in discriminating genuine civilian PTSD among 41 adult victims of child sexual abuse from a group of 39 students instructed to simulate PTSD. Analyses demonstrated Fptsd's incremental validity over F but not over Fp. Based on the two studies examining Fptsd and other validity scales (Elhai et al., 2002, 2004), it was suggested that the Fptsd scale may be more appropriate for combat trauma victims, and the Fp scale may be more appropriate for civilian trauma victims.

Greiffenstein et al. (2004) reported that the MMPI-2 Fake Bad Scale (FBS; Lees-Haley et al., 1991; see Chapter 16, Malingering: Traumatic Brain Injury) distinguished between litigants reporting "implausible symptoms" long after "minor frights or soft tissue injuries" and nonlitigants clinically-referred following severe stressors with "probable posttraumatic syndrome." The F, Fp and F−K scales showed poor utility in discriminating between these groups. Some of the "implausible" symptoms in the litigating sample were that there were multiple diagnoses (93.5% with three or more comorbid diagnoses), delayed symptom onset of one month or more, claims of both mild TBI and PTSD, and symptoms being nonresponsive to psychotropic medications. We would question how improbable such symptoms are. Moreover, although there was little specific information concerning pain problems, it appeared that at least 50 of 57 of the litigating sample had some significant pain problems. Of the nonlitigating sample, it appeared that robbery was the most common stressor and that there were few, if any, participants with significant pain problems. It was also noted that the mean FBS score for the nonlitigating trauma patients was above that initially suggested by Lees-Haley et al. (1991) as a cut-off. FBS cutting scores derived from logistic regression were applied to a third group made up of litigants with histories of undeniably severe trauma. A substantial number of this third group scored above cutoffs for exaggeration, and it was acknowledged that interpretation of this result was ambiguous, that is, higher scores may have been due to effects associated with trauma vs. exaggeration associated with compensation seeking status. Indeed, we do not think that this study provides any useful information concerning the utility of the FBS scale to distinguish between individuals presenting with sequelae associated with actual trauma (especially when this involves pain and related problems) and individuals who may be exaggerating associated with compensation-seeking status.

Elhai et al. (2005) recently examined the Trauma Symptom Inventory's (TSI) ability to discriminate between student simulators and genuine PTSD outpatients. Whereas results demonstrated between-group differences on several TSI clinical scales, few were in the expected direction, that is, the PTSD patients scored higher than simulators on several scales. The Atypical Response validity scale was found to be inadequate in correctly classifying simulators and patients. It was noted that this scale was not developed as a measure of malingering but, instead, was intended to be a general validity screen.

Noting the problem of the applicability of simulation studies for real-world clinical and forensic settings, and that simulators may be better able to avoid detection when informed about validity scales (Walters & Clopton, 2000), Eakin et al. (2006) studied the utility of the MMPI-2 and the PAI in distinguishing between students meeting criteria for PTSD and students who had been exposed to a traumatic event in the past three years but who did not screen positive for PTSD and who were either responding honestly or simulating. All subjects were coached about the presence of validity scales, and simulators were provided with detailed information about PTSD. Results indicated that the validity scales and selected clinical scales of the MMPI-2 and PAI were generally comparable in their ability to distinguish PTSD subjects from healthy controls. However, the PAI was not nearly as effective in discriminating between simulators and PTSD cases. In contrast, all of the MMPI-2 fake-bad validity scales (the FBS scale was not used in this study) and PTSD-relevant clinical scales significantly discriminated simulators and PTSD cases. The MMPI-2 scales demonstrated very good specificity, that is, not identifying a true PTSD case as a simulator, but poor sensitivity using established cutting scores, that is, many of the simulators avoided detection. Importantly, it was noted that whereas students meeting criteria for PTSD had been well diagnosed using the CAPS (Blake et al., 1995) or other criteria, these were not a treatment seeking group and were all undergraduate university students who were likely not as severely affected as may be the case with many others with PTSD.

Depression is another disorder or psychoemotional difficulty that is common not only in the general population but, also, in medicolegal claims or disability assessments, and which may be especially vulnerable to feigning given that most people have some familiarity with symptomatology or ready access to such information (Bagby et al., 2000; Griffin et al., 1996; Nicholson & Martelli, 2006; Steffan et al., 2003). Several studies, most all of which have utilized the MMPI-2, have attempted to determine whether those feigning depression can be detected.

Bagby et al. (1997) compared the MMPI-2 profiles of college students simulating depression or Schizophrenia with profiles produced by actual patients, and found that the MMPI-2 F and Fp validity scales were better able to detect feigned schizophrenia than depression, whereas Fb was better at identifying simulated depression. Bagby et al. (2000) subsequently studied the ability of mental health professionals (psychiatrists, nurses, social workers) with advanced degrees and considerable clinical experience in assessing or treating depression to feign depression while completing the MMPI-2. It was concluded that the clinical experts were unable to successfully simulate depression although they were better than were the student simulators in the Bagby et al. (1997) study. Bagby et al. (2000) found that the Fb validity scale best discriminated between groups, followed closely by F. Neither the Ds nor the FBS scales contributed uniquely to explaining the variance. The feigners also scored higher than clinical cases on six of the nine MMPI-2 clinical scales.

Other studies have found that knowledge of depression or questionnaire validity scales has an effect on the ability of simulators to escape detection. Walters and Clopton (2000) found that simulators who were provided with information about depression or the MMPI-2 validity indices were significantly more successful in simulating depression than participants who were not provided with such information. Viglione et al. (2001) found that subjects simulating depression who had been cautioned to avoid grossly exaggerating their responses produced smaller elevations on MMPI-2 scales and, therefore, had more realistic profiles than simulators who were not so cautioned. None of the validity indices adequately identified simulators who had been cautioned. It was suggested that many real-life malingerers are likely cautious, so that real-life malingering effect sizes may be much smaller than those in simulation studies. Crawford et al. (2006) compared the MMPI-2 records of (1) sophisticated student simulators who had been presented with a scenario about a worker who suffered facial trauma and who were to then feign depression, with (2) the archival records of depressed in-patients.

They found that the FBS scale was the only validity scale that successfully discriminated between groups.

Rogers et al. (2003), as discussed in Chapter 16, conducted a meta-analysis of MMPI-2 studies involving malingering or feigning of mental disorder with an emphasis on distinguishing real from feigned disorder. With respect to depression, it was found that those with genuine depression may have extreme elevations on scales F and Fb. Ds appeared to provide the best discrimination between those who were genuinely depressed and all feigners, but none of the existing MMPI-2 validity scales provided very good discrimination.

Steffan et al. (2003) developed the Malingered Depression (Md) scale from 32 MMPI-2 items that distinguished between college students who feigned depression and those who reported at least mild to moderate depression. A cross-validation study with sophisticated (i.e., provided with information about MMPI-2 validity scales) and naive simulators, and a sample of students in counseling (and presumably depressed) indicated that the Md scale was well able to discriminate between those who were feigning and those who were not, and that this scale provided incremental validity in differentiating sophisticated simulators from depressed persons. However, it was noted that a higher cut-off score may be necessary with patients who are more depressed. Bagby et al. (2005) subsequently examined the incremental validity of the Md scale in comparison with the F, Fb, and Fp scales to detect feigned depression. Although the Md scale did successfully discriminate cases of feigned depression from patients with bona fide mild–moderate or severe depression, the Fb scale and the F/Fp scale combination were the best single predictors. It was suggested that the Md scale may not provide incremental validity over the existing MMPI-2 F, Fb, and Fp scales. Again, there was large overlap between the validity scale scores of the genuine patients and simulators.

Mogge and Lepage (2004) have recently developed the Assessment of Depression Inventory (ADI), which assesses both depression and response bias. In studies that have included cross-validation of the initial findings, it has been found that the measure of depression correlates with other well-validated measures, and that the feigning scale discriminates between simulators and actual patients. One other technique that has begun to be explored in the detection of malingered depression is that of computerized content analysis of speech (Cannizzaro et al., 2004). Although this technique needs further study and development, as do various electrophysiological or other neuroimaging techniques, it may become very useful in many clinical endeavors in the future.

References

Bagby, R. M., Marshall, M. B., & Bacchiochi, J. R. (2005). The validity and clinical utility of the MMPI-2 Malingering Depression scale. *Journal of Personality Assessment, 85*, 304–311.

Bagby, R. M., Nicholson, R. A., Buis, T., & Bacchiochi, J. R. (2000). Can the MMPI-2 validity scales detect depression by feigned experts. *Assessment, 7*, 55–62.

Bagby, R. M., Rogers, R., Buis, T., Nicholson, R. A., Cameron, S. L., Rector, N. A., Schuller, D. R., & Seeman, M. V. (1997). Detecting feigned depression and schizophrenia on the MMPI-2. *Journal of Personality Assessment, 68*, 650–664.

Barrows, H. S. (1971). *Simulated patients*. Charles C. Thomas, Springfield, Il.

Blake, D. D., Weathers, F. W., Nagy, L. M., Kaloupek, D. G., Gusman, F. D., Charney, D. S., & Keane, T. M. (1995). The development of a clinician-administered PTSD scale. Journal of Traumatic Stress, *8*, 75–90.

Briere, J. (1995). *Trauma Symptom Inventory professional manual*. Odessa, FL: Psychological Assessment Resources.

Butcher, J. N., Dahlstrom, W. G., Graham, J. R., Tellegen, A., & Kaemmer, B. (1989). *Minnesota Multiphasic Personality Inventory-2 (MMPI-2): Manual for administration and scoring*. Minneapolis: University of Minnesota Press.

Cannizzaro, M., Reilly, N., & Snyders, P. J. (2004). Speech content analysis in feigned depression. *Journal of Psycholinguistic Research, 33*, 289–301.

Crawford, E. F., Greene, R. L., Dupart, T. M., Bongar, B., & Childs, H. (2006). MMPI–2 assessment of malingered emotional distress related to a workplace injury: A mixed group validation. *Journal of Personality Assessment, 86*, 217–221.

DeViva, J. C., & Bloem, W. D. (2003). Symptom exaggeration and compensation seeking among combat veterans with Posttraumatic Stress Disorder. *Journal of Traumatic Stress, 16*, 503–507.

Eakin, D. E., Weathers, F. W., Benson, T. B., Anderson, C. F., & Funderburk, B. (2006). Detection of feigned Posttraumatic Stress Disorder: A comparison of the MMPI-2 and PAI. *Journal of Psychopathology and Behavioral Assessment, 28*, 145–155.

Edens, J. F., Otto, R. K., & Dwyer, T. J. (1989). Susceptibility of the Trauma Symptom Inventory to malingering. *Journal of Personality Assessment, 71*, 379–392.

Elhai, J. D., Gray, M. J., Naifeh, J. A., Butcher, J. J., Davis, J. L., Falsetti, S. A., & Best, C. L. (2005). Utility of the Trauma Symptom Inventory's atypical response scale in detecting malingered Post-traumatic Stress Disorder. *Assessment, 12*, 210–219.

Elhai, J. D., Naifeh, J. A., Zucker, I. S., Gold, S. N., Deitsch, S. E., & Frueh, B. C. (2004). Discriminating malingered from genuine civilian Posttraumatic Stress Disorder: A validation of three MMPI-2 Infrequency scales (F, Fp, and Fptsd). *Assessment, 11*, 139–144.

Elhai, J. D., Ruggiero, K. J., Frueh, B. C., Beckham, J. C., Gold, P. B., & Feldman, M. E. (2002). The Infrequency-Posttraumatic Stress Disorder scale (Fptsd) for the MMPI-2: Development and initial validation with veterans presenting with combat-related PTSD. *Journal of Personality Assessment, 79*, 531–549.

Frueh, B. C., Elhai, J. D., Gold, P. B., Monnier, J., Magruder, K. M., Keane, T. M., & Arana, G. W. (2003). Disability compensation seeking among veterans evaluated for Posttraumatic Stress Disorder. *Psychiatric Services, 54*, 84–91.

Greiffenstein, M. F., Baker, W. J., Axelrod, B., Peck, E. A., & Gervais, R. (2004). The fake bad scale and MMPI-2 F-family in detection of implausible psychological trauma claims. *The Clinical Neuropsychologist, 18*, 573–590.

Griffin, G. A., Normington, J., May, R., & Glassmire, D. (1996). Assessing dissimulation among Social Security disability income claimants. *Journal of Consulting and Clinical Psychology, 64*, 1425–1430.

Guriel, G., & Fremouw, F. (2003). Assessing malingered Post-traumatic Stress Disorder: A critical review. *Clinical Psychology Review, 23*, 881–904.

Hathaway, S. R., & McKinley, J. C. (1967). *Minnesota Multiphasic Personality Inventory manual*. New York: Psychological Corporation.

Lees-Haley, P. R., English, L. T., & Glenn, W. J. (1991). A Fake Bad Scale on the MMPI-2 for personal injury claimants. *Psychological Report, 68*, 203–210.

Mogge, N. L., & Lepage, J. P. (2004). The Assessment of Depression Inventory (ADI): A new instrument used to measure depression and to detect honesty of response. *Depression and Anxiety, 20*, 107–113.

Morel, K. R. (1998). Development and preliminary validation of a forced-choice test of response bias for Posttraumatic Stress Disorder. *Journal of Personality Assessment, 70*, 299–314.

Morey, L. C. (1991). *Personality Assessment Inventory: Professional Manual.* Odessa, FL: Psychological Assessment Resources.

Nicholson, K., & Martelli, M. (2006). The confounding effects of pain, psychoemotional problems or psychiatric disorder, premorbid ability structure, and motivational or other factors on neuropsychological test performance. In G. Young, A. Kane & K. Nicholson (Eds.) *Psychological Knowledge For Court: PTSD, Chronic Pain and TBI*, pp. 335–351. Springer Science+Business Media: New York.

Rogers, R. (1992). *Structured Interview of Reported Symptoms*. Odessa, FL: Psychological Assessment Resources.

Rogers, R. (1997). Introduction. In R. Rogers (Ed.), *Clinical Assessment of Malingering and Deception* (2nd ed., pp. 1–19). Guilford Press, New York.

Rogers, R., Kropp, P. R., Bagby, R. M., & Dickens, S. E. (1992). Faking specific disorders: A study of the Structured Interview of Reported Symptoms (SIRS). *Journal of Clinical Psychology, 48*, 643–648.

Rogers, R., Sewell, K. W., Martin, M. A., & Vitacco, M. (2003). Detection of feigned mental disorders: A meta-analysis of the MMPI-2 and malingering. *Assessment, 10*, 160–177.

Rosenhan, D. L. (1973). On being sane in insane places. *Science, 179*, 250–258.

Sparr, L., & Pankratz, L. (1983). Factitious Posttraumatic Stress Disorder. *American Journal of Psychiatry, 140*, 1016–1019.

Steffan, J. S., Clopton, J. R., & Morgan, R. D. (2003). An MMPI-2 scale to detect malingered depression (Md Scale). *Assessment, 10*, 382–392.

Viglione, D. J., Wright, D. M., Dizon, N. T., Moynihan, J. E., DuPuis, S., & Pizitz, T. D. (2001). Evading detection on the MMPI-2: Does caution produce more realistic patterns of responding? *Assessment, 8*, 237–250.

Walters, G. L., & Clopton, J. R. (2000). Effect of symptom information and validity scale information on the malingering of depression on the MMPI-2. *Journal of Personality Assessment, 75*, 183–199.

19

Malingering: Summary and Conclusions

KEITH NICHOLSON AND MICHAEL F. MARTELLI

Malingering is often of concern within the context of personal injury litigation or other medicolegal situations in which compensation or disability benefits for traumatic brain injury (TBI), chronic pain, Posttraumatic Stress Disorder (PTSD), and other psychoemotional problems may be at issue. Although there has been extensive study, there is still very poor understanding of what the incidence or prevalence of malingering may be in such situations. Estimates of incidence or prevalence vary widely, mitigating against the use of base rates in determining the utility or most appropriate cutting scores of any diagnostic sign or test result. Overall, there is generally only moderate and often inconsistent evidence that litigation or compensation status (i.e., those involved in litigation, applying for compensation or receiving compensation) by itself is associated with increased symptomatology or disability and there are many possible explanations for such a relationship independent of malingering.

There are many constructs that are often confused with malingering, for example, response bias, poor effort, and symptom validity. Some of these sometimes represent a thinly veiled euphemism for malingering. However, the determination of malingering requires careful consideration of what may be involved in the differential diagnosis. There may be particular difficulty distinguishing between what appears to be exaggerated or excessive problems due to malingering vs. a variety of other reasons that may account for the behavior or results identified.

There has been difficulty studying malingering because there are so few actual malingerers who are unambiguously identified and available for study. Most of the research involves simulation studies, often with students or community volunteers instructed to simulate the problems associated with the disorder or condition of interest, but the performance of subjects instructed to malinger may not represent how actual malingerers behave and, more importantly, such studies may not include relevant comparison groups. Despite a proliferation of methods and assessment techniques, there is still no "gold standard" or unambiguous "test" of malingering. Indeed, catching one "in flagrante delicto" may be the most clear cut evidence of malingering but this is uncommon and there are many possible explanations for less striking discrepancies between reported accident or injury related problems and observed behaviors.

The field of neuropsychology has generated the most interest and research related to malingering, especially with regard to the differential diagnosis of mild TBI, the postconcussive syndrome, and related problems. It is often suspected that the person who does unusually poorly on neuropsychological examination or tests of symptom validity may be malingering, but there are many reasons why this can occur including that the person has other problems (e.g., pain, psychoemotional distress, sleep disturbance) that interfere with performance. Similarly, it is often suspected that the person who presents with unusually severe symptoms or disability may be malingering. With respect to chronic pain, a number of factors such as fear or pain avoidance, undue concern about the significance of bodily sensations, hypersensitivity associated with neurobiological or psychosocial factors, or other central sensitization effects may result in self-report of pain and related disability disproportionate to expectation on the basis of known pathology. It is often suspected that examinees who produce unusual elevations on psychological test indices, including the validity scales of multiscale personality inventories, may be malingering. However, persons with genuine PTSD or other psychoemotional problems responding honestly often produce such elevations, indicative of actual symptomatology including possible exaggeration or magnification of complaint for psychological reasons other than malingering. In such cases, validity scale elevations should be considered as yellow or red flags, indicating the need to further look for data to support or contradict the hypothesis that the person may be exaggerating or malingering.

Despite a proliferation of proposed measures and extensive study, individual psychological techniques can only suggest the possibility of malingering, and the differential diagnosis must involve careful consideration of multiple sources of information and other possible explanations for the behavior. Nonetheless, the results obtained from some techniques, for example, significantly below chance levels of performance on symptom validity testing, provide strong evidence of conscious dissimulation and possible malingering although such findings may sometimes represent a false positive result. Most of the measures utilized for the identification of malingering in TBI or other neuropsychological assessment rely upon below cut-off levels of performance on various symptom validity tests or actual measures of neuropsychological function. However, again, there is evidence that a variety of other problems may interfere with performance on such instruments resulting in poor scores, and interpretation should therefore also consider all reasonably possible causes.

Although there are important caveats, unusually poor performance on symptom validity or standard neuropsychological measures should alert the examiner to the possibility of malingering. In this regard, within the context of neuropsychological examinations, we would recommend use of relatively well studied measures such as the Digit Memory Test, the Portland Digit Recognition Test, the Test of Memory Malingering, the Word Memory Test, the Amsterdam Short Term Memory Test, the Victoria Symptom Validity Test, and the Reliable Digit Span index, to name just a few. Readers are referred to Chapter 16 (Malingering: Traumatic Brain Injury) and the original sources for further information. Whereas some of these measures may be relatively sensitive or specific, further work is required to better establish their relative utility.

If an examinee does score below recommended cut-offs specified in the test manuals or otherwise in the literature, then the examiner needs to decide why this may be. Malingering is only one of several possible explanations. Other possible explanations include deliberately poor performance for the purposes of assuming the "sick role" (i.e., Factitious Disorder), poor effort due to a wide variety of reasons (e.g., disinterest in the assessment process, passive-aggressive or oppositional behavior), and actual interference effects on level of performance (e.g., due to pain, sleep disturbance, medication side effects, psychiatric disturbance, neurologic disorder). A number of other observations or sources of information may help to clarify the diagnosis. If there are unusual or improbable symptoms, not explainable on the basis of other causes, then the index of suspicion may be raised. However, it should be realized that there are numerous symptoms that continue to defy explanation, many of which may represent some somatization or psychophysiological process. Discrepancies in behavior, such as reporting that one is unable to do something but demonstrating capacity in another context, may also be indicative of malingering, but such discrepancies may also be explainable on the basis of various other causes, for example, the generally poor correspondence between self-report and actual capabilities. Examiners need to be familiar with the range of behaviors that may be presented within a medicolegal context, including very good familiarity with the specific presenting problems (e.g., TBI, chronic pain, PTSD), and be able to assess whether behavior is unusual and suggestive of malingering. Similarly, unusual patterns of neuropsychological performance (e.g., better delayed than immediate recall or even recognition memory) may raise the suspicion of possible malingering, but such unusual patterns of performance may be seen for other reasons. In contrast with several other conditions (e.g., PTSD), the validity scale indices of the MMPI-2 are not generally highly elevated in TBI and so, if unusual elevations are observed, increased suspicion that the person may be malingering is warranted. However, if there are comorbid problems such as significant PTSD or depression, there may be more significant validity scale elevations that do not indicate malingering. Furthermore, if these psychoemotional difficulties exist or if there is a significant pain problem, then clinical scale elevations would also be expected. The MMPI-2 FBS validity scale has been suggested to be more sensitive to malingering than other MMPI-2 validity scales with personal injury claimants but we, and others, think that this scale primarily assesses psychological states other than malingering although, in at least some cases, it may also be sensitive to malingering.

In some cases there will be clear and consistent evidence that the person is malingering, for example, all available medical information indicates that there had been little if any physical or psychological injury at all or, occasionally, that the person had not even been involved in the accident, injury, or trauma in question; the person presents with quite improbable or even absurd symptoms, readily discernible as such to the experienced assessor; the person is observed to engage in activities that have clearly been reported to be impossible; the person appears manipulative and evasive when asked about material that may reveal that he or she is malingering; the person scores at significantly below chance levels of performance on symptom validity testing or well below accepted cut-offs, with no other plausible reason for failure; the person performs extremely poorly on standard neuropsychological testing, with no other plausible reason for failure, and is observed to engage in activities that are markedly discrepant with results of formal testing; the person produces elevations on multiscale inventories such as the MMPI-2 that are suggestive of malingering and that could not be explained on the basis of other indicators of significant psychopathology. In many cases, however, there will be less clear evidence of possible malingering in the assessment of TBI. When the evidence is less obvious, the assessor must carefully weigh the convergent (i.e., indicating possible malingering) and divergent (i.e., not indicating malingering) evidence to decide how strong a statement may be made concerning the possibility of malingering.

There has also been considerable study of what may be useful signs of malingering in chronic pain, but several reviewers have concluded that there are no reliable or valid indicators. In contrast, there is growing realization of the complicated interplay of psychosocial and biomedical factors contributing to presentation in chronic pain that may make the differential diagnosis of malingering especially difficult. Some indicators, for example, the Waddell signs, have often been misinterpreted as indicative of malingering. Caveats concerning interpretation of other clinical signs should be considered carefully. Various pharmacological agents, for example, sodium amytal, may be helpful in distinguishing various aspects of pain problems including central sensitization, but none provide a "truth serum."

Whereas detailed analysis of facial behavior in those experiencing actual pain or simulating pain has revealed some differences, for example, that the simulation of pain is often a caricature of the real behavior, differences are typically not clear cut, and many or most observers can only rather poorly distinguish between real and simulated pain on this basis. Signal detection theory indices of response bias and discriminability have demonstrated a number of psychosocial or biomedical effects on the self-report of pain, but this methodology has not yet been applied to the determination of malingering. Unlike many psychiatric disorders, but similar to TBI, multiscale validity indicators in chronic pain are often within normal limits and not indicative of "faking bad," exaggeration, malingering, or related response sets. In contrast, many chronic pain patients present with a socially desirable response set (sometimes interpreted as "faking good") and a tendency to view themselves and others in a positive manner. If the "fake bad" validity scales are significantly elevated (e.g., using cutting scores as recommended by Rogers, Sewell, Martin, & Vitacco, 2003), and there are not significant comorbid psychiatric problems, these may be useful in identification of possible malingering. Other self-report techniques may elicit unusual responses (i.e., unusually high rates of symptom endorsement) in those simulating chronic pain, but further study is required to better establish what may be reliable and valid cutting scores.

Measures of performance using various indicators of strength, effort, or functional ability testing had been widely utilized in assessing chronic pain patients, but reviews of the literature indicate that these techniques generally lack validity or are not reliable, and that findings may be accounted for by reasons other than poor effort or malingering, for example, by fear or pain avoidance behaviors. It has recently been suggested that symptom validity testing, as is widely used in neuropsychological assessment, may usefully be applied to the detection of malingering, poor effort, or related constructs with chronic pain patients. Whereas significantly below chance levels of performance may be strong evidence of conscious dissimulation in chronic pain, we would otherwise strongly caution against the use of such techniques for determination of malingering (poor effort, etc.) with this population until it can be determined whether a variety of chronic pain and related problems might not be associated with poor performance due to actual interference effects, and what should be appropriate cutting scores.

As with TBI, there may be clear evidence of malingering in chronic pain in some cases. There may be evidence that the person had not actually been injured or, that any injuries incurred could not possibly account for presentation; there may be gross discrepancies between reported disability and observed (often surreptitiously) abilities; pain behavior may be obviously insincere on clinical observation; there may be significantly below chance levels of performance on symptom validity testing; or there may be elevation of MMPI-2 validity scale indices (e.g., using cut-offs suggested by Rogers et al., 2003) in the absence of evidence of any more severe psychopathology. However, in many cases, there will not be such clear cut evidence, and the psychologist must carefully assess all possible indicators. Given that operant reinforcement of pain behavior associated with solicitous significant others, or many other psychological mechanisms, may be instrumental in the presentation of chronic pain patients, these must carefully be considered in the differential diagnosis. Readers are referred to Chapter 17 (Malingering: Chronic Pain) for further information.

The detection of malingering in PTSD or depression has relied much more exclusively upon elevation of multiscale validity indicators, in particular, the several MMPI-2 validity scales. Whereas these scales may effectively distinguish between experimental subjects simulating disorder and actual patients, patients who are more severely affected or have comorbid problems often also have marked elevations on validity scales. As such, these indicators may provide information about possible malingering, but one must very carefully consider all relevant information including whether the person had actually experienced a traumatic event, to what degree symptoms actually interfere in life activity, behavior during interview, independent sources of information about the person's behavior, and other psychometrics. Again, in some cases, there may be clear evidence that the person is malingering but, in many or most cases, it may be less apparent. In ambiguous cases, as is true for TBI and chronic pain patients, it may be helpful to have the benefit of closely monitored behavioral interventions and extended observation in order to determine what may be the relevant causal factors. Readers are referred to Chapter 18 (Malingering: Posttraumatic Stress Disorder and

Depression) as well as Chapter 11 (Conducting a Psychological Assessment) by Kane in this volume for further information.

Ongoing research into the utility or refinement of existing measures, as well as development of new measures, is expected to produce better psychometric indicators of malingering and clearer distinction between malingering and other constructs or behaviors that may be involved in the presentation of persons undergoing forensic or other evaluations. Techniques that are currently experimental (e.g., fMRI, electrophysiological indices, computerized speech analysis) may well become more widely utilized with further study and development.

Whereas the possibility of malingering should be considered in all forensic evaluations, any conclusions about this being the reason for a person's presentation must be considered carefully. Of course, the possibility that a person is malingering should not be raised on the basis of frivolous or poorly considered information for the purposes of raising doubt about the person's integrity. Professional and other guidelines caution about ethical transgressions (Martelli, 2005; Martelli & Zasler, 2002; Nicholson, 2005). However, we believe that the forensic psychologist or other mental health assessor should comment on this issue if appropriate, rather than only letting the courts decide as others have suggested. Indeed, the complexity of behavioral issues involved in the differential diagnosis of malingering strongly argues for explicit professional opinion, when appropriate. The psychologist who suspects malingering or related behavior in an assessee must provide an opinion based on a comprehensive evaluation, use of appropriate psychological instruments, and a reasoned logic evaluating all of the available evidence. Any specific conclusions about malingering, one way or another, risk *Daubert* challenges or cross-examination in court, and the psychologist should be well prepared to justify the science in the assessment undertaken, the instruments used, and the literature supporting the conclusions offered.

References

Martelli, M. F. (2005). Ethical challenges in the neuropsychology of pain, Part 1. In S. S. Bush (Ed.), *A casebook of ethical challenges in neuropsychology* (pp. 113–123). New York: Swets & Zeitlinger.

Martelli, M. F., & Zasler, N. D. (2002). Ethics and objectivity in medicolegal contexts: Recommendations for experts. In R. B. Weiner (Ed.), *Pain management: A practical guide for clinicians* (6th ed., pp. 895–908). Boca Ratan, FL: St. Lucie Press.

Nicholson, K. (2005). Ethical challenges in the neuropsychology of pain, Part 2. In S. S. Bush, (Ed.), *A casebook of ethical challenges in neuropsychology* (pp. 124–129). New York: Swets & Zeitlinger.

Rogers, R., Sewell, K. W., Martin, M. A., & Vitacco, M. (2003). Detection of feigned mental disorders: A meta-analysis of the MMPI-2 and malingering. *Assessment, 10*, 160–177.

Section IV

Causality, Psychology, and Law

20

Causation, Psychology, and Law

DANIEL W. SHUMAN AND JENNIFER L. HARDY

Is There Order to the Universe?

Does psychological distress result from an orderly, comprehensible, and predictable process, or is there unpredictable, incomprehensible randomness to the experience of psychological distress? These are the extreme points of view which bracket the complex question whether a psychological order to the universe exists. Sometimes, asking the right question is the critical endeavor, however, it is critically important not only to ask this grand question but also to answer it correctly as well. The answer to this question matters to psychology in its effort to reduce psychological distress from traumatic events and to law in its effort to assess responsibility for the consequences of wrongful events. The answer is not intuitively obvious and, unfortunately, has been the subject of precious little critical analysis from the lens of law and psychology. Using the question of the existence of a psychological order to the universe to anchor the analysis, this chapter first explores the legal rules that govern proof of causation of psychological harm in personal injury actions and their rationale. It then critically explores alternative models that the courts have applied for proof of psychological harm. Finally, after consideration of the psychological, moral, and economic imperatives served by the requirement of causation, it offers a new perspective for assessing the admissibility of expert evidence providing a causal link between tortious behavior and compensable psychological harm.

Although traumatic events and psychological distress may appear intuitively linked, there is much evidence to suggest that there is a significant element of randomness and incomprehensibility to the causes of psychological distress. Some people who experience horrific events suffer psychological scars that significantly and permanently diminish their lives. Others who experience events of equivalent severity do not suffer equivalent psychological scars, raising fundamental questions about how integrally horrific events and psychological harm are linked. Some of the most striking evidence of the difference in psychological responses to horrific events is found in the research addressing Posttraumatic Stress Disorder (PTSD), a mental disorder whose etiology is explicitly linked to a traumatic event. Although many people exposed to traumatic events develop PTSD, most do not (Bonanno, 2004). Contrary to commonly held beliefs, traumatic events do not inevitably and invariably lead to serious psychological distress (Lilienfeld, 2002). Child sexual abuse, a horrific act that is commonly thought to produce profound psychological scars in all of its victims, provides a thought provoking example of the problem of linking traumatic events and psychological harm. Recent review of the research on the psychological consequences of child sexual abuse reveals a less robust correlation between abuse and psychopathology than had been commonly assumed (Rind, Tromovitch, & Bauserman, 1998; but see Dallam et al., 2001). Studies of college students who were sexually abused as children revealed that they were only slightly less well adjusted than control groups. While these findings should not be understood to suggest that the consequence of child sexual abuse is invariably harmless or benign, they do suggest that the causal relationship between abuse and psychopathology is less well understood than previously thought.

It follows from this brief review of the research that we must rethink our ability to predict the psychological scars (i.e., the monetary damages that should be awarded to compensate for consequential psychological harm) that child sexual abuse will produce in any individual case. If the consequences of similar horrific acts of child abuse do not inevitably produce psychopathology, what does that imply for the ability to predict the psychological consequences of less horrific, less similar acts? And, if we cannot accurately predict the psychological consequences of horrific events in individual cases, how can we explain or postdict the causes of psychological trauma in people who have been exposed to horrific events (Simon & Shuman, 2002)?

Looking at psychological distress that occurs in the absence of horrific events is also enlightening. Many people who experience psychopathology that significantly diminishes their lives have not experienced horrific events but are dealing with daily stresses, past issues, relationship stresses, work difficulties, family issues, and so on. The absence of trauma does not invariably lead to the absence of psychological distress, and, conversely, the presence of psychological distress does not provide any assurance that it was preceded by a traumatic event. Some people not exposed to horrific events experience severe psychopathology (Thompson, 2004). Many other factors seem to play a significant role in psychopathology apart from traumatic events. The multiplicity and interaction of these factors make it difficult to predict or postdict why one person succumbs to inevitable stressors, another rises above her circumstances, and yet another fails to take advantage of his station in life. Understanding this perplexing causal conundrum is fundamental to the goals of both psychology and law.

Why We Should Care about Order in the Universe

For mental health clinicians and researchers, understanding the causal relationship between traumatic events and psychopathology plays an important role in preventing and treating psychological harm. To "innoculate" against psychological harm from traumatic events it is important to understand why some exposed to traumatic events develop psychopathology and others do not. Exposure to traumatic events is not a rare occurrence in our society. Numerous surveys reveal that nearly three-quarters of the U.S. population have been exposed to one or more traumatic events including rape, sexual molestation, child abuse and neglect, robbery, life threatening accidents and natural disasters, and combat (Green & Kaltman, 2003). As noted above, although many people exposed to traumatic events develop PTSD, most people exposed to traumatic events do not develop PTSD. Understanding the relationship between traumatic events and their psychological sequela is critical to mitigate the harm that traumatic events may produce. Should we encourage everyone to talk about their exposure to traumatic events (as litigation implicitly encourages) to reduce the likelihood of psychological distress from these events (Neria & Solomon, 1999)? Or, as some research suggests, is it preferable, at least for some people who have experienced traumatic events, to avoid talking about unpleasant experiences (implicitly discouraging litigation) (Bonanno, Keltner, Holen, & Horowitz, 1995)? What explains why some people exposed to traumatic events experience severe psychological distress and others do not? Given the incidence of traumatic events, these are not idle inquiries.

When psychological harm associated with traumatic events result, do all those exposed to the events need to be treated? Should the same treatment be used for all? What distinguishes the need for treatment and whether pharmacological (Sutherland & Davidson, 1999), behavioral (Saigh, Yasik, Oberfield, & Inamdar, 1999), cognitive-behavioral (Meadows & Foa, 1999), or group therapy (Shay & Munroe, 1999) best reduces the duration and severity of psychological distress? And what does the success or failure of a particular treatment suggest about the cause of the harm?

For the researcher, these questions address matters of general causation, not specific causation. Researchers do not attempt to ascertain, for example, what caused psychological harm in any particular case, but instead study questions of general causation, the kinds of harm that groups of people exposed to particular events experience (i.e., nomothetic approach). For the clinician, what matters is specific causation. The clinician is concerned with what caused this particular patient's psychological distress (i.e., idiographic approach). For clinicians, the determination of specific causation may be an evolving process subject to revision, even after the initial assessment.

Causation also plays a fundamental role in affixing responsibility, the business of the law. Thus, the question of whether there is a psychological coherence to the universe matters to the law as well as psychology. Unless psychological distress occurs in an orderly, comprehensible process for the group (i.e., general causation) and therefore for the individual (i.e., specific causation), it is not logically possible to affix responsibility for causing that distress. If the cause of psychological harm is unknown or unknowable, what might justify holding a defendant responsible to compensate the plaintiff for that harm in a fault-based liability system? Our jurisprudence does not entitle someone who has been injured to be compensated merely because injury occurred. To the contrary, the default answer in our legal system is that accidental injury is not to be compensated by a third party and that its costs are to borne by the person who was injured. "The general principle of our law is that loss from accident must lie where it falls." (Holmes, 1946, p. 76). What justification is there for the law to shift the burden of loss from the person on whom it has fallen to another person if the responsibility for causing the harm through wrongful conduct is unknown or unknowable?

However its specific legal requirements are framed, causation is fundamental to a fault-based system of liability. The specific formulation of the legal requirements of causation presents challenges that are as or more perplexing than those faced by researchers and clinicians addressing the causation of psychological distress. Unlike the researcher who only addresses general causation, the law must address both general causation (i.e., this incident is capable of causing this category of harm) and specific causation (i.e., this incident caused the harm in this case). And, unlike the clinician whose assessment can be continually modified in light of new information, the legal doctrine of preclusion (i.e., *res judicata*, claim preclusion) requires that the law determine causation in ways that are not subject to revision at a later date, in claims that must be initiated in a timely manner as dictated by the applicable statute of limitations (typically 1 to 2 years after the claim arises for personal injury claims). Thus, the legal task is demanding and inevitably poses choices that will determine which cases may proceed in the face of uncertainty.

Using a Thought Disorder to Think More Clearly about Causation, Psychology, and Law

In examining the approaches to the requirement for proof of causation of psychological harm that the law has taken, it is useful to compare different approaches to similar harm, or one exemplar, to reduce confounding variation that may explain a difference in approach. For this reason, the analysis begins by comparing judicial decisions about proof of causation for psychological harm in personal injury cases asserting a single unique claim that the defendant's tortious conduct caused the plaintiff to develop Schizophrenia. Although it is generally not necessary in a personal injury action, or necessarily advisable, for the plaintiff to offer or the court to admit expert testimony in support of the claim grounded in a specific mental disorder (Greenberg, Shuman, & Meyer, 2004), let alone Schizophrenia, it occurs. When it does occur, it coincidentally presents an interesting vehicle to study a set of cases addressing psychological testimony about causation addressing allegations of similar harm. Because the assertion that the defendant caused the plaintiff to develop Schizophrenia is so unusual in the personal injury setting, it brings a fresh perspective to the analysis of causation, psychology, and law. Schizophrenia is a well researched mental disorder, which has a common diagnostic definition amongst mental health professionals, thereby facilitating research on the disorder and its etiology (Heinrichs, 2001), and, in particular, the role that stressful events may play in its development (Walker & Diforio, 1997). Although it is a well researched disorder, the purpose of the focus on Schizophrenia in this chapter is not to ascertain whether existing research supports the conclusion that tortious behavior can cause Schizophrenia, but rather to examine the different ways in which courts address the admissibility of expert evidence on its causation in personal injury claims.

The Diagnostic and Statistical Manual of Mental Disorders (*DSM IV-TR*) (American Psychiatric Association, 2000), which describes diagnostic features; subtypes; recording procedures; associated features; culture, age, and gender features; prevalence; course; family pattern; and differential diagnosis of mental disorders but not their etiology (except in the case of PTSD), categorizes Schizophrenia as a psychotic disorder with characteristic symptoms of cognitive and emotional dysfunction including perception, thought, language, volition, and attention. The *DSM* describes the important diagnostic aspects of Schizophrenia as a combination of characteristic symptoms and signs comprised of a range of cognitive and emotional dysfunctions that include delusions, hallucinations, disorganized speech, grossly disorganized or catatonic behavior, and negative symptoms (i.e., affective flattening, alogia, or avolition). These signs and symptoms are related to impaired social or occupational functioning. The *DSM* specifies a durational requirement for the symptoms to justify the diagnosis; they should be present for a lengthy amount of time during a 1-month period, with continuous signs of the disorder lasting for at least 6 months.

A diagnosis of Schizophrenia is not warranted if the disturbance is better accounted for by Schizoaffective Disorder or a Mood Disorder with Psychotic Features or is due to the direct physiological effects of a substance or a general medical condition. In individuals with a previous diagnosis of a Pervasive Developmental Disorder, the additional diagnosis of Schizophrenia is warranted only if prominent delusions or hallucinations are present for at least 1-month.

Whatever skepticism exists about whether mental illness is real, whether psychiatric nosology rests on science or whether it has been misshaped by values, politics, or economics (Gorenstein, 1984; Sadler, 2004), there is a consensus amongst mainstream mental health professionals that Schizophrenia describes a genuine mental disorder. As contrasted with less severe, transitory forms of mental distress that may invoke doubts about the subjectivity or verifiability of a plaintiff's claim of mental or emotional loss, a claim that the defendant's conduct caused the plaintiff to develop Schizophrenia presents an assertion of a severe disorder with agreed diagnostic criteria, as well as a body of research on the use of diagnostic tools (Munley, Busby, & Jaynes, 1997). It is easier to test ideas about the cause of Schizophrenia because of an understanding about what it is and reliability data on its diagnosis.

Importantly, there is no apparent reason to tolerate different levels of rigor necessary to support causal links to the same mental disorder in personal injury litigation. No cogent policy exists to suggest that all claims asserting that the defendant's wrongful conduct caused the plaintiff to develop Schizophrenia should not be required to satisfy the same level of threshold scrutiny across cases. Attempts to prove the same effects should, logically, be subject to the same admissibility requirements (Shuman, 2003). Thus, it is interesting that courts have taken two contrasting positions in their threshold scrutiny of expert testimony seeking to link tortious events and Schizophrenia. One approach has demanded that the expert provide scientific research to support the linkage between the tortious event and Schizophrenia. The other approach has asked only that the expert be qualified and has left scrutiny of the linkage between the tortious event and Schizophrenia to the fact finder.

The Scientific Model

Newton v. Roche Laboratories, Inc. (2002) is a federal district court decision that illustrates the approach demanding scientific research to support linking the defendant's conduct and the Schizophrenia the plaintiff claims it caused. The plaintiff in *Newton* claimed that her use of Accutane, a drug manufactured and sold by Roche Laboratories for the treatment of severe acne, caused her to develop Schizophrenia. The plaintiff offered two expert witnesses to support her assertion of a causal linkage between Accutane and Schizophrenia. The first witness, Dr. James O'Donnell, would have testified regarding general causation that Accutane was pharmacologically capable of causing Schizophrenia. The trial court granted the defendant's motion to exclude O'Donnell's testimony, not only because of its doubts about his qualifications (he was neither an M.D. nor Ph.D.), but also because of its doubts about the science underlying his opinion:

> Although the Court's decision that O'Donnell is not qualified to render an opinion on general causation in this case is enough to grant the motion to exclude his testimony, the Court will also briefly discuss the reliability of O'Donnell's testimony. O'Donnell's first contention is that Accutane is "an analog of Vitamin A" and, therefore, it will "share many of the side-effects experienced with Vitamin A." … . In his report, O'Donnell lists the "typical" side effects he believes result from ingesting too much Vitamin A, including "acute Schizophrenia or remitting psychosis." Id. at 4–5. For this opinion to be admissible, O'Donnell must have a reliable scientific basis to support not only (1) a causal relationship between Vitamin A and psychiatric side-effects, but also (2) his assertion that Accutane will also produce these side-effects. He has shown neither … .The only support O'Donnell cites for his opinion that ingestion of large doses of Vitamin A causes "acute Schizophrenia and remitting psychosis" comes in the form of isolated anecdotal case reports, including an Arctic explorer's journal from the mid-nineteenth century. He admittedly relies on no epidemiological or clinical studies (pp. 679–680).

The plaintiff offered a second expert, Dr. Lyle Rossiter, a clinical psychiatrist, to address the issue of specific causation. This expert opined that Accutane caused this plaintiff's Schizophrenia. The trial court also excluded Dr. Rossiter on the defendant's motion finding that his opinion based on a temporal association between the use of Accutane and the Schizophrenia, and the package inserts warnings provided by the defendant, as well as the Physician's Desk Reference, was insufficient to support the claimed causal linkage in the absence of controlled studies.

> The Court finds this opinion inadmissible because Dr. Rossiter had no reliable basis for it. To establish specific causation (that a product was the cause-in-fact of plaintiff's injury), an expert must demonstrate a "specific train of medical evidence" connecting the illness to the product. *Black, 171 F.3d at 314*. In his attempt to provide this "specific train of medical evidence," Dr. Rossiter admits that he is unable to rely upon any controlled studies showing that Accutane causes psychosis. [*See* Rossiter Rep. at 6.] In fact, he readily agreed that it is not generally accepted in the medical community either that Accutane serves as a "biochemical insult" to the brain or that Accutane causes or aggravates Schizophrenia. (p. 682)

In addition, to support its exclusion of Dr. Rossiter, the district court noted the expert's failure to account for the plaintiff's family background and history, which presented alternative "accepted" risk factors for the development of Schizophrenia.

Newton v. Roche Laboratories, Inc. illustrates a threshold requirement for expert testimony about proof of causation of psychological harm grounded in the demands of science, which assumes that qualifications are necessary but not a substitute for well designed research examining the linkage between the defendant's wrongful act and the plaintiff's harm. It assumes that proof of causation of psychological harm, in this case Schizophrenia, requires the existence of a comprehensible, predictable psychological order to the universe (i.e., Schizophrenia does not occur randomly but only occurs in response to specific causes, and whether Schizophrenia can be caused by Accutane is a discernable scientific question), and that without rigorous scientific proof of that order and the defendant's role in it, it is not appropriate for an expert to offer an opinion regarding the defendant's responsibility for discrete psychological harm. See also *Blanchard v. Eli Lilly* (2002).

The Qualifications Model

The qualifications model is illustrated by the decision of the Supreme Court of Pennsylvania in *Smith v. German* (1969). The plaintiff in *Smith* claimed he developed Schizophrenia as the result of an automobile accident caused by the defendant's negligence. Without demanding evidence that a body of scientific research exists demonstrating that automobile accidents or equivalent traumatic events can result in Schizophrenia in all or some well defined subset of the population that there is some way to ascertain whether this accident was the cause of this plaintiff's Schizophrenia, let alone whether *DSM-II* (1968), as well as its diagnostic category for Schizophrenia, rests on good science, the court concerned itself exclusively with whether expert testimony would be required to support this link and not whether any experts, however well qualified, could scientifically link automobile accidents and Schizophrenia. *Smith* was decided in 1969, and much has occurred in the law of evidence since then. But lest there be any doubt about its continued viability, *Smith* was extensively quoted and cited with approval by the Pennsylvania Supreme Court in *Montgomery v. Bazaz-Sehgal* (2002). See also *Green v. K-Mart Corp.* (2003); *Taylor v. Burlington Northern Railroad Co.* (1986); *Steinhauser v. Hertz* (1970).

Smith does not purport to address inquiries regarding universal psychological coherence but focuses on practical problems facing the trial court. In a case in which the jury is permitted to award damages for proximately caused psychological harm, the court viewed its choice to be to require the jury to be assisted by qualified experts or to permit the jury to sort these matters out on their own. For the *Smith* court, once there was a legally cognizable claim of psychological harm, the important question was whether expert testimony was required to support this claim and, if so, who is a qualified expert to address the harm, not the reliability of the science underlying the expert's testimony.

There may, of course, be something to be said for the adoption of each model. Certainly, neither model is devoid of logic. However, it is difficult to understand why we should simultaneously tolerate both approaches to proof of causation of Schizophrenia in personal injury actions. Schizophrenia is a well researched mental disorder. There is no cogent reason to demand that some, but not all experts offering testimony regarding some causes of Schizophrenia, be grounded in rigorous scientific research. Whether the claimed cause of the plaintiff's Schizophrenia is a drug, an automobile accident, or workplace sexual harassment, each of these causal attributions present the same kinds of questions of general and specific causation—what is known about the cause(s) of Schizophrenia that should lead us to think that this act or event is capable of causing Schizophrenia and why should we think it caused the plaintiff's Schizophrenia? The decision to adopt one of these models, or even a third model, as a foundational requirement to address causation has important implications for law as well as forensic psychology and psychiatry, which requires explorations of the role of causation in the law and its relation to psychological harm.

Why Causation Matters to the Law

Causation matters to the law, in part, for tangible, utilitarian reasons. It is important that tort judgments deter those defendants, but only those defendants, whose wrongful conduct has caused harm and, that tort judgments compensate those plaintiffs, but only those plaintiffs, who experienced harm that was caused by the defendant's wrongful conduct (Shuman, 1993; Shuman, 1994). Imposing tort sanctions that deter defendants who have not caused harm risks dissuading people from engaging in socially useful activities. Failing to impose tort sanctions that deter defendants who have caused harm risks encouraging people to engage in socially harmful activities. Awarding tort damages that compensate plaintiffs who have not experienced harm caused by the defendant's wrongful conduct takes money from the wrong person and may give it to the wrong person. Failing to award tort damages that compensate plaintiffs who experience harm caused by the defendant's wrongful conduct leaves the plaintiff to bear the costs of an injury caused by the wrongful conduct of another or to seek compensation from another who did not cause the harm. In addressing these concerns with deterrence and compensation, causation matters to the law in ways that dollars account.

But causation also matters to the law in other important ways for which dollars do not account. This other framework to understand the legal role of causation in tort law arises instead from a focus on matters of blame and moral responsibility. "Attributing blame is a pervasive human phenomenon. It is one way in which we order and make sense of social experience and it is reflected in our language and social practices" (Kadish, 1985, p. 329). In our everyday lives we make moral judgments about blameworthiness for harm (Hart & Honoré, 1985). Assigning blame entails a judgment about responsibility. These moral judgments assigning blame for harm have broad social consequences as well as deeply personal implications, which, unrequited, risk social and personal upheaval. To quell the primal desire for vengeance and to facilitate the balm provided by a sense of moral symmetry, apart from the exchange of money that furthers compensation and deterrence, tort law offers those injured by negligent or intentional wrongdoing a forum for assessing blame and assigning responsibility for harm.

Evidence of the significance of this role of tort law for which dollars do not account can be found in the behavior of litigants. Some plaintiffs institute tort claims and obtain a judgment finding the defendant's conduct to be wrongful, even where there is little chance of financially satisfying any judgment obtained (Feldthusen, 1993). And, some tort plaintiffs who do collect large damage awards assert that they find the process for assessing responsibility more beneficial than the receipt of the monetary award (Shuman, 1994). For many who suffer injury, tort law's process for assessing blame and responsibility for causing harm is much more than an effort to obtain a monetary award for its own sake.

Legal decisions, and in particular tort decisions, provide a structured process to craft moral judgments about responsibility that mollify societal and personal discord, helping to justify the law and legitimize its authority. It is a critical aspect of why we obey the law. In exchange for forsaking tribal blood feud, we agree, without knowing whether we will find ourselves playing the role of an alleged wrongdoer or victim, to participate in a litigation process that offers victims (and wrongdoers) a voice, respect, and control (Tyler, 1990). Legal judgments must correctly determine causation for wrongdoing not merely because it produces a just outcome in a particular case, but because causation is central to the legitimization of the law's role as a therapeutic alternative to vengeance (Wexler & Winick, 1991).

These moral, psychological, as well as economic imperatives, highlight why it is important that the law be confident in the accuracy of its conclusions regarding the harm that a defendant's conduct has caused. Wrongdoers must be held accountable for the psychological harm they have caused and, conversely, must not be held accountable for psychological harm they have not caused. This necessitates a trustworthy mechanism to sort out psychological distress suffered which can be attributed to a wrongdoer and that which cannot, grounded in the general legal rules for causation and the special rules that govern recovery for psychological harm.

How the Law Has Ordered Psychological Causation

To recover damages under tort law for an injury, a plaintiff must prove, among other things, that the defendant's wrongful (i.e., negligent or intentional) act or omission, more likely than not, was a cause-in-fact of plaintiff's injury. In most jurisdictions, this cause-in-fact requirement is satisfied by proof that the plaintiff's injury would not have occurred "but for" the defendant's wrongful conduct (*Cole v. Shell Petroleum Corp.*, 1939). This elemental requirement is a cornerstone of modern tort law. "The 'but for' test occupies such a position of prominence because it is thought to mark the line between mere temporal succession and true causation" (Moore, 2003, p. 1184). This test poses the question of causation in the negative. Does the evidence support the conclusion that if the defendant's conduct had not occurred, the same result would have obtained? Only if the result would have differed had the negligence not occurred, does the defendant's negligence satisfy the requirement for the cause-in-fact of the injury.

An interesting example of the "but for" rule's application in the case of a tort claimant seeking to recover damages for psychological harm is provided by the case of *Jeffress v. Reddy* (2003). In *Jeffress*, a former patient sued a psychiatric center, physician, and nurse for negligence in the treatment of PTSD which she claimed resulted in numerous injuries including nausea, headaches, insomnia, and anxiety. The trial court granted the defendants' motion for summary judgment and dismissed the case without trial on causation grounds that are commonly asserted in mental health malpractice cases. The trial court found, and the appellate court agreed, that even if the jury found that the defendants had been negligent in their care of the plaintiff, the plaintiff had not offered competent expert testimony from which the jury could find that the defendants' negligence, rather than her preexisting problems that brought her to treatment, was the cause of her suffering.

> Plaintiff wanted to call Dr. Edward Wolpert and Dr. Nicolas Stratas as her expert witnesses. First we note that neither Dr. Wolpert nor Dr. Stratas examined or diagnosed the plaintiff. Both expert witnesses relied upon her past medical records and her own declaration of her conditions. Both Dr. Wolpert and Dr. Stratas expressed that if the defendants had properly managed Mr. Jeffress's bipolar disorder, the plaintiff would not have suffered as she did. However, neither expert took into account the additional "stressors" in the plaintiff's life at the time of her treatment—her embezzlement trial, her other financial difficulties, and her own pre-existing mental problems. Dr. Wolpert stated that the plaintiff's prosecution, and conviction, and her preexisting or existing Post Traumatic Stress Disorder, "[were] problems" and that Mr. Jeffress's mania "led to the difficulties" the Jeffresses experienced. The district court found, and we agree, that this testimony was insufficient to establish the causal link between the defendants' treatment of the plaintiff and any alleged injuries. Similarly, Dr. Stratas had only "vague general notions" of the other problems. To characterize these opinions on causation as within a reasonable degree of medical certainty when neither expert considered all of the surrounding circumstances would be improper. A jury would be forced to speculate that the defendants' treatment, and not the multitude of other possible causes, more likely than not, caused the plaintiff's alleged injuries (p. 632).

According to the "but for" test of causation, which the court determined that the plaintiff did not meet, to permit the fact finder to find in favor of the plaintiff, she was required to offer competent expert testimony that had the defendants not been negligent in her care, she would, more likely than not, have experienced a significantly better outcome in the treatment of her PTSD. If the outcome would not have differed even if the defendant was not negligent (i.e., competent treatment would have yielded the same outcome), the required causal linkage is not satisfied. This requirement that the plaintiff's harm be causally linked in this manner to the defendant's negligent act is captured in an oft quoted phrase: "Proof of negligence in the air, so to speak, will not do" (*Palsgraf v. Long Island R. Co.*, 1928, p. 99).

Because wrongful acts or omissions may have temporally and spatially remote consequences, the courts have concluded that it is not sufficient for a plaintiff merely to establish that a defendant has breached a duty to the plaintiff that was the cause-in-fact of the plaintiff's injuries. In negligence actions, as a matter of policy, courts recognize the necessity to draw a line limiting recovery to some proportional, but not all consequential harm, which the defendant's wrongful acts or omission caused (Schwartz, 1999). The formal application of this policy-based limitation requires that to recover, a plaintiff must also prove that in addition to being the cause-in-fact of the plaintiff's injuries, the defendant's culpable conduct was also the proximate cause of the plaintiff's injuries (*Doe v. Baxter Healthcare Corp.*, 2004).

Although there are numerous formulations of the test for proximate cause (Page, 2003), at their essence most use the lens of foreseeability, providing that the defendant is not responsible for harm caused by his or her wrongful conduct where that harm was not reasonably foreseeable because it is not a proximate cause of the plaintiff's injuries. Using this test, a court asks whether the defendant should have reasonably foreseen that as a result of his or her conduct that the general harm the plaintiff experienced would occur. Thus, the foreseeability test requires (i) a reasonably foreseeable harm and (ii) no superseding, intervening forces (i.e., new unforeseeable forces which join with the defendant's negligence to harm a plaintiff) (*Holmes v. Sec. Investor Prot. Corp.*, 1992).

The California Supreme Court's decision in *Molien v. Kaiser Found. Hospital* (1980) colorfully illustrates this foreseeability principle and its application to psychological harm. As the result of a laboratory error, Mrs. Molien's physician incorrectly informed her that she had a sexually transmitted disease. To ascertain how she could have contracted the disease, Mrs. Molien confronted her husband, he confessed to extra-marital relations, and the couple soon divorced. In an effort to give new meaning to the term chutzpah, when the defendant notified Mrs. Molien that it had erroneously informed her that she had a sexually transmitted disease, Mr. Molien sued the health care provider for his mental and emotional distress which he alleged was caused by the negligent disclosure. Although the defendant's pretrial motion to dismiss did not challenge whether its negligence met the requirements of a cause-in-fact of Mr. Molien's harm, it did move to dismiss asserting that any harm to Mr. Molien was not proximate to their acts with regard to Mrs. Molien. The trial court found these consequences too remote and dismissed without trial, but the Supreme Court of California reversed, finding that the connection was foreseeable, and to that extent presented a cognizable legal claim for harm whose cause the jury would be required to assess:

> In the case at bar the risk of harm to plaintiff was reasonably foreseeable to defendants. It is easily predictable that an erroneous diagnosis of syphilis and its probable source would produce marital discord and resultant emotional distress to a married patient's spouse; Dr. Kilbridge's advice to Mrs. Molien to have her husband examined for the disease confirms that plaintiff was a foreseeable victim of the negligent diagnosis. Because the disease is normally transmitted only by sexual relations, it is rational to anticipate that both husband and wife would experience anxiety, suspicion, and hostility when confronted with what they had every reason to believe was reliable medical evidence of a particularly noxious infidelity (p. 817).

Molien is an entertaining reminder that foreseeability is an elastic concept whose practical application may expand as well as contract the scope of liability.

A special aspect of the foreseeability requirement commonly known as the "egg-shell skull" rule also applies to psychological injury. Although the defendant is not responsible to compensate the plaintiff for preexisting harm or harm resulting from unforeseeable intervening causes, the defendant takes the plaintiff as he finds him or her (*Brackett v. Peters*, 1993). Thus, if the defendant drives negligently and collides with a person who has an unusually thin skull causing severe harm that this impact would not have caused to most others of sturdier build, the defendant is nonetheless liable for the severe, unforeseeable harm. Similarly, although the defendant is not required to compensate the plaintiff for the consequences of traumatic events caused by others' negligence, if the plaintiff is unusually sensitive and suffers severe psychological distress from a negligent event that others would not be foreseeably likely to experience, the negligent defendant is liable for causing this harm.

Lancaster v. Norfolk & Western Ry. Co. (1985) provides a useful example of the egg-shell skull rule and how it applies to psychological injuries. In *Lancaster*, another case involving Schizophrenia, the plaintiff, Gary Lancaster, claimed that he was threatened and assaulted by his supervisors at work and that his mental condition deteriorated, resulting in Schizophrenia. A defense psychological expert opined that the plaintiff was predisposed to developing Schizophrenia that would have been precipitated by some other traumatic event absent the supervisors' behavior. All of the expert witnesses in the case agreed that each incident with the supervisors built upon previous incidents and "precipitated a descent into madness from which Lancaster will never recover" (*Lancaster v. Norfolk & Western Ry. Co.*, 1985, p. 812). The railroad argued that the plaintiff's susceptibility to mental illness may have been exacerbated by earlier acts for which the railroad might not have been responsible and thus it should not be found to have caused the plaintiff's injuries. The Court of Appeals rejected this argument, concluding "under the 'thin skull', or more colorfully the 'egg-shell skull', rule, the railroad would be fully liable for the consequences of [a supervisor's] assault" (*Lancaster v. Norfolk & Western Ry. Co.*, 1985, p. 807). According to the Court of Appeals, the defendant took the plaintiff as it found him—including his predisposition to mental illness—and was therefore liable for the resulting Schizophrenia.

The History of the Special Rules Governing Proof of Cause of Mental and Emotional Harm

Not all harm caused by tortious wrongdoing is compensable. As a matter of policy, certain classes of harm, including claims for mental and emotional harm, have historically been singled out for disparate treatment. Courts in the United States have long been reticent to entertain claims for psychological harm. Based on a belief that claims for psychological harm are easy to feign, difficult to verify, potentially limitless in frequency and amount, or somehow less deserving, these claims have faced barriers not placed in the path of compensation claims for physical harm (*Mitchell v. Rochester Ry.*, 1896).

Reflecting a world view that distinguishes physical and mental disorder even as scientific discoveries blur this distinction (Bremner, 2003), courts have historically been hesitant to value a tort claimant's interest in peace of mind, as contrasted with corporal integrity (Bohlen, 1902; Prosser, 1971). When the defendant's intentional or negligent acts have been proved more likely than not to have been both the cause-in-fact and proximate cause of the plaintiff's physical harm (e.g., medical expenses, property damage) that loss is generally compensable without special limitation; mental or emotional harm is not. When the only result of a defendant's negligence is emotional distress (i.e. if there is neither physical harm nor any other separate source of tort liability) courts have been reluctant to permit recovery (*Mitchell v. Rochester Ry.*, 1896).

A striking contemporary example of this reticence to recognize claims for mental or emotional distress is found in the decision of the Supreme Court of Texas in *Boyles v. Kerr* (1993). The plaintiff and defendant were students who had dated and were sexually intimate. Unbeknownst to the plaintiff, the defendant videotaped their consensual sexual activities and distributed copies of the tape to friends and fellow university students which the plaintiff claimed, understandably, caused her embarrassment and emotional distress. She instituted a claim for negligent (i.e., careless) infliction of emotional distress rather than intentional (i.e., purposeful) infliction of emotional distress, apparently because of the intentional act exclusions contained in any relevant insurance policies that might otherwise have provided coverage. The trial court permitted the negligence case to proceed to the jury, which found for the plaintiff, but the Supreme Court of Texas reversed. Given the controversy that the high court's initial opinion provoked, it withdrew its first opinion and reissued another reaching the same result:

> In rejecting negligent infliction of emotional distress as an independent cause of action, we stated in the original opinion that "tort law cannot and should not attempt to provide redress

for every instance of rude, insensitive, or distasteful behavior, even though it may result in hurt feelings, embarrassment, or even humiliation." We made clear, however, that we did not consider Boyles' conduct to fall into that category, stating in part as follows.

The tort system can and does provide a remedy against those who engage in such conduct. But an independent cause of action for negligent infliction of emotional distress would encompass conduct far less outrageous than that involved here, and such a broad tort is not necessary to allow compensation in a truly egregious case such as this (pp. 601–602).

Within the hostile parameters toward claims for mental or emotional distress which judicial decisions like *Boyles v. Kerr* manifest, a series of exceptions has developed permitting recovery for psychological harm. One of the first exceptions to arise was in the case of intentional wrongdoing. A plaintiff may claim damages for purely psychological injuries if the defendants acted in a gross and wanton, malicious, willful, or indifferent manner and if such conduct was directed at the plaintiff (*Nwakpuda v. Falley's, Inc.*, 1998). Emotional distress claims in intentional tort cases are viewed with less skepticism than emotional distress claims in negligence cases. There are fewer intentional tort cases than negligence based claims, thereby limiting the number of such claims. There is also less concern with protecting the defendant from the financial consequences of intentional wrongdoing. And, courts intuit that psychological injuries are more likely to be genuinely experienced in the case of intentional torts. In the words of one court: "when a tortfeasor engages in extreme and outrageous intentional invasions of the plaintiff's mental and emotional tranquility, the outrageous conduct affords the necessary assurance of the validity of the claim" (*Seminole Pipeline Co. v. Broad Leaf Partners, Inc.*, 1998, p. 756).

Although intentional tort cases permit recovery of mental and emotional distress caused by the defendant's wrongful behavior, they present a number of practical difficulties that militate their potential for the recovery of these damage claims. Proving that the defendant's wrongdoing was intentional rather than merely negligent imposes a heavy burden on the plaintiff that often presents insurmountable problems of proof. And, liability insurance policies typically exclude coverage for intentional wrongdoing, making it impracticable to bring suit against judgment-proof wrongdoers (Pryor, 1997). Thus, the theoretical opportunity to pursue mental or emotional distress under an intentional tort claim is often impaired by practical considerations.

Rather than maintain an absolute rule barring claims for psychological harm in all negligence cases, ultimately most jurisdictions have sought to articulate practicable rules that permitted some narrow class of credible claims to proceed without deluging the courts. To accomplish this, from the impact rule to the zone of danger rule, the courts have wrestled with requirements for allowing recovery for emotional trauma in negligence claims based on the nexus of mental distress to the risk of physical injury. These categories of recovery sought to limit the number of cases in which such claims might be presented to those in which mental harm seemed verifiable and intuitively more likely.

The impact rule first permitted recovery of mental or emotional distress in negligence cases. Its structure relied upon the proximity of some negligence-based claims for mental or emotional distress to claims for physical injury. *Mitchell v. Rochester Ry.*, an 1896 New York case, is a frequently cited example of the impact rule. In *Mitchell*, the plaintiff was startled when the defendant's driver negligently drove a horse-drawn wagon up to plaintiff, stopping just short of colliding with her. Although the horses did not actually strike the plaintiff, she was frightened and suffered a miscarriage. At the trial, the plaintiff's medical expert offered testimony that the fright the plaintiff suffered was sufficient to cause the miscarriage. The trial court dismissed the plaintiff's claim and the Court of Appeals affirmed that dismissal. It concluded that in the absence of a physical impact, permitting the plaintiff's injury claim presented not only insurmountable problems of proof, but also risked a flood of litigation.

> If the right of recovery in this class of cases should be once established, it would naturally result in a flood of litigation in cases where the injury complained of may be easily feigned without detection, and where the damages must rest upon mere conjecture or speculation. The difficulty which often exists in cases of alleged physical injury, in determining whether they exist, and if so, whether they were caused by the negligent act of the defendant, would not only be greatly increased, but a wide field would be opened for fictitious or speculative claims. To establish such a doctrine would be contrary to principles of public policy (pp. 354–355).

The impact rule was at one time controlling in a majority of states. It limited recovery to a finite class of cases in which physical impact had occurred, and in which genuine emotional harm or fright seemed, to the sensibilities of those courts, intuitively more likely.

The impact rule was, however, subject to harsh criticism from those critics who viewed its limitations as artificially and wrongfully constrained. One criticism pointed to the weakness in the rule's justification in cases in which recovery was allowed but the physical impact was minor and the plaintiff's injuries were better explained by fright (Chamallas & Kerber, 1990). Another criticism challenged the concept that injuries resulting from fear are something other than another category of physical injury (Bohlen, 1902). "The fright is not the ground of action—the physical injury is the damage alleged; the fright is but stated as indicating a causal connection between the wrong and the injury" (Bohlen, 1902, p. 172). In a related vein, another critic of the impact rule argued that fear is "more than a purely emotional matter" (Goodrich, 1922, p. 497). As long as we can trace the physical effects of fright, the law should allow for recovery (Goodrich, 1922).

As these criticisms mounted, the impact rule lost favor in many jurisdictions. While the physical impact test artificially limited credible claims for psychological harm, it had the advantage of being an easy test to apply, which produced consistent results in like cases. Struggling to find a practicable test that permitted courts to distinguish credible claims, many courts adopted a zone of danger test, which was also tied to physical injury, albeit more flexibly than the impact rule. The zone of danger rule expanded the scope of liability, but maintained the impact rule's skepticism as to the validity of claims for psychological harm.

The zone of danger rule asks whether the plaintiff's psychological harm resulted from being placed in peril or fear of physical impact by the defendant's wrongful conduct. A commonly cited application of the test is the Supreme Court of Wisconsin's decision in *Waube v. Warrington* (1935). *Waube*, a mother, was watching through the kitchen window as her child dashed into the street in front of the house. As the mother watched, the defendant's car struck and killed the child. Shortly after, the mother died from the emotional shock of witnessing her child's death. The husband brought a survival action to claim the recovery to which his wife would have been entitled had she lived. The Wisconsin Supreme Court ultimately rejected the plaintiff's claims for emotional distress reasoning that it was too unusual and would not be expected by a negligent driver as a likely consequence of an accident. The court emphasized the risk of physical peril to the mother rather than the source of her emotional distress as the critical consideration in whether to permit the claim to proceed (Chamallas & Kerber, 1990).

> Fundamentally, defendant's duty was to use ordinary care to avoid physical injury to those who would be put in physical peril, as that term is commonly understood, by conduct on his part falling short of that standard. It is one thing to say that as to those who are put in peril of physical impact, impact is immaterial if physical injury is caused by shock arising from the peril. It is the foundation of cases holding to this liberal ruling, that the person affrighted or sustaining shock was actually put in peril of physical impact, and under these conditions it was considered immaterial that the physical impact did not materialize. It is quite another thing to say that those who are out of the field of physical danger through impact shall have a legally protected right to be free from emotional distress occasioned by the peril of others, when that distress results in physical impairment. The answer to this question cannot be reached solely by logic, nor is it clear that it can be entirely disposed of by a consideration of what the defendant ought reasonably to have anticipated as a consequence of his wrong. The answer must be reached by balancing the social interests involved in order to ascertain how far defendant's duty and plaintiff's right may justly and expediently be extended. It is our conclusion that they can neither justly nor expediently be extended to any recovery for physical injuries sustained by one out of the range of ordinary physical peril as a result of the shock of witnessing another's danger (pp. 500–501).

Seeking to expand the scope of liability for genuine claims in a manner that could be managed by the courts, the *Waube* court sought to draw a clear line for liability in the bystander context—even when the bystander outside the zone of danger was a close family member (Chamallas & Kerber, 1990).

This clear line for liability in the bystander context drew criticism in cases where one witnessing family member was within the zone of danger and another was just outside the zone of danger, and demonstrated the artificiality of the rule:

> [the courts could] hardly justify relief to the sister for trauma which she suffered upon apprehension of the child's death and yet deny it to the mother merely because of a happenstance that the sister was a few yards closer to the accident (*Dillon v. Legg*, 1968, p. 733).

The zone of danger rule and the underlying concern that emotional disturbance was difficult to measure and easy to fake also drew criticism as the fields of psychiatry and psychology evolved. These criticisms led some courts to adopt a proximate cause-oriented approach to the recovery of damages for psychological harm.

In 1968, a landmark California Supreme Court decision precipitated changes in the rule for bystander recovery leading to a more pragmatic approach to analyzing the nexus between the defendant's wrongful conduct and the plaintiff's psychological harm (*Dillon v. Legg*, 1968). *Dillon v. Legg* permitted a mother who had witnessed the negligent injuring of her child, but was herself outside the zone of danger, to recover damages for her own mental anguish and emotional distress (Chamallas & Kerber, 1990). In *Dillon*, the plaintiff's daughter was crossing the street when the defendant's vehicle collided with the daughter. Although the plaintiff was not in the zone of danger, the court held that she could recover for her emotional trauma and physical injury from witnessing the death or injury to her child since she was "in close proximity to" the accident. In deciding the case, the court stated that allowing a mother to recover from a negligent tortfeasor is a compelling proposition. The California Supreme Court directed courts using *Dillon* as a guideline to decide on a case-by-case basis whether an injury to a plaintiff was reasonably foreseeable addressing three pragmatic considerations—physical proximity, temporal proximity, and relational proximity (Chamallas & Kerber, 1990). Since the *Dillon* case, some, but not all, jurisdictions have allowed a parent who witnesses the negligent injuring of his or her child to recover for the parent's own fright-induced damages (Chamallas & Kerber, 1990).

Dillon moved some courts away from the rigid categories for recovery of psychological harm imposed by the physical impact or zone of danger rule to a broader range of cases limited by proximate cause and the principles that underlie it. It encourages a more pragmatic examination of all the circumstances of an event when determining causation and recovery for psychological harm than the impact or zone of risk rule to determine deserving claims for psychological harm.

However, even where recovery for meritorious claims of psychological harm is allowed, the ambivalence about permitting recovery for this harm as well as concerns regarding the frequency and amount of recovery have resulted in another policy-driven limitation on intangible damage claims but not tangible damage claims. Various formulations of caps on intangible damages (i.e., noneconomic losses) specific to personal injury and/or medical malpractice claims have been enacted in many states which limit the intangible or noneconomic damages that can be awarded, without regard to the merits of the claim or the gravity of the harm.

Lawmakers remain wary that plaintiffs will institute and juries will accept specious claims for emotional distress or those juries will overvalue valid claims. Therefore, in cases where claims for psychological harm are permitted, another manifestation of the physical vs. emotional harm dichotomy that has determined which injuries can be compensated, has been an arbitrary upper limit on recovery for noneconomic damages (Ruda, 1993). Typical of this damage cap enacted in many jurisdictions is an upper limit of $250,000 for combined noneconomic damages [Idaho, 2004; See, for example, Oklahoma, 2003 (placing a limit on noneconomic damages in the healthcare setting)]. These caps are an ongoing manifestation of the suspicion with which states continue to regard claims for emotional distress and psychological harm.

Frye and *Daubert*—When Qualifications Are Not Enough

When claims for psychological harm are legally cognizable, proof of that harm is not limited to expert testimony. A claimant may offer lay testimony about the source and severity of his or her psychological distress [See, for example, *Ruttger Hotel Corp. v. Wagner*, 1997 (allowing plaintiff to testify about his distress manifested in nightmares and "daymares.")]. Although claims for damages are not invariably required to be supported by expert testimony, litigants may be permitted, and in some cases may be required, to offer expert testimony to support or defeat damage claims (Shuman, 2002). Two basic rules guide when expert testimony may and when expert testimony must be presented. Expert testimony is permitted when it helps the fact finder to understand the evidence or determine a fact in issue (Fed. R. Evid. 702). Expert testimony is required when it is necessary for the fact finder to address matters which are beyond lay competence.

Because the role of the expert witness is to assist the fact finder to understand matters beyond its sphere of lay competence, courts have always imposed a threshold requirement for expert witnesses beyond what is imposed on lay witnesses (e.g., taking the oath). The earliest test applied for the admissibility of an expert witness's testimony focused exclusively on the expert's qualifications. "On questions of science or skill, or relating to some art or trade, persons instructed therein by study or experience may give their opinions" (Lawson, 1900, p. 2). Thus, the expert's testimony was to be admitted based on the witness's qualifications and not based on an independent assessment of the validity or reliability of the theory or technique underlying the testimony.

As the fields of science evolved, however, it became apparent that the qualifications model was not always adequate. The growth of science provided ample evidence that being an expert provided no assurance of expertise grounded in science. Change in the approach to the admissibility of experts is often thought to be reflected in the 1923 D.C. Court of Appeals decision in *Frye v. United States* (1923). Although *Frye* now evokes much controversy among courts and commentators, there is little doubt that its concern with the reliability of the theory or technique underlying the expert's opinion, in addition to the expert's qualifications, was an important evidentiary advance (Shuman, 2002).

In *Frye*, the D.C. Circuit Court of Appeals first considered the admissibility of polygraph evidence. Although the court acknowledged the qualifications of the expert who offered to testify about the polygraph results, it addressed the validity of the technique he sought to apply as a separate inquiry and applied an approach to do so that reflected the court's linear view of how scientific knowledge evolves (But see Kuhn, 1970):

> Just when a scientific principle or discovery crosses the line between the experimental and demonstrable stages is difficult to define. Somewhere in this twilight zone the evidential force of the principle must be recognized, and while courts will go a long way in admitting expert testimony deduced from a well-recognized scientific principle or discovery, the thing from which the deduction is made must be sufficiently established to have gained general acceptance in the particular field in which it belongs (*Frye v. United States*, 1923, p. 1014).

Frye required more than a qualified expert testifying that a novel technique is valid to justify its admission. It imposed a new threshold scrutiny requirement that the technique have gained general acceptance in the relevant scientific community, seeking the opinion of fellow scientists to guide the court's assessment of the reliability of the evidence (Giannelli & Imwinkelried, 1986). Although not a widely hailed decision when it was decided, *Frye* came into vogue in the 1960s and 1970s as the courts struggled with increased number of offers of scientific evidence. But as *Frye* was applied more frequently, it came under increased criticism. Not only did the general acceptance test direct the judge to defer uncritically to the judgments of a third party about science, it was unclear what had to be generally accepted, who had to generally accept it, and by what degree of consensus it meant to be generally accepted, let alone why general acceptance was an appropriate proxy for scientific validity or reliability. To further complicate matters, when the Federal Rules of Evidence were enacted in 1975, they contained no reference to *Frye*, leaving the federal courts to disagree amongst themselves whether the silence should be interpreted to mean that *Frye* had been incorporated or rejected in the new rules.

Not until nearly 20 years later did the Supreme Court answer the question of *Frye's* survival under the Federal Rules of Evidence. In *Daubert v. Merrell Dow Pharmaceuticals* (1993), the Court held that the Federal Rules of Evidence had superseded *Frye* and established a relevancy plus reliability test for the admissibility of expert testimony in the federal courts, which some but not all states that had adopted evidence rules patterned after the federal rules followed. *Daubert* involved mothers who, after taking Bendectin for morning sickness during their pregnancy, gave birth to children with serious limb reduction birth defects. The mothers and their children sued Merrell Dow Pharmaceuticals, the makers of Bendectin. The defendant presented evidence, which plaintiffs did not dispute, that none of the numerous epidemiological studies on Bendectin had found a correlation between it and birth defects. Instead the plaintiff offered highly qualified scientists who had utilized other techniques such as animal studies, chemical structure analyses, and unpublished reanalysis of previously published studies to determine that Bendectin was a teratogen. Relying on *Frye*, the trial court ruled that the plaintiffs' expert testimony was inadmissible as it was not based on generally accepted scientific techniques. The Supreme Court of the United States granted review and concluded that *Frye* did not survive the adoption of the Federal Rules of Evidence, which were intended to liberalize admissibility of evidence:

> General acceptance is not a necessary precondition to the admissibility of scientific evidence under the Federal Rules of Evidence, but the Rules of Evidence—especially Rule 702—do assign to the trial judge the task of ensuring that an expert's testimony both rests on a reliable foundation and is relevant to the task at hand. Pertinent evidence based on scientifically valid principles will satisfy those demands (*Daubert v. Merrell Dow Pharmaceuticals*, 1993, p. 597).

Daubert instructed the lower courts to apply a pragmatic set of considerations to guide scientific expert admissibility determinations. Justice Blackmun's majority opinion noted that many factors will bear on the inquiry of admissibility. And, though the Court refused to set out a definitive test or checklist, it did detail four noteworthy factors. First, the Court stated "a key question to be answered in determining whether a theory or technique is scientific knowledge that will assist the trier of fact will be whether it can be (and has been) tested" (*Daubert v. Merrill Dow Pharmaceuticals*, 1993, p. 593). The Court also stated that it is important to consider whether the theory or technique has been subjected to peer review and publication. Additionally, the Court identified a third factor, the known or potential rate of error of the technique and procedures for correcting it. Finally, breathing new life into *Frye*'s recently rejected criteria, the Court noted that general acceptance in the relevant scientific community can be useful in the admissibility inquiry.

For psychologists and psychiatrists, *Daubert* left numerous questions unanswered. Was *Daubert's* application restricted to the hard science context in which it arose; if so what test applied in the social science context? Did *Daubert* apply to experts whose expertise was not grounded in science; if not what test applied in its stead? Before these questions were to be answered by the Court, however, it decided another case regarding the admissibility of expert testimony under the Federal Rules of Evidence, *General Electric Company v. Joiner* (1997). *Joiner* was a technical, but nonetheless extremely important decision, addressing the standard of review that federal appellate courts should apply when reviewing federal trial court decisions on the admissibility of expert evidence. The Court decided that as is the case for appellate review of all other evidentiary determinations, federal appellate courts should apply an abuse of discretion standard when reviewing a trial court's decision to admit or exclude expert testimony. Although *Joiner*'s construction of federal procedural law does not bind state courts, most follow a similar rule.

The abuse of discretion standard is intended to give trial courts broad grant of authority to manage trials. Thus, *Joiner* sends a strong signal that trial courts are likely to have the first and, in most instances, final say in decisions regarding the admissibility of experts. This has a number of important implications. One implication is the importance of the presentation on the admissibility of expert testimony to the trial court judge, which is practically likely to be the last word on the issue. Another important implication of this deference is that it might leave standing lower court admissibility decisions that are conflicting and result in an absence of consistency or certainty about the admissibility of certain proffered expertise from court to court.

Two years later, in *Kumho Tire Co., Ltd. v. Carmichael* (1999), the Court decided that *Daubert*'s pragmatic criteria apply to the admissibility of all offers of expert testimony whether grounded in scientific, technical, or other specialized expertise, but that trial courts have broad discretion in their application:

> We also conclude that a trial court may consider one or more of the more specific factors that Daubert mentioned when doing so will help determine that testimony's reliability. But, as the Court stated in *Daubert*, the test of reliability is "flexible," and *Daubert's* list of specific factors neither necessarily nor exclusively applies to all experts or in every case. Rather, the law grants a district court the same broad latitude when it decides how to determine reliability as it enjoys in respect to its ultimate reliability determination. See *General Electric Co. v. Joiner*, 522 U.S. 136, 143, 118 S.Ct. 512, 139 L.Ed.2d 508 (1997) (courts of appeals are to apply "abuse of discretion" standard when reviewing district court's reliability determination) (pp. 141–142).

Kumho Tire, read together with *Joiner*, applies *Daubert* to all offers of expert testimony in federal court, but emphasizes the trial court's flexibility in applying *Daubert's* pragmatic considerations.

Of the expectations and fears surrounding *Daubert*, much has been written, although its final legacy is still unclear. One thing is clear, however. The *Daubert* trilogy has provided an important tool for judges and lawyers to impose rigorous threshold relevance and reliability demands on experts, while simultaneously providing trial judges virtually unlimited latitude as to how to use this tool in any particular case.

What has the *Daubert* trilogy meant for the admissibility of psychological and psychiatric evidence? The available evidence indicates that in the federal courts and the state courts that have adopted them, in the main, *Daubert, Joiner*, and, *Kumho Tire* have not had a significant across-the-board impact for the admissibility of expert testimony by mental health professionals (Shuman & Sales, 1999). Although specific instances of courts excluding psychiatric and psychological evidence after applying *Daubert* rigorously exist, in general, psychiatric and psychological evidence that was admitted before the *Daubert* trilogy was decided is admitted now, and psychiatric and psychological evidence that was excluded before the *Daubert* trilogy was decided, is excluded now. Where differences in admissibility on particular categories of evidence exist over time, other political, scientific, or legal factors seem to explain the difference in result more effectively than the announcement of these decisions (Shuman & Sales, 1998).

On the matter of psychological or psychiatric evidence of causation for psychological harm, in particular, there are few reported post *Daubert* decisions. Ultimately, these few decisions have not demanded rigorous scientific proof to admit expert testimony regarding the cause of psychological harm. One such post *Daubert* decision, *Jenson v. Eveleth Taconite Co.* (1996), was a class action sex discrimination case presenting claims for psychological harm that had to be disentangled from other potential causes of the claimants' psychological harm.

Jenson presented competing examples of rigorous and nonrigorous applications of *Daubert* to causation of psychological harm, in which the nonrigorous approach ultimately prevailed. The Special Master in *Jenson* initially applied *Daubert* rigorously to reject attempts by the plaintiffs' experts to apportion the psychological harm, finding an absence of a scientific foundation for their methodology, which (temporarily) doomed the plaintiffs' damage claims:

> This Court is persuaded by unanimous testimony of psychiatrists and psychologists, called by both sides, that there is no scientific method for determining the cause of a mental disorder or for allocating proportionate cause when more than one possible cause exists (p. 23).

Most other judges approaching causation for psychological harm, however, like the panel of the Eighth Circuit Court of Appeals that reversed this finding by the Special Master, in a pre*Kumho Tire* opinion, have not been so demanding in their application of *Daubert* (*Jenson v. Eveleth Taconite Co.*, 1997, p. 1297):

> The Special Master made two questionable observations which we believe are at the root of his rulings excluding the opinions of plaintiffs' expert witnesses. First, the court found: "There is, therefore, no scientifically developed psychiatric model or procedure for determining whether a particular stress caused a particular symptom or mental state." ... Second, the court, perhaps misled by its erroneous application of principles of causation, found ... "that there is no scientific method for determining the cause of a mental disorder or for allocating proportionate cause when more than one possible cause exists."

The Court of Appeals attributed the Special Master's erroneous decision to an overly broad reading of *Daubert* and antipathy to psychiatry and psychology:

> The record strongly suggests the Special Master foreclosed consideration of the evidence based on his own preconceived notions relating to psychiatric proof. The Special Master did not attempt to hide his hostility toward psychological evidence in sexual harassment claims, stating: " 'Experts' ... know no more than judges about what causes mental changes—which is to say that they know almost nothing." To the extent the Special Master relied upon *Daubert v. Merrell Dow Pharmaceuticals, Inc.*, 509 U.S. 579, 125 L. Ed. 2d 469, 113 S.Ct. 2786 (1993) to support his rulings, we find his rulings to be in error. n. 15 In Daubert, the Supreme Court addressed the standards of admissibility for specific evidence under *Federal Rules of Evidence 702*. n. 16 There is some question as to whether the Daubert analysis should be applied at all to "soft" sciences such as psychology, because there are social sciences in which the research, theories, and opinions cannot have the exactness of hard science methodologies. *See Daubert,* 509 U.S. at 590 n. 8 ("Rule 702 also applies to technical, or other specialized knowledge. Our discussion is limited to the scientific context because that is the nature of the expertise offered here."). However, the question of whether Daubert should be applied to the psychological evidence excluded here does not affect our ruling in this case, because we find that under either *Daubert* or under the more general parameters of Rule 702, the proffered testimony was both reliable and relevant, and should have been admitted into evidence (pp. 1297–1298).
>
> (See also, *Blanchard v. Eli Lilly & Co.*, 2002).

Reflecting the unfulfilled potential of *Daubert* to generate a critical discussion of what the law should demand of psychological and psychiatric experts, few other decisions addressing minimum reliability requirements for expert testimony seeking to link tortious conduct and psychological harm are to be found. Although not overtly hostile to the demands of good science, most lawyers and judges continue to assume, without critical analysis, that the knowledge possessed by qualified psychologists and psychiatrists about causation of psychological harm is sufficiently relevant and reliable to be admitted without rigorous scrutiny of how these witnesses know what they claim to know. There is a better way.

Reordering the Universe: Models for Acceptable Expert Testimony about Psychological Causation

How then are we to better reconcile the importance of the role of causation in the law, the law's skepticism about recovery for psychological harm, the mixed signals about scrutinizing the reliability underlying expert testimony as a condition of its admissibility, and the gaps in our knowledge about the relationship between trauma and psychological harm? In particular, what is the appropriate role for psychological and psychiatric experts to play when offering to assist the fact finder to connect the dots between a defendant's wrongful conduct and a plaintiff's psychological harm? How can the need for reliable sources of information and the opportunity for litigants to be heard be balanced in a fair and consistent manner?

To assist in this task, we return to the scientific and qualifications models illustrated by the attempts to prove that the defendant's tortious actions caused the plaintiff to develop Schizophrenia, discussed earlier. One significant problem that we identified in those cases was the use of disparate standards for threshold scrutiny of expert testimony attempting to link a tortious event and the claimant's Schizophrenia. Any reconciliation of the importance of the role of causation in the law must address attempts to identify causal links between wrongdoing and psychological harm with similar scrutiny.

What should that similar scrutiny of the causal link between wrongful events and psychological harm entail? Given the importance of these causal attributions for psychology and law, when psychological or psychiatric experts are offered to identify and explain those causal links, there is no cogent justification to permit them to do so in the absence of good science. The moral, psychological, and economic imperatives that underlie our interest in causation are simply too important to permit an expert to venture where science does not provide good grounds to know what the expert claims to know about a causal attribution. To do otherwise, fails to give these considerations their due.

But what of the causal questions for which science lacks relevant information? Where gaps in scientific knowledge of the relationship between the wrong and the psychological harm claimed exist, whether the claimant need be denied his or her day in court should turn, at least in part, on whether courts would permit the fact finder to assess that linkage in any event relying on lay testimony (i.e., is the claimant permitted but not required to prove the linkage between the wrong and the harm with expert rather than lay testimony?) (Veilleux, 1994).

That should not be understood to suggest that relevant testimony grounded in good science should, on that ground alone, be admissible. Other considerations that bear on the use of the science must play a crucial role as well. For example, gathering accurate and complete information to which to apply scientifically validated techniques properly is but one of many other requirements that must precede the admissibility of relevant and reliable expert testimony. Where that is absent, admissibility should be denied.

With these considerations in mind, properly qualified mental health experts may appropriately offer to assist the fact finder in assessing causation for psychological harm in a number of ways. Without implying that they are an exclusive enumeration, we consider here only two for illustrative purposes. In particular, properly qualified mental health experts may offer *descriptive clinical testimony* or *specific causal attributions*. Each approach offers different types of expert assistance to the fact finder and each demands different foundational requirements that reflect an appropriate balance of the considerations bounding causation, psychology, and law.

Where the expert offers a *specific causal attribution*, explicitly linking the defendant's wrongful conduct as the cause-in-fact and proximate cause of the claimant's psychological distress, the necessity for a reliable scientific foundation as a condition of admissibility, in addition to the requirement of appropriate qualifications, is compelled to address the important role of causation in the law and, particularly, in light of the law's skepticism about recovery for psychological harm. By way of example, where the expert asserts that the plaintiff's exposure to the defendant's sexual harassment (or automobile collision or sexual assault or prescription drug) caused the Schizophrenia from which plaintiff now suffers, it is appropriate to apply the *Daubert* qualifications plus good science model or its state equivalent, as a prerequisite for the admissibility of the opinion about causation, to ask how the expert knows what he or she claims to know.

Expert psychological or psychiatric testimony asserting a specific causal nexus necessarily implies a conclusion based in science for which the expert has reliable knowledge that, for example, sexual harassment can cause Schizophrenia, and that it caused this plaintiff's Schizophrenia. How does the expert know that these events are capable of causing Schizophrenia, and did cause this plaintiff's Schizophrenia, and why should we accept that this is so? If the expert chooses to address this *specific causal attribution* (or is required to do so to meet a party's burden of proof), science is in play and must be addressed as a condition of admissibility, demanding more than the *ipse dixit* of the expert (*General Electric Co. v. Joiner*, 1997). Qualifications alone are not a sufficient ground for expert testimony which purports to find the causal nexus between the defendant's wrongdoing and the plaintiff's psychological distress. "[T]he underlying predicates of any cause-and-effect medical testimony are that medical science understands the physiological process by which a particular disease or syndrome develops and knows what factors cause the process to occur." (*Black v. Food Lion, Inc.*, 1999, p. 314). If cause-and-effect psychological testimony is not held to an equivalently demanding standard, it undermines psychology's claim to be grounded in the scientific study of human behavior.

What of the attempt to link the defendant's tortious behavior as the cause of the claimant's emotional harm where that harm is not described as a particular disorder but is instead presented only descriptively, for example, as a profound sadness or a deep sense of loss of enjoyment, without a causal attribution to the defendant's actions? No difference in the threshold reliability requirement result is called for where the *specific causal attribution* is not tied to a particular disorder. Where, for example, the expert offers to testify that the defendant's sexual harassment (or collision or assault or prescription drug) caused the plaintiff to experience emotional distress, manifested in feelings of hopelessness and despair, proof grounded in more than the *ipse dixit* of the expert is also necessary (*General Electric Co. v. Joiner*, 1997). Expert evidence of cause-and-effect demands the existence of a reliable methodology which must be demonstrated as a foundation for the admissibility of that linkage.

For *descriptive clinical testimony*, in which the psychological or psychiatric expert functions as a keen behavioral photographer gathering and presenting oral and visual snapshots of a party, without seeking to link these snapshots in a causal chain, a different sort of threshold is required. Depending on the level of inference sought to be drawn, all that may be necessary as a predicate for admissibility is a demonstration of the expert's qualifications (as well as compliance with customary techniques of the field). Consider first *descriptive clinical testimony* in a sexual harassment case that, based on an examination of the plaintiff and review of the available historical records including the plaintiff's health, financial, and employment records, the plaintiff was an active, happy, and outgoing person in the decade before the alleged harassment, but in the year following the alleged harassment has been inactive, sad, and introverted, stopping there, and leaving it to the fact finder to assess the cause as well as the compensatory value of this behavioral change. In contrast, in the same case, consider expert testimony resting on the same factual basis, that the plaintiff displays symptoms of Schizophrenia now; that there is no evidence that she displayed any of these symptoms prior to the dates that the harassment is alleged to have occurred and, that there is no evidence of known risk factors for Schizophrenia or of the plaintiff having been exposed to other traumatic events, leaving it to the fact finder to infer whether the necessary causal linkage between the defendant's alleged wrongful conduct and the plaintiff's Schizophrenia has been proved to the level of confidence required to support their verdict.

Given the minimal inferential leap drawn by the expert in the first example from clinical observation to description, a demonstration of the scientific link between the tortious event and the psychological harm is not a sensible predicate for this *descriptive clinical testimony*. The expert's opinion neither assumes nor asserts a link between the tortious event and the psychological harm and the expert should not be asked to establish one as a requirement of her testimony. Admissibility requirements address minimum thresholds, leaving anything more to the crucible of the adversary system. Thus, for example, while decision-making errors or heuristics (Kahneman, Slovic, & Tversky, 1982) may distort the expert's clinical lens, and in an ideal world the use of procedures to correct or address heuristics would always be addressed as a condition of admissibility (Beecher-Monas 2000), courts have relegated such issues to the weight rather than the admissibility of expert testimony (i.e., a matter appropriately addressed through cross-examination or opposing expert testimony). There is no sign that *Daubert* has or is likely to change this approach. Some might argue that particularly without the use of techniques specifically designed to address heuristics, that this clinical description is nothing more than lay testimony with an expert veneer. And that may be so. But if the expert's observations are "helpful" to the fact finder who may not have the opportunity to gather information or the sensitivity to identify critical behaviors, that characterization is not legally problematic (Fed. R. Evid. 702).

Certainly, in the second example, where the expert offers a diagnostic snap shot, the distinction between lay and expert input and the requirements for admissibility are clearer. Only qualified mental health professionals are permitted to offer expert testimony regarding a diagnosis of Schizophrenia (*Reese v. Naylor*, 1969). Thus, sorting through an array of information to determine whether the plaintiff does now or did previously display the symptoms of Schizophrenia requires a demonstration of those qualifications. In the case of *descriptive clinical testimony*, as suggested here, the expert's testimony does not imply a scientific linkage between the harassment and Schizophrenia based on a unique fund of knowledge that the expert possesses. Rather it offers to the fact finder information gathered through the expert's time and specialized acumen. While the use of a *DSM* diagnosis raises issues about its reliability that should be addressed as a condition of its admissibility (*United States v. Scholl*, 1997), just as the use of psychological tests raises another set of reliability issues (Shuman, 2002a), purely *descriptive clinical testimony* avoids those issues.

A properly qualified psychological or psychiatric expert is useful to gather and describe information (e.g., behavior, affect, cognition) which lay judges and jurors might not otherwise perceive, let alone have the opportunity to observe within the formalities of trial (Litwack, Gerbert, & Fenster, 1980). Indeed, that descriptive function may be the role best suited to treating experts who may have spent much time with the patient-litigant but who lack the perspective or expertise necessary to reach reliable causal attributions (Greenberg & Shuman, 1997). These clinical observations do not masquerade as science and are not likely to be understood to convey professional knowledge immune from challenge. An opposing party can easily challenge and the jury can easily assess the accuracy and completeness of the information gathered. Certainly, when the plaintiff's lay testimony describing her thoughts, feelings, or behaviors would be admissible absent a scientific foundation to support her damage claim, the clinical observations of a qualified expert comprehensively gathering and presenting that category of information to the fact finder should be admissible in the absence of a scientific foundation.

There are several points to recommend this approach to the admissibility of expert evidence regarding causation of psychological harm. Adopting the wisdom shared by both *Frye* and *Daubert*, this approach distinguishes experts from their expertise, addressing the grounds which support the inferences they seek to draw. Reliable clinical descriptions require clinical competence; reliable causal attributions require the appropriate professional competence as well as the science supporting the attribution. The clarity of the standard proposed is likely to produce similar results in like cases avoiding the existing discordance. Its substance encourages courts to respond to changes in scientific knowledge and is likely to improve the evidentiary reliability of information about causation for psychological harm. Parties wishing to offer more persuasive proof must provide more rigorous science, not merely a more confident expert. Where the expert gathers and presents descriptive clinical information to assist the fact finder, the expert's clinical skills determine the reliability of the information provided and should be the centerpiece of the foundational requirements of the expert's testimony. Where the expert goes beyond this clinical information gathering and reporting function and attributes causation, as a condition of admissibility, the court is entitled to demand to know why we should accept that is so and to require science to satisfy this link. And, that requirement reflects necessary conditions for the admissibility of expert testimony as well as the proper balance underlying causation and its role in the law.

Conclusion

Is there a psychological order to the universe? Having raised the question of whether a psychological order to the universe exists at the outset of this chapter to aid in the analysis of what should be required of experts seeking to link tortious wrongs and psychological harm, we now return to this thorny issue to consider a fundamental dilemma it poses for the structure of accident and injury compensation law. This systemic inquiry is necessary because the contour, as well as the very existence of tort law, is a volatile topic.

There is no right to tort compensation for psychological harm grounded in the U.S. Constitution. The growth and development of tort law, which varies significantly from state to state, has been the product of common law decisions fashioned by judges acting within the constraints of state laws. However, as the creation of no-fault compensation systems such as Workers Compensation (Johnson, 2002) and the National Vaccine Injury Compensation Program (42 USCS § 300aa-11, 2004) that supplanted judge-made state tort law demonstrate, within their respective spheres of authority that, the states and the federal government are empowered to replace the common law of torts with a compensation system that alters the substantive standard for compensation (e.g., no-fault), the mode of trial (e.g., no trial by jury), as well as the damages that are awarded (e.g., no award for punitive damages) (*Mountain Timber Co. v. Washington*, 1917). Given the harsh and widely shared contemporary critiques of the operation of tort law (Berman, 2003), it would be unrealistic to fail to consider the implications of the answer to the psychological order to the universe inquiry for the future of tort law. It is far from clear that fault-based tort law as it now exists, which permits intangible as well as tangible damage awards, will continue without substantial change in the foreseeable future. What form those changes will take is unclear, but psychologists and psychiatrists may have an important role to play in the design of an alternative system of compensation.

The fault-based U.S. tort system's decision to permit an award of damages for psychological harm in a carefully cabined category of cases is bottomed on the assumption that a demonstrable psychological order to the universe exists. The legal principles of causation discussed above are premised on this universal order. Only if the cause of psychological harm follows a known, comprehensible order can an award finding a defendant responsible for causing harm and directing that a defendant compensate a plaintiff for a particular loss be justified.

What is that psychological order to the universe? What psychological process do people undergo as they are transformed from a normal to an abnormal mental state? How is that process affected by the exposure to tortious conduct or its absence? If, as in the case of Schizophrenia as well as many other mental disorders, there is reason to conclude that there is some genetic predisposition to the abnormal mental state, what can science offer to explain the role of traumatic events in bringing about the disorder, whether the stress of a tortious event can cause the abnormal mental state in someone who lacks the genetic predisposition, or whether there are qualitative differences in the abnormal mental state when it is precipitated by the stress of a tortious event as contrasted with its "natural" occurrence? Can we identify those individuals in whom the abnormal mental state would have occurred without the stress of a tortious event and those in which it would not? Answers to these and many similar questions lie at the heart of the decision to compensate for psychological harm. We do not purport to offer answers to these questions in this chapter, but rather seek to identify fundamental questions and their role in this debate.

What if, at the end of the day, after all the relevant theory and research is carefully analyzed, an eminent, independent review panel concludes that we lack a satisfactory understanding of the existence of a psychological order to the universe to answer these fundamental questions confidently? What if a significant portion of the variation in psychological harm lacks a coherent, empirically grounded explanation, leaving us to speculate about the role that trauma plays in causing psychological harm in specific cases? What should that psychological incoherence imply for the structure of a compensation system?

There is much insight to be gained in thinking about this question by considering compensation systems that do not compensate for psychological harm. For economic, as well as scientific reasons, no-fault compensation systems such as Workers Compensation do not award damages to compensate for psychological harm, avoiding the cost of compensating psychological harm as well as the necessity to address the question of whether a psychological order to the universe exists or what that order would portend for the psychological injury claimed in an individual case.

Compensatory damages are awarded to make the claimant whole (Shuman, 1994). The decision to permit an award of damages to compensate for psychological harm presents unique theoretical problems as well as intractable practical problems. Because it is difficult to understand how a monetary award for psychological harm restores the plaintiff to his or her preaccident psychological state in the way that a monetary award restores the plaintiff's lost wages or damaged property to a preaccident state, some argue that tort law should reject compensation claims for psychological harm for jurisprudential reasons (King, 2004).

Tangible damage claim awards, which are finite, are generally both smaller in size and also less subject to dispute over their amount than intangible damage claim awards, which are not finite. Absent claims for intangible psychological harm, the fault-based tort system is less threatening to its critics and, ultimately, is less economically distinct from no-fault compensation schemes, which have the advantage of compensating claimants more swiftly with less administrative expense (O'Connell, 1971). Compensation for psychological harm, tied to findings of fault, presents a host of challenges for a compensation system.

How should these scientific, jurisprudential, and economic challenges to compensation for psychological harm be resolved? Ideally, a policy decision to recognize fault-based tort claims for psychological harm should rest on a determination of whether the importance of the process of making visible these intangible losses substantially outweighs the scientific, jurisprudential, and economic challenges they present, as well as evidence of the litigation induced harm experienced by emotionally vulnerable claimants who bring claims for psychological harm in an adversary setting (Shuman, 1994). There is much to ponder in assessing the wisdom of a compensation system's decision to permit claims for psychological harm. A determination that good grounds exist for a scientific linkage between wrongful acts and psychological harm that has predictive value in individual cases is critical to the decision to permit claims for psychological harm as well as the decision to cling to a fault-based compensation system. Psychologists and psychiatrists are more than interested observers in this debate. The challenge to psychology and psychiatry, as researchers as well as clinicians, is to address the validity of the assumption that underlies the system which permits these claims, by advancing the science that explains the causal relationship between wrongful events and psychological harm.

Acknowledgments. The Dedman School of Law provided generous support for the preparation of this chapter. John Edens, Stuart Greenberg, William Foote, Andrew Kane, Ellen Pryor, Bruce Sales, John Zervopolous, and Gerald Young provided helpful comments on an earlier version of this chapter that are gratefully acknowledged.

References

American Psychiatric Association (1968). *Diagnostic and statistical manual of mental disorders* (2nd ed.). Washington, DC: Author.

American Psychiatric Association (2000). *Diagnostic and statistical manual of mental disorders* (4th ed.). Washington, DC: Author (Text Revision).

Beecher-Monas, E. (2000). The heuristics of intellectual due process: a primer for triers of science. *New York University Law Review, 75*, 1563–1657.
Berman, P. (2003). Dow's pocket has a hole. *Forbes*. March 31, 2003, Business, p. 78.
Black v. Food Lion, Inc. 171 F.3d 308 (5th Cir. 1999).
Blanchard v. Eli Lilly, 207 F. Supp. 2d 308 (D. Vt. 2002).
Bohlen, F. (1902). Right to recover for injury resulting from negligence without impact. *The American Law Register, 50*, 141–173.
Bonanno, G. A. (2004). Loss, trauma, and human resilience: Have we underestimated the human capacity to thrive after extremely aversive events. *American Psychologist, 59*, 20–28.
Bonanno, G. A., Keltner, D., Holen, A., & Horowitz, M. J. (1995). When avoiding unpleasant emotions might not be such a bad thing: Verbal-autonomic response dissociation and midlife conjugal bereavement. *Journal of Personality and Social Psychology, 69*, 975–989.
Boyles v. Kerr, 855 S.W.2d 593 (Tex. 1993).
Brackett v. Peters, 11 F.3d 78 (7th Cir. 1993).
Bremner, J. D. (2003). Does stress damage the brain? Understanding trauma-related disorders from a mind-body perspective. *American Journal of Psychiatry, 160*(5), 1020–1021.
Chamallas, M., & Kerber, L. (1990).Women, mothers, and the law of fright: A history. *Michigan Law Review, 88*, 814–864.
Cole v. Shell Petroleum Corp., 86 P.2d 740 (Kan. 1939).
Dallam, S. J., Gleaves, D. H., Cepeda-Benito, A., Silberg, J. L., Kraemer, H. C., & Spiegel, D. (2001). The effects of child sexual abuse: Comment on Rind, Tromovitch, and Bauserman (1998). *Psychological Bulletin, 127*, 715–733.
Daubert v. Merrell Dow Pharmaceuticals, Inc. 509 U.S. 579, 113 S.Ct. 2786, 125 L.Ed. 2d 469 (1993).
Dillon v. Legg, 441 P.2d 912 (Cal. 1968).
Doe v. Baxter Healthcare Corp., 380 F.3d 399 (8th Cir. 2004).
Fed. R. Evid. 702.
Feldthusen, B. (1993). The civil action for sexual battery: Therapeutic jurisprudence?, *Ottawa Law Review, 25*, 203–324.
Frye v. United States, 293 F. 1013, 34 ALR 145 (D. C. Cir. 1923).
General Electric Co. v. Joiner, 522 U.S. 136, 118 S.Ct. 512 (1997).
Giannelli, P. C., & Imwinkelried, E. J. (1986). *Scientific Evidence. Contemporary Litigation Series*. Charlottesville, VA: The Mitchie Company.
Goodrich, H. (1922). Emotional disturbance as legal damage. *Michigan Law Review, 20*, 497–513.
Gorenstein, E. (1984). Debating mental illness: Implications for science, medicine, and social policy. *America Psychologist, 39*, 50–56.
Green v. K-Mart Corp., 849 So. 2d 814 (La. Ct. App. 2003).
Green, B. L., & Kaltman, S. I. (2003). Recent research findings on the diagnosis of PTSD. In R. Simon (Ed.), *Posttraumatic stress disorder in litigation* (2nd ed., pp. 19–39). Washington, DC: American Psychiatric Publishing, Inc.
Greenberg, S. A., & Shuman, D. W. (1997). Irreconcilable conflict between therapeutic and forensic roles. *Journal of Professional Psychology: Research and Practice, 28*, 50–57.
Greenberg, S. A., Shuman, D. W., & Meyer, R. G. (2004). Unmasking forensic diagnosis. *International Journal of Law and Psychiatry, 27*, 1–15.
Hart, H. L. A., & Honoré, T. (1985). *Causation in the law* (2nd ed.). Oxford, England: Clarendon Press.
Heinrichs, R. W. (2001). *In search of madness: Schizophrenia and neuroscience*. New York, Oxford University Press.
Holmes, O. W. Jr. (1946). *The common law*. Boston, MA: Little Brown.

Holmes v. Sec. Investor Prot. Corp., 503 U.S. 258 (1992).
Idaho Code § 6-1603 (Mitchie 2004).
Jeffress v. Reddy, 77 Fed. Appx. 627 (4th Cir. 2003).
Jenson v. Eveleth Taconite Co., 1996 U.S. Dist. LEXIS 17617.
Jenson v. Eveleth Taconite Co., 130 F.3d 1287 (8th Cir. 1997).
Johnson, H. (2002). *Workers' compensation law and practice* (4th ed.). St. Paul, MN: Thompson West.
Kadish, S. H. (1985). Complicity, cause, and blame: A study in the interpretation of doctrine. *California Law Review, 73*, 323–410.
Kahneman, D., Slovic, P., & Tversky, A. (Eds.). (1982). *Judgment under uncertainty: Heuristics and biases*. Cambridge, MA: Cambridge University Press.
King, J. H. Jr. (2004). Pain and suffering, non-economic damages, and the goals of tort law. *Southern Methodist University Law Review, 57*, 163–210.
Kuhn, T. S. (1970). *The structure of scientific revolutions* (2nd ed.). Chicago, IL: University of Chicago Press.
Kumho Tire Co. v. Carmichael, 526 U.S. 137, 119 S.Ct. 1167 (1999).
Lancaster v. Norfolk & W. Ry., 773 F.2d 807 (7th Cir. 1985).
Lawson, J. D. (1900). *The law of expert opinion evidence reduced to rules with illustrations from adjudged cases*. Chicago, IL: T. H. Flood & Co.
Lilienfeld, S. O. (2002). When worlds collide: Social science, politics, and the Rind et al. (1998) *child sexual abuse* meta-analysis. *American Psychologist, 57*, 176–188.
Litwack, T. R., Gerber, G. L., & Fenster, C. A. (1980). The proper role of psychology in child custody disputes. *Journal of Family Law, 18*, 269–300.
Meadows, E. A., & Foa, E. B. (1999). Cognitive-behavioral treatment of traumatized adults. In P. A. Saigh & J. D. Bremner (Eds.), *Posttraumatic stress disorder: A comprehensive text* (pp. 376–390). Boston, MA: Allyn & Bacon.
Mitchell v. Rochester Ry., 45 N.E. 354 (N.Y. 1896).
Molien v. Kaiser Found. Hospital, 616 P. 2d 813 (Cal. 1980).
Montgomery v. Bazaz-Sehgal, 798 A.2d 742 (Pa. 2002).
Moore, M. (2003). Symposium: For what must we pay? Causation and counterfactual baselines. *San Diego Law Review, 40*, 1181–1273.
Mountain Timber Co. v. Washington, 243 U.S. 219, 37 S.Ct. 260 (1917).
Munley, P. H., Busby, R. M., & Jaynes, G. (1997). MMPI-2 findings in schizophrenia and depression. *Psychological Assessment, 9*, 508–511.
Neria, Y., & Solomon, Z. (1999). Prevention of posttraumatic reactions: Debriefing and frontline treatment. In P. A. Saigh & J. D. Bremner (Eds.), *Posttraumatic stress disorder: A comprehensive text* (pp. 376–390). Boston, MA: Allyn & Bacon.
Newton v. Roche Laboratories, Inc. 243 F. Supp. 2d 672 (W.D. Tex. 2002).
Nwakpuda v. Falley's Inc., 14 F. Supp. 1213 (D. Kan. 1998).
O'Connell, J. (1971). *The injury industry and the remedy of no-fault insurance*. New York, Commerce Clearing House.
63 Okl. St. Ann. § 1-1708. 1F (2003).
Page, J. A. (2003). *Torts: Proximate Cause*. New York: Foundation Press.
Palsgraf v. Long Island Rwy., 162 N.E. 99 (N.Y. 1928).
Prosser, W. L. (1971). *Handbook of the law of torts* (4th ed.). St. Paul, MN: West Publishing Co.
Pryor, E. S. (1997). The stories we tell: Intentional harm and the quest for insurance funding. *Texas Law Review, 75*, 1721–1764.
Reese v. Naylor, 222 So.2d 487 (Fla. Dist Ct. App. 1969).
Rind, B., Tromovitch, P., & Bauserman, R. (1998). A meta-analytic examination of assumed properties of child sexual abuse using college samples. *Psychology Bulletin, 124*, 22–53.

Ruda, L. (1993). Caps on noneconomic damages and the female plaintiff: heeding the Warning signs. *Case Western Reserve Law Review, 44*, 197–240

Ruttger Hotel Corp. v. Wagner, 691 So.2d 1177 (Fla. App. 1997).

Sadler, J. Z. (2004). *Values and psychiatric diagnosis*. Oxford: Oxford University Press.

Saigh, P. A., Yasik, A. E., Oberfield, R., & Inamdar, S. C. (1999). Behavioral treatment of child-adolescent posttraumatic stress disorder. In P. A. Saigh & J. D. Bremner (Eds.), *Posttraumatic stress disorder: A comprehensive text* (pp. 353–375). Boston, MA: Allyn & Bacon.

Schwartz, V. E. (1999). The remoteness doctrine: A rational limit on tort law, *Cornell Journal of Law & Public Policy, 8*, 421–443.

Seminole Pipeline Co. v. Broad Leaf Partners, Inc., 979 S.W.2d 730 (Tex. App. 1998).

Shay, J., & Munroe, J. (1999). Group and milieu therapy for veterans with complex posttraumatic stress disorder. In P. A. Saigh & J. D. Bremner (Eds.), *Posttraumatic stress disorder: A comprehensive text* (pp. 391–413). Boston, MA: Allyn & Bacon.

Shuman, D. W. (1993). The psychology of deterrence in tort law. *The University of Kansas Law Review, 42*, 115–168.

Shuman, D. W. (1994). The psychology of compensation in tort law. *The University of Kansas Law Review, 43*, 39–77.

Shuman, D. W. (2002). *Psychiatric and Psychological Evidence. Evidence Series* (2nd ed.). Colorado Springs, CO: Shephard's/McGraw-Hill, Inc.

Shuman, D. W. (2002a). The role of mental health experts in custody decisions: Science, psychological tests, and clinical judgment. *Family Law Quarterly, 36*, 135–162.

Shuman, D. W. (2003). Science, law, and mental health policy. *Ohio Northern University Law Review, 29*, 587–605.

Shuman, D. W., & Sales, B. D. (1998). The admissibility of expert testimony based on clinical judgment and scientific research. *Psychology Public Policy and Law, 4*, 1226–1252.

Shuman, D. W., & Sales, B. D. (1999). Daubert and behavioral and social science evidence: One case but many meanings. *Psychology Public Policy and Law, 5*, 3–17.

Simon, R. I., & Shuman, D. W. (Eds.). (2002). *Retrospective assessment of mental states in litigation: Predicting the past*. Washington, DC: American Psychiatric Publishing, Inc.

Smith v. German, 253 A.2d 107 (Pa. 1969).

Steinhauser v. Hertz, 421 F.2d 1169 (2nd Cir. 1970).

Sutherland, S. M., & Davidson, J. R. T. (1999). Pharmacological treatment of posttraumatic stress disorder. In P. A. Saigh & J. D. Bremner (Eds.), *Posttraumatic stress disorder: A comprehensive text* (pp. 327–353). Boston, MA: Allyn & Bacon.

Taylor v. Burlington Northern Railroad Co., 787 F.2d 1309 (9th Cir. 1986).

Thompson, G. M. (2004). Happiness and chance: A reappraisal of the psychoanalytic conception of suffering. *Psychoanalytic Psychology, 21*, 134–153.

Tyler, T. R. (1990). *Why people obey the law*. New Haven, CT: Yale University Press.

United States v. Scholl, 959 F. Supp. 1189 (D. Ariz. 1997).

Veilleux, D. R. (1994). Necessity of expert testimony on issue of permanence of injury and future pain and suffering. *American Law Reports 5th, 20*, 1–63.

Walker, E. F., & Diforio, D. (1997) Schizophrenia: A neural diathesis-stress model. *Psychological Review, 104*, 667–685.

Waube v. Warrington, 258 N.W. 497 (Wis. 1935).

Wexler, D. B., & Winick, B. J. (1991). *Essays in therapeutic jurisprudence*. Durham, NC: Carolina Academic Press.

42 USCS § 300aa-11, 2004.

21

Causality, Psychological Injuries, and Court: Conclusions

GERALD YOUNG, ANDREW W. KANE, AND KEITH NICHOLSON

In this concluding chapter, we review the different sections of the book, as well as respond to the challenge launched by Daniel Shuman and Jennifer Hardy in Chapter 20—to demonstrate the efficacy of the science of psychology in the area of causality in psychological injury. We include practice recommendations, and indicate directions for future conceptualization and research. Finally, we anticipate future trends in the law and how, in the area of psychological injury and law, psychology must keep its focus if it is to adapt and increase its capacity to present reliable, valid, trustworthy, and relevant evidence in court.

Psychological Order in the Universe

In their chapter, Shuman and Hardy ask us to examine carefully whether there is "psychological order in the universe." They suggest that prediction of who will develop psychological "scars" after traumatic events is a most difficult task, and that such events lead to "significant and permanent" scars only in a minority of individuals. They pose the essential quandary about causality in psychological evidence offered to court; that is, they indicate that "[u]nless psychological distress occurs in an orderly, comprehensible process for the group (i.e., general causation) and therefore for the individual (i.e., specific causation), it is not logically possible to affix responsibility for causing that distress" (Chapter 20, p. 519), Shuman and Hardy add that the law needs to be confident in psychological experts' conclusions about causality. There must be a "cause-in-fact," "proved" as a "proximate cause" by showing that the plaintiff's psychological harm would not have occurred "but for" the defendant's negligent act. Should the defendant have "reasonably foreseen" that her or his act would have led to the harm? If found negligent regarding an injury to a plaintiff who had an "eggshell skull," that is, one that is unusually sensitive causing more severe psychological distress than could have been foreseen, "the defendant is not responsible to compensate the plaintiff for preexisting harm" (p. 528), according to one legal principle, yet still must "take" the plaintiff as she or he is "found," according to another.

Shuman and Hardy insist that in identifying and explaining causal links, along with other factors such as undertaking comprehensive assessments involving "scientifically" validated techniques, "good" science must be used. A reliable "scientific" foundation or basis is necessary to explicitly link the event in question to the psychological distress purportedly induced. Experts who follow this procedure, using "reliable methodology," are offering to the court "specific causal attributions," asserting a specific causal "nexus." Psychologists must be able to demonstrate in their "cause and effect" evidence that they "understand" the psychological "process" resulting in the harm from the act in question, and "know" the factors that "caused" the process to occur. The explanation must be coherent, empirically grounded, and have "predictive value" in individual cases. Shuman and Hardy conclude by challenging psychologists to "advance" their "science" by explaining the "causal relationship" between negligent acts and psychological harm.

Our Response to the Challenge: The Science of Psychological Assessment and Causality

The authors of this book maintain that, along with the roster of internationally respected contributors to the first volume of this pair of books (see Young, Kane, and Nicholson, 2006), we have risen to the challenge, pertaining to causality, presented to the discipline of psychology by Shuman and Hardy. On the one hand, we have explained the concept of causality and related constructs, and their confusion and conflicts across the disciplines. Therefore, we have taken steps to facilitate the disciplines beginning to use a common language. Should this happen, psychology and law can more readily traverse their disciplinary boundaries. On the other hand, we have presented an up-to-date literature review on the three main areas germane to psychological injury and law, those of Posttraumatic Stress Disorder (PTSD), chronic pain, and mild Traumatic Brain Injury (TBI), including analysis of physiological and psychological mechanisms that serve to promote the persistence of the symptoms into chronic and disabling conditions. At the same time, we have provided cautions about threats to validity in individual assessments. We have examined confounds in interpretations, the need to consider alternative interpretations the need for comprehensive assessments with appropriate instruments, and the problems with current diagnostic categories such as PTSD, chronic Pain Disorder, and postconcussive syndrome (PCS).

We recommend that, in order to meet admissibility requirements for court, psychologists and other mental health professionals undertake, at all levels, scientifically informed assessments. They should base their work on multicausal, biopsychosocial models yet, at the same time, realize that, in extreme individual cases, there may be so much preexisting psychopathology, so many vulnerabilities and lifetime stresses, that it is difficult to determine the degree to which an index event in question has contributed to an individual's presentation of psychological difficulties. The science of psychology is continually improving its knowledge base, both in terms of describing psychopathological conditions and associated behavioral problems, and in terms of the mechanisms that underlie them in an interaction of biological, psychological, and social processes. Also, we are continually improving our understanding of the law, and our ability to translate its concepts into psychological terms that may be tested and analyzed utilizing psychological criteria. At the same time, we are aware of our limits in doing so, needing to couch our conclusions about the evidence that we present to court with appropriate qualifications and admission of limitations. The challenge that psychologists need to make to themselves is to ensure that we engage in sufficient education, training, research, and professional development in order to ensure that all of our assessments meet the highest standards of our profession, as well as what the courts expect of us in terms of impartial, comprehensive, relevant, and reliable evidence that aids the trier of fact.

The Science of Causality and Recommendations for Scientific Practice

In his section of the book, Young, with colleagues, further highlights the need for a scientific approach to causality assessment by making suggestions about the research in the field, and by specifying practice suggestions that optimize the use of scientific reasoning in arriving at defensible conclusions on causality.

In Chapter 2, the first chapter of Section I, Young and Kane review various concepts in the field of psychology and law in civil cases. For example, they present the psychological concepts of reliability and validity. These terms relate, respectively, to the replicability and to the soundness or trustworthiness of research data and related matters. The terms are applicable to psychological instruments, diagnostic categories, and individual observations, including those for court purposes. In evaluations of catastrophic cases involving the AMA Guides, Young and Kane suggest that we need to differentiate degrees of psychological impairment in terms of approximate percentages, following models presented in *Desbiens* (2004), to facilitate arriving at reliable and valid judgments of whole body impairments. They point out the quandaries facing psychologists attempting to specify in their evidence for court the degree and nature of functional impairments and disabilities, including their permanent and catastrophic nature, where applicable.

In Chapter 3, Young makes several proposals that may help lead to more carefully framed evaluations of individuals in psychological injury cases, especially in terms of causality. First, he differentiates among the concepts of symptom magnification, symptom exaggeration, and symptom exacerbation. The last is considered a fundamental mechanism that can lead to worsening of symptoms. This can happen due to a variety of reasons, such as the effect of stress derived from psychological injuries but, also, due to factors related to litigation and compensation issues. In addition, he formulates a five-point ordinal causality scale that specifies five possible degrees of causality that a psychologist or other mental health professional might attribute to an index event after evaluating an individual's claimed psychological condition. The scale is comprised of the following points: Sole Cause, Preponderant Cause, Partial Cause, Minor Cause, and Absent Cause. The concepts of "thin" and "crumbling" skulls, derived from legal parlance, have been embedded in the scale. Also, Young presents a 25-item list of possible factors, rationales, considerations, or explanations that may be used by psychologists and other mental health professionals in arriving at their conclusions and formulations about causality. The recommendations made by Young to assist in the assessment of individuals may provide more uniformity in the process of causality evaluations, and may help attorneys in cross-examination to ascertain the scientific quality of evidence proffered to court.

In Chapter 4, written with Ronnie Shore, the authors present a dictionary of terms with respect to causality, causation, and related terms, from the perspective of the law, medicine, and psychology, in particular. Young and Shore not only compare and contrast the definitions, pointing out their similarities and overlaps, but also present their contradictions, the gaps in the nexus of terms in each field, and the ambiguities and difficulties in translating from one field to another. After this analysis, they provide a table that extracts from the disciplines under review a simplified network of terms that eliminates many of the contradictions, gaps, ambiguities, and translation difficulties inherent in the lists of terms within the disciplines. To summarize the table of key terms given in this chapter, first, the legal field has contributed relevant terms such as: proximate, concurrent, contributing, intervening, material, superseding. Other useful terms can be added from medicine, such as: component, exacerbation, predisposing, primary, secondary. Additional terms that are judged relevant ones from psychology include: catalytic, latent, maintaining, mediating, multiple. Together, these terms permit a more refined understanding of multiple causality, and many aspects of the psycho-legal process, reducing ambiguities in communicating across disciplines. As indicated by Wecht and Koehler (2005), the attorney and the scientist, or clinician, require, "the ability to communicate effectively and to comprehend and serve each other's needs" (p. 530). In addition, Young and Shore recommend that when there is a chain of causation, the temporally initial, intermediate, and more recent components should be specified, without using more ambiguous terms, such as "immediate" and "remote."

In Chapters 5–7, Young reviews recent scientific research on the three major areas of psychological injury—PTSD, chronic pain, and mild TBI. The review incorporates salient points from the chapters written for the companion book by Young et al. (2006), but adds important findings from the professional literature since the time those chapters were written, because it is our intent to provide to the reader the state of the art in the professional literature related to psychological injury.

The biopsychosocial model is the most integrative in the field of psychological injury. To conclude the three chapters on the recent literature on PTSD, chronic pain, and mild TBI, Young presents an integrative account of the biopsychosocial model that cuts across the three areas, and relates it to causality. The literature review includes presentation of physiological mechanisms that may be active in all three areas, as well as presenting physiological mechanisms in the stress process, in general, which are common to the three areas. At the same time, the psychosocial factors that act to exacerbate, worsen, maintain, and render chronic PTSD, pain, and the effects of mild TBI appear to be powerful forces that account for much of the individual variation in the three areas. When evaluating individual cases of psychological injury, forensic and other assessors need to consider how the biopsychosocial model can help explain causality in terms of preevent, event, and postevent factors.

In Chapter 8, devoted to chronic pain, Young and Chapman explore a nonlinear dynamical systems model of pain experience. The chapter presents a theoretical model that is expanding in importance in psychology, and indeed in all sciences, and shows how it can help explain phenomena in pain that otherwise may seem difficult to explain. For example, the pain patient may become "stuck" in her or his mental landscape in "attractors" related to pain, even resisting change despite optimal effort, or she or he may show sudden reversal to experiencing less pain, in what is called the "butterfly effect."

The model has been applied to help explain the intimate connection between pain and affect. The model readily applies to PTSD and TBI, for it is a general model of how systems work. The authors indicate that comorbidity across the three areas of psychological injury, along with other disorders such as depression, may reflect unified superordinate systems, accounting for their persistence, chronicity, and the increased difficulty encountered in treating them. Young and Chapman also present a five-step stage model equally applicable to both the development of chronic pain and the response to therapy for pain. The passage through these steps may include nonlinear dynamical system self-organization. Chronic pain may involve successive transition processes consistent with cyclic attractors, chaotic attractors, gravitating to the region between order and disorder, and Complex Adaptive Systems. Overall, the nonlinear dynamical systems model presented may help psychology to further understand pain and its links to affect and comorbid conditions, and underscores the general principle of multicausality in the determinants of psychological injuries due to traumatic and related events. At the practice level, Young and Chapman suggest that the psychological diagnosis of chronic Pain Disorder should be changed to "Chronic Pain Complications Disorder."

In their chapter, Salmon, Celinski, and Young present a dynamic model of causality, which expands on the traditional stage model of chronic pain developed by Gatchel. They review the literature on rehabilitation measurements. They emphasize that for pain patients in rehabilitation treatment, assessors should monitor treatment adherence by using reliable and valid instruments amenable to repeated administration, to facilitate measuring patients' recovery curves, monitoring their obligation to mitigate their losses.

Overall, the chapters in this section provide clarification concerning terminology used to describe causal relationships, describe theoretical models related to the three areas of psychological injury, that is, those of PTSD, chronic pain, and TBI, and critically review the literature related to the areas and the models. Moreover, the chapters make practical suggestions to improve the scientific basis of psychological injury assessments, especially pertaining to causality. They advise that psychologists who undertake individual assessments for court purposes should maintain a rigorous scientific process, both in considering the professional literature related to the cases at hand, and in evaluating the individuals being assessed in a comprehensive manner using scientific reasoning. Finally, the chapters advise prudence with respect to factors such as malingering and other threats to validity of individual assessments. In all these regards, the section of the book written by Young and colleagues has met the challenge launched by Shuman and Hardy to improve the science in psychology with respect to causality evaluation in psychological assessment, and to improve the scientific process in arriving at judgments about causality in individual assessments.

The Prudence of Psychological Practice and Proffering Evidence to Court

In his section of the book, Andrew Kane has presented what psychologists need to know for court. When these recommendations are followed, the court can be more confident of the relevance and reliability (psychological validity) of evidence and conclusions on causality offered by psychologists.

In his first chapter, Kane discusses in detail the United States' Supreme Court decision in *Daubert v. Merrell Dow Pharmaceuticals, Inc.* and the Canadian Supreme Court decision in *R. v. Mohan*, and their progeny, providing the psychologist and attorney with essential information about those cases and how the requirements of the cases affect testimony by experts in most trial courts. Kane also reviews critical concepts such as error rates, base rates, diagnosis, bases for expert opinions, the role of learned treatises, and thresholds for admissibility of psychological assessments in evaluations undertaken for court. An expert who is not familiar with all of these areas may have difficulty passing a *Daubert/Mohan* challenge, which refers to attempts to prevent the admission of evidence to court via a motion *in limine*.

In his second chapter, Kane presents the requirements for undertaking a comprehensive evaluation as part of preparing to present a case in court. The forensic psychologist must undertake a very substantial historical review, including reviewing numerous types of records, in an effort to establish the pretrauma psychological status of the individual. Similarly, a number of collateral interviews of people with first-hand knowledge about the plaintiff's or complainant's pretrauma psychological status should be conducted, assuming people with such information can be identified and are willing to be interviewed. In addition to an in-depth interview of the individual, the psychological assessment process also includes psychological testing with reliable and valid instruments appropriate to the referral question and the individual being assessed, assessment of response style and malingering, and utilization of various information-gathering instruments. Kane makes specific recommendations regarding psychological tests and other instruments. He strongly indicates the need for the evaluator to be familiar with the state of the art in assessments of the type he or she is conducting by reviewing relevant articles and books from the professional literature. Further, the evaluator needs to be skilled at taking information from the nomothetic database (the professional literature) and applying it appropriately to the idiographic situation (the specific case).

Kane's third chapter discusses other issues that are essential to the psycholegal assessment process. The assessing expert must be extremely familiar with the professional literature relevant to all aspects of a given case. Evaluations must have ecological, incremental, and other types of validity in order to be of significant value to the court process. Evaluators must avoid a number of types of bias in order to ensure the accuracy of the assessment. Kane discusses a number of reasons why therapists should rarely if ever serve as experts in cases involving their clients.

Whereas the Rorschach inkblot test may be of value in an evaluation, Kane reviews the current controversy regarding the Comprehensive System for the Rorschach, the dominant scoring system in use. Until there are new guidelines based on further research, psychologists should avoid making strong statements, including predictions, based on interpretive criteria from the Comprehensive System.

In this chapter, Kane also reviews the concepts of "thin skulls" and "eggshell personalities," which concern varying degrees of preexisting psychological vulnerabilities, psychopathologies, and so on.

Because many experts accept cases outside of the jurisdiction in which they are licensed or certified, Kane provides information regarding the requirements of every state and province for the practice of psychology by individuals not holding a license or certification in the jurisdiction in which the evaluation and testimony are to take place, and cautions experts to ensure that, when accepting referrals outside of their home jurisdictions, they respect the law in the "foreign" jurisdiction. For example, in the state of South Carolina (the most extreme example), a violation of the statute governing the practice of psychology carries a maximum penalty of a $50,000 fine and/or one year in prison. Numerous ethical issues are discussed in the chapter, and numerous practice recommendations are made.

Although the U.S. Supreme Court emphasizes the importance of peer review of published studies, Kane discusses the fact that there are many problems with the peer review process, and ample proof that peer review does not guarantee quality. He notes, however, that peer review remains an important means of addressing quality issues, despite its problems.

Finally, there is evidence that tort cases that are prolonged may in themselves harm plaintiffs, so that appropriate speed in reaching resolution is important. Kane also discusses common errors by evaluators. Kane concludes by indicating that the best means of meeting a *Daubert* or *Mohan* challenge is for the psychologist to conduct a comprehensive, multimethod assessment that is impartial and is thoroughly grounded in scientific and/or accepted clinical methodology.

Causality and the Differential Diagnosis of Malingering: An Examination of Methods and Findings

In their section, Keith Nicholson and Michael Martelli present a detailed and critical review of the literature concerning malingering and related phenomena, highlighting the need for psychologists (and others) to be aware of the many possible explanations, both biomedical and psychosocial, for behavior and test findings. Psychologists and others must critically examine the methods that are utilized in arriving at conclusions, being aware of the limitations of techniques.

Malingering is often a prominent concern in medicolegal situations in which there may be considerable financial incentives. However, despite extensive study, there are still no simple methods for the determination of malingering, and all available information and alternative hypotheses must be carefully considered in the differential diagnosis. Malingering is often confused with other behaviors, and there have been particular problems distinguishing among malingering, exaggeration or accentuation of complaint, or symptomatology for other reasons, and what may be genuine symptoms or difficulties associated with several different and often comorbid conditions such as TBI, chronic pain, PTSD, or other psychoemotional problems.

Although caution must be exercised in arriving at conclusions, assessors and clinicians must be cognizant of the possibility of malingering and be able to investigate this possibility further, if suspected. It is widely agreed that the possibility of malingering should be considered in any situation in which there may be significant financial or other external incentives. Some psychometric techniques, observations, or other information may provide relatively strong evidence of malingering, but evidence is usually less clear, and no single test result, observation, or piece of information can provide unambiguous evidence of malingering. Some methods or techniques remain very controversial, with some practitioners or researchers being avid proponents of them, whereas others argue that such procedures are inappropriate. Research continues to explore the utility of existing techniques or methodologies, and new ones are continually being developed, which should provide for increasing confidence in the differential diagnosis of malingering and related behaviors. Nicholson and Martelli offer pragmatic and prudent approaches to follow in addressing evaluation of malingering and related behaviors.

Conclusions

Psychological Causality in the Legal Universe

Shuman and Hardy's challenge to psychologists is to undertake state of the art evaluations that address the legal questions as thoroughly as possible in given cases. Whereas they initially suggest that it is essential to be able to predict who will (and who will not) have a significant psychological injury from a specified type of trauma, for example, child abuse or a motor vehicle accident (MVA), they later note, correctly, that there are many factors other than the nature of the trauma that determine whether an individual will experience significant dysfunction or will be resilient in the face of the trauma. For any one individual being assessed, it is the comprehensive, impartial, multifactorial, and biopsychosocial nature of the evaluation that will address the relative contributions of the trauma experienced by the individual, the individual's pretrauma state, and the consequences of the traumatic event for the individual. While our legal system attempts to make the victim whole by awarding an amount of money, Shuman and Hardy indicate, correctly, that the money is secondary for many plaintiffs. Rather, a plaintiff may primarily be seeking the assignment of responsibility to the defendant, or may be seeking justice in some other form. The psychologist or other mental health expert contributes to this process by undertaking a complete and competent evaluation that will produce, in Shuman and Hardy's terminology, *descriptive clinical testimony, specific causal attributions*, or other means of assessing causation of psychological harm. The context for every evaluation, as Shuman and Hardy indicate, and as Kane's chapters describe in detail, is a thorough knowledge of the relevant professional literature, application of the appropriate means of assessing the alleged psychological injury, and the expert's impartial, accurate, comprehensive presentation of the data addressing the causal nexus among the trauma, and the individual's pretrauma and individual's posttrauma condition, and other relevant factors. Whether focusing on the expert's clinical skills, the descriptive clinical testimony, the scientifically-based methodology utilized, or conclusions about specific causal attributions, the expert's evidence presented to court greatly facilitates the complex task of the fact finder.

Psychology and other mental health professions aspire to attain a goal analogous to that of physics: to move toward finding a more cohesive theory that helps explain everything pertinent about determinants or causes of behavior, a master theory that will provide a context for understanding causality and causation regarding every observation about individuals in their past, present, and future. It is over 100 years since Einstein first made this attempt to arrive at a relevant global explanatory theory in physics via his Theory of Relativity, which has been included in the current (but still incomplete) Standard Model. Theoretical physicists today posit that a theory of everything may lie in string theory and/or supersymmetry, and researchers are actively exploring these theories and others. Similarly, psychologists have elaborated explanations of behavior that englobe multiple determinants, labeling them multicausal, interactive, biopsychosocial, and so on. Relative to physicists, psychologists may not be as close to a solution in finding an integrative theory, but we are making advances in understanding the complexity of behavior. For example, psychological researchers address biological aspects such as genetic influence, personal aspects such as personality characteristics, coping skills and resilience, and social and environmental aspects such as family support or lack thereof, and developmental and learning aspects, such as classical and operant conditioning. Although neither science can yet explain everything, each is actively pursuing that goal at many levels, including, as specified for psychology by Shuman and Hardy in the last sentence of their chapter, "by advancing the science that explains the causal relationship between wrongful events and psychological harm (p. 545)."

Practice Recommendations

In the following, we highlight some specific concerns that psychologists should consider in their assessments with respect to evaluations of causality.

(a) Some of the outstanding issues in the field relate to the proper evaluation of preexisting factors involved in presentation of complainants. Examinees may be poor historians, engage in withholding of information or impression management, or otherwise make it difficult to assess their pre-incident history. The records on their education, military service, work performance, and so on, may be spotty. Prior medical and mental health documentation may not be sufficiently available or accurate (See, e.g., Koch, O'Neill, & Douglas, 2005).
(b) We emphasize that the psychologist must adhere to a scientific stance and a comprehensive approach throughout the forensic or related evaluation process, from critical appraisal of the recent literature, to selecting instruments with acceptable reliability and validity, to gathering all the relevant data. All relevant hypotheses must be explored, using appropriate critical reasoning to arrive at conclusions that are justified according to the data gathered and the relevant professional literature. With respect to malingering and related constructs, we note that they are difficult to define and difficult to assess; the assumption should be that they may exist in any case in one form or another, and they, therefore, should be addressed carefully in every case. The task of the assessor is to parse out what can be legitimately ascribed to the effects of the index event and its sequelae, if anything, and what can be attributed to a host of factors unrelated to the event, if present, such as a preexisting personality disorder or other psychopathology powerful enough to negate or obscure any additional effects that could derive from the event at issue.
(c) Any assessment in the area of psychological injury needs to be informed by the multifactorial causal perspective in order to improve its validity or trustworthiness. For example, it will be difficult to establish whether assessments have been comprehensive and unbiased if the multifactorial causal model does not guide the approaches taken by assessors. Are the conclusions offered in evidence presented to court consistent with the current trends in the scientific literature concerning multifactorial causal models? Do conclusions to assessments consider possible complexity in the causality underlying the psychological presentation of the individuals assessed, avoiding the pitfalls of overly simplistic explanations?

Suggested Directions for Research

Greenberg, Otto, and Long (2003) decry the lack of research undertaken on forensic assessments in personal injury cases. For example, there have been few studies that systematically review assessment practices, work products, reports, or testimony in psychological injury evaluations. There are few specialized forensic assessment instruments, including in the area of psychological injury, often making it necessary to use instruments designed for other purposes rather than having been validated for use in forensic evaluations. Boccaccini and Brodsky (1999) conducted a survey of 80 psychologists on the psychological instruments that they typically use in their examinations. Although informative, this type of research should be expanded to foster use of the very best instruments available. Also, research can be undertaken to investigate whether for any individual for whom both plaintiff and defense psychological experts have undertaken evaluations, are there similar psychometric instruments used and results obtained, yet the defense and plaintiff psychological experts reach opposing conclusions? In this regard, Large and Neilssen (2001) did report that, in MVA cases, psychiatric reports for the opposing sides generally mirrored the referral sources' expectations.

Zillmer (2003) reminds us that forensic psychologists should adhere to the scientific process and methodology, but this obligation is rendered more difficult without scientific study of how biases come into play and can be detected and controlled. Commons, Miller, and Gutheil (2004) researched bias among forensic psychiatrists, with results indicating that experts need to receive further training in recognition and avoidance of bias, and that further research in this area is needed (see the sections by Kane and by Nicholson and Martelli).

Research is also needed to confirm and expand the utility of psychometric instruments typically used in psychological injury evaluations. For example, the MMPI-2 (Minnesota Multiphasic Personality Inventory, Second Edition, Butcher, Dahlstrom, Graham, Tellegen, & Kaemmer, 1989) is used in 94% of such assessments, according to Boccaccini and Brodsky (1999), yet more research is needed "to demonstrate how the test's assessment of response style functions in personal injury" (Greenberg et al., 2003, p. 416). Certainly, better research is needed in the area of forensic assessment instruments, in general, although, increasingly, this type of research is being undertaken and a body of good instruments with supporting data is being developed (Kane, 1999). For example, there are two existing instruments that are widely used and well-researched—the validity scales of the MMPI-2, and the SIRS (Structured Interview of Reported Symptoms; Rogers, Bagby, & Dickens, 1992). In this regard, Rogers and Shuman (2005) provide strong documentation for both the MMPI-2 and the SIRS, although we echo Greenberg's concern that continuing research on the MMPI-2 and other instruments is needed. For example, the most common use of the SIRS relates to criminal cases, although it is also being utilized in personal injury cases (Franklin & Thompson, 2005; Rogers, 1997).

In terms of the need for research on malingering and related response styles, research along these lines is continuing (see the Nicholson and Martelli section), but there is still poor understanding of the affect of confounding factors, such as that of chronic pain or more severe psychopathology, on measures of malingering and response style.

Kulich et al. (2003) decry that "malingering assessment" packages are being marketed for pain and disability, even though there is "scant" scientific literature in this area. Users of the instruments risk not only *Daubert* admissibility challenges but, also, professional sanctions for ethical infractions.

Research should be undertaken on the recovery process from psychological effects induced by traumatic and other legally-relevant events. We need to know how individuals attempt to mitigate their losses, comply with proposed treatment regimens, demonstrate adequate effort, and so on. In this regard, Otto and Heilbrun

(2002) recommend that we need to ascertain the expected length of treatment for recovery after a traumatic experience, though it will be difficult to determine a meaningful average, given the wide range of individual variation. We need to learn more about what factors work against recovery in cases of psychological injury, what promotes recovery, and what factors influence resilience. For example, most trauma victims, even those severely traumatized, do not develop PTSD (Bonanno, 2004; Christopher, 2004; McNally, 2004; Pledger, 2003). There is much published work regarding therapy for victims of diverse forms of trauma, but until more controlled research is undertaken, the optimal manner for rehabilitating victims of trauma will remain uncertain.

A pressing need in research on psychological injury is for prospective research on functional outcome with a sufficiently long period of follow-up so that we may improve our ability to determine causal relationships underlying long-term psychological impairments, disorders, and disabilities. This research must be multifactorial in nature, considering relevant biological, psychological, and social factors, and preevent, event, and postevent factors, in a complex, interactive model. Simultaneously, it must address malingering, response biases, and other confounds or threats to validity, and, at the same time, address effort to recover and the effects of therapy, in a comprehensive approach to understanding long term psychological dysfunction. The research program should address the three major areas of psychological injury (PTSD, chronic pain, and TBI), including the effects of their interactive concurrent comorbidity. The ultimate goal of the research program would be to both predict better and facilitate better individual, long-term, functional outcome.

Changes in Personal Injury Law

As indicated by Shuman and Hardy, plaintiffs have been able to sue for decades in order to try to obtain compensation for the psychological effects of traumatic incidents. A substantial body of research has documented the nature and degree of psychological injuries possible as the result of traumatic incidents. Specific tests and structured interviews address the diagnostic criteria and phenomenology for PTSD, TBI (including the persistent PCS), chronic pain, and other disorders, as well as for malingering. Nevertheless, these constructs are not universally accepted at face value, and their validity has been questioned. For example, a few authors have questioned the construct of PTSD as a valid entity (McNally, 2003; Rosen, 2004), the persistent PCS may be readily explainable by confounds such as pain and other factors unrelated to brain injury (Nicholson & Martelli, 2006), and the concept of chronic pain as a mental disorder is debated (Melzack & Katz, 2006). If all these syndromes and diagnoses were judged inadmissible in court, this would limit access to the court by individuals having valid, debilitating psychological injuries. Therefore, a great deal remains to be learned about these psychological injuries and related ones. The authors of this text hope and expect that researchers will address these issues and related ones in future work.

Concluding Comment

To meet *Daubert/Mohan* and similar challenges to admissibility of evidence in court, psychologists must be knowledgeable of their field, and apply their knowledge judiciously in comprehensive assessments of individuals. The knowledge base that psychological assessors need is expanding, and practitioners should keep abreast of these developments.

Yet psychologists should expect to encounter continued difficulties when functioning at the intersection of law and psychology. The two professions do not always translate readily across their boundaries. Krauss and Sales (2003) suggest that, "When psychologists are asked to provide psychological assessments and testimony in court, their services must often address legal questions and constructs that are defined in the law, but which do not directly correspond to psychological constructs, assessment instruments, and nomenclature" (p. 545). The authors indicate that a legal standard is of limited value in operationalizing which components of the standard are appropriate to test, as well as the nature of the specific psychological assessment that should be undertaken to respond to it. Translation is also an issue when considering the specific *Daubert/Mohan* standards for admissibility of evidence. Although criteria are described in relation to the reliability and relevance of the evidence with respect to a case at hand, in particular, "it is difficult to nearly impossible to directly translate some of the *Daubert* pragmatic considerations to clinical testimony" (p. 554).

One concern relates to combining clinical testimony and science-based testimony. Assessment instruments and actuarial predictions are based on research on group data (i.e., are nomothetic in nature). In contrast, in individual (idiographic) prediction, there could be some element in a particular case that leads to questions about use of the research base. In order to arrive at valid conclusions about causality, psychologists and other mental health professionals need to respect that the causality evaluation process functions at the level of group data in science and individual data in assessments. Psychologists need to navigate well this interface between research and practice if they are to navigate well the interface between psychology and the law.

This book explains the myriad concepts related to causality and causation, particularly in law and psychology, facilitating work involving both fields. At the same time, in a multicausal perspective, this book explicates the biopsychosocial model, the role of stress in psychological injury, and the role of possible confounds and threats to validity such as malingering and response bias in symptom presentation. Because this book emphasizes the scientific approach—from understanding terms, translating them across fields, knowing the current, relevant scientific literature, grasping the multiple factors in causal relationships, undertaking comprehensive assessments to address individuals' complaints, using reliable and valid instruments in doing so, and arriving at well-supported conclusions in individuals' diagnoses, recommendations, prognoses, and statements about disability—this book, along with its companion volume by the present co-authors (Young et al., 2006), help the psychologist and other assessors prepare better for court-related purposes.

References

Boccaccini, M. T., & Brodsky, S. L. (1999). Diagnostic test use by forensic psychologists in emotional injury cases. *Professional Psychology: Research and Practice, 31*, 251–259.

Bonanno, G. A. (2004). Loss, trauma, and human resilience: Have we underestimated the human capacity to thrive after extremely aversive events. *American Psychologist, 59*, 20–28.

Butcher, J. N., Dahlstrom, W. G., Graham, J. R., Tellegen, A., & Kaemmer, B. (1989). *Minnesota Multiphasic Personality Inventory-2 (MMPI-2): Manual for administration and scoring*. Minneapolis: University of Minnesota Press.

Christopher, M. (2004). A broader view of trauma: A biopsychosocial-evolutionary view of the role of the traumatic stress response in the emergence of pathology and/or growth. *Clinical Psychology Review, 24*, 75–98.

Commons, M. L., Miller, P. M., & Gutheil, T. G. (2004). Expert witness perceptions of bias in experts. *The Journal of the American Academy of Psychiatry and the Law, 32*, 1–10.

Daubert v. Merrell Dow Pharmaceuticals, Inc. 509 U.S. 579, 113 S.Ct. 2786, 125 L.Ed. 2d 469 (1993).

Desbiens v. Mordini, 2004 CanLII 41166 (ON S.C.).

Franklin, C. L., & Thompson, K. E. (2005). Response style and Posttraumatic Stress Disorder (PTSD): A review. *Journal of Trauma & Dissociation, 6*, 1005–1123.

Greenberg, S. A., Otto, R. K., & Long, A. C. (2003). The utility of psychological testing in assessing emotional damages in personal injury litigation. *Assessment, 10*, 411–419.

Kane, A. W. (1999). Essentials of malingering assessment. In M. J. Ackerman (Ed.), *Essentials of forensic psychological assessment* (pp. 78–99). New York: Wiley.

Koch, W. J., O'Neill, M., & Douglas, K. S. (2005). Empirical limits for the forensic assessment of PTSD litigants. *Law and Human Behavior, 29*, 121–149.

Krauss, D. A., & Sales, B. D. (2003). Forensic psychology, public policy, and the law. In I. B. Weiner (Series Ed.) & A. M. Goldstein (Vol. Ed.), *Handbook of psychology: Vol. 11, Forensic psychology* (pp. 543–560). Hoboken, NJ: Wiley.

Kulich, R. J., Driscoll, J., Prescott, J. C. Jr., Pelletier, N. J., Driscoll, S., Cooke, W. et al. (2003). The *Daubert* standard: A primer for pain specialists. *Pain Medicine, 4*, 75–80.

Large, M., & Nielssen, O. (2001). An audit of medico-legal reports prepared for claims of psychiatric injury following motor vehicle accidents. *Australian & New Zealand Journal of Psychiatry, 35*, 535–540.

McNally, R. J. (2003). *Remembering trauma*. Cambridge, MA: Belknap Press.

McNally, R. J. (2004). Conceptual problems with the DSM-IV criteria for Posttraumatic Stress Disorder. In G. M. Rosen (Ed.), *Posttraumatic Stress Disorder: Issues and controversies* (pp. 1–14). Chichester, UK: Wiley.

Melzack, R., & Katz, J. (2006). Pain in the 21st century: The neuromatrix and beyond. In G. Young, A. W. Kane, & K. Nicholson (Eds.), *Psychological knowledge in court: PTSD, pain, and TBI* (pp. 129–148). New York: Springer Science+Business Media.

Nicholson, K., & Martelli, M. F. (2006). The confounding effects of pain, psychoemotional problems or psychiatric disorder, premorbid ability structure, and motivational or other factor on neuropsychological test performance. In G. Young, A. W. Kane, & K. Nicholson (Eds.), *Psychological knowledge in court: PTSD, pain, and TBI* (pp. 335–351). New York: Springer Science+Business Media.

Otto, R. K., & Heilbrun, K. (2002). The practice of forensic psychology: A look toward the future in light of the past. *American Psychologist, 57*, 5–18.

Pledger, C. (2003). Discourse on disability and rehabilitation issues: Opportunities for psychology. *American Psychologist, 58*, 279–284.

R. v. Mohan [1994] 2 S.C.R. 9, 1994 CanLII 80 (S.C.C.).

Rogers, R. (1997). Structured interviews and dissimulation. In R. Rogers (Ed.), *Clinical assessment of malingering and deception* (2nd ed.) (pp. 301–327). New York: Guilford Press.

Rogers, R., Bagby, R. M., & Dickens, S. E. (1992). *Structured Interview of Reported Symptoms: Professional manual*. Lutz, FL: Psychological Assessment Resources.

Rogers, R., & Shuman, D. W. (2005). *Fundamentals of forensic practice: Mental health and criminal law*. New York: Springer Science+Business Media.

Rosen, G. M. (Ed.). (2004). *Posttraumatic Stress Disorder: Issues and controversies*. Chichester, UK: Wiley.

Wecht, C. H., & Koehler, S. A. (2005). Effective expert witnessing, Fourth edition: Practices for the 21st century. *The Journal of Legal Medicine, 26*, 529–534.

Young, G., Kane, A.W., & Nicholson, K. (Eds.). (2006). *Psychological knowledge in court: PTSD, pain, and TBI*. New York: Springer Science+Business Media.

Young, G., & Yehuda, R. (2006). Understanding PTSD: Implications for court. In G. Young, A. W. Kane, & K. Nicholson (Eds.), *Psychological knowledge in court: PTSD, pain, and TBI* (pp. 55–69). New York: Springer Science+Business Media.

Zillmer, A. E. (2003). Introduction to a special issue on psychological and neuropsychological assessment in the forensic setting: Art or science? *Assessment, 10*, 318–320.

Acknowledgment of Sources of Citations, and Permissions Granted

Chapter 1. Causality, Psychological Injuries, and Court: Introduction

The Two Introductory Quotes

Sales, B. D., & Shuman, D. W. (2005). *Experts in court: Reconciling law, science, and professional knowledge.* Reprinted with permission of the American Psychological Association and Dr. B. Sales.

Chapter 2. Causality in Psychology and Law

Reliability

Urbina, S. (2004). *Essentials of psychological testing.* Reprinted with permission of John Wiley & Sons, Inc.

Chapter 4. Dictionary of Terms Related to Causality, Causation, Law, and Psychology

Key Legal Terms Related to Causality and Causation

Causa

Reprinted from *Black's law dictionary;* Garner, B. A. (Ed.), 8th edition (2004). With permission of the West Group.

Causa Scientiae

Reprinted from *Black's law dictionary;* Garner, B. A. (Ed.), 8th edition (2004). With permission of the West Group.

For all quotes, we consulted the publisher involved, and either we were requested to acknowledge the source, and the author, as well, where applicable, or it was indicated to us that using the quote was "fair use." Some sources are credited in the ways indicated by publishers; all others are in APA style.

Causal

Reprinted from *Black's law dictionary;* Garner, B. A. (Ed.), 8th edition (2004). With permission of the West Group.

Causality

Reprinted from *Black's law dictionary;* Garner, B. A. (Ed.), 8th edition (2004). With permission of the West Group.

By permission from *Merriam-Webster's Collegiate® Dictionary, 11th Edition* Copyright 2003 by Merriam-Webster, Incorporated (www.Merriam-Webster.com).

Causation

Reprinted from *Black's law dictionary;* Garner, B. A. (Ed.), 8th edition (2004). With permission of the West Group.

Reprinted from Jewell, E. J., & Abate, F. (Eds.). (2001). *The new Oxford American dictionary.* With permission of the Oxford University Press.

By permission from *Merriam-Webster's Collegiate® Dictionary, 11th Edition* Copyright 2003 by Merriam-Webster, Incorporated (www.Merriam-Webster.com).

Reprinted from Romano, J. F. (1999). Cause yourself to understand the intricacies of causation. *Trial Lawyer, 22*, 101–103. With permission of the Aspen Publishers.

Medical Causation

Reprinted from Romano, J. F. (1999). Cause yourself to understand the intricacies of causation. *Trial Lawyer, 22*, 101–103. With permission of the Aspen Publishers.

Proof of Causation

Reprinted from Romano, J. F. (1999). Cause yourself to understand the intricacies of causation. *Trial Lawyer, 22*, 101–103. With permission of the Aspen Publishers.

Reprinted from Solomon, R. M., Feldthusen, D. P., & Kostal, R. W. (1996). *Cases and materials on the law of torts* (4th ed.). Reprinted by permission of Carswell, a division of Thomson Canada Limited.

Proximate Causation

Reprinted from Koocher, G. P. (1998). Glossary of legal terms of special interest in mental health practice. In G. P. Koocher, J. C. Norcross, & S. S. Hill III (Eds.), *Psychologist's desk reference* (pp. 509–513). With permission of the Oxford University Press.

Cause

Reprinted from *Black's law dictionary;* Garner, B. A. (Ed.), 8th edition (2004). With permission of the West Group.

Reprinted from Jewell, E. J., & Abate, F. (Eds.). (2001). *The new Oxford American dictionary.* With permission of the Oxford University Press.

By permission. From *Merriam-Webster's Collegiate® Dictionary, 11th Edition* Copyright 2003 by Merriam-Webster, Incorporated (www.Merriam-Webster.com).

But-for Cause

Reprinted from *Black's law dictionary;* Garner, B. A. (Ed.), 8th edition (2004). With permission of the West Group.

Reprinted from Cocchiarella, L., & Lord, S. J. (Eds.). *Master the AMA Guides, Fifth Edition*, Copyright 2001, American Medical Association.

Reprinted from *The international handbook of road traffic accidents and psychological trauma: Current understanding, treatment and law* E. J. Hickling & E. B. Blanchard (Eds.), Posttraumatic Stress Disorder stemming from motor vehicle accidents: Legal issues in Canada and the United States; Douglas, K. S., Huss, M. T., Murdoch, L. L., Washington, D. O., & Koch, W. J. (pp. 271–289) Copyright (1999). With permission from Elsevier.

Cause in Fact

Reprinted from *Tort law dictionary*. (n.d.). Retrieved July 2, 2003, from http://lexnet.bravepages.com/tortdict.htm. With permission of author Eric Engles.

Concurrent Cause

Reprinted from *Black's law dictionary;* Garner, B. A. (Ed.), 7th edition (1999). With permission of the West Group.

Contributing Cause

Reprinted from *Black's law dictionary;* Garner, B. A. (Ed.), 8th edition (2004). With permission of the West Group.

Immediate Cause

Reprinted from *Black's law dictionary;* Garner, B. A. (Ed.), 8th edition (2004). With permission of the West Group.

Intervening Cause

Reprinted from *Black's law dictionary;* Garner, B. A. (Ed.), 8th edition (2004). With permission of the West Group.

Dependent Intervening Cause

Reprinted from *Black's law dictionary;* Garner, B. A. (Ed.), 8th edition (2004). With permission of the West Group.

Independent Intervening Cause

Reprinted from *Black's law dictionary;* Garner, B. A. (Ed.), 8th edition (2004). With permission of the West Group.

Material Cause

Reprinted from *Tort law dictionary*. (n.d.). Retrieved July 2, 2003, from http://lexnet.bravepages.com/tortdict.htm. With permission of author Eric Engles.

Reprinted from *The international handbook of road traffic accidents and psychological trauma: Current understanding, treatment and law* E. J. Hickling & E. B. Blanchard (Eds.), Posttraumatic Stress Disorder stemming from motor vehicle accidents: Legal issues in Canada and the United States; Douglas, K. S., Huss, M. T., Murdoch, L. L., Washington, D. O., & Koch, W. J. (pp. 271–289) Copyright (1999). With permission from Elsevier.

Necessary Cause

Reprinted from *Black's law dictionary*; Garner, B. A. (Ed.), 8th edition (2004). With permission of the West Group.

Proximate Cause

Reprinted from *Black's law dictionary*; Garner, B. A. (Ed.), 8th edition (2004). With permission of the West Group.

Reprinted from Koocher, G. P. (1998). Glossary of legal terms of special interest in mental health practice. In G. P. Koocher, J. C. Norcross, & S. S. Hill III (Eds.), *Psychologist's desk reference* (pp. 509–513). With permission of the Oxford University Press.

Reprinted from Solomon, R. M., Feldthusen, D. P., & Kostal, R. W. (1996). *Cases and materials on the law of torts* (4th ed.). Reprinted by permission of Carswell, a division of Thomson Canada Limited.

Reprinted from Slovenko, R. I. (2003). Introduction. In R. I. Simon (Ed.), *Posttraumatic Stress Disorder in litigation: Guidelines for forensic assessment* (2nd ed., pp. ixx–xxiv).

Reprinted by permission of American Psychiatric Publishers.

Reprinted from Wecht, C. H. (1995). Medicolegal causation: The heart of medicolegal litigation. *Trauma, 37*, 69–78. With permission of Lippincott Williams & Wilkins.

Remote Cause

Reprinted from *Black's law dictionary;* Garner, B. A. (Ed.), 8th edition (2004). With permission of the West Group.

Reprinted from Solomon, R. M., Feldthusen, D. P., & Kostal, R. W. (1996). *Cases and materials on the law of torts* (4th ed.). Reprinted by permission of Carswell, a division of Thomson Canada Limited.

Sole Cause

Reprinted from *Black's law dictionary;* Garner, B. A. (Ed.), 8th edition (2004). With permission of the West Group.

Reprinted from Wecht, C. H. (1995). Medicolegal causation: The heart of medicolegal litigation. *Trauma, 37*, 69–78. With permission of Lippincott Williams & Wilkins.

Superseding Cause

Reprinted from *Black's law dictionary;* Garner, B. A. (Ed.), 8th edition (2004). With permission of the West Group.

Sufficient Cause

Reprinted from *Tort law dictionary*. (n.d.). Retrieved July 2, 2003, from http://lexnet.bravepages.com/tortdict.htm. With permission of author Eric Engles.

Cause of Action

Reprinted from *Black's law dictionary;* Garner, B. A. (Ed.), 8th edition (2004). With permission of the West Group.

Reprinted from Koocher, G. P. (1998). Glossary of legal terms of special interest in mental health practice. In G. P. Koocher, J. C. Norcross, & S. S. Hill III (Eds.), *Psychologist's desk reference* (pp. 509–513). With permission of the Oxford University Press.

Auxiliary Legal Terms Associated with Causality and Causation

Admissibility (according to *Daubert*)

Reprinted from Krauss, D. A., & Sales, B. D. (2003). Forensic psychology, public policy, and the law. In I. B. Weiner (Series Ed.) & A. M. Goldstein (Vol. Ed.), *Handbook of psychology: Vol. 11, Forensic psychology* (pp. 543–560).With permission from John Wiley & Sons, Inc.

Bystander Proximity Rule

Reprinted from *Introduction to forensic psychology: Clinical and social psychological perspectives* (2003). Walker, L. E. A., & Shapiro, D. L. Copyright Kluwer Academic/Plenum Publishers, New York, 233 Spring Street, New York, 10013. With kind permission from Springer Science and Business Media.

Complaint

Reprinted from Koocher, G. P. (1998). Glossary of legal terms of special interest in mental health practice. In G. P. Koocher, J. C. Norcross, & S. S. Hill III (Eds.), *Psychologist's desk reference* (pp. 509–513). With permission of the Oxford University Press.

Contributory Negligence or Comparative Negligence

Reprinted from Koocher, G. P. (1998). Glossary of legal terms of special interest in mental health practice. In G. P. Koocher, J. C. Norcross, & S. S. Hill III (Eds.), *Psychologist's desk reference* (pp. 509–513). With permission of the Oxford University Press.

Crumbling Skull Rule

Reprinted from *The international handbook of road traffic accidents and psychological trauma: Current understanding, treatment and law* E. J. Hickling & E. B. Blanchard (Eds.), Posttraumatic Stress Disorder stemming from motor vehicle accidents: Legal issues in Canada and the United States; Douglas, K. S., Huss, M. T., Murdoch, L. L., Washington, D. O., & Koch, W. J. (pp. 271–289) Copyright (1999). With permission from Elsevier.

Reprinted from Bogoroch, R. M., & Chandler, T. S. (2002). How Canadian courts have turned "Thin Skull" damages into "Crumbling Skulls" damages: What are the implications? (Available from the Canadian Institute Advanced Forum on Litigation Damages: Bogoroch & Associates, 150 King Street West, Suite 1707, Toronto, ON M5H 1J9).

Damages

Reprinted from Koocher, G. P. (1998). Glossary of legal terms of special interest in mental health practice. In G. P. Koocher, J. C. Norcross, & S. S. Hill III (Eds.), *Psychologist's desk reference* (pp. 509–513). With permission of the Oxford University Press.

Reprinted from *The international handbook of road traffic accidents and psychological trauma: Current understanding, treatment and law* E. J. Hickling & E. B. Blanchard (Eds.), Posttraumatic Stress Disorder stemming from motor vehicle accidents: Legal issues in Canada and the United States; Douglas, K. S., Huss, M. T., Murdoch, L. L., Washington, D. O., & Koch, W. J. (pp. 271–289) Copyright (1999). With permission from Elsevier.

General Damages

Reprinted from *The international handbook of road traffic accidents and psychological trauma: Current understanding, treatment and law* E. J. Hickling & E. B. Blanchard (Eds.), Posttraumatic Stress Disorder stemming from motor vehicle accidents: Legal issues in Canada and the United States; Douglas, K. S., Huss, M. T., Murdoch, L. L., Washington, D. O., & Koch, W. J. (pp. 271–289) Copyright (1999). With permission from Elsevier.

Future Damages

Reprinted from *The international handbook of road traffic accidents and psychological trauma: Current understanding, treatment and law* E. J. Hickling & E. B. Blanchard (Eds.), Posttraumatic Stress Disorder stemming from motor vehicle accidents: Legal issues in Canada and the United States; Douglas, K. S., Huss, M. T., Murdoch, L. L., Washington, D. O., & Koch, W. J. (pp. 271–289) Copyright (1999). With permission from Elsevier.

Pecuniary Damages

Reprinted from *The international handbook of road traffic accidents and psychological trauma: Current understanding, treatment and law* E. J. Hickling & E. B. Blanchard (Eds.), Posttraumatic Stress Disorder stemming from motor vehicle accidents: Legal issues in Canada and the United States; Douglas, K. S., Huss, M. T., Murdoch, L. L., Washington, D. O., & Koch, W. J. (pp. 271–289) Copyright (1999). With permission from Elsevier.

Special Damages

Reprinted from *The international handbook of road traffic accidents and psychological trauma: Current understanding, treatment and law* E. J. Hickling & E. B. Blanchard (Eds.),

Posttraumatic Stress Disorder stemming from motor vehicle accidents: Legal issues in Canada and the United States; Douglas, K. S., Huss, M. T., Murdoch, L. L., Washington, D. O., & Koch, W. J. (pp. 271–289) Copyright (1999). With permission from Elsevier.

Reprinted from Slovenko, R. I. (2003). Introduction. In R. I. Simon (Ed.), *Posttraumatic Stress Disorder in litigation: Guidelines for forensic assessment* (2nd ed., pp. ixx–xxiv). Reprinted by permission of American Psychiatric Publishers.

Reprinted from Geistfeld, M. (2001). Scientific uncertainty and causation in tort law. *Vanderbilt Law Review, 54*, 1011–1037. With permission of Vanderbilt Law Review & Vanderbilt Journal of Entertainment Law & Practice.

Defendant

Reprinted from Koocher, G. P. (1998). Glossary of legal terms of special interest in mental health practice. In G. P. Koocher, J. C. Norcross, & S. S. Hill III (Eds.), *Psychologist's desk reference* (pp. 509–513). With permission of the Oxford University Press.

Deposition

Reprinted from *Black's law dictionary;* Garner, B. A. (Ed.), 8th edition (2004). With permission of the West Group.

Reprinted from Koocher, G. P. (1998). Glossary of legal terms of special interest in mental health practice. In G. P. Koocher, J. C. Norcross, & S. S. Hill III (Eds.), *Psychologist's desk reference* (pp. 509–513). With permission of the Oxford University Press.

Direct Verdict

Reprinted from Greenberg, S. A. (2003). Personal injury examinations in torts for emotional distress. In I. B. Weiner (Series Ed.) & A. M. Goldstein (Vol. Ed.), *Handbook of psychology: Vol. 11, Forensic psychology* (pp. 233–257). With permission of John Wiley & Sons, Inc.

Evidence

Reprinted from "Amendment to Federal Rule of Evidence 702" by C.E. Brixen & C.E. Mies, published in *Jurimetrics*, Volume 40, No. 4, Summer 2000. Copyright 2000 by the American Bar Association. Reprinted with permission.

Expert Witness

Reprinted from Reid, W. H. (1999). *A clinician's guide to legal issues in psychotherapy: Or proceed with caution*. With permission of Zeig, Tucker & Co., Inc.

Fit

Reprinted from Krauss, D. A., & Sales, B. D. (2003). Forensic psychology, public policy, and the law. In I. B. Weiner (Series Ed.) & A. M. Goldstein (Vol. Ed.), *Handbook of psychology: Vol. 11, Forensic psychology* (pp. 543–560).With permission from John Wiley & Sons, Inc.

Reprinted from "Amendment to Federal Rule of Evidence 702" by C.E. Brixen & C.E. Mies, published in *Jurimetrics*, Volume 40, No. 4, Summer 2000. © 2000 by the American Bar Association. Reprinted with permission.

Full Recovery Rule

Reprinted from *Introduction to forensic psychology: Clinical and social psychological perspectives* (2003). Walker, L. E. A., & Shapiro, D. L. Copyright Kluwer Academic/Plenum Publishers, New York, 233 Spring Street, New York, 10013. With kind permission from Springer Science and Business Media.

Gatekeeping Controls

Reprinted from Weissman, H. N., & DeBow, D. M. (2003). Ethical principles and professional competencies. In I. B. Weiner (Series Ed.) & A. M. Goldstein (Vol. Ed.), *Handbook of psychology: Vol. 11, Forensic psychology* (pp. 33–53). With permission of John Wiley & Sons, Inc.

Malpractice

Reprinted from Koocher, G. P. (1998). Glossary of legal terms of special interest in mental health practice. In G. P. Koocher, J. C. Norcross, & S. S. Hill III (Eds.), *Psychologist's desk reference* (pp. 509–513). With permission of the Oxford University Press.

Negligence

Reprinted from Koocher, G. P. (1998). Glossary of legal terms of special interest in mental health practice. In G. P. Koocher, J. C. Norcross, & S. S. Hill III (Eds.), *Psychologist's desk reference* (pp. 509–513). With permission of the Oxford University Press.

Pain and Suffering

Reprinted from Koocher, G. P. (1998). Glossary of legal terms of special interest in mental health practice. In G. P. Koocher, J. C. Norcross, & S. S. Hill III (Eds.), *Psychologist's desk reference* (pp. 509–513). With permission of the Oxford University Press.

Physical Impact Rule

Reprinted from *Introduction to forensic psychology: Clinical and social psychological perspectives* (2003). Walker, L. E. A., & Shapiro, D. L. Copyright Kluwer Academic/Plenum Publishers, New York, 233 Spring Street, New York, 10013. With kind permission from Springer Science and Business Media.

Probative

Reprinted from *Black's law dictionary;* Garner, B. A. (Ed.), 8th edition (2004). With permission of the West Group.

Reasonable Medical Certainty

Reprinted from Koocher, G. P. (1998). Glossary of legal terms of special interest in mental health practice. In G. P. Koocher, J. C. Norcross, & S. S. Hill III (Eds.), *Psychologist's desk reference* (pp. 509–513). With permission of the Oxford University Press.

Reprinted from Weissman, H. N., & DeBow, D. M. (2003). Ethical principles and professional competencies. In I. B. Weiner (Series Ed.) & A. M. Goldstein (Vol. Ed.), *Handbook of psychology: Vol. 11, Forensic psychology* (pp. 33–53). With permission of John Wiley & Sons, Inc.

Relevance

Reprinted from *Forensic psychology: From classroom to courtroom*; B. Van Dorsten (Ed.), (2002) (pp. 17–33). The mental health professional in court: Legal issues, research foundations, and effective testimony; Brodsky, S. L., Caputo, A. A., & Domino, M. L. Copyright Kluwer Academic/Plenum Publishers, New York, 233 Spring Street, New York, 10013. With kind permission from Springer Science and Business Media.

Reprinted from Krauss, D. A., & Sales, B. D. (2003). Forensic psychology, public policy, and the law. In I. B. Weiner (Series Ed.) & A. M. Goldstein (Vol. Ed.), *Handbook of psychology: Vol. 11, Forensic psychology* (pp. 543–560).With permission from John Wiley & Sons, Inc.

Reliability

Reprinted from *Forensic psychology: From classroom to courtroom*; B. Van Dorsten (Ed.), (2002) (pp. 17–33). The mental health professional in court: Legal issues, research foundations, and effective testimony; Brodsky, S. L., Caputo, A. A., & Domino, M. L. Copyright Kluwer Academic/Plenum Publishers, New York, 233 Spring Street, New York, 10013. With kind permission from Springer Science and Business Media.

Reprinted from Greenberg, S. A. (2003). Personal injury examinations in torts for emotional distress. In I. B. Weiner (Series Ed.) & A. M. Goldstein (Vol. Ed.), *Handbook of psychology: Vol. 11, Forensic psychology* (pp. 233–257). With permission of John Wiley & Sons, Inc.

Reprinted from "Amendment to Federal Rule of Evidence 702" by C. E. Brixen & C. E. Mies, published in *Jurimetrics*, Volume 40, No. 4, Summer 2000. Copyright 2000 by the American Bar Association. Reprinted with permission.

Reprinted from Krauss, D. A., & Sales, B. D. (2003). Forensic psychology, public policy, and the law. In I. B. Weiner (Series Ed.) & A. M. Goldstein (Vol. Ed.), *Handbook of psychology: Vol. 11, Forensic psychology* (pp. 543–560).With permission from John Wiley & Sons, Inc.

Settlement

Reprinted from Koocher, G. P. (1998). Glossary of legal terms of special interest in mental health practice. In G. P. Koocher, J. C. Norcross, & S. S. Hill III (Eds.), *Psychologist's desk reference* (pp. 509–513). With permission of the Oxford University Press.

Sufficiency

Reprinted from "Amendment to Federal Rule of Evidence 702" by C. E. Brixen & C. E. Mies, published in *Jurimetrics*, Volume 40, No. 4, Summer 2000. Copyright 2000 by the American Bar Association. Reprinted with permission.

Reprinted from *The international handbook of road traffic accidents and psychological trauma: Current understanding, treatment and law* E. J. Hickling & E. B. Blanchard

(Eds.), Posttraumatic Stress Disorder stemming from motor vehicle accidents: Legal issues in Canada and the United States; Douglas, K. S., Huss, M. T., Murdoch, L. L., Washington, D. O., & Koch, W. J. (pp. 271–289) Copyright (1999). With permission from Elsevier.

Theory of the Case

Reprinted from Wecht, C. H. (1995). Medicolegal causation: The heart of medicolegal litigation. *Trauma, 37*, 69–78. With permission of Lippincott Williams & Wilkins.

Thin Skull Rule

Reprinted from *Black's law dictionary;* Garner, B. A. (Ed.), 8th edition (2004). With permission of the West Group.

Reprinted from Bogoroch, R. M., & Chandler, T. S. (2002). How Canadian courts have turned "Thin Skull" damages into "Crumbling Skull" damages: What are the implications? (Available from the Canadian Institute Advanced Forum on Litigating Damages: Bogoroch & Associates, 150 King Street West, Suite 1707, Toronto, ON M5H 1J9).

Reprinted from *The international handbook of road traffic accidents and psychological trauma: Current understanding, treatment and law* E. J. Hickling & E. B. Blanchard (Eds.), Posttraumatic Stress Disorder stemming from motor vehicle accidents: Legal issues in Canada and the United States; Douglas, K. S., Huss, M. T., Murdoch, L. L., Washington, D. O., & Koch, W. J. (pp. 271–289), Copyright (1999). With permission from Elsevier.

Reprinted from Klimchuk, D. (1998). Causation, thin skulls and equality. *Canadian Journal of Law and Jurisprudence, 11*, 115–141. With permission of the Faculty of Law at the University of Western Ontario.

Reprinted from Greenberg, S. A. (2003). Personal injury examinations in torts for emotional distress. In I. B. Weiner (Series Ed.) & A. M. Goldstein (Vol. Ed.), *Handbook of psychology: Vol. 11, Forensic psychology* (pp. 233–257). With permission of John Wiley & Sons, Inc.

Reprinted from Bogoroch, R. M., & Chandler, T. S. (2002). How Canadian courts have turned "Thin Skull" damages into "Crumbling Skulls" damages: What are the implications? (Available from the Canadian Institute Advanced Forum on Litigation Damages: Bogoroch & Associates, 150 King Street West, Suite 1707, Toronto, ON M5H 1J9).

Tort

Reprinted from Koocher, G. P. (1998). Glossary of legal terms of special interest in mental health practice. In G. P. Koocher, J. C. Norcross, & S. S. Hill III (Eds.), *Psychologist's desk reference* (pp. 509–513). With permission of the Oxford University Press.

Reprinted from Greenberg, S. A. (2003). Personal injury examinations in torts for emotional distress. In I. B. Weiner (Series Ed.) & A. M. Goldstein (Vol. Ed.), *Handbook of psychology: Vol. 11, Forensic psychology* (pp. 233–257). With permission of John Wiley & Sons, Inc.

Trier of Fact

Reprinted from *Black's law dictionary;* Garner, B. A. (Ed.), 8th edition (2004). With permission of the West Group.

Ultimate Issue

Reprinted from Ewing, C. P. (2003). Expert testimony: Law and practice. In I. B. Weiner (Series Ed.) & A. M. Goldstein (Vol. Ed.), *Handbook of psychology: Vol. 11, Forensic psychology* (pp. 55–66). With permission of John Wiley & Sons, Inc.

Reprinted from Krauss, D. A., & Sales, B. D. (2003). Forensic psychology, public policy, and the law. In I. B. Weiner (Series Ed.) & A. M. Goldstein (Vol. Ed.), *Handbook of psychology: Vol. 11, Forensic psychology* (pp. 543–560).With permission from John Wiley & Sons, Inc.

Wanton

Reprinted from Koocher, G. P. (1998). Glossary of legal terms of special interest in mental health practice. In G. P. Koocher, J. C. Norcross, & S. S. Hill III (Eds.), *Psychologist's desk reference* (pp. 509–513). With permission of the Oxford University Press.

Wilful

Reprinted from Koocher, G. P. (1998). Glossary of legal terms of special interest in mental health practice. In G. P. Koocher, J. C. Norcross, & S. S. Hill III (Eds.), *Psychologist's desk reference* (pp. 509–513). With permission of the Oxford University Press.

Zone of Danger

Reprinted from *Introduction to forensic psychology: Clinical and social psychological perspectives* (2003). Walker, L. E. A., & Shapiro, D. L. © Kluwer Academic/Plenum Publishers, New York, 233 Spring Street, New York, 10013. With kind permission from Springer Science and Business Media.

Key Medical Terms Relating to Causality and Causation

Causal

Reprinted from *Dorland's illustrated medical dictionary* (30th ed.), Dorland, I., & Newman, W. A. p. 311; Copyright 2003. With permission of Elsevier.

Causal Treatment

Reprinted from *Attorney's Dictionary of Medicine and Work Finder* with permission. Copyright 2002, Matthew Bender & Company, Inc., a member of the LexisNexis Group. All rights reserved.

Causality

Reprinted from Stedman, T. L. (2000). *Stedman's medical dictionary* (27th ed.). With permission of Lippincott Williams & Wilkins.

Cause

Reprinted from *Dorland's illustrated medical dictionary* (30th ed.), Dorland, I., & Newman, W. A. p. 311; Copyright 2003. With permission of Elsevier.

Reprinted from Stedman, T. L. (2000). *Stedman's medical dictionary* (27th ed.). With permission of Lippincott Williams & Wilkins.

Component Cause

Reprinted from Cocchiarella, L., & Lord, S. J. (Eds.). *Master the AMA Guides Fifth Edition*, Copyright 2001, American Medical Association.

Constitutional Cause

Reprinted from *Dorland's illustrated medical dictionary* (30th ed.), Dorland, I., & Newman, W. A. p. 311; Copyright 2003. With permission of Elsevier.

Reprinted from Stedman, T. L. (2000). *Stedman's medical dictionary* (27th ed.). With permission of Lippincott Williams & Wilkins.

Exciting Cause

Reprinted from *Dorland's illustrated medical dictionary* (30th ed.), Dorland, I., & Newman, W. A. p. 311; Copyright 2003. With permission of Elsevier.

Reprinted from Stedman, T. L. (2000). *Stedman's medical dictionary* (27th ed.). With permission of Lippincott Williams & Wilkins.

Immediate Cause

Reprinted from *Dorland's illustrated medical dictionary* (30th ed.), Dorland, I., & Newman, W. A. p. 311; Copyright 2003. With permission of Elsevier.

Local Cause

Reprinted from *Dorland's illustrated medical dictionary* (30th ed.), Dorland, I., & Newman, W. A. p. 311; Copyright 2003. With permission of Elsevier.

Necessary Cause

Reprinted from Stedman, T. L. (2000). *Stedman's medical dictionary* (27th ed.). With permission of Lippincott Williams & Wilkins.

Precipitating Cause

Copyright 1998 from *The concise dictionary of medical-legal terms* by Bailey, J. A., II. Reproduced by permission of Routledge/Taylor & Francis Group, LLC.

Predisposing Cause

Reprinted from *Dorland's illustrated medical dictionary* (30th ed.), Dorland, I., & Newman, W. A. p. 311; Copyright 2003. With permission of Elsevier.

Reprinted from Stedman, T. L. (2000). *Stedman's medical dictionary* (27th ed.). With permission of Lippincott Williams & Wilkins.

Copyright 1998 from *The concise dictionary of medical-legal terms* by Bailey, J. A., II. Reproduced by permission of Routledge/Taylor & Francis Group, LLC.

Primary Cause

Reprinted from *Dorland's illustrated medical dictionary* (30th ed.), Dorland, I., & Newman, W. A. p. 311; Copyright 2003. With permission of Elsevier.

Copyright 1998 from *The concise dictionary of medical-legal terms* by Bailey, J. A., II. Reproduced by permission of Routledge/Taylor & Francis Group, LLC.

Proximate Cause

Reprinted from *Dorland's illustrated medical dictionary* (30th ed.), Dorland, I., & Newman, W. A. p. 311; Copyright 2003. With permission of Elsevier.

Reprinted from Stedman, T. L. (2000). *Stedman's medical dictionary* (27th ed.). With permission of Lippincott Williams & Wilkins.

Remote Cause

Reprinted from *Dorland's illustrated medical dictionary* (30th ed.), Dorland, I., & Newman, W. A. p. 311; Copyright 2003. With permission of Elsevier.

Secondary Cause

Reprinted from *Dorland's illustrated medical dictionary* (30th ed.), Dorland, I., & Newman, W. A. p. 311; Copyright 2003. With permission of Elsevier.

Specific Cause

Reprinted from *Dorland's illustrated medical dictionary* (30th ed.), Dorland, I., & Newman, W. A. p. 311; Copyright 2003. With permission of Elsevier.

Reprinted from Stedman, T. L. (2000). *Stedman's medical dictionary* (27th ed.). With permission of Lippincott Williams & Wilkins.

Sufficient Cause

Reprinted from Stedman, T. L. (2000). *Stedman's medical dictionary* (27th ed.). With permission of Lippincott Williams & Wilkins.

Reprinted from Cocchiarella, L., & Lord, S. J. (Eds.). *Master the AMA Guides Fifth Edition*, Copyright 2001, American Medical Association.

Ultimate Cause

Reprinted from *Dorland's illustrated medical dictionary* (30th ed.), Dorland, I., & Newman, W. A. p. 311; Copyright 2003. With permission of Elsevier.

Reprinted from *Attorney's Dictionary of Medicine and Work Finder* with permission. Copyright 2002, Matthew Bender & Company, Inc., a member of the LexisNexis Group. All rights reserved.

Exacerbation

Reprinted from *Dorland's illustrated medical dictionary* (30th ed.), Dorland, I., & Newman, W. A. p. 651; Copyright 2003. With permission of Elsevier.

Hill's Causation Criteria (Epidemiology)

Reprinted from Cocchiarella, L., & Lord, S. J. (Eds.). *Master the AMA Guides Fifth Edition*, Copyright 2001, American Medical Association.

Pathogenesis

Copyright 1998 from *The concise dictionary of medical-legal terms* by Bailey, J. A., II. Reproduced by permission of Routledge/Taylor & Francis Group, LLC.

Auxiliary Medical Terms Associated with Causality and Causation

Diagnosis

Reprinted from Goldstein, A. M. (2003). Overview of forensic psychology. In I. B. Weiner (Series Ed.) & A. M. Goldstein (Vol. Ed.), *Handbook of psychology: Vol. 11, Forensic psychology* (pp. 3–20). With permission of John Wiley & Sons, Inc.

Disability

Reprinted from Cocchiarella, L., & Andersson, G. B. J. (Eds.), *Guides to the Evaluation of Permanent Impairment Fifth Edition*, Copyright 2001, American Medical Association.

Etiology

Copyright 1998 from *The concise dictionary of medical-legal terms;* Bailey, J. A., II. Reproduced by permission of Routledge/Taylor & Francis Group, LLC.

Functional Limitation

Reprinted from Cocchiarella, L., & Andersson, G. B. J. (Eds.), *Guides to the Evaluation of Permanent Impairment Fifth Edition*, Copyright 2001, American Medical Association.

Handicap

Reprinted from Cocchiarella, L., & Andersson, G. B. J. (Eds.), *Guides to the Evaluation of Permanent Impairment Fifth Edition*, Copyright 2001, American Medical Association.

ICD-9 (and *ICD-10*)

Reprinted from Johnson, S. B., Perry, N. W., Jr., & Rozensky, R. H. (2002). Introduction to volume 1: Medical disorders and behavioral applications. In T. J. Boll (Series Ed.), S. B. Johnson, N. W. Perry Jr., & R. H. Rozensky (Vol. Eds.), *Handbook of clinical health psychology: Vol. 1. Medical disorders and behavioral applications* (pp. 4–5). With permission of the American Psychological Association

Impairment

Reprinted from Cocchiarella, L., & Andersson, G. B. J. (Eds.), *Guides to the Evaluation of Permanent Impairment Fifth Edition*, Copyright 2001, American Medical Association.

Key Psychological Terms Related to Causality and Causation

Catalytic Variable

Reprinted from Haynes, S. N. (1992). Models of causality in psychopathology: Toward dynamic, synthetic and nonlinear models of behavior disorders. With permission of author Stephen Haynes.

Causal Connection

Reprinted from *Southern California Law Review, 51* (1978a) 527–654; Crazy behavior, morals, and science: An analysis of mental health law. Morse, S. *Professional Psychology*, 9 (1978b) 389–399; Law and mental health professionals: The limits of expertise. Morse, S. © Kluwer Academic/Plenum Publishers, New York, 233 Spring Street, New York, 10013. With kind permission from Springer Science and Business Media.

Causal Discontinuity

Reprinted from Haynes, S. N. (1992). Models of causality in psychopathology: Toward dynamic, synthetic and nonlinear models of behavior disorders. With permission of author Stephen Haynes.

Causal Latency

Reprinted from Haynes, S. N. (1992). Models of causality in psychopathology: Toward dynamic, synthetic and nonlinear models of behavior disorders With permission of author Stephen Haynes.

Causal Mechanism

Reprinted from Haynes, S. N. (1992). Models of causality in psychopathology: Toward dynamic, synthetic and nonlinear models of behavior disorders. With permission of author Stephen Haynes.

Causal Model

Reprinted from Haynes, S. N. (1992). Models of causality in psychopathology: Toward dynamic, synthetic and nonlinear models of behavior disorders. With permission of author Stephen Haynes.

Causal Variable

Reprinted from Haynes, S. N. (1992). Models of causality in psychopathology: Toward dynamic, synthetic and nonlinear models of behavior disorders. With permission of author Stephen Haynes.

Causality

Copyright 2002 from *The dictionary of psychology*; Corsini, R. J. Reproduced by permission of Routledge/Taylor & Francis Group, LLC.

Reprinted from Reber, A. S., & Reber, E. S. (2001). *The Penguin dictionary of psychology* (3rd ed.). With permission of Arthur S. Reber and Penguin Group.

Causation

Reprinted from Reber, A. S., & Reber, E. S. (2001). *The Penguin dictionary of psychology* (3rd ed.). With permission of Arthur S. Reber and Penguin Group.

Copyright 2002 from *The dictionary of psychology*; Corsini, R. J. Reproduced by permission of Routledge/Taylor & Francis Group, LLC.

Causation and Correlation

Copyright 2002 from *The dictionary of psychology*; Corsini, R. J. Reproduced by permission of Routledge/Taylor & Francis Group, LLC.

Multiple Causation

Reprinted from Reber, A. S., & Reber, E. S. (2001). *The Penguin dictionary of psychology* (3rd ed.). With permission of Arthur S. Reber and Penguin Group.

Simple Causation

Reprinted from Reber, A. S., & Reber, E. S. (2001). *The Penguin dictionary of psychology* (3rd ed.). With permission of Arthur S. Reber and Penguin Group.

Cause

Reprinted from Haynes, S. N. (1992). Models of causality in psychopathology: Toward dynamic, synthetic and nonlinear models of behavior disorders With permission of author Stephen Haynes.

Efficient Cause

Reprinted from Haynes, S. N. (1992). Models of causality in psychopathology: Toward dynamic, synthetic and nonlinear models of behavior disorders With permission of author Stephen Haynes.

False Cause

Reprinted from *Handbook of forensic neuropsychology* A. M. Horton Jr. & L. C. Hartlage (Eds.). (2003). pp. 113–136. Diagnostic decision making in neuropsychology; Williams, A. D. © Kluwer Academic/Plenum Publishers, New York, 233 Spring Street, New York, 10013. With kind permission from Springer Science and Business Media.

Latent Cause

Reprinted from Haynes, S. N. (1992). Models of causality in psychopathology: Toward dynamic, synthetic and nonlinear models of behavior disorders. With permission of author Stephen Haynes.

Intermediate Effect

Reprinted from Haynes, S. N. (1992). Models of causality in psychopathology: Toward dynamic, synthetic and nonlinear models of behavior disorders. With permission of author Stephen Haynes.

Maintaining Cause

Reprinted from Haynes, S. N. (1992). Models of causality in psychopathology: Toward dynamic, synthetic and nonlinear models of behavior disorders. With permission of author Stephen Haynes.

Original Cause

Reprinted from Haynes, S. N. (1992). Models of causality in psychopathology: Toward dynamic, synthetic and nonlinear models of behavior disorders. With permission of author Stephen Haynes.

Triggering Cause

Reprinted from Haynes, S. N. (1992). Models of causality in psychopathology: Toward dynamic, synthetic and nonlinear models of behavior disorders. With permission of author Stephen Haynes.

Determinant

Reprinted from Reber, A. S., & Reber, E. S. (2001). *The Penguin dictionary of psychology* (3rd ed.). With permission of Arthur S. Reber and Penguin Group.

Functional Relationship

Reprinted from Haynes, S. N. (1992). Models of causality in psychopathology: Toward dynamic, synthetic and nonlinear models of behavior disorders. With permission of author Stephen Haynes.

Mediating Variable

Reprinted from Haynes, S. N. (1992). Models of causality in psychopathology: Toward dynamic, synthetic and nonlinear models of behavior disorders. With permission of author Stephen Haynes.

Necessary Condition

Reprinted from Haynes, S. N. (1992). Models of causality in psychopathology: Toward dynamic, synthetic and nonlinear models of behavior disorders. With permission of author Stephen Haynes.

Necessary Causal Variable

Reprinted from Haynes, S. N. (1992). Models of causality in psychopathology: Toward dynamic, synthetic and nonlinear models of behavior disorders. With permission of author Stephen Haynes.

Proximate Cause

Reprinted from Alcock, J. (2001). *Animal Behavior: An evolutionary approach* (7th ed.); With permission of Sinauer Associates, Inc.

Reprinted from Koocher, G. P. (1998). Glossary of legal terms of special interest in mental health practice. In G. P. Koocher, J. C. Norcross, & S. S. Hill III (Eds.), *Psychologist's desk reference* (pp. 509–513). With permission of the Oxford University Press.

Risk Factor

Reprinted from Haynes, S. N. (1992). Models of causality in psychopathology: Toward dynamic, synthetic and nonlinear models of behavior disorders. With permission of author Stephen Haynes.

Vulnerability

Reprinted from Haynes, S. N. (1992). Models of causality in psychopathology: Toward dynamic, synthetic and nonlinear models of behavior disorders. With permission of author Stephen Haynes.

Auxiliary Psychological Terms Associated with Causality and Causation

Biopsychosocial Model

Reprinted from Thompson, R. J Jr., & Van Loon, K. J. (2002). Mental disorders. In T. J. Boll (Series Ed.) S. B. Johnson, N. W. Perry Jr., & R. H. Rozensky (Vol. Eds.). *Handbook of clinical health psychology: Vol. 1. Medical disorders and behavioral applications* (pp. 143–172). With permission of Robert Thompson, Suzanne Bennett Johnson and American Psychological Association.

Reprinted with permission from Keefe, F. J., Smith, S. J., Buffington, A. L. H., Gibson, J., Studts, J. L., & Caldwell, D. S. (2002). Recent advances and future directions in the biopsychosocial assessment and treatment of arthritis. *Journal of Consulting and Clinical Psychology, 70*, 640–655.FIX

Reprinted from Weissman, H. N., & DeBow, D. M. (2003). Ethical principles and professional competencies. In I. B. Weiner (Series Ed.) & A. M. Goldstein (Vol. Ed.), *Handbook of psychology: Vol. 11, Forensic psychology* (pp. 33–53). With permission of John Wiley & Sons, Inc.

Cognitive Behavioral Model

Reprinted from *The Corsini encyclopedia of psychology and behavioral science* (3rd ed.), Craighead, W. E., & Nemeroff, C. B. (Eds.). Copyright 2001. Reprinted with permission of John Wiley & Sons Inc.

Reprinted from Kazdin, A. E. (Ed.). (2000). *Encyclopedia of psychology*. (Vol. 2). With permission of Oxford University Press.

Diathesis-Stress Model

Reprinted from Zuckerman, M. (1999). *Vulnerability to psychopathology: A biosocial model*. With permission of author Marvin Zuckerman and the American Psychological Association.

Reprinted from *Dictionary of theories, laws, and concepts in psychology*. Roeckelein, J. E. Copyright 1998 by Greenwood Press. Reproduced with permission of Greenwood Publishing Group, Inc., Westport, Ct.

Dynamical Systems

Reprinted from Lewis, M. D., & Granic, I. (2000). Introduction: A new approach to the study of emotional development. In M. D. Lewis & I. Granic (Eds.), *Emotion, development, and self-organization: Dynamic systems approaches to emotional development* (pp. 1–12). Reprinted with the permission of Cambridge University Press.

Reprinted from Smith, L. B., & Thelen, E. (Eds.). (1993). *A dynamic systems approach to development: Applications*. With permission of The MIT Press.

Determinism

Reprinted from Haynes, S. N. (1992). Models of causality in psychopathology: Toward dynamic, synthetic and nonlinear models of behavior disorders With permission of author Stephen Haynes.

Reprinted from Reber, A. S., & Reber, E. S. (2001). *The Penguin dictionary of psychology* (3rd ed.). With permission of Arthur S. Reber and Penguin Group.

Ecological Model

Reprinted from *The Corsini encyclopedia of psychology and behavioral science* (3rd ed.), Craighead, W. E., & Nemeroff, C. B. (Eds.). Copyright 2001. Reprinted with permission of John Wiley & Sons, Inc.

Freedom of Will

Reprinted from Reber, A. S., & Reber, E. S. (2001). *The Penguin dictionary of psychology* (3rd ed.). With permission of Arthur S. Reber and Penguin Group.

Individual Differences

Reprinted from Haynes, S. N. (1992). Models of causality in psychopathology: Toward dynamic, synthetic and nonlinear models of behavior disorders. With permission of author Stephen Haynes.

Information Processing Model

Reprinted from *Dictionary of theories, laws, and concepts in psychology*. Roeckelein, J. E. Copyright 1998 by Greenwood Press. Reproduced with permission of Greenwood Publishing Group, Inc., Westport, Ct.

Learning Theory

Reprinted from *The Corsini encyclopedia of psychology and behavioral science* (3rd ed.), Craighead, W. E., & Nemeroff, C. B. (Eds.). Copyright 2001. Reprinted with permission of John Wiley & Sons, Inc.

Levels of Proof

Reprinted from Goldstein, A. M. (2003). Overview of forensic psychology. In I. B. Weiner (Series Ed.) & A. M. Goldstein (Vol. Ed.), *Handbook of psychology: Vol. 11, Forensic psychology* (pp. 3–20). With permission of John Wiley & Sons, Inc.

Reprinted from Weissman, H. N., & DeBow, D. M. (2003). Ethical principles and professional competencies. In I. B. Weiner (Series Ed.) & A. M. Goldstein (Vol. Ed.), *Handbook of psychology: Vol. 11, Forensic psychology* (pp. 33–53). With permission of John Wiley & Sons, Inc.

Medical Model in Psychology

Reprinted from *The Corsini encyclopedia of psychology and behavioral science* (3rd ed.), Craighead, W. E., & Nemeroff, C. B. (Eds.). Copyright 2001. Reprinted with permission of John Wiley & Sons, Inc.

Mind/Body Problem

Reprinted from *The Corsini encyclopedia of psychology and behavioral science* (3rd ed.), Craighead, W. E., & Nemeroff, C. B. (Eds.). Copyright 2001. Reprinted with permission of John Wiley & Sons, Inc.

Person-Environment Transactions

Reprinted from Caspi, A., & Roberts, B. W. (1999). Personality continuity and change across the life course. In L. A. Pervin, & O. P. John (Eds.). *Handbook of personality: Theory and research* (2nd ed, pp. 300–326). With permission of the Guilford Press, Inc.

Positivism

Reprinted from Reber, A. S., & Reber, E. S. (2001). *The Penguin dictionary of psychology* (3rd ed.). With permission of Arthur S. Reber and Penguin Group.

Reasonable Degree of Psychological Certainty

Reprinted from Goldstein, A. M. (2003). Overview of forensic psychology. In I. B. Weiner (Series Ed.) & A. M. Goldstein (Vol. Ed.), *Handbook of psychology: Vol. 11, Forensic psychology* (pp. 3–20). With permission of John Wiley & Sons, Inc.

Reductionist

Reprinted from Reber, A. S., & Reber, E. S. (2001). *The Penguin dictionary of psychology* (3rd ed.). With permission of Arthur S. Reber and Penguin Group.

Reliability

Reprinted from *Handbook of psychological assessment* (4th ed.), Groth-Marnat, G. Copyright 2003. Reprinted with permission of John Wiley & Sons, Inc.

Reprinted from *The Corsini encyclopedia of psychology and behavioral science* (3rd ed.), Craighead, W. E., & Nemeroff, C. B. (Eds.). Copyright 2001. Reprinted with permission of John Wiley & Sons, Inc.

Sensitivity

Reprinted from *Handbook of psychological assessment* (4th ed.), Groth-Marnat, G. Copyright 2003. Reprinted with permission of John Wiley & Sons, Inc.

Specificity

Reprinted from *Handbook of psychological assessment* (4th ed.), Groth-Marnat, G. Copyright 2003. Reprinted with permission of John Wiley & Sons, Inc.

Systems Theory

Reprinted from *Encyclopedia of psychology*. (Vol. 2); Kazdin, A. E. (Ed.). (2000). With permission of Oxford University Press.

Ultimate Cause

Reprinted from Alcock, J. (2001). *Animal Behavior: An evolutionary approach* (7th ed.); With permission of Sinauer Associates, Inc.

Validity

Reprinted from *Handbook of psychological assessment* (4th ed.), Groth-Marnat, G. Copyright 2003. Reprinted with permission of John Wiley & Sons, Inc.

Philosophical Terms

Aristotle's Four Causes: Material, Formal, Efficient, and Final

From *Dictionary of the history of ideas* by Wiener, P. P. (Ed.). Vol. 1. Gale Group, © 1973, Gale Group. Reprinted by permission of The Gale Group.

Reprinted from Haynes, S. N. (1992). Models of causality in psychopathology: Toward dynamic, synthetic and nonlinear models of behavior disorders. With permission of author Stephen Haynes.

Reprinted from Cocchiarella, L., & Lord, S. J. (Eds.), *Master the AMA Guides Fifth Edition*, Copyright 2001, American Medical Association

Copyright 1998 from *Routledge encyclopedia of philosophy*; Craig, E. (Ed.). Reproduced by permission of Routledge/Taylor & Francis Group, LLC.

Reprinted from Flew, A., & Priest, S. (Eds.), *A dictionary of philosophy*, (2002), Pan books an imprint of Pan Macmillan Ltd. Pan Macmillan, 20 New Wharf Road, London N1 9RR, Basingstoke and Oxford Associated companies throughout the world. Reproduced with permission of Palgrave Macmillan.

Causal Law

Copyright 2001 from *Dictionary of world philosophy*; Iannone, A. P. Reproduced by permission of Routledge/Taylor & Francis Group, LLC.

Causal Nexus

Reprinted from Blackburn, S. (1994). *The Oxford dictionary of philosophy*; With permission of Oxford University Press.

Causation

Denier of Causation

Reprinted from Psillos, S. (Ed.). (2002). *Causation and explanation*. With permission of McGill-Queen's University Press.

Determinism

Etiology

Chapter 9. Considering Course and Treatment in Rehabilitation: Sequential and Dynamic Causality

Figure 9.1

Table of Cases

Case Law	Chapters including this case reference
Antoine-Tubbs v. Local 513 Air Transp. Div., 50 F. Supp. 2d 601 (N.D. Tex. 1998).	3, 10
Athey v. Leonati [1996] 3 S.C.R. 458.	3, 4, 12
Barefoot v. Estelle, 463 U.S. 880 (1983).	10
Black v. Food Lion, Inc. 171 F.3d 308 (5th Cir. 1999).	3, 20
Blanchard v. Eli Lilly, 207 F. Supp. 2d 308 (D. Vt. 2002).	20
Boyles v. Kerr, 855 S.W.2d 593 (Tex. 1993).	20
Brackett v. Peters, 11 F.3d 78 (7th Cir. 1993).	20
Burke v. Town of Walpole, 405 F.3d 66 (1st Cir. 2005).	10
Chaney v. Smithkline Beckman Corp., 764 F.2d 527 (8th Cir. 1985).	4
Cole v. Shell Petroleum Corp., 86 P.2d 740 (Kan. 1939).	20
Cooper v. Smith & Nephew, 259 F.3d 194 (4th cir. 2001).	10
Crick v. Mohan (sub nom.) [1993] 142 A.R. 281 (Q.B.).	3
Daubert v. Merrell Dow Pharmaceuticals, Inc. 509 U.S. 579, 113 S.Ct. 2786, 125 L.Ed. 2d 469 (1993).	1, 2, 3, 4, 10, 13, 20, 21
Daubert v. Merrell Dow Pharmaceuticals, Inc., 43 F.3d 1311 (1995).	10
Deatherage v. Board of Psychology, 134 Wn.2d 131, 948 P.2d 828 (Wn. Sup. Ct. 1997).	11
Desbiens v. Mordini, 2004 CanLII 41166 (ON S.C.).	1, 2, 21
Dillon v. Legg, 441 P.2d 912 (Cal. 1968).	2, 20
Doe v. Baxter Healthcare Corp., 380 F.3d 399 (8th Cir. 2004).	20
Estelle v. Smith, 451 U.S. 454, 101 S.Ct. 1866 (1981).	11
Frye v. United States, 293 F. 1013, 34 ALR 145 (D. C. Cir. 1923).	2, 3, 4, 11, 10, 20
General Electric Co. v. Joiner, 522 U.S. 136, 118 S.Ct. 512 (1997).	1, 2, 3, 10, 20
Green v. K-Mart Corp., 849 So. 2d 814 (La. Ct. App. 2003).	20
Harris v. Forklift Systems, Inc., 114 S.Ct. 367 (1993).	10

Case Law	Chapters including this case reference
Heller v. Shaw, 167 F.3d 146 (3d Cir. 1999).	3
Hertenstein v. Kimberly Home Health Care, Inc., 189 F.R.D. 620 (Kan. 1999).	11
Holland v. United States, 182 F.R.D. 493 (D.S.C. 1998).	11
Holmes v. Sec. Investor Prot. Corp., 503 U.S. 258 (1992).	20
In Matter of Athans, 107 Wis.2d 331 (Ct. App. 1982).	4
In re: Air Crash at Tapei, Taiwan on October 31, 2000 (C.D. Cal. 2003).	11
Janiak v. Ippolito [1985] 1 S.C.R. 146, 1985 CanLII 62 (S.C.C.).	3
Jeffress v. Reddy, 77 Fed. Appx. 627 (4th Cir. 2003).	20
Jenkins v. United States, 307 F.2d 637 (D.C. Cir. 1962).	2
Jenson v. Eveleth Taconite Co., 1996 U.S. Dist. LEXIS 17617.	20
Jenson v. Eveleth Taconite Co., 130 F.3d 1287 (8th Cir. 1997).	20
Kumho Tire Co. v. Carmichael, 526 U.S. 137, 119 S.Ct. 1167 (1999).	1, 2, 3, 10, 20
Lancaster v. Norfolk & W. Ry., 773 F.2d 807 (7th Cir. 1985).	20
Miramon v. Bradley, 701 So.2d 475 (La. App. 1 Cir. 1997).	3, 12
Mitchell v. Rochester Ry., 45 N.E. 354 (N.Y. 1896).	20
Molien v. Kaiser Found. Hospital, 616 P. 2d 813 (Cal. 1980).	20
Montgomery v. Bazaz-Sehgal, 798 A.2d 742 (Pa. 2002).	20
Mountain Timber Co. v. Washington, 243 U.S. 219, 37 S.Ct. 260 (1917).	20
Newton v. Roche Laboratories, Inc. 243 F. Supp. 2d 672 (W.D. Tex. 2002).	20
Nwakpuda v. Falley's Inc., 14 F. Supp. 1213 (D. Kan. 1998).	20
Padget v. Gray, 727 S.W.2d 706 (Tex. App. 1987).	3, 4
Palsgraf v. Long Island Rwy., 162 N.E. 99 (N.Y. 1928).	20
R. v J-L.J. [2000] 2 S.C.R. 600, 2000 SCC 51 (CanLII).	2
R. v. Mohan [1994] 2 S.C.R. 9, 1994 CanLII 80 (S.C.C.).	1, 2, 3, 10, 13, 21
Ragge v. MCA/Universal Studios, 165 F.R.D. 605 (C.D. Cal. 1995).	11
Reese v. Naylor, 222 So.2d 487 (Fla. Dist Ct. App. 1969).	20
Ruttger Hotel Corp. v. Wagner, 691 So.2d 1177 (Fla. App. 1997).	20
Seminole Pipeline Co. v. Broad Leaf Partners, Inc., 979 S.W.2d 730 (Tex. App. 1998).	20
Sheehan v. Daily Racing Form, Inc., 104 F.3d 940 (7th Cir. 1997).	10

Case Law	Chapters including this case reference
Shirsat v. Mutual Pharmaceuticals Co., 169 F.R.D. 68 (E.D. Pa. 1996).	11
Siharath v. Sandoz Pharmaceuticals Corp., 113 F.Supp.2d 1347 (N.D. Ga. 2001).	12
Smith v. German, 253 A.2d 107 (Pa. 1969).	20
Snell v. Farrell [1990] 2 S.C.R. 311, 1990 CanLII 70 (S.C.C.).	3
Steinhauser v. Hertz, 421 F.2d 1169 (2nd Cir. 1970).	20
Stevens v. Okrainec [1997] 210 A.R. 161 (Alta. Q.B.).	3
Taylor v. Burlington Northern Railroad Co., 787 F.2d 1309 (9th Cir. 1986).	20
Theriault v. Swan, 588 A.2d 369 (Me. 1989).	3, 4
Tomlin v. Holocek, 150 F.R.D. 628 (D. Minn. 1993).	11
United States v. Scholl, 959 F. Supp. 1189 (D. Ariz. 1997).	20
Waube v. Warrington, 258 N.W. 497 (Wis. 1935).	20
Zinermon v. Burch, 494 U.S. 113, 110 S.Ct. 975 (1990).	11

Index

Printed in the United States
70014LV00001B/46-138